Read this first!

Here's how to find the incredible wedding and special event information in *Here Comes The Guide:*

• Event Locations

Sites are organized by region and city, with illustrated descriptions and details about capacities, fees and services. To find a specific site, see the index starting on page 675.

• Event Services

We feature Northern California's best event professionals—caterers, coordinators, photographers, florists, DJs and more. To review all of them, see pages 643–673. And to find out how they qualified to be in *Here Comes The Guide,* read page 637.

• Bridal Salons We Love

Looking for a fabulous wedding dress or bridesmaid dresses? Find our list of recommended bridal salons on pages 691–694.

• Useful Questions to Ask Venues & Event Professionals

Not sure what to ask a potential event location, photographer, caterer, etc.? Our lists of questions on pages 17–38 will make it easier for you to interview them and help you decide who to hire.

Don't forget to check out HereComesTheGuide.com!

HereComesTheGuide.com has the most up-to-date information on event sites, services, bridal salons and bridal fairs—as well as lots of photos and virtual tours. And if you have a certain type of location, event professional or wedding dress designer in mind, you'll really appreciate our amazingly useful search engine. We make it easy to find exactly what you're looking for.

Our Cover Photographer

milou + olin

Our cover photo was shot by Caroline Winata of Milou + Olin. We think it effortlessly captures this couple in a relaxed, intimate moment, and the connection between them draws you in.

To find out more about Caroline and her work, Here Comes The Guide's editor had a conversation with her:

Q *What an intriguing company name! Who are Milou and Olin?*

A Milou is my amazing Portuguese Water Dog and best buddy. She's been in my life for 12 years, and she's the reason I got started in photography. We used to do agility competitions together and spent a lot of time waiting around for the action to start. At some point I decided to take pictures of her during the down time. It was a lot of fun, and I discovered that I have a knack for photography.

Olin is the name my grandparents gave me when I was a little girl. They were from Indonesia and had trouble pronouncing "Caroline." Somehow, the "Car" and the "e" got dropped, and what was left was "Olin." The nickname stuck!

Q *So how did you go from photographing dogs to shooting weddings?*

A After years of agility competitions, I got tired of that side of the dog world. But I still wanted to do photography and thought weddings would be perfect for me. I love how each wedding has a story that I can tell with my camera. My photos mix editorial and photojournalistic styles with my own quirky take on things. I have a background in graphic design (a BFA and MFA in New Media Design), which comes into play when I shoot photos or create wedding albums—my images reflect strong design elements in their composition and tonality.

Plus wedding photography lets me travel to different parts of the world—I get to meet new people and see how the light changes wherever I go. And I take Milou with me whenever I can!

Q *Why do you think couples like working with you?*

A Well, for one thing, I seem to attract couples with dogs (laughs). They can tell that I'm comfortable with their pets, so that puts them at ease. But couples who don't have dogs hire me, too. What I hear a lot is that they picked me because when they looked at my photos, they felt like they were walking into an intimate moment or seeing a little secret revealed. And while I'm shooting an engagement session or the wedding itself, couples often say that they like my laid-back, unposed approach.

Q *Tell me a little more about what makes you tick...*

A I'm free-spirited, and I love adventure, really good fashion and all things romantic. I'm obsessed with design and beautiful lighting, not to mention big cocktail rings and sashimi. I'm genuinely interested in my clients, and the connection between us helps them be themselves when I'm taking their picture. I truly feel that I'm not just a photographer, I'm an artist. I'm not doing this for a career or money. I do it because it's my passion.

Back cover photos also provided by milou + olin (formerly Tinywater Photography).

What Makes Us Different?

We do most of your homework for you.

1. **We actually visit the locations in *Here Comes The Guide*.**

   We check out 95% of our event sites in person before we include them in *The Guide*.

2. **We write every location description with you in mind.**

   Each site description is based on our personal experience, so it's informative, accurate and often entertaining.

3. **We provide real pricing for venues, along with nitty-gritty details about capacity, site services and amenities.**

   This makes it easy to create a list of your top contenders, and by the time you call or visit a location you're totally informed!

4. **We prescreen all of our event professionals so you don't have to.**

   All of the photographers, floral designers, caterers and other vendors in our Service Directory have been **CERTIFIED BY THE GUIDE.** That means we've thoroughly checked them out, so you don't have to worry about hiring them. Every one is outstanding—we're honored to represent them.

5. **We save you a ton of time.**

   By putting so much comprehensive information all in one place, we save you hours…days…maybe months of searching for event locations and professionals. And, you can actually do most of your planning without leaving home!

HereComesTheGuide.com has it ALL:

- **Virtual Tours**

  Most of the event sites we feature on **HereComesTheGuide.com** have virtual tours! It's *the* way to explore wedding locations on your own time (and in your pajamas).

- **Photos of Hundreds of Wedding Venues, Services & Salons**

  Each location, event professional and bridal salon has their own photo gallery.

- **Fee Info for Every Venue**

  HereComesTheGuide.com provides pricing for facility rental, catering and other costs.

- **CERTIFIED BY THE GUIDE Event Services**

  We don't just feature any old caterer or DJ. We've carefully checked out each event professional.

- **Local Bridal Shows**

  Find out what events are happening near you, like fab food tastings and fashion shows. Did you have something better to do this weekend?

- **Handpicked Bridal Salons**

  You may never walk a runway, but you'll walk down the aisle as the glittering fashionista you were born to be! We've scoped out the shops that'll make it all happen (and we've spoken with brides and industry professionals who recommend them, too).

- **Wedding Dress Trunk Shows and Samples Sales Calendar**

  Want to browse an entire collection of the latest designer wedding dresses? How about a discount on an in-stock bridal gown? This is the place to find special designer and sales events.

- **MyGuide**

  Log in to organize your **HereComesTheGuide.com** search results. You can save and share your favorite locations and event services (and we won't give out your email address—period).

Our website also includes many locations, services and bridal salons that are so new they aren't even in this book!

What People Say

"I went out and spent the money on your book without hesitation. I'm so glad I did! I've gotten some great ideas and was able to create an outline for my budget. Not only did I find great reception locations in your book, but I think I found my rehearsal dinner place as well. It was a gold mine!"

—*Liz Davis, Bride*

"I went to about ten locations that are in your book and found that the site descriptions were pretty accurate. I'm amazed at how well you were able to capture the feeling of a place and put it into words."

—*Stephanie Stevensen, Bride*

"I'm in the process of helping my daughter research sites for her wedding reception and your site has been hugely helpful! The location information is thorough and consistent, making comparing the different locations so easy. We have found places to check out that we never would have thought of on our own. Thanks so much for all the work you must have done to put all this information together!"

—*Gail C., Mother of the Bride*

"Having recently gotten married, I have a special appreciation for *Here Comes The Guide.* It was extremely helpful during my time of planning. The quick descriptions painted a beautiful picture of each and every location, and were very helpful in narrowing down the search by budget, criteria and location. I feel this is a very important tool for every busy bride and still recommend it to all my engaged friends."

—*A Southern California Bride*

"I got married in August and cannot stress how much help *Here Comes The Guide* was to me. I was often able to receive more information from your site than from my contact with the actual locations and vendors! Especially since I was planning a Northern California wedding from Southern California, you saved me A TON of legwork."

—*Jamie Juster, Bride*

"I have finally found a website that has it all! I'm planning my wedding from out of state and your event locations search is the best! I've been looking for a website that has all the information in one place. Thank you!!!"

—*Sarah, Bride*

About Here Comes The Guide

"I just had to let you know how WON-DERFUL your website is. I was amazed to finally find a website with REAL information. Other wedding web-sites just gave me names and phone numbers, and I still had to do all the research on my own. Yours gave me all the nitty-gritty stuff I needed to know to find locations and vendors. With only two sessions at your website, my wedding was planned. Amazing!"

—Christina R., Bride

"I have to tell you, I was blown away by your website. It's so beautiful and pro-fessionally done. The detail you pro-vide is just enough so that the browser doesn't get bogged down in minutiae. Your site is such a great resource that I've started telling everybody about it. I've seen tons of wedding sites, so I know that you've come up with something that's really different."

—Kimberly P., Bride

"I completely love your website and look forward to the book. This is the only resource that is so detailed on California sites, and it makes it so much easier to plan from a long dis-tance. *Here Comes The Guide* is the best source of information."

—Jocelyn, Bride

"I absolutely love your new website. It's warm, feminine and has what one might call 'simple elegance.' Great job! I refer friends to your website all the time—for weddings, showers and of course, birthdays. Keep up the fabu-lous work."

—Maria, Bride

"I love your site! Most other sites that I visited seemed to have a hidden agenda to steer me towards only what benefited them. This site is non-biased and easy to use. Thank you!"

—Elisa Parra, Bride

"Thanks for providing this invaluable resource! I'll be using the site for cor-porate event planning—I don't know what I did without it!"

—Mary, Corporate Planner

"This is a wonderful website, with all the details that a bride looks for when she's searching for a reception location. It's well organized and in-credibly useful. I wish there were more sites like this one. THANK YOU!!!"

—Amy, Bride

We Need Your Help

- **Tell venues and event professionals that you're using *Here Comes The Guide*.**

  When you call the places, services and salons we feature, let them know that you heard about them through *The Guide*.

- **Help us keep our information current.**

  We'd appreciate it if you'd contact us with your comments, corrections, suggestions and complaints. Your feedback helps us maintain the accuracy of our information.

- **Let us know if you discover a great location, event professional or bridal salon that's not featured in *Here Comes The Guide*.**

  Please call or email us if you find an event site, vendor or bridal boutique you think we should include in our book and on our website.

Hopscotch Press, Inc.

930 Carleton Street, Berkeley CA 94710

510/548-0400   fax 510/548-0144

info@HereComesTheGuide.com
www.HereComesTheGuide.com

Information Is Always Changing

Everything changes: pricing, services, décor, landscaping and even ownership.

We've tried to make the information in this book completely accurate, but it's not possible. Locations give us incorrect facts and figures, change ownership or management, revamp their pricing and policies and sometimes go out of business. Truth is, things in the event industry can turn upside down overnight.

So how can you make sure that you're getting correct information? It's simple:

- When you tour locations, bring your book with you (or printouts from **HereComesTheGuide.com**).

- When you contact a location, show or read the information in *Here Comes The Guide* to the facility's representative to verify that it's still current.

- Get everything that's been agreed on in writing, and review it carefully before you sign any contract!

Here Comes The Guide

Thirteenth Edition

Copyright © 2013–2014
Published by Hopscotch Press, Inc.
Printed in the U.S.A.

Here Comes The Guide, Northern California®

Thirteenth Edition

Jan Brenner, *Co-Author/Editor-in-Chief*
Jolene Rae Harrington, *Co-Author/Editor*

Meredith Monday Schwartz, *Managing Director, Hopscotch Press, Inc.*
Sharon Carl, *Production Director*
Lisa Edd, *Managing Editor*
Denise Auerbach, *Director of Vendor Sales*
Jennifer Ahearn, *Online Media Director*
Julia Snippen, *Regional Sales Manager*
Jenna Miller, *Vendor Sales Manager*
Angela Mullan, *Regional Sales Manager*
Maggie Munki, *Production*

Lynn Broadwell, *Publisher*

Inside Illustrations: *Jon Dalton and Michael Tse*

Library of Congress Control Number: 2012949415
ISBN 978-1-885355-20-1

Here Comes The Guide ®

Thirteenth Edition

Acknowledgments

Our deepest appreciation goes to our writers, Jolene Rae Harrington (also an invaluable editor) and Laurie Turner. Without them none of our books would ever get written.

Our artist, Jon Dalton, penned all the new illustrations for this edition of *Here Comes The Guide*. Using both computer graphics and fine art skills, he transformed photographs of the facilities into the distinctive line drawings that give *The Guide* its unique style.

And as always, we are eternally grateful to our clients and our readers. Your support year in and year out keeps *Here Comes The Guide* a popular resource.

Table of Contents

Really, Really Important Information

Questions To Ask

Part One: Event Locations

Regional Areas and Cities

South Bay

Tri-Valley and Livermore Wine Country

East Bay

Solano County

Maps

Part Two: Event Services

Bridal Salons

Indexes

Preface

When I graduated from college, I thought I'd never have to do another endless research project again. Boy, was I wrong. Compared to looking for a place to get married, term papers were a piece of cake. I began my quest optimistically enough, but after a couple of days of frantic and fruitless networking (my wedding date was a mere three months down the road!), the enormity of my task started to sink in. It had taken me 33 years to find the right guy, and it was beginning to look like it might take an equally long time to find the right place.

Going into high gear, I reached out and touched just about everyone I knew, along with quite a few total strangers. Friends and friends of friends didn't have any recommendations that suited our particular needs, and although wedding consultants had information, they were reluctant to part with their lists of sites unless I hired them to plan my wedding. I even called some caterers, florists and cake makers, but they were usually too busy to give me in-depth descriptions of places over the phone. Some chambers of commerce had organized wedding location lists ready to mail out; others had nothing and knew nothing.

After days of phoning, all I had was a patchwork quilt of information. I still hadn't found *the* place, and finally had to face the painful truth: there was no central resource or comprehensive, detailed list. I became anxious. With a full-time job I was hardly free to conduct an exhaustive search, and I realized that I would never be able to find out about the vast majority of interesting or unusual wedding sites, let alone thoroughly evaluate them! My frustration was exacerbated by the fact that it was August and the wedding date in October was drawing closer with each passing day.

As luck would have it, my sister mentioned that her hairdresser had gotten married on a yacht in San Francisco Bay. Hallelujah! That's it! I cried. What a great idea! I'd never even thought about a floating wedding and had no idea you could do such a thing.

We got married on a hot, sunny day behind Angel Island in San Francisco Bay. The captain performed the ceremony on the bow, and afterwards the yacht tooted its horn, the crew let loose multicolored balloons, and a "Just Married" sign was thrown over the stern. As we swept past Alcatraz Island, Sausalito and the Golden Gate and Bay Bridges, our guests relaxed in the sun, enjoying drinks and hors d'oeuvres. What a wonderful day! Even my parents' friends had a great time, and wrote us after the wedding to let us know how much they'd loved their outing on the water.

Serendipity was largely responsible for making my wedding memorable, but you don't have to rely on luck. I created *Here Comes The Guide* so that others wouldn't have to experience what I went through, and I hope it makes your search for the perfect location easy and painless.

Lynn Broadwell
Publisher

Really, Really Important Information

Introduction

Little did we know when we wrote *Here Comes The Guide, Northern California* in 1989 that we would receive such an overwhelming response from our readers. The first edition sold out in less than a year, and as public demand grew we hustled to get the second edition in print. Thanks to our enthusiastic readership of engaged brides, savvy party hostesses and event planners, *The Guide* continues to be a bestseller!

So what makes this book so popular?

We've done most of your homework for you.

We present comprehensive, solid information: a full description and illustration of each location, plus details about fees, capacities and services. Our wide selection of facilities includes delightful places that you might not have found on your own.

This book cuts your search time by 90%.

Instead of having to call dozens of facilities and ask the same questions over and over again, you can look up many of the answers in *The Guide*. Once you've narrowed down your list of potential sites, you can contact them to schedule an in-person visit. Not only does *The Guide* save you time, it often saves you money by letting you comparison shop!

We screen our locations.

We personally evaluate almost every property in *Here Comes The Guide,* sending a professional writer to 95% of our sites to make sure they meet our criteria. (Yes, we actually turn down locations that don't satisfy our requirements.)

All our service professionals are *Certified By The Guide.*

Our goal is to represent only the best event professionals in the industry. In order to achieve this, we thoroughly screen all of the service providers in *Here Comes The Guide.* That means you don't have to take a chance on some anonymous photographer or caterer. Every one of our vendors has been carefully checked out and *Certified By The Guide.*

Our rigorous certification process requires each vendor to submit 30 references, half wedding industry professionals and half recent brides. Then we contact each person and get their honest feedback. Only if the company gets a rave review do we accept them as a client.

(Even though we've checked out all of our professionals very carefully, we can't guarantee their performance. Here Comes The Guide is not responsible for the contract you ultimately sign with them, or for how your event goes. Our best advice is to be thorough, careful consumers and get every single thing in writing. This is what we tell our sisters and best friends, so this is what we're telling you.)

All our bridal salons come highly recommended.

We've handpicked the bridal boutiques that we think offer a combination of style and service for today's brides, whether you want the full princess experience, a custom couture bridal gown, or just friendly service and a good bargain. We've also talked to real brides and industry professionals to discreetly inquire about their experience with these shops. And you know what? If they didn't rave, the salons didn't make our list.

We're experienced.

We've been writing and publishing *Here Comes The Guide* since 1989. We're proud that our publication has become the essential resource for weddings—and just about any kind of event in California.

If you can't find the perfect venue, service or bridal salon in *Here Comes The Guide,* check out our website at HereComesTheGuide.com.

You'll have access to all the information in the *Here Comes The Guide* book online and a lot more:

- **More Northern California locations,** along with photo galleries, virtual tours and slide shows. You'll be able to tour hundreds of sites in your pajamas.

- **Even more locations** in other regions of the U.S., like Southern California, New England, Chicago and Hawaii, just to name a few.

- **More services** with lots of photos of floral designs, cakes, makeup and hair, you name it!

- **More bridal salons** with gorgeous dress images and insider info.

- **Trunk Shows & Sample Sales Calendar** for the latest styles and savings.

- **Bridal Fair Calendar** with deets about upcoming extravaganzas and wedding showcases.

- **Guest accommodations/room block options** plus photos and details.

- **Honeymoon destinations,** including romantic images and practical info.

Navigation is a snap, and our searchable database lets you find event sites by city, type, capacity, view, etc., and event professionals by company name, region or service category. You can even search our recommended bridal salons to find wedding and bridesmaid dresses by a particular designer! A special *MyGuide* feature lets you save your favorites and share them with friends and family.

And check back often—we regularly update our website with event locations, services and salons that are not featured in the book!

Understanding Our Information

Explanation of Main Headings

Each venue description in *Here Comes The Guide* follows the same format. To help you understand the information presented, we've provided an explanation of the main headings in the same order as they appear.

Description

Once you've selected a geographical area and you're clear about your needs, then thoroughly review all the sites listed in your area of preference. The descriptions are written to give you a sense of what places are like, from ambiance to physical layout. However, before reading the descriptions, you may want to check the *Capacity* and *Fees & Deposits* sections to determine which places seem to be a good fit from a size and budget perspective. If a facility is still a viable option after you've read the entire two-page editorial, mark it with a ✔ or flag it for easy reference when planning phone calls and site visits later on.

Ceremony Capacity

Standing and seated capacities are included for ceremonies since these numbers may be totally different than the corresponding numbers for receptions.

Reception Capacity

By now you should have a rough idea of how many people will be attending. If not, it's time to zero in on the number, since many facilities want a deposit based on an estimated head count. Look at the capacity figures for each event location. Seated or sit-down capacity refers to guests seated at tables. Standing capacity refers to a function where the majority of guests are not seated, such as a champagne/hors d'oeuvres reception. Put a ✔ next to those facilities that are compatible with your guest count. If you're planning well in advance and don't have your guest list whittled down yet, then you'll just have to estimate and refine the count as the date draws near. There is a world of difference in cost and planning effort between an intimate party of 60 and a large wedding with over 200 guests. Pin down your numbers as soon as you can.

Meeting Capacity

In general, the seated capacity for meetings is listed as a range or a maximum. Sometimes, specific spaces are named along with their individual capacities. Occasionally, seating configurations are also provided: *theater-style* (auditorium row seating with chairs arranged closely together), *classroom-style* (an organized table-and-chair arrangement, usually in rows) and *conference-style* (seating around tables).

Fees and Deposits

We've tried to make the information regarding costs as accurate as possible. However, keep in mind that we can't list the fees for all of the services a venue offers. Also, while packages tend to be more inclusive, they may not cover the full cost of your event—especially when you add in extras like appetizers or rentals. It's important to find out as soon as possible exactly what is—and isn't—included with any service or package you're considering in order to accurately assess how your venue choice will impact your budget.

It's a good idea to confirm it with the facility you're calling, just to make sure it's still valid. If you're planning far in advance, anticipate price increases by the time you contract with a venue. Once you're definite about your location, lock in your fees in a contract, protecting yourself from possible rate increases later. Make sure you ask about every service provided and are clear about all of the extras that can really add up. Facilities may charge you for tables, chairs, linens, plateware and silverware, glassware and additional hours. Don't be surprised to see tax and service charges in fixed amounts applied to the total bill if the facility provides restaurant or catering services. Although it may seem redundant to include the phrase "tax and service charges are additional" in each entry, we find that most people forget (or just don't want to accept the painful reality) that 23%–33% will be applied to the food and beverage total.

Sometimes a deposit is nonrefundable—a fact you'll definitely want to know if the deposit is a large percentage of the total bill. And even if it's refundable, you still need to read the cancellation policy thoroughly. Also make sure you understand the policies that will ensure you get your cleaning and security deposit returned in full and again, get everything in writing.

> **Look at the information regarding fees and deposits and remember that these figures change regularly and usually in one direction—up!**

Food costs vary considerably. Carefully plan your menu with the caterer, event consultant or chef. Depending on the style of service and the type of food being served, the total food bill can vary dramatically—even if you're getting quotes from the same caterer. If, for example, you're having a multi-course seated meal, expect it to be the most expensive part of your event.

Alcohol is expensive, too, and you may be restricted in what you can serve and who can serve it. A facility may not allow you to bring your own alcoholic beverages, and if it does it may limit you to wine or champagne. Many places discourage you from bringing your own (BYO) by charging an exorbitant corkage fee to remove the cork and pour. Other places have limited permits that don't allow them to serve alcohol or restrict them from serving certain kinds; some will let you or the caterer serve alcohol, others require someone with a license. Make sure you know what's allowed. Decide what your budget is for alcohol and determine what types you're able to provide. And keep in mind that the catering fees you are quoted rarely include the cost of alcohol. If you provide the alcohol, make sure you keep your purchase receipts so you can return any unopened bottles.

So how much will your event cost? Hopefully not more than you can afford! There are a lot of variables involved in coming up with an estimated total for your event. Just make sure you've included them all in your calculations and read all the fine print before you sign any contract.

Availability

Some facilities are available 7am to 2am; others offer very limited "windows." If you'd like to save some money, consider a weekday or weeknight reception, or think about having your event in the off-season (often November, or January through March, but varies depending on the region). Even the most sought-after places have openings midweek and during non-peak months—and at reduced costs. Facilities want your business and are more likely to negotiate terms and prices if they have nothing else scheduled. Again, read all the fine print carefully and ✔ those facilities that have time slots that meet your needs. If the date you have in mind is already booked, it doesn't hurt to ask if someone actually confirmed that date by paying a deposit or signing a contract. If they haven't, you may be in luck.

Services/Amenities and Restrictions

Most facilities provide something in the way of services and many have limitations that may affect your function. For instance, they may not allow you to have amplified music outdoors or bring your own caterer.

We've attempted to give you a brief description of what each venue has to offer and what is restricted. Because of space limitations, we've shortened words and developed a key to help you follow our abbreviated notations. Once you're familiar with our shorthand, you'll be able to read through all the data outlined at the bottom of each entry and put a ✔ next to each facility that meets your requirements.

Services/Amenities Key

CATERING
- **provided:** the facility provides catering (for a fee)
- **provided, no BYO:** the facility provides catering; you cannot bring in your own
- **preferred list:** you must select your caterer from the facility's approved list
- **provided or BYO:** the facility will provide catering or you can select an outside caterer of your own
- **BYO, licensed:** arrange for your own licensed caterer

KITCHEN FACILITIES
- **ample** or **fully equipped:** large and well-equipped with major appliances
- **moderate:** medium-sized and utilitarian
- **minimal:** small with limited equipment; may not have all the basic appliances
- **setup** or **prep only:** room for setup and food prep, but not enough space or utilities to cook food
- **n/a:** not applicable because facility provides catering or doesn't allow food

TABLES & CHAIRS
- **some provided** or **provided:** facility provides some or all of the tables and chairs
- **BYO:** make arrangements to bring your own

LINENS, SILVER, ETC.
- same as above

RESTROOMS
- **wheelchair accessible** or
- **not wheelchair accessible**

DANCE FLOOR
- **yes:** an area for dancing (hardwood floor, cement terrace, patio) is available
- **CBA, extra charge:** you can arrange for a dance floor to be brought in for a fee

BRIDE'S & GROOM'S DRESSING AREA
- **yes:** there is an area for changing
- **no:** there's no area for changing
- **limited:** smaller space, not fully equipped as changing room
- **CBA:** can be arranged

PARKING
- **CBA:** can be arranged
  other descriptions are self explanatory

ACCOMMODATIONS
If overnight accommodations are available on site, the number of guest rooms is listed.
- **CBA:** the facility will arrange accommodations for you

TELEPHONE
- **restricted:** calls made on the house phone must be local, collect or charged to a credit card
- **guest phones:** private phones in guest rooms
- **house phone:** central phone used by all guests
- **emergency use only:** self-explanatory

OUTDOOR NIGHT LIGHTING
- **yes:** there is adequate light to conduct your event outdoors after dark
- **access only** or **limited:** lighting is sufficient for access only

OUTDOOR COOKING FACILITIES

- **BBQ:** the facility has a barbecue on the premises
- **BBQ, CBA:** a barbecue can be arranged through the facility
- **BYO BBQ:** make arrangements for your own barbecue
- **n/a:** not applicable

CLEANUP

- **provided:** facility takes care of cleanup
- **caterer:** your caterer is responsible
- **caterer or renter:** both you and/or your caterer are responsible for cleanup

MEETING EQUIPMENT

- **full range:** facility has a full range of audiovisual equipment, including projectors, overhead screens, etc.

Restrictions Key

ALCOHOL

- **provided, no BYO:** the facility provides alcoholic beverages (for a fee) and does not permit you to bring your own
- **BYO:** you can bring your own alcohol
- **corkage, $/bottle:** if you bring your own alcohol, the facility charges a fee per bottle to remove the cork and pour
- **WCB only:** *(or any combination of these three letters)* only wine, champagne and beer are permitted
- **licensed server:** the server of alcohol must be licensed

SMOKING

- **allowed:** smoking is permitted throughout the facility
- **outside only:** smoking is not permitted inside the facility
- **not allowed:** smoking is not permitted anywhere on the premises
- **designated areas:** specific areas for smoking have been designated

MUSIC

Almost every facility allows acoustic music unless stated otherwise. Essentially, restrictions refer to amplified music.

- **amplified OK:** amplified music is acceptable without restriction
- **outside only:** no amplified music allowed inside

- **no:** no equipment is available
- **BYO:** bring your own meeting equipment
- **CBA:** equipment can be arranged
- **CBA, extra fee:** equipment can be arranged for an extra fee

VIEW

We've described what type of view is available for each facility.

- **no:** the facility has no views to speak of

OTHER

Description of any service or amenity that is not included in above list.

- **inside only:** no amplified music permitted outside
- **amplified OK with limits or restrictions:** amplified music is allowed, but there are limits on volume, hours of play, type of instruments, etc.

WHEELCHAIR ACCESS

Accessibility is based on whether the event areas (not necessarily the restrooms) of a facility are wheelchair accessible or not.

- **yes:** the facility is accessible
- **limited:** the facility is accessible but with difficulty (there may be a step at the entrance, for example, but all of the rooms are accessible)
- **no:** the facility is not accessible

INSURANCE

Many facilities require that you purchase and show proof of some insurance coverage. The type and amount of insurance varies with the facility, and some facilities offer insurance for a minimal charge.

- **liability required, certificate required** or **proof of insurance required:** additional insurance is required
- **not required:** no additional insurance is required
- **may be required:** sometimes additional insurance is required

Valuable Tips

Selecting an Event Location

Before you jump into the venue descriptions in *Here Comes The Guide,* identify what kind of celebration you want and establish selection criteria early. Here are some basics:

Is Your Site Geographically Desirable?

Your first big decision is to select a location that will make geographical sense to you, your family and the majority of your guests. Most people have special events close to home or office, so there's not much to consider. But if you pick a spot out of town, you need to think about the logistics of getting everyone to your event site.

Special Considerations in Northern California

Guests may be traveling a considerable distance by car to get to your party destination. Given the Northern California freeway system and traffic congestion, you'll save them lots of time and trouble if you provide, along with the invitation, specific directions on a separate map drawn to scale. Include symbols indicating directions (north, south, etc.) and the names of the appropriate off-ramps. If you're not sure about exits, landmarks or street names, take a dry run of the route to make sure everything on your map is accurate and easy to follow. If your function occurs after dark, do the test drive at night so you can note well-lit landmarks that will prevent your guests from getting lost—both coming to your event and going home.

If you're having a Friday evening event, take commuters into account, especially if your venue is in an area that gets bumper-to-bumper traffic. One solution is to schedule your get-together after 7pm when freeways are less congested.

Even if you have few constraints when picking a location, it's still worth considering the total driving time to and from your destination. When it's over two hours, an overnight stay may be necessary and you may be limited to a Saturday night event, since your nearest and dearest won't be able to spend hours on the road during the week. If you have guests arriving by plane, it's certainly helpful if there's an airport nearby, and if your co-workers, friends or family enjoy drinking try to house them close to the event site.

There's no reason why you can't contemplate a special event in the Santa Cruz Mountains or in a wine cave in Calistoga. Just remember that if you're planning a wedding that's not local, a venue's on-site coordinator or a wedding planner can really help: Many are experienced in handling destination events and can be a great asset.

Budget

Many couples aren't very experienced with event budgeting and don't know how to estimate what locations, products and services will ultimately cost. If you're not sure what you can realistically afford, we recommend talking to a professional event planner or wedding consultant early in the planning stages. You don't have to make a big financial or time commitment to use a professional; many will assist you on an hourly basis for a nuts-and-bolts session to determine priorities and to assign costs to items on your wish list.

Part of being realistic involves some simple arithmetic. Catering costs, for example, are usually calculated on a per-person basis. The couple who has $10,000 and wants to invite 250 guests should know that $40 per guest actually won't go very far. Tax and gratuity combined usually consume 23–33% of the food and beverage budget. If you subtract 30% from $40, you have $28 left. If you also serve alcohol at $10/person, you're down to $18/person for food. That's usually not enough for appetizers and a seated meal, let alone location rental fees, entertainment, flowers, printed invitations, photography, etc.

Before you make any major decisions or commit any of your funds for specific items, take a serious look at your total budget, make sure it can cover all your anticipated expenses, and leave a little cushion for last-minute items. If your budget doesn't cover everything, it's time for some hard decisions. If you have a very large guest list and a small pocketbook, you may need to shorten the list or cut back on some of the amenities you want to include. No matter who foots the bill, be advised that doing the homework here really counts. Pin down your costs at the beginning of the planning stage and get all estimates in writing.

> **The important point is that if you know what kind of event you want and are clear about your budget, your search will be made faster and easier.**

Style

Do you know what kind of event you want? Will it be formal or informal? A traditional wedding or an innovative party? Will it be held at night or during the day? Indoors or outdoors? Is having a garden ceremony or gourmet food a deal breaker? By identifying the geographical area and the most important elements of your dream wedding before you start looking for a venue, you can really narrow down your search.

Guest Count

How many people are anticipated? Many facilities request a rough estimate 60 to 90 days in advance of your function—and they'll want a deposit based on the figure you give them. A confirmed guest count or guarantee is usually required 72 hours prior to the event. It's important to come up with a solid estimate of your guest list early on in order to plan your budget and select the right ceremony or reception spot.

It's also important to ensure that the guest count you give the facility *before* your event doesn't change *during* your event. Believe it or not, it's possible to have more people at your reception than you expected. How? Some folks who did not bother to RSVP may decide to show up anyway. In one case we know of, the parents of the bride got an additional bill for $1,200 on the event day because there were 30 "surprise" guests beyond the guest count guarantee who were wined and dined. To prevent this from happening to you—especially if you're having a large reception where it's hard to keep track of all the guests—it's a good idea to phone everyone who did *not* RSVP. Let them know as politely as possible that you will need to have their response by a given date to finalize food and beverage totals.

Seasonal Differences

Northern California, for all its (pardon the expression) faults, has got some great advantages weather-wise. Outdoor special events, ceremonies and receptions can take place throughout most of the year, and from September to November you can anticipate sunny skies and warm temperatures. However, when the mercury rises in inland areas, watch out. A canopy or tables with umbrellas are essential for screening the sun. In fact, you should ask each facility manager about the sun's direction and intensity with respect to the time of day and month your event will take place. Guests will be uncomfortable facing into the sun during a ceremony, and white walls and enclosed areas bounce light around and can hold in heat. If your event is scheduled for midday in July, for example, include a note on your location map to bring sunglasses, hat and sunscreen. If you also mention words like "poolside," "yacht deck" or "lawn seating" on the map, it will help guests know how to dress. In summer, you might want to consider an evening rather than a midday celebration. Not only is the air cooler, but you may also get an extra bonus—a glorious sunset.

If you're arranging an outdoor party November through April, or in the foothills or mountain areas, expect cooler weather and prepare a contingency plan. Despite our region's favorable Mediterranean climate, it has rained in May, June and July, so consider access to an inside space or a tent.

Special Requirements

Sometimes, places have strict rules and regulations. If most of your guests smoke, then pick a location that doesn't restrict smoking. If alcohol is going to be consumed, make sure it's allowed and find out if bar service needs to be licensed. If dancing and a big band are critical, then limit yourself to those locations that can accommodate them and the accompanying decibels. Do you have children, seniors or disabled guests, vegetarians or folks who want kosher food on your list? If so, you need to plan for them, too. It's essential that you identify the special factors that are important for your event before you sign a contract.

Locking in Your Event Date

Let's say it's the first day of your hunt for the perfect spot, and the second place you see is an enchanting garden that happens to be available on the date you want. You really like it but, since you've only seen two locations, you're not 100% sure that this is *the* place. No problem. You decide to keep your options open by making a tentative reservation. The site coordinator dutifully pencils your name into her schedule book and says congratulations. You say thanks, we have a few more places (like 25) to check out, but this one looks terrific. Then off you go, secure in the knowledge that if none of the other sites you visit pans out, you still have this lovely garden waiting for you.

The nightmare begins a couple of weeks, or perhaps months, down the road when you've finished comparison-shopping and call back the first place you liked to finalize the details. So sorry, the coordinator says. We gave away your date because a) oops, one of the other gals who works here erased your name by mistake (after all, it was only *penciled* in), b) we didn't hear back from you soon enough, or c) you never confirmed your reservation with a deposit.

For the tiniest instant you picture yourself inflicting bodily harm on the coordinator or at least slapping the facility with a lawsuit, but alas, there's really not much you can do. Whether a genuine mistake was made or the facility purposely gave your date to another, perhaps more lucrative party (this happens sometimes with hotels who'd rather book a big convention on your date than a little wedding), you're out of luck. To avoid the pain (and ensuing panic) of getting bumped, here's what we suggest: Instead of just being penciled in, ask if you can write a refundable $100–250 check to hold the date for a limited time. If the person in charge is willing to do this but wants the full deposit up front (usually nonrefundable), then you'll need to decide whether you can afford to lose the entire amount if you find a more appealing location later on. Once the coordinator or sales person takes your money, you're automatically harder to bump. Make sure you get a receipt that has the event date, year, time and space(s) reserved written on it, as well as the date your tentative reservation runs out. Then, just to be on the safe side, check in with the facility weekly while you're considering other sites to prevent any possible "mistakes" from being made. When you finally do commit to a place, get a signed contract or at least a confirmation letter. If you don't receive written confirmation within a week, hound the coordinator until you get it, even if you have to drive to the sales office and stand there until they hand it over to you. And even after you've plunked down your money and have a letter and/or contract securing your date, call the coordinator every other month to reconfirm your reservation. It pays to stay on top of this, no matter how locked in you think you are.

> **If you try to pick a location before you've made basic decisions, selection will be a struggle and it will take longer to find a spot that will make you happy.**

Parking

Parking is seldom a critical factor if you get married outside an urban area, but make sure you know how it's going to be handled if you're planning a party in a parking-challenged place like downtown San Francisco, San Jose or Berkeley.

A map is a handy supplement to any invitation, and there's usually enough room on it to indicate how and where vehicles should be parked. Depending on the location, you may want to add a note suggesting carpooling or mention that a shuttle service or valet parking is provided. If there's a fee for parking, identify the anticipated cost per car and where the entry points are to the nearest parking lots. The last thing you want are surprised and disgruntled guests who can't find a place to stash their car, or who are shocked at the $20–$40 parking tab.

Professional Help

If you're a busy person with limited time to plan and execute a party, pick a facility that offers complete coordination services, from catering and flowers to decorations and music. Or better yet, hire a professional event or wedding consultant. Either way, you'll make your life much easier by having someone else handle the details. And often the relationships these professionals have with vendors can end up saving you money, too.

Food and Alcohol Quality

Food and alcohol account for the greatest portion of an event's budget; consequently, food and beverage selections are a big deal. Given the amount of money you will spend on this category alone, you should be concerned about the type, quantity and quality of what you eat and drink. If in-house catering is provided, we suggest you sample different menu options prior to paying a facility deposit. If you'd like to see how a facility handles food setup and presentation, ask the caterer to arrange a visit to someone else's party about a half hour before it starts. It's wise to taste wines and beers in advance, and be very specific about hard alcohol selections.

Hidden Costs

This may come as a surprise, but not all services and event equipment are covered in the rental fee, and some facilities hide the true cost of renting their space by having a low rental fee. It's possible to get nickeled and dimed for all the extras: tables, chairs, linens, dance floor, cake cutting, valet service and so forth. You can also end up paying more than you expected for security and cleanup. All these additional charges can really add up, so save yourself a big headache by understanding exactly what's included in the rental fee and what's not before you sign any contract.

Bonus Info

If you're not sure what to ask potential venues and event professionals, check out our "QUESTIONS TO ASK" section starting on page 17. We've put together lists of questions that come in very handy when you're interviewing potential event locations, photographers, caterers, etc.

Tips for Previewing a Location

Make Appointments.

If you liked what you read about a venue in *The Guide,* then we recommend you make an appointment to see that location rather than just driving by. Sometimes an unremarkable-looking building will surprise you with a secluded garden or hidden courtyard. And sometimes the opposite is true—you'll love the stunning façade, but the interior isn't your style.

Incidentally, we've withheld the addresses of privately owned properties. Should you happen to know where any of these facilities is located, we urge you to respect the owner's or manager's privacy and make an appointment instead of stopping by.

When you do call for an appointment, don't forget to ask for specific directions, including cross streets. You can also look up the location on *HereComesTheGuide.com* and print out a detailed street map. Try to cluster your visits so that you can easily drive from one place to another without backtracking. Schedule at least an hour per facility and leave ample driving time. You want to be efficient, but don't over-schedule yourself. It's best to view places when you're fresh and your judgment isn't clouded by fatigue.

Bring along *The Guide* or printed pages from the website.

We've listed the street address for each site, and our illustrations in the book often make it easier to identify the buildings you're planning to see. And if you bring the book or web pages into the facilities with you, you can double-check our information with the site representative and jot down changes.

Bring a notebook—paper or digital!

You can make notes in your copy of *Here Comes The Guide,* but have a small notebook or digital device handy, too. Keep track of the date, time and name of the person relating the information, and then read back the info to the site representative to confirm that what you heard is correct. Remember to have your notes with you when you review your contract, and go over in detail what you were told versus what's in the contract before you sign anything.

Take pictures.

Video is particularly useful for narrating your likes, dislikes and any other observations while you're shooting a venue. However, if you're just taking still photos, make sure you have a system for matching shots to their respective locations. You'd be surprised how easy it is to confuse photos. And bring extra batteries and whatever else you need to make your gear work properly.

File everything.

Many facilities will hand you pamphlets, menus, rate charts and other materials. Develop a system for sorting and storing the information that keeps your notes, photos and handouts together, clearly labeled and easily accessible.

Bring a checkbook or credit card.

Some of the more attractive venues book a year to 18 months in advance. If you actually fall in love with a location and your date is available, plunk down a deposit to hold the date.

Working With a Location

Confirm All the Details

When you make the initial phone call, confirm that the information presented in *Here Comes The Guide* is still valid. Show or read the information in our book to the site's representative, and have him or her inform you of any changes. If there have been significant increases in fees or new restrictions that you can't live with, cross the place off your list and move on. If the facility is still a contender, request a tour.

Once you've determined that the physical elements of the place suit you, it's time to discuss details. Ask about services and amenities or fees that may not be listed in the book and make a note of them. Outline your plans to the representative and make sure that the facility can accommodate your particular needs. If you don't want to handle all the details yourself, find out what the facility is willing and able to do, and if there will be an additional cost for their assistance. Venues often provide planning services for little or no extra charge. If other in-house services are offered, such as flowers or wedding cakes, inquire about the quality of each service provider and whether or not substitutions can be made. If you want to use your own vendors, find out if the facility will charge you an extra fee. For more help with working with a location, see our "Questions to Ask an Event Location" on page 22.

The Importance of Rapport

Another factor to consider is your rapport with the person(s) you're working with. Are you comfortable with them? Do they listen well and respond to your questions directly? Do they inspire trust and confidence? Are they warm and enthusiastic or cold and aloof? If you have doubts, you need to resolve them before embarking on a working relationship with these folks—no matter how wonderful the facility itself is. Discuss your feelings with them, and if you're still not completely satisfied, get references and call them. If at the end of this process you still have lingering concerns, you may want to eliminate the facility from your list even though it seems perfect in every other way.

On the other hand, don't let your rapport with a banquet coordinator or site rep sway you to book a venue you aren't in love with—there's a lot of turnover in the hospitality industry, and you may call Brittany one day only to—surprise!—be referred to Brian. So if Brittany was your main reason for choosing this place, you could be in for a big disappointment if you and Brian don't hit it off and suddenly the venue's shortcomings really stand out.

Signing a Contract

It's easy to get emotionally attached to a location, but remember that it's not a done deal until you sign a contract. Now's the time to be businesslike and put your emotions aside. If you can't do that, get a non-emotional partner, friend or relative to help you review the small print and negotiate changes before you sign. Remember all those notes you took when you first visited the site? Compare them with what's actually written in the contract. No matter what someone told you about the availability of a dance floor, the price of pastel linens, or the ceremony arch, you can't hold the facility to it until the contract is signed. Places revise their prices and policies all the time, so assume that things may have changed since you originally saw the site or talked to a site representative.

If you're not happy with the contract, prepare to negotiate. Before your appointment with whoever has the power to alter the contract, make an itemized list, in order of importance, of the changes you want. Decide what you're willing to give up, and what you can't live without. If in the end the most important things on your list cannot be addressed to your satisfaction, this is probably not the right place for you. It's better to find another location than to stay with a facility that isn't willing to work with you.

Insurance Considerations

Nowadays, if someone gets injured at an event or something is damaged at or near the event site, it's likely that someone will be sued.

In order to protect themselves and spread the risk among all parties involved, facilities often require additional insurance and/or proof of insurance from service professionals and their clients.

Event sites and service professionals (such as caterers) are very aware of their potential liability and all have coverage of one kind or another. Many of the properties we represent will also require you, the renter, to get extra insurance.

What's funny (or not so funny) is that as more and more event sites require extra liability and/or a certificate of insurance, fewer insurance companies are willing to issue either one—even if you're covered under a homeowner's policy. At this point, insurance carriers don't want to attach extra clauses to your policy to increase coverage for a single event, and most, if not all, companies are unwilling to add the event site's name to your existing policy as an additional insured.

Don't despair. Even though it's hard to come by, you can get extra insurance for a specified period of time, and it's relatively inexpensive.

Obtaining Extra Insurance

- **The first thing to do is read your rental contract carefully.** Make sure you understand exactly *what's* required and *when* it's required. Most facilities want $1,000,000–2,000,000 in extra liability coverage. If you don't pay attention to the insurance clauses early in the game, you'll have to play catch-up at the last moment, frantically trying to locate a carrier who will issue you additional insurance. And, if you don't supply the certificate to the facility *on time,* you may run the risk of forfeiting your event site altogether.

- **The second thing is to ask your event site's representative if the site has an insurance policy through which you can purchase the required extra coverage.** If the answer is yes, then consider purchasing it—that's the easiest route (but not necessarily the best!). The facility's extra insurance coverage may not be the least expensive and it may not provide you with the best coverage. What you need to ask is: "If one of my guests or one of the professionals working at my event causes some damage to the premises or its contents, will this extra insurance cover it?" If the answer if yes, get it in writing.

- **The third thing, if the answer is no, is to find your own coverage.** We suggest you avoid the *Yellow Pages* and call:

  R.V. Nuccio & Associates, Inc. at 1-800-ENGAGED (1-800-364-2433) or www.rvnuccio.com. They specialize in insuring special events, and can send you a brochure detailing what's offered.

Coverage starts at $95 for a wedding; the total cost will depend on what you want. Rob Nuccio's coverage is underwritten by Fireman's Fund.

Here are some of the items a typical policy might cover:

- Cancellation or postponement due to: weather, damage to the facility, sickness, failure to show of the caterer or officiant, financial reasons — even limited change-of-heart circumstances!

- Photography or videography: failure of the professional to appear, loss of original negatives, etc.

- Lost, stolen or damaged gifts

- Lost, stolen or damaged equipment rentals

- Lost, stolen or damaged bridal gown or other special attire

- Lost, stolen or damaged jewelry

- Personal liability and additional coverage

- Medical payments for injuries incurred during the event

If you use this service, let us know whether you're happy with them. Call us. We'd love to get your feedback.

It Can't Happen To Me

Don't be lulled into the notion that an event disaster can't happen to you. It could rain when you least expect it. Or your well-intentioned aunt might melt your wedding dress while ironing out a few wrinkles. Wouldn't it be nice to know that your dress, wedding photos, equipment rentals and gifts are covered? Naturally, a New Year's Eve party or a high school prom night is riskier than a wedding, but we could tell you stories of upscale parties where something did happen and a lawsuit resulted.

So even if extra insurance is not required, you may still want to consider additional coverage, especially if alcohol is being served. *You are the best predictor of your guests' behavior.* If you plan on having a wild, wonderful event, a little additional insurance could be a good thing.

Recycling

Do Your Part!

If you're wondering why we're including a brief item about recycling in a book like *Here Comes The Guide,* it's because parties and special events often generate recyclable materials and leftover food that the bride and groom don't want to take home. Nowadays, you and the caterer can feel good by donating the excess, and recycling plastic bottles, glass, metal and paper. An added benefit is that food donations are tax deductible for either you or the caterer. And if you recycle, the cost for extra garbage containers (bins) can be eliminated or reduced. To recycle, call your local recycling center to arrange a pickup.

Food donations are distributed to teenage drop-in centers, youth shelters, alcoholic treatment centers, AIDS hospices, senior centers and refugee centers throughout the region.

IMPORTANT: There are regulations that apply to the kinds of foods that can be donated and how they need to be packaged. If you plan to donate your leftovers, it's best to talk to your caterer about it or call your local food bank prior to your event to find out what their requirements for preparation and drop-off are.

We've provided a list of some well-known Northern California food banks, but you can also look online or through your phone book to find others that may be more convenient for you.

For more valuable tips about going green, read our article "It's A Nice Day for a Green Wedding." You'll find it in the "Green Weddings" category on the Wedding Checklist page on HereComesTheGuide.com.

Donation Organizations

- **San Francisco**

  Food Runners   415/929-1866
  www.foodrunners.org

  Food Bank   415/282-1900
  www.sffoodbank.org

- **Marin County**

  Food Bank   415/883-1302
  www.marinfoodbank.org

- **San Mateo/Santa Clara Counties**

  Second Harvest   650/610-0800
  www.2ndharvest.net

- **Concord**

  Food Bank of Contra Costa
  & Solano   925/676-7543
  www.foodbankccs.org

- **Oakland**

  Alameda County
  Food Bank   510/635-3663
  www.accfb.org

  Oakland Potluck   510/272-0414

- **Sacramento**

  Food Bank   916/456-1980
  www.sfbs.org

  Loaves & Fishes   916/446-0874
  www.sacloaves.org

- **Santa Cruz Area**

  Second Harvest   831/722-7110
  www.thefoodbank.org

Questions To Ask
Locations and Event Professionals

(including The Guide Bride's Wedding Checklist)

The Guide Bride's Wedding Checklist

10–12 Months To Go...

☐ Visit HereComesTheGuide.com and start planning your wedding!

☐ Work out your budget and establish your top priorities—where to save/where to splurge.

☐ Find ideas. Start browsing bridal blogs and magazines to identify your wedding style and color palette.

☐ Compile your preliminary guest list (you'll need that guest count!).

☐ Choose your wedding party—who do you want by your side at the altar?

☐ Find a venue for your ceremony and reception, and reserve your date.

☐ Now that you have a date, tell everyone to save it! For destination weddings or weddings around a holiday, consider sending out Save-the-Date cards or emails. Or create your own wedding website, and let your invitees know about it.

☐ Find a dress and begin assembling the perfect accessories. Need inspiration? Visit a bridal fair.

☐ Already feeling overwhelmed? Consider hiring a Wedding Coordinator.

☐ Assemble an all-star vendor team, maybe starting with your:
  • Caterer
  • Photographer/Videographer
  • Officiant
  When you hire a vendor, get all the details in writing!

☐ Another way to minimize stress: Start dreaming up your honeymoon...and check out our Plan A Honeymoon section on HereComesTheGuide.com.

6–9 Months To Go...

☐ Continue researching, interviewing and booking vendors. And don't forget: When you hire one make sure to put everything in writing!

  • Decide on arrangements with your Floral Designer.
  • Do a tasting and choose your wedding cake with your Cake Designer.
  • Hire the DJ/Entertainment for your ceremony, cocktail hour and reception.
  • Discuss the style and wording of your wedding invitations with a Stationer.

☐ Create your gift registry (and don't forget to update your wedding website!).

☐ Arrange hotel room blocks for out-of-town guests and book your own suite for the wedding night.

☐ Shop for bridesmaid/flower girl dresses and give your attendants clear instructions on how to place their orders.

☐ Arrange and book any necessary transportation.

☐ Go over bridal shower/bachelorette details and the guest list with your Maid of Honor/hostess.

3–5 Months To Go...

☐ Book the rehearsal and rehearsal dinner location(s). If you're including entertainment or specialty details like a groom's cake, now's the time to lock in these elements.

☐ Put together your rehearsal dinner guest list.

☐ Make childcare arrangements for your guests' kids.

☐ Reserve all necessary party rentals and linens.

☐ Order wedding favors for your guests.

☐ Shop for and reserve men's formalwear.

☐ Concentrate on finalizing the:
  • Guest list. Get everyone's mailing address.
  • Invitation wording. Confirm your invitation text with the Stationer, and consider additional stationery (programs, menu cards, place cards, thank-you cards, etc.). Schedule a pickup date for your invites.
  • Ceremony readings and vows.
  • Menu, beverage and catering details.
  • Timeline of the reception formalities.

☐ Do a Makeup & Hair trial and book your stylists. While you're at it, come up with your own beauty and fitness regimen to be camera-ready for the big day.

☐ Shop for and purchase your wedding rings.

☐ Finalize honeymoon plans and obtain all necessary documents (are you sure your passports are up to date?).

6–8 Weeks To Go...

☐ You're getting close…. Mail out those invitations! Have a game plan for recording the RSVPs and meal choices.

☐ Touch base with your vendors to confirm date, deposits and details.

☐ Start researching marriage license requirements and name-change paperwork.

☐ Begin your dress fittings. Be sure to buy the appropriate undergarments beforehand.

☐ So you think you *can't* dance? Consider taking a dance lesson with your fiancé—a good way to break in your bridal shoes!

☐ Give the wedding party a nudge—make sure they've ordered all necessary attire.

☐ Write thank-you cards for shower gifts and any early wedding gifts received.

3–5 Weeks To Go...

☐ Send out rehearsal dinner invitations. If your get-together will be informal, feel free to send an Evite.

☐ Finalize and confirm:
  • Wedding vows and readings with your Officiant.
  • Shot list with your Photographer/ Videographer.
  • Song list for ceremony, cocktail hour and reception with your DJ and/or Band/ Musicians.
  • Timeline for the reception and who's giving the toasts.
  • Wedding night and honeymoon accommodations.

☐ Obtain marriage license and complete name-change documents, if applicable.

☐ Pick up your wedding rings and proofread any engraving!

☐ If you're the traditional type, do you have something old, new, borrowed and blue?

☐ Purchase your guest book, toasting flutes, cake servers, unity candle, and all that good stuff.

☐ Have your final dress fitting. Bring your shoes and accessories for the full impact.

☐ Sigh. Hunt down whoever hasn't RSVP'd yet.

1–2 Weeks To Go...

☐ Give your caterer/venue the final guest count.

☐ Arrange seating and create the seating chart and/or place cards.

☐ Pick up your gown. Swoon.

☐ Confirm arrival times and finalize the wedding timeline with vendors and the wedding party—make sure your MOH has a copy, too.

☐ Put together your own Bridal Emergency Kit.

☐ Speaking of emergencies: Check the weather report, and if things look iffy contact your venue to make sure a contingency plan is in place.

☐ Start packing for your honeymoon. (See "weather report" above.)

☐ In desperate need of a facial or massage? Now's the time to squeeze one in.

The Day Before...

☐ Make sure all wedding-day items are packed/ laid out and ready to go! (Don't forget the rings and marriage license!)

☐ Figure out tips and final payments for vendors. Put them in clearly marked envelopes and give them to the Best Man or another person you trust to hand out at the reception.

☐ Assign someone to pack up your gifts/ belongings after the reception (don't forget the top tier of your cake!).

☐ Thank your BFF for agreeing to return your groom's tux and other rental items the day after the wedding.

☐ Enjoy a mani-pedi.

☐ Attend the rehearsal and dinner. Now's the time to give out wedding party gifts.

☐ Try to go to bed early…you need your beauty sleep tonight.

Here Comes The Guide Bride!

☐ Allow plenty of time for the bride beautification process.

☐ Do the rounds at your wedding—greet everyone and thank them for coming.

☐ Take a deep breath. Stop to appreciate your new spouse and the day that you spent so much time planning!

After the Honeymoon/Back to Reality...

☐ Write and send thank-you cards. (Don't procrastinate!)

☐ Complete your registry and exchange any unwanted or duplicate gifts.

☐ Have your wedding dress cleaned and preserved by a reputable company.

☐ Keep in touch with your Photographer/ Videographer to work on albums, DVDs, etc.

☐ Enjoy wedded bliss…

Questions to Ask an Event Location

Here Comes The Guide is a fantastic resource to help you find the location to host your wedding, rehearsal dinner or company party. Even with all the info we provide, though, you'll need to address your specific needs with each venue you visit to come up with a winner.

The following list of questions and tips will help you navigate through your location search. Print them out and use them as a guide while you're talking with a site contact or reviewing a site information packet. Feel free to add questions that relate to your particular event (e.g. "Can my dog be the ring bearer in my ceremony?") Make sure to get everything in writing in your final contract! **Don't forget to have a notebook or your planning binder handy so that you can record answers to all these questions.**

1. What dates are available in the month I'm considering?

2. How many people can this location accommodate?

3. What is the rental fee and what is included in that price? Is there a discount for booking an off-season date or Sunday through Friday?

4. How much is the deposit, when is it due, and is it refundable? What's the payment plan for the entire bill?

5. Can I hold my ceremony here, too? Is there an additional charge? Is the ceremony site close to the reception site? Is there a bride's changing area? How much time is allocated for the rehearsal?

6. Is the site handicap accessible? (To be asked if you have guests with mobility issues.)

7. What's the cancellation policy? *NOTE: Some places will refund most of your deposit if you cancel far enough in advance (often 60 days), since there's still a chance they can rent the space. After a certain date, though, you may not be able to get a refund—at least not a full one.*

8. What's your weather contingency plan for outdoor spaces?

9. How long will I have use of the event space(s) I reserve? Is there an overtime fee if I stay longer? Is there a minimum or maximum rental time?

10. Can I move things around and decorate to suit my purposes, or do I have to leave everything as is? Are there decoration guidelines/restrictions? Can I use real candles? *TIP: Keep the existing décor in mind when planning your own decorations so that they won't clash. If your event is in December, ask what the venue's holiday décor will be.*

11. What time can my vendors start setting up on the day of the wedding? Is it possible to start the setup the day before? How early can deliveries be made? How much time will I have for décor setup? Does the venue provide assistance getting gifts or décor back to a designated car, hotel room, etc. after the event has concluded?

12. Do you provide a coat check service (especially important for winter weddings)? If not, is there an area that can be used and staffed for that purpose?

13. Is there an outdoor space where my guests can mingle, and can it be heated and/or protected from the elements if necessary? Is there a separate indoor "socializing" space?

14. Do you have an in-house caterer or a list of "preferred" caterers, or do I need to provide my own? Even if there is an in-house caterer, do I have the option of using an outside caterer instead?

15. If I hire my own caterer, are kitchen facilities available for them? *NOTE: Caterers charge extra if they have to haul in refrigerators and stoves.*

16. Are tables, linens, chairs, plates, silverware and glassware provided, or will I have to rent them myself or get them through my caterer?

17. What is the food and beverage cost on a per/person basis? What is the service charge?

18. Can we do a food tasting prior to finalizing our menu selection? If so, is there an additional charge?

19. Can I bring in a cake from an outside cake maker or must I use a cake made on the premises? Is there a cake-cutting fee? If I use a cake made on site is the fee waived? Do you provide special cake-cutting utensils?

20. Can I bring my own wine, beer or champagne, and is there a corkage fee if I do? Can I bring in other alcohol?

21. Are you licensed to provide alcohol service? If so, is alcohol priced per person? By consumption? Are there additional charges for bar staff? Is there a bar minimum that must be met before the conclusion of the event? What is the average bar tab for the number of people attending my event? *NOTE: Some facilities (private estates and wineries in particular) aren't licensed to serve hard alcohol. You may need to get permission from the location to bring in an outside beverage catering company.*

22. Are there restrictions on what kind of music I can play, or a time by which the music must end? Can the venue accommodate a DJ or live band? *TIP: Check where the outlets are located in your event space, because that will help you figure out where the band can set up and where other vendors can hook up their equipment. You don't want the head table to block the only outlet in the room.*

23. Is there parking on site? If so, is it complimentary? Do you offer valet parking, and what is the charge? If there is no parking on site, where will my guests park? Are cabs easily accessible from the venue?? If a shuttle service is needed, can you assist with setting it up? *TIP: You should have the venue keep track of the number of cars parked for your event and add the total valet gratuity to your final bill so that your guests won't have to tip.*

24. How many restrooms are there? *TIP: You should have at least 4 restrooms per 100 people.*

25. Do you offer on-site coordination? If so, what services are included and is there an additional charge for them? Will the coordinator supervise day-of? How much assistance can I get with the setup/décor?

26. What security services do you offer? Do I need to hire my own security guards, or does the site hire them or have them on staff? *TIP: In general, you should have 2 security guards for the first 100 guests and 1 more for every additional 100 guests.*

27. Does the venue have liability insurance? *NOTE: If someone gets injured during the party, you don't want to be held responsible—if the site doesn't have insurance, you'll need to get your own. For info on insurance go to www.rvnuccio.com.*

28. Can I hire my own vendors (caterer, coordinator, DJ, etc.), or must I select from a preferred vendor list? If I can bring my own, do you have a list of recommended vendors? *TIP: Check out the pre-screened vendors featured in this book and on HereComesTheGuide.com. They're all top event professionals who have passed our extensive reference check and been Certified By The Guide.*

29. What overnight accommodations do you provide? Do you offer a discount for booking multiple rooms? Do you provide a complimentary room or upgrade for the newlyweds? What are the nearest hotels to the venue? *TIP: Some venues have partnerships with local hotels that offer a discount if you book a block of rooms.*

30. Do you have signage or other aids to direct guests to my event?

31. Do you have a recycling policy?

More Tips:

- If you really love the site, ask the venue representative to put together a proposal with all the pricing and policies—including the tax and service charge—so you have an idea of the basic cost.

- Bring a digital or video camera with you when you visit locations. You can mention each location and its event spaces as you video a site; if you're using a digital camera you'll need to organize the photos by location name when you get home. After seeing a series of places it's easy to confuse them. Having a photographic record will help you remember what was special about each site.

- Pay attention to the venue as a whole: Check out everything, including the restrooms, the foyer, the dressing rooms, the outdoor lighting and even the kitchen. You want to be sure your vision can be realized at this location. If possible, make arrangements with the site representative to visit the venue when it's set up for a wedding.

- GET EVERYTHING IN WRITING. Your date is not officially reserved until you sign a contract and, in many cases, give a deposit—even if a site contact says you don't need to worry about it. Once you've found THE PLACE, make sure you ask what is required to get your booking locked in and then follow through on satisfying those requirements. And don't assume that just because the site coordinator said you can have 4 votive candles per table you'll get them. Before you sign a contract, read the fine print and make sure it includes everything you and the site contact agreed on. As new things are added or changed in your contract, have the updated version printed out and signed by you and the site representative. Also, document all your conversations in emails and keep your correspondence.

For PDF versions of these QUESTIONS TO ASK, visit www.HereComesTheGuide.com

Questions to Ask a Wedding Planner

In the first flush of joy after your engagement, you'll probably begin browsing magazines and wedding websites…and soon feel buried by a blizzard of checklists and a daunting array of decisions. That's when you and your fiancé might want to think about hiring a professional wedding planner.

Good idea. Depending on your budget and needs, you can contract:

- a full-service planner to arrange every detail

- someone to assist you only in choosing your wedding location and vendors

- a day-of coordinator (which really means 30 days before your wedding)

NOTE: Many locations have in-house coordinators, but make sure you're clear on exactly what level of service they provide. Venue coordinators usually just handle day-of issues and offer a list of their preferred vendors, so having your own planner may still be a great help.

Even though hiring a planner is an added cost, they often end up saving you money in the long run. And no doubt about it—the right wedding planner can definitely save you time and stress (priceless!).

Before interviewing potential wedding planners, you and your fiancé should have an idea of:

- How much money you have in your budget

- How many people you would like to invite

- Your preferred wedding date

- Your vision for your wedding (*NOTE: If you aren't sure yet don't worry—getting help with this is one of the reasons why you're hiring a wedding planner!*)

After each interview is complete, ask yourselves:

- Did we feel heard?

- Does the planner understand our vision?

- Did we get a strong sense she will work with our budget?

- Was there a good connection and did our personalities mesh well?

Listen to your gut. If an interview doesn't feel right, then maybe that person just isn't a good fit for you. Your wedding planner is the vendor you'll be spending the most time with, so it's important to pick someone who's compatible with you and your fiancé.

Now, here are THE QUESTIONS!

Getting to Know a Planner

1. Do you have our wedding date open? If so, do you anticipate any issues with the date such as weather, travel for our guests, difficulty booking a venue, etc.?

2. What made you want to be a wedding planner?

3. Describe the most challenging wedding you planned and how you handled the problems that came up.

4. How would you rate your problem-solving skills?

5. How would you rate your communication skills?

6. Are you a certified wedding planner? If so, where did you get certified? What is your educational background?

7. Are you a member of any wedding association(s)? If so, does your association require you to satisfy yearly education requirements?

8. How long have you been in business? Do you have a business license?

9. How many full-scale weddings have you planned? When was your last one?

10. How many wedding clients do you take on in a year? How many do you expect to have during the month of our wedding?

11. Is wedding planning your full-time job? If it's part-time, what is your other job?

Working With the Venue

12. Have you ever worked at the venue we've chosen?

13. If our event is outdoors, what contingency plan would you have for bad weather? (Describe an event where you had weather issues and how you resolved them.)

Hiring Other Vendors

14. Are we required to book only the vendors you recommend or do we have the freedom to hire someone even if you haven't worked with them before?

15. Do you take a commission or discount from any of the vendors you would refer us to?

16. Will you be present at all of the vendor meetings and will you assist us in reviewing all of the vendor contracts and making sure everything is in order?

17. Will you invoice us for all the vendor fees or will we need to pay each one of them ourselves?

18. For the vendors who will be on site the day of our wedding, can I provide you with checks for final payment that you will distribute to them?

19. If issues arise with the vendors before, during or after our wedding, will you handle them or are we responsible for this?

Scope of Work

20. What kind planning do you offer? Logistical only (i.e. organizational—handling things like the timeline and floor plan) or Design and Logistical (i.e. bringing a client's vision to life as well as taking care of all the organizational aspects of the wedding)?

21. If you just do logistical planning, can you refer us to a vendor who can assist us with event design? *(NOTE: Floral designers often do full event design, as do vendors who specialize in design.)*

22. Will you handle every aspect of the planning or can we do some things on our own? In other words, what parts of the planning will we be responsible for?

23. Will you be the person on site the day of our wedding or will it be another planner? How many assistants will you have?

24. In case of an emergency that prevents you from being at our wedding, who will be the backup planner? What are their qualifications?

25. What time will you arrive and depart on the day of our wedding?

26. Will you stay on site after our wedding to make sure everything has been broken down and all vendors have left the location?

27. Will you provide us with a timeline of the wedding and a floor plan of the wedding venue?

28. Do you offer different package options or is everything customized based on what we're looking for?

29. How many meetings and phone calls are included in our package?

30. Is the wedding day rehearsal included in your services?

31. Do any of your packages include planning the rehearsal dinner and/or post-wedding brunch? If not, would you provide that service and what would be the extra cost to include it in our contract?

32. Do any of your packages include honeymoon planning? If not, would you provide that service and what would be the extra cost to include it in our contract?

33. Do any of your packages include assistance with finding my wedding dress and wedding party attire? If not, would you provide that service and what would be the extra cost to include it in our contract?

Getting Down to Business

34. Once we book with you, how quickly can we expect to receive the contract?

35. After we give you our budget, will you provide us with a breakdown of how the money is going to be allocated?

36. As changes are made to our plans, will you update us with a revised estimate and updated contract?

37. How do you charge for your services? Hourly, percentage of the wedding cost, or flat rate?

38. Can you provide a detailed list of all the items included in your fee?

39. What is your payment policy? Do you accept credit cards?

40. How much of a deposit is required to book your services? When is the final payment due?

41. Are there any fees that won't be included in your proposal that we should be aware of?

42. What is your refund or cancellation policy?

43. Can you provide a list of references? *NOTE: Any experienced coordinator should be able to give you plenty of references. For a list of Coordinators/ Wedding Planners you can trust, see the ones we've featured in this book and on HereComesTheGuide. com. They've all passed our difficult certification process with flying colors! Brides told us how much they loved working with them, so we wanted to recommend them to you.*

44. Can you provide us with a portfolio and/or video of weddings you have done?

Questions to Ask a Wedding Photographer

You've put so much time and effort into planning your wedding you'll want every special moment captured for your photo album. But how do you know which photographer is right for you? Whether you're considering any of our *Certified By The Guide* wedding photographers or another professional, you need to do your homework.

Here are the questions you should ask those photographers who've made your short list, to ensure that the one you ultimately choose is a good fit for you and your wedding.

The Basics

1. Do you have my date available? *NOTE: Obviously, if the answer is NO and you're not willing or able to change your date, don't bother asking the rest of these questions.*

2. How far in advance do I need to book with you?

3. How long have you been in business?

4. How many weddings have you shot? Have you done many that were similar to mine in size and style?

5. How would you describe your photography style (e.g. traditional, photojournalistic, creative)? *NOTE: It's helpful to know the differences between wedding photography styles so that you can discuss your preferences with your photographer. For descriptions of the various styles, see the next page.*

6. How would you describe your working style? *NOTE: The answer should help you determine whether this is a photographer who blends into the background and shoots what unfolds naturally, or creates a more visible presence by taking charge and choreographing shots.*

7. What do you think distinguishes your work from that of other photographers?

8. Do you have a portfolio I can review? Are all of the images yours, and is the work recent?

9. What type of equipment do you use?

10. Are you shooting in digital or film format or both? *NOTE: The general consensus seems to be that either format yields excellent photos in the hands of an experienced professional, and that most people can't tell the difference between film and digital images anyway.*

11. Do you shoot in color and black & white? Both? Infrared? *NOTE: Photographers who shoot in a digital format can make black & white or sepia versions of color photos.*

12. Can I give you a list of specific shots we would like?

13. Can you put together a slideshow of the engagement session (along with other photos the couple provides) and show it during the cocktail hour? What about an "instant" slideshow of the ceremony?

14. What information do you need from me before the wedding day?

15. Have you ever worked with my florist? DJ? Co-ordinator, etc.? *NOTE: Great working relationships between vendors can make things go more smoothly. It's especially helpful if your videographer and photographer work well together.*

16. May I have a list of references? *NOTE: The photographer should not hesitate to provide this.*

The Shoot

17. Are you the photographer who will shoot my wedding? If so, will you have any assistants with you on that day? If not, who will be taking the pictures and can I meet them before my wedding? *NOTE: You should ask the questions on this list of whoever is going to be the primary photographer at your event, and that photographer's name should be on your contract.*

18. Do you have backup equipment? What about a backup plan if you (or my scheduled photographer) are unable to shoot my wedding for some reason?

19. If my wedding site is out of your area, do you charge a travel fee and what does that cover?

20. Are you photographing other events on the same day as mine?

21. How will you (and your assistants) be dressed? *NOTE: The photographer and his/her staff should look professional and fit in with the style of your event.*

22. Is it okay if other people take photos while you're taking photos?

23. Have you ever worked at my wedding site before? If not, do you plan to check it out in advance? *NOTE: Photographers who familiarize themselves with a location ahead of time will be prepared for any lighting issues or restrictions, and will know how best to incorporate the site's architectural elements into the photos.*

24. What time will you arrive at the site and for how long will you shoot?

25. If my event lasts longer than expected, will you stay? Is there an additional charge?

Packages, Proofs and Prints

26. What packages do you offer?

27. Can I customize a package based on my needs?

28. Do you include engagement photos in your packages?

29. What type of album designs do you offer? Do you provide any assistance in creating an album?

30. Do you provide retouching, color adjustment or other corrective services?

31. How long after the wedding will I get the proofs? Will they be viewable online? On a CD?

32. What is the ordering process?

33. How long after I order my photos/album will I get them?

34. Will you give me the negatives or the digital images, and is there a fee for that?

Contracts and Policies

35. When will I receive a written contract? *TIP: Don't book a photographer—or any vendor—who won't provide a written contract.*

36. How much of a deposit do you require and when is it due? Do you offer a payment plan?

37. What is your refund/cancellation policy?

38. Do you have liability insurance?

Questions to Ask Yourself:

1. Do I feel a connection with this photographer as well as his/her photos? Are our personalities a good match?

2. Am I comfortable with this person's work and communication style?

3. Has this photographer listened well and addressed all my concerns?

Check references. *Ask the photographer for at least 5 references, preferably of couples whose weddings were similar to yours in size and/or style. Getting feedback from several people who have actually hired the photographer in question can really help you decide if that person is right for you. Be sure to check out the photographers in this book and on HereComesTheGuide. com. They're some of the best in the business and have all been Certified By The Guide.*

Photography Style Glossary

Though there are no standard "dictionary definitions" of photographic styles, it's still a good idea to have an understanding of the following approaches before you interview photographers:

Traditional, Classic: The main idea behind this timeless style is to produce posed photographs for display in a portrait album. The photographer works from a "shot list," ensuring he or she covers all the elements the bride and groom have requested. To make sure every detail of the shots is perfect, the photographer and her assistants not only adjust their equipment, but also the background, the subject's body alignment, and even the attire.

Photojournalism: Originally favored by the news media, this informal, reality-based approach is the current rage in wedding photography. Rather than posing your pictures, the photographer follows you and your guests throughout the wedding day, capturing events as they unfold in order to tell the story of your wedding. The photographer has to be able to fade into the background and become "invisible" to the crowd in order to get these candid or unposed shots. Since the photojournalist does not give direction, he'll need a keen eye and a willingness to "do what it takes to get the shot."

Illustrative Photography: This style, which is often used for engagement photos, is a pleasing blend of traditional and photojournalistic, with an emphasis on composition, lighting and background. The photographer places subjects together in an interesting environment and encourages them to relax and interact. Illustrative captures some of the spontaneity of candids, while offering the technical control of posed shots.

Portraiture: Traditional photographers generally excel at the precision required in portraiture—formal, posed pictures that emphasize one or more people. Couples interested in a more edgy result may prefer Fine Art Portraiture, with its dramatic lighting, unique angles and European flavor.

High Fashion: Commercial photographers excel at creating striking, simple photographs that dramatize the subject—and, of course, her clothes! Though not a style generally included in wedding photography, you may want to choose a photographer with high fashion experience if looking artsy and glamorous while showing off your dress is important to you.

Natural Light: Rather than using a camera flash, photographers use the natural light found in a setting, usually daylight. The look is warm and, well, natural—yet the photographer must be skilled to deal with shadows and other lighting challenges.

Questions to Ask a Caterer

Besides your location, the food and drink for your wedding bash will probably consume the largest portion of your wedding budget. Catering costs are usually presented as "per-person" charges, sometimes abbreviated in wedding brochures as "pp" after the amount. But be aware—the per-person charge often doesn't include everything: Tax and the gratuity (sometimes called the "service charge") might be extra, and there may also be separate per-person charges for the meal, drinks, hors d'oeuvres, and even setup. So your actual per-person charge might end up being considerably more than you expect. Bring your calculator along when meeting with potential caterers to help you arrive at the real bottom line.

There's more to consider. Nowadays, many caterers offer a range of services in addition to catering. Some are actual "event producers," providing props, special effects, décor—in other words, complete event design. They might also be able to assist in finding a location, coordinating your affair, or lining up vendors. One thing a caterer can't do, however, is cook up a 5-course Beef Wellington dinner for $20 per person. When planning your menu, be realistic about what you can serve given your budget and the size of your guest list.

A lot of factors come into play when selecting a caterer, so don't be afraid to ask as many questions as you need to. You can refer to the following list, whether your potential caterer works at your event facility or you're hiring them independently.

The Basics

1. Do you have my date open?

2. How many weddings do you do per year, and how long have you been in business?

3. Have you done events at my location? *TIP: If you haven't chosen your location yet, ask the caterer if they can help you select one.*

4. Are you licensed by the state of California? Are you licensed to serve alcohol?

5. Will I need any permits for my event? If so, will you handle obtaining them?

6. Will you provide a banquet manager to coordinate the meal service or an on-site coordinator who will run the entire event?

7. Can you assist with other aspects of the wedding like selecting other vendors, event design (e.g. specialty lighting, elaborate décor, theme events, etc.)?

Food & Presentation

8. Given my budget, guest count and event style, what food choices would you recommend? Do you specialize in certain cuisines?

9. Do we have to work off a preset menu or can you create a custom menu for our event? If I have a special dish I'd like served, would you accommodate that?

10. Do you offer event packages or is everything à la carte? What exactly do your packages include?

11. Do you use all fresh produce, meat, fish, etc.? Can you source organic or sustainably farmed ingredients?

12. Can you accommodate dietary restrictions, such as kosher, vegan, etc.?

13. What décor do you provide for appetizer stations or buffet tables?

14. Do you offer package upgrades such as chocolate fountains, ice sculptures, cappuccino machines or specialty displays?

15. Can you do theme menus (e.g. barbecue, luau, etc.)? Would you also provide the décor?

16. What's the difference in cost between passed appetizers and appetizer stations? What's the price difference between a buffet and a sit-down meal? If we have a buffet, are there any stations that cost extra, like a carving station? *NOTE: Don't automatically assume that a buffet is going to be the less expensive option. Ask your caterer which type of service is more affordable for you, given the menu you're planning.*

17. How much do you charge for children's meals?

18. How much do you charge for vendor meals?

19. Do you do wedding cakes? If so, is this included in the per-person meal price or is it extra?

20. Can you show me photos of cakes you've done in the past?

21. If I decide not to serve cake, can you provide a dessert display instead?

22. If we use an outside cake designer, do you charge a cake-cutting fee?

23. Do you do food tastings and is there an extra charge for this?

24. Do you handle rental equipment such as tables, chairs, etc.?

25. What types of linens, glassware, plates and flatware do you provide? *NOTE: Some low-budget caterers have basic packages that use disposable dinnerware instead of the real thing, so make sure you know exactly what you'll be getting.*

26. Can you provide presentation upgrades such as chair covers, lounge furniture, Chiavari chairs, etc.? What would be the additional fees?

27. What is your policy on cleanup? *TIP: Be very clear about what "cleanup" means and who's responsible for handling it—and be sure to get it in writing. We've heard many tales about caterers that left dirty dishes, trash and uneaten food behind. In most cases, when you rent a location it will be YOUR responsibility to leave the place in acceptable condition. You want to spend your wedding night with your honey, not picking up empty bottles from the lawn!*

28. If there is leftover food from my event, can we have it wrapped up for guests to take home or have it delivered to a local shelter?

Drink

29. Do you provide alcoholic beverages and bartenders? Can you accommodate specialty cocktails?

30. What brands of alcohol will be served?

31. Can we provide the alcohol and you provide the bar labor?

32. Do you charge a corkage fee if we provide our own wine or champagne?

33. How do you charge for alcoholic and non-alcoholic beverages? Per consumption or per person? Which is more cost-effective?

34. Is the champagne toast after the ceremony included in your meal packages or is it extra?

35. Will your staff serve the wine with dinner?

36. How long will alcohol be served?

37. Is coffee and tea service included with the per-person meal charge? What brands of each do you offer and do they include decaf and herbal tea options?

Business Matters

38. What is the ratio of servers to guests?

39. How will the servers be dressed?

40. How is your pricing broken down (e.g. food, bar, cake-cutting, tax, gratuity)? *NOTE: Usually tax and a service charge are tacked on to your final cost. The service charge, which can range 18–23%, is used to tip the staff. And in many states, the service charge itself is taxable.*

41. How much time do you require for setting up and breaking down my event, and are there extra fees for this?

42. If my event runs longer than contracted, what are your overtime fees?

43. What is the last date by which I can give you a final guaranteed guest count?

44. What is your payment policy? Do you accept credit cards?

45. How much of a deposit is required to hold my date? When is the final payment due?

46. Are there any fees that won't be included in the proposal that we should be aware of?

47. Once we book with you, how quickly can we expect a contract? And if we make changes to menu choices or other items, will you update us with a revised estimate and contract?

48. What is your refund or cancellation policy?

49. Can you provide a list of recent references? *TIP: See the caterers we feature in this book and on HereComesTheGuide.com. These pre-screened companies provide great food and service, and they all passed our rigorous certification process with flying colors.*

Questions to Ask a Floral Designer

Floral designers do much more than just supply the bouquet! They help create the look and mood for your wedding ceremony, as well as centerpieces and other table decorations for the reception. They add the floral flourishes for the wedding party (don't forget that corsage for Grandma!), and some may even work with your cake designer to provide embellishments.

Before sitting down with a floral designer, you should already have reserved your ceremony and reception venue. That way you'll be able to discuss how much additional floral décor will be needed to either achieve a specific look at your site or complement an existing garden and/or room aesthetic.

Another must: Don't design the wedding bouquet until you've ordered your wedding dress. Since that task will hopefully be completed at least 6 months before your wedding date (hint, hint!), you should have plenty of time to work out the details of both your accessories and floral décor.

So where to start? Do a little research prior to interviewing floral artists by visiting the websites or shops of vendors you're considering. You want to know that whomever you hire can create bouquets and arrangements that suit your style. (And do explore our "Brides Want to Know: Bouquet Brainstorm" for more GUIDElines and inspiration.)

Once you've compiled your short list of contenders, use these questions to zero in on your final choice:

The Basics

1. Do you have my date open?

2. Have you done events at my ceremony and reception location(s) before? If not, are you familiar with the sites?

3. How long have you been in business?

4. How many weddings have you done?

5. Where did you receive your training?

6. How many other weddings or events will you schedule on the same day?

7. Will you be doing my arrangements yourself or would it be another floral designer?

8. What design styles (e.g. ikebana, traditional, modern, trendy, European, Oriental) do you work in?

9. Can you work with my budget?

10. What recommendations can you give me to maximize my budget?

11. Do you offer specific packages or is everything customized?

12. Can you provide me with 3–4 recent brides that I can contact for references?

The Flowers

13. What flowers are in season for the month I am getting married?

14. Based on my color scheme and budget, what flowers do you recommend?

15. Is there a difference in price if I use one type of flower vs. a mixed arrangement or bouquet?

16. If I request it, can you provide any organic, pesiticide-free or sustainably grown varieties? *TIP: Organic roses cost more, but last so much longer!*

17. What are the different kinds of wraps (called "collars" in florist-speak) you can do for my bouquet?

18. What about coordinating boutonnières, bridesmaid flowers, and centerpieces? Can you suggest anything special to coordinate with the theme/venue/season of my event?

19. What other décor can you provide (aisle runner, candelabras, trees, arches, votives, mirrors, etc.)? How will these items affect the overall cost?

20. If I give you a picture of a bouquet and/or arrangement that I like, can you recreate it?

21. Do you have photos or live examples of florals designed in the style I want?

22. Can you do sketches or mockups of the arrangements you've described before I sign the contract?

23. Will you work with my cake designer if I decide to add flowers to my wedding cake? If so, is there an additional setup fee for this?

24. How far in advance of the wedding will you create the bouquets and arrangements, and how are they stored?

25. Can you assist me in the preservation of my bouquet after the wedding? If not, can you recommend someone?

The Costs

26. Do you charge a delivery fee?

27. Do you have an extra charge for the setup and breakdown of the floral décor?

28. Is there an extra fee if I need you to stay throughout the ceremony to move arrangements to the reception site?

29. Are there any additional fees that have not already been taken into account?

The Contract

30. How far in advance do I need to secure your services? What is the deposit required to secure my date?

31. Will you provide me with an itemized list of all the elements we've discussed, along with prices?

32. When can I expect to receive my contract from you?

33. What is your refund policy if for some reason I need to cancel my order?

Useful Tips:

• Prior to meeting with potential floral designers, have your color scheme finalized; create a list of the kinds of flowers you like; and have some examples (pictures from magazines or photos) of the kind of bouquets and arrangements that appeal to you.

• After you've met with each floral designer ask yourself, "Did the florist answer all my questions to my satisfaction?" "Do I feel like the florist really listened and understood my vision?" "Am I comfortable with this person?"

• Once you've booked your floral designer you'll want to provide them with a picture of your dress and swatches or photos of the bridesmaids dresses and the linens you'll be using.

Don't forget to browse our Floral Designers in this book and on HereComesTheGuide.com! They all got rave reviews during our rigorous certification process, and received the Certified By The Guide seal of approval.

Questions to Ask a Cake Designer

Next to your dress, the cake is probably a wedding's most important icon. And whether you want a traditional multi-tiered confection, a miniature Statue of Liberty (hey, that's where he proposed!) or a cupcake tower, your wedding cake should reflect your personality. Use the following questions as a guide when evaluating a potential cake designer. If you're not familiar with cake terms, please see the cake glossary on page 29.

Business Matters

1. Do you have my wedding date open?

2. How many wedding cakes do you schedule on the same day? *NOTE: You want to feel comfortable that your designer is sufficiently staffed to handle the number of cakes they've scheduled to deliver and set up on your date.*

3. How do you price your cakes? By the slice? Does the cost vary depending on the design and flavors I choose?

4. What is your minimum per-person cake cost?

5. What recommendations can you give me to maximize my budget?

6. Do you have a "menu" of cakes and prices that I can take with me?

7. What are the fees for delivery and setup of the cake? Do you decorate the cake table, too?

8. What do you do if the cake gets damaged in transit to or at my reception site?

9. Do you provide or rent cake toppers, a cake-cutting knife, cake stands, etc.? What are the fees?

10. How far in advance should I order my cake?

11. How much is the deposit and when is it due?

12. When is the final payment due?

13. Are there any additional fees that I should be aware of?

14. What is your refund policy if for some reason I need to cancel my order? What if I'm not happy with the cake?

15. When can I expect to receive my contract from you?

Background Check

16. How long have you been in business? Are you licensed and insured?

17. How many weddings have you done?

18. Where did you receive your training?

19. Can you provide me with 3–4 recent brides that I can contact for references? *TIP: Check out the cake vendors featured in this book and on HereComesTheGuide.com. They're some of the best cake designers in Northern California and they've all been Certified By The Guide.*

The Cake

20. Do you have a portfolio of your work I can view, and did you make all the cakes in it?

21. What are your specialties?

22. Can you design a custom cake to match my theme, dress or color scheme, or do I select from set designs?

23. If I provide you with a picture of what I'd like, can you recreate it? Does it cost extra for a custom design?

24. I have an old family cake recipe. Can you adapt it for my wedding cake design?

25. If I don't have a clear vision of what I would like, can you offer some design ideas based on my theme and budget?

26. What flavors and fillings do you offer?

27. What are the different ingredients you typically use? Do you offer all organic or vegan options? *TIP: Quality ingredients cost more, but the investment is worth it—the cake will taste better.*

28. Do you have cake tastings? Is there a charge?

29. Do you do both fondant and buttercream icing?

30. Are there any other icing options I should consider? Which do you recommend for my cake design?

31. Can you create sugar paste, gum paste or chocolate flowers? If I decide to have fresh flowers on my cake will you work with my florist or will you obtain and arrange the flowers yourself?

32. Will you preserve the top tier of my cake for my first wedding anniversary or do you provide a special cake for the occasion?

33. Can you make a groom's cake? Is this priced the same as my wedding cake?

34. How much in advance of the wedding is the cake actually made? Do you freeze your cakes? *NOTE: Wedding cakes usually take at least a couple of days to make.*

Useful Tips:

- Arrange a consultation with your potential cake designer in person, and do a tasting before you sign a contract. *NOTE: Not all cake tastings are complimentary.*

- Make sure your cake designer specializes in wedding cakes. A wedding cake is generally much more elaborate than a birthday cake from your local bakery Your cake professional should have special training in constructing this type of cake.

- In general, you should order your cake 6–8 months prior to your wedding.

- You might be able to save money by choosing one overall flavor for your cake, or by having a small cake for display and the cake cutting accompanied by a sheet cake to serve to your guests.

Wedding Cake Glossary

Icings

Buttercream: It's rich and creamy, is easily colored or flavored, and is used for fancy decorations like shells, swags, basketweaves, icing flowers, etc. Since it's made almost entirely of butter (hence the name), buttercream has a tendency to melt in extreme heat, so it's not recommended for outdoor weddings.

Fondant: Martha Stewart's favorite. This icing looks smooth and stiff and is made with gelatin and corn syrup to give it its helmet-like appearance (it's really very cool looking). It looks best when decorated with marzipan fruits, gum paste flowers, or a simple ribbon, like Martha likes to do. Although not as tasty as buttercream or ganache, fondant does not need refrigeration so it's the perfect icing to serve at your beach wedding.

Royal Icing: A mix of confectioner's sugar and milk or egg whites, royal icing is what the faces of gingerbread men are decorated with. It's white, shiny and hard, and does not need to be refrigerated. It's used for decorations like dots and latticework.

Ganache: This chocolate and heavy cream combination is very dark, and has the consistency of store-bought chocolate icing. It can be poured over cakes for a glass-like chocolate finish or used as filling (it stands up wonderfully between cake layers). Due to the ingredients, however, it's unstable—don't use it in hot or humid weather or the icing will slide right off the cake.

Whipped Cream: Delicious, but by far the most volatile, fresh whipped cream is usually not recommended for wedding cakes because they have to be out of the fridge for so long. If you really want to use it (it looks extremely white and fresh, which goes beautifully with real flowers) just keep it in the fridge until the very last second.

Decorations

Marzipan: An Italian paste made of almonds, sugar and egg whites that is molded into flowers and fruits to decorate the cake. They're usually brightly colored and very sugary. Marzipan can also be used as icing.

Gum Paste: This paste, made from gelatin, cornstarch, and sugar, produces the world's most realistic, edible fruit and flower decorations. Famous cake designers like Sylvia Weinstock are huge fans of gum paste. One nice benefit: these decorations last for centuries in storage.

Piping: Piping is ideal for icing decorations like dotted Swiss, basketweave, latticework, and shells. It comes out of a pastry bag fitted with different tips to create these different looks, which can range from simple polka dots to a layered weave that you'd swear is a wicker basket.

Pulled Sugar: If you boil sugar, water, and corn syrup it becomes malleable and the most beautiful designs can be created. Roses and bows that have been made from pulled sugar look like silk or satin—they're so smooth and shiny.

Dragees: These hard little sugar balls are painted with edible gold or silver paint, and they look truly stunning on a big ol' wedding cake.

Questions to Ask a DJ or Live Entertainment

Too often choosing the entertainment is left to the end of your overwhelming "Wedding To Do List"—but it shouldn't be. Not only does music set the appropriate mood, but a skilled Master or Mistress of Ceremonies will gracefully guide your guests from one spotlight moment to another. And practically speaking, the best performers are often booked well in advance—so shake your groove thing, or you may be stuck doing the chicken dance with Uncle Edgar.

To get you started, we've put together this list of questions that will help you evaluate a DJ, band, or other entertainer. Note that rather than interviewing a specific performer or DJ yourself, you might be dealing with an entertainment agency rep.

The Basics

1. Do you have my date open?

2. Have you done events at my ceremony and/or reception location before? If not, are you familiar with them?

3. How long have you been in business? *NOTE: If you are interviewing a live band, you'll want to ask how long the musicians have played together. However, if you work with a reputable agency, instead of booking a specific band you'll most likely be getting seasoned professionals brought together for your event. Even though all the band members may not have played together before, they're professional musicians who are able to work together and sound fantastic anyway. The key is to make sure you book the specific singer and/or bandleader that you liked in the demo. The players will take their cues from them.*

4. How many weddings have you done? How many do you do in an average weekend?

5. What sets you apart from your competition?

6. Are there any other services that you provide, such as lighting design?

7. How far in advance do I need to secure your services?

8. Can you provide me with 3–4 recent brides that I can contact for references?

Pricing and Other Business Details

9. What is your pricing? Does this include setup and breakdown between ceremony and reception locations?

10. How much is the deposit and when is it due? When is the final payment due?

11. If the event lasts longer than scheduled, what are the overtime charges?

12. What is the continuous music charge? *NOTE: For bands, bookings traditionally run for 4 hours divided into 4 sets, each lasting 45 minutes with a 15-minute break. If you want "continuous music," i.e. with band members trading breaks, there is usually an additional charge.*

13. When can I expect to receive my contract from you?

14. Are there any additional fees that could accrue that I am not taking into account, like travel expenses or charges for special musical requests? (One performer was asked to prepare an entire set of songs from *Phantom of the Opera!* Yes, he charged extra.)

15. What is your refund policy if for some reason I need to cancel or alter my date?

16. Do you carry liability insurance? *NOTE: This usually only applies to production companies that also supply lighting, effects, etc.*

17. If I hire musicians for the ceremony and want them to play at the wedding rehearsal, what is the extra charge?

The Music

18. Do you have a DVD of your music or a video from a prior wedding where you performed?

19. Can you assist me in choosing the music for my processional, recessional, father-daughter dance, etc.?

20. How extensive is your music library or song list? What genres can you cover? Can I give you a specific list of songs I want or don't want played?

21. Are we guaranteed to have the performer(s) of our choice at our event? *SEE NUMBER 3 ABOVE. As mentioned, many bands hired by an agency are made up of members who may not play together regularly. Even set bands often have substitute players. If there are specific performers (singer, harpist, guitarist, etc.) that you want, make sure that your contract includes them. Of course, illness or other circumstances may still preclude their being able to perform at your event.*

22. If the DJ or one of the band members scheduled for my event is unable to perform for some reason, do you have a backup replacement ready to go?

23. Can you provide wireless mics for the ceremony?

24. Does any of your equipment require special electrical outlets that I need to inform my wedding site about?

25. Do you bring backup equipment?

26. What kind of space or stage do you require for the DJ or band? If my site doesn't provide what you need, will you make arrangements for the stage or am I responsible for renting it? *NOTE: a band will require a specific amount of square feet per band member.*

27. How much time will you need for setup, sound check and breakdown on the day of the event?

28. What music will be provided during the breaks? *NOTE: If you have a preference, make it known. If you want them to play your home-burned CD mix, be sure to test it on their equipment first because not all CDs will play on every system.*

29. How many people will you staff for my event?

Useful Tips:

- Discuss with your site manager any restrictions that might affect your event, like noise limits, a music curfew and availability/load of electrical circuits. Also check with your facility and caterer about where and what to feed the performers.

- All professional entertainers have access to formalwear (if they don't, that's your first clue they're not professionals!) However, it is YOUR responsibility to be specific about how you expect your performers to be dressed. Any extraordinary requests (period costumes, all-white tuxes, etc.) are normally paid for by the client.

- Make notes of your general music preferences before you meet with your DJ, bandleader, etc. For example: "Classical for the ceremony, Rat Pack-era for the cocktail hour and a set of Motown during the reception." Not only will this help you determine which entertainment professionals are a good match for you, it will guide them in preparing your set list. *TIP: The DJs and Entertainers in this book and on HereComesTheGuide. com are first-rate. They all got great reviews during our certification process, and we're happy to recommend them.*

For PDF versions of these QUESTIONS TO ASK, visit www.HereComesTheGuide.com

Questions to Ask When Ordering Your Wedding Invitations

Letterpress, thermography, engraved, matte, jacquard, glassine... ordering invites will mean learning a few new vocabulary words (see page 34). You'll also need to learn about all the components that you might want to include in your invitation, as well as what other printed materials could be part of your wedding scenario. With so many details to consider, you'll depend on a creative wedding invitation professional to clue you in on the jargon, and guide you in choosing invites that reflect your wedding style. After all, nothing sets the tone for an event like an impeccably designed wedding invitation.

Bring this list of must-ask questions to the stationery boutique or graphic designer you're considering to ensure that no detail is left unaddressed (no pun intended).

Getting To Know Your Invitation Professional

1. How long have you been in business?

2. What is your design background? *NOTE: This may or may not involve formal training. Remember, "good taste" isn't necessarily something that can be taught!*

3. What types of printing processes do you offer and which do you specialize in? Which do you recommend for my budget and style?

4. Is your printing done in-house or do you outsource it? *NOTE: Printing is usually less expensive if it's outsourced. However, a possible benefit of in-house printing is a quicker turnaround time, which could come in especially handy if any reprinting (say, due to an error) is required.*

5. Do you offer custom invitations as well as templated styles? Is there a fee if I want to order a sample of either an existing invitation style or a custom design? If so, how much?

6. If I choose a custom wedding invitation, what are my options for color, paper type, ink and fonts? What is the word limit for the text?

7. Can I also order my table numbers, place cards, escort cards, ceremony programs, menus, etc. from you?

8. Do you offer a package or a discounted price if I order all of the invitation components at the same time? (For a complete list of what might be included, see the next page.)

9. If I want to include a picture or graphic on my save-the-date card or invitation, can you accommodate that? If so, does the image need to be saved in a specific format? Do you have photo retouching available, and if so, what is the price range? Can your photo specialist also convert color images to black & white or sepia? Is there an additional cost?

10. Are there any new styles, trends and color combinations I might consider? Which are the most popular? What kinds of handmade or artisanal paper do you offer? *NOTE: The answers to these questions will give you a sense of how creative and up-to-the-minute your invitation professional is.*

11. Can my invitations be printed on recycled paper and/or with soy-based ink?

12. Based on the paper I select and the number of pieces involved, what would it cost to mail my wedding invitation? *NOTE: If you use a non-standard sized envelope, postage may be more expensive.*

Getting Down To Business

13. Once I place my order, how long will it take to have the completed invitations delivered? Do you have rush-order available and what are the extra fees? If you are ordering from an online company, ask: What are the shipping methods available to me, and their respective costs?

14. If the invitation involves multiple pieces, can you assemble them? If so, is there an additional fee? How will the assembly affect my delivery date?

15. Do you offer an invitation addressing service? If so, what is the charge for this? What lettering style options are available? Will the lettering push back my delivery date?

16. When is payment due?

17. I will have an opportunity to sign off on my invitation proof before you send my order to print, right?

18. Once I've signed off on the proof, I expect the printed invitations to match the approved sample. If they don't (i.e. an error was made after I signed off on the proof), will my invitations be corrected and reprinted at no additional cost? How much additional time will it take to redo my order if there is a problem with it?

19. What is your refund policy if for some reason I need to cancel my order?

20. When can I expect to receive my contract from you?

21. Can you provide me with the contact information of 3–4 recent brides who I can call or email for references?

Possible Printed Invitation Components

(Don't panic … most of the extra elements are OPTIONAL!!)

- Save-the-Date Cards

- Wedding Announcement

- Wedding Invitation Components:
  - Outer Envelope
  - Optional Inner Envelope
  - Optional Belly Band
  - Invitation
  - Reception Card, if held at a different location than the ceremony
  - Directions/Map
  - Response Card & SASE

- Thank-You Cards

- Shower Thank-You Cards

- Other Invites:
  - Engagement Party
  - Shower
  - Bachelor/Bacherlorette Party
  - Rehearsal Dinner
  - After Party

- Wedding Program

- Pew Cards

- Place Cards

- Table Cards

- Menus

- Napkins, Matchbooks or Labels for favors

Useful Tips:

- Ordering your invitations over the phone increases the possibility of mistakes, so order in person if possible. If you order your invitations from an online company, make sure your contract states that they will correct mistakes they make for free.

- Insist on getting a proof. Have at least two other people review all your proofs before you sign off on them—it's amazing what a fresh pair of eyes will see!

- If ordering online, remember that color resolution can vary drastically between computers. The best way to guarantee the exact color you want is to ask that a sample be snail mailed to you.

- Order 20–30 extra save-the-dates and/or invitations with envelopes in case you have to add to the guest list or you make a mistake when assembling or addressing the envelopes.

- Save-the-date cards should be sent out 6–9 months prior to your wedding.

- Invitations should be sent out 6–9 weeks prior to your wedding.

- Consider working with one stationer or graphic designer for all of your printed materials. She'll guide you in making sure all of the components convey a consistent design concept. Not that they have to be identical, but as Joyce Scardina Becker observes in *Countdown to Your Perfect Wedding,* "It's like making a fashion statement: All of the accessories in your wardrobe should coordinate and fit together nicely."

- To Evite or not to Evite? For the main event, even we progressives at *Here Comes The Guide* come down on the side of tradition and say go with real paper and snail mail—even if your budget determines that you have to DIY. However, if your overall wedding style is relaxed and casual, then we think Evites are fine for the supporting events, such as your Bachelorette Party. We like Evite's built-in RSVP system and creative style options.

Invitations Glossary

A glossary of common printing terms.

Printing Terms

Letterpress: Letterpress printing dates back to the 14th century, and involves inking the raised surface of metal type or custom-engraved plates and then applying the inked surface against paper with a press. When used with the right paper (thick, softer paper results in a deeper impression), typefaces and colors, letterpress creates an elegant product with a stamped, tactile quality. This process offers lots of options, but can cost more than other methods. Also, photographs and metallic inks generally don't work well with letterpress.

Embossing: Using a metal die, letters and images are pressed into the paper from behind, creating a raised "relief" surface, imparting added dimension to the invitation design. Usually used for large initials or borders. Ink or foil may be applied to the front of the paper so that the raised letters and images are colored.

Blind embossing: No ink or foil is applied, so the embossed (raised) image is the same color as the paper.

Thermography: This popular printing method uses heat to fuse ink and resinous powder, producing raised lettering. Though it looks almost exactly like engraved printing, thermography is much less expensive. This process will not reproduce detail as sharply as engraving will. The powder is added after the ink is applied, generally with an offset press, so the use of paper or metal offset plates affects quality here, too.

Engraving: Engraving is generally the most formal and expensive printing option. The image is etched into a metal plate, and the ink held in the etched grooves is applied to the paper with a press. The resulting raised image is comprised entirely of ink sitting on the surface of the paper. The ink applied is opaque, making it possible to print a lighter colored ink on a darker colored paper. Engraving is not the best printing choice if you have a photo or illustration that requires a screen.

Offset printing: Most printing these days is offset, which means the original image is transferred from a plate to a drum before it is applied to the paper. This process produces print that sits flat on the surface. There are many levels of quality with this method: If your printer uses paper printing plates, the job will cost less but the result may be fuzzy, inconsistent lettering. Metal plates yield much sharper, crisper type.

Digital printing: In this method the computer is linked to the printing press and the image is applied to paper or another material directly from a digital file rather than using film and/or plates. Digital is best for short-run, quick jobs. This can also be a good option if you want to use full color.

Foil stamping: Foil is applied to the front side of the paper, stamped on with a metal die. Foils can be metallic or colored, shiny or dull. They are usually very opaque, and this is a great way to print white on a dark colored paper.

Calligraphy: This is the perfected art of writing by hand. Often associated with fancy, curlicue script, calligraphy can be done in several genres and styles.

Paper Terms

Matte: A paper coating that's flat and non-reflective (no gloss).

Jacquard: Screen-printed paper that creates an illusion of layering; for example, paper that looks like it's overlaid with a swatch of lace.

Parchment paper: This paper is somewhat translucent and often a bit mottled to mimic the appearance of ancient, historical documents made out of animal skin. It's excellent for calligraphy.

Linen finish: Paper with a surface that actually mimics linen fabric. If you look closely, you see lines of texture going both horizontally and vertically on the surface.

Rice paper: Not actually made of rice, this paper is extremely thin and elegant.

Glassine: A very thin, waxy paper. Thinner than vellum (see below), its surface is slick and shiny, whereas vellum is more translucent. Glassine is best suited for envelope use, while vellum is sturdy enough to be printed on directly for invitation use.

Vellum: A heavier, finely textured, translucent paper made from wood fiber. Similar to parchment, it was originally made from the skin of a calf, lamb or baby goat and used for writing and painting during the pre-printing age.

www.HereComesTheGuide.com

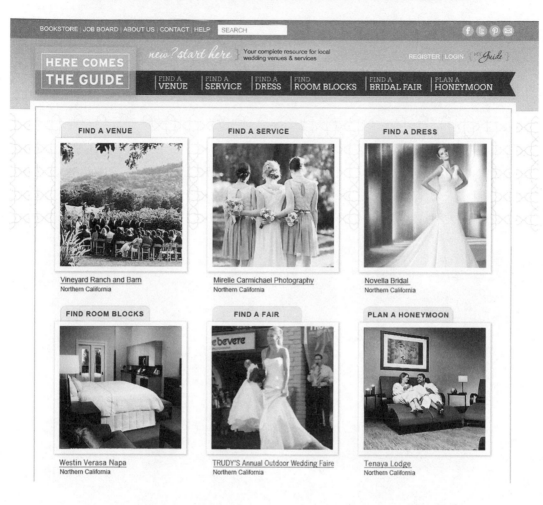

You've gotta visit our website! Here's what you'll find:

- A fast and easy way to search for the perfect locations, wedding services and bridal salons.

- Information about new locations that aren't in the book!

- More great wedding dress salons and special event services!

- Direct links to the event locations, services and salons we feature.

- Tons of photos and videos.

- Virtual tours of most locations.

- Information about wedding fairs.

Part One: Event Locations

Northern California

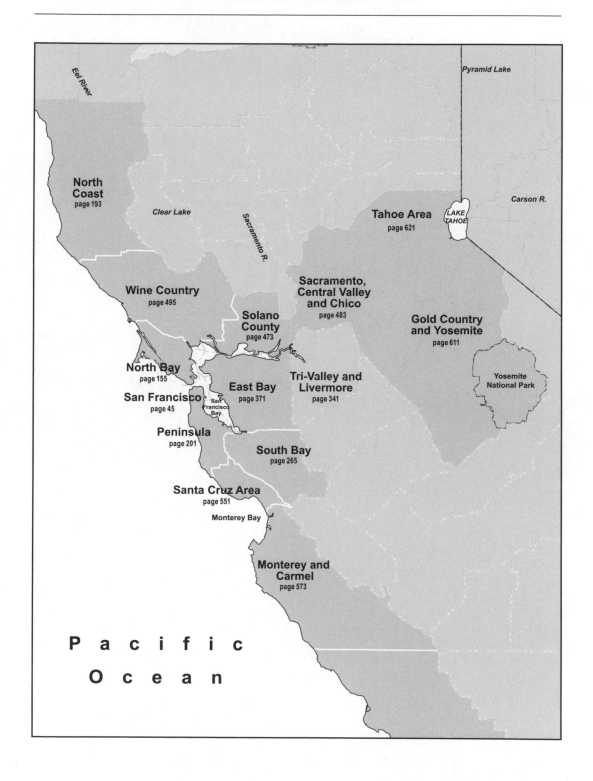

Eel River

Pyramid Lake

North Coast
page 193

Clear Lake

Sacramento R.

Carson R.

Tahoe Area
page 621

LAKE TAHOE

Wine Country
page 495

Solano County
page 473

Sacramento, Central Valley and Chico
page 483

Gold Country and Yosemite
page 611

North Bay
page 155

East Bay
page 371

Tri-Valley and Livermore
page 341

Yosemite National Park

San Francisco
page 45

San Francisco Bay

Peninsula
page 201

South Bay
page 265

Santa Cruz Area
page 551

Monterey Bay

Monterey and Carmel
page 573

P a c i f i c

O c e a n

San Francisco

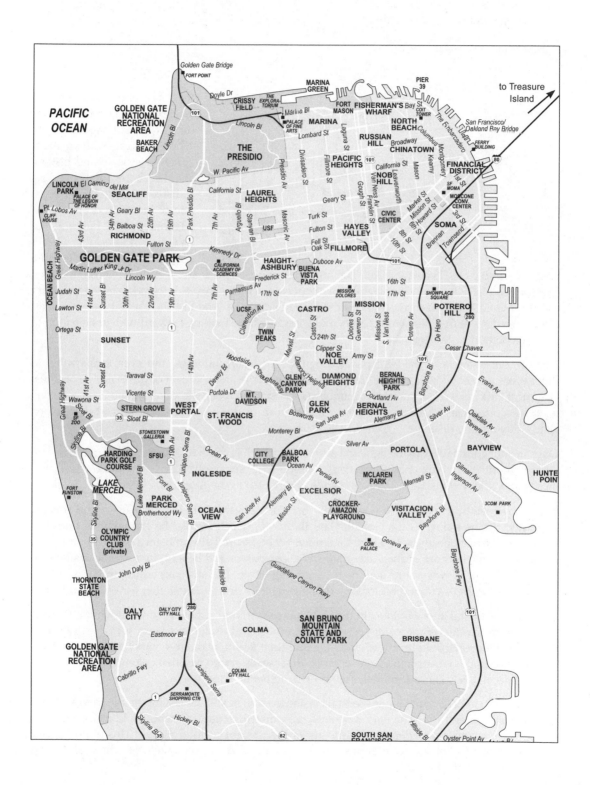

Argonaut Hotel

Waterfront Hotel

495 Jefferson Street, San Francisco
415/345-5552 Catering Department
www.argonauthotel.com
jordan.nimura@argonauthotel.com

- Rehearsal Dinners
- Ceremonies
- Wedding Receptions
- Corp. Events/Mtgs.
- Private Parties
- Accommodations

As befits its prime waterfront location on Fisherman's Wharf, the Argonaut Hotel easily seduces visitors with an abundance of seaside and historic charm. A recent makeover has transformed the Argonaut—one of the main occupants of a landmark 1907 building that had once housed the wharf's largest fruit and vegetable cannery—into a chic boutique hotel. The building's exposed brick and wooden beams have been incorporated into the interior's playful design concept, which takes its inspiration from the luxury cabins of Gold Rush-era steam ships bound for San Francisco. And like the excited passengers arriving here for the first time, your family and friends will be looking forward with anticipation to your celebration at the Argonaut.

First off, out-of-towners will be captivated by the iconic surroundings, and even locals will find themselves rediscovering its allure. The hotel overlooks the green stretch of the Maritime National Historical Park, as well as numerous antique vessels docked along the water's edge. Everyone will want to capture classic photos in front of a cable car, or the bay with Alcatraz and the Golden Gate Bridge in the distance.

Once inside, guests relax in the light and airy lobby, which is a playful interpretation of the ocean-journey motif. Navy blue deck chairs flank antique-style steamer trunks, and a working astronomer's clock above the stately fireplace mantle contributes to the Argonaut's nostalgic character.

The lobby's nautical theme is echoed in the prefunction foyer, where guests enjoy the cocktail hour. Receptions follow in the Golden Gate Ballroom, which recalls the formality of first-class ocean travel when one always dressed for dinner. Yet be assured, the ambiance is neither stuffy nor ho-hum: Chandeliers are shaped like giant ships' compasses and beautifully textured wall coverings reminiscent of woven jute add exotic, seafaring flavor. The spacious ballroom has a flexible layout, and can be sectioned off for a wedding ceremony or used altogether for one grand gala.

You can also tie the knot outdoors in the Del Monte Courtyard, landscaped with twinkle-lit trees. The bride makes her entrance down a brick staircase, and exchanges vows with her groom in front of the legendary skyline. The adjoining Maritime Room, with large windows and lofty ceilings, hosts social hours or intimate receptions. Brick walls, rough wooden columns and maritime-inspired accents lend an informal though no less authentic atmosphere.

All the hotel's events feature superb coastal cuisine from its next-door restaurant, the Blue Mermaid Chowder House and Bar. The chef welcomes customized menus, but who could resist including one of the signature chowders and fresh, sustainably caught seafood dishes? This trendy dining spot is also available for private events, and has a patio that can be tented for rehearsal dinners or casual get-togethers.

Want more novelty? The hotel's first floor houses the San Francisco Maritime National Historical Park Museum Visitors Center, a unique social hour venue. Interactive displays of nautical memorabilia let guests drink in the neighborhood's storied past along with their champagne. The Argonaut's event pros can even arrange an intimate soiree aboard the tall ship Balclutha moored nearby.

After the festivities, guests retire to luxuriously outfitted accommodations, most with postcard views. Together with its 4-diamond service and amenities, the Argonaut offers an epic destination wedding experience.

CEREMONY CAPACITY: The Argonaut holds up to 270 seated guests both indoors and outdoors.

EVENT/RECEPTION CAPACITY: The hotel accommodates 320 seated or 450 standing guests indoors (270 with a dance floor).

MEETING CAPACITY: With over 8,500 square feet of private space, the Argonaut can accommodate groups ranging from 10–300 guests.

FEES & DEPOSITS: An initial $2,000 deposit is required to confirm the date and time. A second deposit is due 60 days prior to the event. The estimated final balance is due 3 days prior to the event. Any overages or additional requests will be billed at the conclusion of the event. Ceremony and setup fees range $250–$1,000. Wedding packages start at $115/person for evening events and $100/person for daytime events. Non-package, à la carte meals range $50–85/person. Five-hour wedding packages include passed hors d'oeuvres, 1-hour open house bar, and the option of a 3-course meal, lunch or dinner buffet or heavy appetizer reception. Wine is included for 2 hours with the meal service, and a champagne toast is offered as well. Wedding packages also include chair covers and sashes, and complimentary accommodations for the night of the event. Special guest room rates may be negotiated. A 23% service charge and tax are additional.

AVAILABILITY: Daily until midnight. Early morning hours by arrangement. Closed on Thanksgiving, Christmas, and New Year's Day.

SERVICES/AMENITIES:

Catering: provided, approved outside catering allowed
Kitchen Facilities: n/a
Tables & Chairs: provided
Linens, Silver, etc.: provided
Restrooms: wheelchair accessible
Dance Floor: provided
Bride's & Groom's Dressing Areas: yes
Meeting Equipment: full range

Parking: valet or public garage
Accommodations: 252 guest rooms
Telephone: pay phones
Outdoor Night Lighting: yes
Outdoor Cooking Facilities: no
Cleanup: provided
View: SF cityscape, SF Bay and park
Other: event coordination

RESTRICTIONS:

Alcohol: provided
Smoking: outside only
Music: amplified OK indoors with volume restrictions

Wheelchair Access: yes
Insurance: not required but recommended
Other: no glitter, rice or birdseed

This is important! Tell locations you're reading HERE COMES THE GUIDE and ask if our information is still current.

Asian Art Museum

Museum

200 Larkin Street, San Francisco
415/581-3777
www.asianart.org/facilityrentals.htm
facilityrentals@asianart.org

- ● Rehearsal Dinners
- ● Ceremonies
- ● Wedding Receptions
- ● Corp. Events/Mtgs.
- ● Private Parties
- ☐ Accommodations

The historic and regal building that houses San Francisco's Asian Art Museum is as captivating as the art inside. A massive stone Beaux-Arts structure—which was built in 1917 and functioned as the city's main library for decades—stands four stories high with columns, stairs, and inscriptions completing its stately façade. Gleaming marble surfaces, beautifully carved stone arches, and antique light fixtures greet visitors in the lobby and grace the sophisticated special event spaces beyond.

The stunning transformation from book repository to museum was masterminded by Italian architect Gae Aulenti, who is perhaps best known for taking a defunct train station in Paris and turning it into the award-winning Musée D'Orsay.

Through the central archway leading off the lobby, guests encounter the opulent Grand Staircase and Loggia, which still retain an early 1900s elegance. Three flights of gently ascending travertine marble steps lead up to the Loggia, an airy arcade that overlooks the staircase and has a decorative barrel-vaulted ceiling. The glass cases that line its walls display an array of distinctive Asian ceramics, and remind us that this is indeed a museum. Some couples have married on the stairs, which look amazing when decorated with candles and flowers; with this setup, wedding attendees observe the ceremony from the Loggia above, as if gazing upon royalty. Once the service concludes, cocktails, passed champagne and hors d'oeuvres are served in the Loggia, where tall tables, candles and special linens personalize the space. During this time, your guests can explore the art galleries situated on either side of the Hall, where a world-class collection of works from China, Japan and Korea awaits.

For an elegant sit-down dinner and dancing, the adjacent Samsung Hall is equally classy. Vast and square-shaped, it continues the visual theme of columns and plenty of marble, but also boasts enormous windows crisscrossed with intricate metalwork. A huge bronze chandelier illuminates the festivities from high above. When you add linen-clad tables, mood lighting and the dulcet sounds of a string quartet, the hall feels positively palatial.

If you prefer a contemporary setting, the museum has a pair of almost identical courts on the lower level that are connected by two open hallways. Known as the North and South Courts, they were completely remodeled during the museum construction, and present a striking contrast to the historic sections of the facility. Their thoroughly modern and minimalist design features clean lines, a marble floor, and an angular ceiling of skylights nearly three stories above. Because of their considerable size, the courts lend themselves to a wide range of event options: wedding ceremonies, sit-down dinners, buffets with food stations, and cocktail parties. You can even create a lounge atmosphere by bringing in a bar, conversational groupings of couches, and tables and chairs.

Before the festivities begin, brides who want a secluded spot in which to get ready or relax can utilize the lovely Peterson Room on the first floor. A lavish private room, it has Oriental rugs and Asian-inspired décor that's very Zen.

There are many advantages to planning an event at the Asian Art Museum, but the main one is this: No matter where you hold your celebration, you're surrounded by beauty. The building has so much style and history (not to mention its world-renowned art collection) that you don't have to add much to make your celebration dazzling.

CEREMONY, EVENT/RECEPTION & MEETING CAPACITY: The Museum accommodates a maximum of 400 seated or 1,500 standing guests, though not all in one room. Samsung Hall and the Loggia hold up to 250 seated guests (225 when including space for a dance area), and up to 350 standing. Each Court holds up to 200 seated or 250 standing guests. The Galleries may be rented with event spaces. Food and beverages are not permitted in the galleries.

Please inquire about outdoor tent options to increase maximum capacity.

FEES & DEPOSITS: A $5,000 nonrefundable deposit is required to reserve your date. The balance is due 30 days prior to event. Rental fees range $3,500–20,000 depending on space rented.

AVAILABILITY: Weddings are contracted from 5:15pm–1:30am (including setup, event, and load-out) year-round, except Thursday nights.

SERVICES/AMENITIES:

Catering: select from list

Kitchen Facilities: prep only

Tables & Chairs: through caterer

Linens, Silver, etc.: through caterer

Restrooms: wheelchair accessible

Dance Floor: built-in or BYO through caterer

Bride's Dressing Area: yes

Meeting Equipment: CBA, extra charge

Parking: valet or public garage

Accommodations: no guest rooms

Telephone: pay phones

Outdoor Night Lighting: yes

Outdoor Cooking Facilities: yes

Cleanup: through caterer

View: artwork

Other: in-house audiovisual

RESTRICTIONS:

Alcohol: BYO, licensed server

Smoking: outside only

Music: amplified OK

Wheelchair Access: yes

Insurance: liability required

Other: no glitter, rice or birdseed

Bently Reserve and Conference Center

Historic Bank Foyer

301 Battery Street, San Francisco
415/294-2226
www.bentlyreserve.com
vivian.perez@bentlyreserve.com

● Rehearsal Dinners   ● Corp. Events/Mtgs.
● Ceremonies   ● Private Parties
● Wedding Receptions   Accommodations

We always get asked about mansions in San Francisco, and to tell you the truth, there aren't many that can accommodate large wedding receptions indoors. Although the Bently Reserve is not a mansion, it possesses the stately, elegant and understated grandeur you'd expect from a palatial estate. And it can handle quite a crowd.

Originally part of the lobby of the 1924 Federal Reserve Bank of San Francisco, the event space has been fully restored and the building in which it's housed is included in the National Register of Historic Places. The Bently Reserve is a fine example of San Francisco's "banking temple" tradition and the government's penchant for monumental classical architecture during that era. Inside, you'll find one of the most dramatic staircases we've ever seen. If you'd like to make a theatrical entrance, descend the bronze and marble double stairway, which starts from two separate places and curves seamlessly down onto the gleaming marble floor below. Everywhere you look you'll see French and Italian marble (or a close facsimile). Expertly painted faux marbling has transformed the two rows of 25-foot-tall Ionic columns that flank the room into "rock-solid" architectural elements. The entry doors are solid bronze, and two original bronze chandeliers (designed by the architect) draw your eyes up to the awe-inspiring 34-foot ceiling overhead. All in all, if you have an extended guest list and are searching for a grand location in the City, you couldn't ask for a better spot.

CEREMONY CAPACITY: The main hall holds 350 seated guests. The Conference Center holds up to 70 seated guests.

EVENT/RECEPTION & MEETING CAPACITY: The Banking Hall holds 250 seated theater-style, 350 seated banquet-style or up to 650 standing guests; the Conference Center holds up to 70 guests and has 8 separate meeting spaces.

FEES & DEPOSITS: The Banking Hall rental fee ranges $5,800–10,900 depending on the day of your event. A $1,000 refundable security deposit is payable with the signed license agreement. On-site facility security services are required and are an additional charge. The Conference Center's rental fee for special events is contingent on the time and day of the event, the size of the group, and is subject to availability.

AVAILABILITY: Sunday–Thursday, 8am–midnight; Friday and Saturday events until 1am. Tours of the facility are by appointment only.

SERVICES/AMENITIES:

Catering: select from preferred list
Kitchen Facilities: fully equipped
Tables & Chairs: caterer
Linens, Silver, etc.: caterer
Restrooms: wheelchair accessible
Dance Floor: yes
Bride's Dressing Area: yes
Meeting Equipment: full range CBA
Other: coat check room

Parking: adjacent garage, discounted on evenings and weekends
Accommodations: hotels nearby
Telephone: no
Outdoor Night Lighting: yes
Outdoor Cooking Facilities: no
Cleanup: renter
View: no

RESTRICTIONS:

Alcohol: exclusive bar service through *Best Beverage Catering*
Smoking: outside only
Music: amplified OK indoors

Wheelchair Access: yes
Insurance: liability required
Other: no glitter or confetti

California Academy of Sciences

Museum

Golden Gate Park, 55 Music Concourse Drive, San Francisco
415/379-5868
www.calacademy.org/visit/plan_an_event/wedding/
weddings@calacademy.org

- Rehearsal Dinners
- Ceremonies
- Wedding Receptions
- Corp. Events/Mtgs.
- Private Parties
- Accommodations

There's only one place on the planet where you can get married in front of a coral reef, dine in the company of penguins, and stroll through a rainforest. We're talking about the California Academy of Sciences, San Francisco's world-renowned, eco-friendly natural history museum. Whether you're hosting a private dinner for 30, a wedding for 300 or a corporate extravaganza for 3,000, it will be as green as it is memorable.

The California Academy of Sciences building is one of the most innovative and environmentally conscious structures in the world. Not only does it house an aquarium, planetarium and rainforest, but it also has a living roof, whose undulating contours mirror the seven hills of the city and are covered with millions of plants. Hosting a wedding here is truly a once-in-a-lifetime experience. You have access to the main floor as well as the Aquarium on the lower level, and you can even pose for pictures on the roof before your family and friends arrive. Your coordinator will help you choreograph your celebration, while top Bay Area caterers create your menu—featuring organic, sustainable foods, of course.

With a dozen areas to choose from, your event can flow seamlessly from one part of the museum to another. You might serve cocktails in the elegantly columned Swamp, famously inhabited by an albino alligator, then move on to a gourmet five-course repast in the African Hall. Here you'll be flanked by 21 meticulously crafted dioramas depicting wild animals like lions, antelope, baboons, leopards and mountain gorillas in their natural settings. The best spot for the head table has to be at the end of the room, where permanently "tuxedoed" penguins frolic in the water, observing the festivities from their glassed-in habitat.

Several exhibits offer immersive and interactive activities that will engage your guests. Just add a bar and cocktail tables throughout for a unique social hour. Or serve hors d'oeuvres in the Aquarium itself—the popular "touch tidepool" provides an unusual icebreaker.

Have your ceremony here, too, and prepare to be dazzled: There's nothing like exchanging vows against a 25-foot-high backdrop of turquoise water, filled with a glimmering confetti of neon-colored fish…unless it's saying "I do" with the misty greenery of the four-story Rainforest dome behind you. If you prefer an outdoor option, the East and West Gardens are lovely during warm weather. For an intimate rehearsal dinner that's literally out of this world, reserve the Planetarium anteroom, which can be transformed into a starry galaxy by the state-of-the-art media system.

At the California Academy of Sciences, the "décor" often flies, swims or grows before your very eyes. Let the museum take your guests to beautiful and amazing places they've never seen and inspire them with wonder. An event here is so much more than an event—it's an adventure.

CEREMONY CAPACITY: The site accommodates 280 seated guests indoors.

EVENT/RECEPTION CAPACITY: The museum holds 280 seated or 3,000 standing guests indoors.

MEETING CAPACITY: The facility accommodates 300 seated guests.

FEES & DEPOSITS: 50% of the rental fee is required to confirm your date. The balance is due 30 days prior to the event. For your wedding event, you'll have access to the entire Academy, including use of the following spaces: Rainforest, Aquarium, Swamp, Piazza, African Hall, East Pavilion, West Pavilion, Forum and Main Lobby. Also included are a Wedding Ready Room with adjoining restroom, plus additional services such as security for the museum, coat check, custodial services, and docents for the Academy living exhibits (as available). Please contact the Special Events Department for details. The all-inclusive use fee is $18,500 for up to 3,000 standing guests.

AVAILABILITY: Year-round, 7pm–midnight, every day except Thursday.

SERVICES/AMENITIES:

Catering: select from list
Kitchen Facilities: prep only
Tables & Chairs: through caterer
Linens, Silver, etc.: through caterer
Restrooms: wheelchair accessible
Dance Floor: CBA
Bride's Dressing Area: yes
Meeting Equipment: CBA

Parking: garage nearby
Accommodations: no guest rooms
Telephone: pay phone
Outdoor Night Lighting: no
Outdoor Cooking Facilities: no
Cleanup: caterer or renter
View: cityscape, park, landscaped grounds

RESTRICTIONS:

Alcohol: BYO licensed server
Smoking: not allowed
Music: amplified OK with restrictions

Wheelchair Access: yes
Insurance: liability required

Overwhelmed? Use the search criteria on www.HereComesTheGuide.com to narrow down your choices.

53

The Century Club of California
and the Julia Morgan Ballroom

1355 Franklin Street, San Francisco
415/673-7117
www.thecenturyclubofcalifornia.org
manager@thecenturyclubofcalifornia.org

Historic Women's Club

● Rehearsal Dinners	● Corp. Events/Mtgs.
● Ceremonies	● Private Parties
● Wedding Receptions	Accommodations

Having exclusive access to a splendid Edwardian mansion for your big day is just one of the reasons why The Century Club of California is such a coveted event venue. Built in 1905 as the "clubhouse" for a women's social organization that still meets here, the venerable establishment has opened its doors to nonmembers, making its gorgeous rooms available for weddings and other special occasions.

When you step into the expansive foyer of this historic building, you feel like you've taken a trip back in time. Antique furniture, a handsome grandfather clock, and handmade light fixtures create a warm, old-fashioned feeling. Carved, dark wood chairs—from Shakespeare's Church in England—and a rich set of Oriental rugs complete the picture.

A pair of French doors open into the Reception Room, an intimate banquet space with seafoam green carpet, white walls and a gold-toned Japanese screen covering one wall. Brides often decorate this charming room with flowers, and host a luncheon or shower here. Two adjacent lounges offer the bride and groom ample space for getting ready or just relaxing before, during or after the ceremony.

If you're having a larger event, ascend the stairs to the second floor, passing by colorful stained-glass windows on your way. The cozy foyer on this level is shared by two grand spaces, the Drawing Room and the Ballroom. In the luxurious Old World atmosphere of the Drawing Room, couples marry in front of the monumental marble fireplace. Guests gather 'round, either standing or sitting on the many overstuffed couches and chairs. When the ceremony concludes, friends and family enjoy cocktails and hors d'oeuvres while admiring the interesting artwork and built-in bookshelves (which also make a lovely backdrop for a tea or luncheon).

Seated dinners and buffets are held in the Ballroom. Designed by renowned architect Julia Morgan, it features a vaulted ceiling, white walls and decorative wainscoting. Add plants, flowers, linens and candlelight, and this spacious room takes on a magical glow. The small stage at one end accommodates a DJ or a band quite easily, and the polished wood floor is ready-made for dancing.

If the bride wants a moment or two alone, she can steal away to the "bride's room" on the third floor. Accessible via a somewhat hidden back staircase or the elevator, it's a comfortable and feminine living room that provides total privacy and has its own bathroom next door.

Standing in any of The Century Club's many rooms, the past doesn't seem distant at all. You can almost imagine the stylish club members taking tea in front of the fireplace or fêting city luminaries in the Ballroom. Close your eyes and you might even hear the horse-drawn carriages that used to carry the ladies to and from this elegant clubhouse. Inside The Century Club, tradition, history and the beauty of a bygone era still exist, enriching every celebration that takes place here.

CEREMONY CAPACITY: The Drawing Room accommodates small ceremonies for up to 75; the Ballroom holds up to 150.

EVENT/RECEPTION CAPACITY: The Ballroom accommodates up to 225 guests, the Drawing Room holds 60–125, and the Reception Room holds 50–100 depending on type of event. The Dining room accommodates 70 seated guests.

MEETING CAPACITY: The Ballroom accommodates up to 225 guests seated theater-style.

FEES & DEPOSITS: 50% of the rental fee along with a signed contract are required to secure your date. The rental balance and a $750 refundable security deposit are due 60 days prior to the event. Rental fees range $700–5,000 depending on space rented and level of building access. A kitchen use fee may also apply. The club is beautifully decorated for the holidays in December. The rental price of the Ballroom includes one free daytime rehearsal.

AVAILABILITY: Year-round, daily, 8am–midnight.

SERVICES/AMENITIES:
Catering: select from list or BYO
Kitchen Facilities: prep only
Tables & Chairs: some provided, more CBA
Linens, Silver, etc.: BYO or through caterer
Restrooms: not wheelchair accessible
Dance Floor: yes
Bride's Dressing Area: yes
Meeting Equipment: limited A/V equipment

Parking: public lots nearby
Accommodations: no guest rooms
Telephone: emergency use only
Outdoor Night Lighting: access only
Outdoor Cooking Facilities: no
Cleanup: caterer or renter
View: no

RESTRICTIONS:
Alcohol: BYO, licensed server
Smoking: outside only
Music: amplified OK with restrictions

Wheelchair Access: limited
Insurance: liability required
Other: no rice, confetti or birdseed

City Club of San Francisco

Historic Club

155 Sansome Street, San Francisco
415/362-2480
www.cityclubsf.com
catering@cityclubsf.com

- Rehearsal Dinners
- Corp. Events/Mtgs.
- Ceremonies
- Private Parties
- Wedding Receptions
- Accommodations

Just walking into the lobby of this former Stock Exchange Tower, situated in the heart of the Financial District, gives you an inkling of what's to follow. One glance at the highly polished black-and-green marble floors, black-and-white marble walls and gold ceiling and you feel instantly surrounded by glamour.

Elevators whisk you up to the 10th floor, and the entrance to The City Club itself. Here, even the elevator doors—framed in bronze and decorated in silver, bronze and brass appliqué— offer an elegant example of this facility's attention to detail. The club (which occupies the 10th and 11th floors) features one of the most striking and exquisite Art Deco interiors we've seen, including a remarkable stairwell painted with an original 30-foot-high Diego Rivera fresco. Furnishings are original Art Deco pieces and appointments are generously clad in black marble, silver and brass. The ceiling is stunning, covered with burnished gold leaf squares. Sophisticated with just the right amount of glitz, this is an exceptional place for a wedding reception or corporate special event.

CEREMONY CAPACITY: The 10th floor (Cafe) can accommodate 220 seated or 300 standing; the 11th floor (Main Dining Room) 240 seated or 300 standing guests. The 9th floor suites can accommodate 120 seated or 150 standing.

EVENT/RECEPTION & MEETING CAPACITY: For receptions, the entire club (10th and 11th floors) may be reserved. The club holds 20–460 seated or up to 500 for a standing reception on two floors.

FEES & DEPOSITS: For special events, the rental fee for a 5-hour block of time is $2,500 for Saturday and $2,000 for Sunday. Food and beverage minimums range $10,000–23,000. Curfew is 2am and the overtime charge is $500/hour. On weeknights, Monday–Friday, food and beverage minimums range $6,000–12,000 and rental fees are waived. Minimums vary depending on the month and day of the event. Tax and a 22% service charge are additional. Member sponsorship and benefits are available.

AVAILABILITY: Year-round, Monday–Friday, 7:30am–2am. On Saturdays and Sundays, 8am–2am.

SERVICES/AMENITIES:

Catering: provided, no BYO
Kitchen Facilities: n/a
Tables & Chairs: provided, styles and quantities vary
Linens, Silver, etc.: provided
Restrooms: wheelchair accessible
Dance Floor: yes
Bride's Dressing Area: yes
Meeting Equipment: full A/V services available

Parking: CBA
Accommodations: no guest rooms, affiliate club hotels
Telephone: guest phones
Outdoor Night Lighting: access only
Outdoor Cooking Facilities: no
Cleanup: provided
View: San Francisco skyline

RESTRICTIONS:

Alcohol: provided
Smoking: in smoking room only
Music: amplified OK

Wheelchair Access: yes
Insurance: not required

Cliff House

1090 Point Lobos, San Francisco
415/666-4027

www.cliffhouse.com
virginia@cliffhouse.com

Historic Waterfront Restaurant

- Rehearsal Dinners
- Ceremonies
- Wedding Receptions
- Corp. Events/Mtgs.
- Private Parties
- Accommodations

For nearly a century and a half, the Cliff House has been one of The City's most familiar and beloved landmarks. Generations of San Franciscans have brought visiting friends and relatives to this spot to show off the glorious westernmost part of the city. Drawn here by the spectacular ocean views and the waves crashing along the rocky shore, they often stopped in at the restaurant for a hot meal after a blustery walk on Ocean Beach, or to watch a particularly lovely sunset over a glass of wine.

What most people don't realize is that the Cliff House is also a remarkable place for a wedding or special event. Originally built in 1863, it's gone through a number of incarnations in its long and illustrious life and is now more captivating than ever.

The 1909 building at the core of the current venue has been uncovered and restored, and the new Sutro Wing on the north side (named for the famous public bathhouse that flourished on this site in the early 1900s) has been designed as an upscale restaurant. This clever addition's two-story windows frame the truly breathtaking views, while an opalescent floor-to-ceiling sea-glass mosaic reflects the shimmery light of the ocean and evokes the pearly inside of an abalone shell. An exhibition kitchen, which expands the open feeling, is visible from nearly everywhere in the room. Two large Italian ceramic panels, which depict ladies bathing and once hung in the Sutro Baths, have been restored and now grace the restaurant.

The completely separate Terrace Room in the 1909 section, however, is the place for weddings. All of the glories of a Pacific sunset to the west and misty Ocean Beach stretching southward can be viewed through floor-to-ceiling windows on two sides. If you hold your ceremony on the private Terrace, you'll have the beach and the Pacific as your backdrop while you face Seal Rock. Afterwards, invite your guests inside the Terrace Room for cocktails followed by dinner and dancing. A palette of muted sand dune tones is carried through the chairs, carpet and window treatments; seven large framed mirrors run along the wall opposite the windows, brightening the room and reflecting the view. (Consider having your cake table in front of one of the mirrors.) There's often an extended dusk here—the kind you get when you're out at sea. With any luck, that lingering glow will illuminate the room all during your reception. An adjacent dedicated kitchen turns out updated classic cuisine for your private party, so there's no conflict with restaurant dining.

Come rediscover this uniquely San Franciscan treasure. Its mesmerizing clifftop location and exceptional sea (and seal!) views make it well worth the trip.

CEREMONY CAPACITY: The Terrace Deck and Terrace Room each accommodate 70 seated guests.

EVENT/RECEPTION & MEETING CAPACITY: The Terrace Room can accommodate 120 seated or 180 standing guests.

FEES & DEPOSITS: To reserve for events, a $3,500 nonrefundable deposit (which is applied to wards the final bill) is required when reservations are confirmed. 75% of the estimated event total is due 5 weeks prior to the event; the balance payable at the end of the function. A guest count confirmation is due 2 weeks in advance. Food service is provided. Per person costs run $65–75 for buffets, $49–75 for seated dinners. Beverages, tax and a 20% service charge are additional.

For business meetings, a room rental fee may apply. The fee will vary depending on day of week, event duration and food and beverage total.

AVAILABILITY: Year-round, daily, 8am–1:30am. The Terrace Room is not available Sunday before 6pm or on major holidays.

SERVICES/AMENITIES:

Catering: provided, no BYO
Kitchen Facilities: n/a
Tables & Chairs: provided
Linens, Silver, etc.: provided
Restrooms: wheelchair accessible
Dance Floor: yes
Bride's Dressing Area: no
Meeting Equipment: CBA, extra charge

Parking: nearby lots
Accommodations: no guest rooms
Telephone: emergency use only
Outdoor Night Lighting: no
Outdoor Cooking Facilities: no
Cleanup: provided
View: ocean
Other: wedding and event coordination

RESTRICTIONS:

Alcohol: provided
Smoking: outdoors only
Music: amplified OK indoors

Wheelchair Access: yes
Insurance: not required

The professionals in the back of this book are the best in the business. How do we know? Read page 637.

Commodore Cruises & Events

Yachts

Boarding at Alameda, Pier 40 SF, and 19 other ports in the Bay Area
510/337-9000
www.commodoreevents.com
events@commodoreevents.com

- Rehearsal Dinners
- Ceremonies
- Wedding Receptions
- Corp. Events/Mtgs.
- Private Parties
- Accommodations

If you're a lover of ocean liners, cruise ships, yachts, and all the grandeur and pampering they imply, why not charter one of Commodore Cruises' six luxury yachts for your milestone event? Boarding from their home port in Alameda, Pier 40 and 19 other ports in the San Francisco Bay area, their fleet has maintained the fine tradition of white glove entertaining at sea for over 30 years.

The *Cabernet Sauvignon* is the Grande Dame of San Francisco Bay. It possesses four enormous decks: a spacious lounge deck, a dining deck for sit-down dinners or buffets, a large dance-floor deck equipped with an excellent sound system and magnificent bar, and an open-air sky deck that's perfect for viewing the city skyline. A private stateroom provides a changing space for brides and bridesmaids.

Commodore's trio of Mega Yachts is extremely versatile. The *Pinot Noir,* with its long white bar and mirrored ceilings resembles a chic set straight out of a James Bond movie. Its equally stunning sister yacht, the *Chardonnay,* boasts a large dance floor on the second deck. Couples who desire an intimate outdoor ceremony might want to consider the *Merlot.* Popular because it serves groups large and small, it has a dance floor on the second deck that spills out onto the open-air deck, creating a wonderful indoor/outdoor flow.

The *Fumé Blanc,* a three-deck replica of a New York State steamship, features a 30-foot dance floor, roomy viewing platforms on the bow, and a 340-guest capacity. And lastly, the *Zinfandel* treats guests to fabulous 360-degree views from a dining deck with floor-to-ceiling windows.

All vessels offer well-appointed settings for dining, gorgeous wraparound views of the bay, and multiple menu options for a wide variety of social and corporate functions. Plus Commodore Cruises & Events works with a selection of highly rated vendors to help you create the wedding or special event of your dreams. Before booking any other venue, make reservations for one of Commodore's open houses where you can "Meet the Fleet." *Bon Voyage!*

CEREMONY, EVENT/RECEPTION & MEETING CAPACITY: Maximum capacity is 340 guests aboard the *Fumé Blanc* and 350 aboard the *Cabernet Sauvignon.* Many events are hosted with 20–130 guests aboard smaller yachts.

FEES & DEPOSITS: A nonrefundable deposit of 25% of the estimated event total is required to reserve your date. Another 25% is due 120 days prior to the event. The balance is due 14 days prior to the event. Fees, including meals, a full bar and 3–4 hours aboard, range $65–200/person. The yachts are also available à la carte.

AVAILABILITY: Year-round, anytime.

SERVICES/AMENITIES:

Catering: provided or BYO
Kitchen Facilities: fully equipped
Tables & Chairs: provided
Linens, Silver, etc.: provided, upgrades available
Restrooms: some wheelchair accessible
Dance Floor: yes
Bride's Dressing Area: yes
Meeting Equipment: provided

Parking: large free lot
Accommodations: guest rooms nearby
Telephone: onboard radio and cellular phones
Outdoor Night Lighting: yes
Outdoor Cooking Facilities: n/a
Cleanup: provided
View: entire San Francisco Bay
Other: wedding cakes, florals, referrals

RESTRICTIONS:

Alcohol: provided, or BYO with corkage fee
Smoking: on open-air decks only
Music: sound system and in-house DJs available

Wheelchair Access: yes
Insurance: not required

Conservatory of Flowers

100 John F. Kennedy Drive, San Francisco
415/831-2090

www.conservatoryofflowers.org/events/weddings
rentals@sfcof.org

Historic Conservatory

- Rehearsal Dinners
- Ceremonies
- Wedding Receptions
- Corp. Events/Mtgs.
- Private Parties
- Accommodations

If you're looking for a symbolic place to begin your marriage, you can't beat the Conservatory of Flowers in Golden Gate Park. This seemingly fragile, multi-faceted gem of a building with a thriving, ever-growing, organic heart, has suffered fire, earthquakes and windstorms—and yet, it's still standing after 130 years.

In December 1995, a Pacific storm with 100-mile-an-hour winds shattered 40 percent of the frosty white glass panels, and damaged the framework so badly that the entire structure had to be dismantled and reassembled using a mixture of old and replacement wood beams. Luckily, a rebuilt and thoroughly revitalized Conservatory was able to reopen in the fall of 2003.

The Vestibule is the entry to the Conservatory and a lovely entrée to your event. While you're serving cocktails in this peaked roof section, take a look at the surrounding glass: It's not all white or clear, but punctuated by jewel-like insets of green, tiger lily orange, ruby and delphinium blue.

From the Vestibule, go through the Lowland Tropics, the large central gallery with the gorgeous pointed cupola housing the enormous century-old philodendron and a dense mix of other tropical plants. The cool Highland Tropics gallery contains a collection of delicate high-altitude orchids. The Aquatic Plants gallery has a water lily pond with little waterfalls and fantastic *Victoria amazonica* lily pads—the kind that grow so large they're depicted in fairy-tale books with children sitting on them.

Inside Potted Plants, the wooden arbor is tailor-made for exchanging vows. It's flanked by potted palms, and the vines overhead drip with star-shaped lavender flowers. Throughout this gallery are hibiscus plants with showy blooms in yellows, pinks, oranges and reds, and orchids in all the crazy variety of sizes, shapes and colors that orchids exhibit. Huge pots of Dr. Suessian, spiky-stemmed Madagascar Palms sit here, and two banks of plants with a mesmerizing diversity of leaf textures, shapes and patterns run the length of the room.

Just past Potted Plants is Special Exhibits, a large open gallery dominated by the ethereal, spun-sugar look of the Conservatory's structure. Depending on the availability of this space, ceremonies take place here among changing exhibits that always include a variety of plants.

In 2008, a new event space adjacent to the Aquatic Plants gallery was added for larger, sit-down dinner functions, events or meetings. Outdoor ceremonies and tented events for up to 300+ people can be held on the Conservatory's lawn or platform.

Flower lovers will find no better place for a celebration than this Conservatory. It's a uniquely beautiful San Francisco landmark.

CEREMONY CAPACITY: The Conservatory can accommodate 150 seated guests indoors and 300 seated outdoors.

EVENT/RECEPTION & MEETING CAPACITY: The Conservatory holds up to 288 seated or 400 standing guests total. Smaller celebrations as well as larger tented events can be accommodated; call for details.

FEES & DEPOSITS: 25% of the rental fee is required to reserve your date. The balance is due 30 days prior to event date. Rental fees range $2,500–10,000 depending on space, day and length of time rented.

AVAILABILITY: Year-round, daily, 5pm–midnight. Daytime hours are available with some restrictions.

SERVICES/AMENITIES:

Catering: select from list
Kitchen Facilities: prep only
Tables & Chairs: white wooden folding chairs included, tables through vendor
Linens, Silver, etc.: BYO or through caterer
Restrooms: wheelchair accessible
Dance Floor: wood flooring throughout
Bride's Dressing Area: no
Meeting Equipment: BYO or through vendor

Parking: reserved parking included, street parking available
Accommodations: no guest rooms
Telephone: emergency use only
Outdoor Night Lighting: access only
Outdoor Cooking Facilities: no
Cleanup: caterer
View: landscaped grounds, Golden Gate Park

RESTRICTIONS:

Alcohol: BYO, licensed server
Smoking: not allowed
Music: amplified OK indoors with restrictions

Wheelchair Access: yes
Insurance: liability required

de Young Museum

Landmark Museum

50 Hagiwara Tea Garden Drive, Golden Gate Park, San Francisco
415/750-3683
www.famsf.org
deyoungevents@famsf.org

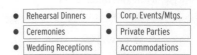

- Rehearsal Dinners
- Ceremonies
- Wedding Receptions
- Corp. Events/Mtgs.
- Private Parties
- Accommodations

For an event as captivating as a work of art, the de Young Museum is unquestionably the right venue. Founded in 1895 and situated in the heart of San Francisco's Golden Gate Park, the completely redesigned museum has been transformed into an ultra-cool contemporary frame for fine art and outstanding functions.

Entrance is through the courtyard installation by famed sculptor Andy Goldsworthy. An invitingly lit lobby, featuring Italian stone floors and Ruth Asawa sculptures, is a fitting place to greet guests with champagne before whisking them up nine stories to the Hamon Observation Tower. Here, surrounded by walls of glass, delighted celebrants can savor cocktails, hors d'oeuvres and music. While mingling, they'll admire unimpeded 360-degree panoramic views of San Francisco's downtown skyline, the Golden Gate Bridge, the sparkling Pacific, and Golden Gate Park.

Your guests will also be impressed by the spectacular architecture of the concourse-level event spaces and galleries. The walls soar two stories high in dramatic Wilsey Court, a perfect fit for an über-elegant wedding reception, dinner dance or upscale corporate affair. Designed by renowned Swiss architects Herzog & de Meuron, its inspired use of angles, openness and art gives the space a fluid vitality. A grand staircase to the upper galleries is ideal for regal entrances and photo ops. And don't forget that you can include the de Young's exciting exhibits in your event, if you choose. The adjacent Piazzoni Murals Room, with burnished Italian landscapes adorning its walls, can serve as a special lounge, a separate bar and entertainment area, or an exclusive private chamber for more intimate gatherings.

But why stop here? For an artsy vibe with a whimsical twist, take your party to the de Young Café, de Young Terrace, and Barbro Osher Sculpture Garden, which can be used separately or in combination. Have your ceremony on the broad sculpture garden lawn amid playful artworks and fanciful landscaping, host cocktails on the adjacent terrace, then dine and dance in the café. One of the museum's most popular event spaces, it transforms to suit your mood: casual, formal, festive or even sultry. Striking touches like the colorful hand-blown glass lamps suspended over-head remind you that no matter where you go in the de Young art is everywhere, contributing a dynamic dimension to your celebration.

CEREMONY & MEETING CAPACITY: Indoors, spaces hold up to 400 seated guests. Outdoors, the Garden holds up to 200 seated guests for a ceremony.

EVENT/RECEPTION CAPACITY: Indoors, spaces hold up to 400 seated or 2,500 standing guests.

FEES & DEPOSITS: 50% of the rental fee is due at the time of booking. Rental fees start at $5,000 and vary depending on the space rented.

AVAILABILITY: Year-round, daily. Special events take place in a 4-hour window between 6:30pm and 1am. Daytime rental is available in limited spaces during museum hours. Overtime fees are additional.

SERVICES/AMENITIES:

Catering: preferred list
Kitchen Facilities: fully equipped
Tables & Chairs: some provided
Linens, Silver, etc.: through caterer
Restrooms: wheelchair accessible
Dance Floor: provided
Bride's & Groom's Dressing Areas: no
Meeting Equipment: some provided

Parking: valet or public garage
Accommodations: no guest rooms
Telephone: pay phones
Outdoor Night Lighting: access only
Outdoor Cooking Facilities: no
Cleanup: provided
View: park, garden, pond, cityscape
Other: event coordination, A/V equipment

RESTRICTIONS:

Alcohol: BYO
Smoking: not allowed
Music: amplified OK

Wheelchair Access: yes
Insurance: liability required

Want to know WHAT TO ASK a potential location or vendor? Check out our Questions to Ask starting on page 17.

E&O Asian Kitchen

314 Sutter Street, San Francisco
415/693-0303
www.eosanfrancisco.com
cnewman@eosanfrancisco.com

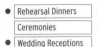

Restaurant

● Rehearsal Dinners		● Corp. Events/Mtgs.
Ceremonies		● Private Parties
● Wedding Receptions		Accommodations

One of San Francisco's favorite dining and event spaces just got even better. Located amid galleries, boutiques and topnotch hotels just a block from Union Square, the tremendously popular restaurant formerly known as E&O Trading Company has been re-envisioned and re-introduced to fans and new customers as E&O Asian Kitchen.

Tonya Bellusci, designer of San Francisco's District and Oakland's Pican restaurants, was commissioned to update the environment with a more relaxed Southeast Asian feel. Inspired by the beaches of Bali, Thailand and Sri Lanka, the new vibe incorporates shades of earth, gray and gold along with subtle tropical accents.

The spacious foyer, which leads seamlessly to the long open bar, is airy and inviting and creates a lounge area ideal for music, cocktails and plenty of guest interaction. This is no doubt the perfect place to sample the wondrous concoctions of the venue's expert mixologist—how about a Gazebo… or a Sea Witch…or perhaps a Blushing Geisha? Guests can mingle effortlessly here, nibbling on an inventive array of appetizers or simply sipping a glass of wine or champagne.

The hip new floor plan encourages flow, and everyone will be able to move freely through the restaurant as they dine on treats like succulent wood-grilled satays, ahi poke, plump little dumplings, and other delicious Pacific Rim specialties. You'll find all the design elements E&O is known for—sleek bar, exhibition kitchen, soaring ceilings—here in the main dining area.

Planning an intimate affair? A new private dining room has been added on the ground floor. It features Asian-influenced décor, a flat screen TV and a fabulous antiqued carved wooden door to ensure that your party will not be disturbed.

Downstairs in the Cinnabar Room, so named for the distinctive red color of the walls, the atmosphere is decidedly den-like and clubby. The wood-beamed ceiling, black marble bar, and velvet and leather chairs add to the aura of comfort and privacy.

For extra-large company dinners or smaller family gatherings, the mezzanine level is ideal. Past the shimmering, waterfall-like wall mosaic, up the stairs or elevator, the handsome U-shaped mezzanine affords a dazzling command of the main floor dining room, attractive Sutter Street views, and private and semiprivate dining in the E&O Room and North Mezzanine.

The flexible layout allows you to use individual spaces or combine them to suit your celebration. However, if you're hosting a large event or you just want the whole restaurant to yourself, you have the option of entertaining and dining on all three levels.

E&O is easy to reach via public transportation, and the adjacent Stockton-Sutter Garage makes parking convenient. Guests staying in nearby hotels will love the fact that everything is within walking distance—they can do a little shopping or visit a few galleries on their way to your event.

CEREMONY CAPACITY: Ceremonies do not take place at this facility.

EVENT/RECEPTION CAPACITY: Private dining spaces hold up to 275 seated or 300 standing guests.

MEETING CAPACITY: The restaurant accommodates up to 200 seated guests.

FEES & DEPOSITS: 50% of the estimated event total is required to reserve your date. The balance is due at the end of the event. Meals range $42–78/person. Tax, alcohol and a 20% service charge are additional.

AVAILABILITY: Year-round, daily, 11:30am–midnight.

SERVICES/AMENITIES:

Catering: provided, no BYO
Kitchen Facilities: n/a
Tables & Chairs: provided
Linens, Silver, etc.: provided
Restrooms: wheelchair accessible
Dance Floor: CBA
Bride's Dressing Area: no
Meeting Equipment: some provided

Parking: public garage
Accommodations: no guest rooms
Telephone: house and office phones
Outdoor Night Lighting: no
Outdoor Cooking Facilities: no
Cleanup: provided
View: SF cityscape
Other: event coordination, on-site florals

RESTRICTIONS:

Alcohol: provided, no BYO
Smoking: outside only
Music: amplified OK indoors

Wheelchair Access: yes
Insurance: not required

Exploratorium

Pier 15, San Francisco
415/528-4500
www.exploratorium.edu/rentals
events@exploratorium.edu

Landmark Museum

● Rehearsal Dinners	● Corp. Events/Mtgs.
● Ceremonies	● Private Parties
● Wedding Receptions	Accommodations

For a jaw-dropping event that will wow young and old, you simply must consider the Exploratorium in its all-new venue at Pier 15 on San Francisco's Embarcadero. Packed with exciting exhibits and exhilarating event spaces, the new Exploratorium is making a huge splash—creatively—on our ever-popular Bayscape.

The totally re-envisioned 100,000-square-foot facility is situated right on the water between Fisherman's Wharf and the Ferry Building. Set on a nine-acre campus that encompasses Pier 17, the super-popular interactive museum of science, art and human perception includes a Forum, Restaurant, Café, Museum Shop, numerous indoor Galleries, an Outdoor Gallery, an Observatory Gallery and an Outdoor Terrace—all of which can be used alone or in combination for your spectacular celebration.

What we love about this venue is that, true to its mission, it was designed with the latest developments in sustainable architecture. With a goal of being the largest net-zero energy museum in the U.S., it offsets its energy use with "green" features like solar panels and a bay water heating and cooling system. We also like the way it allows for so much movement and flow. You can thread your event through the exhibits in a manner that entertains and engages. Whether you're planning a wedding, gala, corporate extravaganza, product launch, film screening, dinner-dance or any other kind of gathering, you'll find just the right spot in this tremendously flexible and dynamic setting.

Weddings, for example, might begin with a ceremony in the Observatory Gallery, a gorgeous glass-walled jewel box of a room on the second floor of the only entirely new structure on the pier. This exquisite chamber affords nearly 360-degree views that include Treasure Island, the Bay Bridge, the Transamerica Pyramid and Coit Tower, and it contains an oculus—a giant glass eye in the ceiling from which to view the heavens. Sliding glass doors open onto the Outdoor Terrace, where more soothing bay views frame cocktails, passed hors d'oeuvres, dinner or dancing under a tent or a canopy of sky.

Three more galleries offer unique entertainment experiences. Your guests can chat, stroll, dine and dance their way through one or all of them, depending on your vision. The Life Sciences come alive in the East Gallery, a beautiful space for an intimate seated dinner or reception with enormous windows overlooking the bay. The expansive Central Gallery is perfect for larger affairs where the exploration of sight, sound and perception is sure to stimulate interaction. In the exciting West Gallery, you'll find the museum's iconic Tactile Dome and a "black box" for immersive installations. It can be used in tandem with the adjacent Forum—which has a stage, a state-of-the-art sound and projection system, theater- or cabaret-style seating and a permanent bar—or with other galleries to engender the sense of wonder, amazement, joy and play that makes an event here unforgettable.

And do remember: The Exploratorium's expertise in interaction and perception extends to its energetic and imaginative event staff. Whether it's picking out party favors from the Museum Shop, inventing new ways to utilize the galleries and exhibits, or carefully orchestrating a festive flow, they'll know how to transform your great ideas into a truly inspiring celebration.

CEREMONY CAPACITY: Indoor ceremony spaces can accommodate 50–400 seated guests. The outdoor Observatory Terrace holds up to 150 guests.

EVENT/RECEPTION CAPACITY: Individual galleries hold 150–450 seated or 250–1,200 standing. The entire facility can accommodate up to 1,600 seated or 4,000 standing.

MEETING CAPACITY: Meeting spaces hold up to 220 seated.

FEES & DEPOSITS: 50% of the rental fee is required to reserve your date. The balance is due 3 months prior to the event. Rental fees start at $12,000 and vary depending on galleries rented, number of guests and total contracted hours.

AVAILABILITY: Year-round, daily except Wednesday and Thursday, starting at 5:15pm.

SERVICES/AMENITIES:

Catering: select from approved list
Kitchen Facilities: prep only
Tables & Chairs: through caterer
Linens, Silver, etc.: through caterer
Restrooms: wheelchair accessible
Dance Area: provided or through caterer
Bride's Dressing Area: CBA
Meeting Equipment: CBA, extra charge
Other: A/V equipment, access to hundreds of hands-on exhibits

Parking: valet, public lots or on street
Accommodations: no guest rooms
Telephone: office phone
Outdoor Night Lighting: access only
Outdoor Cooking Facilities: no
Cleanup: caterer
View: cityscape of Transamerica Pyramid and Coit Tower; bay views including Bay Bridge and Treasure Island

RESTRICTIONS:

Alcohol: through caterer, licensed server required
Smoking: outdoors only
Music: amplified OK with restrictions

Wheelchair Access: yes
Insurance: liability required

The Fairmont Hotel

Hotel

Atop Nob Hill, San Francisco

415/772-5000

www.fairmont.com/sanfrancisco
emilie.rekart@fairmont.com

● Rehearsal Dinners	● Corp. Events/Mtgs.
● Ceremonies	● Private Parties
● Wedding Receptions	● Accommodations

As the first hotel to open after the 1906 earthquake, the Fairmont San Francisco became the main gathering place and grand centerpiece of the City by the Bay. Since then, this extraordinary hotel continues to be a mecca for guests from all over the world and one of San Francisco's most treasured landmarks.

Over the last century, The Fairmont has undergone many changes, but an $85 million restoration not only brought back architect Julia Morgan's stunning turn-of-the-century interior, it added all the modern amenities you'd expect in a world-class hotel.

The lobby is now both larger and lighter in tone, and is splendidly understated with rich plum and gold hues. The original white-and-gray marble floor (lifted out slab by slab, cleaned and meticulously replaced) has been given a high sheen. The gold leaf on the 26-foot-high ceilings has been enhanced, and the ornate moldings have been cleaned and restored. Multiple pilasters and columns, painted in a *trompe l'oeil* marble finish, are highlighted with gold leaf accents. Informal clusters of period-style furniture, rich in detail with lots of tassels and trim, dot the lobby. The adjacent Laurel Court has become a warm and elegant restaurant and bar where your guests will enjoy mingling over drinks and hors d'oeuvres.

Two of the most grand and glamorous spaces in the Fairmont are the Venetian and Gold Ballrooms. Both are light and airy, with elaborately ornamented vaulted ceilings, gold leaf detailing, and crystal chandeliers. The Pavilion Room has picture windows that overlook The Fairmont's rooftop garden, a sublime spot for exchanging vows. The Crown Room, named for its spectacular location on the top floor of the Fairmont Tower, is a soothing environment in soft celadon, sage, pale violet and gold highlights. The room's most remarkable feature, however, is the view. Tall wraparound windows reveal a sweeping 270-degree panorama of the Golden Gate and Bay Bridges, Coit Tower, Alcatraz, Downtown and the Twin Peaks. The setting here is impressive enough, but if you really want to have the ultimate reception, opt for the Presidential Service: Each table has its own waiter, and everyone is served at exactly the same time.

The ultimate place to hold your event may be the 6,000-square-foot Penthouse, a palatial residence spanning the entire eighth floor of the main building following a $2 million enhancement. This extraordinary suite features a living room with a grand piano, a formal dining room that seats 50, a two-story circular library, a billiard room, a breathtaking terrace with sweeping views of the San Francisco skyline and bay, and three oversized bedrooms. When you reserve the Penthouse, you and your guests have exclusive use of it and are free to flow from one space to another throughout the celebration.

If your event is on a more intimate scale, the Fairmont has many beautiful smaller banquet rooms from which to choose. For a more casual rehearsal dinner or post-wedding gathering, the Tonga Room consistently receives awards for hosting San Francisco's best happy hour and offers exceptional Pacific Rim Asian cuisine in a tropical setting.

This is one historic hotel that's also quite forward thinking. Their Green Weddings program includes hundreds of options from organic, locally produced foods and biodynamic wines to recyclable favors and confetti. Guest rooms are also totally up to date, with flat screen TVs, MP3 docking stations, Frette linens and pillow-top beds. There is no question that The Fairmont's combination of exquisite classic décor, first-rate amenities and personalized service puts this deluxe five-star hotel in a category of its own.

CEREMONY CAPACITY: Seven indoor ceremony sites accommodate 50–500 seated guests. The Roof Garden holds 150 seated.

EVENT/RECEPTION CAPACITY: The hotel's event spaces can accommodate 40–900 seated or 150–2,500 standing guests indoors.

MEETING CAPACITY: There are 19 rooms that hold 35–1,500 seated guests theater-style or 12–1,000 seated classroom-style.

FEES & DEPOSITS: A nonrefundable deposit is required when reservations are confirmed. 20% of the estimated event total is due 90 days prior to the event. An additional deposit of 60% of the estimated total is due 30 days prior, with the remaining balance due 14 days before the event. Wedding packages range $140–350/person. Tax, alcohol and service charge is additional. For ceremonies, a $3,500–15,000 fee may be charged depending on room(s) selected and extent of setup. Bride and groom receive a complimentary suite for the night of the event. Group rates for overnight guests can be arranged.

AVAILABILITY: Year-round, daily, 8am–2am.

SERVICES/AMENITIES:

Catering: provided, no BYO
Kitchen Facilities: n/a
Tables & Chairs: provided
Linens, Silver, etc.: provided
Restrooms: wheelchair accessible
Dance Floor: provided
Bride's & Groom's Dressing Areas: yes
Meeting Equipment: full range CBA
Other: event planning, on-site florist

Parking: adjacent garages, valet CBA
Accommodations: 591 guest rooms
Telephone: guest phones
Outdoor Night Lighting: yes
Outdoor Cooking Facilities: no
Cleanup: provided
View: SF Bay, city skyline, Bay and Golden Gate Bridges

RESTRICTIONS:

Alcohol: provided, no BYO
Smoking: outdoors only
Music: amplified OK indoors

Wheelchair Access: yes, elevator
Insurance: not required

Want to find more venues and services? Check out our informative website, www.HereComesTheGuide.com.

71

First Unitarian Universalist Church of San Francisco   *Historic Church*

1187 Franklin Street, San Francisco
415/776-4580 x202
www.uusf.org
reservations@uusf.org

● Rehearsal Dinners	● Corp. Events/Mtgs.
● Ceremonies	● Private Parties
● Wedding Receptions	○ Accommodations

As you drive past the bustling corner of Geary and Franklin Streets, you'll notice a beautiful old building that contrasts sharply with its modern neighbors. Built of sandstone in the Gothic Revival-Romanesque style, the First Unitarian Universalist Church of San Francisco looks as if it has existed for over a hundred years—and it has.

Although this is the church's third location in the city, it has occupied this corner since 1889. The First Unitarian Universalist Church marries all loving couples, and does not discriminate based upon gender or spiritual belief.

In the sanctuary, Gothic and modern design elements create an atmosphere that is open and airy, yet visually stimulating. White plaster walls, set with exquisite stained-glass rose windows, soar up to meet the tracery of the carved beam ceiling hung with wrought-iron and gilt chandeliers. On the chancel, the imposing carved Gothic chairs, pulpit and lectern are lightened by a delicate abstract metal candelabra hung on the wall behind them. A custom-built 3,100-pipe organ—said to be one of the best on the West Coast—sits regally in the choir loft. For an extra touch of magic, six-foot-tall candelabras can be fitted into brackets at the ends of the pews, giving an ethereal glow to your ceremony.

The 70-seat Chapel is ideal for smaller weddings. Octagonal in shape, its tall concrete walls are inset with narrow, stained-glass windows in shades of blue and gold, and hung with Oriental rugs and wall hangings. What makes the Chapel truly unique, however, is its fabulous acoustics. Not only do they enhance every type of music from harp to string quartet, they give the Chapel a feeling of real intimacy, and ensure that your guests will hear even your softest-spoken words.

The 35-seat Fireside Room, with fireplace, beamed ceilings and wood paneling is a cozy spot for intimate weddings, receptions or business functions. A favorite place for wedding photos and outdoor celebrations is the Allyne Courtyard, a sunny space whose focal point is a free-form bronze fountain, surrounded by flowering trees and plants.

For indoor events, the Church has two large function areas. The Thomas Starr King Room is named after the Church's beloved minister from 1860 to 1864. This spacious room has a parquet floor, impressive pyramidal beamed skylight hung with wood-and-opaque-glass light fixtures, and a recessed stage area that is perfect for a bride's table or DJ setup. The artwork on the walls is changed monthly. The adjacent Martin Luther King Room, named after the civil rights leader, is a smaller version of the Starr King Room, and sliding doors allow you to combine the two if desired.

Perhaps the most impressive thing about the First Unitarian Universalist Church is its acceptance of diverse faiths, cultures and lifestyles. You are invited to work with their clergy to create a ceremony that celebrates your values and the unique commitment you are making. So, whether you want a traditional wedding with organ music accompanying your procession, or a less conventional ceremony, you're sure to find a warm welcome at the First Unitarian Universalist Church.

CEREMONY CAPACITY: The Sanctuary can accommodate up to 350 seated guests.

EVENT/RECEPTION & MEETING CAPACITY: The church's two reception rooms combined hold up to 270 seated or 300 standing guests indoors.

FEES & DEPOSITS: 50% of the rental fee is required to reserve your date; the balance is due 30 days prior to the event. A $550–1,950 ceremony fee includes an hour for rehearsal, 2 hours for setup, an hour for photos after the ceremony, the organist, and an event coordinator. Rental fees for receptions and business functions range $700–1,500 depending on guest count and space rented. Events running past 10pm incur additional fees.

AVAILABILITY: Year-round, daily, 8am–10pm.

SERVICES/AMENITIES:

Catering: BYO
Kitchen Facilities: prep only
Tables & Chairs: provided
Linens, Silver, etc.: BYO
Restrooms: wheelchair accessible
Dance Floor: yes
Bride's & Groom's Dressing Areas: provided
Meeting Equipment: TV/VCR, microphones, sound system, CD/DVD capability

Parking: nearby garages
Accommodations: no guest rooms
Telephone: emergency use only
Outdoor Night Lighting: n/a
Outdoor Cooking Facilities: n/a
Cleanup: through caterer
View: inner courtyard
Other: event coordination

RESTRICTIONS:

Alcohol: BYO
Smoking: outdoors only
Music: amplified OK indoors only

Wheelchair Access: yes
Insurance: not required

Foreign Cinema

Restaurant

2534 Mission Street, San Francisco
415/648-7600 X24

www.foreigncinema.com
janine@foreigncinema.com

- Rehearsal Dinners
- Ceremonies
- Wedding Receptions
- Corp. Events/Mtgs.
- Private Parties
- Accommodations

Dinner and a movie…it's the quintessential first date that's probably launched more relationships than any other activity. So what could be more perfect than celebrating the most important day of your relationship by playing out your own romantic wedding scene at Foreign Cinema in San Francisco?

This dynamic and thoroughly original venue in the Mission District has become a magnet for foodies, cinephiles, and loyal locals by artfully editing together critically acclaimed cuisine with several unique dining environments—including a glorious courtyard where films are projected on an exterior wall. If you buy out the restaurant, all of these spaces become yours for the Big Night.

A small marquee-style awning marks the entrance to the restaurant, where two stainless steel doors usher you down a seductively lit hallway, flickering with votive candles. If you're having your ceremony here, your guests will be invited outside to the canopied center Courtyard, which provides a nice long aisle for a dramatic bridal entrance. After the service, friends and family can enjoy a sumptuous cocktail reception in the Modernism West Gallery, a loft-like space with a two-story ceiling. Lining the crisp white walls is an impressive display of visually exciting artwork, which gives the setting a cultural edge and provides a great backdrop for photos. There's a chic bar at one end, and along the other are floor-to-ceiling windows inset with glass doors that lead to a cozy Zen-like Upper Patio. Some couples opt to host their entire event in the Gallery.

For larger groups, the festivities continue across the Courtyard with dinner in the rustically elegant Dining Room, whose wood-framed windows open to the outdoors, creating a nice connection between the two spaces. Burgundy banquettes, a stainless steel bar, fireplace, the rich patina of the wood floor and very cool chandeliers made of hanging light bulbs with their cords tied together give the room a warm, yet trendy feel.

Overlooking it all is the Mezzanine, which can serve as a VIP lounge, an intimate rehearsal dinner spot, or a retreat for the bride and groom…all with great views of the action below. And part of that action is the open kitchen, because Foreign Cinema, being chef-owned, is very focused on maintaining the high level of its popular California-Mediterranean dishes, which use only fresh, organic ingredients in inventive ways.

Finally, top off a wonderful evening with dancing in the Gallery and nightcaps in the Courtyard, as your favorite movie or a slideshow of your own love story is projected on the wall.

CEREMONY CAPACITY: The facility holds 100 seated guests indoors or outdoors.

EVENT/RECEPTION CAPACITY: The venue can accommodate up to 175 seated or 400 standing guests.

MEETING CAPACITY: Meeting rooms hold 70 seated guests.

FEES & DEPOSITS: A deposit of varying amounts is required to reserve your date, and the balance is due at the conclusion of the event. Food and beverage minimums range $1,500–35,000 depending on the space reserved and the day of the week of the event. Menus range $55–100/person. Tax, alcohol and a 20% service charge are additional. A facility fee may apply.

AVAILABILITY: Year-round, daily. Call or email for specifics on times available.

SERVICES/AMENITIES:

Catering: provided
Kitchen Facilities: n/a
Tables & Chairs: provided
Linens, Silver, etc.: provided
Restrooms: wheelchair accessible
Dance Floor: provided
Bride's Dressing Area: no
Meeting Equipment: CBA

Parking: on street, valet, garage nearby
Accommodations: no guest rooms
Telephone: house phone
Outdoor Night Lighting: provided
Outdoor Cooking Facilities: none
Cleanup: provided
View: garden courtyard
Other: on-site florals, event coordination, film projection available

RESTRICTIONS:

Alcohol: provided
Smoking: not allowed
Music: amplified OK with restrictions

Wheelchair Access: yes
Insurance: not required

Fort Mason Center

Historic Event Center

Landmark Building A, Fort Mason Center, San Francisco

415/345-7500

www.fortmason.org
www.fortmason.org/venuerental/rfp

Rehearsal Dinners	●	Corp. Events/Mtgs.
● Ceremonies	●	Private Parties
● Wedding Receptions		Accommodations

Fort Mason Center embodies what most people love about San Francisco—a nearness to nature (especially the bay), novel architecture and a sense of the past. Located on some of the most prime real estate in the city, the center's historic buildings sit adjacent to the Marina Green, right on the water, with postcard-worthy vistas of the Golden Gate Bridge, Alcatraz, and the Marin Headlands. Its well-preserved structures and piers recall its military past, but in the 1970s the site was re-purposed as an urban national park and Fort Mason Center was established. It's since become a hub for nonprofit arts organizations, and also houses galleries, bookstores and restaurants. In addition, the center has more than 17 venues that host events of all types and sizes.

Among the most popular sites for intimate weddings is the Firehouse, a lovely freestanding hall tucked away in the far northeast corner of the complex. Considered a hidden gem thanks to its near complete privacy and divine views, it edges right up to the bay on one side and a pine-covered hill on the other. Naturally, couples often choose to marry outdoors on its cozy waterfront patio, with Marin's rolling hills in the distance. Add a tent and heat lamps for evening get-togethers, or retreat inside where high-ceilinged rooms dress up nicely for seated dinners, buffets and dancing.

For larger festivities, the Conference Center—comprised of three adjoining rooms—offers spectacular seascape vistas. In the Golden Gate Room, an entire wall of windows faces the marina. During the day, glittering blue water contrasts with white sailboats and the signature orange-red of the Golden Gate Bridge. At night, the view becomes a galaxy of twinkling lights from the city, yachts and bridge. Guests dine and dance beneath a vaulted ceiling, while a band or DJ plays on the elevated stage.

Recently, the General's Residence—which has entertained luminaries such as General MacArthur and two presidents—has been restored to its former splendor. A sprawling lawn behind the building hosts ceremonies with sweeping bay views, while floor-to-ceiling windows throughout the interior bring those legendary panoramas indoors. The Residence is an intriguing blend of past and present: The Foyer evokes nostalgic grandeur with a fireplace and magnificent crystal chandelier, yet the Dining Room and Ballroom both have a breezy, contemporary simplicity.

At each of these distinctive venues, you can tailor an event to your taste and budget. The managers of the property embrace couples who want a do-it-yourself potluck as much as those planning an elaborate catered affair. And because of the undeniably beautiful location, you don't need to add much in the way of fancy décor.

The nondenominational Chapel, located near the General's Residence, can be used in combination with any venue at the center and features stained-glass windows, a historic bell tower, and a choir loft.

Though Fort Mason Center effortlessly accommodates those tying the knot, it also has a strong mission to serve the local community. Booking an event here helps ensure that this landmark—and its affiliated arts organizations—remains for future generations to enjoy. This added benefit is not lost on socially conscious couples who realize that it's possible to get married in high style and support a nonprofit in the process.

CEREMONY CAPACITY: The Golden Gate Room can accommodate up to 300 seated guests, the Firehouse 125 seated, the General's Residence 160 seated, and the Chapel up to 200 seated.

EVENT/RECEPTION CAPACITY: The Conference Center holds 180 seated or 225 standing guests, the Firehouse holds 85 seated or 100 standing, and the General's Residence holds 160 seated in the dining room or 400 standing in the entire venue.

MEETING CAPACITY: The Conference Center holds 285 guests indoors, seated theater-style.

FEES & DEPOSITS: 50% of the rental fee is required to reserve your date. The balance is due 45 days prior to the event. Rental fees range $1,000–8,000 depending on the time of the event and the space rented.

AVAILABILITY: Year-round, daily, 8am–midnight.

SERVICES/AMENITIES:

Catering: BYO
Kitchen Facilities: limited
Tables & Chairs: provided
Linens, Silver, etc.: some provided
Restrooms: wheelchair accessible
Dance Floor: portable provided
Bride's Dressing Area: CBA
Meeting Equipment: some provided
Other: picnic area, A/V equipment, event coordination

Parking: large lot, on street, valet CBA
Accommodations: no guest rooms
Telephone: emergency use only
Outdoor Night Lighting: access only
Outdoor Cooking Facilities: BBQ CBA
Cleanup: renter
View: panorama of San Francisco Bay, Alcatraz Island, cityscape and coastline

RESTRICTIONS:

Alcohol: BYO
Smoking: not permitted
Music: amplified OK indoors

Wheelchair Access: yes
Insurance: liability required

This is important! Tell locations you're reading HERE COMES THE GUIDE and ask if our information is still current.

77

Galleria at the San Francisco Design Center

Event Facility

101 Henry Adams Street, San Francisco
415/490-5861
www.sfvenues.com
jwagner@sfdesigncenter.com

● Rehearsal Dinners	● Corp. Events/Mtgs.
● Ceremonies	● Private Parties
● Wedding Receptions	Accommodations

The exterior of the Galleria building at the San Francisco Design Center gives you no clue as to what's inside—all you see is sky and trees, reflected in a gleaming, four-story façade of more than 700 individual glass panes. Walk through the front doors, however, and you see the world as it would be if top designers were in charge.

The main event space is directly ahead of you, and it becomes immediately clear that the building's architects have made excellent use of the four stories they had to play with. They've created a soaring atrium with a retractable skylight that literally brings the outdoors inside: On nice days, fresh air and sunshine flood in. The whole space radiates warmth and contemporary sophistication with its open, airy feel, Italian tile floor and exposed brick walls.

Just about any kind of event would feel at home here. The polished light maple hardwood floor in the center can be used for dining or dancing; the elevated stage is right for presentations, a performance or a band, and there's a built-in beverage bar as well. Rising on all sides are three levels of balconies, where *tête-à-tête* tables provide an excellent vantage for people-watching.

On weekdays the Galleria showcases designer furniture, but on weeknights and weekends it comes into its own as a party venue. With its state-of-the-art sound and light system, its stage and dance floor, and its versatile seating options, it's especially suitable for corporate galas, creative receptions and cocktail parties. Not surprisingly, the Galleria has been discovered by high tech, multimedia companies and the media, who love the possibilities it offers. They frequently bring in incredible props and produce large-scale audiovisual presentations to launch a new website or product. Other "transformations" have included a Casablanca Night and a White Christmas party complete with "snow."

There are so many pluses to this unique space, you can do almost anything with it! Entertain an intimate gathering of 100, or throw a bash for 1,600. Take advantage of the full-scale sound system, which allows a DJ to hook right in, or experiment with the theatrical lighting to make a dramatic statement on the dance floor and stage. For some truly festive sparkle, set the Tivoli lights on "chasing." Guests can mingle with the crowd on the main floor, or steal away to an upper tier for a quiet conversation, and still feel part of the event.

While this facility is terrific for high-end corporate and private parties, don't overlook the inventive possibilities for a wedding ceremony or reception. Picture the atrium awash in rose petals... or maybe palm trees and toucans for that tropical island ambiance...or a snow motif for winter nuptials. So go ahead and fantasize—truth is, for any event where you want a quality production with endless possibilities, the Galleria has the resources, the space and, above all, the style.

CEREMONY CAPACITY: The Galleria holds 400 seated guests.

EVENT/RECEPTION & MEETING CAPACITY: The Galleria can accommodate up to 750 seated or 1,600 standing guests; the first floor holds 350 seated or 1,000 standing, and 3 additional floors hold 150 more seated guests per floor.

FEES & DEPOSITS: 50% of the rental fee is required as a deposit to secure your date; the balance is payable 90 days prior to the event. The rental fee starts at $6,000 and varies depending on guest count and floors rented. Sound and light technicians (at $50/hour per technician) are available. A facility manager and security guards are required; call for specific rates.

AVAILABILITY: Year-round, weekday evenings 6pm–2am, and weekends 8am–2am.

SERVICES/AMENITIES:

Catering: select from list or BYO with approval
Kitchen Facilities: no
Tables & Chairs: provided for up to 300 guests
Linens, Silver, etc.: through caterer
Restrooms: wheelchair accessible
Dance Floor: yes
Bride's Dressing Area: yes
Meeting Equipment: podium, mic, sound system

Parking: on-street, pay lots
Accommodations: no guest rooms
Telephone: no
Outdoor Night Lighting: access only
Outdoor Cooking Facilities: CBA
Cleanup: basic janitorial cleanup included in rental fee
View: no

RESTRICTIONS:

Alcohol: provided, no BYO
Smoking: outside only
Music: amplified OK

Wheelchair Access: yes
Insurance: liability insurance required

Great American Music Hall

Historic Music Hall

859 O'Farrell Street, San Francisco
415/255-7395
www.gamh.com
amie@slims-sf.com

- Rehearsal Dinners
- Ceremonies
- Wedding Receptions
- Corp. Events/Mtgs.
- Private Parties
- Accommodations

Standing beneath marble columns, ornately gilded balconies and an elaborate frescoed ceiling, it's easy to imagine this building's allure when it first came on the scene as a flashy French restaurant and San Francisco's grandest nightclub. Opening in 1907 on the heels of the great earthquake, the 5,000-square-foot concert hall symbolized the city's renewed optimism. The popular club flourished for a quarter century in this incarnation, then became the Music Box, where Sally Rand performed her famous fan dances, and later served as a Moose Lodge and yet another French restaurant.

In 1972 it was reborn as the Great American Music Hall, and in 1994 a complete facelift restored the club to its original rococo grandeur. For more than 25 years the hall has showcased the talents of music and comedy greats such as Ray Charles, the Grateful Dead, Bonnie Raitt, Jay Leno, Whoopi Goldberg and Robin Williams. Its intimate setting and wonderful acoustics continue to make it a favorite among locals, as well as with their devoted following throughout the Bay Area.

In addition to countless concerts, the Hall has hosted corporate bashes, fundraisers, holiday parties, product launches and weddings. Its flexible layout—one large room with balconies, a stage, huge oak dance floor and two full bars—makes it party-friendly, and there's not a bad seat in the house. The Music Hall also comes equipped with a state-of-the-art lighting and sound system and all the necessary staff.

Couples getting married here use the stage for the ceremony, with their "audience" seated in chairs on the dance floor and up in the balconies. Once the knot has been tied, the rows of chairs are removed and the Hall is ready for the next phase of the celebration. Tables have been set up for dining all around, and even on the balconies if you like. With a band or a DJ making music on the stage and your guests dancing in the center of the room, the festivities can carry on into the night.

The Great American Music Hall offers a couple of very cool options that take the fun factor up a notch: They'll put the name of your company, your group, your families, or a special message on their marquee (who wouldn't get a kick out of seeing your name in lights?). Considering a theme event? The Hall is the perfect setting for a glitzy casino night, a Barbary Coast bash, or a Phantom of the Opera Night. Swing or '60s dance parties work well here, too.

Close to Union Square and only 10 blocks from Moscone Center, the Music Hall is conveniently situated for post-convention events. The space adapts comfortably to the size of your group, whether you have 100 or 600 guests, and the in-house coordinator will help you book just the right band or DJ.

While you can enhance the mood here with candles or uplighting the columns, the Great American Music Hall is really quite scintillating all by itself. The only building of its kind in The City, it provides a unique window into San Francisco's colorful, exuberant past.

CEREMONY & EVENT/RECEPTION CAPACITY: The Hall can accommodate 50–350 seated and up to 600 standing guests for a reception. Ceremonies can take place on the stage.

MEETING CAPACITY: Up to 250 seated guests with an unobstructed view of the stage.

FEES & DEPOSITS: Half the required event minimum plus a $500 refundable security deposit are due when reservations are confirmed; the balance is payable 2 business days prior to the event. Facility rental rates are as follows: Sunday–Wednesday $6,500, with an additional food and beverage minimum of $3,000. The rental rate for Thursday–Saturday is $8,000, with an additional food and beverage minimum of $5,000. Food and beverage minimums are subject to a service charge and current sales tax. Holiday rates may be subject to an additional surcharge.

There are additional fees for miscellaneous services and various rental items. Evening rental rates include a house manager, bartenders, cocktail waitresses, sound and lighting technicians, security staff, an on-site event coordinator and more. If you use the in-house catering, all servers and culinary staff are included and meal pricing is as follows: hors d'oeuvres start at $20/person, dinners at $45/person; alcohol, tax and service charge are additional.

AVAILABILITY: Year-round, daily, 6am–3pm or 3pm–2am. Other blocks of time can be arranged.

SERVICES/AMENITIES:

Catering: provided or BYO
Kitchen Facilities: fully equipped
Tables & Chairs: cocktail tables and chairs are provided or BYO
Linens, Silver, etc.: call for details
Restrooms: wheelchair accessible
Dance Floor: yes
Bride's Dressing Area: 3 dressing rooms
Meeting Equipment: microphones, screen, built-in stage

Parking: valet, garage, nearby lots, on street
Accommodations: no guest rooms
Telephone: house phone
Outdoor Night Lighting: access only
Outdoor Cooking Facilities: no
Cleanup: provided
View: no
Other: event coordination, state-of-the-art sound and lighting systems, entertainment bookings

RESTRICTIONS:

Alcohol: provided
Smoking: no
Music: amplified OK

Wheelchair Access: yes
Insurance: required
Other: no birdseed, rice or confetti; no stick-on name tags

Greens

Fort Mason Center, Building A, San Francisco
415/771-7955 X114
www.greensrestaurant.com
events@greensrestaurant.com

Waterfront Restaurant

- Rehearsal Dinners
- Ceremonies
- Wedding Receptions
- Corp. Events/Mtgs.
- Private Parties
- Accommodations

Greens is a special restaurant, not just because of its waterfront location at Fort Mason, or because it's owned by a Zen Buddhist organization, or because it serves gourmet vegetarian fare with flair. This place is special because the space makes you feel so good.

Greens has enormous multipaned windows extending the entire length of the restaurant. These windows have superb views of the Golden Gate Bridge and of the boat harbor just beyond the building. At sunset, the waning light reflected off the bridge and boats is a stunning sight to see. And for smaller events, Greens can serve you in their private room which features the same wonderful views. The interior of Greens is exceptional, with excellent original artwork, unusual carved wood seating and tables, and a high vaulted ceiling. The overall impression is light, airy and comfortable.

And just in case you think Greens serves bean sprouts and tofu, think again. Their menus are diverse, with wide-ranging entrées that appeal to vegetarians and nonvegetarians alike. Mouthwatering hors d'oeuvres, savory vegetable tarts, hearty pasta and filo dishes and an extensive wine list help make Greens one of the most popular places in San Francisco. We have a feeling that long after the party's over, your wedding guests will return to sample Greens' other culinary delights on their own.

CEREMONY CAPACITY: The Main Dining Room holds 200 standing.

EVENT/RECEPTION CAPACITY: The entire restaurant is available as a buyout for up to 140 guests for a seated meal and up to 200 for a standing reception; the Private Dining Room holds up to 50 guests for a seated meal and up to 65 for a standing reception.

FEES & DEPOSITS: A $1,500 deposit and signed contract with credit card is required to reserve a date. A buyout starts at $8,000 and the Private Dining Room rental fee starts at $175. Prices vary depending on the date rented. Full meal service is provided. Three-course meals start at $35/person for lunch and $50/person for dinner in the private room. All events include linens, printed menus, small flowers and votive candles. Alcohol, tax and a 20% service charge are additional.

AVAILABILITY: Year-round, daily, anytime. Call for details.

SERVICES/AMENITIES:

Catering: provided, no BYO

Kitchen Facilities: n/a

Tables & Chairs: provided

Linens, Silver, etc.: provided

Restrooms: wheelchair accessible

Dance Floor: CBA, extra cost

Bride's Dressing Area: CBA

Meeting Equipment: CBA

Parking: large lot

Accommodations: no guest rooms

Telephone: pay phone

Outdoor Night Lighting: access only

Outdoor Cooking Facilities: no

Cleanup: provided

View: Golden Gate Bridge, Marin Headlands, San Francisco Bay and Marina

RESTRICTIONS:

Alcohol: provided, wine, beer or champagne only

Smoking: outside only

Music: amplified OK

Wheelchair Access: yes, ramp

Insurance: not required

Overwhelmed? Use the search criteria on www.HereComesTheGuide.com to narrow down your choices.

83

Haas-Lilienthal House

2007 Franklin Street at Washington, San Francisco
415/441-3000 X14

www.sfheritage.org
broldan@sfheritage.org

Historic Home

- Rehearsal Dinners
- Ceremonies
- Wedding Receptions
- Corp. Events/Mtgs.
- Private Parties
- Accommodations

The 1886 Haas-Lilienthal House is a Pacific Heights treasure and unique museum. Owned and operated by San Francisco Architectural Heritage, this stately Queen Anne-style Victorian has been meticulously preserved, complete with period furnishings. Largely unchanged since it was built, it offers an unparalleled Victorian experience that will transport you and your guests back in time.

An abundance of rich woodwork and architectural detail throughout create a warm, intimate environment that's perfect for weddings. The main floor features 13-foot ceilings, two large parlors, a formal dining room and a foyer and hall. A spacious ballroom is available downstairs for larger parties. Exuding the grace and comfort of a bygone era, this historic house provides a delightful setting for your celebration.

In the city of "Painted Ladies," the Haas-Lilienthal House is the only residential Victorian whose interior is open to the public. Tours are held Wednesday, Saturday and Sunday afternoons, and docent-led tours can be arranged for special events.

If you're looking for a one-of-a-kind wedding, the Haas-Lilienthal House is an excellent choice—and proceeds help ensure that the house will remain a San Francisco landmark for decades to come!

CEREMONY CAPACITY: The front and middle parlors, combined, hold 50 seated or up to 100 seated and standing.

EVENT/RECEPTION CAPACITY: The house accommodates 90 guests for a seated meal or 100 for a standing reception.

MEETING CAPACITY: The house holds up to 65 seated guests.

FEES & DEPOSITS: A $500 refundable security deposit is required and is returned 30 days after the event. The rental fee runs $2,350–3,400 and includes use of the entire museum, tables and chairs, and dressing rooms. During December the house is festively decorated for the holidays. For wedding rehearsals, there is an extra $250 fee.

Rates for business functions and meetings vary depending on services selected; call the Haas-Lilienthal House for specific details.

AVAILABILITY: Year-round, daily. Sunday–Thursday until 10pm; Friday and Saturday until 11pm.

SERVICES/AMENITIES:

Catering: select from preferred list, or BYO with approval
Kitchen Facilities: moderately equipped
Tables & Chairs: some provided
Linens, Silver, etc.: through caterer or BYO
Restrooms: not wheelchair accessible
Dance Floor: yes
Bride's Dressing Area: provided
Meeting Equipment: fax, copier, WiFi

Parking: on street, valet CBA
Accommodations: no guest rooms
Telephone: emergency only
Outdoor Night Lighting: access only
Outdoor Cooking Facilities: with approval
Cleanup: caterer
View: garden

RESTRICTIONS:

Alcohol: through caterer or BYO, must be served by licensed catering staff
Smoking: outside only
Music: amplified OK with restrictions

Wheelchair Access: limited
Insurance: liability required, BYO or ask for application, extra charge

Hamlin Mansion

2120 Broadway, San Francisco
415/389-8069

www.parties-sf.com
moira@parties-sf.com

Historic Pacific Heights Mansion

● Rehearsal Dinners	● Corp. Events/Mtgs.
● Ceremonies	● Private Parties
● Wedding Receptions	Accommodations

Now and then you may come across a school that occupies a mansion, but only the Hamlin School has a Pacific Heights address with a spectacular panoramic view of the Golden Gate and San Francisco Bay.

The mansion in this case is Stanwood Hall, one of three buildings that make up the school. Designed by Julius Kraft, the 24-room house was constructed in 1901 for James Leary Flood, son of the Nevada silver king, and was part of the last wave of mansion building in The City. Its Italian Baroque exterior is distinguished by Ionic columns, pilasters and pedimented windows arranged in formal symmetry, characteristic of the early 1900s Revival style that succeeded the late Victorians.

Granite steps, flanked by two gray marble lions (nicknamed Leo and Leona by Hamlin students), lead to a mosaic and marble vestibule and a pair of oak-and-plate-glass doors. Beyond the vestibule is the two-story Great Hall, a space with columns and wall-to-wall oak paneling that's practically custom-made for ceremonies. The bride makes her entrance by walking down a magnificent staircase, illuminated by a large art glass window with four chipped glass "jewels" embedded in it. Guests are seated throughout the hall, and there's room on the balcony above for an additional group of onlookers.

Cocktails are usually served after the ceremony, giving guests an opportunity to explore the entire house, upstairs and down. Directly beyond the Great Hall is the Library, a warm room with a dark mahogany-paneled interior, striking black marble and gold fireplace and great bay views. Note the carved wood garland over the doorway as you enter. In contrast to the Library is the adjacent Solarium. This mosaic-and-glass space, filled with light and capped by three small Tiffany glass cupolas, also overlooks the bay and Marin County. Upstairs, there's a mezzanine that overlooks the Great Hall.

Receptions are held on the level below the main floor in the new Dining Area, whose East and West Dining Rooms can be reserved individually or combined for large parties. The décor is simple, yet elegant, with ivory walls and maple floors. Large windows provide bay views and natural light during the day, while wall sconces cast soft light at night. If you'd like a more romantic ambiance, candles are permitted.

For over a century, the Hamlin Mansion has impressed all who enter its doors with its classic lines and rich appointments. You'll find that these qualities also make it a wonderful place for an upscale wedding, party or corporate event.

CEREMONY CAPACITY: The Great Hall holds 100 seated, with space around the balcony for an additional 80 standing guests.

EVENT/RECEPTION & MEETING CAPACITY: The Mansion accommodates a maximum of 200 seated guests in two adjoining dining rooms. The largest one, the West Dining Room, holds up to 150 seated.

FEES & DEPOSITS: A refundable $1,000 security/cleaning deposit is required when the contract is signed. For weddings, a $6,000 rental fee covers use of the facility for 5 hours and is payable 2 months prior to the event. Food services are provided: an hors d'oeuvres buffet starts at $60/person, buffet dinners at $65/person and seated dinners at $70/person. Prices do not include equipment. Tax, staff and alcohol are additional. Brunch and luncheon menus and full event-planning services are also available. Valet service runs $450–2,800 and a security guard $360/8 hours; both prices depend on guest count.

For corporate events, the rental fee runs $6,000 for groups under 100 guests or $6,500 for groups over 100 guests.

AVAILABILITY: Year-round, weekdays after 6:30pm, weekends and school holidays all day.

SERVICES/AMENITIES:

Catering: provided, no BYO
Kitchen Facilities: n/a
Tables & Chairs: some provided
Linens, Silver, etc.: provided, extra charge
Restrooms: wheelchair accessible
Dance Floor: yes
Bride's Dressing Area: yes
Meeting Equipment: no

Parking: valet required, extra charge
Accommodations: no guest rooms
Telephone: CBA
Outdoor Night Lighting: access only
Outdoor Cooking Facilities: no
Cleanup: caterer
View: panorama of SF Bay
Other: baby grand piano, coordination, lawn area

RESTRICTIONS:

Alcohol: BYO or CBA
Smoking: outdoors only
Music: amplified OK; music curfew 10pm Sunday–Thursday, 11:30pm Friday–Saturday; bands have 5-piece instrument maximum

Wheelchair Access: elevator
Insurance: recommended
Other: no rice, rose petals or bubbles

Hornblower Cruises & Events

Yachts

San Francisco and Berkeley
415/438-8300

www.hornblowerweddings.com
sfsales@hornblower.com

● Rehearsal Dinners	● Corp. Events/Mtgs.
● Ceremonies	● Private Parties
● Wedding Receptions	Accommodations

Offering some of the most stunning views in the world, the San Francisco Bay is a wedding destination in itself. When you're out on its vibrant blue waters, there are picture-perfect panoramas wherever you look: landmarks like the Bay and Golden Gate Bridges and sun-washed Alcatraz Island; the forested Marin headlands; and San Francisco's famous skyline. One of the best ways to merge these scenic glories with a topnotch celebration is with Hornblower Cruises & Events. From glamorous yachts to a replica of a turn-of-the-century coastal steamer, Hornblower's wide range of vessels combine the facilities of a fine hotel with the excitement of a bay cruise. Whether you're planning a fabulous formal affair or a blowout blast for 2,200 of your closest friends, one of Hornblower's San Francisco Bay-based fleet will provide a spectacular setting.

The *Commodore Hornblower,* a 90-foot custom-built wood yacht, comes with two decks and two bars. The *Empress Hornblower,* docked in Sacramento, is a 100-foot vessel reminiscent of river ferryboats. Outfitted with the rich woods and shining brass typical of the Hornblower fleet, she features indoor decks, an awning-covered outdoor deck, two dance floors and two bars. The *Sunset Hornblower* is a 100-foot charter ship that was recently refurbished. She has two decks appointed with mahogany and brass, as well as two bars.

The newest addition to the Hornblower fleet is the 150-foot, sleek and modern *San Francisco Spirit.* Live large on this 400-person craft, with marble dance floors and elegant appointments that create a luxurious atmosphere.

The 183-foot *California Hornblower* is patterned after early 19th-century steamships and is the flagship of the Hornblower fleet. Boasting three decks, dining salons and mahogany bars, spacious promenade decks and multiple dance floors, she can handle even the largest gathering with style. For a dockside event, the *Ferryboat Santa Rosa* combines the charm of being on the water with the convenience of being able to come and go as you please.

One of the most impressive vessels is the 292-foot *San Francisco Belle.* Originally a casino riverboat, she's been remodeled to accommodate sizable groups for special events. She's designed with three large interior decks and an expansive sundeck.

For the ultimate green wedding, reserve the *Hornblower Hybrid,* an eco-showpiece powered by solar panels, wind turbines and fuel-efficient engines. At 64 feet, this re-engineered former dive boat is a fun choice for parties of 100 or fewer.

All Hornblower events include linens, china and silver. Their staff can handle as many of your wedding details as you desire, from personalized menus and invitations to photography and custom floral displays. If you get married on board, note that all of Hornblower's captains are licensed ministers. With more than 50,000 special events and private parties to their credit, Hornblower Cruises & Events knows how to make the most of an unforgettable setting, and provide all the finery to make your celebration truly memorable.

CEREMONY, EVENT/RECEPTION & MEETING CAPACITY: Depending on the vessel selected, Hornblower's fleet can accommodate 32–1,600 seated or 50–2,200 standing guests. The largest seated meeting capacity on one deck is 560 people.

FEES & DEPOSITS: 50% of the estimated total is required to book a vessel. A confirmed guest count is due 14 working days prior to the event; the final balance is due 7 working days prior. Custom weddings and wedding packages are available. Packages start at $69/person and include a 2 to 4½-hour cruise, meal, bar program, champagne, wedding cake, tax, service charge and landing fee. The captain performs ceremonies at no extra charge.

AVAILABILITY: Year-round, daily, anytime.

SERVICES/AMENITIES FOR ALL VESSELS:

Catering: provided

Kitchen Facilities: n/a

Tables & Chairs: provided

Linens, Silver, etc.: provided

Restrooms: wheelchair accessibility varies per vessel

Dance Floor: available

Bride's Dressing Area: CBA

Meeting Equipment: full range CBA

Other: full event planning

Parking: various locations

Accommodations: no guest rooms

Telephone: varies per vessel

Outdoor Night Lighting: varies

Outdoor Cooking Facilities: no

Cleanup: provided

View: the entire San Francisco Bay and skyline, Alcatraz and all bridges

RESTRICTIONS:

Alcohol: provided with packages, or corkage $15/bottle

Smoking: allowed on outside decks

Music: provided or BYO; amplified OK

Wheelchair Access: varies per vessel

Insurance: not required

Other: no rice or fire on boats

The professionals in the back of this book are the best in the business. How do we know? Read page 637.

Hotel Kabuki

Hotel

1625 Post Street, San Francisco
415/922-3200 Catering Department
www.hotelkabuki.com or www.jdvhotels.com
rbacon@jdvhotels.com

- Rehearsal Dinners
- Ceremonies
- Wedding Receptions
- Corp. Events/Mtgs.
- Private Parties
- Accommodations

Elegantly balancing both Western and Eastern influences, the Hotel Kabuki is a serene retreat in the heart of historic Japantown. This Joie de Vivre property has a modern, sophisticated interior, filled with elements that also reflect the refined beauty of the past.

A distinctively Japanese tone is set by the Summer Garden, a calm enclave featuring a koi pond and waterfall surrounded by a perfectly manicured landscape. This is a lovely spot for a small ceremony and wedding photos.

On every floor you'll discover displays of priceless art, some of it dating back to the 1700s. Downstairs on the Garden Level, the impressive Imperial Ballroom features hand-painted Japanese murals, custom-made chandeliers and sconces, and a parquet dance floor. Through a large picture window you have a view of the Spring Garden, an artful arrangement of white rocks and lush ferns. Prefunction cocktails are often served in the Imperial Ballroom Foyer, whose walls are lined with exquisite, one-of-a-kind Japanese artworks.

Back up on the Lobby level is the hotel's junior ballroom, the Sakura Room. This space is notable for its shoji-coffered ceiling and view of the Summer Garden through a floor-to-ceiling window. Natural light flows into the room during the day, and at night adjustable lighting allows you to create whatever ambiance you like. The Garden, softly lit in the evening, is a tranquil addition to the mood you've created. Additional rooms, some with garden vistas, are available for smaller functions.

If you stay overnight here, you'll enjoy services unique to this premier hotel. Bathing, for example, is taken to a luxurious new level: In guest rooms, deep-soaking tubs are ergonomically designed to let you immerse your entire body up to the neck in hot water enhanced by whatever soothing bath product you've chosen from the inspired bath menu. Just a block and a half away from the hotel is Kabuki Springs and Spa—and hotel guests receive a complimentary pass to the Spa's communal baths, the only facility of its kind in the city. So here's a fun idea: Why not incorporate this Japanese ritual into your bachelorette party festivities? Follow it up with one or two exotic body treatments (think green tea wrap and Javanese Frangipani oil massage) and even an acupuncture session, and you and your friends will look and feel cool, calm and collected for your trip down the aisle.

The Hotel Kabuki is pet-friendly, and its central location puts you within walking distance to shopping, dining, a new Sundance film theater complex, and a variety of music venues. Union

Square, the Golden Gate Bridge, Golden Gate Park, Chinatown and the famed cable cars, as well as the Fillmore district, are also nearby.

Whether you're planning an intimate rehearsal dinner, a gala reception or a post-wedding brunch, Hotel Kabuki's variety of options, multilingual staff and emphasis on personalized service will make it a success.

CEREMONY CAPACITY: Several ceremony spaces can accommodate 100–400 seated guests indoors.

EVENT/RECEPTION CAPACITY: The hotel holds 15–400 seated or 30–1,200 standing guest indoors.

MEETING CAPACITY: Meeting spaces can accommodate 12–400 seated guests.

FEES & DEPOSITS: A deposit is required to reserve your date and is applied to the balance. Per-person food costs, not including wine, start at $40 for lunch or $50 for dinner. Alcohol, tax and a 20% service charge are additional.

AVAILABILITY: Year-round, daily, anytime.

SERVICES/AMENITIES:

Catering: provided; Indian, kosher and other cuisine also available
Kitchen Facilities: n/a
Tables & Chairs: provided
Linens, Silver, etc.: provided
Restrooms: wheelchair accessible
Dance Floor: yes
Bride's & Groom's Dressing Areas: yes
Meeting Equipment: full-service A/V and business center

Parking: Japan Center garage or valet, extra charge (low rates)
Accommodations: 218 guest rooms
Telephone: guest phones
Outdoor Night Lighting: access only
Outdoor Cooking Facilities: n/a
Cleanup: provided
View: Japanese tea gardens
Other: full-service event coordination, piano, stage

RESTRICTIONS:

Alcohol: provided, corkage negotiable
Smoking: outside only
Music: amplified OK

Wheelchair Access: yes
Insurance: not required

Hotel Nikko San Francisco

Hotel

222 Mason Street, San Francisco
415/394-1111
www.hotelnikkosf.com
sales@hotelnikkosf.com

- Rehearsal Dinners
- Ceremonies
- Wedding Receptions
- Corp. Events/Mtgs.
- Private Parties
- Accommodations

Hotel guests stroll across the vast, high-ceilinged, art-filled lobby. Visitors from all over the world lounge in its velvet chairs. Through enormous windows hotel guests can watch the city bustle by, as the soothing sound of a cascading fountain provides a calming contrast to the whirl of activity outside.

High-rise hospitality and a reputation for service and style have long been the hallmarks of the popular Hotel Nikko, a sophisticated downtown hostelry that can quite literally look down on its neighbors. A favorite spot for grand gatherings, its 25 floors of public and private spaces offer opportunities for entertaining that most smaller establishments can't match. In addition to the 510 tastefully appointed guest rooms and 22 suites, there are good-sized, subdividable meeting rooms, which are great for social and corporate functions.

But the Nikko Grand Ballroom on the third floor is a real show-stopper; at over 6,600 square feet, it's immense. Its Asian contemporary décor, featuring burnished wall coverings, dark carpeting with a subtle overlay of cherry blossoms, and amber ceiling and wall fixtures, lends it a warmth that is generally lacking in rooms large enough to accommodate a Viennese waltz at full tilt. Subdividable, like so many of the hotel's other meeting and banquet rooms, it breaks down into three smaller chambers, each of which is still suitable for a fairly large function and offers a sense of grandeur in a somewhat cozier setting.

For high-profile parties with a clubbier feel, ascend to Hotel Nikko's 25th floor where an elegant aerie of glass showcases panoramic bay views in an atmosphere of style and restraint. From the floor-to-ceiling windows of the Golden Gate Room one can see Marin County and the Golden Gate Bridge. Bay View Room vistas include the hotel's Financial District and Union Square neighbors, the wooded East Bay hills, and the silvery Bay Bridge. The Peninsula Room looks south, past AT&T Park, all the way to San Bruno Mountain. Night or day, this spectacular pageant of round-the-clock bayscapes is a hard-to-beat backdrop for glamorous wining and dining. Rooms can be combined to accommodate varying numbers of guests, and there are three boardrooms, as well, on this level. Each of these provides an equally stunning western perspective of the surrounding city, plus fax capability, high-speed internet access and other high-tech amenities.

ANZU Restaurant and Bar lends itself beautifully to an intimate wedding, rehearsal dinner, post-wedding brunch or bridal shower. It can be reserved exclusively for your affair, and the dramatic bar and upscale modern furnishings create a captivating setting so no other decoration is needed.

But the strongest suit of this excellent downtown hotel is service. Legendary Asian hospitality has always been a big part of its legacy, and decades of experience show in the way the expert staff custom caters and creates events with the kind of flair and focus that has earned lofty accolades. From sophisticated menu design and the careful arrangement of flowers to the care and feeding of its distinguished clientele, the attention to detail is exacting. It's no wonder Hotel Nikko partygoers and guests often book return engagements.

CEREMONY CAPACITY: The Nikko Ballroom holds 600 seated guests and the Golden Gate Room holds 120 seated guests. Various other spaces are available with capacities ranging 10–200 seated guests.

EVENT/RECEPTION CAPACITY: The hotel can accommodate 70–600 seated or 100–1,000 standing guests indoors. ANZU Restaurant and Bar holds up to 90 seated or 150 for a standing reception.

MEETING CAPACITY: 16 different spaces (20,000+ sq. ft.) hold up to 600 seated guests.

FEES & DEPOSITS: 10% of the estimated event total is required to reserve your date. 50% of the estimated event total is due 3 months prior to the event, and the balance is due the week of the event. Several wedding packages are offered, and include hors d'oeuvres, meal, wedding cake, champagne toast, and complimentary suite for bride and groom. Also included are floor-length linens, silver service, mirror and votive candles on tables. Packages start at $90/person. Tax, alcohol and service charge are additional.

AVAILABILITY: Year-round, daily, 6am–2am.

SERVICES/AMENITIES:

Catering: provided, no BYO
Kitchen Facilities: n/a
Tables & Chairs: provided
Linens, Silver, etc.: provided
Restrooms: wheelchair accessible
Dance Floor: yes
Bride's & Groom's Dressing Areas: yes
Meeting Equipment: full range

Parking: valet CBA or several garages nearby
Accommodations: 532 guest rooms
Telephone: pay phones
Outdoor Night Lighting: no
Outdoor Cooking Facilities: no
Cleanup: provided
View: panoramic cityscape and SF Bay
Other: event coordination

RESTRICTIONS:

Alcohol: provided or BYO, corkage fees apply
Smoking: not allowed
Music: amplified OK

Wheelchair Access: yes
Insurance: not required

Hotel Vitale

Hotel

8 Mission Street, San Francisco
415/278-3719

www.hotelvitale.com
syassin@jdvhotels.com

- Rehearsal Dinners
- Ceremonies
- Wedding Receptions
- Corp. Events/Mtgs.
- Private Parties
- Accommodations

At the Hotel Vitale, the luxury is subtle. A member of the Joie de Vivre family, this boutique hotel along the revitalized Embarcadero strikes the hard-to-find balance between contemporary and warm—think reclaimed wood and river stones mixed with sleek minimal design and you get the idea. The hallmark Joie de Vivre finesse is everywhere, from the swanky circular bar downstairs to the terraces on the upper floors, making this a chic setting for a wedding, reception or post-wedding brunch.

The overall feeling of serenity and vibe of cool permeates every space in the hotel. On the first floor, just off the street-level lobby, the Amalfi Coast Room offers an ultrastylish backdrop for seated dinners and lounging. Almost sheer, platinum-colored curtains filter in daylight (or the city lights at night) but keep the room private, and thanks to its neutral palette the Amalfi Coast dresses up beautifully. Formal dinners here shine, with brocade linens, Chiavari chairs, and candlelight; it also makes an excellent lounge with a bar in the corner, overstuffed white couches and large potted palms.

The hotel's signature restaurant, Americano, provides several options for parties. A circular room at one end works well for private cocktail receptions or brunches; warmth comes from wood floors and buttery club chairs, which are arranged so that guests can look out the abundant windows to the palm-lined Embarcadero beyond. In the intimate private dining room at the opposite end of the restaurant, a curtain separates rehearsal dinners from the main dining area. An expansive patio right outside is a harmonious counterpart to the adjacent Embarcadero: Tall bamboo and wooden furniture—plus the requisite heat lamps—create a relaxed, yet civilized, ambiance.

Take the elevator to the hotel's peaceful upper levels, and you'll find the terraces and spa that make this place truly special. The fifth-floor terrace overlooks the Ferry Building and bay, and is an excellent spot for a cozy ceremony, cocktail party or small seated dinner. The two-tiered terrace on the seventh and eighth floors is also a stellar location to tie the knot or host a standing reception. With its slightly higher vantage point maximizing the view of the Ferry Building, Embarcadero and the Bay Bridge, this outdoor aerie transforms into a gorgeous above-city party scene.

On the hotel's penthouse level, the Vitale Spa pampers bridal parties in style before—and after—the wedding. Who can say no to an infinity soaking tub set amid a rooftop bamboo garden, where all you have to do is "look up at the sky and imagine where your skin ends and the water begins?"

Couples can enjoy a side-by-side massage (with a view of the Bay Bridge), not to mention daily private yoga classes.

In the Hotel Vitale, every element is designed with a commitment to subtle visual pleasure and pure comfort. Soft and sultry lighting, fresh lavender scattered throughout, and warm wood accents soothe the senses and make this San Francisco getaway an unlikely urban oasis.

CEREMONY & EVENT/RECEPTION CAPACITY: Indoor spaces can accommodate 100 seated or 150 standing guests. Outdoors, five terraces each hold up to 60 seated or 100 standing.

MEETING CAPACITY: Several spaces accommodate 2–100 guests.

FEES & DEPOSITS: Half of the estimated event total is required to reserve your date. The balance is due 30 days prior to the event. Rental fees range $500–3,000 depending on the space, day and time rented and guest count. Meals range $35–100/person. Tax, alcohol and a 21% service charge are additional.

AVAILABILITY: Year-round, daily. Please call for details on event spaces and availability.

SERVICES/AMENITIES:

Catering: provided
Kitchen Facilities: n/a
Tables & Chairs: provided
Linens, Silver, etc.: provided
Restrooms: wheelchair accessible
Dance Floor: CBA
Bride's Dressing Area: CBA
Meeting Equipment: CBA, extra charge

Parking: valet required
Accommodations: 200 guest rooms
Telephone: house phones
Outdoor Night Lighting: CBA
Outdoor Cooking Facilities: no
Cleanup: provided
View: SF Bay and cityscape
Other: event coordination, spa services, A/V equipment

RESTRICTIONS:

Alcohol: provided
Smoking: outdoors only
Music: amplified OK with restrictions

Wheelchair Access: yes
Insurance: liability required

Want to know WHAT TO ASK a potential location or vendor? Check out our Questions to Ask starting on page 17.

Hotel Whitcomb

Hotel

1231 Market Street, San Francisco
415/487-4439, 415/487-4478
www.hotelwhitcomb.com
schism@hotelwhitcomb.com

● Rehearsal Dinners	● Corp. Events/Mtgs.
● Ceremonies	● Private Parties
● Wedding Receptions	● Accommodations

Walking through the doors of the Hotel Whitcomb, you leave behind bustling Market Street and enter the relaxed and sophisticated atmosphere of this unique turn-of-the-century boutique hotel.

As soon as you step into the lobby you're surrounded by historic grandeur, from the polished marble foyer and the Austrian crystal chandeliers adorning the reception area to the hand-carved wood paneling gracing the high, beamed ceiling. Completed just after the 1906 earthquake, the Whitcomb was chosen by city leaders to serve as a temporary City Hall from 1912 to 1915, a shining stand-in for the building that was destroyed. The words "City Hall" were faintly etched above the hotel's entrance for years, and some of the original jail cells are still intact in the basement.

While the hotel's historic elements captivate visitors, contemporary amenities also abound: a Starbucks coffee shop in the lobby, free high-speed WiFi internet in guest rooms, an internet café and a fitness room. The hotel also features over 17,000 square feet of event space, with free internet access in each meeting room.

Just off the main lobby are the Whitcomb Ballroom and the Ghirardelli Room, the hotel's two main function spaces. With its magnificent crystal chandeliers, a grand staircase for a dazzling bridal entrance, and the largest parquet dance floor in the city, the ballroom is a dream setting for a ceremony and reception. There's even a mezzanine level from which to snap those signature photos of your celebration. The smaller, more intimate Ghirardelli Room, which is popular for rehearsal dinners, features warm, wood paneling and gold leaf accents throughout.

These rooms, however, are not just for weddings. If you're hosting a business function, the ballroom is ideal for large keynote speeches, while the Ghirardelli Room works well for board meetings. Six smaller meeting rooms are also available.

Regardless of the type of event you hold, your guests will appreciate the hotel's experienced catering staff, comfortable, updated guest rooms, and proximity to everything San Francisco is known for: Union Square, Ghirardelli Square, Fisherman's Wharf, the Embarcadero, Chinatown, and Civic Center, which is just steps away from the hotel's main entrance. The Hotel Whitcomb really does offer the perfect mix of vintage charm, modern amenities and world-class hospitality.

CEREMONY CAPACITY: The Whitcomb Ballroom holds 400 seated, and the Ghirardelli Room 100 seated guests. Some standing guests can also be accommodated.

EVENT/RECEPTION CAPACITY: The Whitcomb Ballroom holds 400 seated or 600 standing guests, and the Ghirardelli Room up to 100 seated or standing guests.

MEETING CAPACITY: There are 6 rooms that accommodate 8–400 seated guests.

FEES & DEPOSITS: For weddings, a deposit is required to reserve your date. The event balance is payable 14 business days prior to the event along with a guest count guarantee. Wedding packages start at $35/person; some packages include champagne toast. Menus can be customized.

For other special events and business functions, a deposit is required and varies depending on the services and menu selected. Room rental/setup fees may apply. Call for more specific information.

AVAILABILITY: Year-round, daily, anytime including holidays.

SERVICES/AMENITIES:

Catering: provided, no BYO

Kitchen Facilities: n/a

Tables & Chairs: provided

Linens, Silver, etc.: provided

Restrooms: wheelchair accessible

Dance Floor: provided

Bride's & Groom's Dressing Areas: suite provided with package

Meeting Equipment: full range, extra charge

Parking: garage or adjacent parking

Accommodations: 447 guest rooms, 12 suites

Telephone: pay or guest phones

Outdoor Night Lighting: n/a

Outdoor Cooking Facilities: n/a

Cleanup: provided

View: no

RESTRICTIONS:

Alcohol: provided

Smoking: outside only

Music: amplified OK, midnight curfew

Wheelchair Access: yes

Insurance: may be required

InterContinental Mark Hopkins

Hotel

One Nob Hill, San Francisco
415/616-6959 Catering Department
www.intercontinentalmarkhopkins.com
sfoha.sales@ihg.com

- Rehearsal Dinners
- Ceremonies
- Wedding Receptions
- Corp. Events/Mtgs.
- Private Parties
- Accommodations

Since it opened in 1926, the InterContinental Mark Hopkins has been one of San Francisco's premier hotels. Poised at the crest of Nob Hill, it rises nineteen stories and is as much a San Francisco icon as the cable cars that clang past its grand entrance. So it's no surprise that it evokes lots of romance and history. During WWII, the Top of the Mark was the site of many farewell rendezvous where couples met for a last drink before the men shipped out. Wives and girlfriends stayed behind to watch from the top-story windows as their sweethearts' ships slipped through the Golden Gate.

The InterContinental Mark Hopkins is still a perfect place for a romantic rendezvous—happily without a tearful farewell. Hold your wedding in the Room of the Dons, notable for its 26-foot ceiling and nine vibrant murals (by Maynard Dixon and Frank Van Sloun) depicting scenes from early California. Painted in a rich medley of reds, blues and browns against gold leaf, they were completed in 1926 for the hotel's grand opening. The seven-foot-high murals, set off by the subtle cream-and-taupe walls and ceiling, create a colorful banner around the room's perimeter. While you're admiring their artistry, say your vows in front of a towering arched window, which is gracefully draped in silk brocade.

Receptions are often held in the Peacock Court, a light, palatial ballroom befitting a grand hotel. Complete with its own stage, its classical details include gold and ivory walls framed by delicately carved plaster moldings, arched windows draped in layers of amber and bronze silk brocade, and a ceiling with intricate plasterwork.

The InterContinental Mark Hopkins has many smaller event rooms as well, which reflect the hotel's grace and elegance and provide flexible event-planning options. Or for a world-class treat, reserve the Top of the Mark, a glass-walled sky lounge on the 19th floor with a breathtaking 360-degree panorama of San Francisco and much of the Bay Area. The Art Deco theme features dark woods and wrought-iron balustrades, while a 20-foot vaulted ceiling and split-level floor offer unobstructed views from virtually every seat. Let the staff transform the upper terrace for your wedding ceremony with a floor-to-ceiling mirrored backdrop that adds extra glitz. You can choose to have your guests seated so that they overlook either the bay and Golden Gate Bridge or the glittering downtown skyline. Literally one of The City's high points, the sky lounge is also an exceptional spot for impressive receptions and rehearsal dinners—or even a bridal shower brunch. (Famous for its 100 Martini menu, the room hosts great bachelorette parties, too.)

Whatever type of event you have, the Mark Hopkins will leave you and your guests walking on air.

CEREMONY CAPACITY: Six rooms hold 45–500 seated or 30–900 standing guests.

EVENT/RECEPTION CAPACITY: The hotel can accommodate 90–450 seated or 150–800 standing guests indoors.

MEETING CAPACITY: The hotel has 20 rooms with over 19,000 square feet of meeting space and can accommodate 10–500 seated guests.

FEES & DEPOSITS: A 30% deposit is payable when the contract is submitted; the event balance along with a guest count guarantee are due 3 business days prior to the event. Rental fees may apply to corporate meetings and wedding ceremonies, depending on room(s) selected, catering fees, guest count and season. Any menu can be customized. Luncheons start at $52/person, buffets range $43–95/person, and dinners start at $64/person; alcohol, tax and a 22% service charge are additional. Several wedding packages are available that include hors d'oeuvres, open bar, 3-course seated meal, wine with dinner, wedding cake, champagne toast, and suite for the bride and groom. Prices start at $135/person. Tax and service charges are additional. Seasonal discounts may be available for group accommodations.

AVAILABILITY: Year-round, daily, anytime. Weddings take place in 5-hour blocks, with additional time negotiable.

SERVICES/AMENITIES:

Catering: provided
Kitchen Facilities: n/a
Tables & Chairs: provided
Linens, Silver, etc.: provided
Restrooms: wheelchair accessible
Dance Floor: provided
Bride's & Groom's Dressing Areas: yes
Meeting Equipment: full range

Parking: limited hotel garage, nearby garages
Accommodations: 382 guest rooms, 32 suites
Telephone: pay and guest phones
Outdoor Night Lighting: n/a
Outdoor Cooking Facilities: no
Cleanup: provided
View: Nob Hill, San Francisco and Bay
Other: baby grand, ice sculptures, event coordination

RESTRICTIONS:

Alcohol: provided, no BYO
Smoking: outdoors in designated areas
Music: amplified OK with volume restrictions

Wheelchair Access: yes, elevator
Insurance: not required
Other: decorations restricted

InterContinental San Francisco

Hotel

888 Howard Street, San Francisco
415/616-6628
www.intercontinentalsanfrancisco.com
matteo.chiari@ihg.com

- Rehearsal Dinners
- Ceremonies
- Wedding Receptions
- Corp. Events/Mtgs.
- Private Parties
- Accommodations

The chic InterContinental San Francisco has pulled off the nearly impossible: It charms like a boutique hotel, while providing all of the amenities and luxuries you expect from an internationally renowned brand. Towering over the burgeoning South of Market district, this 32-story newcomer with its gleaming blue-glass façade makes a streamlined, very modern statement. However, the interior spaces have an unexpected warmth, featuring details that evoke a sense of place...an essence of San Francisco. With all of its assets, this InterContinental is a superb choice for local couples looking to get married in The City, as well as those planning a sophisticated destination wedding.

The hotel offers an array of event spaces on the 3rd, 4th and 5th floors that can accommodate nearly any size or type of wedding imaginable. The Grand Ballroom on floor 3 works best for very large parties: Guests dine at elegantly dressed rounds encircling a generous dance floor, while the bride and groom often sit at a long table in front of floor-to-ceiling windows at one end of the room. The city views beyond add to the expansive feeling, as do the 20-foot-high ceilings. Florists regularly fashion tall, dramatic centerpieces to play up the verticality of the Ballroom, which opens onto a foyer that's perfect for cocktails.

More intimate events are held on all three floors. Floor number 4 boasts the Pacific Terrace, where fair-weather ceremonies and small parties take place outside against a backdrop of the city's angular and colorful skyline. The Terrace can be tented, and it has its own sunny foyer. Up on 5, the InterContinental Ballroom is a smaller version of the Grand Ballroom. Like its counterpart, a wall of windows supplies abundant light and a San Francisco vista. Here, too, the neutral décor allows receptions to shine when set up with copious florals and crisp linens. Breakout rooms on all three floors are excellent for smaller celebrations of any kind; natural light and city views make them distinctive.

The InterContinental San Francisco has been designed throughout with guests' comfort in mind. Abstract fine art on the walls, soothing color schemes and modern furniture create an atmosphere of calm and ease. Each floor is limited to 22 guest rooms and one natural light-filled hallway instead of the usual maze of corridors you find in a large hotel. The rooms themselves are outfitted with extra outlets, an iPod docking station, flat screen TVs and WiFi, plus spectacular vistas. And then there's the skylit indoor lap pool, and the personalized pampering at the Spa.... Who wouldn't be happy staying here?

Opened in 2008, the InterContinental is the proverbial new kid on the block in San Francisco, and it's actually the newest high-rise hotel downtown. But it joins the ranks of InterContinental hotels sprinkled across the globe in Paris, Tokyo, Nairobi, and Tahiti and, like them, expertly melds world-class service, impeccable facilities, and gourmet cuisine.

CEREMONY CAPACITY: The hotel holds 840 seated indoors and 400 seated outdoors.

EVENT/RECEPTION CAPACITY: The hotel can accommodate 440 seated or 1,000 standing guests indoors and 300 seated or 773 standing outdoors.

MEETING CAPACITY: The hotel holds 840 seated guests.

FEES & DEPOSITS: 30% of the estimated event total is required to reserve your date. The balance is due 7 days prior. Rental fees range $1,000–5,000 depending on the space rented. Meals range $75–175/person. Tax, alcohol and a 22% service charge are additional.

AVAILABILITY: Year-round, daily, anytime. Call for details.

SERVICES/AMENITIES:

Catering: provided
Kitchen Facilities: n/a
Tables & Chairs: provided
Linens, Silver, etc.: provided
Restrooms: wheelchair accessible
Dance Floor: portable provided
Bride's & Groom's Dressing Areas: CBA
Meeting Equipment: provided

Parking: valet required
Accommodations: 550 guest rooms
Telephone: house phone
Outdoor Night Lighting: CBA
Outdoor Cooking Facilities: no
Cleanup: provided
View: cityscape
Other: grand piano, on-site wedding cake, on-site florals, spa services, A/V equipment, event coordination

RESTRICTIONS:

Alcohol: provided
Smoking: not allowed
Music: amplified OK indoors

Wheelchair Access: yes
Insurance: liability required

Want to find more venues and services? Check out our informative website, www.HereComesTheGuide.com.

101

James Leary Flood Mansion

2222 Broadway, San Francisco

415/292-3142

www.floodmansion.org
info@floodmansion.org

Historic Mansion

● Rehearsal Dinners		● Corp. Events/Mtgs.	
● Ceremonies		● Private Parties	
● Wedding Receptions		Accommodations	

The Flood Mansion is a symphony of classical styles—Italian Renaissance, Rococo, Tudor and Georgian. This elegant building, constructed in 1915, has remained well preserved since Mrs. Flood donated her home to the Religious of the Sacred Heart in 1939. Although the building is now used as a private school, it's available for special events after school hours and on weekends.

The Mansion is impressive: Its Grand Hall is 140 feet long with marble floors and great views of the bay; the Adam Room, near the entry, has a high, ornate ceiling, specially designed wood tables and chairs, and a marble fireplace; the architecturally complex Reception Room boasts a magnificent coffered ceiling, painted murals in golds, blues and greens, and a parquet floor. And, weather permitting, a pretty enclosed courtyard off of the Grand Hall is available for outdoor gatherings. The Flood Mansion is definitely the place for a stately and elegant party.

CEREMONY CAPACITY: The courtyard holds 180 seated and the Grand Hall 200 seated.

EVENT/RECEPTION CAPACITY: The entire main floor can hold 200 seated or 300 standing guests for cocktail receptions. The courtyard holds 200 standing guests.

MEETING CAPACITY: The main floor can accommodate 200 seated.

FEES & DEPOSITS: 50% of the rental fee is required to secure your date, the rental balance and a certificate of insurance are due one month prior to the event date. The rental fee starts at $8,500.

AVAILABILITY: Year-round, weekdays after 4pm, Saturday and Sunday all day. Guests and catering staff must vacate the premises by 11pm Sunday–Thursday, or midnight Friday and Saturday.

SERVICES/AMENITIES:

Catering: select from preferred list
Kitchen Facilities: ample
Tables & Chairs: BYO
Linens, Silver, etc.: BYO
Restrooms: wheelchair accessible
Dance Floor: yes
Bride's Dressing Area: CBA
Meeting Equipment: BYO

Parking: valet parking required
Accommodations: no guest rooms
Telephone: emergency use only
Outdoor Night Lighting: access only
Outdoor Cooking Facilities: no
Cleanup: caterer
View: SF Bay, Golden Gate Bridge and Alcatraz
Other: grand piano

RESTRICTIONS:

Alcohol: BYO, must use licensed server
Smoking: outside only
Music: amplified OK indoors, Sunday–Thursday until 9:30pm; Friday–Saturday until 10:30pm

Wheelchair Access: yes
Insurance: extra liability required

Jewish Community Center of San Francisco

Community Center

3200 California Street, San Francisco
415/292-1269
www.jccsf.org/privateevents
privateevents@jccsf.org

- Rehearsal Dinners
- Ceremonies
- Wedding Receptions
- Corp. Events/Mtgs.
- Private Parties
- Accommodations

If you remember the old Spanish-style red brick Jewish Community Center of San Francisco, you'll be impressed by the new center, which opened in 2004. Though it's three times the size of its predecessor (and has lots more to offer), this new building of sand-colored brick and tawny Jerusalem limestone still manages to fit gracefully into the neighborhood.

The heart of the building is the light-filled three-story Atrium. An airy mobile, appropriately named *Ruach* (Bridge of Breath) sails overhead. Its slender steel arches are fitted with panels of dichroic glass that shine different colors depending on how the light strikes them. There are various interpretations of the sculpture, but many like to think it symbolizes the bridge joining the bride and groom and connecting their two families. The floor is paved with more Jerusalem limestone in tones ranging from light almond to amber. If you would like to be married on site, you can descend the glass-walled staircase from the second floor and have your ceremony in front of the two curved walls where life-affirming values are written in Hebrew and English. Or, if you're tying the knot elsewhere, use this space as a prefunction area for cocktails. There is a platform for musicians, and you can set up a bar here as well.

Both of the center's reception rooms open to the Atrium. Kanbar Hall, the larger of the two, has a dramatically high ceiling, walls of rich paprika-red fabric, tall soundproof windows and a full-sized stage. It's also outfitted with state-of-the-art lighting and sound systems (a technician can be arranged, too). The theater seating normally used for performances or lectures is fully retractable and disappears during events. Place your head table on the stage, or have the band here paired with a dance floor set right below.

Smaller receptions are held in the Fisher Family Hall, brightened by white and papyrus-colored walls and light filtering in from the Atrium through one wall of frosted glass. Like Kanbar Hall, it has a complete audiovisual system, and its blond parquet sprung-wood floor is perfect for dancing.

Note that other conference rooms are available on the second floor if you're planning a Ketubah signing, Bedecken or Tisch. Also, there are three separate kitchens, one of which will suit your event: a kosher meat kitchen (under strict rabbinical supervision; kosher meat tableware is available), a dairy/vegetarian kitchen and a non-kosher kitchen.

The JCCSF has some perks you will love: First and foremost in this parking-challenged town is that the center has its own parking garage. Second, the performer's Green Room makes a terrific dressing room. With plenty of mirrors and a sitting room (even a mini-fridge), you and your bridesmaids have ample space for prep and touch-ups.

The JCCSF, organized in 1877, is the oldest Jewish center on the West Coast, and while its mission is specifically to foster a Jewish community, it is open to all. So come and build a little community of your own.

CEREMONY CAPACITY: The Atrium holds up to 250 seated guests.

EVENT/RECEPTION CAPACITY: The Center holds up to 330 seated or 474 standing guests.

MEETING CAPACITY: The Center can accommodate 470 seated guests.

FEES & DEPOSITS: 50% of the rental fee is required to reserve your date, the balance is due 30 days prior to the event. Rental fees range $125–4,400 depending on space rented and day and time rented. A refundable security deposit is required in addition to the rental fee.

AVAILABILITY: Year-round, daily, 8am–midnight.

SERVICES/AMENITIES:

Catering: select from list
Kitchen Facilities: 3, including supervised kosher meat kitchen and tableware
Tables & Chairs: provided
Linens, Silver, etc.: BYO or through caterer
Restrooms: wheelchair accessible
Dance Floor: CBA
Bride's Dressing Area: yes
Meeting Equipment: CBA

Parking: parking garage
Accommodations: no guest rooms
Telephone: pay phone
Outdoor Night Lighting: access only
Outdoor Cooking Facilities: no
Cleanup: caterer or renter
View: no
Other: full sound and lighting

RESTRICTIONS:

Alcohol: BYO, must use licensed server
Smoking: outside only
Music: amplified OK

Wheelchair Access: yes
Insurance: not required

Julia Morgan Ballroom
at the Merchants Exchange

465 California Street, San Francisco

415/421-7730

www.juliamorganballroom.com
info@juliamorganballroom.com

Historic Landmark

- Rehearsal Dinners
- Ceremonies
- Wedding Receptions
- Corp. Events/Mtgs.
- Private Parties
- Accommodations

The Julia Morgan Ballroom at the Merchants Exchange is an architectural treasure and one of San Francisco's most coveted private event spaces. Designed by Willis Polk and the renowned Julia Morgan, its classic Beaux-Arts style echoes that of Hearst Castle, Morgan's most famous building.

As you pass through the street-level doors, you're immediately transported to another era, one of lavish detail and impeccable taste. The barrel-vaulted lobby sparkles with marble, gold leaf and bronze, while the curved glass ceiling washes the space in abundant natural light.

An elevator takes you up to the 15th floor, where that sense of time travel continues in the Julia Morgan Ballroom. Here, there are no busy hotel corridors to contend with, no intrusions from the outside world. Looking out across the city, the elegant 4,300-square-foot ballroom envelopes you with warmth and sophistication.

You enter via a classic foyer and proceed naturally through the richly appointed bar and lounge, featuring gilded ceilings and fireplaces of carved stone at each end. The 27-foot curved marble bar sweeps you toward the ballroom and a breathtaking reveal: Light flows in through a wall of soaring floor-to-ceiling arched windows that afford a view of the heart of San Francisco's skyline, while mirrors on the opposite wall reflect the light. The overhead view is also impressive—the ceiling is a honeycomb of painstakingly crafted mahogany octagonals. The paneled walls continue this aesthetic commitment with classic columns worked directly into the wood. At the far end, a 20-foot stone fireplace provides an iconic backdrop and a final touch of grandeur.

When you reserve the Julia Morgan Ballroom, you enjoy use of the entire 15th floor including the bar and lounge, coat check, full catering kitchen, and several smaller rooms that are perfect for bridal dressing areas or other activities. Exclusive access to these fluid spaces affords the utmost flexibility in planning your event, as well as complete privacy.

The ballroom's professional production team boasts decades of combined experience in producing the finest San Francisco weddings. In addition, they've hosted numerous successful high-level events, from lunches with both First Lady and President Obama to galas showcasing the brightest stars of film, music and sports. With its incomparable setting and distinguished track record, the Julia Morgan Ballroom offers more than a remarkable wedding venue; it also offers peace of mind.

CEREMONY & EVENT/RECEPTION CAPACITY: Ceremonies and receptions can be held in the Lobby, Ballroom or Lounge. The Julia Morgan Ballroom holds up to 350 seated or 800 standing. The lounge area holds 60 seated or 350 standing.

MEETING CAPACITY: For large meetings, the Ballroom holds approximately 450 theater-style or 350 conference-style. There are 2 smaller seminar rooms that can accommodate 12–20 seated conference-style.

FEES & DEPOSITS: The rental fee for use of the entire 15th floor starts at $9,500. The rental fee for only the lounge area is $4,500, and for smaller meeting rooms, the fee starts at $600. To secure your date, half the rental fee is required. There is special pricing for Friday and Sunday celebrations, call for details. Meals start at $75/person. Tax, alcohol and service charge are additional.

AVAILABILITY: Year-round, daily. Hours are by arrangement.

SERVICES/AMENITIES:

Catering: provided by in-house chef; choose from preferred list; or BYO licensed, insured and bonded

Kitchen Facilities: fully equipped

Tables & Chairs: provided, mahogany Chiavari chairs and barstools available

Linens, Silver, etc.: BYO or CBA

Restrooms: wheelchair accessible

Dance Floor: provided (mahogany)

Bride's & Groom's Dressing Areas: yes

Meeting Equipment: available

Parking: street parking, nearby garages or valet

Accommodations: no guest rooms

Telephone: pay phones

Outdoor Night Lighting: access only

Outdoor Cooking Facilities: no

Cleanup: provided

View: downtown San Francisco cityscape

Other: full-service event production, WiFi, event lighting, stage, setup and breakdown

RESTRICTIONS:

Alcohol: provided

Smoking: outdoors only

Music: amplified OK

Wheelchair Access: yes

Insurance: certificate required

Other: no rice, birdseed, glitter or sparklers

This is important! Tell locations you're reading HERE COMES THE GUIDE and ask if our information is still current.

Legion of Honor Museum

Landmark Museum

100 34th Avenue, Lincoln Park, San Francisco
415/750-3698
www.famsf.org
legionevents@famsf.org

● Rehearsal Dinners	● Corp. Events/Mtgs.
● Ceremonies	● Private Parties
● Wedding Receptions	Accommodations

Whether you're seeing the Legion of Honor for the first time or the tenth, you can't help but be a little awe-struck. The majestic neoclassical building, standing on the highest point of Lincoln Park, represents San Francisco at its absolute best: great architecture, fine art, romance, and stunning coastal views.

Weddings often begin with a ceremony on the Balustrade Lawn, a promontory where couples exchange vows against a breathtaking panorama of the Golden Gate Bridge, the Marin Headlands, and the Pacific Ocean. Or, if palatial is your preference, get married in the regal Court of Honor. Sunrise to sunset, the light is forever changing in this expansive piazza with its soaring wraparound colonnade. August Rodin's famous sculpture, *The Thinker,* sits alone at the entrance, animating the space with its dynamic form.

The Legion of Honor is home to more than 70 Rodin sculptures, and it's the only place on earth where you and your guests may dine and dance sumptuously among the sculptor's masterpieces. They reside in three adjacent galleries with vaulted ceilings—a series of event spaces of princely proportions. Celebrating in any one of these chambers will give your gathering a luxurious feel. But combine all three for unprecedented grandeur: Have cocktails in one gallery, dining in another and dancing in the third. However, you'll probably want to have that first dance, center stage, under the museum's magnificent rotunda, whose gorgeous marble floor is available for just that purpose. You might also opt to include a favorite musical selection played by the museum's designated organist on the Legion's very own walnut, ivory and ebony Skinner pipe organ—one of the finest in the world and a working work of art. Its 4,500 pipes have been seamlessly integrated into the very structure of the museum.

Downstairs on the Terrace Level other interesting choices await. How about a cocktail reception amid the treasures in the dramatic Hall of Antiquities? Guests can meet and mingle surrounded by pottery, sculpture, glass vessels and metalwork created by early artists from Greece, Rome, Egypt and the Ancient Near East. There's room for a large bar, and waiters can serve up champagne and passed hors d'oeuvres here before celebrants step into the adjoining Legion Café to dine.

The Legion Café, with its abundant windows and glass doors, and art-accented walls is an inviting environment for any affair. You can use the whole room or just a section of it for a more intimate atmosphere. Doors open onto the herb-scented Café Terrace. Attractive brickwork grounds the airy space, an elegant stone balustrade frames it, and silvery olive trees create a natural canopy.

It feels so removed from the stresses and pressures of everyday life, you might well imagine that you've been spirited away to Paris's Luxembourg Gardens or some other leafy paradise.

The Legion of Honor houses some of the most beautiful art in the world, which elevates every event that's held here. No matter what your occasion—wedding, corporate gala or private party—it will unfold brilliantly in this exquisite Beaux-Arts setting.

CEREMONY CAPACITY: The Balustrade Lawn, to the right of the museum entrance, and the Court of Honor, each hold up to 275 seated guests. The indoor Rodin Gallery can accommodate 120 seated, and the Florence Gould Theater seats 300.

EVENT/RECEPTION CAPACITY: The Café holds 220 seated or 300 standing guests. An additional 140 guests may be added to that capacity by tenting the sculpture garden at an additional charge. There are three Rodin Galleries, together they hold 225 seated or 250 standing. 130 guests may be seated in the central Rodin Gallery.

MEETING CAPACITY: The museum's Florence Gould Theater holds 316 seated theater-style, plus 3 wheelchair spaces and 2 companion seats.

FEES & DEPOSITS: 50% of the facility fee and a signed agreement are due at the time of booking. Rental fees start at $5,000 and vary depending on the rental package selected. The balance and final guest count are due at least 60 days prior to the event.

AVAILABILITY: Year-round, daily, starting at 6:30pm. Additional hours are available for an extra fee.

SERVICES/AMENITIES:

Catering: select from preferred list
Kitchen Facilities: setup or prep only
Tables & Chairs: some provided
Linens, Silver, etc.: BYO
Restrooms: wheelchair accessible
Dance Floor: provided
Bride's Dressing Area: CBA, extra fee
Meeting Equipment: CBA, extra fee

Parking: large lot
Accommodations: no guest rooms
Telephone: pay phones
Outdoor Night Lighting: yes
Outdoor Cooking Facilities: n/a
Cleanup: provided
View: Lincoln Park, Pacific Ocean, Golden Gate Bridge and Marin Headlands

RESTRICTIONS:

Alcohol: BYO
Smoking: not allowed
Music: amplified OK with volume restrictions

Wheelchair Access: yes
Insurance: certificate required

Mandarin Oriental, San Francisco

Hotel

222 Sansome Street, San Francisco
415/276-9619

www.mandarinoriental.com
tgarcia@mohg.com
mosfo-reservations@mohg.com

- Rehearsal Dinners
- Ceremonies
- Wedding Receptions
- Corp. Events/Mtgs.
- Private Parties
- Accommodations

Mandarin Oriental, San Francisco creates a soothing and sophisticated environment where guests lack for nothing. Borrowing elements from other acclaimed Mandarin Oriental hotels in Hong Kong, Thailand and Paris, this one manages to be both modern and luxurious.

A feeling of calm envelopes guests as they enter the dramatic new Italian travertine marble lobby. From here, a striking grand staircase, outfitted with curved glass and mapa burlwood veneer, leads them up to the main event spaces on the second level. With more than 5,000 square feet of beautifully designed, versatile, and technologically enhanced function rooms, the hotel easily accommodates lavish weddings, business meetings, and private parties.

For a spectacular ceremony, host it on the 40th-floor Sky Deck. At this height you're presented with a postcard panorama normally only enjoyed by birds: views of the Golden Gate Bridge, Coit Tower and Alcatraz Island. There are plenty of options for tying the knot indoors, too.

Receptions follow in your choice of two completely different function rooms. The more classic Embassy Room features French-influenced décor, while the recently added California Room has an upscale, contemporary look. Its elegant beige and white palette complements the color scheme of any event, and natural light flowing in through a wall of windows fills the space during the day. Of course, wherever you celebrate in the hotel, their professional planners will ensure that your affair is executed with the uncompromising attention to detail for which Mandarin Oriental is renowned.

Executive Chef Adam Mali and his culinary team, who base much of their cuisine on fresh, local ingredients, are happy to customize your menu. You also have an extensive array of cocktails to choose from, as well as a selection of over 600 wines.

The guest rooms and suites occupy the top 11 floors of this 48-story building (the third tallest in San Francisco), and afford expansive vistas of the bay, both bridges, Alcatraz Island, Marin, the East Bay and the city itself. Two of their signature suites have large terraces, where the newlyweds can enjoy breakfast the next morning. Another recent addition to the hotel is The Spa, an 8,000-square-foot spa and fitness center with a couple's suite and three treatment rooms. An array of flexible packages allow you to personalize your treatments and enjoy a rejuvenating experience before and after your event.

Although it has plenty of international glamour, Mandarin Oriental, San Francisco offers the personality and attentive service of a boutique hotel. We think it's a wonderful choice, not only for a special occasion, but for a romantic getaway any time of the year.

CEREMONY & EVENT/RECEPTION CAPACITY: The California Room holds 70 seated or 100 standing, the Embassy Room holds 120 seated or 130 standing and the Library 60 seated or 70 standing guests. The Boardroom holds 40 seated or 50 standing.

MEETING CAPACITY: Several spaces accommodate 15–120 seated guests.

FEES & DEPOSITS: 50% of the food and beverage minimum plus the applicable room rental fee is required to reserve your date. The balance is due 10 days prior to the event. Rental fees start at $1,500 and vary depending on space, day and time rented. Wedding packages range $135–$200/person. Tax, alcohol and a 20% service charge are additional. A cleanup/setup fee may apply. A complimentary guest room is available if the event minimum is met.

AVAILABILITY: Year-round, daily, anytime.

SERVICES/AMENITIES:

Catering: provided, no BYO

Kitchen Facilities: n/a

Tables & Chairs: provided

Linens, Silver, etc.: provided

Restrooms: wheelchair accessible

Dance Floor: yes

Bride's Dressing Area: CBA

Meeting Equipment: full range, extra fee

Parking: valet or nearby garages

Accommodations: 158 view guest rooms

Telephone: guest phones

Outdoor Night Lighting: no

Outdoor Cooking Facilities: no

Cleanup: provided

View: San Francisco

Other: event coordination, spa services

RESTRICTIONS:

Alcohol: provided

Smoking: not allowed

Music: amplified OK indoors

Wheelchair Access: yes, elevator

Insurance: not required

Other: decorations require approval

Marines' Memorial Club

Historic Club and Hotel

609 Sutter Street, San Francisco
415/441-8562

www.marineclub.com
jenniferchin@marineclub.com

- Rehearsal Dinners
- Ceremonies
- Wedding Receptions
- Corp. Events/Mtgs.
- Private Parties
- Accommodations

The Marines' Memorial Club is a hidden jewel in the heart of San Francisco's Union Square. This Beaux-Arts beauty was built in 1926, and in 1946 was dedicated as a memorial to the Marines who lost their lives during World War II. Today, the landmark is a nonprofit club for veterans and their families—and also a fine hotel and special event facility.

The club's rich architectural heritage, first-class food and service, and nostalgically elegant décor bring extra dimensions to any celebration. The entire 10th and 11th floors of the building are fitted out with wonderful banquet spaces. Weddings on the 11th floor might begin with a ceremony in the exquisite, take-your-breath-away Crystal Ballroom. A vaulted hand-painted ceiling holds three massive crystal chandeliers. Their ornate prisms shimmer over the gleaming candelabra, and the ballroom's oval shape lends a soft intimacy to the magnificent space. For ceremonies, the staff sets up a raised dais flanked by a pair of ficus trees festooned with twinkle lights. After the service, guests retire to the Crystal Lounge, connected to the ballroom by a foyer. Everyone toasts the happy couple, while taking in the sweeping city view from the Lounge's wall of vaulted windows. (Tear your eyes away from the luminous cityscape for a moment, and admire the Lounge's gold-leafed and frescoed ceiling.) When it is time to dine, guests return to the Crystal Ballroom, which has been transformed with white linens and silver candelabra centerpieces. The ballroom also has a built-in dance floor that runs the length of the room, so everyone has plenty of space to kick up their heels.

An equally impressive option awaits on the 10th floor. There's a stately majesty about the Commandant's Ballroom, thanks to a 22-foot-high intricately painted and coffered ceiling, wood detailing, and striking iron chandeliers with matching sconces. Enhancing this ballroom's splendor are vaulted east-facing windows that capture a sparkling city vista. Just as with the Crystal Ballroom, the Commandant's serves as the setting for both ceremonies and lavish receptions. During the cocktail hour, the nearby Heritage and Regimental Rooms, which are connected by an adjoining foyer, are set for cocktail service. Guests can get their drinks from bars set up in either room, then relax at cocktail tables holding flickering votive candles. The Regimental Room looks out toward Nob Hill, and is clad in mahogany paneling. A built-in bar comes in handy during a cocktail hour or rehearsal dinner, and a working fireplace adds to the clubby atmosphere. The Heritage Room enjoys views of Nob Hill and downtown, and Art Deco chandeliers convey a bit of whimsy. Returning to the Commandant's Ballroom for the reception and dancing completes the evening's revelry.

Events at the Club are catered in-house, and feature gourmet contemporary American cuisine. Renovated guest rooms and suites provide a comfortable overnight stay. Newlyweds love Suite #403's oversized tub-for-two; its spacious living room and wall of mirrors are great for pre-wedding primping. The Leatherneck Steakhouse on the 12th floor showcases a stunning panorama with glimpses of the bay over towering skyscrapers—what a dynamic spot for a rehearsal dinner! Though shopping and nightlife is right outside the Club's door, the Marines' Memorial is marvelously self-contained: it also has a health club, an indoor pool, a library, a museum, and its own theater! Whether you are a veteran or civilian, you're sure to find a warm welcome at this timeless club.

CEREMONY & EVENT/RECEPTION CAPACITY: The club holds 25–280 seated guests indoors.

MEETING CAPACITY: Several spaces can accommodate 30–300 seated guests.

FEES & DEPOSITS: For weddings, a nonrefundable deposit is required to reserve the banquet room. There's no rental fee if you meet a food and beverage minimum; however, house catering is required. A guest count along with the estimated event balance is required 7 business days prior to the event. Wedding packages, which include open bar, hors d'oeuvres, champagne and wine service, salad and entrée service and cake cutting range $69–135/person. Seated luncheons start at $29/person and dinners at $40/person. Hors d'oeuvres start at $20/person and buffets (min. 50 people) at $54/person. Tax and a service charge are additional.

For meetings and business functions, rental fees for meeting rooms vary depending on room(s) and/or services selected. Call for additional information regarding food and beverage charges.

AVAILABILITY: Year-round, daily, 7am–11pm. There are overtime charges for events running more than 5 hours.

SERVICES/AMENITIES:

Catering: provided, no BYO
Kitchen Facilities: n/a
Tables & Chairs: provided
Linens, Silver, etc.: provided
Restrooms: wheelchair accessible
Dance Floor: yes
Bride's Dressing Area: CBA
Meeting Equipment: CBA

Parking: nearby garage
Accommodations: 138 guest rooms
Telephone: pay and guest phones
Outdoor Night Lighting: access only
Outdoor Cooking Facilities: no
Cleanup: provided
View: Nob Hill, SF cityscape and Union Square
Other: full event coordination; ethnic cuisine available upon request

RESTRICTIONS:

Alcohol: provided
Smoking: not allowed
Music: amplified OK

Wheelchair Access: yes, elevator
Insurance: required for DJs and entertainers

Overwhelmed? Use the search criteria on www.HereComesTheGuide.com to narrow down your choices.

113

McCormick & Kuleto's

Restaurant

900 North Point, Suite H301 (at Beach & Larkin), San Francisco

415/929-8374

www.mccormickandkuletos.com
mssfcsm@ldry.com
mssfcsm2@ldry.com

● Rehearsal Dinners	● Corp. Events/Mtgs.
● Ceremonies	● Private Parties
● Wedding Receptions	Accommodations

If it's true that good food tastes even better when it's served up with a great view, then eating at McCormick & Kuleto's is bound to be a delectable experience. This three-tiered restaurant in Ghirardelli Square specializes in impeccably fresh seafood from all over the world. It overlooks the bay—which just happens to be right across the street—and almost every diner has an unobstructed view of Alcatraz, Marin and a variety of historical ships that are docked at Hyde Street Pier.

The interior scenery is also captivating. In the Main Dining Room, fantastic tortoise shell "boat" chandeliers drop from the vaulted ceiling. Wood-and-copper railings flow from tier to tier, defining each level. The Captain's Room derives its warmth from sumptuous burled redwood paneling throughout and elegant hand-crafted glass lighting fixtures. For larger receptions, this space may be reserved with the Bay View Room and can be used either for cocktails or additional banquet seating. The Dolphin Room, with its modern décor, adjoining patio and views of the bay, is a nice spot for intimate rehearsal dinners and receptions. It features Italian mosaic tiles on the center columns and archways. For smaller receptions or bridal showers, the Alcatraz Room is a more informal space with redwood paneling and pictures of historic ships decorating the walls.

Suffused with sunlight or enhanced by the nighttime glitter of boats docked below, McCormick & Kuleto's provides a generous helping of visual as well as gastronomic appeal.

CEREMONY CAPACITY: Ceremonies for 60–80 guests can be arranged.

EVENT/RECEPTION CAPACITY: The restaurant holds 20–220 seated or 80–220 standing guests in various rooms.

MEETING CAPACITY: Event spaces can accommodate 20–220 seated guests. Buyouts are available for larger groups.

FEES & DEPOSITS: A $500–1,000 deposit is due when reservations are made. For weddings, 80% of the estimated event total is due 3 days prior to the event and the balance is payable the day of the event. Any menu can be customized. Catering costs run $35–40/person for luncheons and $60–80/person for dinners. Tax and a 21% service charge are additional.

AVAILABILITY: Year-round, daily, 11:30am–11pm.

SERVICES/AMENITIES:

Catering: provided, no BYO
Kitchen Facilities: n/a
Tables & Chairs: provided
Linens, Silver, etc.: provided
Restrooms: wheelchair accessible
Dance Floor: CBA, extra charge
Bride's Dressing Area: no
Meeting Equipment: CBA, extra charge
Other: event coordination

Parking: garage, on street
Accommodations: hotels nearby
Telephone: emergency use only
Outdoor Night Lighting: in Ghirardelli Square
Outdoor Cooking Facilities: no
Cleanup: provided
View: SF Bay, Maritime Museum, historic ships, Angel Island and Alcatraz

RESTRICTIONS:

Alcohol: provided
Smoking: outdoors only
Music: amplified OK until 11pm, with volume restrictions

Wheelchair Access: yes
Insurance: not required

Mission Bay Conference Center

1675 Owens Street, Suite 251, San Francisco
866/431-8273

www.acc-missionbayconferencecenter.com
mbccsales@aramark.com

Conference Center

● Rehearsal Dinners		● Corp. Events/Mtgs.
Ceremonies		● Private Parties
● Wedding Receptions		Accommodations

Exciting and dramatic in scale, the Mission Bay Conference Center is almost as striking as the Golden Gate Bridge and San Francisco Bay from which it draws much of its distinctive orange-red and ocean-blue color palette. Dominating the handsome UCSF campus in the recently developed Mission Bay neighborhood, this contemporary structure represents a brilliant 21st-century standard in event planning options. A seamless mixture of large and intimate public and private spaces, the venue provides everything you need to take your event—wedding, corporate or community function, performance or social gathering—to the next level.

The entrance is through the doors of the William J. Rutter Center and a softly lit hall gallery that opens almost immediately onto the expansive Fisher Atrium, where windowed walls, an open mezzanine, and skylights high overhead create a sense of soaring dimension. Have your cocktail reception here—there's plenty of room for guests to circulate. And while they're sipping champagne and sampling passed hors d'oeuvres, they'll be admiring the clean lines and captivating use of light, shadow and geometry achieved by world-renowned architect Ricardo Legorreta.

For your sit-down reception or dinner-dance, the adjacent Fisher Banquet Room is a splendid setting. The room, which can be used in its entirety or divided into two smaller sections, is enhanced by mood lighting and a built-in sound system and projector. Glass doors in a wall of floor-to-ceiling windows lead out to a pair of terraces framed by greenery. The Bank of America Terrace has a campus vista and offers a lovely way to take part of your celebration outdoors. If you feel your guests need still more room to relax, the ground floor lounge with a terrace view is just the spot.

But that isn't all. We said the center would take your event to another level and we meant it. Moving up to the glass-walled mezzanine that looks out over the Fisher Atrium on one side and the campus grounds on the other, you'll find yourself in the airy Robertson Auditorium Foyer, another spacious entertainment area. Bright and open, with a roomy outdoor deck, it's large enough for a cocktail reception, food stations, photo booths, or any creative combination of activities. The Robertson Auditorium itself has a grand, state-of-the-art stage and projection system, as well as a beautiful *Architectural Digest*-style surround warmed with rich walnut colors—perfect for framing any special affair.

Ready to rise to an even higher level? Head for the roof, where surprising features include a little "lawn" area and a rock-climbing wall. On the way, check out the boardroom and the additional conference rooms before stepping out onto the Pink and Brown Patios with their awesome Bay and City skyline views.

CEREMONY CAPACITY: Ceremonies do not take place at this location.

EVENT/RECEPTION CAPACITY: The site holds 300 seated or 600 standing guests indoors and 300 seated or 600 standing outdoors.

MEETING CAPACITY: Meeting spaces accommodate 600 seated guests.

FEES & DEPOSITS: 50% of anticipated event total is required to reserve your date. The balance is due 30 days prior to the event. Rental fees range $1,800–5,000 depending on the space rented. Receptions and dinners starting at $35/person. Tax, alcohol and a 20% service charge are additional.

AVAILABILITY: Year-round, daily, 6am–11pm.

SERVICES/AMENITIES:

Catering: provided
Kitchen Facilities: n/a
Tables & Chairs: provided
Linens, Silver, etc.: provided
Restrooms: wheelchair accessible
Dance Floor: CBA
Bride's Dressing Area: yes
Meeting Equipment: provided, A/V equipment

Parking: on site, garage nearby
Accommodations: no guest rooms
Telephone: office phone
Outdoor Night Lighting: CBA
Outdoor Cooking Facilities: BBQ CBA
Cleanup: provided
View: cityscape, garden courtyard, bay
Other: in-house florals, picnic area, event coordination

RESTRICTIONS:

Alcohol: provided
Smoking: not allowed
Music: amplified OK

Wheelchair Access: yes
Insurance: liability required

The Omni San Francisco Hotel

Historic Luxury Hotel

500 California Street at Montgomery, San Francisco
415/677-9494
www.omnisanfrancisco.com
kcroff@omnihotels.com

● Rehearsal Dinners	● Corp. Events/Mtgs.
● Ceremonies	● Private Parties
● Wedding Receptions	● Accommodations

The clang of a cable car bell adds just the right touch of romance to the ambiance at the Omni San Francisco Hotel, located in San Francisco at the foot of ever-fashionable Nob Hill. Movie-set perfect, this opulent venue is the result of a painstaking restoration of the old Financial Center Building, one of the city's architectural icons. Completed in 2002 at a cost of $100 million, this 362-room luxury hotel recaptures the bygone grace and Florentine Renaissance style of its illustrious 1926 predecessor.

The elegance of old money still wreaths the interior where the two-story atrium lobby combines the well-upholstered intimacy of a private club and the glamour of a grand salon. Bronzed washed torchères, dark cherrywood and mahogany accents, deep brown Italian marble, dreamy jazz and the scent of exotic blooms ease guests into a world of refined sophistication.

From the lobby, a dramatic grand staircase winds up to a broad wrought-iron-balconied mezzanine just made for receptions. From this airy perch, guests can look out through 20-foot windows curtained by the cascade of Czechoslovakian crystal that twinkles in the lobby's chandeliers. On the same floor, the Union Square Room offers hush-hush views of the corner of California and Montgomery through its seven arched, draped and betasseled windows. The portrait-friendly lighting and intimate dimensions of this setting make it ideal for everything from rehearsal dinners to brunches to well-arranged seminars. The North Beach Room next door, with its floor-to-ceiling windows and Italian pastoral feel, is another fine choice for smaller functions.

For large parties, guests ascend to the third floor. Here the plushly carpeted and appointed foyer hints at the glamour of a vast Grand Ballroom, outfitted in the rich patterns and tasteful gold tones of the Florentine Renaissance. Lit with chandeliers and wall sconces and paneled in silk, its 2,800 square feet can easily accommodate the most extravagant affair. With acoustics and a sound system that woos divas and DJs alike, it's got what it takes to keep any function from flagging. On the same floor, a terrace (cut into the heart of the building and shielded by the fortress-like walls of the hotel) allows guests to mingle outdoors, free from the wind and fog that bedevil most outdoor events in the city.

When the band has played its last tune, out-of-town and local visitors alike may find it hard to abandon all of this sophistication and style. Not a problem. They can book into recently renovated guest rooms that feature damask wall coverings, polished brass, Italian marble, Chinese granite, plush terry robes, down duvets and other upscale amenities. And should they want to step out, Chinatown, North Beach, Union Square and the Embarcadero are among the many San Francisco treats to be found mere minutes away.

CEREMONY CAPACITY: The Ballroom holds 200 seated guests, 170 with a dance floor.

EVENT/RECEPTION CAPACITY: The hotel holds 100–200 seated or 125–300 standing guest indoors.

MEETING CAPACITY: 9 meeting rooms are available that can accommodate up to 200 seated guests.

FEES & DEPOSITS: Rental fees range $0–5,000. Lunches range $53–90/person; dinners $65–195/person. Tax, alcohol and a 21% service charge are additional.

AVAILABILITY: Year-round, daily, 6am–midnight.

SERVICES/AMENITIES:

Catering: provided, no BYO
Kitchen Facilities: n/a
Tables & Chairs: provided
Linens, Silver, etc.: provided
Restrooms: wheelchair accessible
Dance Floor: provided
Bride's & Groom's Dressing Areas: yes
Meeting Equipment: CBA, extra charge

Parking: valet or nearby garages
Accommodations: 362 guest rooms, 15 suites
Telephone: pay phones
Outdoor Night Lighting: access only
Outdoor Cooking Facilities: no
Cleanup: provided
View: no
Other: event coordination

RESTRICTIONS:

Alcohol: provided
Smoking: outdoors only
Music: amplified OK

Wheelchair Access: yes
Insurance: required for vendors
Other: decorations require prior approval

The professionals in the back of this book are the best in the business. How do we know? Read page 637.

119

Parc 55 Wyndham Hotel

Hotel

55 Cyril Magnin Street, Market at Fifth, San Francisco
415/403-6651

www.parc55hotel.com
catering@parc55.com

- Rehearsal Dinners
- Ceremonies
- Wedding Receptions
- Corp. Events/Mtgs.
- Private Parties
- Accommodations

Sophisticated, fashion-forward wedding couples are drawn to Parc 55 Wyndham, unquestionably one of the best and most exciting downtown hotels. Events held at this venue, located on a chic little street off of Union Square in the heart of the city's premier shopping, dining and arts district, are truly one hundred percent San Francisco. All of your guests—especially those coming from out of town—will appreciate the center-of-the-action locale, as well the impressive level of personal service, apparent right from the doorman's greeting.

Encompassing four levels of dynamic event options, Parc 55 thrives with the energy and pizzazz of its neighborhood. Guests are admitted through the first-floor gallery, where a sculpted contemporary art wall makes a striking backdrop for wedding photos. A dramatic staircase climbs up to the bustling lobby, a spectacular two-story atrium with floor-to-ceiling windows that flood the space with natural light. Hallways lead to an oasis of cozy gathering spots, each named for a city street or landmark. Also on this level is the hotel's restaurant, Cityhouse, a local hotspot that welcomes rehearsal dinners, cocktail receptions or wedding brunches.

The third level features two junior ballrooms, though with capacity for up to 200 of your nearest and dearest, these spaces are plenty grand indeed. The handsomely appointed Market Street Room, for example, can easily accommodate a well-attended wedding ceremony. Stunning modern fixtures with sculptural elements evoke movement without overwhelming, so that the bride in all her glory still takes center stage. A spacious prefunction area is marvelous for cocktails overlooking the atrium, and it serves as a bridge to the larger Embarcadero Room, a lovely, airy reception choice with large arched windows on two sides.

An ascent to the fourth floor brings guests to the spacious Ballroom Foyer, whose 14-foot windows framing vibrant city vistas entice some couples to stage their ceremony here. Three sets of double doors open to the magnificent 5,600-square-foot Cyril Magnin Ballroom, which is ideal for a gala wedding reception catered to perfection. With a warm yet stately presence, the Cyril Magnin boasts a wall mural collage of San Francisco landmarks. The mural's soft, burnished tones harmonize with almost any style reception. The ballroom can be sectioned into three smaller salons, perhaps with a ceremony held in one and dining and dancing unfolding in the other two.

Up on the 31st floor, the Executive Club Lounge has sleek décor and a panoramic view of the city lights. The Lounge is a snappy setting for a rehearsal dinner or cocktail hour...or for the newlyweds to savor a few minutes of alone time.

After such an epic celebration, no one—least of all the bride and groom—will want their sublime experience to end when the party is over. This stunningly renovated 32-floor property is lavished with high-class amenities, and friends and family should opt to overnight in one of the 1,015 deluxe rooms. Newlyweds deserve the splurge of a Sunset Suite with a parlor, dining room and Jacuzzi bath, or one of the Club Rooms on the top six floors. That way, they can relax on their wedding night and romance each other in the lap of luxury.

CEREMONY CAPACITY: The hotel seats 400 guests indoors.

EVENT/RECEPTION CAPACITY: The hotel holds 400 seated or 900 standing guests indoors.

MEETING CAPACITY: The hotel can accommodate 400 seated guests.

FEES & DEPOSITS: 50% of the estimated event total is required to reserve your date. The balance is due 2 weeks prior to the event. Rental fees range $500–7,500 depending on the day and time of the event and the size of the event space and setup needed. Wedding packages range $95–150/person. Tax, alcohol and a 21% service charge are additional.

AVAILABILITY: Year-round, daily, anytime. Call for details.

SERVICES/AMENITIES:

Catering: provided
Kitchen Facilities: n/a
Tables & Chairs: provided
Linens, Silver, etc.: provided
Restrooms: wheelchair accessible
Dance Floor: provided
Bride's Dressing Area: yes
Meeting Equipment: provided
Other: event coordination

Parking: on street, valet required, garage nearby
Accommodations: 1,015 guest rooms
Telephone: pay, house and guest phones
Outdoor Night Lighting: access only
Outdoor Cooking Facilities: no
Cleanup: provided
View: no

RESTRICTIONS:

Alcohol: provided, or BYO with corkage fee
Smoking: not allowed
Music: amplified OK indoors

Wheelchair Access: yes
Insurance: not required

Pavilion By The Bay

Waterfront Event Facility

291 Avenue of the Palms, Treasure Island, San Francisco
415/274-2013
www.winevalleycatering.com
lynn@winevalleycatering.com

- Rehearsal Dinners
- Ceremonies
- Wedding Receptions
- Corp. Events/Mtgs.
- Private Parties
- Accommodations

Banners, kites, fireworks, pleasure barges floating by—the festive spirit of Treasure Island will sweep you away when you set eyes on this spectacular venue. Situated on broad lawns next to the bay, this enormous, white, high-peaked, Genesis tent pavilion is one of the most captivating properties imaginable.

It's the perfect backdrop for all types of events, and has hosted many themed or ethnic celebrations like traditional Indian or Russian weddings and bar mitzvahs. And because it can be used in combination with other nearby Treasure Island venues, it's a particularly good choice for a large party or one that lasts all day. For example, an extended Indian wedding began with pre-ceremony mingling in the charming salon and courtyard of Casa de la Vista, followed by the groom's arrival on a horse. Then everyone was seated in the pavilion for the ceremony, after which they gathered in yet another building on the island for dinner and dancing.

The pavilion itself is completely expandable, heated or cooled, and it has glass walls on three sides to let the views in, which in this case means an eye-level panorama of the San Francisco cityscape, all three bridges and the glittering face of the bay. The interior dimensions and details can be easily modified to suit your occasion, and the sky's the limit as far as lighting goes. Eight huge double doors open onto the landscaped grounds, giving events that oh-so-desirable indoor-outdoor flow. For an intimate ceremony, you can also exchange vows in the lovely little chapel next to the Casa de la Vista.

If ever there was a place made for parties this is it. Treasure Island, a man-made body of land created from imported fill on the shoals of Yerba Buena Island, was "built" by the U.S. Government for the 1939–40 Golden Gate International Exposition. Truly a treasure—the island was christened after the Robert Louis Stevenson novel of the same name—it's situated around mid-span of the San Francisco-Oakland Bay Bridge in one of the most picturesque points on the bay. Recently voted the hippest spot to be married by *InStyle Weddings* magazine, it's a terrific site for any social or commercial event in which a stellar setting is a factor.

But here's the best part: What you get when you book Pavilion By The Bay is far more than a gorgeous location. The acclaimed professionals at *Wine Valley Catering* are the creative masterminds behind the development and management of this property, so you know that whatever you plan the execution will be flawless. There's a full kitchen on site to ensure that every menu is prepared to their exacting standards. The food is fresh, organic, locally raised, carefully composed, exquisitely presented and can be paired with the very best Napa and Sonoma Valley wines. Naturally the service is impeccable; what else would you expect from a management team with over 125 years of experience between them?

It's no wonder *7x7 Magazine* calls this the best place to tie the knot. We have to agree and add that whatever the event, it's certain to be the talk of the town if it's held here.

CEREMONY CAPACITY: The facility holds 300–600 seated guests, indoors or outdoors.

EVENT/RECEPTION & MEETING CAPACITY: The facility accommodates 350 seated with a dance floor, 400 seated with no dance floor, or 900 standing guests indoors.

FEES & DEPOSITS: A 50% venue deposit is required to reserve your date. The balance is due 30 days prior to the event. The rental fee ranges $3,500–5,500 depending on the day of the event. Meals range $52–95/person. Tax, alcohol and a 20% service charge are additional.

AVAILABILITY: Year-round, daily, anytime.

SERVICES/AMENITIES:

Catering: provided, no BYO
Kitchen Facilities: yes
Tables & Chairs: through caterer
Linens, Silver, etc.: through caterer
Restrooms: wheelchair accessible
Dance Floor: through caterer
Bride's Dressing Area: CBA
Meeting Equipment: CBA
Other: event coordination

Parking: large lot
Accommodations: no guest rooms
Telephone: emergency use only
Outdoor Night Lighting: provided
Outdoor Cooking Facilities: no
Cleanup: provided
View: panorama of cityscape and San Francisco Bay

RESTRICTIONS:

Alcohol: provided
Smoking: outdoors only
Music: amplified OK

Wheelchair Access: yes
Insurance: liability required
Other: no rice, glitter, confetti, rise petals or sparklers

Presidio Chapel

Historic Chapel

130 Fisher Loop, San Francisco Presidio
415/561-5444
www.presidio.gov
events@presidiotrust.gov

Rehearsal Dinners	Corp. Events/Mtgs.
● Ceremonies	Private Parties
Wedding Receptions	Accommodations

On a forested hillside overlooking the bay, this elegant Spanish Mission-style chapel is an inspirational place for a wedding. Appealing architecture and panoramic views are only part of what makes the Presidio Chapel so popular. Couples also value the venue's convenient location, secluded setting and affordability. And unlike many houses of worship, here you're welcome to use your own officiant, musicians and cultural style.

In fair weather, gather for pre-ceremony socializing in the memorial garden, a flower-lined tiled patio that faces the Presidio grounds and the bay. This is a wonderful spot for photos, thanks to a stunning backdrop of Angel and Alcatraz Islands framed by sweeping branches of pine and eucalyptus. Here guests await the peal of the church bell summoning them to the sanctuary for the ceremony. Inside the chapel, a soaring redwood-beamed ceiling hung with wrought-iron chandeliers, twelve arched stained-glass windows, and heavy oak doors all contribute to a strong Old World flavor.

Adjacent to the sanctuary, the Mural Room feels like a long, glass-enclosed sun porch. It looks out onto the garden and hillside, but its most notable feature is the mural from which it derives its name. Painted by the same artist who created the famed Coit Tower murals, it depicts St. Francis at its center—a fitting picture considering the variety of wildlife that lives around the chapel and the fact that St. Francis is the patron saint of San Francisco and animals. The room makes a tranquil spot for an intimate reception or post-wedding mingling, while the bride and groom have their photos taken in the picturesque memorial garden.

Couples who get married in the Presidio Chapel often have their reception at one of several other venues within the Presidio. Many newlyweds also stay the weekend at the new Inn at the Presidio, a historic 1903 Georgian Revival-style building that has been remodeled into an elegant lodge. It features an inviting front porch with rocking chairs, a dining room, and an outdoor deck with a fire pit. The inn makes a great home base for exploring everything the Presidio has to offer, including miles of hiking trails, wild open spaces and public and cultural events.

CEREMONY CAPACITY: The chapel holds 150–185 seated guests.

EVENT/RECEPTION CAPACITY: Receptions are not held on site. However, they can be hosted at a variety of other venues nearby.

FEES & DEPOSITS: A nonrefundable $340 reservation fee is required to secure your date and will be applied to the total rental fee. The balance of the fee is payable within 6 months of the event date. A $250 insurance fee and a refundable $500 security deposit are due with the signed contract. The rental fee for ceremonies ranges $1,200–1,500 depending on the day of the week. Rehearsals are $150/hr. A surcharge may apply for use of the courtyard and/or events with food and beverages.

AVAILABILITY: Year-round, daily, 7am–11pm.

SERVICES/AMENITIES:

Catering: BYO, licensed and insured
Kitchen Facilities: no
Tables & Chairs: BYO or through caterer
Linens, Silver, etc.: BYO or through caterer
Restroom: limited wheelchair accessible
Dance Floor: no
Bride's & Groom's Dressing Areas: yes
Meeting Equipment: n/a

Parking: large lot, free on weekends
Accommodations: Inn at the Presidio
Telephone: no phone
Outdoor Night Lighting: access only
Outdoor Cooking Facilities: no
Cleanup: renter
View: panorama of San Francisco and bay

RESTRICTIONS:

Alcohol: BYO, server must be licensed and insured
Smoking: outside only
Music: amplified OK

Wheelchair Access: yes
Insurance: required for aisle runner only
Other: no glitter, confetti, birdseed, rice or balloon releases; some decoration restrictions

Presidio Chapel of Our Lady

Historic Chapel

45 Moraga Avenue, SF Presidio, San Francisco
415/561-5444
www.presidio.gov
events@presidiotrust.gov

Rehearsal Dinners	Corp. Events/Mtgs.
● Ceremonies	Private Parties
● Wedding Receptions	Accommodations

For soldiers stationed at the Presidio during its early years as a military garrison, this little white church was known as the "Ivy-Covered Chapel" for the abundance of vines on its walls. The simple wooden building, with its gabled roof and steeple, was built in 1864 to serve as a place of worship for a small group of military officers and their families. These days, both the ivy and the soldiers are gone, but the Chapel of Our Lady has endured and is now a nondenominational church for ceremonies of all religions.

Although the Presidio is only minutes from downtown San Francisco, it's completely removed from the "urban-ness" of The City, and it encompasses some of the most beautiful real estate in Northern California. In fact, this former military base is now part of the Golden Gate National Recreation Area.

To get to the church, we followed Presidio Boulevard from the Marina, but it doesn't matter which road you take through the Presidio—it's a lovely drive from every direction. Our route curved through woods and past old officers' houses and military buildings, all neatly maintained and painted off-white with red roofs. The Chapel of Our Lady is set back from the sidewalk, surrounded by a grove of eucalyptus trees and shrubs. Standing on the front steps, you can see snippets of San Francisco Bay and the Golden Gate Bridge through the trees.

From the outside, the little chapel is still reminiscent of an old country church, but renovations have widened its original footprint and added decidedly modern elements. The chapel has been expanded with side aisles, a baptistery, a dressing room, a choir room, and a sanctuary.

Standing in the chapel on a sunny day, you notice right away how warm and bright it is. The main room is filled with light, flowing in through two walls of windows, constructed entirely of clear and multicolored glass block panels. The altar stands in front of a huge floor-to-ceiling window, which lets in even more light. Contemporary-styled wooden pews flank the center aisle, and wooden beams support the vaulted ceiling. Small iron chandeliers and wall sconces provide ambient lighting for ceremonies in the evening or on a misty day.

When the weather is glorious, consider extending the celebration onto the chapel grounds. Guests can gather in the front courtyard to congratulate the happy couple as they emerge from the chapel, then walk over to the side courtyard for champagne and light hors d'oeuvres. For a festive touch, add a few umbrella-shaded tables, clad with linens and flowers.

Many couples who get married in the Chapel of Our Lady make life easy on themselves by having their reception at the Presidio Officers' Club, Golden Gate Club or the Log Cabin which are popular for all types of celebrations.

After the wedding, consider staying the weekend at the new Inn at the Presidio. Formerly the bachelor officers' quarters, this historic 1903 Georgian Revival-style building has been remodeled into an elegant lodge. It features an inviting front porch with rocking chairs, a dining room, and an outdoor deck with a fire pit. From here you can enjoy everything the Presidio has to offer, including miles of hiking trails, wild open spaces and public and cultural events.

CEREMONY CAPACITY: The Chapel holds 200 seated guests for ceremonies or 100 seated guests in the Courtyard.

RECEPTION CAPACITY: The Chapel Courtyard holds 100 standing for a cocktail reception.

MEETING CAPACITY: The Chapel can accommodate 200 seated.

FEES & DEPOSITS: A $340 reservation fee is required to secure your date. A $250 insurance fee and a refundable $500 security deposit are required. The Chapel rental fee for ceremonies is $1,000.

For ceremonies with Courtyard receptions, there is an additional $100 charge. A 1-hour rehearsal runs $150.

AVAILABILITY: Year-round, daily, 10am–2pm or 3pm–7pm for ceremonies. Not available on national holidays, Christmas Eve or Day, or New Year's Eve or Day.

SERVICES/AMENITIES:

Catering: BYO, licensed and insured
Kitchen Facilities: no
Tables & Chairs: BYO or through caterer
Linens, Silver, etc.: BYO or through caterer
Restrooms: not wheelchair accessible
Dance Floor: no
Bride's Dressing Area: yes
Meeting Equipment: BYO

Parking: large lot nearby, restrictons may apply
Accommodations: Inn at the Presidio
Telephone: no phone
Outdoor Night Lighting: access only
Outdoor Cooking Facilities: no
Cleanup: caterer or renter
View: courtyard and landscaped grounds

RESTRICTIONS:

Alcohol: BYO, licensed and insured server
Smoking: outside only
Music: amplified OK until 7pm with volume restrictions

Wheelchair Access: no
Insurance: extra liability required ($250)
Other: decorations require prior approval

Presidio Golden Gate Club

Historic Club and Event Facility

135 Fisher Loop, Presidio, San Francisco
415/561-5444
www.presidio.gov
events@presidiotrust.gov

- Rehearsal Dinners
- Ceremonies
- Wedding Receptions
- Corp. Events/Mtgs.
- Private Parties
- Accommodations

Something magical must have come over the army architects who designed the many fine structures that dot the Presidio of San Francisco. Instead of fashioning plain barracks or no-frills buildings for the enlisted men and officers, they constructed some of the most exciting examples of Mission-style architecture on California's northern coast.

The Presidio's Golden Gate Club—which once functioned as the Non-Commissioned Officers Club—is no exception. With its red-tiled roof, white stucco walls and arcaded courtyard, it's the very picture of rich, Spanish-inspired design. Today, weddings and special events take place in this well-preserved 1940s-era club, and the sense of history and period details add real pizzazz to each celebration.

Nestled amongst towering cypress trees, the club's white-and-red exterior pops in sharp contrast to the deep greens that surround it. As you approach, the wide-open courtyard of the U-shaped building reveals palm trees and a fancy, tropical tile-and-grass patio. When it's set up with cock-tail tables covered in bright linens, this area can accommodate a standing reception beautifully.

After the mingling and champagne sipping have concluded, guests drift past large white columns and through double-glass doors into the stately Ventana Room, undoubtedly the property's most dazzling asset. A two-story wall of windows overlooks a grove of trees, and the bay shimmers in the distance. When you dress up this ballroom for dinner and dancing, that incredible view remains the focal point. Here, you'll also find a cathedral ceiling, a sizable wood dance floor, and a huge fireplace at one end. As you look around and experience the warmth of this space and your closeness to nature, you feel an overwhelming sense of serenity.

If you want to split up the party or you need more room, the Hawthorn and Cypress rooms are at your disposal. They provide two more options for wedding ceremonies and cocktail receptions, as well as quiet areas for children to play and older guests to relax. They're also ideal for hosting a dessert and/or espresso bar. Up on the second floor, there are breakout rooms for additional space and a small mezzanine that overlooks the Ventana Room.

It's worth mentioning that two charming chapels are within walking distance of the Golden Gate Club. Saying "I do" at either one of them and then proceeding with all your guests over to the club is fun and exhilarating—plus you can take advantage of photo opportunities along the way.

Although it may be hard to imagine soldiers once partying in such an elegant place, it's quite easy to picture your own festivities here. Whether you're planning a wedding, an anniversary bash or another special event, consider yourself lucky that the Golden Gate Club has passed out of army hands and into the public domain, where you can fully appreciate its tranquil, sophisticated setting.

And when your fabulous wedding has ended, extend your stay through the weekend at the new Inn at the Presidio. Formerly the bachelor officers' quarters, this historic 1903 Georgian Revival-style building has been remodeled into an upscale lodge. It features an inviting front porch with rocking chairs, a dining room, and an outdoor deck with a fire pit. From here you can enjoy everything the Presidio has to offer, including miles of hiking trails, wild open spaces and public and cultural events.

CEREMONY CAPACITY: The Golden Gate Club holds up to 200 seated guests depending on room selection and layout.

EVENT/RECEPTION & MEETING CAPACITY: With a buyout, the Golden Gate Club can accommodate up to 450 seated or 850 standing guests. Many configurations are available to accommodate groups of varying sizes; call for details.

FEES & DEPOSITS: A $1,000 reservation fee is required to secure your date. A $250 insurance fee and a $1,500 security deposit are required. Rental fees range $4,500–6,500, depending on the day of the week.

AVAILABILITY: Year-round, daily, 8am–midnight. Weddings are held in 10-hour blocks. Not available on national holidays or Christmas and New Year's Days and Eves.

SERVICES/AMENITIES:

Catering: BYO, licensed and insured
Kitchen Facilities: limited, prep only
Tables & Chairs: BYO or limited CBA
Linens, Silver, etc.: BYO or through caterer
Restrooms: wheelchair accessible
Dance Floor: yes, in Ventana Room
Bride's Dressing Area: CBA
Meeting Equipment: BYO or limited CBA

Parking: 60 spaces and large lot nearby, restrictions may apply
Accommodations: Inn at the Presidio
Telephone: house phone
Outdoor Night Lighting: access only
Outdoor Cooking Facilities: no
Cleanup: caterer or renter
View: SF Bay, Golden Gate bridge, cypress trees

RESTRICTIONS:

Alcohol: BYO, licensed and insured server
Smoking: outside only
Music: amplified OK indoors with volume restrictions until 11:30pm

Wheelchair Access: yes
Insurance: extra liability required ($250)
Other: decorations require prior approval

Presidio Golf Course and Clubhouse

Golfcourse & Clubhouse

300 Finley Road at Arguello Gate, San Francisco Presidio
415/561-4661 X207

www.presidiogolf.com
presidiobanquets@palmergolf.com

- Rehearsal Dinners
- Ceremonies
- Wedding Receptions
- Corp. Events/Mtgs.
- Private Parties
- Accommodations

Since 1776, the year Lieutenant Colonel Juan Bautista de Anza was dispatched to establish a garrison to protect the harbor of St. Francis, the Presidio has guarded the narrow mouth of San Francisco Bay, first for Spain, then Mexico, and finally for the United States. Then, as now, the Presidio was one big beautiful piece of California real estate. Today, its 1,500 acres of eucalyptus, cypress, pine forest, coastal wild flowers, and ocean and bay views belong not to the army, but to the National Park Service, and the 7,000-square-foot Clubhouse just inside the old Arguello Gate is a fine place to host a wide spectrum of events.

Set on a rise at the end of a stately drive, the Clubhouse has a casually refined look that makes you want to step inside. The interior, a blend of Mission-style architecture and Maybeck-inspired, landscape-friendly details, features cathedral ceilings, exposed fir beams, cherrywood trim and paneling, and a large limestone fireplace. Five French doors extend its largest dining area, the Presidio Cafe, onto a spacious wood-trellised patio with an excellent view of the final green of the Presidio's historic 18-hole golf course. President Theodore Roosevelt reviewed the command on the Presidio Golf Links in 1903, and many a golfer of note—including TR himself, Dwight Eisenhower, Bing Crosby and Arnold Palmer—has played through on its fairways. The patio, with its verdigris tables and chairs, is perfect for any style of function from barbecue to black-tie.

Of course, the close proximity of Bentgrass greens and well-maintained parklands is a powerful lure. Party plans could easily include a bit of golf practice or a short, ranger-led walk. But more likely, guests will simply want to sit back and enjoy the fresh air and the vista—lush green lawns, pine and eucalyptus groves, the blue-roofed towers of distant USF, and the comely neighborhood mansions, all looking very low-rise from this vantage point on a gentle crest.

If those wide open vistas are a tad too distracting, the Palmer Room (named for Arnold Palmer, of course!), provides cozier quarters just right for smaller meetings, breakfasts, luncheons or dinners, and the Palmer Terrace and lawn with its garden setting and pine-curtained bay views allows celebrants once again to take the dining and good times outdoors.

CEREMONY CAPACITY: The Outdoor Terrace holds up to 150, the South Lawn accommodates 220 and the Palmer Lawn holds 130 seated guests.

EVENT/RECEPTION CAPACITY: The Cafe holds 80 seated or 125 standing guests, the Palmer Room 40 seated or 50 standing guests, and the entire Clubhouse 130 seated or 150 standing guests. The Clubhouse and a tented outdoor terrace combined holds 200 seated.

MEETING CAPACITY: The Palmer Room accommodates up to 50 guests seated theater-style or 30 guests seated conference-style. The entire facility holds 120 seated.

FEES & DEPOSITS: For events, 50% of the estimated event total is required to reserve your date; the balance is due 10 days prior to the event. Room rental fees range from $250 for a daytime event in the Palmer Room to $4,000 for use of the Clubhouse and Tented Terrace. Lunches range $20–40/person. Dinners range $55–115/person. Tax, alcohol and a 21% service charge are additional, as is a $2/person cake-cutting fee.

AVAILABILITY: Year-round, daily, dawn until midnight.

SERVICES/AMENITIES:

Catering: provided, no BYO
Kitchen Facilities: n/a
Tables & Chairs: provided
Linens, Silver, etc.: provided
Restroom: wheelchair accessible
Dance Floor: provided
Bride's Dressing Area: no
Meeting Equipment: CBA, extra charge

Parking: large lot, complimentary
Accommodations: no guest rooms,
Telephone: emergency use only
Outdoor Night Lighting: yes
Outdoor Cooking Facilities: no
Cleanup: provided
View: fairways, park
Other: event coordination

RESTRICTIONS:

Alcohol: provided or corkage $15/bottle
Smoking: outside only
Music: amplified OK indoors

Wheelchair Access: yes
Insurance: not required

Want to find more venues and services? Check out our informative website, www.HereComesTheGuide.com.

131

Presidio Log Cabin and Log Cabin Lawn

Historic Log Cabin & Lawn

1299 Storey Avenue, The Presidio, San Francisco
415/561-5444
www.presidio.gov
events@presidiotrust.gov

● Rehearsal Dinners	● Corp. Events/Mtgs.
● Ceremonies	● Private Parties
● Wedding Receptions	● Accommodations

The name might suggest a humble little structure, but the Presidio Log Cabin is anything but. Although it is made of logs, it's more like a grand hunting lodge, with its solid fieldstone foundation and spacious interior.

Formerly the NCO Club for the army's Airborne Division, this unique 1937 building has seen its share of festivities. And luckily for us, its sturdy timbers have always been beautifully maintained. Ceiling beams and columns are made of actual tree trunks, and there are giant wagon wheel chandeliers overhead. The Old West flavor feels authentic here, and adds a fun element to parties without being over the top. Casual events like company picnics often play up the country-western theme by incorporating cowboy costumes, country music and square dancing. However, for wedding receptions and formal dinner parties, all it takes is candles and flowers to make the place glow with a rustic elegance. In fact, when the huge fireplace is lit and the room is warmed by guests dancing and celebrating, the ambiance is downright cozy.

During warm weather, the Log Cabin is great for an indoor/outdoor event. Get married on the expansive front lawn, either under a tent or in the open sunshine surrounded by nature. From here you have a view of the woods, the San Francisco skyline, and snippets of San Francisco Bay. Afterwards, host a cocktail reception on the large covered patio at the entrance of the Log Cabin. Often set up with small tables and chairs, it's a wonderful spot for mingling. When it's time for the reception, just invite your guests inside for dining and dancing.

You don't come across many log cabins in a sophisticated city like San Francisco, and this may be the only one where you can have a smashing party. It's also probably the only place where you can wear a tux or a cowboy hat and feel equally at home.

After the wedding there's no need to rush off—consider staying the weekend at the new Inn at the Presidio. Formerly the bachelor officers' quarters, this historic 1903 Georgian Revival-style building has been remodeled into an upscale lodge. It features an inviting front porch with rocking chairs, a dining room, and an outdoor deck with a fire pit. From here you can enjoy everything the Presidio has to offer, including miles of hiking trails, wild open spaces and public and cultural events.

CEREMONY & EVENT/RECEPTION CAPACITY: The Log Cabin holds 150 seated or 200 standing, and the Log Cabin Lawn up to 150 seated or 200 standing.

MEETING CAPACITY: Many room configuration options are available to accommodate groups of varying sizes. Call for details.

FEES & DEPOSITS: A $1,000 reservation fee is required to secure your date. A $250 insurance fee and a $1,500 refundable security deposit are required. Rental fees range $2,500–3,500 depending on the day of the event.

AVAILABILITY: Year-round, daily, 8am–midnight. Weddings are held in 10-hour blocks. Not available on national holidays or Christmas and New Year's Days and Eves.

SERVICES/AMENITIES:

Catering: BYO, must be licensed and insured
Kitchen Facilities: limited, prep only
Tables & Chairs: BYO, CBA or through caterer
Linens, Silver, etc.: BYO or through caterer
Restrooms: wheelchair accessible
Dance Floor: hardwood floor
Bride's Dressing Area: no
Meeting Equipment: BYO or limited CBA

Parking: 40 spaces on site, restrictions may apply
Accommodations: Inn at the Presidio
Telephone: no
Outdoor Night Lighting: access lighting only
Outdoor Cooking Facilities: no
Cleanup: caterer or renter
View: SF Bay and San Francisco Skyline

RESTRICTIONS:

Alcohol: BYO, licensed and insured server
Smoking: outdoors only
Music: amplified OK with volume restrictions; indoors until 11:30pm, outdoors until 6pm

Wheelchair Access: yes
Insurance: extra liability required ($250)
Other: decorations and any tent or equipment on lawn requires prior approval

Rincon Atrium & Yank Sing Restaurant

Banquet, Event Facility & Restaurant

101 Spear Street, San Francisco
415/781-7888

www.yanksing.com
sales@yanksing.com

- ● Rehearsal Dinners
- ● Ceremonies
- ● Wedding Receptions
- ● Corp. Events/Mtgs.
- ● Private Parties
-   Accommodations

If you're passionate about Chinese food, and your guest list doesn't exceed 1,000, the Rincon Atrium and Yank Sing Restaurant are a unique combination of event spaces in the Financial District. Both are part of the Rincon Center, an impressive historic building that houses everything from businesses to federal offices to apartments.

The Atrium is at the heart of the center, and Yank Sing is one of the marquee establishments around its perimeter. Anyone who reads restaurant reviews knows about Yank Sing's scrumptious food. And for those foodies out there, Yank Sing is the recipient of the highly coveted James Beard Award. What's rarely mentioned, however, is that the restaurant also has access to the Atrium for special events.

In contrast to its serious Financial District setting, the Atrium is a vibrant indoor courtyard that soars five stories and is topped with a glass ceiling. Built of polished granite with rich wood touches, its contemporary design is softened by an abundance of greenery: potted palms all around, and lush plants cascading off the balconies above. The focal point is a remarkable "rain column" fountain, whose five-story free fall begins at the ceiling and ends in a simple pool, set flush with the floor. And while this is a public use area, a sense of privacy is created by having the storefronts (all done in polished cherrywood) tucked unobtrusively around the outer circumference of the space. Four separate eating areas off the main walk-through also provide intimate gathering places. Events here have included everything from corporate holiday parties and elegant civic functions to weddings staged in front of the dramatic backdrop of the fountain.

Yank Sing is just steps from the Atrium. At the entrance, a picture of Alice Chan, the restaurant's gracious founder, reminds you that this is a family business and welcomes you inside. The large open dining room is designed so that everyone can see each other, and the courtyard is visible through a wall of glass. Diners are surrounded by pale peach silk walls hung with Chinese brush paintings. A black granite bar flecked with copper picks up the warmth from the pastel walls, and gleams in the soft light cast by alabaster chandeliers. The room can be configured any way you want, with movable partitions made of wood and etched glass. In one corner, a glass-enclosed section of the room is often used for a traditional wedding tea ceremony. Hidden shades can be pulled down for complete privacy, so this area can be used as a bridal dressing area or for gifts.

Yank Sing and the Atrium are available separately or together. Some couples have used the Atrium's unconfined space to advantage by having a troupe of lion dancers perform for their guests.

Whether you're planning to serve just dim sum or a complete Chinese banquet, the menu will be customized to your tastes. Yank Sing uses only the freshest ingredients in its award-winning food, and offers hundreds of options, from delicate translucent dumplings and tender noodle dishes to time-honored favorites like Peking Duck and Honey Walnut Prawns. Chinese couples often schedule their wedding by picking a lucky day from the lunar calendar. In our opinion, any day you choose to celebrate at Yank Sing and the Rincon Atrium is a lucky day.

CEREMONY CAPACITY: The Atrium can accommodate up to 350 seated.

EVENT/RECEPTION & MEETING CAPACITY: The Atrium holds 750 seated or 1,000 standing. Yank Sing Restaurant accommodates 220 seated or 300 standing guests.

FEES & DEPOSITS: A $5,000 nonrefundable deposit is required when the date is reserved and the event is booked. The balance is payable 2 weeks prior to the event. The Atrium rental fee ranges $1,000–4,000 plus a $500 cleaning fee; there's no rental fee for Yank Sing Restaurant. Meals start at $35/person; alcohol, tax and service charges are additional.

AVAILABILITY: Yank Sing and the Atrium, year-round.

SERVICES/AMENITIES:

Catering: provided by *Yank Sing Catering*
Kitchen Facilities: n/a
Tables & Chairs: provided up to 400 guests
Linens, Silver, etc.: provided
Restrooms: wheelchair accessible
Dance Floor: CBA
Bride's Dressing Area: yes
Meeting Equipment: CBA

Parking: free parking in underground garage
Accommodations: no guest rooms
Telephone: emergency use only
Outdoor Night Lighting: access only
Outdoor Cooking Facilities: n/a
Cleanup: provided
View: indoor waterfall
Other: event coordination, entertainment CBA

RESTRICTIONS:

Alcohol: provided, or wine corkage $15/bottle
Smoking: not allowed
Music: amplified OK with volume limits

Wheelchair Access: yes
Insurance: additional may be required
Other: no glitter or confetti

The Ritz-Carlton

Historic Hotel

600 Stockton at California Street, San Francisco

415/296-2354

www.ritzcarlton.com
erin.mccommon@ritzcarlton.com

● Rehearsal Dinners	● Corp. Events/Mtgs.
● Ceremonies	● Private Parties
● Wedding Receptions	● Accommodations

Set atop prestigious Nob Hill, The Ritz-Carlton is housed in one of San Francisco's finest examples of neoclassical architecture. Originally built in 1909, the block-long structure has an impressive and stately façade. When you step inside, you're greeted by an updated version of The Ritz-Carlton's signature style. An expansive marble-clad lobby sets a sleek, modern tone, while crystal chandeliers and enormous fresh floral arrangements add understated sophistication. The adjoining lounge is both contemporary and supremely elegant, with floor-to-ceiling windows that frame the bustling Financial District and bring in natural light.

The first level also holds a magnificent setting for large celebrations—the Ballroom and adjacent galleries. With high vaulted ceilings, ornate woodwork, large oil paintings, and gold-toned silk-covered walls, the spacious galleries provide a luxurious area for cocktails and hors d'oeuvres. Seated receptions follow in the Ballroom, a regal yet warm venue that can be partitioned into smaller sections. Light glows from spectacular crystal chandeliers suspended from a recessed oval ceiling, and walls are softened by panels of patterned, muted gold silk brocade. The hotel's second and third levels offer additional event spaces, each of which can be used for a private rehearsal dinner or intimate receptions. All are tastefully designed with light wood molding and wainscoting.

Then there's the Terrace Room, the Ritz-Carlton's newest place to party. It enjoys abundant natural light and opens to the Terrace Bar, a roomy and convenient spot for social-hour mingling. The Terrace Room's most exciting attribute, however, is its direct access to the red-bricked Terrace Courtyard. Enclosed by an impeccably manicured garden of roses, lavender, ivy and flowers, the fragrant courtyard also boasts a striking cityscape, making it a sublime choice for outdoor gatherings. Glass-topped tables with umbrellas and chairs dot the courtyard, and the central portion can be tented to accommodate a ceremony or dining if the weather doesn't cooperate.

Remember, The Ritz Carlton has a long tradition as hospitality experts, so ask your event professional about arranging for a bridal shower afternoon tea, a martini night for the bachelor party or a day-after brunch.

And after the festivities there's no need to rush off—the bride and groom can unwind in one of the hotel's two Presidential Suites, and be whisked to the airport the next day by a hotel-arranged limousine service.

CEREMONY CAPACITY: The hotel can accommodate 10–750 seated or 50–1,100 standing guests indoors.

EVENT/RECEPTION CAPACITY: The site holds 16–700 seated or 26–1,100 standing guests indoors.

MEETING CAPACITY: There are 13 spaces that accommodate 26–826 guests seated theater-style, 12–122 conference-style or 16–475 classroom-style.

FEES & DEPOSITS: For weddings, a deposit of 25% of the estimated event charges is due when your contract is submitted. The ceremony setup charge is approximately $4,000. For receptions, buffet luncheons run $63–73/person, seated luncheons $65–70/person and seated dinners $90–100/person. Tax and service charges are additional. The estimated food and beverage total is payable 10 days prior to the event.

For business functions or meetings, fees vary depending on rooms and services selected. Call for specifics.

AVAILABILITY: Year-round, daily, 8am–2am, including holidays.

SERVICES/AMENITIES:
Catering: provided
Kitchen Facilities: n/a
Tables & Chairs: provided
Linens, Silver, etc.: provided
Restrooms: wheelchair accessible
Dance Floor: provided
Bride's Dressing Area: yes
Meeting Equipment: full range CBA

Parking: valet at $35/car for event parking
Accommodations: 336 guest rooms, 59 suites
Telephone: guest phones
Outdoor Night Lighting: CBA
Outdoor Cooking Facilities: CBA
Cleanup: provided
View: SF Bay and skyline from upper floors
Other: event coordination

RESTRICTIONS:
Alcohol: provided
Smoking: designated areas only
Music: amplified OK indoors

Wheelchair Access: yes
Insurance: not required
Other: no rice indoors

This is important! Tell locations you're reading HERE COMES THE GUIDE and ask if our information is still current.

137

St. John's Presbyterian Church

Historic Church

25 Lake Street, San Francisco
415/751-1626
www.sfchurchweddings.com
smoore@stjohnssf.org

Rehearsal Dinners	Corp. Events/Mtgs.
● Ceremonies	Private Parties
● Wedding Receptions	Accommodations

Lovely homes and the bustling Richmond and Presidio Heights neighborhoods have replaced the sand dunes that once surrounded St. John's Presbyterian Church, but things inside the church haven't changed. A welcoming spirit of fellowship and friendship still fills the gracefully turreted 1906 structure, and permeates all of its activities.

The cordiality begins at the bright and airy entrance, where you and your guests can gather for greetings and farewells. From here, turn left into the Narthex, the burgundy-carpeted gallery that opens onto the Sanctuary. In this intimate space, two beautiful stained-glass windows let in filtered daylight, making it an ideal location for a gift table or guest book. During the ceremony, the room can also serve as a retreat for parents with fussy children: They can mind the kids and still watch the wedding through a long row of interior windows.

Step from the Narthex into the Sanctuary, a "wow"-inspiring hall with soaring arches, gothic detailing and rows of burgundy-upholstered pews. Ten stained-glass windows and a large chandelier illuminate the darkly wooded interior, lending it a feeling of grandeur that is equal parts solemnity and warmth. Behind the pulpit and ample stage, an elegant choir loft and magnificent, newly restored Johnson organ (purchased by the church in 1870), suggest the significant role that music has always played in this institution's ministry. A Steinway grand piano is also on hand, and the recently restored original hardwood floors further add to the room's superior acoustics.

Around the corner from the Sanctuary, the white and cheerful Fireside Room offers a contrast to ecclesiastical grandeur. Outfitted with a fireplace, this spacious, light-drenched chamber has been used for tea ceremonies, small receptions and as a haven for the bride, the groom and their families. The adjacent Library, a small room with closet and full-length mirror, offers yet another level of privacy.

If needed, additional reception space is available downstairs in two large community rooms. The Fellowship Hall can accommodate anything from a dinner dance to a luncheon buffet. In this room, as in all the others under the church's roof, an atmosphere of amiability and versatility governs. It's an attitude mirrored by the staff, who imbue every event here with the same gracious care and attention that has endeared St. John's to its community for nearly a century.

CEREMONY CAPACITY: The Sanctuary holds 300 seated, the Chapel 50 seated guests.

EVENT/RECEPTION CAPACITY: The reception room can accommodate 100 seated or 200 standing guests indoors.

FEES & DEPOSITS: For weddings, a partially refundable $450 security deposit is required to confirm your date. For ceremonies, the rental fee (Sanctuary $1,600; Chapel $650) is payable 2 weeks prior to the event, and includes an hour for the rehearsal, 2½ hours for the ceremony, plus some coordination. For receptions, room rental fees run $200/hour plus a $250 refundable security deposit. Minister and musician services are extra, as is coordination for receptions.

AVAILABILITY: Year-round, daily. Weddings take place Sundays after 6pm, Saturdays 11am–10pm or weekdays, 9am–10pm. The church is available most holidays, depending on the social schedule, with an additional charge.

SERVICES/AMENITIES:
Catering: BYO
Kitchen Facilities: prep only
Tables & Chairs: some provided, remainder BYO
Linens, Silver, etc.: BYO or caterer
Restrooms: wheelchair accessible
Dance Floor: Fellowship Hall
Bride's & Groom's Dressing Areas: CBA
Meeting Equipment: n/a

Parking: nearby garage or on street
Accommodations: no guest rooms
Telephone: emergency use only
Outdoor Night Lighting: no
Outdoor Cooking Facilities: no
Cleanup: renter or caterer
View: no
Other: event coordination, minister, grand piano, pipe organ

RESTRICTIONS:
Alcohol: BYO wine and nonalcoholic beverages only
Smoking: not allowed
Music: amplified OK with volume limits

Wheelchair Access: yes, ramp
Insurance: not required
Other: no rice, birdseed or petals

St. Mark's Lutheran Church

Landmark Church

1111 O'Farrell Street, San Francisco
415/928-7770 x258
www.stmarks-sf.org
baldridge@stmarks-sf.org

● Rehearsal Dinners		Corp. Events/Mtgs.
● Ceremonies		● Private Parties
● Wedding Receptions		Accommodations

Known for its welcoming spirit, this landmark brick-and-stone church has been flinging wide its doors to celebrations of life and love since its inception. Designed with an artful blend of Romanesque style and Gothic elements by German-American architect Henry Geilfuss and built to last in 1895, St. Mark's has easily weathered shakeups of every kind—including major earthquakes. In June of 2005, it underwent an $11-million renovation and complete restoration inside and out, as well as an expansion of its rooms and facilities. Such great care was taken in the process that the church received a Preservation Design Award by the California Preservation Foundation in 2007.

The sanctuary is a stunner. Guests can meet and mingle in the eclectically furnished foyer beneath frosted-glass chandeliers before stepping through the three double doors that lead inside. In the sanctuary, cream-colored walls soar to a sky-blue vaulted ceiling and ten floor-to-ceiling stained-glass windows sparkle with a jewel-like brilliance. Honey-colored floors and pews cushioned in amber velvet add to the beauty of the interior. The lighting—from shafts of sunlight, chandeliers, sconces or the soft aura of candlelight—is exquisite and much of it is adjustable. As for the acoustics, they're so phenomenal that even Grammy Award-winning musicians love performing here and you can be sure everyone will be able to hear your vows.

For your reception or any other type of gathering, take the staircase with the beautiful mahogany balustrade down to the homey Heritage Hall. Also accessible through a separate entrance at the side of the church, this flexible and extremely affordable family-oriented space includes a roomy salon with grand piano, A/V capability, and mood lighting. It also comes with a full catering kitchen; a nursery with tiny tables, toys, and playhouses for the kiddies; and a roomy ladies' room with a shower. The vibe is comfortable and casual here, but the expert and accommodating staff can help you create a more formal setting if that's your preference. You can also opt to either keep the festivities indoors or use adjacent St. Mark's Square for meet and greets, cocktails, as a tented addition to your event area, or simply as a place for guests to relax on seating beneath the olive trees.

Across the square, the Urban Life Center Auditorium can be rented alone or as another way to expand your celebration. Large and extremely utilitarian, it's suitable for dances, dinners, party games—just about anything where the atmosphere is low-key and the emphasis is on simplicity and ease. The little fireside room next door, outfitted with a piano, fireplace and TV, could be the ideal hangout for the bride and her attendants, staff or entertainers.

St. Mark's is such a gorgeous church that even if you're not a religious person you're likely to have a spiritual experience.

CEREMONY CAPACITY: The facility holds 470 seated guests indoors and 350 seated outdoors.

EVENT/RECEPTION CAPACITY: The site can accommodate 175 seated or 250 standing indoors and 350 seated or standing outdoors.

MEETING CAPACITY: Meetings do not take place at this facility.

FEES & DEPOSITS: A $400 deposit is required to reserve your date and the balance is due 30 days prior to the event. Rental fees range $500–3,000 depending on the day and time of the event, guest count and the amenities required.

AVAILABILITY: Year-round, daily. Only one wedding booked per day.

SERVICES/AMENITIES:

Catering: BYO
Kitchen Facilities: fully equipped
Tables & Chairs: provided
Linens, Silver, etc.: provided
Restrooms: wheelchair accessible
Dance Floor: CBA
Bride's & Groom's Dressing Areas: yes
Meeting Equipment: n/a

Parking: large lot
Accommodations: no guest rooms
Telephone: emergency use only
Outdoor Night Lighting: CBA
Outdoor Cooking Facilities: no
Cleanup: renter or caterer
View: garden, landscaped grounds
Other: event coordination, grand piano, clergy on staff, expert vendor referrals

RESTRICTIONS:

Alcohol: BYO
Smoking: outside only
Music: amplified OK with restrictions

Wheelchair Access: yes
Insurance: not required

San Francisco Film Centre

Film Center

39 Mesa Street, Suite 107, The Presidio, San Francisco
415/561-3456
www.sffilmcentre.com
propmgr@sffilmcentre.com

● Rehearsal Dinners		● Corp. Events/Mtgs.	
● Ceremonies		● Private Parties	
● Wedding Receptions		Accommodations	

It's always interesting to learn how something built for one purpose ends up being used in a completely different and unforeseen way. The San Francisco Film Centre is a perfect case in point: It occupies one of two attractive Mission-style structures originally designed to house enlisted men and officers stationed at the Presidio. Although the Centre's building never fulfilled its function as a military residence, it has found another calling. In 1999, the Film Centre undertook a historic renovation of the elegantly appointed edifice, and today it's a multi-use facility, providing a variety of resources to the film and media community.

You don't have to be affiliated with the film or media industry, however, to have your event in the Palm Room, the Centre's amazingly versatile event space. Fresh white walls and columns and honey-colored hardwood floors, polished to a mirror finish, give the room a natural sophistication. During the day sunlight streams in through attractively shaded multipaned windows, illuminating the room and making the floors gleam (subtle track lighting at night makes them shimmer). East and west windows provide views of the parade ground, the Golden Gate Bridge and the Presidio's meticulously landscaped sylvan setting. On the eastern side, floor-to-ceiling French doors open onto a beautiful Mexican-tile veranda, distinguished by 13 graceful arches and wrought-iron railings. When the weather is warm (or with heaters), you can serve cocktails or dine outdoors.

We think the Palm Room is quite inviting, even if you do nothing at all to it. But with a little imagination, you can transform it in innovative ways. Wrap the columns with green garlands studded with flowers, or make a "hanging" photo album by putting favorite pictures around the room. Many partygivers take full advantage of the state-of-the-art lighting. One bride used copper and yellow uplights on walls and columns to pick up the colors in her floral centerpieces. For a corporate soirée, brown leather banquettes, round red carpets and red tablecloths were brought in to create a rich, clubby feeling. Red uplighting throughout gave the atmosphere just the right touch of sultriness.

The room's excellent acoustics are great for DJs, bands and—as has been demonstrated by previous events—for anything from film screenings to interactive art installations. Twenty-four electrical outlets and internet connections at both ends of the room allow the Palm Room to go high tech.

Also part of the large property and available for rental are the pale yellow Conference Room and Spanish-style Boardroom. They offer breakout arrangements during business functions, or private quarters for bride, groom and attendants. Downstairs, a professionally equipped catering kitchen adds to the marvelous versatility of this venue. The intimate Screening Room, located downstairs as well, seats 24 in a combination of plush leather and comfy theater seating. You can imagine the creative party possibilities: a place to enjoy a pre-dinner film or screen that award-winning montage of the bride and groom from childhood to matrimony. Capture your memorable Palm Room celebration on tape, and it might just provide you with the perfect excuse to book a return engagement.

CEREMONY CAPACITY: Outdoor lawn areas hold up to 150 seated guests. Small ceremonies may be held on the Veranda.

EVENT/RECEPTION CAPACITY: The Palm Room accommodates up to 180 seated, 150 with dancing or 250 standing guests; the Veranda holds up to 96 seated or 150 standing.

MEETING CAPACITY: The Palm Room seats up to 250 guests theater-style or 100 classroom-style

FEES & DEPOSITS: 50% of the facility rental fee is required to reserve your date, the balance is due 30 days prior to the event. The rental fee ranges $700–5,000. Rental rates are for an 8-hour time frame, extra time is $250/hour.

AVAILABILITY: Year-round, daily, 7am–midnight.

SERVICES/AMENITIES:

Catering: select from preferred list
Kitchen Facilities: fully equipped
Tables & Chairs: BYO or through caterer
Linens, Silver, etc.: BYO or through caterer
Restrooms: wheelchair accessible
Dance Floor: hardwood floor
Bride's Dressing Area: yes
Meeting Equipment: CBA, extra charge

Parking: large lot
Accommodations: no guest rooms
Telephone: emergency use only
Outdoor Night Lighting: yes, on veranda
Outdoor Cooking Facilities: CBA
Cleanup: caterer
View: Main Post and Golden Gate Bridge, Presidio Officers' homes

RESTRICTIONS:

Alcohol: provided
Smoking: outside only
Music: amplified OK indoors only

Wheelchair Access: yes
Insurance: liability required

Overwhelmed? Use the search criteria on www.HereComesTheGuide.com to narrow down your choices.

Sir Francis Drake Hotel

Hotel

450 Powell Street, San Francisco
415/395-8526

www.sirfrancisdrake.com
catering@sirfrancisdrake.com

- Rehearsal Dinners
- Ceremonies
- Wedding Receptions
- Corp. Events/Mtgs.
- Private Parties
- Accommodations

The Sir Francis Drake Hotel's 21-story, Gothic-style tower just off Union Square and its Beefeater-attired doormen have been beloved San Francisco attractions since 1928.

Stepping into the Drake's opulent Italian Renaissance lobby is just like stepping back into the 1920s: Marble staircases, walls and pillars convey a stately air; crystal chandeliers shine and the lofty, ornately detailed ceiling sparkles with gold leaf. The main event spaces, the Empire Ballroom and the Franciscan Room, have a high-society, Age of Innocence ambiance. In the gold-and-ivory Empire Room, beautiful hand-painted murals turn the walls into works of art. Overhead, three crystal chandeliers suspended from a vaulted ceiling painted with ribbons of gold leaf give the room a delicate amber glow. The adjoining wood-paneled Walnut Room, with its club-like, Edwardian atmosphere and built-in bar, makes a great prefunction space.

Located just off the mezzanine, the spacious and grand Franciscan Room is an excellent choice for a formal wedding. It's a regal setting, featuring a 21-foot ceiling with intricate gold embossing, chandeliers, windows draped with blue silk curtains, and columns with carved gold capitals. Guests can enjoy cocktails and hors d'oeuvres on the adjacent mezzanine, which offers a cozy fireplace and a bird's-eye view of the vibrant hotel lobby below.

And for those who have a yen for a panoramic 180-degree view of San Francisco, try Harry Denton's Starlight Room on the 21st floor. It not only has a built-in dance floor and shiny baby grand piano, it features floor-to-ceiling windows that wrap around the room, making it seem like you're floating in the clouds. The Starlight Room will be renovated in July 2011.

Steeped in 80 years of history, the Drake is a true classic. Brides may fall in love with its enchanting vintage architectural details, but they'll also appreciate the modern amenities and personal service this landmark hotel has to offer.

CEREMONY & EVENT/RECEPTION CAPACITY: The hotel can accommodate 50–220 seated or 200–350 standing guests indoors.

MEETING CAPACITY: The Hotel has 17,000 square feet of meeting and conference space with 14 different rooms accommodating groups from 10 to 350 people.

FEES & DEPOSITS: For weddings, a nonrefundable deposit is required to confirm your date. Half the total food and beverage payment is payable 4 months prior to the event; the balance and guest count guarantee are due 3 days prior. Wedding packages range $125–160/person and include open bar, passed hors d'oeuvres, champagne, wine, wedding cake and a 3-course dinner. Tax, and a 23% service charge are additional. Per-person prices for seated meals are as follows: luncheons start at $55, dinners at $65, luncheon buffets at $60, and dinner buffets at $75. Alcohol, tax and a 23% service charge are additional. Bride and groom receive a complimentary suite, and group discounts for overnight guests can be arranged.

Fees for meetings and business functions vary depending on rooms and services selected; call for specifics.

AVAILABILITY: For special events and business functions, year-round, daily, 6am–midnight. Weddings usually take place on Saturdays 11am–5pm or 6pm–midnight; other days have more flexible time frames. The Starlight Room is available Saturday 3pm–8pm, and Sunday 6pm–midnight. Contact the wedding consultant for specifics.

SERVICES/AMENITIES:
Catering: provided, no BYO
Kitchen Facilities: n/a
Tables & Chairs: provided
Linens, Silver, etc.: provided
Restrooms: wheelchair accessible
Dance Floor: provided
Bride's & Groom's Dressing Areas: no
Meeting Equipment: A/V
Other: event coordination, baby grand piano

Parking: nearby garages or valet, extra fee
Accommodations: 416 guest rooms
Telephone: guest and pay phones
Outdoor Night Lighting: n/a
Outdoor Cooking Facilities: n/a
Cleanup: provided
View: Starlight Room has 180-degree view of San Francisco skyline

RESTRICTIONS:
Alcohol: provided, no BYO
Smoking: designated areas
Music: amplified OK

Wheelchair Access: yes, elevator
Insurance: liability required
Other: no rice, open flames or fog machines

Terra Gallery and Event Venue

511 Harrison Street, San Francisco
415/896-1234
www.terrasf.com
info@terrasf.com

Art Gallery & Event Venue

- Rehearsal Dinners
- Ceremonies
- Wedding Receptions
- Corp. Events/Mtgs.
- Private Parties
- Accommodations

The collective creativity of entre-preneurs, artists and tech whiz-zes has made SOMA the hippest neighborhood in The City, vibrat-ing with a diversity of businesses, restaurants, clubs and galleries.

One of the most intriguing of these is Terra Gallery & Event Venue, a collection of newly renovated galleries and event spaces that epitomizes the syn-ergy of art and technology. At this urban-chic venue, just blocks from the Bay Bridge, you're en-couraged to turn your celebration into a work of art—literally. The whole place is like a big blank canvas on which you can paint whatever vision you have in mind. Terra's two diverse levels have separate entrances, so you can reserve a floor individually or take over all the galleries and offer your guests multiple environments.

Terra Gallery's upper floor has a spacious, open feeling thanks to 5,000 square feet of Brazilian cherry hardwood floors, white brick walls and support columns rising 20 feet to the ceiling. The most arresting feature is at the end of the room, where 40 feet of floor-to-ceiling windows show-case the downtown skyline. Light pours in during the day, and at night city lights turn the wall of glass into a vast glittering tableau—a dreamy backdrop for a wedding ceremony. A carpeted area with leather furniture and a baby grand piano lets guests relax and enjoy the view.

Equally impressive is Mer, a lounge-style space on the lower floor that gives off the ultra-hip vibe of a private club. Serpentine bars inlaid with glass tiles let the staff serve up signature cocktails with style and ease. A built-in oak stage at one end holds your entertainment, while guests dance on the gleaming hardwood floor. Mer adjoins a 3,000-square-foot landscaped patio, which can be left open to the stars or elegantly tented. Bamboo, lush foliage and water features evoke a garden atmosphere for cocktails or an outdoor ceremony.

Terra's staff will work with you and your planners to ensure that your wedding is seamlessly choreographed. You're welcome to incorporate the current exhibit's paintings and sculptures into your event, or turn Terra into your own personal gallery by exhibiting blown-up photos of the bride and groom on the walls, or projecting a slide show set to music. Terra's state-of-the art Bose sound system, in-house TerraPod photo booth, gallery lighting and multimedia capabilities allow for the ultimate in customization. And if you're having a destination wedding here, they're able to provide a live feed to guests who can't attend.

You're free to bring your own licensed caterer, and there's plenty of nearby parking with valet service available upon request. To make it easy for out-of-town guests who want to take advantage of nearby museums, entertainment and sightseeing, Terra has partnered with local hotels for special group rates.

Terra's versatility makes it an inspired choice for just about any type of event. Whether you desire a quiet and refined affair or a totally theatrical experience, Terra has all the elements.

CEREMONY CAPACITY: Terra Gallery holds up to 250 guests seated; Mer accommodates 200 guests seated.

EVENT/RECEPTION CAPACITY: Terra Gallery holds 250 guests seated, 725 standing; Mer accommodates 200 guests seated, 740 standing.

MEETING CAPACITY: Terra Gallery holds 250 guests seated; Mer accommodates 200 guests seated; or using both floors—400 theater-style with breakout area for 200.

FEES & DEPOSITS: A $1,000 deposit is required to reserve your date. The balance is due 30 days prior to the event. Rental fees range $4,500–11,000 depending on date of event, guest count, facility usage and type of organization.

AVAILABILITY: Year-round, daily. Weekdays 10am–4am, weekends 10am–6am.

SERVICES/AMENITIES:

Catering: BYO or CBA
Kitchen Facilities: 2 prep kitchens
Tables & Chairs: BYO or CBA
Linens, Silver, etc.: BYO or CBA
Restrooms: wheelchair accessible
Dance Floor: provided at no charge
Bride's & Groom's Dressing Areas: yes
Meeting Equipment: CBA, extra fee

Parking: garages nearby or valet CBA
Accommodations: hotels nearby
Telephone: house phone
Outdoor Night Lighting: provided
Outdoor Cooking Facilities: yes
Cleanup: provided
View: cityscape, landscaped grounds
Other: contemporary art on display; increased bandwidth in/out available at competitive rates

RESTRICTIONS:

Alcohol: provided
Smoking: outside only
Music: amplified and live music OK indoors

Wheelchair Access: yes
Insurance: required, CBA

The University Club of San Francisco

Historic Social Club

800 Powell Street, San Francisco
415/781-0900 x133
www.univclub.com
events@univclub.com

- Rehearsal Dinners
- Ceremonies
- Wedding Receptions
- Corp. Events/Mtgs.
- Private Parties
- Accommodations

Nob Hill is one of the city's premier addresses, and you can celebrate at the very top of the hill in an equally premier event venue. Clubby, intimate and estate-like, The University Club of San Francisco is a place where your guests can not only party, but also relax for days on end with the whole city virtually at their feet. Whatever the affair—wedding, birthday party, fundraiser or corporate gala—your entourage will feel right at home in the club's members only-style environment.

Once inside the striking brick building, you might want to pause in the handsome wood-paneled lobby with its antiques, Oriental carpet and hardwood floors before taking the elevator upstairs to the third and fourth floors where the festivities unfold.

More elegant than ever after recent renovations, the fourth floor features a spacious lounge with huge picture windows that afford stunning views of some of the best parts of the skyline—including Coit Tower, Telegraph Hill and the TransAmerica Pyramid—as well as a game room, bar, boardroom, and library. Consider planning a ceremony, cocktail reception or dinner in the lounge, a small rehearsal dinner in the book-lined library (also a great sitting room for the bride and bridesmaids), and after-dinner drinks in the bar. Two small, old-fashioned phone compartments in the hall have Romeo and Juliet-style windows that open onto the carpeted stairwell, providing a super-romantic photo op. The boardroom, with its hidden wet bar, might be the perfect hideaway for the groom and his men.

Of course you could always have the ceremony and cocktails on the fourth floor and dinner on the third, where you'll find more nicely appointed areas for entertaining such as the Main Dining Room, which has a built-in dance floor as well as chandeliers, a fireplace, and views that mirror the lounge's upstairs. It opens onto the South Main Dining Room, which can provide extra space, be used on its own, or be combined with the ever-so-cozy Black Cat Bar.

It's all so delectably inviting, your guests won't want to depart…and they needn't. Charming boutique hotel-style guest rooms and five queen suites offer all the comforts of home and then some, including a continental breakfast. Tuesday through Friday, lunch and dinner are also served up with panache by the club's inimitable staff. Plus, the on-site fitness center gives guests additional space to unwind or wind up with a bracing match on the squash courts.

Family and friends can check in, check out the city and congregate in the club's cozy corners to chat away about what a fabulous time they're having and how brilliant you were to book your special event here.

CEREMONY CAPACITY: The Fourth Floor Lounge holds up to 150 seated guests.

EVENT/RECEPTION & MEETING CAPACITY: The Dining Rooms accommodate 180 seated or 300 standing guests.

FEES & DEPOSITS: A deposit is required to reserve your date. The balance is due 2 weeks prior to the event. The site fee for a ceremony and reception is $5,000 for Saturday, Sunday or Monday. The site fee for reception only is $3,500 for Saturday, Sunday or Monday. Please inquire for special rates for corporate meetings, events, or Friday weddings. Catering menus start at $75/person. Tax, alcohol and a 21% service charge are additional, as is a $5/person fee for cakes or other desserts brought in from the outside.

AVAILABILITY: Year-round, daily.

SERVICES/AMENITIES:

Catering: provided, no BYO
Kitchen Facilities: n/a
Tables & Chairs: provided
Linens, Silver, etc.: provided
Restrooms: wheelchair accessible
Dance Floor: provided
Bride's Dressing Area: yes
Meeting Equipment: some provided, more CBA

Parking: garage nearby
Accommodations: 16 guest rooms
Telephone: emergency use only
Outdoor Night Lighting: access only
Outdoor Cooking Facilities: no
Cleanup: provided
View: panorama of SF cityscape and SF Bay
Other: event coordination, grand piano

RESTRICTIONS:

Alcohol: provided, no BYO
Smoking: outside on balconies or street only
Music: amplified OK

Wheelchair Access: limited
Insurance: liability required

The professionals in the back of this book are the best in the business. How do we know? Read page 637.

W San Francisco

Hotel

181 Third Street, San Francisco
415/817-7881
www.whotels.com/sanfrancisco
wsanfrancisco.weddings@whotels.com

- Rehearsal Dinners
- Ceremonies
- Wedding Receptions
- Corp. Events/Mtgs.
- Private Parties
- Accommodations

Hip, fresh, stylish and vibrant, this multifaceted boutique hotel in San Francisco's artistic epicenter offers floor after floor of entertaining options for your extraordinary upcoming event.

It all begins at the lobby level, where the eclectic and electric mix of iconic design and contemporary luxury that characterizes W Hotels World-wide is immediately apparent. Arranged more like a home than a lobby, W's capacious Living Room brings suggestions of the cityscape and the artsy SF MOMA ambiance indoors in the sophisticated use of black and gray, the silvery and neon accents, and lighting that transitions naturally from day to night. This clubby, lounge-like setting with its chic metal-and-glass fireplace and racy black bar is a guaranteed ice-breaker, so start the party with a DJ and cocktails here…or use the restaurant, TRACE, with its focus on sustainability and innovation, for cocktails and dining. An outdoor lounge area further extends the ground-floor possibilities.

But don't stop here. A swift ascent by stair or elevator will take you to the next dazzling level—the ultra-sexy mezzanine-style floor that overlooks the Living Room. A delicate fiber-optic chandelier waterfalls from the third-floor ceiling down through both spaces tying them together. In the Up-stairs Drink Boutique, your guests can sip cocktails while watching the scene below. The long, all white LED-lit bar is a showstopper. Silver bead-curtained cabanas with Living Room views and private seating are a very subtle nod to San Francisco in the '60s and lend this sleek space a sultry charm. Need more room to mingle? How about dinner, dancing or cocktails in the Industry Room and its intimate prefunction area, another great spot from which to view the first-floor action.

There's more. The third floor features two glamorous Great Rooms with a chocolate and teal color scheme, recessed lighting, floor-to-ceiling windows, full A/V capability and a generous prefunction foyer. Both rooms can be combined for banquets and galas. Or consider the three Workrooms, which can also be used together if the occasion warrants, along with their own prefunction space. For certain celebrations you might want to book the whole floor, which also includes a Strategy Room and a Studio. Even the halls here are suitable for entertaining. You could wander around them for hours, relaxing in club and wingback chairs or chilling to music in the unusual chair pod—try it; it's a cool backdrop for photos.

Want to take your affair to still greater heights? On the fourth floor you'll find the marvelous rooftop Terrace for dining, dancing and ceremonies, as well as a pool called WET, a gym called SWEAT, and the very fittingly named BLISS Spa.

Really, this is a venue so mind-blowing in possibilities you will just have to see it to believe it. So, check it out. The youthful and experienced event staff are poised and eager to help you invent an unforgettable affair. And when the party is over, your next adventure can begin here. You and your guests will love unwinding in one of the fanciful guest rooms or suites and sampling W Hotels' famous Whatever/Whenever service.

CEREMONY CAPACITY: The hotel holds 360 seated guests indoors.

EVENT/RECEPTION CAPACITY: This facility holds 200 seated or 350 standing indoors.

MEETING CAPACITY: Meeting spaces hold 400 seated.

FEES & DEPOSITS: 25% of the estimated event total is required to reserve your date. The balance is due two weeks before the event. Rental fees range $500–2,000 depending on space rented and guest count. Meals range $125–145/person. Tax, alcohol and a 22% service charge are additional.

AVAILABILITY: Year-round, daily, call for details.

SERVICES/AMENITIES:

Catering: provided
Kitchen Facilities: n/a
Tables & Chairs: provided
Linens, Silver, etc.: provided
Restrooms: wheelchair accessible
Dance Floor: provided
Bride's Dressing Area: yes
Meeting Equipment: provided, A/V equipment

Parking: valet required
Accommodations: 404 guest rooms
Telephone: house phone
Outdoor Night Lighting: CBA
Outdoor Cooking Facilities: BBQ CBA
Cleanup: provided
View: cityscape
Other: in-house florals, spa services, DJ booth stylized bars, event coordination

RESTRICTIONS:

Alcohol: provided
Smoking: designated areas only
Music: amplified OK

Wheelchair Access: yes
Insurance: not required

The Westin St. Francis San Francisco
On Union Square

Historic Hotel

335 Powell Street, San Francisco
415/774-0126

www.westinstfrancis.com
robin.lewis@westin.com

- Rehearsal Dinners
- Ceremonies
- Wedding Receptions
- Corp. Events/Mtgs.
- Private Parties
- Accommodations

Commonly referred to as the Grand Dame of Union Square, The Westin St. Francis has been a symbol of elegance in San Francisco for more than a century. Its many rooms, some featuring exquisite historic detailing and others reflecting more modern luxury, have hosted beautiful wedding ceremonies, grand receptions, and business events of all types.

In the hotel's turn-of-the-century Landmark Building, you'll find stunning ballrooms with marble floors, gilt pillars, intricately carved ceilings, and a hundred years' worth of history. They include: the Borgia Room, a jewel-box chamber with oak-paneled walls, a six-foot-tall marble fireplace, and a vaulted, delicately painted ceiling (originally the hotel's chapel, it's perfect for a wedding ceremony); the St. Francis Suite (just right for a smaller ceremony and reception); and the Colonial Room, appointed with Italian murals, elaborate candelabras, and gold-leafed columns separating regal opera balconies. Large events are held in the Grand Ballroom, which is easily transformed by your choice of décor and can accommodate up to 800 guests. Receptions often start with cocktails in the Colonial Room, then flow into the adjacent Grand Ballroom for the main affair.

If you prefer a more contemporary ambiance, hold your celebration in the Tower Building. Its two premier spaces, Victor's and Alexandra's, are a pair of sophisticated settings on the 32nd-story Imperial Floor. Five glass elevators overlook spectacular downtown panoramas as they whisk guests up to this sky-high getaway. Boasting breathtaking floor-to-ceiling views that extend from the Bay Bride to the Golden Gate, these private rooms also dazzle at night: Glowing chandeliers and hundreds of sparkling pin-spots provide adjustable lighting to match your mood. Gold Chiavari chairs, custom Wedgwood china and your own Imperial Floor concierge make having an event up here a sublime experience.

The possibilities at The Westin St. Francis are almost endless. Are you looking for Old San Francisco glamour or something more modern? If you can't decide, why not combine the past and the present with a ceremony in the Borgia Room followed by dinner and dancing in Alexandra's. Whatever spaces you select, your event will most certainly be magical.

CEREMONY CAPACITY: The hotel can accommodate 20–1,000 seated guests.

EVENT/RECEPTION CAPACITY: The St. Francis has 32 banquet rooms with 56,000 square feet of event space; some of the larger rooms hold 80–800 seated or up to 1,200 standing guests indoors.

MEETING CAPACITY: The facility has 32 rooms and over 56,000 square feet of meeting space that hold 20–1,500 seated theater-style, 15–800 classroom-style or 10–50 conference-style.

FEES & DEPOSITS: For social events, a nonrefundable deposit based on the estimated event total is required when the contract is signed; the remaining balance and a final guest count are due 72 business hours prior to the event. Wedding packages start at $165/person ($225/person for the Imperial Floor), and include hors d'oeuvres, 4-hour bar, 2-course meal, wedding cake, champagne toast, wine with meal, and a luxury suite for the bride and groom. Tax and a 22% service charge are additional. A ceremony setup fee may be required. Customized wedding and bar mitzvah packages can be arranged; kosher catering under strict rabbinical supervision is available. Persian and Indian catering is also available.

AVAILABILITY: Year-round, daily, anytime, including holidays.

SERVICES/AMENITIES:

Catering: provided
Kitchen Facilities: n/a
Tables & Chairs: provided
Linens, Silver, etc.: provided
Restrooms: wheelchair accessible
Dance Floor: provided
Bride's & Groom's Dressing Areas: suite provided
Meeting Equipment: full range; A/V extra charge
Other: kosher, Indian and Persian catering; wedding cakes

Parking: limited in-house; many nearby garages
Accommodations: 1,195 guest rooms
Telephone: emergency use only
Outdoor Night Lighting: n/a
Outdoor Cooking Facilities: n/a
Cleanup: provided
View: sweeping cityscape from upper floors

RESTRICTIONS:

Alcohol: provided
Smoking: outside of hotel only
Music: amplified OK

Wheelchair Access: yes
Insurance: not required

North Bay

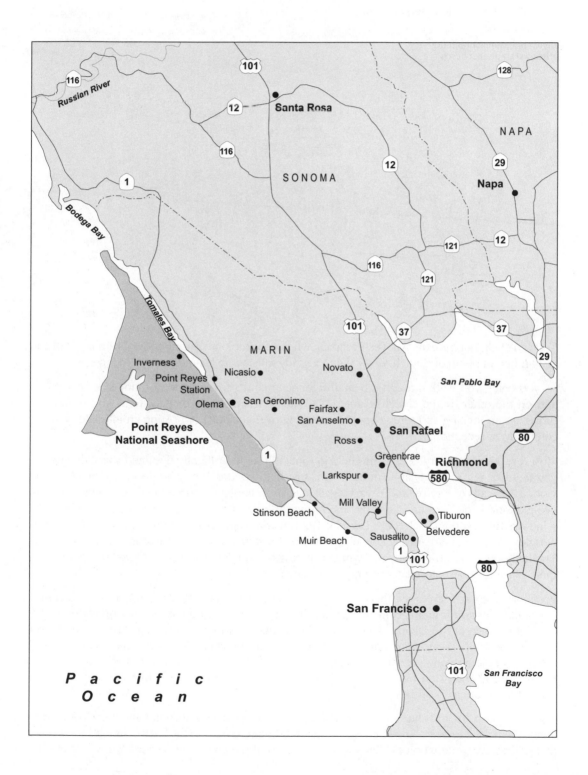

Kimball Hall at
St. Stephen's Episcopal Church

3 Bay View Avenue, Belvedere/Tiburon
415/435-4501

www.ststephenschurch.org
office@ststephenschurch.org

Reception Hall and Church

● Rehearsal Dinners	● Corp. Events/Mtgs.
● Ceremonies	● Private Parties
● Wedding Receptions	Accommodations

You can't help but have an "Ah, yes!" reaction when you step onto the campus of Kimball Hall and St. Stephen's Episcopal Church, nestled into a shady hillside on lush Belvedere Island.

As you enter, you walk through a beautiful fountain courtyard bounded on one side by the hall and on the other by the church. Planted with Japanese maples, camellias, ferns and rhododendrons, it's an inviting and serene spot for mingling over cocktails or hosting an intimate al fresco ceremony or reception.

Most receptions and large events are held in Kimball Hall, a brilliantly designed space that makes you feel like you're inside an exquisite, light-splashed wooden box. The floors are simple blond wood, the walls are softwood in varying shades, and the gently curved ceiling is trimmed with eye-pleasing lattice. Natural light passes through the courtyard-facing glass wall as well as the windows that overlook Belvedere Lagoon, Tiburon and Angel Island, giving the airy room an inner glow. With such an artfully conceived interior, the venue can accommodate any color palette. The hall opens onto the courtyard, which can provide additional seating for large receptions or a quiet place for guests to relax during your celebration.

For a formal church ceremony, the sanctuary at St. Stephen's is ideal. The soaring concrete columns and walls of its gothic architecture suggest a sacred space and eloquently convey a powerful—even tangible—sense of the Divine. A heavenly blue ceiling crowns the long, high nave, and slender vertical bands of stained glass filter sunlight down onto the church's wooden altar. Hand-carved torchières holding votive candles line the aisle, softly lighting the way as the bride walks toward her groom. At the same time, music played on the massive pipe organ fills the building, long noted for its superb acoustics.

The hall, courtyard and church are a lovely combination of spaces that complement each other perfectly. From the pageantry and solemnity of the wedding ceremony to the festive dining and dancing that follow, everyone who celebrates with you here will remember the experience with pleasure.

CEREMONY CAPACITY: The church holds up to 250 seated guests indoors. Please ask about requirements for use of the St. Stephen's Church sanctuary.

EVENT/RECEPTION CAPACITY: Kimball Hall accommodates up to 150 seated guests or 120 with room for dancing. The courtyard provides additional seating for up to 60.

MEETING CAPACITY: Meeting spaces hold 125 seated guests.

FEES & DEPOSITS: A $1,000 deposit is required to book your date. The balance is due 10 days prior to the event. Rental fees range $1,500–$5,000 depending on the number of hours reserved and whether both the church and hall are rented.

AVAILABILITY: Year-round, daily, except the week before Easter and the week before Christmas. The church is available 11am–10pm except Thursdays (11–6pm) and Sundays (3pm–9pm).

SERVICES/AMENITIES:

Catering: BYO
Kitchen Facilities: fully equipped
Tables & Chairs: some provided or through caterer
Linens, Silver, etc.: through caterer
Restrooms: wheelchair accessible
Dance Floor: provided
Bride's & Groom's Dressing Areas: yes
Meeting Equipment: some provided

Parking: large lot, on street, limited
Accommodations: no guest rooms
Telephone: emergency use only
Outdoor Night Lighting: some provided
Outdoor Cooking Facilities: BBQ CBA
Cleanup: renter
View: garden patio, hills, lagoon, fountain
Other: grand piano, clergy on staff, pipe organ, event coordination

RESTRICTIONS:

Alcohol: BYO wine, beer or champagne
Smoking: not allowed
Music: amplified OK with restrictions

Wheelchair Access: yes
Insurance: liability required

Want to know WHAT TO ASK a potential location or vendor? Check out our Questions to Ask starting on page 17.

157

The Tavern at Lark Creek

Restaurant & Garden

234 Magnolia Avenue, Larkspur
415/924-1602

www.tavernatlarkcreek.com
tavernevents@larkcreek.com

● Rehearsal Dinners		● Corp. Events/Mtgs.	
● Ceremonies		● Private Parties	
● Wedding Receptions		○ Accommodations	

The Tavern at Lark Creek, one of the most popular restaurants in the Bay Area, is a delightful place for a wedding or reception. Built in 1888, this former Victorian country home is nestled in a grove of redwoods, next to a flowing creek. Sunlight filters through trees and windows, warming the tables in the Main Dining Room. Overhead, an enormous skylight creates an open, airy ambiance. Muted colors, rich wood paneling and rotating exhibits of original art complete the tasteful interior. Outdoors, the Creekside Patio is perfect for a romantic outdoor ceremony, and the formal front garden with fountain provides a lovely backdrop for photographs.

The Tavern at Lark Creek has received national acclaim as well as local restaurant awards, and we have found the food here to be some of the best we've ever tasted. Note that the special events manager is available to coordinate all aspects of your party, including rehearsal, ceremony and reception. Add to that the outstanding atmosphere and you'll understand why your wedding celebration here will receive rave reviews.

CEREMONY CAPACITY: The Creekside Patio holds 150 seated or 200 standing guests. Indoors, the Inn holds up to 50 seated guests.

EVENT/RECEPTION & MEETING CAPACITY: Private rooms hold 24–40 seated or 40–60 standing guests indoors. The patio holds 60 seated or 100 standing outdoors. The entire restaurant, including the patio, can accommodate 180 seated or 300 standing guests.

FEES & DEPOSITS: A nonrefundable deposit of 25% of the food and beverage minimum is required to book your date. Additional deposits may be required with the remaining balance due on the day of the function. Room rental fees are $150 for the Private Dining Room, $225 for the Sunroom, $500 for the Creekside Patio or $750 for the entire restaurant. Food and beverage minimums for the entire restaurant start at $9,000 and vary depending on the day of the week, time of the event and the time of year. Tax, ceremony fees and service fees are additional.

AVAILABILITY: Year-round, daily.

SERVICES/AMENITIES:

Catering: provided, no BYO
Kitchen Facilities: n/a
Tables & Chairs: provided
Linens, Silver, etc.: provided
Restrooms: wheelchair accessible
Dance Floor: yes
Bride's Dressing Area: yes
Meeting Equipment: CBA, extra fee

Parking: large lot, valet CBA
Accommodations: no guest rooms
Telephone: emergency use only
Outdoor Night Lighting: yes
Outdoor Cooking Facilities: n/a
Cleanup: provided
View: garden, redwoods and creek
Other: in-house pastry chef

RESTRICTIONS:

Alcohol: provided, no BYO
Smoking: designated area only
Music: amplified OK indoors and outdoors with restrictions

Wheelchair Access: yes
Insurance: not required

Mill Valley Community Center

180 Camino Alto, Mill Valley
415/383-1370
www.millvalleycenter.org
sallingham@cityofmillvalley.org

Community Center

- Rehearsal Dinners
- Ceremonies
- Wedding Receptions
- Corp. Events/Mtgs.
- Private Parties
- Accommodations

How blessed is Mill Valley? Let us count the ways: dramatic location at the foot of Mt. Tamalpais; redwood groves; proximity to the bay and San Francisco; sophisticated citizenry and small-town feel.

And, since April 2001, add the Mill Valley Community Center to that list— it's become the town's pride and joy. Every day, from early morning to late evening, people flock here to swim, dance, work out or attend meetings.

The two-building complex, connected by arcades and enclosed walkways, is clad in olive-green wood siding that calls to mind the leaves of the oak trees on nearby hills. While it has the inviting silhouette of an Adirondack-style resort from 100 years ago, this structure deftly combines wood, concrete, painted steel, copper and glass to create a facility with all the light-admitting spaciousness and crispness of good modern architecture.

The center's main event space is the Cascade Room, and to reach it visitors first pass through a dramatic entrance atrium. Their eyes are immediately drawn up to a vaulted ceiling supported by four slender concrete pillars. The atrium's distinctive reddish-gray slate floor is made of stone quarried in China. (The floor generates steady inquiries from landscapers whose clients have fallen in love with the slate and want to know where they can get some for themselves.)

The generous use of glass in the Cascade Room is particularly effective at night, when light pours out through the windows. Motorists on the nearby main road often slow down to look in longingly on its festive scenes, and imagine themselves dancing the night away in this warm, bright place. By day, the two-story space is lit by sunlight falling through the tall windows that run the length of its side walls. The cathedral-style ceiling is supported by laminated wood trusses, an airy architectural element that makes the room soar. Perhaps the nicest touch is the wood floor, left uncarpeted to allow the richness of its eucalyptus floorboards to dazzle the eye. They range along a spectrum of earthy reds, from reddish-browns and near maroons to lighter-colored planks. An adjoining professional kitchen can accommodate any catering operation.

The large patio on the east side of the Cascade Room has no walls or fences, so people don't feel hemmed in. It runs right up to a three-acre lawn (part of a community playing field), so that in one step you can move from stone to grass. This is a well-thought-out design that provides a sense of space, and invites parties to spill happily beyond the patio. The level lawn is a fine place to pitch a tent or two if you want to host an outdoor event.

Smaller rooms are available for wedding-related activities, including the Terrace Room, which can handle a cocktail party or small dinner. Wedding parties can also rent the whole facility if they'd like, including the 25-yard swimming pool, Jacuzzi, giant water slide and adjoining patio.

Mill Valley has always had a nice hum, and this well-maintained facility only adds to it. People instinctively sense it's a great place to hold a celebration.

CEREMONY CAPACITY: The Cascade Room holds 400, and the lawn area 200 seated.

EVENT/RECEPTION CAPACITY: The center can accommodate 12–285 seated or 30–400 standing guests indoors.

MEETING CAPACITY: The facility has 6 rooms which can accommodate 2–400 theater-style, or up to 200 classroom-style.

FEES & DEPOSITS: For special events, a $100–500 refundable deposit is required when the contract is signed. Room rental fees for the Cascade Room range $120–195/hour on weekdays and $2,400–2,900 on weekends (for an 8-hour block). The Terrace Lounge is $45–81/hour on weekdays, and $75–101/hour on weekends. Other rooms range $26–101/hour. An attendant fee runs $15/hour, for weeknights and weekends.

AVAILABILITY: Year-round, daily, 8am–1am.

SERVICES/AMENITIES:

Catering: BYO
Kitchen Facilities: commercial kitchen
Tables & Chairs: provided to 240 guests
Linens, Silver, etc.: BYO or caterer
Restrooms: wheelchair accessible
Dance Floor: hardwood floor in Cascade Room
Bride's Dressing Area: CBA
Meeting Equipment: lectern, TV/VCR, screen, dry erase boards, microphone and sound system, portable stage

Parking: large complimentary lot
Accommodations: no guest rooms
Telephone: CBA
Outdoor Night Lighting: CBA
Outdoor Cooking Facilities: CBA
Cleanup: provided
View: Mt. Tamalpais
Other: baby grand piano

RESTRICTIONS:

Alcohol: BYO
Smoking: outside only
Music: amplified OK indoors, OK outdoors with curfew and volume restrictions

Wheelchair Access: yes
Insurance: certificate required
Other: decorations require approval

Mountain Home Inn

Retreat

810 Panoramic Highway, Mill Valley
415/381-9000

www.mtnhomeinn.com
mountainweddingevents@gmail.com

● Rehearsal Dinners	● Corp. Events/Mtgs.
● Ceremonies	● Private Parties
● Wedding Receptions	● Accommodations

Perched on a forested ridge between the lofty peaks of Mt. Tamalpais and Mill Valley 1,000 feet below, the Mountain Home Inn has been enticing guests with stunning views and rustic charm for almost a century.

This bed and breakfast was built in 1912 as a mountain getaway for San Franciscans seeking an escape to nature, and has since served the entire Bay Area as a welcome stop for hiking enthusiasts, writers, lovers and even celebrities (Jack London and the Grateful Dead have stayed here). An abundance of wood, both inside and out, lends warmth to all the rooms, as do numerous fireplaces and homey details like the vintage photos of the inn framed on guest room doors.

Everyone who comes here is mesmerized by the breathtaking panorama from the Upper Deck: A vast redwood forest flows down and away to the distant foothills of Mt. Tam, and on a clear day you can see past Tiburon and Angel Island to the East Bay. Although the inn is only 25 minutes from The City, it feels like it's at the edge of the wilderness. No wonder so many couples decide to get married here.

When you book your wedding at Mountain Home Inn, you can have exclusive use of the venue, which includes indoor and outdoor event spaces on three levels plus ten guest rooms. You're free to choreograph your day any way you like, but it has to be said that the Upper Deck, with its spectacular vista and endless sky overhead, is the premier spot for any warm-weather ceremony or reception. If the temperature drops, couples get married in front of the fireplace in the cozy Mountain View Room, where large picture windows frame all three peaks of Mt. Tamalpais. Other ceremony options include the nearby woods and beach (permits are required for these sites). The terraced gardens just below the deck are filled with purple Mexican sage, rosemary and salvia, making them a lovely setting for photos.

Cocktails and hors d'oeuvres are generally served either outside right in front of the inn or downstairs in the Bayview Room, which has French doors that open to a view-filled terrace. While your guests are mingling, tables for the reception are set up on the deck or in the Mountain View

Room. Simple decorations such as candles, leaves and tree branches are easy to come by and complement the natural surroundings.

All of the guest rooms face east, so your family and friends will wake up to the sunrise. Some of the rooms also have Jacuzzi tubs, fireplaces and terraces. Mountain Home Inn's sister property, the English Country-style Pelican Inn, is only ten minutes away and offers a convenient place for a rehearsal dinner or post-wedding brunch. A shuttle can be arranged to transport your guests between the inn and any other local lodging.

Mountain Home Inn offers a number of wedding packages, and their on-site wedding coordinator is happy to customize a package for you. She can also assist in organizing activities for your guests, such as hiking on Mt. Tam, cycling, picnicking or going to the beach. Designated a Bay Area Green Business, the inn keeps its grounds pesticide-free, uses eco-friendly cleaning products and supports local farmers and artisans.

CEREMONY CAPACITY: The inn holds 100 seated guests indoors (upstairs and downstairs) and 100 seated outdoors.

EVENT/RECEPTION CAPACITY: The facility accommodates 100 seated or standing outdoors, and 50 seated or standing indoors.

MEETING CAPACITY: Meetings spaces hold up to 30 guests.

FEES & DEPOSITS: 33% of the total event cost is required to reserve your date and the balance is due on the day of the event. Rental fees range $750–2,200 depending on the season. Meals start at $42/person. Tax, alcohol, staff wages and a 20% service charge are additional.

AVAILABILITY: Year-round, daily.

SERVICES/AMENITIES:

Catering: provided
Kitchen Facilities: n/a
Tables & Chairs: provided
Linens, Silver, etc.: provided
Restrooms: wheelchair accessible
Dance Floor: CBA or BYO
Bride's Dressing Area: yes
Meeting Equipment: CBA or BYO
Other: event coordination

Parking: large lot, on street
Accommodations: 10 guest rooms
Telephone: house, office and guest phones
Outdoor Night Lighting: yes
Outdoor Cooking Facilities: no
Cleanup: provided
View: panorama of ocean, mountains, hills, forest, valley and cityscape

RESTRICTIONS:

Alcohol: beer and wine provided
Smoking: not allowed
Music: amplified OK

Wheelchair Access: yes
Insurance: not required

Want to find more venues and services? Check out our informative website, www.HereComesTheGuide.com.

163

Rancho Nicasio

1 Old Rancheria Road, Nicasio
415/662-2219
www.ranchonicasio.com
maxbrown@ranchonicasio.com

Historic Restaurant & Grounds

- Rehearsal Dinners
- Ceremonies
- Wedding Receptions
- Corp. Events/Mtgs.
- Private Parties
- Accommodations

In the Broadway play *Brigadoon*, an enchanted village appears on the Scottish moors for a single day each century, then disappears for another 100 years. In the geographic center of Marin County, the little town of Nicasio must look like a Brigadoon to the frazzled city dwellers who often happen upon it during rambling weekend drives. Fortunately, Nicasio, set in a secluded valley and surrounded by grassy hills, woods and placidly grazing ranch animals, never fades from view (except, perhaps, on the rare foggy day). Although travelers who discover it leave reluctantly, they're consoled by the thought that this little country retreat is only half an hour away from the clamor of Highway 101.

Often they come back to get married, heading straight for Rancho Nicasio, the town's heart and soul. You can't miss it: Set at the north side of Nicasio's New England-style town square, Rancho Nicasio is the busiest and most important building in town. That's because it's the area's all-in-one post office, general store, bar, restaurant and social center. Even without the hubbub surrounding it, Rancho Nicasio's Spanish-style white stucco façade, red trim, sloping tile roof and long porch (where locals invariably gather to schmooze) set it apart from its Victorian neighbors.

Two settings create Rancho Nicasio's appeal for weddings. Indoors, the Rancho Room, with its beautiful wooden ceiling trusses, brass-trimmed fixtures and permanent oak dance floor, has a built-in stage equipped with professional lighting and sound (Rancho Nicasio is West Marin's main live music venue). Curtains on the north wall open to a view of a deep green lawn, a vine-festooned gazebo, a shady grove of pines, and distant pastures, farm buildings and soft-shouldered knolls. There's a touch of whimsy, too: The moose head above the fireplace wears different hats throughout the year.

Just outside the Rancho Room, an open-air deck looks out over Rancho Nicasio's grand lawn, which has been the memorable venue for many a wedding. Remember, Marin has one of the best climates in the world, and Nicasio sits at its sunny center. Couples love exchanging vows outdoors—usually in front of the gazebo—while musicians play across the way on a small stage. Afterwards, guests socialize by the full-service al fresco bar on the lawn's east side, or enjoy the aroma of food cooking on the two big grills next to it. A professional chef provides on-site catering.

Besides the lawn and the Rancho Room, Rancho Nicasio also boasts Marin's quintessential western barroom. There are lots of animal heads on the walls, wagon wheel chandeliers, a long oak bar with glass mirrors, a brick fireplace, dark wood trusses and knotty pine paneling. The bar adjoins a meeting room that has its own private, oak-sheltered deck—a splendid rehearsal dinner location. (There's even a cottage tucked away at the far end of the green that's ideal for the bridal party. It has a tub and shower, full-length mirror, living room and bedroom.)

Locals brag that Rancho Nicasio "is 25 minutes from everywhere." The couples who come here from "everywhere" leave with lifelong memories. They look back on having pledged their love under a canopy of warm country light, enveloped by happy friends and great music. It's just the kind of experience you'd expect to have at Marin's own Brigadoon.

CEREMONY CAPACITY: The lawn holds up to 300 seated guests. Indoors, the Rancho Room holds up to 200 seated guests.

EVENT/RECEPTION CAPACITY: Outdoors, Rancho Nicasio holds up to 300 guests; indoors, up to 200 seated guests.

MEETING CAPACITY: Event spaces hold up to 300 guests for meetings.

FEES & DEPOSITS: A 25% nonrefundable deposit is required to reserve your date and the balance is due on the day of the event. Rental fees start at $500. The rental fees and packages vary depending on the guest count, space rented, the day of the week, time of the event and the time of year. All-inclusive wedding packages range $16,000–20,000 for up to 150 guests. Tax and gratuity are additional.

AVAILABILITY: Year-round, except Christmas and New Year's Day.

SERVICES/AMENITIES:

Catering: provided, no BYO
Kitchen Facilities: n/a
Tables & Chairs: provided
Linens, Silver, etc.: provided
Restrooms: wheelchair accessible
Dance Floor: yes
Bride's Dressing Area: yes
Meeting Equipment: CBA, extra charge
Other: on-site event coordinator, professional sound and lighting technician on staff, on-site music coordinator for assistance with musical entertainment and bands

Parking: on site
Accommodations: no guest rooms
Telephone: pay phones
Outdoor Night Lighting: CBA
Outdoor Cooking Facilities: chefs can prepare buffet on outdoor brick barbecue
Cleanup: provided
View: 5-acre site; landscaped grounds; panorama of hills and valley

RESTRICTIONS:

Alcohol: provided, full bar
Smoking: designated outdoor areas only
Music: amplified OK indoors, outdoors CBA, stages available both inside and outside

Wheelchair Access: yes
Insurance: typically not required

StoneTree Golf Club

Golf Club

9 StoneTree Lane, Novato
415/209-6296
www.stonetreegolf.com
ebugg@stonetreegolf.com

● Rehearsal Dinners	● Corp. Events/Mtgs.
● Ceremonies	● Private Parties
● Wedding Receptions	Accommodations

For years, the tree-studded site at Novato's Black Oak Point was where the Bay Area's Renaissance Faire revelers gathered each September to recreate Elizabethan England. These days the area's beautiful oak woods sweep down to the great clubhouse at StoneTree Golf Club. With its stone columns, picture windows, rafter beams and handsome dark furniture, the clubhouse evokes the grand lines of a mountain lodge.

This is a place carefully designed to host weddings and events, indoors or out. The attractive entrance hall sets an elegant tone with its large window at the far end that drinks in the light, and a floor-to-ceiling stone fireplace. Throughout the building, the walls are a warm yellow accented by dark-stained wood. From the hall, guests can head off to the Black Point Bar & Fireside Lounge or to the Black Oak and Waterfall Salon, the clubhouse's main reception room, or outside to the Sunset Terrace. Some couples use the Black Point Bar & Fireside Lounge for their ceremony, reciting their vows in front of the picture window. This area is especially popular for winter weddings when the warmth of the fireplace adds to the intimate setting.

The Black Oak and Waterfall Salon is named after a spring-fed waterfall just outside it that tumbles down from the woods to one of three ponds near the base of the clubhouse. Every view from this spacious room is pleasant, ranging from nearby ponds and Black Point's oaks to the intricate stonework alongside the club's main road. The Salon, which can be split into smaller sections, has an adjacent arcaded balcony that's visible through tall windows and accessible through French doors. The balcony's sheltering colonnade, formed by tapering wood pillars set on stone bases, reinforces the feeling of being in a grand lodge.

The Sunset Terrace is a generous patio marked by trellises and exquisitely crafted stone walls. Its view takes in the golf course below, and a panorama that extends from Mt. Tamalpais and the San Rafael hills to the south, all the way north to Novato's wooded ridges and Black Point's oak woods. The golf course undulates over terrain that's an artful mix of sharply manicured greens and natural vegetation. Wedding parties often begin with a ceremony and/or cocktail hour on the Sunset Terrace, then move to the Black Oak and Waterfall Salon for dinner. The Sunset Terrace is also perfect for a casual rehearsal lunch or dinner.

With architecture that inspires but never overwhelms, StoneTree Golf Club makes people feel that they're part of a grand occasion. That sensibility, combined with beautiful views and masterful catering, makes this facility a prime prospect among North Bay wedding venues.

CEREMONY CAPACITY: The Terrace holds 250 seated or 300 standing guests.

EVENT/RECEPTION CAPACITY: The Black Oak Salon seats 70 guests; the Waterfall Salon seats 130. Combined they accommodate 200 guests with space for a dance floor.

MEETING CAPACITY: The Black Oak and Waterfall Salon holds up to 220 seated guests.

FEES & DEPOSITS: A nonrefundable retainer of 20% of the estimated total is required when the contract is signed. The balance is due 14 days prior to the event. Wedding packages start at $75/person. Tax, alcohol and service fee are additional. There are no fees for room rental, cake-cutting or dance floor.

AVAILABILITY: Year-round, daily 6am–midnight, except Christmas Day.

SERVICES/AMENITIES:

Catering: provided
Kitchen Facilities: n/a
Tables & Chairs: provided
Linens, Silver, etc.: provided
Restrooms: wheelchair accessible
Dance Floor: portable provided
Bride's & Groom's Dressing Areas: yes
Meeting Equipment: CBA, extra fee

Parking: 2 large complimentary lots
Accommodations: no guest rooms
Telephone: emergency use only
Outdoor Night Lighting: CBA
Outdoor Cooking Facilities: CBA
Cleanup: provided
View: coastal range, Mt. Tamalpais, Mt. Burdell, Big Rock Ridge, golf course

RESTRICTIONS:

Alcohol: provided, or BYO wine and champagne with corkage fee
Smoking: outdoor designated areas
Music: amplified OK indoors, OK outdoors until 10pm

Wheelchair Access: yes
Insurance: not required
Other: no rice, confetti, birdseed or sparklers; limited real flower petals are permitted

Unity Center

600 Palm Drive, Hamilton Center, Novato

415/475-5000

www.unityinmarin.com
events@unityinmarin.org

- Rehearsal Dinners
- Ceremonies
- Wedding Receptions
- Corp. Events/Mtgs.
- Private Parties
- Accommodations

Step back in time to the sun-kissed days when California belonged to Spain and town centers displayed flowing fountains, colonnades, bell towers, gardens and charming baroque façades. The Unity Center invites you to do just that. Nestled in the rolling hills of southern Novato, this Marin County wedding venue includes a multi-use Chapel area, the versatile Unity Hall for receptions, a commercial kitchen, and a lawn and garden courtyard.

The chapel, which blends pleasingly with the Spanish Colonial-style buildings in the adjacent town center, is surrounded by roses, wisteria, palms and a broad lawn. Its soaring interior welcomes ceremonies and/or receptions, with light-colored walls and cushioned chairs for flexible seating. Windows line the top of each side wall, bringing in views of the ever-changing sky. Pendant chandeliers, suspended from a spectacular exposed-wood-beam ceiling, cast up and down lighting. The room's ambiance is further enhanced by an ethereal half-dome ceiling over the maple-floored chancel/stage area.

The balcony is backlit by a colorful stained-glass window with an arch of clear glass beneath it. Old pews from the original Hamilton Chapel have been restored for additional seating. To the side, a state-of-the-art media booth controls a world-class sound system, theater lights and a rear-lit projection screen. The 8' x 10' screen, designed to be a discreet architectural element over the chancel area, appears as an opaque window when not in use. With this sophisticated A/V system, you can project favorite photos, engagement pictures, videos or background images prior to or during the ceremony or reception.

In the vestibule area, there's a soundproof family or "cry" room. This carpeted area has a picture window that allows families with babies or crying children a comfortable place from which to view the ceremony. Adjoining the chapel is a bride's room with its own bathroom and full-length mirror, perfect for treasured moments of privacy and as a place to change before and after the wedding.

Unity Hall is ideal for receptions and banquets, and can also be partitioned into four smaller meeting rooms. Floor-to-ceiling windows and multiple doors offer views of the courtyard, while other windows look out to the back hillside. The countertops and granite serving counter work well for buffets, and the adjacent full-size commercial kitchen can accommodate any caterer.

Garden-style weddings are easily arranged in the courtyard, which has a fountain as its centerpiece. This outdoor space is enclosed by colonnaded walkways that provide shade and can also be used for a buffet or cocktail table setup. With unobtrusive built-in lighting and sound, the courtyard can be used any time of day.

The campus' newest addition is the Meditation Garden, a beautiful backdrop for photos. A wisteria-covered trellis beckons you down a winding path through naturally landscaped gardens. Wooden benches along the way encourage you to relax and enjoy the surrounding native trees, flowers and greenery.

Unity Center is both romantic and spiritually uplifting. When you come by for a visit, take a moment to sit on a bench near the fountain and appreciate how deftly this venue has melded past and present together. We think its combination of carefully rendered classical Mission architecture and cutting-edge facilities is hard to beat.

CEREMONY CAPACITY: Several spaces accommodate 50–300 seated guests.

EVENT/RECEPTION CAPACITY: Unity Center can accommodate 80–210 seated or 150–275 standing guests indoors, and 80–300 seated or 400 standing outdoors.

MEETING CAPACITY: The chapel holds up to 300 seated theater-style, 200 for a sit-down banquet or up to 80 seated classroom-style. Unity Hall holds up to 145 seated theater-style, 120 for a sit-down banquet or 50 seated conference-style.

FEES & DEPOSITS: 50% of the rental fee is required to reserve your event date. The rental balance and a $150–900 refundable security deposit are due 30 days prior to the event. Venue rental fees start at $1,200 and vary depending on spaces selected, date of your event and guest count. Optional catering packages with preferred vendors start at $85/person and include: several menu options to fit your taste and budget; beverage and coffee service; linens; table service; wedding cake; DJ; event waitstaff and banquet coordination.

AVAILABILITY: Year-round, daily, 7am–midnight; extended hours can be negotiated.

SERVICES/AMENITIES:

Catering: provided, or BYO licensed and full-service
Kitchen Facilities: commercial, fully equipped
Tables & Chairs: CBA
Linens, Silver, etc.: BYO or caterer
Restrooms: wheelchair accessible
Dance Floor: CBA
Bride's Dressing Area: yes
Meeting Equipment: WiFi internet access, state-of-the-art A/V, lighting and sound available, extra fee

Parking: ample, complimentary
Accommodations: no guest rooms, hotels nearby
Telephone: office phone
Outdoor Night Lighting: yes
Outdoor Cooking Facilities: no
Cleanup: renter or caterer
View: courtyard and Novato hills
Other: ministers available

RESTRICTIONS:

Alcohol: BYO or through caterer
Smoking: designated areas only
Music: amplified OK indoors, outdoors with limits

Wheelchair Access: yes
Insurance: liability required

This is important! Tell locations you're reading HERE COMES THE GUIDE and ask if our information is still current.

169

Point Reyes Seashore Lodge
and Restaurant

Lodge, Restaurant & Retreat

10021 Coastal Highway One, Olema

415/663-9000

www.pointreyesseashore.com
lodgekeeper@pointreyesseashore.com

● Rehearsal Dinners	● Corp. Events/Mtgs.
● Ceremonies	● Private Parties
● Wedding Receptions	● Accommodations

With a setting you're likely to see in one of those gorgeous photographic coffee table books, the lodge has long maintained a reputation as a terrific romantic hideaway. It's on one of the prettiest sections of the Northern California coast, flanked by giant redwoods and Point Reyes National Seashore Park. Many of its guest rooms feature fireplaces and whirlpool tubs with pastoral views of the lodge's landscaped grounds and the park's meadows and mountains beyond (yes, you can see the view from the tub!). Given its natural appeal, the lodge increases its romantic possibilities by not only hosting weddings and receptions, but by offering your family, friends and guests the opportunity to have an exclusive retreat for a long weekend celebration.

With the lodge as a backdrop and the expansive, sloping lawn and blooming English garden of the hotel grounds before you, outdoor weddings here are a special treat. You can tie the knot under the branches of a blossoming magnolia tree, or beneath any one of the mature olive, oak and shady alder trees that border the grounds.

For smaller weddings consider the lodge's Casa Olema Retreat, which includes a cottage and lawn. Walk down a flagstone path behind the lodge and under a redwood arch, and you'll be in a separate grass-covered area, surrounded by a formal herb and flower garden and apple, fig, pear and magnolia trees. On one side of the lawn is an arbor containing a built-in table and benches. Crafted from the lodge's trademark golden fir and thickly draped with ivy, it's a charming setting. For larger gatherings, you can set up tables and chairs on the lawn itself.

For small weddings held midweek, the delightful Creekside Cottage, located right on Olema Creek, is ideal for up to 10 people.

Adjoining the lodge is the 1865 Historic Farm House Restaurant, Bar and Deli. In addition to being available for rehearsal dinners and post-wedding brunches, it's an option for intimate indoor weddings. When the weather's warm you can also get married outside on the restaurant's Clemente Garden Patio, which is bordered by a lawn and the Olema Creek.

Included with the rental of the main lodge, the Casa Olema cottage provides both a small kitchen for caterers and a bride's dressing room. Plush furnishings, a fir-manteled fireplace and wainscoting create a room as quaint and personable as any one of the lodge's guest rooms. The cottage's eight-person outdoor hot tub, set within an enclosed brick patio, is a relaxing treat for bride and groom or members of the wedding party. You'll have the exclusive use of its cozy breakfast room, where you can warm yourself in front of a massive stone fireplace, and the downstairs game room, outfitted with an antique billiard table. If you're inviting out-of-town guests, there are also 21 quiet and restful rooms, all with private baths. The Point Reyes Seashore Lodge makes it possible to combine getting married and getting away in one of the state's most scenic and secluded areas.

CEREMONY CAPACITY: The main lawn behind the lodge holds 150 seated or standing guests.

EVENT/RECEPTION CAPACITY: The Casa Olema Retreat lawn accommodates 150 seated or standing for a variety of events. Tents may be advisable depending on weather conditions. The Farm House can accommodate up to 100 guests.

MEETING CAPACITY: The Casa Olema Retreat holds 20 seated conference-style or 25 theater-style; the Creekside Cottage holds 10 for meetings. The Farm House Restaurant's Park Room holds 40 guests conference-style and 50 theater-style.

FEES & DEPOSITS: For weddings or special events, 50% of the rental fee is the nonrefundable deposit required to secure your date. The rental fee (which ensures exclusive use of the entire Lodge and grounds for your event) ranges $5,000–6,500 and includes tables and chairs and 2 nights' lodging at the Casa Olema Cottage. A $500 cleaning/damage deposit and a certificate of insurance are due 8 weeks prior to the event. There is some flexibility in fees for midweek ceremonies and receptions. Catering packages can be customized to fit any budget. Buffets start at $37/person. There is a fee if you bring in your own caterer.

For business functions, fees are based upon date reserved, number of rooms booked and services requested. Please call for rates.

AVAILABILITY: Mid-May through mid-October, weather permitting. A 6-hour block (1pm–7pm) is allowed for ceremonies and receptions.

SERVICES/AMENITIES:
Catering: provided by *Farm House Restaurant* or select from preferred list
Kitchen Facilities: prep only
Tables & Chairs: provided
Linens, Silver, etc.: BYO
Restrooms: not wheelchair accessible
Dance Floor: provided, extra charge
Bride's Dressing Area: yes
Meeting Equipment: VCR, TV, projector and screen, flip charts; secretarial services CBA

Parking: ample
Accommodations: 21 guest rooms, 2 cottages
Telephone: in guest rooms; pay phone nearby
Outdoor Night Lighting: access only
Outdoor Cooking Facilities: BBQ
Cleanup: caterer or renter
View: coastal mountains, creek, meadow

RESTRICTIONS:
Alcohol: provided by *Farm House Restaurant*
Smoking: outdoors only
Music: acoustic only

Wheelchair Access: limited
Insurance: certificate required
Other: no confetti, rice or birdseed

Marin Art & Garden Center

Art Center & Garden

30 Sir Francis Drake Boulevard, Ross
415/455-5260 X2
www.magc.org
rental@magc.org

● Rehearsal Dinners	● Corp. Events/Mtgs.
● Ceremonies	● Private Parties
● Wedding Receptions	○ Accommodations

The Marin Art & Garden Center, an 11-acre historic estate in the exclusive town of Ross, is a dream come true for anyone seeking exquisitely landscaped gardens and a serene, private atmosphere. Within these lush grounds are various indoor and outdoor sites available for weddings, parties, celebrations of life, meetings, workshops and other special events.

The Livermore Pavilion is a wonderful venue for large events. Spacious and airy, it offers an uninterrupted view of the gardens through a wall of windows. Rustic stone gas-jet fireplaces add warmth both inside the room and on the adjoining deck, which is shaded by an attractive awning. The Pavilion is air-conditioned and can be divided into two smaller spaces, making it ideal for corporate meetings. Two A/V screens are available on request.

The inviting Garden Room opens to an expansive garden area. When the weather is warm, you won't be able to resist having your event outside. The garden is enclosed by ivy-covered walls, live oaks, redwoods and Japanese maples. Below these trees, huge mossy boulders, heavenly bamboo and flourishing shrubs heighten the woodsy atmosphere. Buffet service or a string quartet can be set up on a slightly raised area, shaded by redwoods. Evening events are made magical by soft lighting and the twinkling stars overhead.

For couples getting married at the center, the grounds offer a host of appealing ceremony sites. The Fountain area is perfect for an outdoor ceremony, reception or party. Here, a large fountain pool sends its glittering spray into the air. A floral rainbow of daylilies, blue catnip, verbena, Santa Barbara daisies and iris blooms around the fountain, all enclosed by an aggregate-concrete path. On one side, a forest of mature elms, Lombardy poplars, deodar cedars and honey locusts forms a backdrop behind a curving wooden bench beneath a pergola. Other spots for ceremonies include the Magnolia Tree Lawn and the Gazebo Lawn, a broad swath of velvety grass graced by a rare dawn redwood, elm and horse chestnut trees.

Though its fabulous gardens and tranquil atmosphere make the Marin Art & Garden Center seem a world away, it's centrally located near Highway 101 and only 20 minutes from San Francisco. When you have your event here, you not only have a chance to "get away from it all," you also experience a little piece of Paradise close to home.

To contact Marin Art and Garden Center by mail, the address is PO Box 437, Ross, CA 94957.

CEREMONY CAPACITY: Indoor and outdoor spaces can seat 300+ guests.

EVENT/RECEPTION CAPACITY: The center can accommodate 200 seated indoors, or 300 seated or standing guests outdoors.

MEETING CAPACITY: The Livermore Pavilion holds 200+ guests seated classroom-style or 225 guests theater-style and the Garden Room seats 80 guests theater-style.

FEES & DEPOSITS: Half of the total rental fee is required to secure your date; the rental balance and a $500 refundable cleaning/security deposit are due 1 month prior to the function. Rental fees range $1,500–4,000 depending on space selected. A buyout wedding package is $7,000 which guarantees full exclusivity on the day of your wedding.

AVAILABILITY: Year-round, weekends, 8am–10pm at the Livermore Pavilion and in the Garden Room.

SERVICES/AMENITIES:

Catering: select from preferred list only
Kitchen Facilities: ample, fully equipped
Tables & Chairs: provided, no extra fee
Linens, Silver, etc.: BYO or through caterer
Restrooms: wheelchair accessible
Dance Floor: yes
Bride's Dressing Area: yes
Meeting Equipment: sound systems, A/V screens, mics, wireless internet

Parking: large lot and on street
Accommodations: no guest rooms
Telephone: emergency use only
Outdoor Night Lighting: access only
Outdoor Cooking Facilities: yes, on asphalt only
Cleanup: through caterer or renter
View: gardens, pond, hills, Mt. Tamalpias
Other: security guard CBA, Chiavari chairs ($4/chair)

RESTRICTIONS:

Alcohol: BYO, must use licensed server
Smoking: outdoors only
Music: amplified OK with restrictions

Wheelchair Access: yes
Insurance: liability required
Other: no rice or birdseed; decorations restricted

San Francisco Theological Seminary

Seminary

105 Seminary Road, San Anselmo
800/447-8820 x843

www.sfts.edu/rentals
dcarey@sfts.edu
hliencres@sfts.edu

● Rehearsal Dinners	● Corp. Events/Mtgs.
● Ceremonies	● Private Parties
● Wedding Receptions	● Accommodations

When they first see a photograph of this place, many people remark that it looks like a castle on a wooded Scottish brae or a medieval village in central Europe. It's easy to understand why this seminary on a hill evokes such romantic associations. First there's Montgomery Memorial Chapel, a graceful stone church near the seminary's main entrance that is one of its two most popular wedding sites. Then, up the hill, there's Stewart Memorial Chapel at Geneva Hall, a splendid white church with an arcade, a soaring campanile, a terrace that overlooks a breathtaking view, and stained-glass windows whose intense colors rival those of Europe's cathedrals.

In between the two ceremony venues is a tree-shaded campus with grand lawns, weathered moss-covered stone walls, classrooms, Victorian homes for faculty members and rock-faced administration buildings that evoke the allure of historic citadels. The most popular reception site is the Geneva Hall terrace, a curving sweep of stone that provides one of the most stunning panoramas in Marin: the north flank of Mt. Tamalpais; Ross Township's redwood-covered ridges; Red Hill; the seminary's signature stone academic buildings; and views down the Ross Valley.

There's a more prosaic form of beauty here, too: Because the seminary is a religious nonprofit entity, it can offer its beautiful grounds and facilities at prices that are considered quite competitive by Marin County standards.

The seminary has another deal sweetener—a Victorian home available for small prenuptial parties or a pre-wedding stay. You can rest overnight at the seminary, then awaken fresh the next morning, knowing you don't have to travel anywhere for the big day. The seminary also has a 28-room dorm-style retreat center, which allows close friends and family to lodge together. Keeping so many of your loved ones nearby makes it easy to turn your wedding into a destination weekend.

Besides a choice of romantic chapels and the campus' overall enticing feel, couples also like the unlimited parking and almost universal accessibility for their disabled guests. This site is like a good day that just keeps getting better. First, the drive here takes you through some of Marin's loveliest, leafiest neighborhoods, and then the campus itself charms you with its meandering lanes, compelling architecture and one-of-a-kind vistas in a county famous for its views. Once it wins you over, any other venue just won't feel as right.

CEREMONY, EVENT/RECEPTION & MEETING CAPACITY: This location holds up to 170 seated or standing guests indoors and up to 170 seated or standing guests outdoors.

FEES & DEPOSITS: A nonrefundable deposit of 50% of the estimated event total is required to reserve your date. The balance is due 2 months prior to the event. Rental fees range $800–3,500 depending on the space rented.

AVAILABILITY: Year-round. Call for details.

SERVICES/AMENITIES:

Catering: select from preferred list
Kitchen Facilities: none
Tables & Chairs: provided
Linens, Silver, etc.: through caterer
Restrooms: wheelchair accessible
Dance Floor: through caterer
Bride's & Groom's Dressing Areas: yes
Meeting Equipment: some provided

Parking: large lot or on-street
Accommodations: 33 guest rooms
Telephone: no
Outdoor Night Lighting: access only
Outdoor Cooking Facilities: no
Cleanup: caterer or renter
View: mountains, meadow, garden, forest
Other: pianos, picnic area

RESTRICTIONS:

Alcohol: through caterer
Smoking: not allowed
Music: amplified OK indoors and outdoors with restrictions

Wheelchair Access: yes
Insurance: liability required

Overwhelmed? Use the search criteria on www.HereComesTheGuide.com to narrow down your choices.

175

Falkirk Mansion

1408 Mission Avenue, San Rafael
415/485-3328
www.falkirkculturalcenter.org
beth.goldberg@ci.san-rafael.ca.us

Historic Mansion

- Rehearsal Dinners
- Ceremonies
- Wedding Receptions
- Corp. Events/Mtgs.
- Private Parties
- Accommodations

Magnificent oaks and magnolias frame the historic Falkirk Mansion, a lovely Queen Anne Victorian in the heart of Marin. Built in 1888, the house is the creation of Clinton Day, the architect who designed the Stanford University campus chapel. In keeping with the style of the day, it has a complex and intriguing roof line of gables and chimneys, variously shaped bays and plenty of decorative details.

The property was purchased in 1906 by Captain Robert Dollar, a Scotsman who'd made his fortune in timber and shipping. He added many features to the estate, including the brick steps and pond, rolling lawns, the greenhouse and a carriage house. A civic-minded man, he donated generously to both San Rafael and his hometown of Falkirk, Scotland—hence the name of the Mansion.

Today, Falkirk Cultural Center serves as a historic site, contemporary art gallery, cultural and educational center, as well as a popular spot for weddings. You can have your ceremony in the outdoor Wedding Garden, on the sprawling lawns or in the parlor. The Mansion's interior is beautifully rendered in rich redwood paneling, and features ornate mantelpieces, hardwood floors and elegant wall coverings. When you reserve the Mansion, you have use of the entire first floor. The foyer has a huge decorative fireplace and floor-to-ceiling stained-glass windows. Have your reception indoors or, during warmer months, dine and dance on the veranda. This secluded wooden porch is enclosed by camellia bushes and an ancient oak. It doesn't matter how you orchestrate your wedding; Falkirk will imbue it with intimacy and a century's worth of Victorian charm.

CEREMONY CAPACITY: The Parlor holds 50 seated or 75 standing; outdoors the site can accommodate 125 seated guests.

EVENT/RECEPTION CAPACITY: October–April, standing capacity is 100; seated capacity 50–60 guests. April–October, the house and veranda hold up to 125 guests.

MEETING CAPACITY: Indoors, the venue holds 60 seated theater-style or 20 seated conference-style; outdoors it holds 80 seated theater-style.

FEES & DEPOSITS: Half of the rental fee is a nonrefundable deposit required to reserve your date. Weekend rates for a 6-hour minimum block are $1,800 from April 15 to October 14, and $1,200 from October 15 to April 14. Additional charges will apply for overtime hours. A refundable $500 security deposit and any remaining balance are payable 45 days in advance of your event. Weekday rates vary; call for more information. Special rates can be arranged for nonprofits.

AVAILABILITY: Year-round, Saturdays and Sundays 1pm–11pm. Weekdays 9am–11pm by arrangement.

SERVICES/AMENITIES:

Catering: select from approved list or BYO

Kitchen Facilities: minimal

Tables & Chairs: provided

Linens, Silver, etc.: BYO

Restrooms: wheelchair accessible

Dance Floor: no

Bride's Dressing Area: yes

Meeting Equipment: limited

Parking: large public lot

Accommodations: no guest rooms

Telephone: emergency use only

Outdoor Night Lighting: yes

Outdoor Cooking Facilities: no

Cleanup: caterer

View: wooded park and grounds

RESTRICTIONS:

Alcohol: BYO

Smoking: restricted area only

Music: amplified OK to 90 decibels

Wheelchair Access: yes

Insurance: extra liability required

Other: no candles, decorations restricted

Maple Lawn Estate

Historic Mansion and Lawn

1312 Mission Avenue, San Rafael
415/295-LAWN (5296)

weddingsmaplelawn.com
maplelawnevents@gmail.com

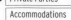

- Rehearsal Dinners
- Ceremonies
- Wedding Receptions
- Corp. Events/Mtgs.
- Private Parties
- Accommodations

A pair of hand-stacked stone pillars mark the entry to Maple Lawn, a rambling Victorian house and grounds that was once the home of one of the area's leading families. Built with 19th-century mining riches, the residence was often the scene for "must attend" social and civic soirées. Happily today, under the current ownership of the San Rafael Elks, this grand estate continues to set a gold standard for gracious events.

Maple Lawn's pièce de résistance is the expansive Magnolia Terrace, an absolute jewel of a garden area off to the side of the blue-and-white mansion. As you enter through an ornate, iron gate, the first thing that greets you is a profusion of colorful blooming hedges. Just ahead is a raised, canopied terrace, and stretching out beyond that is an incredibly lush lawn surrounded on three sides by mature magnolia and camellia trees. Running straight through the center of the grass is a wide brick promenade adorned with two multi-tiered fountains topped dramatically with Greek goddesses.

What a spectacular setting this makes for your ceremony, as friends and family seated on the lawn watch you walk down that center aisle to meet your groom beneath a neoclassical arch. After vows are exchanged, everyone is invited to toast your new life with a glass of bubbly on the terrace. Slightly elevated and separated from the grass by box hedges and flower-filled urns, this shady spot is perfect for enjoying cocktails and hors d'oeuvres. Then dinner is served at tables on the lawn, followed by dancing back on the terrace under the twinkle-lit canopy.

Beautiful as the grounds are, there are pleasures to be found inside the house as well. To start with, you'll surely be smitten with a bride's room that's the epitome of femininity. Large enough for all your attendants to gather and relax, its décor includes an antique Victorian vanity table, a carved white marble fireplace, and high ceilings with lots of crown molding. The groomsmen get to play men of leisure in the "old school" Card Room Lounge with its adjacent wood-paneled Billiards Room.

At the front of the house, there's an airy Solarium and cozy porch overlooking pine trees that would make a delightful spot for a bridal shower or bridesmaid's breakfast. And the clubby Drake's Bar, complete with burgundy leather wingback chairs, early American paintings and a vintage mural of Sir Francis Drake arriving in the Bay Area, could be just right for a rehearsal dinner.

If you'd prefer an indoor reception, check out the regal-sized Boyd Banquet Room, which boasts a coved ceiling with the original brass-and-crystal chandeliers that illuminated many historic parties. But even if you don't entertain inside, do take advantage of the polished wooden doors (replete with brass doorknockers), central staircase and porte-cochère as romantic photo backdrops unique to Maple Lawn.

CEREMONY CAPACITY: The site holds 180 seated guests indoors and 500 seated outdoors.

EVENT/RECEPTION CAPACITY: The facility can accommodate 200 seated or 300 standing indoors and 330 seated or 500 standing outdoors

MEETING CAPACITY: Meeting rooms hold up to 180 seated guests.

FEES & DEPOSITS: A $500 deposit is required to reserve your date and the balance is due 120 days prior to the event or upon contract execution, whichever comes first. Rental fees range $150–2,000 depending on the day and time of the event and the space reserved.

AVAILABILITY: Year-round, daily.

SERVICES/AMENITIES:

Catering: select from preferred list or BYO
Kitchen Facilities: fully equipped
Tables & Chairs: CBA
Linens, Silver, etc.: through caterer
Restrooms: wheelchair accessible
Dance Floor: provided
Bride's Dressing Area: yes
Meeting Equipment: some provided
Other: event coordination available, extra fee

Parking: large lot, garage nearby
Accommodations: no guest rooms
Telephone: emergency use only
Outdoor Night Lighting: yes
Outdoor Cooking Facilities: BBQ on site
Cleanup: renter or caterer
View: forest, fountain, garden, landscaped grounds

RESTRICTIONS:

Alcohol: provided
Smoking: designated areas only
Music: amplified OK with restrictions

Wheelchair Access: limited
Insurance: liability required

Osher Marin Jewish Community Center

Community Center

200 North San Pedro Road, San Rafael

415/444-8084

www.marinjcc.org
pday@marinjcc.org

● Rehearsal Dinners	● Corp. Events/Mtgs.
● Ceremonies	● Private Parties
● Wedding Receptions	Accommodations

When this long-anticipated architectural gem opened in 1991, it was an immediate hit with Marin County residents. It continues to be one of the county's main social hubs, with a constant stream of people attending exercise classes, lectures, dances, theatrical productions and parties. It's also one of Marin's favorite places to hold a wedding, and just one look at this facility's design tells you why.

Set at the base of a high forested ridge, this three-story Craftsman-style building is a masterpiece of exquisite proportions and detailing—including one of the Bay Area's most beautiful interior staircases.

Its façade, screened by maple trees, is faced with brick on the bottom and finished with a smooth, soft beige stucco on the top. Rust-red window sashes and trim complete the building's subdued exterior palette. Inside, past the reception area, are three contiguous spaces that form the nucleus of the JCC's wedding venue: the Hoytt Theater, an enclosed atrium that opens to a garden courtyard and the impressive Main Hall that connects them.

The Theater, with its broad stage, extensive seating area and professional sound and lighting equipment, is a flexible space suitable for ceremonies, receptions and dinners. Its sconces and light fixtures, which resemble white pyramids stacked upside down upon one another, give it an Art Deco look. For event coordinators this place is like catnip: one whiff of its ample size and high-level amenities, and their imaginations start buzzing with ideas. The venue is a classy blank slate that lends itself to almost any theme, and dresses up beautifully for a wedding.

Just outside the Theater, the terracotta-paved Main Hall has a peaked 30-foot ceiling of white tiles, supported by light-colored wood trusses. A row of glass doors along one wall leads into the spacious Kurland Center, which can be used as one large room, or can be closed off with moveable walls to create three separate spaces. The central atrium, filled with natural light, opens onto the intimate garden courtyard.

Then there's the JCC's most compelling interior feature: the Elaine Rosenberg Stairway. This grand staircase has to be one of the Bay Area's loveliest. It curves out in wide welcome at the bottom, then narrows and climbs, first to a spacious mezzanine landing and then up to the facility's lofty top floor. The stairway ascends so steeply (a clever visual trick) that you get the impression it's aspiring to reach Heaven itself. Many brides can't resist descending this remarkable flight of steps during their pre- or post-ceremonial entrances.

Management here is fond of saying, "This isn't your grandmother's JCC," and they're right. Grandma never had access to such an architecturally satisfying, state-of-the-art facility. And her JCC probably didn't have this community center's reputation for hospitality, either. While the Osher Marin JCC is set up to accommodate pre-wedding minyans and other traditional Jewish activities, it is a famously "come one, come all" place. It doesn't matter who you are; when you're here, you *are* somebody.

CEREMONY CAPACITY: The Hoytt Theater holds up to 500 seated guests; outdoors, the courtyard holds up to 200 seated guests.

EVENT/RECEPTION CAPACITY: The Hoytt Theater holds up to 265 seated or 650 standing guests; outdoors, the courtyard holds up to 200 seated or 250 standing guests. The Kurland Center holds up to 185 seated or 200 standing guests.

MEETING CAPACITY: The Hoytt Theater holds up to 500 guests; the Kurland Center accommodates up to 200 guests. Meetings and conferences for nonprofit organizations only.

FEES & DEPOSITS: A $750 deposit is required to reserve your date. The balance is due 1 month prior to the event. Rental fees range $450–4,500 depending on space rented.

AVAILABILITY: Year-round, daily, 4pm–midnight on weekends, 6pm–midnight on weekdays.

SERVICES/AMENITIES:

Catering: BYO
Kitchen Facilities: fully equipped, no catering equipment
Tables & Chairs: provided
Linens, Silver, etc.: BYO or through caterer
Restrooms: wheelchair accessible
Dance Floor: yes
Bride's Dressing Area: yes
Meeting Equipment: yes

Parking: large lot
Accommodations: no guest rooms
Telephone: pay phone
Outdoor Night Lighting: yes
Outdoor Cooking Facilities: no
Cleanup: renter or caterer
View: garden patio
Other: internet access

RESTRICTIONS:

Alcohol: BYO
Smoking: not allowed
Music: amplified OK

Wheelchair Access: yes
Insurance: extra liability required

The professionals in the back of this book are the best in the business. How do we know? Read page 637.

181

Unitarian Universalist Congregation of Marin   *Church*

240 Channing Way, San Rafael
415/479-4131
www.uumarin.org
events@uumarin.org

● Rehearsal Dinners	● Corp. Events/Mtgs.
● Ceremonies	● Private Parties
● Wedding Receptions	Accommodations

Exploring Marin County can be a lifetime passion, especially as you discover the region's wonderful hidden vistas, many of which are seldom publicized in guidebooks and tourist literature. One of those little-known views can be enjoyed at the Unitarian Universalist Congregation of Marin, a place that welcomes couples of any faith or sexual orientation (great for interfaith marriages and same-sex unions).

From its hilltop setting high above Terra Linda, the center offers a grand panorama of the north flank of Mt. Tamal-pais that most people will never see. Superb as the view is, however, the heart of this venue is a simple, tranquil courtyard graced by a grove of mulberry trees whose broad leaves spread bountiful shade over a lush lawn. A curving three-level terrace rises toward an arbor-topped knoll along two sides of the space, and an ornamental pool and fountain in the center teems with goldfish and water lilies. Water gurgles over a sandstone ledge and spills into the pool creating a calming, almost musical sound.

Beginning at the courtyard, a gravel path winds up past flowers, herbs and succulents to a flagstone-paved area on top of the knoll. With a tall oak and an arbor as backdrops, this is a compelling spot for photos. From this height you can see a quintessential Marin panorama: Terra Linda and Mt. Tam to the west and southwest; the wooded hills that run south of Santa Venetia from Civic Center to China Camp; and a commanding view of San Pablo Bay.

The center's Fellowship Hall is the most popular site for dining and dancing (or for winter indoor ceremonies). It has a high ceiling of pine beams and rafters, an oak floor and picture windows on three sides, including one that looks out over Terra Linda and that impressive Mt. Tam view. The more modest Fireside Room is warm and intimate, ideal for a small wedding or reception. Its focal point is a tall sandstone-faced fireplace, flanked by picture windows that look out to a dense oak wood. The room has direct access to the courtyard, and in winter a roaring fire makes it especially inviting. Whichever space you use, your guests can party till 11pm.

Caterers will find counter space galore and a professional range in the large kitchen, and UUCM is happy to refer brides to a preferred list of seasoned vendors.

Their first look at the courtyard is usually all it takes to convince many couples to get married here. But if more reasons are needed, the center's outstanding views, affordability, and beautiful setting quickly clinch their decision.

CEREMONY CAPACITY: The Courtyard holds up to 200 seated guests; the Fellowship Hall up to 200.

EVENT/RECEPTION CAPACITY: The Courtyard accommodates up to 200 seated or 250 standing guests; the Fellowship Hall up to 200 seated or 250 standing.

MEETING CAPACITY: The Fellowship Hall holds 12–200 seated guests.

FEES & DEPOSITS: For a wedding, a $950 deposit is required to reserve your date. The package fee is due 4 weeks prior to the event. Packages range $2,125–2,700 depending on the space rented and the day and time of the event. There is a 25% discount for November–March weddings. Hourly rental of the facility is also available, call for pricing. Packages include use of entire facility, attendant, tables and chairs (for up to 150 guests), custodial service (setup, breakdown and cleanup). The Saturday wedding package includes use of the facility for a half day the Friday before to decorate, rehearse, etc. Outdoor chairs are provided for a nominal fee. For rentals and other services, select from their preferred vendor list.

AVAILABILITY: Year-round, Monday–Saturday, 7am–11pm and Sunday, 2pm–11pm.

SERVICES/AMENITIES:

Catering: select from preferred list
Kitchen Facilities: fully equipped
Tables & Chairs: provided indoors
Linens, Silver, etc.: BYO or through caterer
Restrooms: wheelchair accessible
Dance Floor: provided
Bride's Dressing Area: yes
Meeting Equipment: some provided

Parking: large lot and on-street
Accommodations: no guest rooms
Telephone: office phone
Outdoor Night Lighting: limited, BYO, CBA
Outdoor Cooking Facilities: BBQ CBA
Cleanup: provided
View: panorama of bay, woods and mountains
Other: grand piano, clergy on staff, picnic area, A/V equipment

RESTRICTIONS:

Alcohol: BYO
Smoking: outside only
Music: amplified OK

Wheelchair Access: yes
Insurance: liability required

Cavallo Point
The Lodge at the Golden Gate

601 Murray Circle, Fort Baker, Sausalito
415/339-4709
www.cavallopoint.com
jessica@cavallopoint.com

Historic Landmark

- Rehearsal Dinners
- Ceremonies
- Wedding Receptions
- Corp. Events/Mtgs.
- Private Parties
- Accommodations

It's been awarded honor status by the National Trust for Historic Preservation; it has LEED Gold Certification from the U.S. Green Building Council; and it's on *Condé Nast Traveler's* "Hot List" and *Travel+Leisure's* Top 10 New Green American Landmarks. History, ecology and luxury all seem to come seamlessly together at Cavallo Point Lodge, the meticulously restored Colonial Revival complex tucked away like a gorgeous surprise at the northern foot of the Golden Gate Bridge.

The views are breathtaking from anywhere on this property set on 75,000 acres of sunny national parkland, but especially from the Mission Blue Chapel. Named after an endangered California butterfly, this pristine, cream-colored structure stands high on a hillside covered with tufted grasses and California native plants. Its adjoining terrace is ideal for light-hearted gatherings, and affords a vista of San Francisco, the sparkling bay, and the towers of the Golden Gate Bridge rising above the pines and eucalyptus through tiaras of clouds.

There are no pews in the chapel, which has large picture windows, gleaming honey-colored floors, and a low stage that make it an excellent setting for anything from a meeting of the minds to a wedding ceremony or reception. But perhaps you'll want to take your celebration outdoors to the Mission Blue Lawn, where your guests can enjoy an elegant hilltop affair or an exchange of vows framed by the incomparable natural panorama.

At the foot of the hill, the Callippe Terrace—named for the endangered Callippe butterfly—is another prime party venue. This one comes with a welcoming fire pit, comfortable seating and a lovely view of historic Fort Baker. Team it up with the Callippe Ballroom and the Callippe Foyer for an ultra-grand indoor-outdoor fête. The foyer alone is roomy enough for cocktails and dancing. Large, lounge-like alcoves flanking the doors add to the sense of grandeur. If you need a place for additional activities, the handsome Silverspot Room on the opposite side of the ballroom can be used as a minitheater, a children's playroom and more.

Not enough possibilities? The lodge offers an amazing 14,000 square feet of adaptable function rooms and formal meeting space. Traipse upstairs to where the balconied Verbena Room and Foyer, La Mariposa Borracha Room and the Cavallo Point Cooking School kitchen multiply ways to maximize your event experience. Imagine serving cocktails or dinner in a graceful salon with fireplace and thrilling wraparound views, or a group lesson in the art of fine cuisine in the warmth of a spotless, professionally equipped, wine country-style kitchen.

Added to all this are day-of accommodations for the bride, a luxurious Healing Arts Center & Spa, the award-winning Murray Circle restaurant, the Farley Bar and a dreamy veranda designed for sitting back and soaking up the wild beauty of the surrounding terrain. You won't want to leave the grounds and you don't have to. The magnificently renovated two-bedroom family-friendly suites and guest rooms and glamorous contemporary lodgings are a great place for you and your guests to settle in and relax for a weekend…or embark on an extended stay full of fun-filled exploration. Rest assured, any journey that begins here is bound to be a glorious one.

CEREMONY CAPACITY: The facility holds 208 seated guests, indoors or outdoors.

EVENT/RECEPTION CAPACITY: The site can accommodate 180 seated or 250 standing indoors, and 250 seated or standing outdoors.

MEETING CAPACITY: Meeting rooms hold 200 seated guests.

FEES & DEPOSITS: 50% of the total event cost is required to reserve your date and the balance is due 30 days prior to the event. Rental fees range $6,000–9,000 depending on the season and the number of guests. Meals, including wine, beer and wedding cake range $218–298/person. Tax, alcohol and a 21% service charge are additional.

AVAILABILITY: Year-round.

SERVICES/AMENITIES:

Catering: provided
Kitchen Facilities: n/a
Tables & Chairs: provided, CBA
Linens, Silver, etc.: provided, CBA
Restrooms: wheelchair accessible
Dance Floor: portable provided
Bride's Dressing Area: yes
Meeting Equipment: provided, CBA
Other: on-site wedding cake, spa services, picnic area

Parking: large lot
Accommodations: 142 guest rooms
Telephone: house phone
Outdoor Night Lighting: CBA
Outdoor Cooking Facilities: BBQ CBA
Cleanup: provided
View: garden patio, landscaped grounds; panorama of fields, hills, cityscape, coastline, forest, mountains, ocean and park

RESTRICTIONS:

Alcohol: BYO with corkage fee
Smoking: designated areas only
Music: OK with restrictions

Wheelchair Access: yes
Insurance: not required

The Spinnaker Restaurant
and Banquet Facility

100 Spinnaker Drive, Sausalito
415/332-1500

www.thespinnaker.com
jeff@thespinnaker.com

Waterfront Restaurant

● Rehearsal Dinners	● Corp. Events/Mtgs.
● Ceremonies	● Private Parties
● Wedding Receptions	Accommodations

A well-known landmark along downtown Sausalito's waterfront, The Spinnaker Restaurant has been a favorite dining destination for over 50 years. This popular venue, which sits on piers right over the water, also boasts a delightful banquet facility that offers the same excellent cuisine, topnotch service and spectacular bay views.

Although the banquet facility adjoins the restaurant, it's completely separate from the main dining room and has its own entrance as well as a dedicated kitchen that caters solely to your special event. And like the restaurant, it has plenty of floor-to-ceiling windows and glass doors that let diners savor sweeping vistas of Belvedere, Angel Island, the Bay Bridge and San Francisco's skyline from anywhere in the room.

The warm interior, in shades of cream and rose, is complemented by a high, distinctive, wood-slat ceiling. Sliding glass doors open onto an outdoor deck that provides an additional 1,000 square feet of bayside event space. Sailboats glide past almost close enough to touch, their colorful spinnakers and white sails billowing in the breeze.

The practical attributes of The Spinnaker Banquet Facility are as compelling as the views. This versatile venue is spacious enough to accommodate a large wedding reception or holiday party (with a band and dance floor) or can easily be set up with lecture-style seating, a stage and a podium for business functions. It can also be configured for smaller, more intimate gatherings, such as bridal shower luncheons, anniversary parties or birthday celebrations.

The Spinnaker is known for orchestrating memorable occasions tailored to their clients' individual needs. Their expert event planning services include arranging everything from florals and photography to music or other entertainment. They offer a variety of reception packages, and their signature menus—which feature fresh seafood, gourmet meats, local specialties and savory vegetarian options—cater to every culinary preference.

Quiet and tasteful, The Spinnaker Banquet Facility is an inviting waterfront venue that makes the most of its picturesque surroundings.

CEREMONY & EVENT/RECEPTION CAPACITY: The deck holds 75 seated or 90 standing, the banquet room 160 seated or 220 standing guests.

MEETING CAPACITY: The Banquet Room holds 200 seated theater-style or 160 seated conference-style.

FEES & DEPOSITS: To reserve your date, a $1,500 nonrefundable deposit is required (which is applied towards the event balance). The food and beverage balance is payable at the event's completion. The food and beverage minimum is $2,000 Monday–Thursday daytime, $3,000 Monday–Thursday evening, $4,000 Friday, Saturday and Sunday daytime, and $8,000 Saturday evening. In-house catering is provided. Buffets or seated meals run $45–55/person; alcohol, tax and an 18% service charge are additional. A $1,000 room charge, $175 bartending fee and $225 dance floor fee may apply. For ceremonies, there's a $450 setup charge.

For business luncheons and dinners, or for smaller groups, special rates can be arranged.

AVAILABILITY: Year-round, daily, 7am–midnight, in 4-hour blocks.

SERVICES/AMENITIES:

Catering: provided, no BYO

Kitchen Facilities: n/a

Tables & Chairs: provided

Linens, Silver, etc.: provided

Restrooms: wheelchair accessible

Dance Floor: CBA, extra fee

Bride's Dressing Area: no

Meeting Equipment: PA, microphones

Parking: valet parking

Accommodations: no guest rooms

Telephone: pay phone

Outdoor Night Lighting: on deck

Outdoor Cooking Facilities: no

Cleanup: provided

View: San Francisco Bay and bridges

Other: event coordination, cakes, music CBA

RESTRICTIONS:

Alcohol: provided or corkage $14–16/bottle

Smoking: designated areas

Music: amplified OK

Wheelchair Access: yes

Insurance: not required

Want to know WHAT TO ASK a potential location or vendor? Check out our Questions to Ask starting on page 17.

Stinson Beach Community Center

Community Center & Chapel

32 Belvedere Avenue, Stinson Beach
415/868-1444
www.stinsonbeachcommunitycenter.org
info@stinsonbeachcommunitycenter.org

- Rehearsal Dinners
- Ceremonies
- Wedding Receptions
- Corp. Events/Mtgs.
- Private Parties
- Accommodations

Stinson Beach is one of the Bay Area's natural treasures. This curving stretch of white sand extends three miles along Marin County's Pacific coastline and has a visual advantage many other beaches lack: To reach it, you drive down a scenic mountain road whose views are often as dramatic as those along the French Riviera. But even better than Stinson Beach's gratifying appearance is the little town that has grown up beside it: a quiet seaside community whose very existence is a restorative balm to almost any visitor's hectic life.

This is a beautiful place for a wedding, and the best place to celebrate is at the Stinson Beach Community Center, a building that's been at the heart of Stinson Beach's civic life for decades. Located just off Shoreline Highway, up from the fire station and next door to Stinson Beach Community Church, the center looks like a small lodge. The exterior is finished with brown wood siding with white trim. Wood predominates inside, too: Three impressive trusses under a ceiling of pine rafters span the center's large sunny interior, the walls have four-foot-high wainscoting, and the floors are Canadian maple hardwood. Delightful murals of sunlit clouds are painted on the east and west walls, adding a whimsical touch. Across the room from the entrance, the center's focal point is a tall light-brick fireplace capped with a huge log mantel. On either side of it are large wood-trimmed windows and French doors.

The French doors open out to a patio enveloped by nature. A flower- and bush-lined fence runs along one side, separating it from a gurgling creek edged with fragrant cedars, mulberry trees and pines. While flowerbeds and potted plants adorn the patio, its most compelling visual attribute is a magnificent maple tree whose trunk has grown out horizontally. The trunk—easily 2.5 feet in diameter—runs parallel to the ground for about 20 feet, finally coming to rest on the pavement, where it extends three long branches 30 feet up into the air. It's an impressive conversation piece, to say the least.

Some couples marry on nearby Stinson Beach, while others opt for a ceremony in the church next to the center. The church's bright interior of light fir walls and pews soars to pointed arches, and the altar is backed by floor-to-ceiling glass. A mezzanine accommodates an organ and a choir. The church has an intimate feel inside and a small-town look outside, with its wooden siding and steeply angled roof culminating in a little belfry.

Stinson Beach has a best-of-both-worlds air about it. Although it's only a 45-minute drive from San Francisco, it's just far enough removed to possess an enticing away-from-it-all quality. And, it may be just the place to have a memorable, uncomplicated wedding day.

CEREMONY CAPACITY: The Community Center holds 150–200 seated guests with room for 299 standing. The Chapel holds 115 seated guests and up to 130 including standing guests.

EVENT/RECEPTION & MEETING CAPACITY: The Community Center holds 200 seated or 299 standing. Tenting can be arranged to increase capacity.

FEES & DEPOSITS: For special events, a $500 security deposit is required to secure your date. The rental fee ranges $2,300–2,500 and includes a block of time from 8am to midnight plus full use of the industrial kitchen, basic cleaning, and an event monitor. The Chapel rents for $450/day and includes a rehearsal the day prior to the ceremony.

Please call for affordable meeting rates.

AVAILABILITY: Year-round, daily, 8am–midnight.

SERVICES/AMENITIES:

Catering: BYO or CBA
Tables & Chairs: provided, call for details
Kitchen Facilities: new, fully equipped
Linens, Silver, etc.: BYO
Restrooms: wheelchair accessible
Dance Floor: hardwood floor indoors
Bride's Dressing Area: yes
Meeting Equipment: limited, ask for specifics
Other: grand piano, organ

Parking: Center's parking area and on street
Accommodations: nearby hotels and beach house rentals
Telephone: emergency use only
Outdoor Night Lighting: on porch and patio
Outdoor Cooking Facilities: CBA
Cleanup: caterer, basic cleanup provided
View: Stinson Beach hills, part of Mt. Tamalpais

RESTRICTIONS:

Alcohol: BYO
Smoking: outside only
Music: amplified OK until 11pm, call for details

Wheelchair Access: yes
Insurance: certificate required

Corinthian Yacht Club

Historic Yacht Club

43 Main Street, Tiburon
415/435-4812
www.corinthiancatering.com
leila@cyc.org

● Rehearsal Dinners	● Corp. Events/Mtgs.
● Ceremonies	● Private Parties
● Wedding Receptions	Accommodations

The setting of the Corinthian Yacht Club is truly spectacular. Even its members, who've been coming here for years, never fail to be awed by its sweeping view. It is easily one of the great panoramas in all of California, taking in Tiburon's rustic downtown, the deep waters of Raccoon Strait, Angel Island's wooded profile, the silvery Bay Bridge, the high hills and towers of San Francisco, Alcatraz' ship-like silhouette, and Belvedere Island's leafy slopes and grand mansions. Only steps away, in the club's harbor, spars and spinnakers bob everywhere, and there's a steady flow of craft setting out to ply the bay or return home from it.

This beloved Marin landmark—a Colonial Revival building with a shimmering white façade and soaring 40-foot namesake columns—could be tempted to let its prime waterfront address do all the work. But the club has never rested on its scenic laurels. "Location, location and location" is matched with a high level of service, thanks to a cadre of employees who have worked exclusively for Corinthian for several years. Their experience shows through in their uncanny ability to anticipate guests' desires, providing little touches that may not be much in the larger scheme of things, but are remembered over the years by grateful clients: glasses that get refilled without prompting; a server conjuring up a bobby pin that saves a bride from a hair disaster.

Corinthian's award-winning kitchen team has worked together for years, and is proud of its menu and flexible pricing. Their attitude reflects the club's client-friendly philosophy: Make the venue highly competitive when it comes to cost and value.

Bridal parties can take over the entire second story, an ensemble of four distinctive spaces that tie wonderfully well together to create a terrific flow. People love to circulate here, knowing that each area they stroll to presents its own visual reward. Start with the Grand Ballroom, a redwood-paneled room with a 22-foot-high ceiling, large stage for musicians, imposing stone fireplace and an oak floor that's ready for dancing no matter how you configure the dining tables. Guests often amble into the adjoining solarium, which runs along one side of the ballroom, and take in Corinthian's dramatic bay view through giant picture windows. (With such an impressive backdrop, the solarium is a favorite site for the cake cutting, too.) It accesses an outdoor deck that not only presents a fine harbor and breakwater view, but can function as a bar or reception area. Both the deck and ballroom have doorways to a separate salon that features a granite-topped bar. The bar's nautical-motif plaques, pendants and photos create an enjoyable clubby feel.

Because it offers access to one of the Bay Area's stellar locales at an affordable rate, Corinthian is a "best of both worlds" proposition. It's nice to know that you don't have to choose between the site and service—your guests will take away fond memories of both.

CEREMONY CAPACITY: The Solarium holds 100 seated with additional room for 30 standing guests.

EVENT/RECEPTION CAPACITY: The Ballroom accommodates 250 seated or up to 300 standing guests.

MEETING CAPACITY: The Ballroom seats 300.

FEES & DEPOSITS: A $2,000 deposit is applied towards the total event cost and is required at the time of booking. The facility rental fee ranges $1,600–4,500, depending on your guest count and the date of the event. Fees cover a 5-hour block; extra hours can be negotiated. 80% of the estimated total is due 6 weeks prior to the event, and the balance is due 4 days prior to the event.

Catering is provided; menu prices range $65–85/person, plus a 20% service charge and tax. On average, bar prices range $30–55/person based on consumption, including service and tax.

AVAILABILITY: The Ballroom is available daily 9am–11pm.

SERVICES/AMENITIES:

Catering: provided, no BYO
Kitchen Facilities: n/a
Tables & Chairs: provided
Linens, Silver, etc.: china, silverware, glassware provided; no linens
Restrooms: wheelchair accessible
Dance Floor: yes
Meeting Equipment: limited

Parking: public lot nearby
Accommodations: no guest rooms
Telephone: emergency use only
Outdoor Night Lighting: yes
Outdoor Cooking Facilities: no
Cleanup: provided
View: San Francisco Bay and skyline, Angel Island and Alcatraz

RESTRICTIONS:

Alcohol: provided, or wine and champagne with corkage fee
Smoking: on decks only
Music: amplified OK with volume restrictions

Wheelchair Access: yes, all levels
Insurance: not required
Other: security required

North Coast

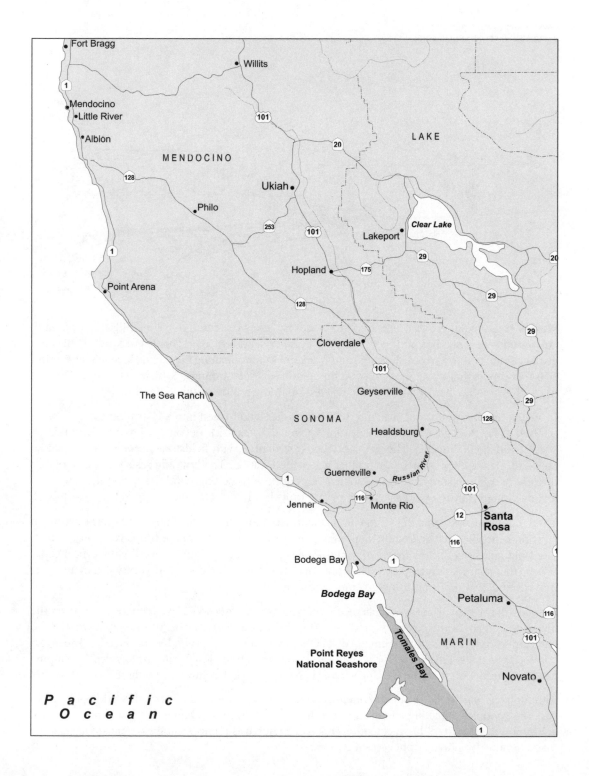

Bodega Harbour Yacht Club

Yacht Club

565 Smith Brothers Road, Bodega Bay
707/875-3519 x40

www.bodegayachtclub.com
avineyard@kempersports.com

● Rehearsal Dinners	Corp. Events/Mtgs.
● Ceremonies	● Private Parties
● Wedding Receptions	Accommodations

West of Petaluma, there's a scenic two-lane road that takes you through rolling hills and past dairy farms and sheep ranches until you reach the coast and Bodega Bay. This is the kind of sheltered estuary small craft owners, fishermen, and weekend sailors all along the Pacific love. It's a beautiful seaside outpost that's been passed by in the "grand scheme of things," which suits the natives just fine—they're quite happy enjoying the relaxed small-town pace of this little port.

In 1970 a historic waterfront structure was refurbished and turned into a charming meeting place dubbed "The Bodega Harbour Yacht Club." Over the years it's become a favorite for wedding parties and special events. The two-story cedar structure, with fieldstone accents, lies beyond a copse of mature cypress trees on a quiet waterside location. The building rests on sturdy pilings directly over the water, so visitors looking out the floor-to-ceiling windows facing the bay often feel as though they're on a vessel slipping out of its berth to go to sea.

These tall windows frame the yacht club's centerpiece stone fireplace. Guests can't resist sitting on its wide hearth to chat and enjoy their champagne, as well as admire the fireplace's construction. The bold fieldstone façade extends from floor to ceiling, and the flue is faced with vertical cedar boards that soar like organ pipes. The entire space is strikingly finished in knotty cedar, an effect that continues in the supporting columns and crossbeams.

Couples often host a pre-wedding reception downstairs, followed by a ceremony next to the fireplace in front of the bayfront windows. Afterwards, the party moves upstairs to a wood-lined mezzanine-style room overlooking the first floor's dramatic glass-and-stone façade. The room comfortably seats 120 guests for a buffet-style dinner. Professional catering services, including food prepared with pride by the club's own chef, are provided exclusively by the Bluewater Bistro.

Although the yacht club is a self-contained building that easily handles both weddings and receptions, couples sometimes hold their ceremony at St. Teresa's church in the town of Bodega, a 10-minute drive from the yacht club. This small church is an appealing Colonial-style building made famous by photographer Ansel Adams.

The club also offers elegant beach ceremonies for couples who want to combine romance and nature. Another amenity is the availability of rental housing and numerous inns in the Bodega Bay area for relatives and guests.

Few places like the yacht club exist on the waterfront between San Francisco and Mendocino. Its architectural beauty, bayside location and scenic harbor views make it a natural for couples seeking a bucolic, yet very civilized, setting.

CEREMONY CAPACITY: The yacht club's ground floor holds 125 seated.

EVENT/RECEPTION CAPACITY: The club holds 120 seated or 200 standing guests.

MEETING CAPACITY: Meetings do not take place at this facility.

FEES & DEPOSITS: A deposit in the amount of $500 is required at the time of reservation. 90% of the estimated total is due within 7 days of the event and the remaining balance is due on the day of the event. These payments are nonrefundable. For receptions only, the club rental fee is $2,500 for a 5-hour period. For receptions with ceremonies, the fee is $3,500 (5 hours plus ceremony time). Buffets range $35–60/person; alcohol, hors d'oeuvres, tax and a 20% service charge are additional.

AVAILABILITY: Year-round, daily, 8am–midnight, including holidays.

SERVICES/AMENITIES:
Catering: provided, no BYO
Kitchen Facilities: n/a
Tables & Chairs: provided
Linens, Silver, etc.: provided
Restrooms: wheelchair accessible
Dance Floor: hardwood floor lower level
Bride's Dressing Area: no
Meeting Equipment: n/a
Other: some coordination

Parking: on-street and complimentary lot
Accommodations: no guest rooms, hotels nearby
Telephone: no
Outdoor Night Lighting: yes
Outdoor Cooking Facilities: no
Cleanup: provided
View: Bodega Bay and marina

RESTRICTIONS:
Alcohol: provided, or wine and champagne corkage $20/bottle
Smoking: outside only
Music: amplified OK indoors until 11pm

Wheelchair Access: yes
Insurance: certificate required

Want to find more venues and services? Check out our informative website, www.HereComesTheGuide.com.

195

Compass Rose Gardens

Private Garden

Corner East Shore & Bay Flat Roads, Bodega Bay

707/875-2343

www.compassrosegardens.com
info@compassrosegardens.com

● Rehearsal Dinners	● Corp. Events/Mtgs.
● Ceremonies	● Private Parties
● Wedding Receptions	Accommodations

When we passed through the Compass Rose Gardens' humble iron gate, we felt as if we had encountered Narnia—the magical, otherworldly kingdom that C.S. Lewis wrote of in his famed children's books. Entering the gardens, you're immersed in a world of unbridled beauty. In every direction the eye is delighted: here the abundant blooms of rhododendrons, irises and camellias; over there delicate Japanese maples, cherry trees and towering redwoods. A year-round running brook unspools the length of the gardens, pausing now and again to calm itself in one of several lovely ponds. It is truly an idyllic place to hold a celebration.

Donna Cook Freeman is the exuberant owner and green thumb responsible for coaxing such beauty from what was once three acres of tangled briars, willows and blackberries. She began work on the grounds in 1986; the foliage was so thick she had to crawl in on her hands and knees to reach the interior. There she sat for hours in contemplation, dreaming her garden into existence. A 10-year labor of love ensued, during which Donna and her family hauled, excavated, pruned and thinned. They built footbridges and cottages, planted flowers and trees, eventually wrangling a magnificent garden from a tenacious coastal jungle. Then in homage to Bodega Bay's long seafaring history, she christened the gardens "Compass Rose" (a compass rose is the starlike insignia found on mariners' maps and compasses).

A variety of scenic spots are available to tie the knot; however, most couples prefer to marry on an oval lawn overlooking the property's largest pond. Guests are seated on the opposite bank (still within earshot) where they are afforded a perfect view of the bride and groom as they exchange vows underneath a venerable willow. After the ceremony, folks can lose themselves along the gardens' meandering paths before joining the feasting and festivities at the handsome pavilion at the far side of the gardens. The newlyweds may want to slip away to share a quiet moment in the meditation garden. Nestled in a ring of redwoods, it's just the place to collect oneself after all the hubbub. Couples are also welcome to participate in what has now become a Compass Rose tradition—the planting of a "wedding" sapling or placing a personalized birdhouse in a nearby tree, which serves as both living memory and future promise for their journey together.

Although the Compass Rose is an ideal spot for outdoor weddings, it is also an excellent gathering place for any number of events—seminars, retreats, bar mitzvahs and anniversaries. For those who desire lodging nearby, there are both luxury hotels and more modest accommodations nearby. And movie buffs will be interested in the gazebo from Hitchcock's famous film *The Birds*. The owners of the gardens, who were extras in the movie, have decided to share their favorite memento by setting it into a hillside where everyone can enjoy it.

The Compass Rose Gardens used to be Bodega Bay's best kept secret, but given their extraordinary beauty, of course word got out. They were also featured in *HGTV, A&E, Town and Country Magazine,* radio and other media! So if your heart is set on a garden party, call sooner rather than later—this is one opportunity you won't want to miss!

CEREMONY & EVENT/RECEPTION CAPACITY: The Ceremony Area holds 200 seated and the Pavilion up to 150 seated guests.

MEETING CAPACITY: Meetings spaces accommodate up to 200 guests.

FEES & DEPOSITS: 50% of the rental fee is required to reserve your date, the balance and a $1,500 refundable security deposit are due 1 month prior to the event. Engagement photos and a 1-hour rehearsal are included. The weekend rental fee starts at $4,900; call for midweek rates. Extra hours are available.

AVAILABILITY: Daily, May through October.

SERVICES/AMENITIES:

Catering: select from preferred list or with approval

Kitchen Facilities: yes, limited outdoor

Tables & Chairs: through caterer

Linens, Silver, etc.: through caterer

Restrooms: not wheelchair accessible

Dance Floor: large dance area

Bride's Dressing Area: yes

Meeting Equipment: BYO

Parking: ample on-street and in private lot

Accommodations: no guest rooms, hotels nearby

Telephone: no

Outdoor Night Lighting: yes

Outdoor Cooking Facilities: yes, area available

Cleanup: caterer or renter

View: gardens, pond, creek and redwoods

RESTRICTIONS:

Alcohol: BYO, insurance required, no corkage fees

Smoking: not allowed

Music: amplified OK until 10pm

Wheelchair Access: limited

Insurance: certificate required

Sea Ranch Lodge

Restaurant & Lodge

60 Sea Walk Drive, The Sea Ranch
800/732-7262, 707/785-2371

www.searanchlodge.com
info@searanchlodge.com

- Rehearsal Dinners
- Ceremonies
- Wedding Receptions
- Corp. Events/Mtgs.
- Private Parties
- Accommodations

In the early morning, a light mist veils the coast. Weathered redwood buildings float into view, hugged by deep green stands of cypress trees. Far below, the sea crashes against the rocks, and the rugged, serpentine coastline fades away into the fog. You blink, half expecting that when you open your eyes it will all disappear. But it doesn't. And you begin to understand why so many people consider The Sea Ranch a magical place.

Perched high on a bluff, the Sea Ranch Lodge is part of a small community of individualists who cherish the soothing solitude of this North Coast haven. And for those who don't have the luxury of living here permanently, the lodge provides a temporary getaway. It's also a coveted location for a wedding.

Getting married outdoors here is an exhilarating experience. The short path down from the lodge that brings you to the two ceremony sites cuts through a meadow of golden grass bordered by wildflowers in purple, yellow and white. As you walk, you hear the surf pounding and smell the ocean's scent in the air. Bihler Point is a breathtaking, secluded spot on the bluffs with a panoramic view of the ocean. However, there's only standing room for 25 people; no chairs or other furniture are permitted. Most ceremonies take place on nearby Black Point Lawn, where you can tie the knot followed by cocktails next to a charmingly rustic 1890s barn that overlooks the shoreline extending for miles in both directions. For a spiritual touch at either site, have a bagpiper or flutist play a special melody.

If you'd rather have your celebration inside the lodge, the facility has two interconnecting spaces, each with redwood walls and ocean views. The two-level Fireside Room is perfect for a cozy reception, elopement, renewal of vows or rehearsal dinner. A large river rock fireplace dominates one wall, while art from the Spindrift Gallery is showcased on another. A huge picture window and a skylight let in natural light. The adjacent Solarium is an intimate atrium used for cocktails, hors d'oeuvres and mingling. Completely enclosed by glass, it affords a floor-to-ceiling view of the meadows, ocean and sky.

Larger receptions are held in a festive party tent, which is set up near the guestrooms. Bordered by a high, weathered fence and fronted by greenery, it feels quite private. The spacious pole tent, included in one of Sea Ranch Lodge's wedding packages, comes with a dance floor, oak bar, flooring, heat, sound, and more. Twinkling perimeter lights add sparkle at night, and you can customize the décor, too, with paper lanterns, crystal chandeliers, long farm tables, or whatever suits the style of your event.

The beauty of The Sea Ranch, aside from its abundant natural attributes, is that you and your guests can stay here long enough to really relax and enjoy it. Recently renovated with stylish contemporary appointments, guest rooms are uncluttered and comfortable; all have ocean views and most have fireplaces (but, to preserve the tranquility, none have televisions). Diversions include exploring the many beaches, hiking along miles of trails, and playing golf on The Sea Ranch's links-style course. Black Point Grill serves all meals, which feature internationally inspired California cuisine with an emphasis on the freshest local ingredients.

Not getting married? Don't let that stop you from coming to the Sea Ranch Lodge. The setting is just as uplifting for a romantic weekend, corporate retreat, or family reunion. Let's face it, when the earth was created, some places ended up much more enchanting than others. This is one of them.

CEREMONY CAPACITY: The outdoor oceanfront ceremony site accommodates 2–125 guests. Indoors, the Fireside Room holds up to 50 seated guests, which makes it perfect for a small wedding, commitment ceremony, elopement or renewal of vows.

EVENT/RECEPTION CAPACITY: The Fireside Room holds 72 seated and tented space can hold 73–125 seated guests.

MEETING CAPACITY: The Fireside Room holds 50 seated theater-style, 33 seated conference- or classroom-style.

FEES & DEPOSITS: To secure your date, a nonrefundable deposit of 50% of the anticipated event total is required, with guest room minimums based on the number of attendees. Site fees range $500–6,900 depending on the guest count. Catering menu starts at $75/person and wedding dinner packages, including food, wine and beverages, start at $149/person with upgrades and customizations available. Room rates run $209–379 based on double occupancy and include a full, prepared-to-order breakfast in the oceanview dining room. Selected dog-friendly rooms are available; there is a one-time charge of $50/pet with a limit of 2 pets per room.

AVAILABILITY: Year-round, daily, anytime.

SERVICES/AMENITIES:

Catering: provided
Kitchen Facilities: n/a
Tables & Chairs: provided
Linens, Silver, etc.: provided
Restrooms: wheelchair accessible
Dance Floor: included in tent package
Bride's & Groom's Dressing Areas: CBA
Meeting Equipment: wireless internet access, easels, projectors

Parking: ample
Accommodations: 19 guest rooms
Telephone: guest phones
Outdoor Night Lighting: access only
Outdoor Cooking Facilities: n/a
Cleanup: provided
View: Pacific Ocean, coastline, meadows, cypress trees
Other: event coordination, spa treatments in private treatment rooms, recreational activity planning and more; call for details

RESTRICTIONS:

Alcohol: provided, or BYO with corkage fee
Smoking: not permitted
Music: amplified OK with restrictions

Wheelchair Access: yes
Insurance: CBA

Peninsula

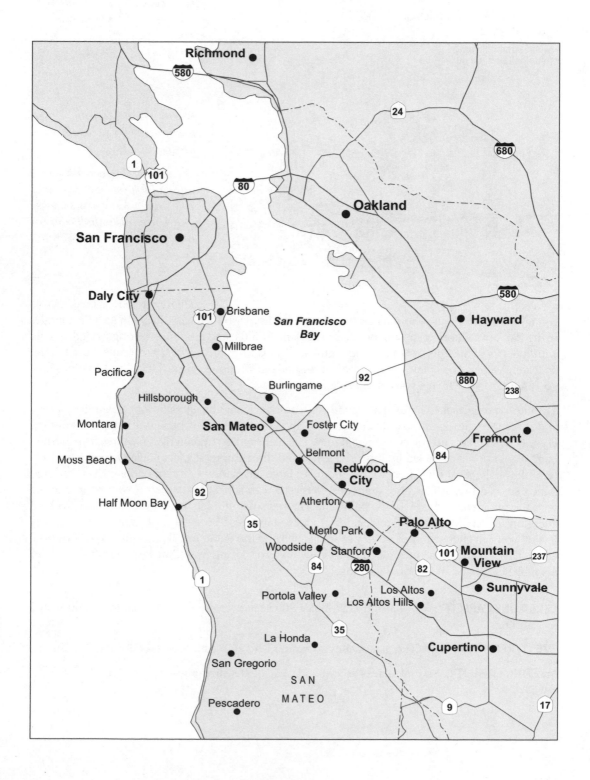

Ralston Hall Mansion
at Notre Dame de Namur University

1500 Ralston Avenue, Belmont
650/508-3501

www.ralstonhall.com
ralstonhall@ndnu.edu

Historic Mansion

- Rehearsal Dinners
- Ceremonies
- Wedding Receptions
- Corp. Events/Mtgs.
- Private Parties
- Accommodations

Ralston Hall Mansion closed temporarily for renovations in April of 2012.

The date of the reopening was unavailable when Here Comes The Guide went to press, so please visit www.ralstonhall.com for information on the venue's current status.

This registered National Historic Landmark is a stunning Victorian mansion, completed in 1867 by William Chapman Ralston, founder of the Bank of California. Ralston purchased the land in 1864, and modified the original Italian villa with touches of Steamboat Gothic and Victorian details to create a lavish and opulent estate. The delicately etched glass panes of the front doors, and the windows dressed in striped awnings give you an indication of what you'll see inside.

The interior reflects the charm of a bygone era, featuring a magnificent ballroom, delightful parlors, and a picturesque opera box gallery. Each room is decorated with beautiful antiques, stunning crystal chandeliers and colorful Oriental rugs. The ballroom is particularly appealing. Its patterned hardwood floor is encircled by mirrored walls, and three impressive chandeliers hang gracefully from the skylight. At the far end of the room is a large bay window, with a curving fabric-covered bench seat and regal matching draperies. Musicians can set up in an alcove without interfering with the grandeur and flow of the ballroom. The spacious dining rooms were decorated with an attention to detail that is unparalleled by today's standards. Because of Ralston Hall's size and layout, you can choose from a variety of setups utilizing the entire first floor or the expansive front lawn. This facility is one of the Peninsula's few mansion locations and makes a terrific venue for a sophisticated and memorable wedding.

CEREMONY CAPACITY: The Ralston lawn holds 200 seated or standing; the ballroom 200 seated or standing.

EVENT/RECEPTION CAPACITY: The facility accommodates 200 seated guests or 275 standing guests.

MEETING CAPACITY: Several spaces accommodate 13–150 seated guests.

FEES & DEPOSITS: For weddings and special events, a $4,500 booking deposit is required to reserve your date. This amount includes a $500 refundable security deposit. For an 8-hour event, the rental fee runs $7,000–9,500 and is payable 6 months prior to the function. Fees include a facility manager and 2 hours for setup and 1 hour for cleanup. The security deposit is returned if the property is left in good condition.

The fee for meetings and other special events is $400/hour, Monday–Thursday, with a 4-hour minimum.

AVAILABILITY: Year-round, daily, 9am–midnight.

SERVICES/AMENITIES:

Catering: select from exclusive list
Kitchen Facilities: moderate
Tables & Chairs: provided
Linens, Silver, etc.: through caterer
Restrooms: wheelchair accessible
Dance Floor: provided
Bride's Dressing Area: yes
Meeting Equipment: BYO

Parking: ample
Accommodations: no guest rooms
Telephone: local calls only
Outdoor Night Lighting: limited
Outdoor Cooking Facilities: BBQ
Cleanup: caterer
View: lawn with fountain
Other: security available

RESTRICTIONS:

Alcohol: through caterer or BYO
Smoking: not permitted inside
Music: amplified OK

Wheelchair Access: yes
Insurance: certificate required
Other: candles not permitted

This is important! Tell locations you're reading HERE COMES THE GUIDE and ask if our information is still current.

203

Mission Blue Center

Community Center

475 Mission Blue Drive, Brisbane
415/508-2143

www.brisbaneca.org/living/community-center
www.ablacktieaffairinc.com
facilities@ci.brisbane.ca.us

● Rehearsal Dinners   ● Corp. Events/Mtgs.
● Ceremonies   ● Private Parties
● Wedding Receptions   Accommodations

Brisbane is like the librarian in romantic comedies whose beauty—until the doofus leading man finally figures out to take off her glasses and undo her hair—remains unseen. It's hidden away in a nook of Mt. San Bruno and isolated by wetlands from the tens of thousands of commuters who pass by it daily on Highway 101.

But those who leave the freeway and do some exploring will find an unspoiled little town that climbs up its hill like an Italian fishing village. Brisbane has its share of wealth, but it has yet to be yuppified or see its main street turned into a stretch of chain stores. You sense right away that this is a tight-knit place that knows it has a good thing going. Part of that good thing is Mission Blue, the community center the town built in 2000. It has everything a building of its type should have, including appealing architecture, a great hillside location with a fine view, and the ability to seamlessly accommodate a wedding and reception. There's a poetic touch, too: Mission Blue is named after a rare butterfly whose preservation inspired the saving of open space on Mt. San Bruno, the imposing palomino-colored ridge that dominates the view from the center's terrace.

Mission Blue's main entrance takes you to a soaring glass-walled foyer that's often used for a post-ceremony champagne reception. It opens into the spacious room at the center's heart, cleverly designed with visual cues that separate it into two distinct areas. The first half of the room, with its hardwood floor and light-colored walls, is perfect for an indoor ceremony or dancing. The second half, carpeted and tiled, and painted a slightly darker color, is ideal for dining. The two areas can be partitioned or used in combination, and are easily accessed from the nearby full-service kitchen.

Glass doors lead from the interior to a beautifully fashioned, stone-finished terrace that runs the length of Mission Blue's west and north sides. It sweeps out from the building toward a well-kept lawn that many couples have used to recite their vows. Standing on the terrace, you can look across a valley to Mt. San Bruno, and south to a view of Brisbane's little houses clambering up the hill. There are fine design touches everywhere, including a wooden pergola at one end of the lawn and a colonnade along the terrace whose eye-catching beams and supports call to mind the sophisticated carpentry of a Chinese temple. Planters and flowerbeds abound, and the simple black railing that stands between the lawn and the hillside is sculptural in form. Even Mission

Blue's exterior colors have a sensual appeal—the olive green, creamy white and light chocolate tones give it an almost luscious appearance.

This site's architects certainly understood how to create a welcoming place: Mission Blue is a harmonious interplay between space and light, colors and materials, indoors and outdoors. But when you have your celebration here, you won't be thinking about how all the elements work so well together—you'll just be having a great time.

CEREMONY CAPACITY: Mission Blue Center holds up to 250 seated indoors and 200 seated outdoors.

EVENT/RECEPTION & MEETING CAPACITY: This location holds 250 seated at tables or 350 guests seated theater-style. The large room can be broken into smaller spaces.

FEES & DEPOSITS: A $500 refundable cleaning deposit is required to reserve your date; the balance is due 21 days prior to the event. The rental fee is $400/hour, discounts are available for Brisbane residents and for partial hall rentals. Meals range $18–26/person. Tax, alcohol and a 15% service charge are additional.

AVAILABILITY: Year-round, daily, 8am–midnight.

SERVICES/AMENITIES:

Catering: preferred caterer is *A Black Tie Affair Catering*
Kitchen Facilities: full kitchen
Tables & Chairs: provided
Linens, Silver, etc.: through caterer
Restrooms: wheelchair accessible
Dance Floor: yes
Bride's Dressing Area: CBA
Meeting Equipment: wall-mounted projection screen, LCD projector, PA system, CD/tape player, DVD/VCR, stage

Parking: 40-space lot and on-street
Accommodations: no guest rooms
Telephone: house phone
Outdoor Night Lighting: access only
Outdoor Cooking Facilities: no
Cleanup: caterer or renter
View: Mt. San Bruno and bay
Other: event coordination, cake, ice carving; chocolate fountain available through caterer

RESTRICTIONS:

Alcohol: provided by caterer
Smoking: outdoors only
Music: amplified OK

Wheelchair Access: yes
Insurance: proof of liability provided by caterer or renter
Other: no wall decorations

Hyatt Regency San Francisco Airport

Hotel

1333 Bayshore Highway, Burlingame
650/696-3025

sanfranciscoairport.hyatt.com
thomas.toomey@hyatt.com

- Rehearsal Dinners
- Ceremonies
- Wedding Receptions
- Corp. Events/Mtgs.
- Private Parties
- Accommodations

Less than half an hour from San Francisco and minutes from the airport, this first-class hotel is popular for high-profile conventions and corporate functions. But brides in search of convenience and lots of options will find the red carpet is rolled out for weddings, too.

First impressions really count, and the Hyatt Regency in Burlingame wows you at the entrance with its soaring, multi-tiered, tropical atrium. Rising skyward more than nine stories, it's filled with plants, trees, a soothing water wall and cafés, making you feel like you're in an outdoor plaza. A refreshing change from the typical hotel lobby, the atrium is not only a great place to "people watch," but it's also a winning spot for a sophisticated cocktail reception.

If you're the kind of person who has as many friends in real life as you do on Facebook and you'd like to invite all of them to share your special day, then the Grand Peninsula Ballroom is for you. Start with cocktails and hors d'oeuvres in the open, airy Grand Foyer, which is separated from the atrium by a bank of banana trees and queen palms. At the appointed hour, four sets of double doors will be opened to reveal the expansive, plush ballroom. With fabric-covered walls, a coffered ceiling and eye-catching chandeliers dripping with crystal beads, this is a fitting backdrop for even the most formal affair. If you'd also like to get married here, you can easily section off part of the room's 18,000 square feet for a lovely ceremony site, complete with its own entrance.

Tucked away in another section of the lobby level is the Regency Ballroom and its adjoining foyer. Sleekly modern in design, it features opaque glass sconces, honey-toned walls and a high ceiling with rows of recessed spotlights. You can use part or all of this space, which has a large rectangular center section and two smaller side sections.

For a celebration site that's a bit less conventional, there's the contemporary, tented Poolside Pavilion. Recently renovated and completely climate controlled, this "bride's favorite" is fronted by a graceful, wisteria-covered arbor and looks out to the shimmering pool.

Need an interesting place for a rehearsal dinner or engagement party? Try Scalini, a private party venue with big-city style. Lots of dark wood, a wraparound bar, Art Deco pendant lights and cool, black & white subway tiles would convince you that you were in Chicago or New York except for one thing: a view of the bay through a wall of windows.

The Hyatt offers a range of packages, and their catering team is happy to custom-tailor a menu for your event, as well as accommodate cultural or ethnic needs. Plus, if you take advantage of their flexible Personal Preference Dining option, your friends and family will be able to select their favorite entrée from among four choices. In addition to having a great time at your wedding, your out-of-town guests will enjoy all the hotel's amenities, including a glass-walled fitness room, pool, lively sports bar and free trolleys to area attractions.

CEREMONY CAPACITY: The hotel holds 2,500 seated guests indoors.

EVENT/RECEPTION & MEETING CAPACITY: The facility can accommodate 1,500 seated or 1,800 standing guests indoors and 250 standing outdoors.

FEES & DEPOSITS: 20% of the total event cost is required to reserve your date and the balance is due 14 days prior to the event. Rental fees range $500–1,500 depending on the space rented. Meals range $53–86/person. Tax, alcohol and a 22% service charge are additional.

AVAILABILITY: Year-round, daily, 6am–2am.

SERVICES/AMENITIES:

Catering: provided
Kitchen Facilities: n/a
Tables & Chairs: provided
Linens, Silver, etc.: provided
Restrooms: wheelchair accessible
Dance Floor: provided
Bride's Dressing Area: CBA
Meeting Equipment: provided

Parking: large lots
Accommodations: 789 guest rooms
Telephone: house or office phone
Outdoor Night Lighting: CBA
Outdoor Cooking Facilities: no
Cleanup: provided
View: garden, landscaped grounds, pool area
Other: A/V equipment, event coordination

RESTRICTIONS:

Alcohol: provided, no BYO
Smoking: outside only
Music: amplified OK

Wheelchair Access: yes
Insurance: not required

Wedgewood Wedding & Banquet Center
at Crystal Springs Golf Course

Event Facility

6650 Golf Course Drive, Burlingame
866/966-3009

www.wedgewoodbanquet.com/crystal-springs
sales@wedgewoodbanquet.com

- Rehearsal Dinners
- Ceremonies
- Wedding Receptions
- Corp. Events/Mtgs.
- Private Parties
- Accommodations

One of the most picturesque wedding sites in the Bay Area has something very few people ever have the privilege of seeing: a bird's-eye view of the protected land around Crystal Springs Reservoir. San Francisco stores its precious drinking water in this jewel of a lake, and the city jealously guards access to the reservoir—only rangers, scientists and certain officials can visit the heavily wooded semi-wilderness surrounding it.

But if you wed outdoors at Crystal Springs Golf Course, you are among the rare outsiders who get to enjoy this vista, and with it comes much more than simple bragging rights. The ceremony site, a city-owned meadow at the southern end of the golf club, has a gazebo that stands on a grassy knoll overlooking the reservoir. The view from here is sensational, with glistening reservoir waters below and tree-covered ridges behind it. In the distance, high hills slope toward the bay. There are no houses in sight, and deer often graze nearby. The backdrop is so spectacular that the gazebo needs little adornment—put some flowers in front or over the entry, and voilà, all eyes are upon it. There's plenty of room for a limo to drop off the bride, and if she wants to add a little more pizzazz to the moment, she can arrive in a horse-drawn carriage. A well-tamped earthen aisle cuts through a beautifully tended lawn to the gazebo, where the couple exchanges vows.

The reception takes place up a tree- and greens-lined road at the Wedgewood Banquet Center. The club's main building, painted creamy white with gray-green trim, is set at the edge of gentle terraces that drop toward the reservoir. To reach its two banquet rooms and deck, you walk along a red-carpeted terrace that has a sweeping view down to the golf course. Best of all is spotting the deer that placidly graze the course.

The Wedgewood's Vista Room is the primary dining-reception area. The entire west wall, which faces the Vista Deck, is glass windows and doors, with airy, white sheers framing the view outside. If you reserve this space, you also get the adjoining Vista Deck, a large glassed-in area shaded by a canopy. The vista looks west toward woods and north toward neighboring hills and the golf course's gorgeous landscape.

Wedgewood's all-inclusive packages offer the best values in the Bay Area, saving time and money, and make planning your event here a breeze. Services range from a basic ceremony at the gazebo with seating (and, of course, the view!), to such amenities as invitations, DJ, food, cake, beverages, florals and the honeymoon suite.

The elements for a fine, fine day are here in splendid array: the gazebo in its unforgettable setting; a personable, attentive staff; good food; fresh, sea-kissed air (the ocean is only a few ridges away); and nature's intense blues and greens. Lastly, nearby Highway 280 makes the course easily accessible from San Francisco, the Peninsula and the South Bay. Now, that's a list that should satisfy anyone.

CEREMONY CAPACITY: This location accommodates up to 300 guests indoors or 400 outdoors.

EVENT/RECEPTION CAPACITY: Indoors, the Vista Room holds 300 seated or 375 standing guests.

MEETING CAPACITY: Event spaces accommodate 50–200 seated guests.

FEES & DEPOSITS: 25% of the estimated event total is required to reserve your date. The next 25% is due 90 days prior to the event; the balance is due 10 days prior. Wedding area fees range $1,000–2,000 depending on services needed. There is no room charge for the reception area. All-inclusive packages start at $40/person. Tax, alcohol and a 20% service charge are additional. There are several wedding packages available.

AVAILABILITY: Year-round, anytime.

SERVICES/AMENITIES:

Catering: provided
Kitchen Facilities: n/a
Tables & Chairs: provided
Linens, Silver, etc.: provided
Restrooms: wheelchair accessible
Dance Floor: yes
Brides Dressing Area: yes
Meeting Equipment: CBA, extra charge

Parking: large lot
Accommodations: no guest rooms
Telephone: emergency use only
Outdoor Night Lighting: yes
Outdoor Cooking Facilities: no
Cleanup: provided
View: fairways, lake, meadows, mountains
Other: event coordination

RESTRICTIONS:

Alcohol: provided
Smoking: outside only
Music: amplified OK with some restrictions

Wheelchair Access: yes
Insurance: not required
Other: no rice, confetti or glitter; no open flames

Overwhelmed? Use the search criteria on www.HereComesTheGuide.com to narrow down your choices.

209

Crowne Plaza Foster City-San Mateo

Hotel

1221 Chess Drive, Foster City
650/295-6129
www.eventscp.com
irene@cpfcc.com

- Rehearsal Dinners
- Ceremonies
- Wedding Receptions
- Corp. Events/Mtgs.
- Private Parties
- Accommodations

"Location, location, location!" may be the byword of people who deal in real estate, but hoteliers are pretty hip to the idea, too. That's certainly the case at the Crowne Plaza Foster City-San Mateo, a bustling 351-room hotel conveniently situated at a major Bay Area crossroads. Right off the western end of the San Mateo Bridge, and just minutes south of San Francisco International Airport, it's easily accessible from The City, South Bay, East Bay and the Peninsula. Free parking and a complimentary airport shuttle to SFO are provided, and nearby restaurants, shopping and parks add even more to the hotel's appeal.

But a great location is only part of what makes the Crowne Plaza a thriving site for weddings. The five-story garden atrium certainly has brides talking. Its most impressive feature has to be the room-length waterfall along the east side: Four streams of water cascade among flower-strewn rocks, creating a soothing and arresting backdrop. For obvious reasons, many couples love having their ceremony in here. The two-level space (split between a bar and café) can be closed off with lattice, and decorated with flowers and an arch. Brides often descend dramatically from above in one of the hotel's glass elevators, then walk to a wooden bridge at the center of the atrium to exchange vows. Palms, ficus and other plants give this glassed-in area a tropical feel.

Receptions usually start in the Magellan Foyer where cocktails are set up, and then move into the adjoining ballroom, which can be divided into four sections depending on the size of your event. Rehearsal dinners and post-wedding brunches are often held on site, too. The Marco Polo Room, directly off the atrium, is especially well suited for smaller gatherings where family and close friends want to mingle and catch up with each other. An abundance of rich wood creates a lot of warmth, and the glass wall facing the atrium can be curtained for privacy or left open for people watching.

Bridal suites, which are a standard part of the hotel's wedding package, are located in the Executive Tower, a twin building reached via a covered driveway. The Crowne Club there has a cocktail and hors d'oeuvre serving area that you can reserve for an intimate reception. The adjacent Bay View Ballroom, which hosts dinners and dancing and is sometimes used for ceremonies, is a favorite with smaller wedding parties. For musical entertainment, bring your own band or DJ or, if your event is on a Friday or Saturday night, you have another option: Accompany your guests over to the Clubhouse Bistro just off the atrium, where the house DJ rocks the crowd three nights a week.

The final component of this hotel's appeal is its experienced wedding staff. They're not only flexible about letting you decorate early so you'll have plenty of time to spare, they also go out of their way to accommodate the needs of almost any ethnic group. For example, when there's a traditional Chinese wedding, which involves a pre-ceremony tea ritual, the staff here always sets aside a proper space for it.

The wedding manager says the first thing she asks any prospective client is, "What is it that you want to do?" When she gets the answer to that question, she and her team quickly go about the business of making each reception reflect the couple's wishes.

CEREMONY CAPACITY: The Atrium holds 70 seated guests.

EVENT/RECEPTION CAPACITY: Various rooms hold up to 650 seated or 800 standing guests. Smaller events can be accommodated; call for detailed configuration options.

MEETING CAPACITY: Event spaces accommodate 25–650 seated guests.

FEES & DEPOSITS: A $2,500 deposit is required to reserve your date and a second deposit, which is equal to 50% of your estimated event total, is due 4 months after the original booking date; the final balance is due 10 days prior to the event. There are no separate room rental fees. Meals range $36–90/person. Packages are available ranging $68–105/person. A 20% service charge and tax are additional. A $4/chair ceremony setup fee and a $3/person cake-cutting fee may also apply. Group room rates are available, as is a complimentary bridal suite for the wedding couple. Call for details about honeymoon packages.

AVAILABILITY: Year-round, daily, 6am–1am.

SERVICES/AMENITIES:
Catering: provided
Kitchen Facilities: n/a
Tables & Chairs: provided
Linens, Silver, etc.: provided
Restrooms: wheelchair accessible
Dance Floor: yes
Bride's & Groom's Dressing Areas: yes
Meeting Equipment: full range

Parking: complimentary self-parking
Accommodations: 351 guest rooms
Telephone: pay phones
Outdoor Night Lighting: CBA
Outdoor Cooking Facilities: no
Cleanup: provided
View: bay views from some spaces
Other: event coordination

RESTRICTIONS:
Alcohol: provided
Smoking: outside only
Music: amplified OK indoors

Wheelchair Access: yes
Insurance: not required

Long Branch Saloon and Farms

Wild West Town

321 Verde Road, Half Moon Bay
650/726-3117
www.longbranchfarms.net
events@longbranchfarms.net

● Rehearsal Dinners	● Corp. Events/Mtgs.
● Ceremonies	● Private Parties
● Wedding Receptions	Accommodations

Hidden away just off Highway 1 south of Half Moon Bay, Long Branch Farms is a 46-acre spread with pastures, paddocks, horses and other assorted critters. That's the "Farms" part. What's got everyone buzzing, though, is "the Saloon" part—or rather, the faux frontier town that includes the Saloon… It all started with local businessman Kevin Palmer, whose lifetime fascination with Americana led to an impressive collection of memorabilia. He also had a dream, shared by his wife Jill, of creating a replica Old West town to serve as a novel party venue. Their vision and hard work paid off, and today the Palmers host weddings that are chock-full of personality.

The first thing guests see when they arrive is a massive open-pit barbecue, usually already crackling with aromatic victuals. Next, they begin their stroll down "Main Street," a wide unpaved avenue flanked by old-fashioned storefronts and pioneer accoutrements: a dressmaker's shop, a smithy, a livery stable, antique barber chairs, the mercantile, and the Hotel NoTell, a wink to bridal couples.

Finally guests reach a barn-style chapel poised against a backdrop of tree-cloaked hills. Beautiful and intimate, the cozy chapel includes original stained-glass windows, exquisite fixtures and pews from one of San Francisco's most historic churches. Ceremonies are usually held like they were in olden times—with the front doors wide open and onlookers gathered on the entryway deck. Alternatively, vows are exchanged with the doorway framing the couple, and guests looking on from the street. An altar can also be set up in a neighboring meadow. All types of ceremonies are welcome here, each embracing the setting's heartwarming simplicity.

While the newlyweds explore the many whimsical photo ops, guests engage in friendly competitions of archery, slingshot, lasso toss or miniature golf. They can even pan for gold! Take the fun inside the spacious Saloon for light-hearted games of chance, or belly up to the massive wood bar that came from *The Quick and The Dead* movie set. Handsomely constructed, the Saloon boasts a rich hardwood floor, vaulted open-beam ceiling and rough-hewn log trim. Gilt-framed mirrors hang on the walls, along with countless Western artifacts that enhance the Saloon's authentic character.

Indoor dining takes place in the glamorous Reception Parlor, reminding you that the West wasn't just about roughing it. High society would approve of the Parlor's centerpiece: the original mirrored bar from San Francisco's posh Palace Hotel. Elegant chandeliers and red-flocked wallpaper lend additional turn-of-the-century élan.

Outdoor receptions in the middle of Main Street take on a rustic charm, whether arranged with traditional rounds or long banquet tables laden with hearty fare (remember that barbecue?). At one end of the street, Adirondack chairs cluster around a roaring campfire, the perfect place for s'mores or snuggling under the wool ponchos and blankets that the Palmers keep on hand.

Some couples play up the Old West theme, while others use Long Branch as their private country-casual gathering spot, relishing the vintage atmosphere. Expressions of personal style are encouraged, like bridesmaids in cowboy boots and table numbers strung on a clothesline. The Palmers have plenty of ideas, as well as several antique vehicles for grand entrances and exits. They also customize wedding packages and connect you with local vendors.

Genuine, imaginative and surprisingly affordable, Long Branch Saloon and Farms is truly one-of-a-kind.

CEREMONY, EVENT/RECEPTION CAPACITY: The site holds 75 seated indoors, and 300 seated guests outdoors. Larger events can also be arranged.

MEETING CAPACITY: The meeting room seats 75 indoors.

FEES & DEPOSITS: 25% of the total event cost is required to reserve your date and the balance is due 14 days prior to the event. Rental fees start at $2,500 and vary depending on the guest count. Meals start at $25/person. Tax and alcohol are additional.

AVAILABILITY: Year-round, daily, until 10pm.

SERVICES/AMENITIES:

Catering: provided, choose from preferred list or BYO
Kitchen Facilities: limited
Tables & Chairs: provided, CBA
Linens, Silver, etc.: provided or BYO
Restrooms: wheelchair accessible
Dance Floor: provided
Bride's Dressing Area: yes
Meeting Equipment: some provided including A/V equipment, more CBA or BYO

Parking: large lot
Accommodations: no guest rooms
Telephone: guest phone
Outdoor Night Lighting: provided
Outdoor Cooking Facilities: BBQ on site
Cleanup: provided
View: landscaped grounds, garden; panorama of forest, hills, fields, mountains and valley
Other: clergy on staff, event coordination

RESTRICTIONS:

Alcohol: provided or BYO
Smoking: designated areas only
Music: amplified OK with restrictions

Wheelchair Access: yes
Insurance: liability required

Oceano Hotel and Spa

Waterfront Hotel and Spa

280 Capistrano Road, Half Moon Bay
650/726-5400

www.oceanohalfmoonbay.com
nancyn@oceanohalfmoonbay.com

- Rehearsal Dinners
- Ceremonies
- Wedding Receptions
- Corp. Events/Mtgs.
- Private Parties
- Accommodations

A quaint, artsy Main Street... miles of shoreside trails and nature habitats...world-class golf, surfing and fishing.... As if there wasn't enough to love about Half Moon Bay, we've discovered another compelling reason to celebrate in this secluded oasis: Oceano Hotel and Spa. Conceived as a cutting-edge model of environmental sensitivity, Oceano is not only one of the greenest hotels in California, it's also one of the most inviting.

First off, consider the location, just a few minutes north of town center overlooking Pillar Point Harbor. Sailboats bob and sway in the marina, dolphins cavort beyond the breakers, and in the distance the Santa Cruz coastline is etched along a watery-blue panorama. The hotel lobby's creamy marble elegance is equally uplifting, and the Great Room just beyond the foyer has all the charm of a luxurious, sun-washed beach house. Three stories of guest rooms encircle this cozy yet airy space, bathed in a natural light from its vaulted atrium ceiling. The magic of the sea whispers at Oceano: A replica of a schooner sits atop a grand fireplace mantle, and overstuffed sofas surround a whimsical glass coffee table that encases starfish, seashells and coastal mementos in a bed of sand. The entire boutique hotel is peppered with such well-chosen decorative details, all of which maintain the seaside motif.

You and your event guests will also be delighted by your spacious accommodations. High ceilings, fireplaces and plantation-style furniture make you want to move right in. Thoughtful amenities like Aveda bath products, super-soft towels and organic bamboo sheets seduce you with plush comfort. Step out to your oceanview balcony and experience Half Moon Bay's dual personality: On an easy, breezy afternoon, sunlight glistens on the waves and brown pelicans dive for their dinner; then in an instant, curls of mist roll in with the setting sun and the bellow of foghorns adds a romantic mystique.

Speaking of romance, ceremonies are utterly picturesque out on the Wedding Garden, a sweep of landscaped lawn facing the harbor. A stone pathway leads to a white gazebo where you can exchange vows. Afterwards, serve cocktails on the adjoining Cypress Courtyard before retiring to the ballroom for the reception.

This beautiful new banquet space is embellished with ornate crown molding, Art Deco wall sconces and a trio of crystal chandeliers. The soothing neutral palette—soft gold, vanilla and a touch of sea-green—lends an upscale ambiance to your wedding dinner. (Incidentally, Oceano has superb cuisine, and their knowledgeable and experienced Executive Chef will sit down with you to design your menu.) When it's time for dancing, five sets of double doors swing open to the Atrium, a stylish annex aglow in moonlight from a skylit ceiling.

Though Half Moon Bay has plenty of diversions, your guests really don't need to leave Oceano at all. There's an on-site spa offering indulgent treatments, and the hotel's shopping promenade, Harbor Village, features select boutiques, cafés and galleries—all with colorful façades reminiscent of a Nantucket village. The enclosed promenade, which is flooded with natural light thanks to a greenhouse roof, is a great place for a stroll year-round and it's also available for events.

Perhaps the most endearing aspect of this sea-inspired sanctuary is its warm and enthusiastic service: The staff is genuinely eager to help you realize your own personal wedding vision. In short, Oceano is a real class act.

CEREMONY CAPACITY: The hotel holds 250 seated indoors and 350 seated outdoors.

EVENT/RECEPTION CAPACITY: The hotel accommodates 350 seated or 450 standing guests indoors and 400 seated or 800 standing outdoors.

MEETING CAPACITY: The hotel holds 350 seated guests.

FEES & DEPOSITS: 30% of the total event cost is required to reserve your date and the balance is due 2 weeks prior to the event. Rental fees range $1,000–5,000 depending on the space rented. Meals range $50–100/person. Tax, alcohol and a 20% service charge are additional.

AVAILABILITY: Year-round, daily, 6am–11pm.

SERVICES/AMENITIES:
Catering: provided
Kitchen Facilities: n/a
Tables & Chairs: provided
Linens, Silver, etc.: provided
Restrooms: wheelchair accessible
Dance Floor: provided
Bride's Dressing Area: yes
Meeting Equipment: provided
Other: spa services, picnic area, A/V equipment, shopping promenade, event coordination

Parking: large lot
Accommodations: 95 guest rooms
Telephone: house, office and guest phones
Outdoor Night Lighting: CBA
Outdoor Cooking Facilities: BBQ CBA
Cleanup: provided
View: landscaped grounds, garden, courtyard; panorama of mountains, ocean/bay and fields

RESTRICTIONS:
Alcohol: provided, or BYO with corkage fees
Smoking: not allowed
Music: amplified OK with restrictions

Wheelchair Access: yes
Insurance: not required
Other: no birdseed, rice, glitter or confetti

The professionals in the back of this book are the best in the business. How do we know? Read page 637.

Sam's Chowder House

Waterfront Restaurant

4210 North Cabrillo Highway, Half Moon Bay
650/712-0245

www.samschowderhouse.com
events@samschowderhouse.com

- Rehearsal Dinners
- Ceremonies
- Wedding Receptions
- Corp. Events/Mtgs.
- Private Parties
- Accommodations

Oh, Sam's Chowder House in glorious Half Moon Bay, how do brides love thee? Let us count the ways! They love thee for your warm, welcoming atmosphere and waterfront setting; they love thee for your fresh, delicious cuisine; they love thee for your savvy, unpretentious service and versatile, ocean-view event spaces. *(Pssst... if you haven't met Sam's yet, be prepared to be swept off your feet!)*

Perched on a beachside bluff, this sublime restaurant, with its Cape Cod-style façade and hearty menu that's more surf than turf, was inspired by the traditional seafood houses of New England. Yet Sam's also evokes a California-casual sensibility that makes even refined celebrations feel relaxed and cheerful. The interior is decked out with wood and windows that frame scenic snapshots in all directions: *seabirds soaring over the blue Pacific...sailboats moored at the neighboring harbor...sweethearts strolling hand in hand along the shore.* A ramble of banquet rooms and refreshing sea-scented terraces (all with windbreaks and heaters) provide an array of mix-and-match event options.

The private Harbor View Room boasts a dark hardwood floor and a fireplace, especially cozy during the cooler seasons. It opens onto its own terrace, lined with Adirondack chairs and fire pits, offering a comfortable vantage for sipping cocktails and admiring sunsets. The South Beach Bar is a private, two-level patio with an informal, beach-shack vibe and built-in bar. While it sports café tables with colorful umbrellas, this festive space has room for long banquet tables, too—and it's also dog-friendly if you tie the knot here and happened to bring your pup along to serve as ring bearer. Planning a large bash? Then consider buying out the entire restaurant, including the Main Dining Room with its marble-topped oyster bar and row of picture windows.

Yet another reason brides love Sam's is for its private Beachfront Lawn, a sand-skimming meadow outfitted with umbrellas, strings of lights, and appropriate event accouterments. The staff will set up your wedding arch for picturesque "I do"s right on the beach, with the gentle whoosh of the waves enhancing the naturally romantic ambiance. Guests then dine at long tables, arranged family-style, on the lawn.

Sam's super-scrumptious menu focuses on sustainable and locally sourced ingredients. With so many culinary temptations to choose from, we have a hot tip: Opt for Sam's famous three-course Lobster Clambake, prepared right in front of your guests. Whole Maine lobsters, clams, mussels,

Andouille sausage, red potatoes and fresh ears of corn layered with seaweed are steamed in authentic New England-style wooden boxes, and served along with clam chowder and other tasty accompaniments. Add a raw seafood bar and margaritas to your cocktail hour, and let the flavorful aroma of the cooking feast create mouth-watering anticipation. *Mmmmm…*

Amazingly, all of this food and fun is value priced—there are no rental fees, just food and beverage minimums. Sam's Director of Special Events will help you sort it all out to match your wedding vision. By the way, wedding couples aren't the only ones that have fallen for Sam's. Since its opening in 2006, the award-winning restaurant has garnered an impressive string of accolades. Which just goes to prove our point that to know Sam's is to love Sam's, for oh so many reasons.

Already found the perfect spot for your celebration? Sam's ChowderMobile, the mobile gourmet catering version of Sam's Chowder House, can also bring a seafood feast right to your location!

CEREMONY CAPACITY: The site can accommodate 60 seated indoors and 200 seated outdoors. Indoor ceremonies are not recommended.

EVENT/RECEPTION & MEETING CAPACITY: Indoors, the entire restaurant holds 200 seated or standing guests, private room Mavericks holds 20 seated, the Ocean Terrace room holds 40 seated, and the Harbor View Room holds 60 seated. Outdoors, the Beachfront Lawn area holds 100 seated or 150 standing, and Sam's South Beach Bar holds 60 seated or 80 standing.

FEES & DEPOSITS: An event date can be held for 4 days without a deposit. 50% of the estimated event total, a signed contract and credit card authorization are required to reserve your date. The balance is due on the day of the event. There is no room rental fee, but food and beverage minimums apply and vary depending on space rented. Lunch and dinner range $35–75/person. Tax, alcohol and a 20% service charge are additional.

Cancellation charges will be applied if notice is given 30 days or less before the confirmed event date.

AVAILABILITY: Year-round daily, 11am–10pm, except major holidays.

SERVICES/AMENITIES:

Catering: provided
Kitchen Facilities: n/a
Tables & Chairs: provided
Linens, Silver, etc.: provided
Restrooms: wheelchair accessible
Dance Floor: CBA
Bride's Dressing Area: yes
Meeting Equipment: CBA, extra charge

Parking: large lot, valet CBA
Accommodations: no guest rooms
Telephone: emergency use only
Outdoor Night Lighting: provided
Outdoor Cooking Facilities: yes
Cleanup: provided
View: harbor and Pacific Ocean
Other: cakes, flowers, music CBA, event coordination

RESTRICTIONS:

Alcohol: provided, full bar, no BYO
Smoking: not allowed
Music: amplified OK

Wheelchair Access: yes
Insurance: not required

Hillsborough Racquet Club

Historic Club

252 El Cerrito, Hillsborough
650/343-2062

www.hillsboroughracquetclub.org
info@hillsboroughracquetclub.org

● Rehearsal Dinners	● Corp. Events/Mtgs.
● Ceremonies	● Private Parties
● Wedding Receptions	○ Accommodations

The Hillsborough Racquet Club has a wonderful ambiance—polished and dignified, but without any stiffness or stuffiness. HRC's members are proud of their private club and enjoy its unique spaces, from the ballroom, patio and bar, to the indoor badminton court. When you host your wedding here, you have exclusive use of the facility during your event, along with an experienced manager to provide discreet assistance.

Built in 1913 as a polo club, the Hillsborough Racquet Club is located in a lovely residential neighborhood surrounded by elms, cypresses and laurel hedges. The entrance faces away from the street, and it's not until you walk around to it that you see the club's beautiful architectural elements. The building's design is based on the classical Greek Doric order with clean, elegant lines. A handsome portico curves along the front, opening to a patio with flowerbeds and the main entrance. Visitors enter a domed, parquet-floored foyer with hallways that lead to a bridal changing room, a servers' entrance, dining and music rooms, and the ballroom.

The ballroom is the heart of the club and it's easy to see why. It's large and airy, but not overwhelming—ideal for dinner and dancing. Interior designers enjoy the room's good "bones"—the walls are finished in off-whites and ornamentation is simple and subdued. The room's main visual focuses are a large working fireplace capped with a Tudor arch on one side, and a wall of windows and French doors on the opposite side that open to the patio. This sunny space, sheltered by a shade tree and lined with flowers and small hedges, is a wonderful spot for cocktails and outdoor dining.

Adjoining the ballroom is a bar and a "domino room." The bar is backed by a mirror that reflects light pouring in from the windows. Next door, the domino room has a very clubby feel with its green plaid-covered cane furniture. Often used as a "quiet room," it's a fine place to sit and relax, or to take a break from the festivities.

The dining room has a fireplace, brass chandelier and "hounds and hunters" prints on the walls. In the adjacent music room, a grand piano stands against a light-loving wall of windows that can serve as a backdrop for small ceremonies. (Couples may wed in the ballroom, too, and HRC is close to several neighborhood churches.) French doors in this room also lead to the patio, creating a nice indoor/outdoor flow.

Other pluses are the large staging kitchen off of the dining room, and the changing room/ladies' lounge next to the foyer—it's spacious enough for a bride and her attendants to get ready in comfort.

The members are happy to share their club with you for your special occasion, whether it be a wedding, anniversary party, or other celebration. What's more, you'll get the attention you deserve, since HRC never hosts more than one function per weekend.

CEREMONY & EVENT/RECEPTION CAPACITY: Indoors, the club holds 225 seated or 322 standing guests; the patio holds up to 50 seated or 60–70 standing guests.

MEETING CAPACITY: The ballroom holds 225 guests seated theater-style.

FEES & DEPOSITS: A $1,000 deposit is required. 50% of the rental fee is due 6 months prior to the event, the balance is due 3 months prior. Rental fees range $4,000–4,500 (depending on guest count) for a 5-hour block of time. An extra hour is allowed for a wedding ceremony ($300 ceremony fee).

AVAILABILITY: Year-round, daily (except Thursdays) until 11pm.

SERVICES/AMENITIES:

Catering: BYO
Kitchen Facilities: warming kitchen
Tables & Chairs: provided
Linens, Silver, etc.: through caterer
Restrooms: wheelchair accessible
Dance Floor: yes
Bride's Dressing Area: yes
Meeting Equipment: BYO
Other: exclusive use of facility during event

Parking: ample on site
Accommodations: no guest rooms
Telephone: no
Outdoor Night Lighting: CBA
Outdoor Cooking Facilities: through caterer
Cleanup: caterer and resident manager
View: landscaped terrace

RESTRICTIONS:

Alcohol: BYO
Smoking: outdoors only
Music: amplified OK indoors with restrictions

Wheelchair Access: yes
Insurance: liability required

Los Altos History Museum

51 South San Antonio Road, Los Altos
650/948-9427 X12

www.losaltoshistory.org
mperry@losaltoshistory.org

History Museum & Special Event Facility

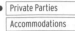

- Rehearsal Dinners
- Ceremonies
- Wedding Receptions
- Corp. Events/Mtgs.
- Private Parties
- Accommodations

Not so very long ago, apricot orchards, vineyards, and walnut groves cloaked the fertile plains of the Peninsula, and dairy farms and greenhouses dotted the hillsides. The transition from pristine agricultural paradise to Silicon Valley hub is skillfully realized at the Los Altos History Museum, where the past comes alive right before your very eyes. We thought this place was so interesting and so lovely that we would come here even if we weren't planning a special event. But make no mistake—there's plenty here to entice party-givers of all types.

In a model of team spirit, a group of Los Altos go-getters banded together to create this local museum, a captivating window in time set among acres of delightful parks and gardens. Open since spring 2001, the History Museum resides in a folksy, wood-plank building. The vaulted entryway and the indoor balcony, which encircles the three-story space, generate an open, welcoming look and feel. Most of the main floor is taken up by the Changing Exhibits Gallery, which features visiting collections, some on loan from notable institutions like the Smithsonian. Up a winding staircase to the permanent exhibit you'll find engaging interactive displays of Los Altos area history. There's more history just across the landscaped courtyard in the landmark J. Gilbert Smith History House. This adorable Craftsman-style shingled farmhouse from 1905 sets a nostalgic tone for your outdoor wedding or special event.

Surrounding both buildings, the pretty museum gardens offer several spots to enjoy the inspiring beauty of flowers in bloom, treetops swaying in the breeze, and squirrels scampering about their natural habitat. Why not exchange marriage vows under the dappled shade of oak trees? The front yard of the History House is a darling scene for memorable photos, the newlyweds framed by an archway wrapped in wild roses, or the wedding party posed on the broad porch steps in an old-fashioned tableau. In fair weather, you may want to hold your reception outdoors too, skillfully arranged by the museum's expert event coordinator.

A more formal outdoor ceremony and reception site is the spacious red-brick courtyard between the main Museum and the quaint façade of the History House. Your walk down the aisle is accented by antique-style verdigris lamps, potted blooms and delicate saplings, and a redwood pergola lets you say your vows while facing the lush garden. Afterwards, you can dine outdoors and even have your first dance under the stars.

Then the party moves through sliding glass doors into the Changing Exhibits Gallery, where polished blond wood floors and works of art lend an air of distinction to your celebration. Here, the cake is served and guests can dance the night away. Those who prefer quieter pursuits might meander upstairs to enjoy the interactive displays, artifacts and vintage clothing, or step outside for a stroll along the moonlit garden lanes. This is the way museums should be—hands-on, fun, and fascinating. To further enhance your event, arrange a guided tour of the History House. The quaintly furnished rooms replicate in amazing detail the lifestyle of a 1930s farm family. You'll feel like you stepped through a time tunnel into the simple, wholesome world of a bygone era.

The Los Altos History Museum is more than just a peek into the past; it's also a vision of the future, a future that embraces family, community, and traditional values, while honoring a connection to the land. When you hold your special celebration here, you'll become part of this ideal tomorrow, because most of the proceeds from your event go towards supporting the museum and its grounds for generations to come.

CEREMONY CAPACITY: The Garden accommodates 200 seated, and the Changing Exhibits Gallery 100 seated guests.

EVENT/RECEPTION CAPACITY: The Garden holds 200 seated or standing, and the Changing Exhibits Gallery 100 seated or 150 standing guests.

MEETING CAPACITY: The Gallery holds 100 seated theater-style or 60 seated classroom-style.

FEES & DEPOSITS: The entire rental fee, along with a $1,000 security deposit and a $500 application fee, are required to reserve your date. Rental fees range $2,000–4,500. Liability insurance is required. There is also an alcohol permit fee required.

AVAILABILITY: Tuesday–Sunday, 4pm–11pm, mid-April through mid-October. Setup access at 3pm.

SERVICES/AMENITIES:

Catering: select from preferred list
Kitchen Facilities: fully equipped, caterer's kitchen
Tables & Chairs: provided; extra fee
Linens, Silver, etc.: BYO or through caterer
Restrooms: wheelchair accessible
Dance Floor: hardwood floor or brick patio
Bride's & Groom's Dressing Areas: yes
Meeting Equipment: full range, extra fee
Other: coordination, docent-led tours

Parking: large lot, complimentary
Accommodations: no guest rooms
Telephone: pay phone at library
Outdoor Night Lighting: yes
Outdoor Cooking Facilities: through caterer
Cleanup: through caterer
View: garden courtyard, Peninsula coastal hills and landscaped grounds

RESTRICTIONS:

Alcohol: BYO, licensed and insured server
Smoking: not allowed
Music: amplified OK indoors and outdoors until 8pm with volume restrictions

Wheelchair Access: yes
Insurance: extra liability required
Other: no rice, birdseed, confetti or glitter

Want to know WHAT TO ASK a potential location or vendor? Check out our Questions to Ask starting on page 17.

Allied Arts Guild

75 Arbor Road at Cambridge, Menlo Park
650/322-2405
www.alliedartsguild.org
events@alliedartsguild.org

Historic Landmark & Garden

● Rehearsal Dinners	● Corp. Events/Mtgs.
● Ceremonies	● Private Parties
● Wedding Receptions	Accommodations

The Allied Arts Guild is an extraordinary place. It hits you instantly as you walk through the entry and gaze at the fountains, the wrought-iron details, colorful frescos and intricate tilework. The beautiful and tranquil gardens draw you further into the central courtyard, where you say to yourself, "I can't believe I'm in Menlo Park."

No wonder. This serene oasis is a historic landmark located amidst three and a half acres that were once part of an original Spanish land grant. Allied Arts is so hidden, you'd never know that it's located here, tucked away in a quiet, residential neighborhood not far from the Stanford University campus. The founders' original dream of a European-style crafts guild was realized in 1929 by California artist Pedro deLemos and architect Gardner Dailey. Both were responsible for creating the gardens, buildings and shops of the complex, and adhering to a romantic palette with a strong Spanish emphasis.

After more than 70 years, the site holds a major place in California history. Luckily for all of us, this jewel-of-a-venue has been recently and completely restored back to its original splendor. The complex is designed in the Spanish Colonial style, with meandering courtyards and terraces, burbling fountains, and handsome buildings with white plaster walls topped by terracotta tiles. The lush gardens were inspired by gardens in Granada, Spain, with an emphasis on color, fragrance and seasonal flowers. During the summer months, a floral profusion of intense color makes a great background for wedding photos. Just imagine getting married outdoors in a spot called "Garden of Delight," encircled by Blue Nile lilies, aster, salvia and hydrangeas or "The Court of Abundance," with splashing fountain surrounded by gold and yellow marigolds, wallflowers and nasturtiums!

If the weather is uncooperative, you can have your ceremony or reception indoors in the Dining Room or Sunset Room. Both have rustic, high-beamed ceilings and wrought-iron chandeliers. The cement floors are worthy of note: They were painstakingly handcarved by Pedro deLemos to look like stone. The homey Spanish fireplaces are made of adobe, and when a fire is burning, they give the rooms a warm glow.

You can rent one part of the complex, or go for broke and celebrate by renting the entire facility. You'd be hard pressed to find a more relaxed and striking setting on the Peninsula with both indoor and outdoor event spaces. And there's an added benefit: Because Allied Arts is a nonprofit organization, all proceeds are donated to the Lucile Packard Children's Hospital at Stanford—which means a significant portion of your rental fees are tax deductible!

CEREMONY & EVENT/RECEPTION CAPACITY: The site accommodates 140 seated or standing indoors and 140 seated or standing outdoors.

MEETING CAPACITY: The site holds 120 seated guests, or up to 44 seated conference-style.

FEES & DEPOSITS: Ceremonies start at $3,000; for receptions the use fee ranges $5,000–8,000. Weekday events range $800–2,000.

AVAILABILITY: Year-round, Monday–Saturday 8:30am–9pm.

SERVICES/AMENITIES:

Catering: select from preferred list
Kitchen Facilities: prep only
Tables & Chairs: some provided
Linens, Silver, etc.: through caterer
Restrooms: wheelchair accessible
Dance Floor: CBA
Bride's Dressing Area: yes
Meeting Equipment: provided
Other: A/V equipment

Parking: on-site lot for 120 cars, and on-street
Accommodations: no guest rooms
Telephone: house phone
Outside Night Lighting: yes
Outdoor Cooking Facilities: CBA
Cleanup: provided
View: garden, landscaped grounds, historic architecture

RESTRICTIONS:

Alcohol: provided
Smoking: designated area only
Music: amplified OK indoors, acoustic only outdoors

Wheelchair Access: yes
Insurance: certificate required
Other: no birdseed or rice; no swimming

Arrillaga Family Recreation Center

Community Center

701 Laurel Street, Menlo Park
650/330-2200
www.menlopark.org/departments/com/parks/reccenter.htm
nsbickel@menlopark.org

●	Rehearsal Dinners	●	Corp. Events/Mtgs.
●	Ceremonies	●	Private Parties
●	Wedding Receptions		Accommodations

There's so much to love at the Arrillaga Recreation Center that it may truly be the rare event venue that has something for everyone. Situated on what was once a sprawling, mid-1800s private estate, this thriving community hub is just blocks from downtown Menlo Park in the Civic Center complex. Thanks to a multimillion-dollar renovation, it boasts light-filled interiors, private landscaped patios, and all the charms of its Burgess Park surroundings—including historic backdrops for memorable photos.

When guests arrive at the redwood-and-glass building, they often gather in its open, airy lobby for prefunction refreshments. Then, if you're having your ceremony here (and most couples do), your family and friends will be ushered through Craftsman-styled double wooden doors to the serene South Patio. This beautiful, crescent-shaped flagstone space wraps around one entire side of the building and features a Zen-like border of Japanese maples, native plants and graceful oaks. Handcrafted ceramic urns are integrated throughout and serve as artful and calming water features.

You can opt to exchange vows in front of those wooden entry doors, or take full advantage of the patio's *pièce de résistance* and say "I do" beneath an asymmetrical canvas canopy that's evocative of a dove spreading her wings. Dramatically tethered by four angled copper posts, this soaring installation is a dynamic focal point.

There's ample room for al fresco cocktails on the patio before everyone moves into the Sequoia Room for dinner. This reception area feels quite spacious, with its cathedral ceiling, polished hardwood floors, and two walls of glass—one that looks out to the main lobby and the other (of glass doors) that opens to the patio and allows lots of natural light to stream in. The neutral décor is compatible with almost any event's color scheme.

If you're planning a more intimate wedding, there's the Oak Room on the other side of the building, complete with a private patio that virtually doubles the square footage of your reception space. A huge oak tree dominates the courtyard patio, creating shade and soft, dappled light, while an impressive set of wooden doors makes an excellent backdrop for your ceremony. This seductive spot also lends itself to rehearsal dinners, as well as bridal party staging and photos.

Speaking of photos, the grounds provide lots of options, from the duck pond and waterfalls to wooden bridges and photogenic trees…but you'd be remiss if you didn't capture a kiss in front of the original Victorian gatehouse and the to-die-for, antique tiered fountain.

Other perks at the center include easy accessibility from several highways, the convenience of a metro station right outside its gates, ample free parking and a totally updated kitchen—where you can bring in the caterer of your choice! Arrillaga does indeed offer something for just about everyone.

CEREMONY & EVENT/RECEPTION CAPACITY: The site holds 200 seated or 250 standing guests indoors and 250 seated or 300 standing outdoors.

MEETING CAPACITY: Meetings spaces hold 300 seated guests.

FEES & DEPOSITS: A $250 refundable security deposit ($500 with alcohol) is required to reserve your date and the balance is due 2 weeks prior to the event. Rental fees range $125–230/hour depending on residency and whether the event is on a weekday or weekend. Monday–Thursday rental rate is $125/hour for residents and $170 per/hour for nonresidents. Friday–Sunday rental rate is $170/hour for residents and $230/hour for nonresidents. 30% discount on any additional room(s) rented at the same time (applies to the lower-cost room).

AVAILABILITY: Year-round, Monday–Thursday 8am–10pm, Friday–Sunday 8am–1am.

SERVICES/AMENITIES:

Catering: BYO
Kitchen Facilities: prep only
Tables & Chairs: provided
Linens, Silver, etc.: through caterer or BYO
Restrooms: wheelchair accessible
Dance Floor: provided
Bride's Dressing Area: CBA
Meeting Equipment: some provided, A/V equipment

Parking: large lot
Accommodations: no guest rooms
Telephone: office phones
Outdoor Night Lighting: provided
Outdoor Cooking Facilities: no
Cleanup: caterer or renter
View: creek, fountain, garden patio, lagoon, landscaped grounds, park

RESTRICTIONS:

Alcohol: BYO
Smoking: not allowed
Music: amplified OK

Wheelchair Access: yes
Insurance: liability required

Westin San Francisco Airport

Hotel

One Old Bayshore Highway, Millbrae
650/872-8118

www.westin.com
vicki.idzal@westin.com

- Rehearsal Dinners
- Ceremonies
- Wedding Receptions
- Corp. Events/Mtgs.
- Private Parties
- Accommodations

The name Westin San Francisco Airport Hotel is a bit of a misnomer, because even though it's close to the airport this venue is really more like an elegant resort. With its refined décor, warm ambiance and long list of amenities, it's one of the Peninsula's most popular places for weddings, receptions and parties.

Set on the cusp of a palm-lined drive near the edge of the bay, and just two minutes from the airport, the Westin is surprisingly quiet and peaceful. Even the lobby has a calming influence, designed in warm natural shades and outfitted with modern, comfortable furnishings and lush floral arrangements.

From here it's a short walk to the banquet rooms, and by the time you reach them, you're expecting something sophisticated and tasteful. You won't be disappointed. The Westin Ballroom, where most weddings, large meetings and special events take place, is very lovely. Brides are usually overjoyed with the décor and have been known to exclaim, "Oh, this will match my dress perfectly!" That's because the walls are papered in a neutral champagne-and-taupe print that gives off a subtle gold sheen, and the coffered ceiling is white. One of the most striking features of this ballroom is the lighting. Instead of traditional chandeliers, there are fixtures fashioned from white globes seemingly "scattered" behind a veil of pearl strands. When the lights are dimmed, you feel like you're gazing at clusters of stars, shining through golden clouds. Additional romantic lighting comes from alabaster-and-brass wall sconces. Although the ballroom can be divided into four sections, only one event at a time is scheduled so you can tailor the size of the space to fit your needs.

The expansive foyer area in front of the ballroom is not only refreshing to the eye, it's large enough to be set up with fountains, plants and an hors d'oeuvre buffet and still have plenty of room left over for a crowd to mingle comfortably. And if you have kids at your event, you'll be ever grateful to the Westin—they make a room with childcare available just off the foyer.

Smaller weddings and meetings are held in the Bayshore Ballroom, an intimate space with crystal chandeliers, alabaster wall sconces, and floor-to-ceiling windows overlooking the pool atrium. The atrium itself is ideal for cocktail parties and more informal receptions. Huge potted ferns and rubber trees, as well as colorful flowers set around the pool, soak up the sunlight from the vaulted skylit "ceiling" and create a tropical ambiance.

Two dozen other rooms are available for functions, and award-winning chefs will create custom, culturally diverse menus. Guests staying overnight sleep well, thanks to the Westin's super-comfy Heavenly Bed and triple-paned windows that create a virtually soundproof environment. There's one more amenity just for weddings: a customized web page for each couple to facilitate reserving guest rooms and providing information to attendees.

The combination of beautiful facilities, excellent food and personal service generates lots of repeat business for the hotel. Their "Letters To The Hotel" binder includes pages of laudatory comments such as, "The Westin is the only place to hold an event in San Mateo County! Period!" and "My daughter's dream of a perfect wedding day came true!" Read them all and you come away with a sense that guests feel quite welcomed here and very well taken care of. It's absolutely clear why they return to the Westin time after time—for many of them it's like coming home.

CEREMONY CAPACITY: The Bayshore Ballroom holds 200, and the Westin Ballroom holds 300.

EVENT/RECEPTION CAPACITY: The hotel can accommodate 48–410 seated or 125–600 standing guests indoors.

MEETING CAPACITY: The Westin has over 22,000 square feet of function space, including 31 flexible rooms, from ballrooms and salons to suites and boardrooms. Spaces can accommodate 4–700 guests for business events.

FEES & DEPOSITS: For weddings, a nonrefundable $5,000 deposit is required to secure your date; the event balance is due 3 days prior to the event. There are 3 wedding packages, ranging $75–125/person, that include centerpieces, champagne reception and toast, 3-course meal, hors d'oeuvres, wine with meal, overnight accommodations and breakfast for the bride and groom. All menus can be customized; wedding menus range $75–120/person. Tax and a 22% service charge are additional. There is a $500 ceremony setup charge.

For other social events or business functions, prices will vary depending on the menu and services selected; call for specific rates. Meeting packages are also available.

AVAILABILITY: Year-round, daily until 1am, including holidays. For Saturday weddings, time frames are 11am–5pm or 6pm–1am.

SERVICES/AMENITIES:

Catering: provided, no BYO
Kitchen Facilities: n/a
Tables & Chairs: provided
Linens, Silver, etc.: provided
Restrooms: wheelchair accessible
Dance Floor: provided
Bride's & Groom's Dressing Areas: guest room CBA
Meeting Equipment: full range and business center, in-room data port lines

Parking: ample, gated and secure lots
Accommodations: 400 guest rooms
Telephone: guest phones
Outdoor Night Lighting: access only
Outdoor Cooking Facilities: no
Cleanup: provided
View: no
Other: event coordination, baby grand piano, ice sculpture, wedding cakes, limo service, customized web page

RESTRICTIONS:

Alcohol: provided, or wine and champagne corkage negotiable
Smoking: outside only
Music: amplified OK

Wheelchair Access: yes
Insurance: not required
Other: no rice, birdseed, glitter or confetti

La Costanera—Contemporary Peruvian Cuisine

Waterfront Restaurant

8150 Cabrillo Highway, Montara
650/728-1600

www.lacostanerarestaurant.com
events@lacostanerarestaurant.com

- Rehearsal Dinners
- Ceremonies
- Wedding Receptions
- Corp. Events/Mtgs.
- Private Parties
- Accommodations

La Costanera, a Michelin-starred culinary destination just north of Half Moon Bay, is an upscale all-in-one event venue with gourmet panache. Perched on a bluff above Montara Beach, this gorgeous restaurant is nothing short of a masterpiece. The three-level, 10,000-square-foot building is shaped like half of a modern Mesoamerican pyramid, with slanting windows and skylights that embrace a breathtaking ocean view. Its overall design reflects a contemporary global aesthetic, artfully blending rustic, natural elements—rich woods, sea shells, distressed metal—into the décor of the geometrically shaped rooms. Cleverly styled furnishings and accents, such as old-fashioned maps inlaid into some of the tabletops and nautically inspired mobiles, convey an antique seafaring flair. The effect is beautifully original.

La Costanera's layout offers supreme event versatility, and whether you buy out the entire restaurant for your event or reserve individual sections, there are no rental fees as long as you meet the food and beverage minimums. The main floor houses the restaurant and a semiprivate dining area called the Greenhouse, with its own fireplace and atrium. Glass doors open to an oceanview patio, complete with fire pit, for outdoor dining or an intimate ceremony. Back inside, a staircase leads to a skylit balcony that overlooks the action on the main floor. This private enclave can host rehearsal dinners, showers or small gatherings.

The lower level holds the bar and lounge, a very cool space for receptions, social hours and after-parties—La Costanera can stay open until 2am. A long bar serves up the drinks (we recommend the house-made sangria or their pisco sour, a Peruvian cocktail that's one of our all-time favorites). Gleaming tile floors and Oriental carpets enhance the space's exotic luxe; a sunken lounge area, normally outfitted with velour couches and club chairs, can be cleared ahead of time for dancing. Glass doors open onto a beachfront patio, whose glorious panorama of sea and sky makes it quite the romantic spot for ceremonies. A footpath leads directly to the sand, so while your guests are sipping sangria, you and your bridal party can pose for photos alongside the waves.

The food and drink is as impressive as the setting. Chef-owner Carlos Altamirano already has two critically acclaimed restaurants to his credit, Mochica and Piqueos, and this latest venture is sure to add to his culinary fandom. Altamirano's fusion dishes reflect his country's Asian and Mediterranean influences, and introduce some fascinating indigenous components like yucca fries, sweet plantains and blue potatoes. Seafood is the star here, but entrées like lamb chops in mint chimichurri sauce will keep carnivores contented, too. La Costanera brilliantly showcases

Peru's national dish, *cebiche,* in a dozen or so provocative interpretations, and they even have a cute cart to serve it up to your guests. Round out the appetizers with an assortment of tapas and *anitcuchos* (South American-style skewers), and you have a cocktail hour that's pure foodie fun. Just don't forget the pisco! La Costanera has an entire menu of pisco variations, ensuring your signature cocktail will be unique (mojitos are so 2008…).

The expert staff will help you navigate the novel food and drink options, and can assist with event extras—entertainment, late-night service, valet parking, flowers, favors and more. With its hip vibe, cutting-edge cuisine and stunning atmosphere, La Costanera is definitely a venue to put on your short-list.

CEREMONY CAPACITY: The restaurant holds 150 seated guests indoors and 100 seated outdoors.

EVENT/RECEPTION CAPACITY: The facility can accommodate 270 seated or 400 standing indoors and 50 seated or standing outdoors.

MEETING CAPACITY: Meeting rooms hold 200 seated guests.

FEES & DEPOSITS: 25% of the total event cost is required to reserve your date. Rental fees range $400–3,500 depending on the space rented. Meals range $50–125/person. Tax, alcohol and a 20% service charge are additional.

AVAILABILITY: Year-round, Tuesday–Sunday, 5pm–midnight.

SERVICES/AMENITIES:

Catering: provided
Kitchen Facilities: fully equipped
Tables & Chairs: provided
Linens, Silver, etc.: provided
Restrooms: wheelchair accessible
Dance Floor: provided
Bride's Dressing Area: CBA
Meeting Equipment: BYO

Parking: large lot
Accommodations: no guest rooms
Telephone: house phone
Outdoor Night Lighting: provided
Outdoor Cooking Facilities: none
Cleanup: provided
View: coastline, mountains, ocean/bay
Other: event coordination

RESTRICTIONS:

Alcohol: provided, or BYO with corkage fee
Smoking: outdoors only
Music: amplified OK with restrictions

Wheelchair Access: yes
Insurance: liability required

Want to find more venues and services? Check out our informative website, www.HereComesTheGuide.com.

229

Cypress Meadows

Private Banquet Facility

343 Cypress Avenue, Moss Beach
650/728-8045

www.cypressmeadows.net
info@cypressmeadows.net

- Rehearsal Dinners
- Ceremonies
- Wedding Receptions
- Corp. Events/Mtgs.
- Private Parties
- Accommodations

Tucked inside a quaint residential neighborhood just north of Half Moon Bay Airport, Cypress Meadows is a welcome addition to the San Mateo coastal scene. This private banquet facility is hidden behind a pretty flower farm, and offers a secluded milieu for your wedding celebration. On these nine pleasant acres, adjacent to the Fitzgerald Marine Reserve, the air is sweet, tinged with a hint of salt from the nearby sea, and the atmosphere mellow and relaxed.

Your congenial proprietors are Randy and Sharon Dardenelle, who designed Cypress Meadows specifically to host social events. They've outfitted meeting areas and guest rooms with the latest modern technology; yet, they've managed to instill the place with a timeless simplicity, beginning with the cedar board-and-batten building. Trimmed with river rock pillars and copper handrails, the structure conveys a comfortable, rustic vibe. Yet it's a fairly new venue, so everything is neat and fresh inside. Guests enter through the foyer, where a trio of skylights, a travertine tile floor, and a gas fireplace in one corner make an inviting first impression. Brides often place their gift table and guest book here.

Indoor gatherings congregate in the Cypress Room, a warm and friendly space bookended by two gas fireplaces glowing beneath tall, stacked-stone hearths. Depending on your preferred setup, the room can accommodate up to 75 guests, with overflow seating on an adjacent terrace (which can be tented in case the weather doesn't cooperate).

The terrace is also a sublime spot for your cocktail hour, with a low trickling waterfall pond and potted plants setting the scene. The most striking feature, however, is the bird's-eye view of a lovely hillside garden, with a sprawling meadow down below. From the terrace, follow a loose gravel path that cascades downward through native plantings—flowering herbs, blooming succulents and fragrant lavender—that spill over low walls. Several stone seating areas built into the landscape entice you to pose for photos, framed by purple salvia and wispy ornamental grasses. Or steal a few moments with your sweetie, snuggling together on the old-fashioned driftwood swing.

At the bottom of the path, a vast green meadow, kissed with bursts of yellow wildflowers, spreads before you. On one side, a copse of lofty cypress trees feathers the sky; on another, a bank of lithe willows bends in the breeze. Opposite, Montara Mountain forms a jagged silhouette against the mercurial skyline. Wedding ceremonies on the meadow take on an informal, country charm coupled with a sense of wild majesty. Little decoration is needed to improve upon what nature provides, which includes peek-a-boo ocean views.

Unlike at some locations, you're free to hire any caterer you wish to take advantage of the commercial kitchen with separate, easy access. Another bonus at this property: two guest rooms on opposite sides of the building, each with its own private entrance. The nicely styled suites—one for the bride, one for the groom—open to a balcony overlooking the meadow. What an inspired spot for tossing your bridal bouquet, as you savor the culmination of your memorable celebration at Cypress Meadows.

CEREMONY CAPACITY: The facility holds 80 seated guests indoors, and 150 seated outdoors.

EVENT/RECEPTION CAPACITY: Cypress Meadows can accommodate 65 seated or 80 standing guests indoors and 100 seated or 150 standing outdoors.

MEETING CAPACITY: The facility holds 60 seated guests.

FEES & DEPOSITS: A $1,000 deposit is required to reserve your date. The balance is due 30 days prior to the event. Rental fees range $1,500–5,000 depending on the day of the week and the type of event.

AVAILABILITY: Year-round, daily, 8am–10pm.

SERVICES/AMENITIES:

Catering: BYO
Kitchen Facilities: fully equipped
Tables & Chairs: some provided
Linens, Silver, etc.: CBA
Restrooms: wheelchair accessible
Dance Floor: provided
Bride's & Groom's Dressing Areas: yes
Meeting Equipment: provided
Other: on-site florals, A/V equipment

Parking: large lot
Accommodations: 2 guest rooms
Telephone: office phone
Outdoor Night Lighting: provided
Outdoor Cooking Facilities: BBQ CBA
Cleanup: caterer & facility
View: forest, fountain, garden, courtyard, meadow, mountains, ocean

RESTRICTIONS:

Alcohol: BYO
Smoking: not allowed
Music: amplified OK with restrictions

Wheelchair Access: yes
Insurance: liability required

Crowne Plaza Cabaña Palo Alto

Hotel

4290 El Camino Real, Palo Alto
650/857-0787
www.cabanapaloalto.com
sales.catering@cabanapaloalto.com

● Rehearsal Dinners	● Corp. Events/Mtgs.
● Ceremonies	● Private Parties
● Wedding Receptions	● Accommodations

What do the Beatles, Frank Sinatra, and President Clinton's security dogs have in common? They've all been guests at the Crowne Plaza Cabaña! Originally owned by movie star Doris Day, the Cabaña Hotel opened its doors in 1962 and immediately became a magnet for Hollywood luminaries. Described by _Life Magazine_ as "one of the best hotels on the West Coast," it's now "the Cabaña reinvented," thanks to a 21st-century makeover that completely updated the décor, event spaces and guest rooms. However, the venue still retains the breezy, relaxed elegance and innovative design elements that made it a California classic.

With the largest event capacity on the Peninsula, the Crowne Plaza Cabaña offers numerous choices for functions, especially weddings and other fabulous fêtes. In the expansive Grand Mediterranean Ballroom, two-toned gold walls painted in a subtle swirling pattern complement the carpet. Overhead, eye-catching half-dome light fixtures made from tortoise shell and opaque glass panels are set into the high, coffered ceiling. Just outside, a spacious and sunny courtyard is perfect for a smaller ceremony or reception. It can be used alone, or as a prefunction area in conjunction with the ballroom. Other first-floor facilities include the intimate Bacchus Room, with a fireplace, new fixtures and plantation-shuttered windows.

On the second floor you'll find the sophisticated Cyprus Room, the hotel's most sought-after venue. With its unique oval shape, wraparound floor-to-ceiling windows and elegant touches, this room's charms are hard to resist. During the day, natural light streams in through the windows, which provide ample views of the trees, courtyard and sparkling swimming pool below. At night, lights may be dimmed for a soft, romantic ambiance.

The Cyprus Room opens to the Sun Deck, which accommodates overflow reception seating and also works well for a wedding ceremony or social hour. Six Cabaña Suites next to the deck provide even more options: For example, you might reserve one for the bride's changing room and another for a hospitality room. One of the suites connects to both the Cyprus Room and the Sun Deck, creating a wonderful indoor-outdoor flow.

A host of smaller rooms are available, too, so you should be able to find a space that perfectly suits your occasion. In addition, the staff is extremely flexible and will work with you to deliver the event you envision. The Crowne Plaza Cabaña has always impressed its guests, and it continues to do so with inspired service, modern amenities and comfortable accommodations.

CEREMONY CAPACITY: The hotel accommodates up to 800 seated guests indoors and 400 seated outdoors.

EVENT/RECEPTION CAPACITY: The facility holds 640 seated and 800 standing indoors; 350 seated and 750 standing outdoors.

MEETING CAPACITY: Event spaces accommodate 800 seated guests.

FEES & DEPOSITS: 25% of the estimated event total is due at contract signing. The balance is payable 30 days prior to the event. Ceremony fees start at $1,000. Wedding packages start at $40/person. Tax, alcohol and a 20% service charge are additional. Room rental fees may apply if certain minimums are not met.

AVAILABILITY: Year-round, daily, 6am–midnight.

SERVICES/AMENITIES:

Catering: provided or approved outside ethnic caterer

Kitchen Facilities: fully equipped

Tables & Chairs: provided

Linens, Silver, etc.: provided

Restrooms: wheelchair accessible

Dance Floor: yes

Bride's & Groom's Dressing Areas: yes

Meeting Equipment: provided

Parking: large lot

Accommodations: 184 guest rooms and 11 suites

Telephone: house phones

Outdoor Night Lighting: yes

Outdoor Cooking Facilities: no

Cleanup: provided

View: pool, courtyard, grounds

Other: event coordination

RESTRICTIONS:

Alcohol: provided

Smoking: outside only

Music: amplified OK indoors

Wheelchair Access: yes

Insurance: not required

Dinah's Garden Hotel

Restaurant & Hotel

4261 El Camino Real, Palo Alto
650/493-2844
www.dinahshotel.com
sales@dinahshotel.com

- Rehearsal Dinners
- Ceremonies
- Wedding Receptions
- Corp. Events/Mtgs.
- Private Parties
- Accommodations

For decades, Dinah's Garden Hotel has been treating guests to their unique brand of hospitality—imaginative accommodations, eclectic art and statuary from around the world, and five luxuriantly landscaped acres. Lured by sparkling waterfalls and serene grottos, sweethearts would head to this Peninsula oasis for a romantic getaway.

Dinah's has now teamed up with The Sea by Alexander's Steakhouse, a new venture from the Michelin-rated restaurant group.

So in addition to the delectable setting, you also get delectable dining. Although seafood is their specialty, you'll be able to choose from among a wide range of dishes, and the culinary team will also be happy to customize your menu.

Receptions unfold in The Sea's ballroom, a sophisticated space dressed with wood trim and Brazilian cherrywood floors polished to a high gleam. Chandeliers suspended from a soaring cathedral ceiling and multipaned clerestory windows lend a luminous grandeur. Paintings of South Pacific scenes accent corners, while banks of French doors open to a spacious L-shaped terrace. Begin with an intimate ceremony on the tiled section beneath the shade of an awning, set off by Chinese lanterns or floral embellishments strung on the rafters. Then toast the momentous occasion in the adjoining open-air section, where ferns, palms and straw umbrellas create a festive atmosphere.

The hotel itself displays the same superior standards and attention to detail as the restaurant. A stroll through Dinah's takes you past gardens brimming with waterfalls, and ponds teeming with giant multicolored koi. Footbridges and Oriental gazebos invite stolen kisses, and statues of Buddha inspire quiet contemplation.

To further enhance your stay, each of Dinah's 129 guest rooms is uniquely decorated with world-class art and priceless collectibles. Lagoon rooms embrace lush greenery and the sound of flowing water. The opulently arrayed Signature Suites take luxury to a new level. With themes like "Bali," "Asian Sunset," and "The Railroad Baron," their deluxe amenities—such as a steam room, antiques, private lagoon decks, and a working model train—pamper, relax and amuse. The morning after, enjoy brunch at Dinah's retro-chic Poolside Grill.

CEREMONY CAPACITY: The facility can accommodate up to 60 seated guests outdoors on the terrace.

EVENT/RECEPTION CAPACITY: Indoors, the facility holds 150 seated with a dance floor, 300 standing; outdoors, 80 seated or 150 standing.

MEETING CAPACITY: Event spaces accommodate 200 seated guests.

FEES & DEPOSITS: A deposit is not required to reserve your date and the event total is due on the day of the event. Rental fees range $1,200–35,000 depending on the day and time of the event, the guest count and the space rented. Meals range $85–115/person. Tax, alcohol and a 20% service charge are additional.

AVAILABILITY: Year-round, daily.

SERVICES/AMENITIES:

Catering: provided
Kitchen Facilities: n/a
Tables & Chairs: provided
Linens, Silver, etc.: provided
Restrooms: wheelchair accessible
Dance Floor: yes
Bride's & Groom's Dressing Areas: yes
Meeting Equipment: provided

Parking: large lots
Accommodations: 129 guest rooms
Telephone: house phone
Outdoor Night Lighting: yes
Outdoor Cooking Facilities: no
Cleanup: provided
View: garden, pool area, waterfall, pond
Other: event coordination; A/V equipment

RESTRICTIONS:

Alcohol: provided, or BYO with corkage fee
Smoking: outside only
Music: amplified OK with restrictions

Wheelchair Access: yes
Insurance: not required

This is important! Tell locations you're reading HERE COMES THE GUIDE and ask if our information is still current.

235

Elizabeth F. Gamble Garden

Historic Home & Garden

1431 Waverley Street, Palo Alto
650/329-1356 X201

www.gamblegarden.org
admin@gamblegarden.org

- Rehearsal Dinners
- Ceremonies
- Wedding Receptions
- Corp. Events/Mtgs.
- Private Parties
- Accommodations

The Elizabeth F. Gamble Garden is one of the most perfect garden ceremony/ reception sites we've seen. Miss Gamble, granddaughter of the co-founder of the Procter & Gamble Company, willed the home and its grounds to the City of Palo Alto. The estate is now run by the Elizabeth F. Gamble Horticultural Foundation.

The main house is a 1902 Colonial/Georgian Revival-style structure built in a lovely, older residential area of Palo Alto. Inside, a dining room, drawing room and library are available for receptions. Each room has been carefully restored using colorful, turn-of-the-century reproduction wallpapers. Dark natural wood wainscoting has been returned to its original splendor and there are graceful, molded ceilings and nicely finished oak floors throughout. Each room has its own fireplace. A set of French doors in the Library opens onto a brick porch that leads down to the first of many beautifully landscaped spaces.

Our favorite spots are the formal and informal gardens—the collective work of a full-time horticulturist and 300 volunteers. Each separately landscaped area feels like a private secret garden: The rose garden (with its 100 species of roses), the wisteria garden, and the Victorian grotto—separately or combined—provide elegant settings for small wedding ceremonies and receptions.

After the ceremony, guests are invited to gather at the Tea House, where hors d'oeuvres and beverages are served. The bride and groom often slip away from the festivities at this time for a quiet moment together in the Gazebo, an Edwardian-inspired garden house.

The reception is usually held at the Carriage House. While the buffet is set up inside, guests are seated on the adjoining brick terrace. Five sets of French doors make it easy for people to move indoors and out, giving them the feeling of being in a garden pavilion.

Miss Gamble succeeded in creating a place of serenity and beauty. We recommend it highly.

CEREMONY CAPACITY: The Wisteria Garden, Rose Garden, Tea House Patio and Carriage House each hold 50 seated or standing guests; the Drawing Room holds 30 seated or standing guests.

EVENT/RECEPTION & MEETING CAPACITY: The facility hosts events for up to 50 guests.

FEES & DEPOSITS: For events, to secure a date the rental fee is due with a signed contract. The rental fee on Saturdays and Sundays is $1,200 for an 8-hour block; Monday–Friday daytime, $100/hour; weekday evenings, $600 minimum.

For meetings and business functions, fees vary based on rooms rented and rental time frames; call for more details.

AVAILABILITY: Year-round, daily. For weddings, Saturdays and Sundays, noon–10pm and Monday–Friday 4pm–10pm. For other weekday functions, Monday–Thursday, 9am–5pm; Friday, 9am–4pm.

SERVICES/AMENITIES:

Catering: BYO
Kitchen Facilities: fully equipped
Tables & Chairs: BYO
Linens, Silver, etc.: BYO
Restrooms: wheelchair accessible
Dance Floor: yes
Bride's Dressing Area: yes
Meeting Equipment: screen, wireless

Parking: lot
Accommodations: no guest rooms
Telephone: emergency use only
Outdoor Night Lighting: yes
Outdoor Cooking Facilities: no
Cleanup: renter or caterer
View: Edwardian gardens

RESTRICTIONS:

Alcohol: BYO wine, beer or champagne; no beer kegs in main house
Smoking: not allowed
Music: acoustic only; no amplified or recorded music

Wheelchair Access: yes
Insurance: required
Other: rose petals only (no rice, birdseed, etc.)

Garden Court Hotel

Hotel

520 Cowper Street, Downtown Palo Alto
800/824-9028, 650/323-1912
www.gardencourt.com
eventservices@gardencourt.com

- Rehearsal Dinners
- Ceremonies
- Wedding Receptions
- Corp. Events/Mtgs.
- Private Parties
- Accommodations

The Garden Court Hotel is one of the few venues on the Peninsula where you can host your wedding ceremony and reception and your guests can stay. Recently remodeled, the hotel provides a warm, relaxed atmosphere combined with modern sensibilities and five-star personalized service.

Designed around a beautiful open-air European-style courtyard, the hotel is visually impressive. The large central fountain and tiers of flower-laden balconies create the feeling of an old Mediterranean town square. Arches abound, planters and urns are filled with colorful flowers and evergreen foliage, and trees are lit with twinkle lights. Celebrations often begin around the fountain in the courtyard with butler-passed champagne and hors d'oeuvres. Then guests are invited into the spacious Courtyard Ballroom for the main event.

The Grove Ballroom on the second floor is another favorite reception space. Floor-to-ceiling arched windows wrap around the room and overlook a lushly landscaped balcony. Here, guests may enjoy an al fresco cocktail hour out on the balcony followed by dinner and dancing inside. Both ballrooms are popular for their indoor/outdoor flow and inviting ambiance.

There are many benefits that contribute to the complete guest experience at the Garden Court. A few of them are exclusively available to wedding couples with a guaranteed guest list of 75 or more: preferred room rates for guests staying at the hotel; a complimentary guestroom for the wedding couple on the night of the event; and a complimentary seven-night "Honeymoon in Spain" that the couple may split between multiple sister hotels. What more could you ask for?

CEREMONY CAPACITY: The Grove Ballroom accommodates 225 seated or 300 standing. The Courtyard Ballroom holds 120 seated or 200 standing.

EVENT/RECEPTION & MEETING CAPACITY: Various rooms can accommodate 8–230 seated or 8–300 standing for a reception. For a meeting, the hotel seats 8–60 conference-style or 8–200 theater-style. Removable dividing walls can vary the room size.

FEES & DEPOSITS: For weddings, a $1,000–3,000 nonrefundable deposit is due at the time of booking, an additional $3,000 nonrefundable deposit is due 6 months prior to your event date, and the final estimated total is due 10 days prior to the event. All deposits are applied to the total cost of the event. Facility fees start at $1,000 and vary depending on the day of the week and space reserved. Menu and beverage packages range $65–95/person. Tax and a 20% service charge are additional. All pricing is guaranteed 90 days prior to the event date, with some specialty items subject to market change.

Facility fees for meetings and corporate events vary based on group size, room(s) selected and catering requirements. Please call for more details. Customized estimate and an event packet will be emailed or mailed directly.

AVAILABILITY: Year-round, daily, 8am–midnight. Please call for specific time frames for events.

SERVICES/AMENITIES:
Catering: provided
Kitchen Facilities: n/a
Tables & Chairs: provided
Linens, Silver, etc.: provided
Restrooms: wheelchair accessible
Dance Floor: provided
Bride's Dressing Area: CBA, extra fee
Meeting Equipment: full range CBA, extra fee

Parking: complimentary valet, large lot
Accommodations: 62 guest rooms and suites
Telephone: pay phones
Outdoor Night Lighting: yes
Outdoor Cooking Facilities: no
Cleanup: provide
View: Mediterranean courtyard and downtown Palo Alto

RESTRICTIONS:
Alcohol: provided or wine and champagne corkage $20/bottle
Smoking: outside only
Music: amplified OK indoors only, outdoors acoustic music only

Wheelchair Access: yes
Insurance: not required
Other: no birdseed or rice

Lucie Stern Community Center

Community Center

1305 Middlefield Road, Palo Alto
650/463-4900
www.cityofpaloalto.org
lscc@cityofpaloalto.org

● Rehearsal Dinners	● Corp. Events/Mtgs.
● Ceremonies	● Private Parties
● Wedding Receptions	○ Accommodations

With its white-stucco archways, red-tile roof and vibrant courtyard, the Lucie Stern Center is a gracious example of Spanish-Mediterranean architecture. Designed by Birge Clark and donated by Lucie Stern, an heir of Levi Strauss, it was originally built in 1931 as a community theater. But since then, the center has matured into a welcoming hacienda that offers a variety of options for weddings.

You can rent individual areas or the whole center. For instance, if your wedding is small and informal, consider having it in the mid-sized Community Room, whose windows overlook a Mission-style promenade. The adjacent patio, which is enclosed by the U-shaped building and a vine-covered brick wall, has a two-tiered lawn bordered by an array of colorful flowers. The upper level is an ideal spot for your ceremony or live entertainment. Another choice for an intimate event is the Fireside Room. It features a large fireplace constructed of brick and stucco, and also adjoins the patio.

One of the most popular areas for gathering during a celebration is the Municipal Courtyard, a brick-paved retreat surrounded by flowers of every conceivable color. Enhancing this picturesque setting is the majestic stucco theater, standing tall in the background—it's evocative of a centuries-old Spanish church.

From the courtyard, guests walk through double glass doors into the Lucie Stern Center Ballroom, a large space complete with beautiful hardwood floors, dark wood wainscoting and two tiled fireplaces. Done in a rustic, early-California style, the room has a cathedral ceiling with exposed wooden beams and six cylindrical chandeliers crafted of black wrought iron. A row of windows overlooks the lush lawn in front of the facility.

From the blooming white roses at the courtyard entry to the open-air promenade and Mission-style rooms, the Lucie Stern Center is a classic Old World setting. And it's this abundance of old-fashioned elements that makes the center such a charming spot for weddings.

CEREMONY CAPACITY: The center holds 300 seated guests indoors or up to 250 seated guest outdoors.

EVENT/RECEPTION & MEETING CAPACITY: The center holds 200 seated or 300 standing guests indoors or up to 150 seated or 200 standing guest outdoors.

MEETING CAPACITY: The center holds up to 300 guests seated theater-style.

FEES & DEPOSITS: A reservation fee is due within 10 days of obtaining an approved permit. The balance is due in 2 payments; the final payment is payable 4 weeks prior to the event. If a cancellation occurs, 33% of the total fees and charges is nonrefundable. Cancellations within 30 days of an event receive no refund. The exclusive use fee ranges $300–350/hour for Palo Alto residents, $450–500/hour for nonresidents. If you don't rent the entire facility, individual rooms can be rented on an hourly basis; call for rates. A $25–30/hour fee is charged for a city employee to be on premises during the event.

AVAILABILITY: Year-round, daily, 6am–1am.

SERVICES/AMENITIES:

Catering: BYO
Kitchen Facilities: fully equipped
Tables & Chairs: most provided or through caterer
Linens, Silver, etc.: BYO or through caterer
Restrooms: wheelchair accessible
Dance Floor: ballroom
Bride's Dressing Area: no
Meeting Equipment: BYO or CBA

Parking: ample on site
Accommodations: no guest rooms
Telephone: emergency use only
Outdoor Night Lighting: yes
Outdoor Cooking Facilities: through caterer
Cleanup: caterer or renter
View: garden patio

RESTRICTIONS:

Alcohol: BYO wine, beer or champagne
Smoking: outside only
Music: amplified OK with restrictions

Wheelchair Access: yes
Insurance: extra liability required

Overwhelmed? Use the search criteria on www.HereComesTheGuide.com to narrow down your choices.

241

Palo Alto Hills Golf & Country Club

Country Club

3000 Alexis Drive, Palo Alto
650/917-5101

www.pahgcc.com
ltbeaton@pahgcc.net

- Rehearsal Dinners
- Ceremonies
- Wedding Receptions
- Corp. Events/Mtgs.
- Private Parties
- Accommodations

Set high in the rolling hills above Silicon Valley and nestled next to the Arastradero Open Space Preserve, the Palo Alto Hills Golf & Country Club boasts spectacular Bay Area vistas. And although this is one of the most prestigious private clubs in the United States, you don't have to be a member to host a special event here.

The country club is known for its welcoming atmosphere, and its Grand Ballroom could not be more inviting. Considered one of the loveliest spaces on the Peninsula, it's an ideal setting for any celebration. Windows on three sides showcase the golf course, signature 18th-hole green and cascading waterfall (a fabulous backdrop for a wedding ceremony and photos). The venue is also spacious enough to accommodate a seated reception for 275 with a dance floor.

The ballroom opens onto a landscaped terrace that's popular for wedding ceremonies, rehearsal dinners or post-ceremony cocktail receptions. Your guests will appreciate both the fresh air and the irresistible view: verdant fairways bordered by majestic redwoods, pine and oak trees. The park-like setting not only brings nature into your event, it offers endless photo opportunities.

For smaller gatherings, reserve the sophisticated Members Dining Room, whose warm cherrywood walls are crisscrossed with a distinctive pattern of brass inlay. In the evening, add a romantic glow with candles on the tables, or simply enjoy the captivating panorama of city lights sparkling against the night sky.

Two meeting rooms, which can be used individually or combined, are available for rehearsal dinners.

The chef takes pride in using the freshest ingredients and supporting many local and organic farms and vendors. He and his staff have created three distinct wedding packages, but if you have something else in mind they're happy to customize a menu for your occasion.

Impeccable service is the top priority at the Palo Alto Hills Golf & Country Club. Whether you're planning an elegant black-tie affair, a casual poolside party or something in between, you'll be impressed with their entire staff, from the valet parking attendants to the professional event coordinator who will help you personalize your festivities.

CEREMONY, EVENT/RECEPTION & MEETING CAPACITY: The clubhouse holds up to 275 seated or 400 standing guests, both indoors and outdoors.

FEES & DEPOSITS: Rental fees range $500–3,000 depending on the day of the week. Meals range $85–130/person. All wedding packages include a 1-hour hors d'oeuvres reception, salad course, entrée, champagne toast and cake-cutting fee. Tax, alcohol and a 20% service charge are additional.

AVAILABILITY: Year-round.

SERVICES/AMENITIES:

Catering: provided
Kitchen Facilities: n/a
Tables & Chairs: provided
Linens, Silver, etc.: provided
Restrooms: wheelchair accessible
Dance Floor: provided
Bride's Dressing Area: yes
Meeting Equipment: provided, extra fee
Other: event coordination

Parking: self-parking or valet, extra fee
Accommodations: no guest rooms
Telephone: emergency use only
Outdoor Night Lighting: yes
Outdoor Cooking Facilities: n/a
Cleanup: provided
View: bay, fairways, grounds, hills, pool, waterfall

RESTRICTIONS:

Alcohol: provided, or BYO wine with corkage fee
Smoking: outdoors only
Music: amplified OK

Wheelchair Access: yes
Insurance: not required

Sheraton Palo Alto

Hotel

625 El Camino Real, Palo Alto
650/328-2800

www.sheraton.com/paloalto
kbowne@pahotel.com

●	Rehearsal Dinners	●	Corp. Events/Mtgs.
●	Ceremonies	●	Private Parties
●	Wedding Receptions	●	Accommodations

Picture a clear, rocky stream running beneath foot bridges, past bushy ferns and flower gardens. Sounds more like a combination of the mountains and a tropical island than Palo Alto, but that's exactly where it is. At the Sheraton Palo Alto, you have a variety of event spaces, each with its own unique look, from the Spanish-tiled, glass-enclosed courtyard to the ballroom decorated with authentic Chinese antiques. The hotel is located on a commercial boulevard within walking distance of downtown Palo Alto, but because it's set back off the road and imaginatively landscaped, the Sheraton maintains an air of exclusivity.

A walk through the mostly glass lobby, suffused with light from windows and skylights, takes you to the large rectangular swimming pool area. It's the perfect spot for a splashy cocktail hour: A brick-paved patio is bordered by trees and gardenias, and at night the pool is illuminated by underwater lights and the trees glow with twinkle lights.

The Reception Room is set in its own wing, and the adjoining lawn is equally suited for ceremonies or stargazing. A semicircular wall encloses the lawn, so only your group can access it. The room itself features two large crystal chandeliers, a dance floor and vaulted ceiling, and fold-out glass doors that open onto the lawn.

Justine's Ballroom is highlighted by a beautiful glass-enclosed interior courtyard between spacious banquet rooms. It has Spanish tile, white stucco archways, arched mirrors and a glass ceiling. The setting makes a picturesque backdrop for your ceremony, photographs and even the cake cutting. Use the banquet room that opens out onto a streamside patio for cocktails, then spread out into both dining rooms for dinner. Beneath Justine's Ballroom is the Cypress Ballroom, an imperial room that features deep burgundy custom carpeting and royal white columns inset in the wall. Works of art from China are displayed in softly lit shadow boxes.

With its variety of event spaces, the Sheraton Palo Alto gives you plenty of options, and their creative and experienced staff guarantee to work wonders on your special day.

CEREMONY CAPACITY: The hotel can accommodate 150–300 seated or 200–350 standing guests indoors, and up to 120 seated or 200 standing outdoors.

EVENT/RECEPTION CAPACITY: The site holds 150–350 seated or up to 500 standing guests indoors.

MEETING CAPACITY: Small meeting rooms and parlors are available in addition to 3 larger spaces that seat 30–300 guests.

FEES & DEPOSITS: For weddings and special events, 25% of the estimated event total is required to secure your date. The balance is due 10 days prior to the event. Lunches start at $45/person and wedding packages start at $72/person. Alcohol, a 20% service charge and tax are extra. Bride and groom receive a complimentary room with champagne. Group rates can be arranged for overnight wedding guests. For meetings, room rental fees start at $400.

AVAILABILITY: Year-round, daily, anytime. Weddings take place on Saturdays and Sundays, 11am–4pm or 6pm–midnight.

SERVICES/AMENITIES:

Catering: provided; some ethnic caterers permitted
Kitchen Facilities: n/a
Tables & Chairs: provided
Linens, Silver, etc.: provided
Restrooms: wheelchair accessible
Dance Floor: portable indoors or Piazza Courtyard
Bride's & Groom's Dressing Areas: CBA
Meeting Equipment: full range CBA

Parking: large lot, valet available
Accommodations: 350 guest rooms and suites
Telephone: emergency use only
Outdoor Night Lighting: yes
Outdoor Cooking Facilities: n/a
Cleanup: provided
View: flower gardens, fountain, koi ponds
Other: event coordination

RESTRICTIONS:

Alcohol: provided, or corkage $15/bottle, $25/magnum
Smoking: outdoors only
Music: amplified OK

Wheelchair Access: yes
Insurance: not required
Other: no birdseed or rice; no fog machines

Westin Palo Alto Hotel

Hotel

675 El Camino Real, Palo Alto
650/321-4422
www.westin.com/paloalto
kbowne@pahotel.com

- Rehearsal Dinners
- Ceremonies
- Wedding Receptions
- Corp. Events/Mtgs.
- Private Parties
- Accommodations

It may look like simply another nice hotel from the outside, but as soon as you step into the marble-clad lobby of the Westin Palo Alto you experience its extraordinary appeal. This boutique-style venue combines clean, harmonious Feng Shui with a cosmopolitan sophistication that is warmed by understated Mediterranean architecture. Facing the entrance, a sleek marble staircase is flanked by a tableau of up-lit Oriental ferns in creamy ceramic vases. Above you, a ceiling inset with a serene shade of sky-blue introduces the hotel's design motif: *celestial.*

The expansive feeling of connection to heavenly elements is most artfully realized in the hotel's peaceful garden courtyards. Each is defined by two five-storied façades, whose guest room windows are embellished with wrought-iron balconies and pastel-hued shutters that recall Old World town squares. The Court of the Moon & Stars is favored by many brides for ceremonies because of its striking water feature: Along one ivy-decked wall, a row of fountain urns the color of cobalt blue overflow with water into a rectangular pool. At night, white globes glow like full moons in the background. Opposite this wall are French doors opening to a luxurious fireplace suite, often reserved by the bridal couple for the perfect grand entrance. Your attendants and overnight guests might stay in the other rooms overlooking the courtyard, turning it into your own private party haven.

But feel free to spread your event out into other delightful enclaves. The Court of the Sun features a bronze sundial at its center, cheerful yellow umbrellas, and a trellis climbing with golden honeysuckle. A large celadon fountain urn gurgles at the center of the Court of the Wind, while reeds and grasses arch along one wall as if bending to a gentle breeze. Either of these are pleasant spots for a social hour or an al fresco reception; or serve cocktails in the Court of Water around the swimming pool!

Indoor receptions are equally charming in the sumptuous Siena-Carrara Ballroom, commodious enough to accommodate your exclusive fête while still keeping things cozy. Leave the doors open, and guests can meander into the tastefully appointed Foyer, furnished with club chairs and sofas for relaxed conversation.

The Westin Palo Alto caters to intimate celebrations, that convivial kind of gathering where you're actually well-acquainted with each guest. Since yours is the one and only event on site, the Westin staff is dedicated to making it quite special indeed.

You would expect a venue with such style and personal service to be very costly; however, Westin offers reasonably priced wedding packages that include champagne and butler-passed hors d'oeuvres for the social hour; plated gourmet dinner with wine; elegant centerpieces; and a complimentary suite for the newlyweds. Speaking of wedding nights: Most of the hotel suites include romantic touches like a fireplace and whirlpool tub, and all rooms have Westin's signature Heavenly Bed, which boasts "10 layers of comfort"...so if you and your new spouse decide to leave the "do not disturb" sign on your door indefinitely, everyone will understand.

CEREMONY CAPACITY: The Courtyard holds 50 seated guests; the Siena-Carrara Ballroom 100.

EVENT/RECEPTION CAPACITY: The Siena-Carrara Ballroom holds up to 60 seated or 100 standing guests; the Courtyard up to 50 seated or 60 standing guests.

MEETING CAPACITY: Event spaces accommodate 12–80 seated guests.

FEES & DEPOSITS: 25% of the estimated event total is required to reserve your date. The balance is due 10 days prior to the event. Rental fees range $300–800 depending on the food and beverage minimum. Lunches start at $45/person, wedding packages start at $76/person. Tax, alcohol and a 20% service charge are additional.

AVAILABILITY: Year-round, daily, anytime. Weddings take place on Saturdays and Sundays, 11am–4pm or 6pm–midnight.

SERVICES/AMENITIES:

Catering: provided
Kitchen Facilities: n/a
Tables & Chairs: provided
Linens, Silver, etc.: provided
Restrooms: wheelchair accessible
Dance Floor: provided
Bride's & Groom's Dressing Areas: CBA
Meeting Equipment: CBA

Parking: large lot, valet available
Accommodations: 184 guest rooms
Telephone: emergency use only
Outdoor Night Lighting: yes
Outdoor Cooking Facilities: no
Cleanup: provided
View: pool, courtyard, fountain, grounds
Other: event coordination

RESTRICTIONS:

Alcohol: provided, or corkage $15/bottle
Smoking: outside only
Music: amplified OK with restrictions

Wheelchair Access: yes
Insurance: not required

The professionals in the back of this book are the best in the business. How do we know? Read page 637.

Woman's Club of Palo Alto

Historic Woman's Club

475 Homer Avenue, Palo Alto
650/321-5821

womansclubofpaloalto.org
rentals@womansclubofpaloalto.org

● Rehearsal Dinners	● Corp. Events/Mtgs.
● Ceremonies	● Private Parties
● Wedding Receptions	○ Accommodations

On June 20, 1894, 24 women gathered to organize the Woman's Club of Palo Alto. Their goals were friendship, self-improvement, and community involvement. Within the first four years of the club's existence, they founded the city's first reading room and library, as well as its first elementary school and high school.

Their dream of having their own clubhouse, however, was not realized until 1916. After 12 years of fundraising, they built their Tudor-Craftsman-style "home" for $10,590. At the time, they worried that it was too far removed from the center of town, but its location in a quiet residential neighborhood has proved a felicitous one.

Weddings are held in the Ballroom, a simply designed space with grand proportions. On two sides, tall windows flood the room with light, which reflects off polished maple floors. Eight brass-and-glass fixtures suspended from the high ceiling, and dark wood wainscoting and trim throughout add period character. Have your ceremony on the stage, which is framed by a red velvet curtain and illuminated by footlights. A Steinway grand piano is available for musical accompaniment. Buffets are usually set up in the adjacent Fireside Room, aptly named for its tiled fireplace, and joined to the Ballroom by folding French doors.

The founders of the Woman's Club of Palo Alto may not have envisioned their clubhouse as a setting for private events, but today the landmark building has become just that. Its elegant ballroom, Japanese garden and chef's kitchen make it a popular and affordable spot for weddings, corporate functions, and other celebrations.

CEREMONY, EVENT/RECEPTION & MEETING CAPACITY: The Ballroom and Fireside Room hold 150 seated guests.

FEES & DEPOSITS: For weekend special events or weddings, the full-day rental fee is $2,300 plus a $500 security deposit and a $125 janitorial fee. Half the rental fee and the security deposit are due with your signed contract; the balance is payable 2 weeks prior to the event.

For weekday meetings and multi-day bookings, the rental fee varies depending on usage. The base rate is $200/hour with a minimum of 6 hours.

AVAILABILITY: Year-round, daily, anytime.

SERVICES/AMENITIES:

Catering: BYO
Kitchen Facilities: fully equipped
Tables & Chairs: provided
Linens, Silver, etc.: BYO
Restrooms: wheelchair accessible
Dance Floor: on stage, in Ballroom
Bride's Dressing Area: yes
Meeting Equipment: WiFi, A/V

Parking: on-street and nearby lots
Accommodations: no guest rooms
Telephone: no phone
Outdoor Night Lighting: access only
Outdoor Cooking Facilities: BYO BBQ
Cleanup: caterer or renter
View: residential neighborhood
Other: air conditioning

RESTRICTIONS:

Alcohol: BYO; wine, beer and champagne only
Smoking: outdoors only
Music: amplified OK indoors only until 10pm

Wheelchair Access: yes
Insurance: liability required

Valley Presbyterian Church

Church

945 Portola Road, Portola Valley
650/851-2848

www.valleypreschurch.org
wedding@valleypreschurch.org

Rehearsal Dinners	Corp. Events/Mtgs.
● Ceremonies	Private Parties
Wedding Receptions	Accommodations

From its breathtaking sanctuary to its wooded grounds, Valley Presbyterian Church draws on the purity of the natural world to enhance your spiritual experience. "There's a sense of peace here," explains one congregant. "You feel like a part of nature, and thus closer to God."

The heart of Valley Presbyterian Church is the awe-inspiring sanctuary. The sanctuary's simplicity and unpretentious beauty evoke serenity and wonder. Guests enter through four heavy wooden doors, richly carved with images of New Testament figures. Flanking each side of the church are stone planters filled with lush greenery. Oak pews are upholstered in green fabric, and the A-frame pine ceiling is accented by dark beams. Polished riverbed stones in the washed aggregate floor echo the sanctuary's earthy aesthetic.

However, it's the soaring sanctuary windows behind the communion table that take your breath away. They frame a grove of majestic redwood trees reaching heavenward, while a filigree of sunbeams streams into the church. Guests face this magnificent forest scene, while from the steps below the communion table the bridal party enjoys its own striking tableau: the six-foot-tall stained-glass panel above the front doors that depicts a simple golden cross in a blue-toned mosaic. When the sun shines through it, the amber cross is reflected across the church onto the view of the redwoods, and seems to float mysteriously in the air—a sparkling vision that heightens the mood of peaceful reverence.

The church comes with the services of a minister, coordinator, organist, wedding hostess and hostess assistant. Every couple that marries at Valley Presbyterian attends a one-day Marriage Preparation Workshop, as well as a separate private meeting with their assigned officiant. All are welcome here, and though a Valley Presbyterian minister will be the main officiant of the wedding, you may invite a guest minister to assist with the ceremony. Also included, but optional, are candelabras and candles, unity candle, silk floral arrangement, pew decorations and aisle runner.

Valley Presbyterian Church believes in giving back to the community, and is known for its outreach and children's programs. This is a church that actively promotes family, community, and spiritual values—a promising environment for starting a new life together.

CEREMONY CAPACITY: The Sanctuary holds 225+ guests. Call for details.

FEES & DEPOSITS: A $1,000 nonrefundable deposit is required to reserve your date. The fee through 2014 is $1,850 for a 2½-hour time frame. Fees subject to change without notice. Couples need not be members of Valley Presbyterian Church; however, it is necessary that the ceremony be a Christian service.

AVAILABILITY: Year-round. Ceremonies on Saturday begin at 10am, noon, 2:30pm and 5pm, and on Sunday at 2:30pm and 5pm. Rehearsals take place on the Friday before the wedding.

SERVICES/AMENITIES:

Catering: n/a

Kitchen Facilities: n/a

Tables & Chairs: n/a

Linens, Silver, etc.: n/a

Restrooms: wheelchair accessible

Dance Floor: n/a

Bride's & Groom's Dressing Areas: yes

Meeting Equipment: n/a

Parking: lot for 175 guests

Accommodations: no guest rooms

Telephone: house phone

Outdoor Night Lighting: yes

Outdoor Cooking Facilities: n/a

Cleanup: provided

View: redwood forest

RESTRICTIONS:

Alcohol: not permitted

Smoking: not allowed

Music: acoustic only

Wheelchair Access: yes

Insurance: not required

Other: no birdseed or rice

San Mateo County History Museum

Museum

2200 Broadway, Redwood City
650/299-0104 x225

www.historysmc.org
sue@historysmc.org

● Rehearsal Dinners		● Corp. Events/Mtgs.	
● Ceremonies		● Private Parties	
● Wedding Receptions		○ Accommodations	

Domes are wondrous things, and there's no end to our fascination with them. Fortunately, you don't have to go to Rome (St. Peter's), Washington, DC (the Capitol) or Istanbul (the Hagia Sophia) to get a great dome fix—or even to get married beneath one. Just take the much shorter trip to Redwood City, where the San Mateo County History Museum has preserved one of the Bay Area's most remarkable domes.

The museum inhabits the venerable 1910 county courthouse, a sandstone structure that retains all of the dignity of that era, with its tile floors, Corinthian columns and tall, stately doors opening to Exhibit Galleries and the beautifully restored Courtroom A. The overwhelming centerpiece, however, is its magnificent dome. A towering concoction of skylit glass panes colored brilliant red, green, amber and opaque white, it rises above sculpted eagles and ornamental arches to a constellation of gold stars on a deep blue background. The dome is a full-tilt, rock-your-head-back-on-your-shoulders-and-stare-at-it-in-wonder kind of thing. Get married under it and you'll be talking about it for years to come.

Many couples also use the rotunda for their ceremony and reception. If your party is a large one, take advantage of the balcony-like second floor, which doubles as another dining space. Here guests not only have a better vantage of the gorgeous glass overhead, they can stroll over to the railing and enjoy a bird's-eye view of the festivities below.

Courtroom A also makes a fabulous setting for a ceremony or sit-down dinner. You reach it via a grand staircase distinguished by marble-topped risers, brass railings and mahogany banisters. Couples love its elegance and often pose for wedding photos on it. The courtroom has rich oak moldings and furnishings, including the traditional long railing that separates the jury and bar members from the public. Overhead, the ceiling features an oblong skylight of green, red and gray-blue glass arranged in abstract floral patterns. Stylized plaster wreaths of fruits and grains border the skylight, and four heavy Federal-style chandeliers with scalloped sconces hang low from the ceiling. Large oak-framed windows along two walls come down almost to the floor, and a Roman-style pediment spans the main entrance. The thick English carpet, red with gold highlights, feels absolutely wonderful underfoot. The original clerk, bailiff and judge's benches are still there, as are the jury chairs. This immensely refined room bestows an extra element of grace on any wedding.

The rotunda is so phenomenal that it needs little decoration, and the same goes for Courtroom A. For an added diversion (and fee), arrange to have the museum's exhibits open to your guests. If you love history or simply want something delightfully unconventional, it would be hard to beat this domed museum.

CEREMONY CAPACITY: Courtroom A holds 100 seated guests and the Rotunda holds 150 seated.

EVENT/RECEPTION CAPACITY: The entire courthouse holds 400 standing guests. Courtroom A accommodates up to 170 for a seated reception.

MEETING CAPACITY: The museum holds up to 120 guests for meetings.

FEES & DEPOSITS: A $750 deposit is required to reserve your date. The balance is due 30 days prior to event. Rental fees range $3,200–5,000 depending on spaces reserved, services selected and staffing needed for the event.

AVAILABILITY: Year-round, daily: Monday all day; Tuesday–Sunday 4pm–midnight.

SERVICES/AMENITIES:

Catering: BYO
Kitchen Facilities: full catering kitchen
Tables & Chairs: tables provided, extra fee
Linens, Silver, etc.: CBA
Restrooms: wheelchair accessible
Dance Floor: yes
Bride's Dressing Area: yes
Meeting Equipment: full range CBA, including teleconferencing and internet access

Parking: on-street or large lot, free after 6pm
Accommodations: no guest rooms
Telephone: no
Outdoor Night Lighting: yes
Outdoor Cooking Facilities: no
Cleanup: caterer and janitorial staff
View: park, hills, fountain, grounds
Other: access to exhibits, extra fee

RESTRICTIONS:

Alcohol: BYO
Smoking: outdoors only
Music: amplified OK indoors

Wheelchair Access: yes
Insurance: required

Want to know **WHAT TO ASK** a potential location or vendor? Check out our Questions to Ask starting on page 17.

Sofitel San Francisco Bay

Hotel

223 Twin Dolphin Drive, Redwood City
650/598-9000

www.sofitel-sanfrancisco-bay.com
sofitel.sanfranciscobay@accor.com

- Rehearsal Dinners
- Ceremonies
- Wedding Receptions
- Corp. Events/Mtgs.
- Private Parties
- Accommodations

Poised on the banks of a serene lagoon, Sofitel San Francisco Bay conveys a contemporary elegance. Sofitel's European heritage and French-inspired cuisine are complemented by a California-style friendliness and an experienced staff that make guests feel right at home.

The marble-clad lobby boasts a striking abstract blown-glass chandelier in shades of sapphire blue, reminiscent of the sun-splashed waters of the bay. Throughout the public spaces, the same vibrant blues play against the interior's muted hues as eye-catching accents—throw pillows on a dove-gray sofa in *bay bar;* painted library alcoves; and restaurant *bay 223's* modern dining banquettes. In fact, the hotel décor is stunning, applied with sleek, fresh brushstrokes befitting its uniquely presented luxury.

Wedding ceremonies sparkle out on the dock, which overlooks a tranquil waterway where egrets and blue herons feed alongside flocks of ducks and geese. Follow up with a cocktail hour on the landscaped patio surrounding the swimming pool, with the glistening lagoon as a picturesque backdrop.

There are plenty of event options indoors as well—15 rooms in all, including Sofitel's 6,200-square-foot Grand Ballroom. Serve cocktails and hors d'oeuvres in the Foyer, adorned with illuminated swags of blue crystals. Inside, the recently renovated Grand Ballroom is done in a refined color scheme of gold, sand and cream with accents of blue. Avant-garde lighting fixtures incorporate wavy sheets of striped glass that are in harmony with shimmery drapes in the same honey and copper earth tones. One wall of floor-to-ceiling windows looks out to a porte-cochère, where water flows from a Mediterranean-style fountain. The Grand Ballroom can be used in its entirety or divided in half, depending on the size of your party.

Wedding showers and rehearsal dinners take on an air of exclusive intimacy in the Grand Salon or Blue Room. Small receptions are held in the Veranda, a room enclosed entirely by glass walls. Marble detailing and floors inlaid with dark wood add extra flair.

Cuisine is not an afterthought at Sofitel—the kitchen has a reputation for superbly prepared gourmet fare, best described as Bay Area French. Creative menus employ fresh local ingredients and the expertise of a French culinary staff for a marvelous dining experience.

To help you relax after the big event, Sofitel offers a complimentary suite for the bride and groom, with champagne and strawberries upon arrival, and special group rates for out-of-town guests.

All the rooms feature Sofitel's signature SoBed, a plush featherbed oasis of comfort. There will be plenty of takers for any overnight accommodations you arrange, as guests will want to extend their visit to this fashionable establishment as long as possible!

CEREMONY CAPACITY: Dockside (next to the lagoon) accommodates up to 175 seated; the Ballroom holds 450 seated guests.

EVENT/RECEPTION CAPACITY: The hotel holds 80–450 seated or 100–700 standing guests indoors.

MEETING CAPACITY: 15 rooms are available, including the Ballroom, the Executive Board Room, and a variety of salons. The facility holds 10–400 classroom-style, 12–30 conference-style, 14–50 in a U-shape and 10–700 seated theater-style.

FEES & DEPOSITS: For events, 10% of the estimated total is required as a nonrefundable deposit when you book your date; 50% of the estimated total is due 6 months prior, and another 25% is due 1 month prior to the event. The remaining balance is required 1 week prior to the event, and a guaranteed guest count is due 3 business days prior. Any remaining charges are payable at the conclusion of your event. Wedding packages range $100–150/person; sales tax and a 20% service charge are additional. The Sofitel offers a discount for Friday and Sunday receptions. For meetings, room rental fees start at $400/day.

AVAILABILITY: Year-round, daily, 11am–1am. Call for details on specific spaces.

SERVICES/AMENITIES:
Catering: provided, or approved outside ethnic caterer
Kitchen Facilities: n/a
Tables & Chairs: provided
Linens, Silver, etc.: provided
Restrooms: wheelchair accessible
Dance Floor: provided
Bride's Dressing Area: yes
Meeting Equipment: CBA, extra fee

Parking: ample parking, valet available
Accommodations: 421 guest rooms
Telephone: private lines CBA
Outdoor Night Lighting: no
Outdoor Cooking Facilities: no
Cleanup: provided
View: lagoon, hills, fountain
Other: complete event coordination and wireless internet available

RESTRICTIONS:
Alcohol: provided
Smoking: designated areas
Music: amplified OK

Wheelchair Access: yes
Insurance: may be required
Other: no rice, birdseed or confetti

CuriOdyssey

Science Center and Zoo

1651 Coyote Point Drive, San Mateo
650/340-7565
www.curiodyssey.org
events@curiodyssey.org

● Rehearsal Dinners	● Corp. Events/Mtgs.
● Ceremonies	● Private Parties
● Wedding Receptions	Accommodations

If you're a lover of nature or innovative architecture, then you're sure to appreciate the unique attributes of CuriOdyssey, a family-friendly science center, zoo, and thoroughly original event venue. Poised at the edge of the Coyote Point Recreation Area and overlooking San Francisco Bay, CuriOdyssey is surrounded by eucalyptus groves and county parkland. Right from the ample parking lot, you're likely to spy some of the local residents: scurrying woodland creatures, wading shorebirds or colorful hummingbirds.

CuriOdyssey's main hub is a contemporary building with an angular portico. Adjacent patios form the entrance to over an acre of gardens and wildlife exhibits. Couples can tie the knot in the Hummingbird Garden, an intimate spot surrounded by trees and flowering plants, while a rescued porcupine and Channel Island fox look on from their enclosure. The neighboring Butterfly Garden can be set up with a portable bar for a lively social hour, and if you'd like your friends and family to experience an up-close encounter with an Animal Ambassador—a boa constrictor or African hedgehog, for example—that can be arranged, too. Guests are free to stroll along the pathways and explore the 25 naturalistic habitats showcasing native flora and fauna, including bobcats and other mammals, and a towering aviary. Another social hour option is to invite everyone indoors to play with the interactive science exhibits.

Receptions are usually held in the stunning Redwood Hall, which has been meticulously crafted from rich, reclaimed wood. Even its foyer, called the Bayview Terrace, is magnificent: Soaring multipaned windows capture a breathtaking panorama of the bay through the trees, from romantic sunset to sparkling nighttime cityscape. The view remains on display from inside the hall, too. The Redwood Hall is made up of four cascading levels that can be used individually or in combination. The upper story features a mirrored cupola with a *trompe l'oeil* cloud-filled sky. On the facing wall, a painting of a full moon complements the celestial motif. Many couples opt to wed facing the bay view, with the faux moon as the ceremony backdrop.

Since the levels are connected by ramps and fan out like tiers on a wedding cake, it's easy to envision your celebration progressing from vows, to cocktail hour, to dinner, to dancing. The ceiling is lined with rows of thin, polished wood beams, and cylindrical wooden columns descending to the floor form a visual counterpoint. In one corner of the hall, an abstract wooden oak tree stretches its boughs overhead. Throughout, artfully arranged nature prints suspended from the rafters seem to float in the air. To truly appreciate the hall's striking design and extraordinary architectural details, we recommend that you see it for yourself.

With such intriguing settings, you'd expect CuriOdyssey to be pricey, but it's not. What's more, holding your event here supports the museum's mission to educate and inspire people to take care of the earth wisely, which makes CuriOdyssey a "natural" choice for a green wedding or other milestone occasion.

CEREMONY CAPACITY: The venue seats 300 indoors and 60 outdoors.

EVENT/RECEPTION CAPACITY: The site accommodates 300 seated or 500 standing indoors, and 60 seated or 300 standing outdoors.

MEETING CAPACITY: Meeting spaces hold 150 seated guests.

FEES & DEPOSITS: A security deposit is required to reserve your date. The balance is due 90 days prior to the event. For events with up to 250 guests, fees begin at $1,800. For events with 250–500 guests, fees begin at $2,400.

AVAILABILITY: Year-round, daily, 5pm–midnight for special events. Call for availability on classroom and theater.

SERVICES/AMENITIES:

Catering: select from preferred list
Kitchen Facilities: prep only
Tables & Chairs: some provided
Linens, Silver, etc.: through caterer
Restrooms: wheelchair accessible
Dance Floor: provided
Bride's Dressing Area: yes
Meeting Equipment: BYO

Parking: large lot
Accommodations: no guest rooms
Telephone: emergency use only
Outdoor Night Lighting: CBA
Outdoor Cooking Facilities: BBQ CBA
Cleanup: provided, extra fee
View: panorama of forest, ocean and park
Other: Animal Ambassador appearance available, extra fee

RESTRICTIONS:

Alcohol: BYO
Smoking: not allow
Music: amplified OK

Wheelchair Access: yes
Insurance: liability required

San Mateo Marriott

Hotel

1770 South Amphlett Boulevard, San Mateo
650/653-6093

www.sanmateomarriott.com
info@marriott-sanmateo.com

- Rehearsal Dinners
- Ceremonies
- Wedding Receptions
- Corp. Events/Mtgs.
- Private Parties
- Accommodations

The intersection of 101 and 92 is the true crossroads of the San Francisco Bay Area, linking east to west, north to south, and bay to coast. At that exact nexus, just minutes from San Francisco International Airport, sits the San Mateo Marriott.

Remodeled in 2007, the hotel's exterior is topped with Spanish-style red-tile roofs, and the interior is decidedly contemporary. The circular marble-clad lobby and many of the lounges sport whimsical wrought-iron chandeliers and sconces with brightly colored, hand-blown glass shades. French doors everywhere open to patios, terraces and courtyards, and there are more windows than usual for such a large hotel, giving the venue a light and airy feel.

Stage your ceremony in the courtyard beneath the white-pillared gazebo with its decorative wrought-iron dome. Afterwards your guests can enjoy cocktails and hors d'oeuvres in the nearby lobby lounge with its full bar and fireplace, while you take advantage of the beautiful courtyard for photographs. From here, make your grand entrance into the spacious Engage Ballroom for the reception. Wood molding, silky gold drapes and a fireplace framed in green stone tiles give this space an almost European flavor. During the day the room is flooded with light, flowing in through French doors.

More event options are available on the second floor. Have cocktails in the Synergy Lobby and your banquet in the Inspire Ballroom, which can be employed as one large space or partitioned for smaller celebrations. Off the grand foyer is the circular Synergy, with unusual, brick-lined walls and massive glass doors. Set the buffet and bar in the boardroom, and let your guests mingle in the foyer, or wander out onto the adjacent terrace for some fresh air.

Windows on both sides of the capacious Convene Ballroom are framed in pale gold drapes, and the room is lit with impressive alabaster and verdigris chandeliers. Invite your guests to sip champagne in the sconce-lit Convene Lobby to the sound of soft music played on the grand piano, before they move into the ballroom for the reception.

If there are many children on your guest list, consider offering them their own kid-friendly banquet in the adjacent Synergy 1, with a child-size (and child-safe) buffet of pizza, chicken tenders and other readily accepted kid fare.

San Mateo Marriott specializes in California cuisine, but the hotel will cater to any preference, be it pork and poi or roast beef and potatoes. They'll handle all the details, from flowers to fire-eaters (really!), or you can plan your whole event yourself.

If your guests are coming from far and wide, San Mateo Marriott is in the single most convenient location possible. It can be reached easily from anywhere in the greater Bay Area, and there are enough luxury rooms and suites (476 to be precise) to accommodate the largest of weddings. There are even brand new bridal suites with lofted bedrooms, Jacuzzi tubs and full-length mirrors. Making everyone happy is a difficult goal to achieve, but San Mateo Marriott does it with ease.

CEREMONY CAPACITY: The hotel seats 600 indoors and 300 outdoors.

EVENT/RECEPTION CAPACITY: The Marriott accommodates 350 seated or 700 standing indoors, and 170 seated, 200 standing outdoors.

MEETING CAPACITY: The hotel holds 600 seated guests.

FEES & DEPOSITS: A $1,000 deposit is required to reserve your date. The balance is due 7 days prior to the event. Rental fees range $1,800–4,500 depending on the space rented. Meals range $70–120/person. Tax, alcohol and a 22% service charge are additional.

AVAILABILITY: Year-round, daily, anytime.

SERVICES/AMENITIES:

Catering: provided or BYO
Kitchen Facilities: minimal
Tables & Chairs: provided
Linens, Silver, etc.: provided
Restrooms: wheelchair accessible
Dance Floor: patio, deck or portable
Bride's Dressing Area: yes
Meeting Equipment: provided

Parking: large lot, valet available
Accommodations: 476 guest rooms
Telephone: house phone
Outdoor Night Lighting: yes
Outdoor Cooking Facilities: BBQ on site
Cleanup: provided
View: hills, pool area, landscaped grounds
Other: A/V equipment

RESTRICTIONS:

Alcohol: provided
Smoking: outside only
Music: amplified OK

Wheelchair Access: yes
Insurance: may be required

Want to find more venues and services? Check out our informative website, www.HereComesTheGuide.com.

259

The Mountain Terrace

17285 Skyline Boulevard, Woodside
650/851-1606

www.themountainterrace.com
info@themountainterrace.com

Special Event Facility

● Rehearsal Dinners	● Corp. Events/Mtgs.
● Ceremonies	● Private Parties
● Wedding Receptions	Accommodations

Whether you're driving down from San Francisco or up from San Jose, the final six miles to The Mountain Terrace are sensational. They ascend a mountainside on state route 84, one of California's most magnificent sections of highway. The winding road is flanked by sturdy old oaks, dense fragrant redwood groves and huge chateau-like mansions. There are spectacular bay and ridge views at several spots along the way and, in a couple of places, imposing trees thrust their branches out across the road to form living archways.

If the last leg of the trip is a revelation, a second surprise awaits at the top. Where Highway 84 meets up with redwood-edged Skyline Blvd., there's a small crossroads settlement. The Mountain Terrace is an unassuming wooden building at the far end of this little village. However, as they say, appearances can be deceiving: The Mountain Terrace's prosaic exterior conceals glories inside. Once you cross the parking lot and pass through a redwood arbor, what you see takes your breath away: a brilliant green acre of lawn, shimmering in the sunlight, rimmed by oaks and dozens of soaring redwoods. At its far boundary, where the mountain begins to slope to the lowlands, it draws your eyes to a sweeping view of the southern part of San Francisco Bay all the way down to the Fremont hills.

By itself, the lawn makes a perfect spot for an outdoor wedding and reception. But there's more—once you've taken in the lawn, you turn to see a large two-level redwood deck. Right away you know it would make a superb setting for a stand-up reception, sit-down dinner or any kind of function in between. On its upper level, a vine-covered trellis shelters half the deck. The lower deck, only a couple of steps down from the upper, has a deftly crafted octagonal-shaped extension that's built around a mature oak tree. Just beyond the deck there are more oaks (one with a tree swing) shading chairs beneath them. The little grove makes a perfect nook partygoers can use to take a break from the main festivities while not losing touch.

There's still more: Glass doors connect the deck to a substantial indoor space, divided into a dining room and a bar/dance area by a large stone fireplace. The antique bar, made of solid oak, has hefty Doric columns carved into it and is backed by a massive three-part mirror. The room's hardwood floor invites carefree dancing (there's an area where a band or DJ can set up). The dining area looks out through picture windows onto the deck and lawn. In winter, with a roaring fire inside and mist-shrouded redwoods outside, it makes a cozy wedding and reception site by itself.

As a facility, The Mountain Terrace is a "three-fer": stunning lawn and view, inviting interior and grand redwood deck. Then there's the drive up, which will put your guests in such a good mood, by the time they arrive they'll be ready to fully enjoy the charms of this very special place.

CEREMONY CAPACITY: The meadow accommodates up to 400 seated guests.

EVENT/RECEPTION & MEETING CAPACITY: Indoors, the site holds 130 seated guests. Outdoors, the patio holds up to 200 seated guests; the decks and lawn seat up to 250. When combined, the indoor and outdoor spaces accommodate a maximum of 330 seated guests.

FEES & DEPOSITS: A $500 refundable security deposit plus half the rental fee is required to reserve your date. The remainder, along with any estimated bar charges, is due 15 days prior to the event, and the balance is payable on the day of the event. Rental fees range $750–4,250 depending on the date and time rented. Meals start at $26/person. Tax, alcohol and service charge are additional.

AVAILABILITY: Year-round, daily.

SERVICES/AMENITIES:

Catering: provided or approved caterer
Kitchen Facilities: fully equipped
Tables & Chairs: provided for up to 150 guests
Linens, Silver, etc.: through caterer
Restrooms: wheelchair accessible
Dance Floor: indoor area
Bride's Dressing Area: yes
Meeting Equipment: CBA

Parking: on-site lot or shuttle
Accommodations: no guest rooms
Telephone: house phone
Outdoor Night Lighting: yes
Outdoor Cooking Facilities: CBA, extra fee
Cleanup: caterer
View: redwoods, partial bay view

RESTRICTIONS:

Alcohol: provided
Smoking: designated areas
Music: amplified OK indoors only, outdoors acoustic only

Wheelchair Access: yes
Insurance: not required

Thomas Fogarty Winery and Vineyards

Hilltop Winery

19501 Skyline Boulevard, Woodside
650/851-6772

www.fogartywinery.com
events@fogartywinery.com

●	Rehearsal Dinners	●	Corp. Events/Mtgs.
●	Ceremonies	●	Private Parties
●	Wedding Receptions		Accommodations

If we were to rate facilities on a scale from 1 to 10, the Fogarty Winery would be a 10! Located off Skyline Boulevard, this has to be one of the best places we've seen, not only for weddings, but for private parties and corporate functions, too.

Commanding an extraordinary panorama of the bay and Peninsula, the winery sits high on a ridge in a quiet vineyard setting. As you drive in, vineyards and a lovely pond come into view. At the top of the ridge is a large lawn, beautifully landscaped around the perimeter—a perfect spot for an outdoor ceremony.

Receptions and special events are held in the Hill House and/or the outdoor Pavilion. True to its name, the former steps down the hill, and is designed with incredible attention to detail, featuring a stone fireplace, fine woodwork, skylights, a wine bar and professional kitchen. From comfortable seating indoors, as well as from the semiglass-enclosed terrace, you can see for miles—past the neighboring vineyard all the way to the distant bay.

Adjacent to the Hill House is the Pavilion, a covered redwood deck suspended over the hillside. Calling it a "covered deck" may be something of an understatement: This 4,000-square-foot architectural treat is constructed of teal-painted columns and beams which support a peaked cedar roof inset with skylights. You have a 270-degree view of the surrounding oak-dotted hills and the Chardonnay vineyards below. The Pavilion is truly the perfect spot for cocktails and hors d'oeuvres or an open-air seated reception—no matter how hot the day is, there's always a breeze blowing here. You can reserve the House or Pavilion individually or use them in combination—they're connected by a deck, so there's a wonderful flow between them.

For small private dinners, the Redwood Room is light and airy, arranged with custom-built "barrel" tables, handcrafted leather chairs, a wood-burning stove and full kitchen. Even the restroom is unique, with a blue-green slate and stone bathtub! And if you'd like to have a meeting in this glorious setting, hold it in the Board Room or the Hill House. A recent landscaping project has covered the hillside with ferns, manzanita and native plantings, not to mention tons of river rock.

The improvements only add to the sense you get that the winery has been designed with taste and sophistication to blend in with its surroundings. We can't recommend this facility highly enough.

CEREMONY CAPACITY: The Garden holds 200 seated or 216 standing.

EVENT/RECEPTION CAPACITY: The Hill House accommodates 216 seated guests without space for dancing, or 180 with dancing. The Pavilion holds up to 216 seated guests.

MEETING CAPACITY: Event spaces accommodate 20–150 seated guests.

FEES & DEPOSITS: For weddings, 50% of the rental fee is required as a nonrefundable deposit, due when reservations are confirmed; the balance is payable 6 months prior to your function. The rental fee includes use of the lawn area, Hill House and the Pavilion for 8 hours. The wedding rental fee for the entire facility is $7,000 Monday–Friday, year-round. The weekend rental fee ranges $4,500–10,000 year-round.

For other special events and business functions, fees vary depending on spaces selected, event duration, day of week and season. Call for rates.

AVAILABILITY: Year-round, daily. For weddings and receptions, weekends 8am–11pm. For corporate events, any day 7am–11pm. Closed Thanksgiving, Christmas and New Year's Days and Eves.

SERVICES/AMENITIES:

Catering: select from preferred list
Kitchen Facilities: fully equipped
Tables & Chairs: some provided
Linens, Silver, etc.: BYO
Restrooms: wheelchair accessible
Dance Floor: inside Hill House
Bride's Dressing Area: yes
Meeting Equipment: full range
Other: site manager, wine tasting

Parking: for weddings, valet included in fee
Accommodations: no guest rooms
Telephone: pay phone
Outdoor Night Lighting: yes
Outdoor Cooking Facilities: CBA
Cleanup: caterer
View: panorama of SF Bay and all major mountain peaks

RESTRICTIONS:

Alcohol: wine and champagne provided, no BYO
Smoking: outside only
Music: must select band or DJ from preferred list; acoustic only in lawn area

Wheelchair Access: yes
Insurance: certificate required

South Bay

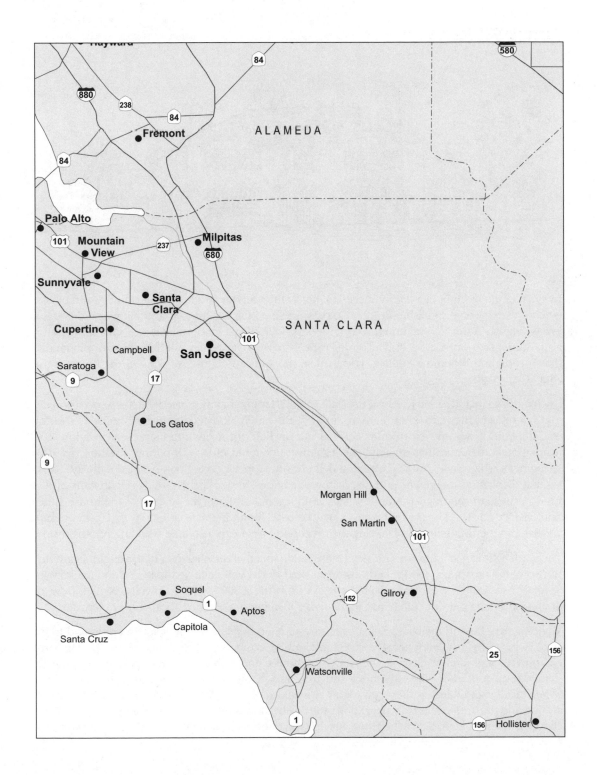

Ainsley House and Gardens

Historic House & Gardens

300 Grant Avenue, Campbell
408/866-2119

www.cityofcampbell.com/museum
kerryp@cityofcampbell.com

● Rehearsal Dinners	● Corp. Events/Mtgs.
● Ceremonies	● Private Parties
● Wedding Receptions	○ Accommodations

In 1925, in the twilight of a highly successful life as the founder of a local fruit cannery and export company, expatriate Englishman John Colpitts Ainsley built for himself and his wife, Alcinda, a lovely English Tudor Revival home. With 15 rooms (including a modern kitchen with a refrigerator, a six-burner two-oven stove, and adjoining maid's quarters), large bay windows, a swooping mock thatch roof, and blooming English-style garden, the Ainsley's home was one of the finest in the Santa Clara Valley.

During the years following JC Ainsley's death in 1937, family members used the house occasionally for Christmas parties and other reunions. In 1989, the family donated the historic house to the city of Campbell. It was moved from its original site on Bascom Avenue to its present location, and restoration was begun immediately. The result is a living museum with period furniture (most of it original to the house), walls covered in delicate silk fabric, glowing oak-paneled hallways, closets that display period gowns and tiny flapper-era shoes, and a kitchen stocked with cans of JC's fruit! Because of the fragile nature of these antiques and artifacts, the interior of the house is not available for parties. The parlor, however, may be used for an intimate ceremony (up to 15 guests), and couples getting married or having their reception here can also take wedding photos inside.

The gardens that now surround Ainsley House retain much of the character of the original gardens. Blossoming crabapples, rhododendrons, irises, and bridal veil encircle the house and back lawn. Several rose bushes were transplanted straight from the Ainsley's 1925 flowerbeds. The front of the house opens onto the Orchard City Green, a lush lawn used for a local concert series.

Weddings are held in the backyard, a large private lawn bordered by flowers and redwood trees, and enclosed by latticed fencing covered in climbing roses. For the ceremony, the bridal party emerges through French doors at the rear of the house, and walks across the lawn to the wisteria-shaded redwood arbor where the bride and groom exchange vows. Afterwards, guests are seated at beautifully set tables on the grass for an al fresco reception. With colorful English gardens all around and the Tudor house as a backdrop, the celebration is infused with considerable Old World charm. Dancing takes place in the arbor, which is romantically lit at night by hanging period lanterns.

Ainsley House provides elegance, beauty and a taste of a time when life was more relaxed. If JC Ainsley could come back for a visit, he would be pleased to see that his home is still one of the finest in the region.

CEREMONY CAPACITY: The garden holds 200 seated guests.

EVENT/RECEPTION & MEETING CAPACITY: The garden holds 200 seated or 250 standing for a cocktail reception.

FEES & DEPOSITS: For special events, a $500 refundable security deposit and half the entire rental fee are required to secure your date. For ceremonies and rehearsals, the rental fee starts at $925 for a 3-hour minimum. For a reception, the fee is $1,425 for a 6-hour minimum; for a ceremony and reception, the fee starts at $1,925 for an 8-hour minimum. For each additional hour, there's a $200/hour charge.

AVAILABILITY: May–October. Call for more information.

SERVICES/AMENITIES:

Catering: BYO

Kitchen Facilities: no

Tables & Chairs: BYO

Linens, China, etc.: BYO

Restrooms: wheelchair accessible

Dance Floor: cement area

Bride's Dressing Area: yes

Meeting Equipment: BYO

Parking: ample, complimentary

Accommodations: no guest rooms

Telephone: emergency use only

Outdoor Night Lighting: yes

Outdoor Cooking Facilities: no

Cleanup: renter or caterer

View: English cottage garden

RESTRICTIONS:

Alcohol: BYO, champagne, wine and beer only

Smoking: restricted

Music: amplified OK, volume limits until 10pm

Wheelchair Access: yes

Insurance: not required

Other: no rice, birdseed, petals or confetti

This is important! Tell locations you're reading HERE COMES THE GUIDE and ask if our information is still current.

Villa Ragusa

Special Events Facility

35 South Second Street, Campbell
408/364-1900
www.delvillas.com
enquiry@delvillas.com

Rehearsal Dinners	●	Corp. Events/Mtgs.
● Ceremonies	●	Private Parties
● Wedding Receptions		Accommodations

Some couples opt for a small wedding, with just their nearest and dearest in attendance. Then there are those exuberant souls who want to share their once-in-a-lifetime experience with everyone, from next of kin and good friends to third cousins twice removed. If you fall into the latter category, we've got a great suggestion for you: Check out Villa Ragusa, located in the historic downtown section of Campbell.

Built in traditional Mediterranean style, with a stucco façade and red-tile roof, Villa Ragusa blends in so seamlessly with its vintage neighbors it's hard to believe it's only been here since 2001. Inside, the simple European-style décor gives the villa an Old World ambiance, yet everything is freshly painted and polished to a high gloss.

When you enter the facility, a grand staircase leads to the Foyer, whose flawless limestone-and-granite floor glistens like a frozen pond. Four wooden double doors lead from the Foyer to the immense room that is the heart of Villa Ragusa. Here, the visual details are spare but carefully chosen. The thick carpeting, patterned in shades of maroon, green, gold and cream, looks as if no one has ever walked on it, and the dark wood bar that occupies one side of the space is immaculate and gleaming. Round frosted-glass-and-brass chandeliers are suspended from the coffered white ceiling, and arched windows let natural light stream in. The walls, painted in soft neutral shades of gray-green and cream, are enlivened by architectural elements such as pilasters, molding and wooden wainscoting. French doors lead to a covered deck that wraps around two sides of the building, making a great place for guests to mingle and enjoy Campbell's salubrious climate.

Although Villa Ragusa can accommodate 600 people, it can be divided into smaller galleries holding from 100 to 400 seated guests. Naturally, they provide portable bars and dance floors, and some of the galleries are available for wedding ceremonies. Villa Ragusa is also more than happy to book other types of events. They've hosted everything from Little League dinners to giant corporate parties, and the City of Campbell is one of their frequent clients. Last, but not least, there's plenty of parking in the 350-space garage just down the street. So go ahead and send a wedding invitation to that cousin from back east that you haven't seen since you were five years old, and anyone else you can think of. There's room for everyone up at Villa Ragusa.

CEREMONY CAPACITY: The Campbell Gallery holds 300, and the West Gallery holds 250 seated guests.

EVENT/RECEPTION & MEETING CAPACITY: Event spaces accommodate 100–600 seated guests.

FEES & DEPOSITS: For events, a nonrefundable deposit of $2,000 is required to hold your date. The final balance is due 10 days prior to the event. Beverage packages range $6–28/person, and include beverages and bar service. The ceremony fee is $750, including chairs, setup and use of the facility.

AVAILABILITY: Year-round; Sunday–Thursday, 7am–11pm; Friday–Saturday, 7am–midnight.

SERVICES/AMENITIES:

Catering: provided
Kitchen Facilities: fully equipped commercial
Tables & Chairs: provided
Linens, Silver, etc.: provided
Restrooms: wheelchair accessible
Dance Floor: hardwood and 2 portable available
Bride's Dressing Area: yes
Meeting Equipment: mic/podium, stage and riser at no additional charge; other A/V equipment CBA for extra fee

Parking: public, free parking nearby
Accommodations: no guest rooms
Telephone: emergency use only
Outdoor Night Lighting: access only
Outdoor Cooking Facilities: no
Cleanup: caterer
View: downtown Campbell
Other: some event coordination

RESTRICTIONS:

Alcohol: provided, or corkage $10/bottle
Smoking: outside only
Music: amplified OK until midnight

Wheelchair Access: yes
Insurance: not required
Other: no confetti or glitter; decorations require approval

Wedgewood Wedding & Banquet Center
at Eagle Ridge Golf Club

Golf Club

2951 Club Drive, Gilroy
866/966-3009

www.wedgewoodbanquet.com/eagle-ridge
sales@wedgewoodbanquet.com

● Rehearsal Dinners	● Corp. Events/Mtgs.
● Ceremonies	● Private Parties
● Wedding Receptions	Accommodations

Mention the town of Gilroy and most people immediately think of farm stands, orchards and, of course—garlic! But ever since the high-tech boom of the 1980s and '90s, Gilroy has quietly been undergoing a transformation from a sleepy farm town to a thriving bedroom community, with fine homes, shopping centers and other amenities. The only thing missing was a sophisticated special event facility, and now, Wedgewood Wedding and Banquet Center at Eagle Ridge Golf Club has filled that niche.

As befits its name, this lovely golf club perches high on the hills above Gilroy, affording a 360-degree view of the surrounding countryside. Closer in, the greens and fairways of the golf course are draped over the golden hills like a cape of emerald velvet. Warm breezes are redolent with the scent of roses, thanks to the dozens of flourishing bushes planted in front of the clubhouse. This graceful, two-story structure was built in the "Monterey Colonial" style, combining elements from both New England and Spanish Colonial architecture. With its white clapboard siding, green shutters and wisteria-twined veranda, it looks as refreshing as a cold glass of lemonade in the summer, and quite cheerful in the midst of winter. But no matter what the time of year, the clubhouse blends in with its surroundings as effortlessly as the 100-year-old oaks that shade the golf course and adjacent countryside.

Inside, the club is every bit as appealing as it is outside. In the Lounge, you'll find a freestanding double fireplace of brick and wood; an impressive marble-and-wood bar; and circular wrought-iron chandeliers hanging from a soaring, vaulted, open-beamed ceiling. Guests can relax in overstuffed leather chairs as they sip cocktails before moving into the dining room for dinner. This space has creamy walls with white trim, carpeting in shades of rust and green, and plenty of windows to showcase the sweeping golf course vista.

Upstairs, the Terrace is ideal for more intimate events, including small ceremonies. For parties or receptions, they can set up a dance floor and portable bar. And since the Terrace is enclosed on three sides and covered, your guests can revel in the fabulous outdoors (and fabulous views) while keeping their cool on hot days; a built-in fireplace adds warmth when the sun goes down.

Just outside the clubhouse, a great swath of lawn serves as the main ceremony site. Exchange vows in a white gazebo, with the golf course as a beautiful backdrop.

Though Eagle Ridge is visually stunning, one of its most valuable assets is the professionalism and service provided by the Banquet Center's expert planning staff. Wedgewood offers the same trademark on-site coordination that has distinguished the company for decades. Five lavish wedding packages include invitations, flowers, cake and music, as well as the DJ, minister and menu—all of which are carefully sampled, screened and priced to ensure top quality, affordability and maximum satisfaction. Menu options are varied and generous, with room for customization.

CEREMONY CAPACITY: The lawn area holds up to 275 seated guests.

EVENT/RECEPTION & MEETING CAPACITY: The banquet room accommodates 275 seated and 375 standing.

FEES & DEPOSITS: 25% of the estimated event total is required to reserve your date. The next 25% is due 90 days prior to the event, and the balance is due 10 days before the event, along with the final guest count. Wedding packages start at $40/person and include rental fee, bartenders, outside ceremony setup and cleanup. Tax, alcohol and a service charge are additional. Customized packages are also available.

AVAILABILITY: Year-round, daily, 6am–11pm.

SERVICES/AMENITIES:

Catering: provided, no BYO
Kitchen Facilities: n/a
Tables & Chairs: provided
Linens, Silver, etc.: provided
Restrooms: wheelchair accessible
Dance Floor: yes, extra charge
Bride's Dressing Area: yes
Meeting Equipment: full range CBA, extra charge

Parking: large lot
Accommodations: no guest rooms
Telephone: emergency use only
Outdoor Night Lighting: yes
Outdoor Cooking Facilities: no
Cleanup: provided
View: fairways, foothills
Other: event coordination

RESTRICTIONS:

Alcohol: provided
Smoking: outdoors only
Music: amplified OK with volume restrictions

Wheelchair Access: yes
Insurance: not required
Other: no rice, confetti or glitter; no open flames

San Juan Oaks Golf Club

Golf Club

3825 Union Road, Hollister
831/636-6125

www.sanjuanoaks.com
dvarner@sanjuanoaks.com

● Rehearsal Dinners	● Corp. Events/Mtgs.
● Ceremonies	● Private Parties
● Wedding Receptions	Accommodations

Old World charm meets modern day amenities at San Juan Oaks Golf Club, a peaceful California-style hacienda and 18-hole championship golf course, set amongst the creeks and foothills near historic San Juan Bautista.

The drive to San Juan Oaks is a relaxing one, meandering through the valley floor, past a green and golden landscape dotted with colorful seasonal flowers. And when you pull into the club's circular brick entranceway with its softly flowing fountain, you realize that this place is as serene as its surroundings. "It's such a beautiful site—people arrive and find themselves in good spirits," says David Varner, Director of Food & Beverage services.

Architecturally, the club takes a nod from the town's 200-year-old Mission, with a tile roof, wide hallways, broad windows and arched entryways. A gorgeous, wraparound terrace spills onto the lush golf course, and offers an unobstructed view of the shimmering lake just beyond. Inside, the club's foyer features tiled floors and comfortable oversized chairs. High ceilings throughout the 19,000-square-foot facility are punctuated by dramatic exposed wooden trusses and sleek, hanging light fixtures.

All three of San Juan Oaks' event spaces open out onto the terrace through a series of French doors, so no matter where you celebrate, you have a clear view of the fairways, lake and distant foothills. Guests can kick off an event with a drink or appetizer at the gorgeous cherrywood bar in the Lounge, then stroll into the adjacent Oaks Room for the main reception. This versatile space accommodates large weddings, showers, rehearsal dinners or corporate functions, and can be divided into two smaller rooms for more intimate events. When the weather's balmy, guests like to dine on the terrace and take in the sunset, and if the evening turns cool, they're quickly warmed by the wood-burning stone fireplace. If you're planning a small conference or meeting, the Fred Couples Room next door is a private space with its own bar and fireplace, and an interesting display of Couples' trophies, photos and memorabilia.

The cuisine at San Juan Oaks is overseen by their talented chef, who incorporates the freshest ingredients into his culinary creations. He and his team specialize in regional California dishes with artistic presentations. Customized menus are available, and may feature wine pairings from the club's wine list, which includes a selection of favorite local wines.

Although you don't have to be a golfer to host your event at San Juan Oaks, lovers of the game will be in heaven here. In a recent ranking of 5,000 North American public and resort courses by *Golf Digest Magazine,* San Juan Oaks received four out of five stars for customer service, value and golf course quality. Designed by PGA great Fred Couples, the Front Nine winds through five lakes and interconnecting creeks on the valley floor; the Back Nine climbs 200 feet into the foothills, and includes elevated tees and fairways with spectacular views. The Pro Shop is experienced in organizing a wide range of golf-related events, including "Shotgun" tournaments, charity events, and golf clinics. Lodging options in neighboring San Juan Bautista, or in the Monterey Bay area (just 35 minutes away), can be arranged.

A great deal of care has gone into making San Juan Oaks blend seamlessly into its natural environment, and an equal amount of effort has been put into providing topnotch facilities and service. Much to the delight of golfers and non-golfers alike, they've succeeded on both counts.

CEREMONY CAPACITY: The Patio holds 300 seated.

EVENT/RECEPTION CAPACITY: The Fred Couples Room holds 50 seated guests, the Adobe Room 80 seated or 100 standing, the Oaks Room 160 seated or 200 standing, and the Oaks and Adobe Rooms together hold 300 seated or 350 standing guests indoors.

MEETING CAPACITY: The Fred Couples Room holds 30 guests seated conference-style. The Oaks Room seats 200 theater-style.

FEES & DEPOSITS: A $1,000 nonrefundable deposit is required to reserve your date and is applied towards the event total. A $2,000 nonrefundable payment is due 90 days prior, and the estimated event balance is payable 5 days prior to the event. Events range $60–100/person depending on the day of the week and guest count; tax, alcohol and an 18% service charge are additional. Facility fees range $250–2,000 depending on the room selected. A $750 ceremony fee is additional.

AVAILABILITY: Year-round, daily, 7am–midnight.

SERVICES/AMENITIES:

Catering: provided, no BYO
Kitchen Facilities: n/a
Tables & Chairs: provided
Linens, Silver, etc.: provided
Restrooms: wheelchair accessible
Dance Floor: yes
Bride's Dressing Area: yes
Meeting Equipment: screen, podium, wireless microphones

Parking: large lot
Accommodations: no guest rooms
Telephone: emergency use only
Outdoor Night Lighting: access only
Outdoor Cooking Facilities: BBQ CBA
Cleanup: provided
View: fairways, rolling hills, lake
Other: event coordination

RESTRICTIONS:

Alcohol: provided
Smoking: patio only
Music: amplified OK

Wheelchair Access: yes
Insurance: not required
Other: no rice or birdseed, no open flames

Overwhelmed? Use the search criteria on www.HereComesTheGuide.com to narrow down your choices.

273

Creekside of Los Gatos

Address withheld to ensure privacy. Los Gatos
408/559-7733, Panetta's Catering
www.creeksidelosgatos.com
lbeesley@msn.com

Private Estate

- Rehearsal Dinners
- Ceremonies
- Wedding Receptions
- Corp. Events/Mtgs.
- Private Parties
- Accommodations

Creekside of Los Gatos was born of the romantic vision of two people in love. Pat and Augusto purchased this view-filled spread with the idea of designing an awe-inspiring wedding location; it was bound to turn out fantastically, since the couple also planned on using it for their own summer wedding.

Though conveniently located near a main highway, Creekside is totally secluded. A private treelined drive takes visitors onto the grounds, a gently sloping hillside surrounded by coastal

oaks. Tucked between unspoiled hills and a forested stream, this exclusive haven feels oh-so-close to nature.

The first part of the couple's dream project involved renovating the 100-year-old genuine log cabin, which is poised atop a narrow plateau. Quaint and welcoming beneath a canopy of leafy boughs, the cabin's burnished redwood façade seems as fresh as if its planks had just been hewn. With a pretty lawn and garden, the cabin's charming front yard is a delightful milieu for pre-party mingling or cocktail gatherings. Inside the cabin, beautifully appointed rooms with plenty of closet space are reserved for the bride and her attendants to prepare in privacy. The Great Room has a picture window that lets a bride preview the unfolding scene before making her grand entrance.

While the cabin's ambiance is warm and down to earth, the event areas are breathtaking and dramatic. Broad steps lead from the cabin to two descending river rock terraces, a popular option for dining. On the other side of the stairs, flagstone and rocks have been artfully arranged into a magnificent tropical waterfall. As the watery cascade glistens in the waning rays of the sun, guests succumb to the hypnotic sound of the water's flow. In front of the terraces stands a spacious open-sided timber pavilion, which usually shelters the wedding cake. A stone fireplace contributes a mood of cozy conviviality, making the pavilion perfect for dancing or even an intimate ceremony.

Another captivating element at Creekside is the view. From the terraces, a vast carpet of manicured lawn makes a gradual descent towards the forest's edge. Through billowy trees, glimpses of a meandering creek seem like a beguiling mirage. The placid vision of sparkling Lexington Reservoir is a sweep of blue in the distance. There are a total of four possible ceremony spots that take advantage of this picturesque tableau, including a lush cathedral of redwood trees and a timbered pergola, which has guests looking on from teak benches.

Pat and Augusto had intended to say their vows beneath the pergola, but a funny thing happened on the day of their wedding. Everything was in place on the grass awaiting the arrival of friends and family. Then Pat was suddenly struck by an adventurous impulse: Why not get married on one of the waterfall's flagstone landings amid the mist and ornamental ferns? Being the bride, her whim was gratified, seating was quickly rearranged, and Pat officially inaugurated the waterfall as a resplendent ceremony option!

Creekside of Los Gatos is available exclusively through *Panetta's Catering,* event pros whose attractively priced, full-service packages expertly pull all the elements together. *Panetta's* joins Pat and Augusto in extending a gracious invitation to bask in this estate's many charms.

CEREMONY, EVENT/RECEPTION & MEETING CAPACITY: The site holds a maximum of 200 seated or 250 standing guests outdoors.

FEES & DEPOSITS: A $1,000 deposit is required to reserve your date. The balance is due 30–90 days prior to the event. Rental fees range $4,000–5,000 depending on the date rented. Meals start at $60/person. Tax, alcohol and an 18% service charge are additional.

AVAILABILITY: Available from late April–early October. Just one event takes place on the property per day. Hours are flexible, and amplified music must be over by 10pm.

SERVICES/AMENITIES:

Catering: provided by *Panetta's Catering*
Kitchen Facilities: n/a
Tables & Chairs: some provided
Linens, Silver, etc.: through caterer
Restrooms: wheelchair accessible
Dance Floor: provided
Bride's & Groom's Dressing Areas: yes
Meeting Equipment: CBA

Parking: limited; shuttles CBA, extra fee
Accommodations: no guest rooms
Telephone: office phone
Outdoor Night Lighting: yes
Outdoor Cooking Facilities: no
Cleanup: renter or caterer
View: meadow, lake, garden, waterfall, hills
Other: event coordination

RESTRICTIONS:

Alcohol: BYO beer, wine and champagne; signature drink CBA for cocktail hour only
Smoking: designated area only
Music: amplified OK outdoors with restrictions

Wheelchair Access: limited
Insurance: required

Hazlwood

Address withheld to ensure privacy. Los Gatos

408/429-4381

www.hazlwood.com
barbarahzwd@yahoo.com
jknipe@yahoo.com

Private Estate

Rehearsal Dinners	●	Corp. Events/Mtgs.
● Ceremonies	●	Private Parties
● Wedding Receptions		Accommodations

Just like every bride is uniquely beautiful, so, too, is each private estate charming in its own way. Hazlwood boasts charm aplenty, beginning with a bucolic and secluded location in the foothills of Los Gatos. It's only a few minutes off the highway, but Hazlwood's congenial, storybook personality makes you feel as if you were dropped into the middle of an enchanted forest.

A driveway lined with birdhouses leads to a parking area bordered by redwoods; a flower-covered archway marks a footpath onto Hazlwood's bi-level grounds, and from here you get an overview of the lush property. On a rise to the left sits a comely wood-frame home, whose broad wraparound deck invites your guests to sit back and enjoy the view. Just beyond this home is a spacious brick patio flanked by a quaint summer house. Abundant fruit trees frame garden lawns that cascade down towards a magnificent site: a waterfall and water garden ringed with river rocks, reedy bamboo and wild grasses. The trickling of water and a breeze whispering through the treetops harmonizes with birdsong, while bullfrogs and fish dart among the water lilies. Below the water garden is the ceremony area, a rambling emerald-green lawn edged with coastal redwoods. A brick-lined aisle makes a gentle descent to a simple white-columned pergola, set against a dense grove of redwood trees, nature's chapel for your wedding vows.

During the social hour, guests can mingle around the water garden, tour the south and west gardens, or have a friendly game of bocce on the two courts near the entrance. Drinks are served on the broad porch of the summer house, while redwood and apple trees provide shade for hors d'oeuvres stations. Dining tables are spread out over the patio and on the lawns; nearby, a petite greenhouse, decorated with café lights and flowers, holds the buffet.

After dinner, guests can enjoy dancing on the patio under the stars or relaxing in the two-room summer house. A vaulted ceiling and tall, multipaned windows create a bright and airy atmosphere. The pretty first room has a polished wood floor, and while it's reserved for the bride's preparations before the ceremony, it's open to guests afterwards. Up a step, an adjoining salon features a fireplace and Italian-tile floor, making it a great choice for after-dinner dancing, as well as cake cutting and coffee service. Both rooms have French doors that are left open to the patio, so guests can easily roam inside and out.

Hazlwood has one more arrow in its quiver of delights: James and Brenda Knipe, who cater many of the events here and are devoted to making your celebration special. We have it on good authority that they cook up a storm; and since James is the brother of owner Robert Knipe, festivities at Hazlwood take on the convivial spirit of a real family affair. Together, they extend a genteel welcome to you and your loved ones.

CEREMONY CAPACITY: The Ceremony Lawn holds 300 seated guests.

EVENT/RECEPTION CAPACITY: The brick and lawn areas accommodate up to 300 guests. The Summer House holds up to 75 seated or 150 standing guests.

FEES & DEPOSITS: 50% of the rental fee is required to secure your date. The balance is due 30 days prior to the event. Rental fees range $3,000–9,000 depending on guest count. Meals start at $35/person. Tax, alcohol and service charge are additional.

AVAILABILITY: May 15–October 15, daily, 10am–10pm.

SERVICES/AMENITIES:

Catering: provided, or BYO approved
Kitchen Facilities: n/a
Tables & Chairs: through *Prestigious Provisions*
Linens, Silver, etc.: through *Prestigious Provisions*
Restrooms: wheelchair accessible
Dance Floor: provided
Bride's Dressing Area: yes
Meeting Equipment: no
Other: coordination available, extra charge

Parking: limited, valet CBA
Accommodations: no guest rooms
Telephone: emergency use only
Outdoor Night Lighting: yes
Outdoor Cooking Facilities: through caterer
Cleanup: caterer
View: flower and water gardens, redwood forest

RESTRICTIONS:

Alcohol: BYO
Smoking: designated areas only
Music: amplified OK with restrictions

Wheelchair Access: limited
Insurance: liability required

Laurel Mill Lodge

Lodge

Address withheld to ensure privacy. Los Gatos

408/353-5851

www.laurelmilllodge.com
proprietors@laurelmilllodge.com

- Rehearsal Dinners
- Ceremonies
- Wedding Receptions
- Corp. Events/Mtgs.
- Private Parties
- Accommodations

Whether you're seeking a place with unspoiled natural beauty for your wedding, a quiet atmosphere for a writer's retreat, or just a place to get in touch with your "inner child," Laurel Mill Lodge has a variety of packages to suit your needs. Nestled in the tall trees of the Santa Cruz Mountains, this delightfully rustic establishment is not only a special event facility, but a virtual summer camp for grown-ups (and their kids, too). The stresses and strains of the everyday world will float away like so much dandelion fluff, as you experience the extraordinary effect of the Laurel Mill Lodge.

This 27-acre facility occupies the site of a lumber mill that operated over a century ago, and part of the lodge dates back to when it was the mess hall for the lumberjacks. Today, the property is equipped to handle any kind of event, from an elegant wedding to a laid-back family reunion. In the lodge itself, you'll find a spacious room that works well for meetings, sit-down dinners or just relaxing. Paneled entirely in very old redwood, with windows along one wall framing views of the surrounding trees, the room features a large fireplace, a baby grand piano and a big screen TV with VCR/DVD player. The adjacent sunny deck, with its umbrella-shaded tables, overlooks a pavilion that can be used as a stage, a dance floor, or for an outdoor luncheon or dinner. The convenient arrangement of event spaces allows you to have your celebration indoors, outdoors or both. And from the commercially equipped and caterer-friendly kitchen, you'll be able to serve gourmet meals to a crowd.

One of Laurel Mill Lodge's most attractive features is a vast verdant meadow, surrounded by magnificent redwoods and bordered by Soquel Creek. This sun-splashed space, carpeted in lush "barefoot grass," can seat a sizeable group for a wedding ceremony, concert or theater production. An octagonal redwood stage with detachable handrails and arch can be placed anywhere on the meadow, which is also an ideal setting for camping, picnics, barbecues and outdoor games. After dining and dancing, guests often soak in the 20-person hot tub, bake in the sauna or gather around a campfire with guitars and marshmallows.

Laurel Mill Lodge specializes in long, leisurely celebrations. In times past, when the mountain residents traveled by horseback, they didn't just get together for an afternoon or an evening—they partied for days! This charming custom is still observed here, thanks to a variety of overnight options. Across the footbridge over Soquel Creek and up a short winding path through redwoods, ferns and forget-me-nots, you will find simple but cozy cabins, each with a king-size sleeping loft and a deck overlooking the creek. Another footbridge leads to six A-frame bunkhouses, each of which sleeps four. Camping is permitted on the meadow. Just think—you could extend your rehearsal, wedding and reception over several days, so that your close friends and family have time to really get to know each other. Guests can stay even longer if they wish. Best of all, when you hold your wedding at Laurel Mill Lodge, you get the entire property to yourself. The same could be said for reunions, parties, bar/bat mitzvahs and retreats.

We could go on and on about the beauty and versatility of Laurel Mill Lodge, but only a visit will convince you how special this facility really is. To protect the privacy of each event in progress, site visits are arranged by appointment only.

CEREMONY, EVENT/RECEPTION & MEETING CAPACITY: The site holds 80 seated banquet-style or 150 standing indoors and 150 seated or standing guests outdoors. Spaces are available for smaller events.

FEES & DEPOSITS: For weddings, 50% of the estimated event total is required to reserve your date; the balance is due 21 days before the event. Rental fees range $3,200–7,900 for 6-hour to 48-hour wedding packages. When you rent the site for a wedding, you have access to the entire facility. Some overnight accommodations are additional. If your event includes more than 5 children, childcare will be provided by the facility at an additional charge.

For business meetings or seminars, rental fees for the conference room range $10–25/person depending on length of time rented. For family reunions, $30–45/person/day includes camping and many other amenities.

AVAILABILITY: Year-round, daily.

SERVICES/AMENITIES:

Catering: BYO
Kitchen Facilities: commercially equipped
Tables & Chairs: provided
Linens, Silver, etc.: CBA, extra charge
Restrooms: narrow wheelchairs OK
Dance Floor: on deck
Bride's & Groom's Dressing Areas: yes
Meeting Equipment: TV with VCR/DVD, whiteboards, projection screen, podium; other CBA, extra charge

Parking: 60 spaces available
Accommodations: 9 cabins, 6 bunkhouses and tent camping
Telephone: available upon request
Outdoor Night Lighting: yes
Outdoor Cooking Facilities: yes
Cleanup: provided
View: redwood trees, creek, meadow, starry night sky
Other: piano, large hot tub, sauna, outdoor fire pit, stage lighting

RESTRICTIONS:

Alcohol: BYO, licensed server
Smoking: outdoors only
Music: amplified OK until 10pm

Wheelchair Access: limited
Insurance: liability required
Other: no fireworks, torches, lighter fluids or pets

The professionals in the back of this book are the best in the business. How do we know? Read page 637.

279

Los Gatos Lodge

Hotel and Garden

50 Los Gatos-Saratoga Road, Los Gatos
408/354-3300

www.losgatoslodge.com
atovar@losgatoslodge.com

- Rehearsal Dinners
- Ceremonies
- Wedding Receptions
- Corp. Events/Mtgs.
- Private Parties
- Accommodations

Los Gatos Lodge is an oasis of serenity, just minutes away from the center of picturesque downtown Los Gatos. Nestled on 10 beautifully landscaped acres, it's an attractive garden setting with a warm, casual atmosphere. Its accessible location—close to three major airports—makes it very convenient for out-of-town wedding guests and business travelers alike.

The two-story lodge has 129 guest rooms, including 13 suites with fireplaces and over 5,000 square feet of banquet facilities featuring five meeting rooms for seminars, retreats, conferences, weddings, and receptions. Among the outdoor event spaces are the Garden Gazebo (designed exclusively for ceremonies), a large pool and patio with ample space for a band or DJ, and emerald-green lawns (great for cocktail receptions, wedding photos, or just a quiet stroll). The Whimsical Lawn, for example, boasts its own garden area that's perfect for private dining and family gatherings.

The Garden Gazebo is a private, covered arbor set slightly outside of the circle formed by the lodge's main buildings. It's available for rental whether you're holding your reception at the lodge or elsewhere, and it nicely combines both natural and decorative elements. Guests are seated on white garden chairs, while the wedding party makes its entrance through a frame of trees and flowers. They walk along an aisle runner, taking their places under a lattice arch. The bride can make a dramatic entrance from a nearby room that has been provided as a changing area.

You can choose the ceremony and reception spaces that best suit your event, and the venue's wedding packages include many amenities such as a custom cake, florals, and a private bar with bartender.

The facilities at Los Gatos Lodge offer many advantages. If you're planning a large wedding with a lot of out-of-town guests, you can reserve a block of rooms. Both wedding and business guests will appreciate the putting green, regulation bocce ball court, and the in-house food and beverage services. Here, your dining experience is enhanced by views of a lush garden through large picture windows. You might consider organizing a post-wedding brunch in one of the smaller banquet rooms, easily arranged by the lodge's experienced Event & Wedding Planner. Their Bar & Grill, which serves lunch and dinner and has live entertainment on Friday and Saturday, is also a great place for an after party!

However you decide to utilize this flexible facility, you'll find the management extremely knowledgeable and accommodating. Their hospitality even extends to your four-footed friends: If you'd like your pooch to be your ring bearer, no problem—the lodge is VERY pet friendly.

CEREMONY CAPACITY: Indoors, the El Gato Room acommodates 150 seated, the Saratoga Room 48 seated guests. Outdoors various areas hold up to 200 seated guests.

EVENT/RECEPTION CAPACITY: Indoors, the El Gato Room seats 120 seated guests, the DeAnza Room 80, the Saratoga Room 40, and the Garden Room 75 seated guests. Outdoors various areas hold up to 200 seated guests.

MEETING CAPACITY: Various rooms seat 15–80 classroom-style or 30–150 theater-style.

FEES & DEPOSITS: For all private events, a deposit in the amount of the room rental fee is due within 7 days of booking your date. The event balance is due 5 days prior to the event. Room rental fees run $300–1200 depending on the space reserved and time rented (half-day or full-day). Wedding packages range $79–119/person (including ceremony and reception space rental fees), and à la carte meals start at $20/person. Tax, alcohol and a 20% service charge are additional. A $1.50/person cake-cutting fee also applies. Wedding packages may include wine, cake, flowers, chair covers, colored linens, and private bar with bartender.

For business functions, a deposit may be required. The event balance is due 5 days prior to the function. Meeting rooms run $200–500 and meals run $15–35/person; tax, alcohol and a 20% service charge are additional.

AVAILABILITY: Year-round, daily, including holidays.

SERVICES/AMENITIES:

Catering: provided, no BYO

Kitchen Facilities: fully equipped

Table & Chairs: provided

Linens, Silver, etc.: provided

Restrooms: wheelchair accessible

Dance Floor: CBA, $200 extra charge

Bride's Dressing Area: yes

Meeting Equipment: CBA, extra charge, WiFi access, business center

Parking: free, ample and on site

Accommodations: 129 guest rooms, including 13 suites with fireplaces

Telephone: guest phones

Outdoor Night Lighting: yes

Outdoor Cooking Facilities: BBQ

Cleanup: provided, extra fee may be applied

View: garden courtyard

Other: event coordination, security provided, pet friendly

RESTRICTIONS:

Alcohol: Provided, or BYO champagne or wine with corkage fee, no beer or hard alcohol

Smoking: outside only

Music: amplified OK outdoors until 7pm, indoors until 1am

Wheelchair Access: yes

Insurance: not required

Other: decorations must have prior approval

Nestldown

Address withheld to ensure privacy. Los Gatos Mountains

408/353-5311

www.nestldown.com
info@nestldown.com

Private Estate

- Rehearsal Dinners
- Ceremonies
- Wedding Receptions
- Corp. Events/Mtgs.
- Private Parties
- Accommodations

A bride at Nestldown descends a broad stairway through redwoods to a lakeside amphitheater where she will say her vows. About halfway down, she experiences a sublime moment when, for a few seconds, it's possible for her to look up to the tops of the soaring trees and down to their bases far below, as though she's suspended in the air among them, a bird waiting to glide to earth.

This is not the only ethereal moment she or her groom and guests will enjoy here. Nestldown, an enchanted hideaway in a mountain forest, evokes magic over and over.

Years ago it was a fruit farm in the Santa Cruz Mountains that grew apples, peaches and kiwis. Its current owners have spent the past decade creating a wonderland of gardens, whimsical sculptures, topiary figures, and fanciful structures on 35 acres at the property's heart. The result is a place where so many things delight and amaze: redwoods standing gray under morning clouds that suddenly blaze cinnamon in sunlight; flowers splashed along every path; barely-there trails and unexpected stairways that lead the curious to bentwood benches and chairs set smack in the middle of the forest. But all of these sensory treats are just preludes to the beauty of Nestldown's outdoor chapel and the breathtaking architecture of its signature building, The Barn.

You reach the chapel on an earth-and-wood staircase that meanders down a forested hillside. Its destination is a flagstone-paved amphitheater, sheltered by trees and ferns, that faces a wisteria-covered pergola. The pergola, set at the edge of a small, forest-fringed lake, is built from redwood saplings with their bark left on. It's so natural in appearance that it looks as though it sprang by itself from the ground. Just beyond it is another grace note, a wooden bridge, Japanese in its simplicity, that arches over a rivulet at the foot of a small waterfall.

Post-ceremony celebrations take place in The Barn and on its adjoining lawn. The Barn is one of the most beautiful wooden structures built in Northern California in recent years. Almost everybody who enters it for the first time gasps at the interior of this soaring glass-and-fir structure. The interior rises to a steep-pitched ceiling, supported by slender wooden columns. The timbers, stained a glowing reddish-amber, still have the wonderful smell of fresh-cut wood lingering about them. Gardens and trees hug two sides of The Barn. Flowers bloom year-round—geraniums, red hot salvias, alyssum, candytufts, begonias, violas, irises and calla lilies—and there are fanciful critters everywhere: A brass bear peers out from one garden and in another a topiary serpent undulates through a sea of long, slender-bladed fescue. A large koi pond in front of The Barn is lined with willows and birch, and embellished by a brass stork. Just off The Barn's terrace, a grand meadow sweeps out to a copse of redwoods where a hand-carved wooden bench reveals the image of three cavorting bears.

Nestldown is sheer exhilaration. You feel a giddy sense of expectation and joy, as you discover nature's best so skillfully combined with the fruit of human imagination.

CEREMONY CAPACITY: The outdoor chapel holds 225 seated guests, the Foxglove Meadow 250 seated guests, The Barn holds 150 seated, and the Main Lawn 250 seated guests.

EVENT/RECEPTION & MEETING CAPACITY: There is one indoor and several outdoor spaces available that hold up to 300 seated guests. Smaller events can also be accommodated.

FEES & DEPOSITS: 50% of the rental fee is required to reserve your date; the balance is due 60 days prior to the event. The rental fees range $3,500–15,000 depending on guest count, space rented and time of year.

AVAILABILITY: Year-round, daily, 8am–10pm. Limited capacities apply December–March.

SERVICES/AMENITIES:

Catering: select from list
Kitchen Facilities: prep only
Tables & Chairs: provided up to 250 guests
Linens, Silver, etc.: through caterer
Restrooms: wheelchair accessible
Dance Floor: yes
Bride's Dressing Area: yes
Meeting Equipment: CBA, extra charge full A/V on site

Parking: on site for up to 125 cars, shuttle CBA
Accommodations: no guest rooms
Telephone: emergency only
Outdoor Night Lighting: some areas
Outdoor Cooking Facilities: CBA
Cleanup: provided
View: pond, meadow, redwoods, garden

RESTRICTIONS:

Alcohol: BYO, licensed server
Smoking: designated area only
Music: amplified OK indoors

Wheelchair Access: limited
Insurance: certificate required
Other: no rice or birdseed; some types of balloons are restricted

Opera House

140 West Main Street, Los Gatos
408/354-1218

www.operahouselosgatos.com
sales@operahouselosgatos.com

Landmark Building

● Rehearsal Dinners	● Corp. Events/Mtgs.
● Ceremonies	● Private Parties
● Wedding Receptions	☐ Accommodations

For large weddings, the Opera House is still the only game in town. Occupying a 1904 landmark brick building with crisp white trim, its 8,000 square feet can seat up to 350 guests!

Enter the downstairs foyer and wind your way up the formal sweeping staircase to the main event floor. Award-winning Bradbury & Bradbury wallpaper in blues, creams and golds adorns the stairwell. Walls and ceilings are covered with original pressed tin in 15 different Victorian motifs, and antique light fixtures abound. The Grand Ballroom has a 24-foot ceiling, with a rectangular skylight in the center that brings in natural light. From the Balcony up above, you can toss your bouquet or watch the dancing below. The lower portion of the room, called the Mezzanine, has a wall of windows facing north. Soft pastels, cream and taupe predominate, and a large mural on an upper wall facing the Ballroom depicts the Opera House's original theater curtain.

Because of the way this facility is configured, groups of 100 or fewer won't feel dwarfed in this space. Additional enhancements are a moveable dance floor and a beautiful turn-of-the-century-style mahogany bar. And if you haven't been able to whittle down your invitation list, we think the Opera House is a must-see.

CEREMONY CAPACITY: The Mezzanine holds 100 seated; the Main Room up to 350 seated.

EVENT/RECEPTION CAPACITY: The site holds 50–350 seated or 110–450 standing guests indoors.

MEETING CAPACITY: The facility holds 39–300 seated conference-style or theater-style.

FEES & DEPOSITS: A nonrefundable $1,000 deposit is required within 1 week of confirming reservations. A second deposit, the amount dependent on size and type of event, is due 180 days prior to the event. The balance for the entire event, including a $500 refundable security deposit, is due 1 week prior to your function. Customized wedding receptions are available. Meals start at $50/person, including tax and service charge. Alcohol is additional.

For weekday functions, the rental fee starts at $1,000. Food and beverage service is provided; rates will vary depending on services requested.

AVAILABILITY: Year-round: Sunday–Thursday until midnight; Friday and Saturday until 1am.

SERVICES/AMENITIES:

Catering: provided or BYO with approval
Kitchen Facilities: prep only
Tables & Chairs: provided for 350 guests
Linens, Silver, etc.: through caterer
Restrooms: wheelchair accessible
Dance Floor: yes
Bride's Dressing Area: yes
Meeting Equipment: CBA
Other: event coordination

Parking: valet or self-parking
Accommodations: no guest rooms, hotels nearby
Telephone: no
Outdoor Night Lighting: access only
Outdoor Cooking Facilities: no
Cleanup: provided
View: Santa Cruz Mtns., Old Town Los Gatos

RESTRICTIONS:

Alcohol: provided, no BYO
Smoking: not allowed
Music: amplified OK

Wheelchair Access: yes, elevator
Insurance: not required
Other: decorations restricted

Want to know WHAT TO ASK a potential location or vendor? Check out our Questions to Ask starting on page 17.

Testarossa Winery

Historic Winery

300-A College Avenue, Los Gatos
408/354-6150
www.testarossa.com
events@testarossa.com

● Rehearsal Dinners	● Corp. Events/Mtgs.
● Ceremonies	● Private Parties
● Wedding Receptions	Accommodations

Located just a half mile off Main Street in downtown Los Gatos, Testarossa Winery is one lovely spot. The road leading up to this site winds through a pleasant residential neighborhood, but once you enter the historic winery's stone and wrought-iron gates, you leave the modern world behind.

It was on top of this knoll that Jesuits began missionary work in California in the late 1860s. The first seminary was built here in 1888, giving way to a more permanent winery building in 1893. Known as the Novitiate Winery in honor of the seminary students (called "novices"), it's a fine example of a 19th-century, three-story, gravity-flow winery, and amazingly, it's still in operation today. The Jesuits stopped making Novitiate wines in 1985 and leased the winery to Testarossa in 2003. The original building still stands, forming the core of the present-day venue.

A variety of options are available for weddings, special events and business functions. Outside, the sunny, flower-lined courtyard patio is a sweet spot to hold an open-air reception in the summer. Trees border one side, and on the other there's a bank of ivy containing a recessed, two-stepped wooden deck that's perfect for ceremonies and musicians.

Indoors, Testarossa has a unique group of spaces. As you pass through the front door, you find yourself in a cool stone tunnel that's one of the most interesting ceremony sites you'll ever see. It feels exactly like a cave, with its century-old limestone walls and vaulted ceiling. A photographic history of the Novitiate is displayed on one wall, and artwork graces the other. Antique chandeliers softly light the way, as the bride walks down the center aisle, flanked on both sides by her seated guests.

The Palazzio Room is spacious enough for dinner and dancing. Rehearsal dinners are cozy and elegant in the Niclaire Room, whose stone walls rise to a wood-beamed ceiling and enclose a grand table that extends the length of the room. Add beautiful linens, crystal and candles to make dining here a romantic affair.

Inside and out, Testarossa Winery conveys warmth and a sense of a rich past. You couldn't ask for a more tranquil and beautiful environment for any kind of event.

CEREMONY CAPACITY: The facility holds 90 seated guest.

EVENT/RECEPTION CAPACITY: Various indoor spaces hold 15–120 seated or 35–150 standing guests. Combined, the Tasting and Palazzio Rooms plus the patio hold up to 200 guests for an appetizer reception. The patio alone accommodates 100 seated or standing guests outdoors.

MEETING CAPACITY: Event spaces accommodate up to 60 guests seated theater-style.

FEES & DEPOSITS: Half of the total purchase is required to reserve your date; the balance is due 2 weeks prior to the event.

Testarossa Winery offers two choices when planning your wedding. One option is to rent the facility and work directly with a preferred caterer to create a menu specialized to your needs. All-inclusive wedding packages range $101–175/person and include the rental fee and a selection of gourmet menus from which to choose. The rental fees for a wedding range $4,000–6,500 depending on the size and day of the event. Weddings may be held on any day of the week.

Corporate packages range $95–185/person, including food, wine and rental. Tax is additional.

AVAILABILITY: Year-round, daily, 6:30pm–11pm. Please call for date availability.

SERVICES/AMENITIES:

Catering: provided or select from approved list
Kitchen Facilities: prep only
Tables & Chairs: provided up to 150 guests
Linens, Silver, etc.: basic linens provided
Restrooms: wheelchair accessible
Dance Floor: yes
Bride's Dressing Area: yes
Meeting Equipment: wireless broadband internet; more CBA, extra charge

Parking: 2 lots
Accommodations: no guest rooms
Telephone: conference phone available
Outdoor Night Lighting: yes
Outdoor Cooking Facilities: no
Cleanup: caterer
View: Los Gatos hills
Other: event coordination

RESTRICTIONS:

Alcohol: wine, beer and champagne by Testarossa; no BYO
Smoking: outside only
Music: amplified OK indoors only

Wheelchair Access: yes
Insurance: certificate required
Other: no rice, birdseed or confetti

Summitpointe Golf Club

Golf Club

1500 Country Club Drive, Milpitas
408/262-2500

www.countryclubreceptions.com
catering@summitpointegc.com

- Rehearsal Dinners
- Ceremonies
- Wedding Receptions
- Corp. Events/Mtgs.
- Private Parties
- Accommodations

Clearly, the designers of Summitpointe Golf Course understood the meaning of the expression "photo op." Nestled in a canyon between rolling East Bay foothills, this Milpitas golf course offers sweeping views in every direction, not to mention an absolutely world-class ceremony site.

Encompassing the far end of the driving range (which is closed whenever events are held) and the huge expanse of lawn beyond, the site adjoins the largest of the course's three natural lakes. Place an arch at the water's edge, and the weeping willows that dip towards the lake provide all the decoration necessary. Brides typically make their entrance via limousine, but for more drama, consider making the journey in a horse-drawn carriage. Golf carts are also available to transport any elderly or physically challenged guests.

In spring and summer months, your entire wedding day can be staged outdoors. Following the ceremony, guests amble over to the broad area in the driving range for an al fresco reception. Have rounds set up in the shade of umbrellas, or long banquet tables arranged beneath a large canopy. Either way, your guests will appreciate the fresh air and beautiful scenery.

If you prefer an indoor celebration (or just indoor dancing), Summitpointe's Lakeview Room will comfortably accommodate most groups. Large windows on two walls reveal views of the hills and lakes. On chilly evenings, a generous mirrored fireplace at one end creates a warmly romantic atmosphere. And guests who need to take a break will enjoy stepping outside onto the roomy brick patio where they can order up their favorite drink from the full-service indoor bar nearby. The patio is also an event site in its own right: It's covered year-round with a canvas tent, whose clear walls can be rolled up for maximum access to balmy afternoon breezes, or rolled down to provide protection from the elements.

Next to its photogenic setting, this golf club's most appealing feature may be its affordability. If you long for a wedding at a country club but don't belong to one, Summitpointe is a wonderful alternative. Their friendly, helpful staff will gladly streamline your to-do list by making arrangements for everything from a champagne fountain to deluxe chair coverings. And with their flexible menu options, you're sure to find a combination of dishes that perfectly suits you and your budget.

CEREMONY CAPACITY: The Lakeview Room holds 130 seated; the Lawn holds 300 seated.

EVENT/RECEPTION CAPACITY: The Lakeview Room accommodates 130 seated or 200 standing guests; the Lawn area holds 250 seated with tent option and the Lakeview Patio holds 200 seated guests.

MEETING CAPACITY: Event spaces accommodate up to 90 seated guests.

FEES & DEPOSITS: A nonrefundable deposit, which is applied to your food and beverage total, is required to reserve your date. The amount of the deposit is equal to 25% of the estimated event total. 50% is due 6 months prior, and 100% of the final estimated balance is due 10 days prior to the event date. Rental fees range $500–1,500 depending on space, day and time rented. Meals range $18–76/person. Tax, alcohol and a 20% service charge are additional.

AVAILABILITY: Year-round, daily, 6am–midnight.

SERVICES/AMENITIES:

Catering: provided, no BYO
Kitchen Facilities: n/a
Tables & Chairs: provided
Linens, Silver, etc.: provided
Restrooms: wheelchair accessible
Dance Floor: CBA, extra charge
Bride's Dressing Area: no
Meeting Equipment: CBA, extra charge

Parking: ample on site
Accommodations: no guest rooms
Telephone: pay phone
Outdoor Night Lighting: yes
Outdoor Cooking Facilities: BBQ CBA
Cleanup: provided
View: panorama of fairways, hills, valley, lakes
Other: event coordination

RESTRICTIONS:

Alcohol: provided, no BYO
Smoking: designated areas
Music: amplified OK indoors

Wheelchair Access: yes
Insurance: not required
Other: no confetti, birdseed or rice

Guglielmo Winery

Winery

1480 East Main Avenue, Morgan Hill
408/779-2145
www.guglielmowinery.com
eventcenter@guglielmowinery.com

● Rehearsal Dinners	● Corp. Events/Mtgs.
● Ceremonies	● Private Parties
● Wedding Receptions	Accommodations

There is practically no event that this versatile venue can't handle. Corporate dinners, private parties and seminars keep this family winery hopping all year long. They even host a Harvest Festival complete with a grape stomping competition, and a Holiday Gift Faire in December. But from the first weekend in May through the second weekend in October, the winery's charming Villa Emile Event Center is most popular for rehearsal dinners and weddings.

Emilio Guglielmo, whose family passed down a winemaking craft for generations in Italy, came to the Santa Clara Valley in 1908 and by 1925 had established his winery in Morgan Hill. Today, Emilio's grandsons run the winery, and their custom-designed event space, Villa Emile, is a pleasing complement to their award-winning winery. Creativity is encouraged here, and the staff will help you custom-design your event, too, including personalized labels for small bottles of wine you can use as favors.

Villa Emile is immediately adjacent to the winery itself. Pass through the iron gates, topped by a stained-glass window with the family name "Guglielmo" encircled by grapevines, and you'll find yourself in the courtyard. This area consists of a cobblestone patio bordered by beds of assorted flowers, an appropriate setting for small parties or pre-dinner drinks and hors d'oeuvres. Nearby is a large granite bar where wine, champagne and beer are served under an arbor covered by a luxuriant 80-year-old grapevine.

A redwood pergola and concrete walkway separate the courtyard from the larger event space, a vast green lawn where tables and chairs can be set up—with umbrellas, if the weather is hot. At one end of the lawn is an enormous covered stage supported by rugged sandstone pillars (perfect for live music or a DJ). In front of the stage, a large dance floor invites you to get out there and boogie. At the other end of the lawn is a charming red-tile-roofed arbor, where couples often exchange wedding vows. To the right, a new building contains a spacious, beautifully appointed dressing room for the bride and her attendants. A small balcony off this room overlooks the vineyard and rolling hills, and is a favorite spot for wedding photos.

The structures here—all built out of terracotta stucco—seem to have sprung from the earth as naturally as the grapevines themselves, and their red-tile roofs are reminiscent of Tuscany. Geraniums, lilies-of-the-Nile, and petunias are colorful accents in front of the stage and along the paths. In this lovely setting, with its relaxed, Old World ambiance, you and your guests will feel that time spent at Guglielmo Winery is time well spent indeed.

CEREMONY, EVENT/RECEPTION & MEETING CAPACITY: Indoors, Guglielmo holds up to 72 seated guests, outdoors up to 450 seated guests.

FEES & DEPOSITS: The rental fee starts at $800 for indoor events, and at $4,500 for outdoor events, and varies depending on space rented, day and time of event and guest count.

AVAILABILITY: Indoors, year-round. Outdoors, May–October.

SERVICES/AMENITIES:

Catering: select from list
Kitchen Facilities: fully equipped
Tables & Chairs: provided
Linens: provided, variety of colors
Restrooms: wheelchair accessible
Dance Floor: cement floor near stage
Bride's & Groom's Dressing Areas: yes
Meeting Equipment: BYO

Parking: ample, lot nearby
Accommodations: no guest rooms
Telephone: no
Outdoor Night Lighting: yes
Outdoor Cooking Facilities: no
Cleanup: caterer or renter
View: vineyards and surrounding hills
Other: event coordination

RESTRICTIONS:

Alcohol: provided, no BYO
Smoking: designated areas
Music: amplified OK

Wheelchair Access: yes
Insurance: certificate required

Want to find more venues and services? Check out our informative website, www.HereComesTheGuide.com.

291

The Corinthian Event Center

Historic Private Club

196 North Third Street, San Jose
408/938-2332

www.corinthiangrandballroom.com
rmendoza@corinthiangrandballroom.com

● Rehearsal Dinners	● Corp. Events/Mtgs.	
● Ceremonies	● Private Parties	
● Wedding Receptions	Accommodations	

Located in the heart of historic downtown San Jose, this 1924 landmark is no ordinary venue. As you walk up the broad granite steps, past the enormous urns and soaring columns, you can't help but be impressed by the stately elegance of its neoclassic design.

That impression carries through to the interior spaces as well. The Corinthian Room is the event center's main ballroom, and it has all the elements of a true ballroom. You enter through a foyer, regally outfitted with a crystal chandelier and a hand-painted wood-beam ceiling. Once inside the Corinthian Room, you're struck by its grand proportions and majestic features. The 60-foot ceiling has massive wood beams, and is inset with alternating panes of blue glass and intricately detailed panels of gold leaf grillwork. Six extraordinary wrought-iron-and-glass lanterns hang from the ceiling like giant luminous earrings, while five 30-foot palm trees embedded with twinkle lights add sparkle. At one end of the room is a stage with a carved stone proscenium arch framing red velvet curtains; at the other end is a carved granite balcony, where just-married couples often dance their first dance. Banquettes along the sides of the room make cozy seating areas, and there's a raised section that's ideal for the head table. The hardwood dance floor is permanently ensconced in front of the stage.

Smaller functions take place in the Gold, Silver and Bronze Rooms. All have crystal chandeliers, cream walls, red carpeting and ceilings baffled for sound. You can reserve these rooms individually, or combine them to make one long room—the perfect space for a wedding ceremony. And all three rooms have access to the Columns Lounge, a more casual space with faux-candle chandeliers and a mix of antiques and contemporary furnishings. The Olympia Room, a large private room with white walls and pastel detailing, is available for small meetings and as a bride's dressing area.

Whether you're getting married or planning a company meeting or party, the center's staff will help you orchestrate it. And if you're inviting out-of-town guests, they'll appreciate being close to many of San Jose's best hotels and cultural activities.

CEREMONY CAPACITY: The Gold, Silver and Bronze Rooms combined hold up to 150 seated guests; the Olympia and Decathlon Rooms hold 60 seated guests each, and the Corinthian Room 300 seated guests.

EVENT/RECEPTION CAPACITY: The facility holds 5–300 seated or up to 500 standing guests indoors. The ballroom can accommodate 300 seated or 500 standing.

MEETING CAPACITY: Event spaces accommodate 5–350 seated guests.

FEES & DEPOSITS: For special events and weddings, a $2,000 nonrefundable deposit secures your date and is required when reservations are made. Full payment is due 5 days prior to your event. For 5 hours' use, the rental fee ranges $500–2,000 depending on the space selected. There is a ceremony setup charge. In-house catering is provided: Meals start at $35/person; alcohol, tax and a 20% service charge are additional. Note that there's a $10,000 minimum for functions held on Saturday evenings. All wedding events have private use of the event center when the food and beverage minimum is met. Off-site catering is also available.

For business functions, weekday morning and afternoon rental rates run $150–500 depending on the room(s) selected. Food prices will vary depending on the type of function, guest count and event duration.

AVAILABILITY: Year-round, daily, 7am–1am. Weddings are in 5-hour blocks; extra hours may be available for an additional $300/hour.

SERVICES/AMENITIES:
Catering: provided
Kitchen Facilities: n/a
Tables & Chairs: provided
Linens, Silver, etc.: provided
Restrooms: wheelchair accessible
Dance Floor: yes
Bride's Dressing Area: CBA
Meeting Equipment: A/V, other CBA, extra fee
Other: event coordination, poolside parties

Parking: on-street or nearby garage, free on weekends and weekdays after 6pm
Accommodations: no guest rooms
Telephone: emergency use only
Outdoor Night Lighting: yes
Outdoor Cooking Facilities: no
Cleanup: provided
View: no

RESTRICTIONS:
Alcohol: provided
Smoking: outside only
Music: amplified OK indoors

Wheelchair Access: yes
Insurance: not required
Other: no helium balloons in Corinthian Room; no confetti, birdseed or rice indoors

Fairmont Hotel San Jose

Hotel

170 South Market Street, San Jose
408/998-1900 x3520
www.fairmont.com
glenn.comp@fairmont.com

- Rehearsal Dinners
- Ceremonies
- Wedding Receptions
- Corp. Events/Mtgs.
- Private Parties
- Accommodations

For almost 100 years, the words "Fairmont Hotel" have represented the *ne plus ultra* in grand hotels, and the Fairmont San Jose lives up to this reputation admirably. Winner of the AAA Four Diamond Award, the Fairmont San Jose offers not only the elegant décor, luxurious accommodations and exemplary service that has made the chain famous around the world, but an entire floor of ballrooms and meeting spaces tailor-made for sophisticated celebrations and business functions.

Planning a sit-down dinner for 1,000 guests, or a banquet for 800? Then you'll want to check out the 13,000-square-foot Imperial Ballroom and the 8,000-square-foot Regency Ballroom. Both of these majestic spaces feature 20-foot molded ceilings with crystal chandeliers, and the Imperial Ballroom is accompanied by a Foyer that's lovely enough for a wedding ceremony or prefunction cocktail party. It's full of natural light, thanks to an enormous arched window overlooking César Chavez Plaza. For ceremonies, a stage is set up beneath the fanciful wrought-iron-and-crystal chandelier that hangs from the Foyer's vaulted ceiling, and guests are seated in a "theater in the round" configuration. A host of smaller rooms are available for more intimate gatherings, whether festive or business oriented. All are similar in décor to the Imperial and Regency Ballrooms, but with more modest 12-foot ceilings. Many of them have large windows with views of the Plaza or the trees lining First Street, giving the rooms an open, airy feel.

One of the most delightful spaces at the Fairmont is the Club Regent. Formerly a dinner theater, its octagonal shape and curtained stage give this room plenty of personality, while split-level seating makes it surprisingly intimate and versatile. It's ideal for sit-down receptions of up to 240, since the room's unique layout allows guests to be seated around a central head table, making everyone feel close to the "action." But it's also a favorite spot for bar and bat mitzvahs, since the kids can cut loose on the main floor, while adults observe the festivities from the relatively sedate upper level (the Club Regent would also be great for a graduation party, or any event where different generations might each like their own "space").

As you would expect from an award-winning hotel, the Fairmont provides much more than just beautifully appointed ballrooms and meeting spaces. They're one of the only hotels in the South Bay to offer kosher catering, and they specialize in Asian, Indian and Persian weddings. Perks for brides and grooms include a complimentary bridal suite and a tulle-draped stage to showcase the wedding cake. The hotel's layout keeps large and small events separate, and solid padded walls mean that your string quartet won't be drowned out by the DJ next door. And the Fairmont's fabulous lobby, with its marble columns, statuary, chandeliers and floral displays, makes an opulent backdrop for your wedding photos.

With all the amenities we've listed above, plus a great central location in the heart of Silicon Valley, it's easy to see why the Fairmont has been awarded such high accolades. Don't be afraid to expect perfection at this first-rate establishment—you won't be disappointed. After all, this is the Fairmont!!

CEREMONY CAPACITY: There are 22 rooms which can accommodate 10–1,000 seated guests.

EVENT/RECEPTION CAPACITY: The hotel has 22 banquet rooms that hold 30–1,000 seated or 50–3,200 standing guests. In addition, the Club Regent holds 240 seated or 300 standing guests.

MEETING CAPACITY: The hotel offers 65,000 square feet of meeting space, with 22 rooms that hold 28–1,400 seated guests.

FEES & DEPOSITS: For weddings, a nonrefundable $3,000 minimum deposit is required to secure your date. 50% of the anticipated total is due 45 days prior, and the balance is payable 5 business days prior to the event. Rental charges vary depending on room size and the event time frame. There are 4 wedding packages ranging $89–120/person, which usually include hors d'oeuvres, a 2-course dinner, wedding cake, champagne toast, and bridal suite. Tax and service charges are extra.

For business functions, all services are customized; call for more information and rates. The hotel has an on-site full-service business center.

AVAILABILITY: Year-round, daily, including holidays until 2am.

SERVICES/AMENITIES:
Catering: provided; outside caterers allowed only for Indian cuisine, and must be approved
Kitchen Facilities: n/a
Tables & Chairs: provided
Linens, Silver, etc.: provided
Restrooms: wheelchair accessible
Dance Floor: provided
Bride's & Groom's Dressing Areas: CBA
Meeting Equipment: full range A/V

Parking: valet or nearby parking lots
Accommodations: 805 guest rooms
Telephone: pay phones
Outdoor Night Lighting: CBA
Outdoor Cooking Facilities: CBA
Cleanup: provided
View: César Chavez Park, Circle of Palms
Other: baby grand pianos, ice sculpture, event coordination, wedding cakes

RESTRICTIONS:
Alcohol: provided, no BYO
Smoking: allowed outdoors
Music: amplified OK until 1am

Wheelchair Access: yes
Insurance: not required
Other: no fog machines

First Unitarian Church of San Jose

160 North Third Street, San Jose
408/841-7542
sanjoseuu.org/AboutUs/Rentals/
rentals@sanjoseuu.org

Reception Facility and Church

● Rehearsal Dinners	● Corp. Events/Mtgs.
● Ceremonies	● Private Parties
● Wedding Receptions	☐ Accommodations

For many brides and grooms, the dream starts with a big church wedding, preferably a place with lots of charm, a sense of history and a warm, inviting atmosphere. Well, dreams can come true, because the First Unitarian Church of San Jose offers all that and more. Built in 1891 and recently restored to its former glory, the venue's Romanesque Revival architecture incorporates graceful domes, arched entryways, a sun-kissed stucco façade and some of the most beautiful stained-glass windows you're likely to find anywhere. Perhaps equally important, the church, with its long tradition of community outreach and social equality, welcomes all couples—regardless of religious affiliation or sexual persuasion—to celebrate their union in its unique circular sanctuary.

Arriving guests enter through three sets of double doors at the top of the terracotta steps (there's a side ramp and elevators, too). Once inside the two-story, domed space, you're struck by the lack of hard edges as one design motif flows into another, reinforcing a sense of continuity. Rows of old wooden seats, their antique patina glowing in the light from dozens of floral stained-glass windows, are arranged in a semicircle on both the main floor and the mezzanine. They face an inspiring stained-glass panel that flanks the graceful, triple-arched altar. Etched right into the carpet below is a large labyrinth, adding a note of contemplation to the spirituality of the surroundings. And speaking of notes, the acoustics in a room without angles are superb for savoring the sound of either the Steinway baby grand or the Galanti organ during your service.

If you have your reception here, you may want to start with cocktails and hors d'oeuvres in the parlor-style Fireside Room, which features an upright piano, wainscoted walls and a barrel ceiling. Dominating one wall is the Arts and Crafts wooden fireplace, while throughout the room there are notable antique touches like an intricately carved buffet. When it's time for dinner, just swing open the French doors and invite your guests into the adjacent Hattie Porter Hall. This spacious, high-ceilinged dinner and dancing area, set off by moss green walls and dark wood floors, is filled with light from more stained-glass windows and twinkling chandeliers. For a quiet moment away from the crowd, retreat to the casual upstairs lounge (which also serves as your bridal room) and enjoy a bird's-eye view of the festivities from windows that look down on the action in the hall below.

Just remember before you leave to take advantage of photo opportunities at the historic St. James Park across the street. Among its illustrious designers was Frederick Olmstead, one of this country's pre-eminent landscape architects and the mastermind behind outdoor treasures such as New York's Central Park.

CEREMONY CAPACITY: The sanctuary holds 237 seated guests.

EVENT/RECEPTION CAPACITY: Indoors the facility holds 150 seated or 200 standing guests.

MEETING CAPACITY: Meeting rooms accommodate 150 seated guests.

FEES & DEPOSITS: A $1,000 refundable deposit is required to reserve your date. The balance is due 3 months prior to the event. Rental fees range $1,200–2,500 depending on the space rented.

AVAILABILITY: Year-round, daily, 9am–midnight.

SERVICES/AMENITIES:

Catering: BYO

Kitchen Facilities: prep only

Tables & Chairs: provided

Linens, Silver, etc.: BYO

Restrooms: wheelchair accessible

Dance Floor: provided

Bride's & Groom's Dressing Areas: yes

Meeting Equipment: some provided

Parking: garage nearby

Accommodations: no guest rooms

Telephone: emergency use only

Outdoor Night Lighting: access only

Outdoor Cooking Facilities: none

Cleanup: provided

View: cityscape

Other: grand piano, A/V equipment

RESTRICTIONS:

Alcohol: BYO

Smoking: allowed outdoors only

Music: amplified OK indoors

Wheelchair Access: yes

Insurance: not required

This is important! Tell locations you're reading HERE COMES THE GUIDE and ask if our information is still current.

297

Hilton San Jose

Hotel

300 Almaden Boulevard, San Jose
408/947-4450 Sales, 408/287-2100 Main
www.sanjose.hilton.com
sales@sanjosehilton.com

- Rehearsal Dinners
- Ceremonies
- Wedding Receptions
- Corp. Events/Mtgs.
- Private Parties
- Accommodations

Given its prominence in downtown San Jose (which is, after all, the heart of Silicon Valley) it's only natural that the Hilton San Jose would embrace the culture of innovation and constant improvement. Their forward-thinking approach is evident in the venue's recent $11.5 million, top-to-bottom transformation that seamlessly integrates leading-edge technology, eye-catching design and an expansion of its public space…all without losing the kind of hands-on, personal touch that makes you and your event feel special.

Drop off your car with the valet and enter the new classic modern lobby where soft, recessed lighting and wall panels in rich earth colors create a soothing atmosphere. Nearby, a dramatic interior fountain features stainless steel sculptures rising from a pool of water in front of the Affinity Lounge, the hotel's casually chic restaurant for meeting, greeting and dining on the chef's inventive European-inspired cuisine.

Just a few steps from the restaurant is the Affinity Patio, an open-air, urban oasis and a great place to start your celebration. Located on the McEnery Convention Center Plaza, this charming spot is shielded from view by an artistically sculpted metal screen. There's a cascading water wall and movable fire pits set amongst the dark rattan sofas and chairs—a perfect locale for your cocktail reception. While many brides opt to have their ceremony at one of the nearby houses of worship, like St. Joseph's Cathedral, you can also exchange vows on the Patio (they even have an officiant on staff!).

Afterwards, invite your guests back inside the hotel to the beautifully proportioned Market Room. Ambient light from skylights gracing the three-story vaulted ceiling along with a series of picture windows that look out towards the Patio give you a sense of the outdoors. White glass chandeliers and billowing swags hung from the high, steel beams add a romantic note.

For a completely different ambiance, or if you have a larger group, begin with cocktails at the Winchester Room on the other side of the lobby. You can get more of a city vibe here with hip, lounge-type, retro-cool furnishings and floor-to-ceiling windows that provide a view of the energetic street scene outside. When you're ready for dinner and dancing, the spacious Almaden

Ballroom is just across the lobby. High ceilings, hanging chandeliers and an optional hardwood dance floor make this an elegant setting for your main reception.

One of the most mesmerizing aspects of the Hilton is the panoramic view you get from the top floors, and there's no better way to appreciate it than from your exquisite bridal suite. Many hotels offer complimentary honeymoon suites, but this one is extraordinary. This VIP space, with full living room and luxurious bedroom, has curving, wraparound walls of windows that offer 90-degree vistas of downtown's twinkling lights and recognizable landmarks...a truly fabulous retreat to cap off a memorable night.

CEREMONY CAPACITY & EVENT/RECEPTION CAPACITY: The Almaden Ballroom holds 200 seated or 400 standing guests. Various other rooms hold 25–150 seated or 30–250 standing. Outdoors, the Affinity Patio holds 100 seated or standing guests.

MEETING CAPACITY: There are 14 meeting rooms which can accommodate 10–190 seated guests, classroom-style.

FEES & DEPOSITS: For weddings, a $1,000 nonrefundable deposit is required when the contract is signed. Half of the anticipated event total is due 3 months in advance, the balance is payable 7 days prior.

There are multiple wedding packages, ranging $80–90/person, which include linen décor package, 1-hour hors d' oeuvres reception, dinner with wine service on the tables, wedding cake, champagne toast and complimentary bridal suite for one night, breakfast in bed the following morning and shuttle service to the airport. Group discounts are available for out-of-town guests. Also included is a complimentary overnight stay on your 1-year anniversary.

AVAILABILITY: Year-round, daily.

SERVICES/AMENITIES:

Catering: provided
Kitchen Facilities: n/a
Tables & Chairs: provided
Linens, Silver, etc.: provided
Restrooms: wheelchair accessible
Dance Floor: portable provided
Bride's Dressing Area: yes
Meeting Equipment: CBA

Parking: valet required, garage nearby
Accommodations: 353 guest rooms
Telephone: house, office and guest phones
Outdoor Night Lighting: CBA
Outdoor Cooking Facilities: BBQ CBA
Cleanup: provided
View: no
Other: on-site wedding cake and florals, clergy on staff, A/V equipment, event coordination

RESTRICTIONS:

Alcohol: provided, or BYO with corkage fee
Smoking: outdoors only
Music: amplified OK indoors, outdoors with limits

Wheelchair Access: yes
Insurance: not required
Other: decorations require approval

Mexican Heritage Plaza

1700 Alum Rock Avenue, San Jose
408/794-6240

www.mhplaza.com
rentals@mhplaza.com

School of Arts & Culture

- Rehearsal Dinners
- Ceremonies
- Wedding Receptions
- Corp. Events/Mtgs.
- Private Parties
- Accommodations

The Mexican Heritage Plaza, a six-acre jewel located in a bustling section of San Jose, is a beacon of neighborhood pride and veritable feast for your senses. Viewed from the street, its distinctive adobe-hued tower and modern building complex barely hint at the treasures you'll find within this dynamic culture and education center. The artfully designed property revels in its mix of vibrant murals, architectural flourishes, tranquil gardens and soothing water features. But it's the whole-hearted homage to family and community, expressed artistically throughout the property, that stirs your soul and makes this exciting venue such a compelling choice for a wedding.

From the moment you arrive, you see the fun and unexpected ways in which Mexico's heritage is celebrated, from the colorful mosaic walkway at the street entry, to the Aztec symbols adorning a fountain at the side entry. A gate here leads to MHP's beautifully landscaped garden and water areas, the place where you'll probably begin your event.

The Main Garden is utterly charming, with a wide lawn planted with rows of stately palms and an adobe brick wall draped in ivy and red trumpetvine flowers. Set into the wall are large niches decorated with handcrafted tiles imprinted with photo transfers of local ancestors and historic events. Woven together, they create a tapestry of life from generation to generation. With your own nearest and dearest gathered to witness your rite of passage, this makes a particularly meaningful ceremony site. As an alternative, you can exchange vows in front of the adjacent Rose Garden. Your guests will be seated beneath a lovely arbor that's covered with an array of blooms and ringed by flowering trees. Separating these two captivating settings is a serene reflecting pool, complete with feathery marsh grass, a small waterfall and surrounding patio.

Either of these areas is also perfect for a cocktail reception, especially at night when twinkle lights or hidden spots add a bit of magic. Or take advantage of the site's modern, state-of-the-art theater building by utilizing the glass-enclosed Theater Lobby. With its massive, brightly painted wooden bar, Day of the Dead figurines and tribal theater masks adorning the walls, it makes for a festive scene.

You're in for a treat when it comes to options for your main reception as well. The dazzling Pavilion has a dramatic, stepped pyramid-style ceiling that reflects more than a nod to Aztec influences. The room's four walls are made up of glass doors that can fold away leaving only the corner pillars, creating an indoor-outdoor feel (with the advantages of a great sound system and climate control). If you're craving a totally al fresco party under the stars, set up your dining and dancing in the Plaza itself. No matter what spaces you choose you can't go wrong here: From expansive backdrops for large groups to unique nooks for more intimate gatherings, every spot at the Mexican Heritage Plaza has its own allure.

CEREMONY CAPACITY: The site holds 300 seated indoors and 200 seated outdoors.

EVENT/RECEPTION CAPACITY: The facility can accommodate 200 seated or 500 standing indoors and 900 seated or 2,000 standing guests ourdoors.

MEETING CAPACITY: Meeting spaces hold 250 seated.

FEES & DEPOSITS: One third of the total event cost is required to reserve your date. The balance is due 90 days prior to the event. Rental fees range $3,900–5,300 depending on the time of year, guest count and space rented.

AVAILABILITY: Year-round, daily in 8-hour increments. Events must end by midnight.

SERVICES/AMENITIES:

Catering: select from preferred list
Kitchen Facilities: prep only
Tables & Chairs: provided
Linens, Silver, etc.: through caterer or BYO
Restrooms: wheelchair accessible
Dance Floor: provided
Bride's & Groom's Dressing Areas: upon request
Meeting Equipment: some provided, CBA
A/V equipment

Parking: large lots, on street
Accommodations: no guest rooms
Telephone: emergency use only
Outdoor Night Lighting: yes
Outdoor Cooking Facilities: no
Cleanup: in-house contractor required
View: fountain, garden courtyard, landscaped grounds

RESTRICTIONS:

Alcohol: BYO, security required
Smoking: outdoors only
Music: amplified OK

Wheelchair Access: yes
Insurance: liability required

Paolo's Restaurant

Restaurant

333 West San Carlos Street, San Jose
408/294-2558

www.paolos.com
carolyn@paolos.com

- Rehearsal Dinners
- Ceremonies
- Wedding Receptions
- Corp. Events/Mtgs.
- Private Parties
- Accommodations

Like a chameleon, Paolo's Restaurant transforms itself into just the right setting for your wedding reception or any special event. Its location in a sleek, granite office tower overlooking the beautiful Guadalupe River Park is surprisingly versatile—add a little creative magic with flowers, linens, and lighting and—voila! You've got a candlelit gala on a terrace overlooking a wooded creek. Or an elegant soirée in the building's gleaming main lobby. Or a cozy get-together in the Wine Room upstairs. Or…you get the idea; Paolo's shapes itself to your personal vision.

There's an understated richness about Paolo's décor. The walls are a soft, burnished gold reminiscent of an old Tuscan village sleeping in the afternoon sun. Quiet lighting and artfully gathered jewel-tone drapes showcase the original, modern paintings and sculptures that grace every room and passageway.

All three dining rooms look out on a sweeping terrace, which also features a stairstep waterfall cascading down to a lower level. The trees along the creek form a pastoral foreground that softens the view of the city's towers, and the bridge across the creek to the Center for the Performing Arts is an irresistibly dramatic entrance point for the bridal party. If you have a large group, consider reserving the entire restaurant. When weather permits, special arrangements can be made to dine outdoors, too.

Paolo's specializes in authentic regional Italian cuisine that emphasizes fresh, seasonal foods and skillful combinations of flavors. When we dined here we had broad maltagliate pasta accompanied by rabbit braised with fresh vegetables until the meat melted off the bone and the vegetables gently disappeared into a luscious sauce. The rabbit, tender and flavorful, was perfectly complemented by the al dente pasta. We also tried a house-made gnocchi, which we declared the best we've ever tasted: soft potato pillows that melted on the tongue, made even more *squisito* by baby wild mushrooms and black truffle butter.

In addition to providing a choice of wedding packages, Paolo's special event coordinator can work with you to custom-design a menu. And if cucina italiana isn't what you have in mind, Chef Carolyn Allen-Samavarchian—daughter of Jack Allen, who founded the restaurant a half a century ago—will exert her considerable culinary talents to accommodate your preferred cuisine. Sommelier/Maitre d' and husband-of-the-chef Jalil Samavarchian has compiled a handpicked, 34-page wine list with selections from Italy, France, and California. For their efforts, Paolo's has been a consistent *Wine Spectator* "Best of Excellence" and *Distinguished Restaurants of Northern America* award winner.

Conveniently located downtown, Paolo's is close to the many churches and upscale hotels of central San Jose. In fact, it's within walking distance of at least three of the best hotels the city has to offer, something your overnight guests will appreciate—especially if they've fully partaken of Paolo's exquisite cuisine and fine wines. Another plus is the validated on-site parking.

A successful and memorable wedding is often about pleasing the greatest number of people possible, which means convenience and flexibility become nearly as important as ambiance, great food and service. This restaurant impresses in all of these areas and possesses one more quality that's often harder to come by: *il cuore,* or "heart." Paolo's puts love into everything they do.

CEREMONY CAPACITY: Ceremonies do not take place at this facility.

EVENT/RECEPTION CAPACITY: The restaurant can accommodate 180 seated or 300 standing indoors and 250 seated or 350 standing outdoors.

MEETING CAPACITY: Meeting spaces hold 110 seated.

FEES & DEPOSITS: For weddings, 25% of the total anticipated event cost or $2,000 (whichever is greater) is required to reserve your date. Call for nonrefundable policy terms and conditions. The balance is due 5 business days prior to the event. Rental fees range $0–2,000 depending on the day and time of the event, guest count and the space rented. Wedding packages range $52–95/person. Tax, alcohol and a 20% service charge are additional.

For private, corporate or special events, a $250–2,500 deposit is required. Contact the Special Events Department for pricing details.

AVAILABILITY: Year-round, Monday–Saturday, 9am–midnight. The restaurant is closed most Sundays and major holidays except by prior arrangement. Call for availability and details.

SERVICES/AMENITIES:

Catering: provided
Kitchen Facilities: n/a
Tables & Chairs: provided
Linens, Silver, etc.: provided
Restrooms: wheelchair accessible
Dance Floor: CBA
Bride's & Groom's Dressing Areas: yes
Meeting Equipment: some provided, CBA
Other: grand piano, event coordination

Parking: validated parking in covered garage on site
Accommodations: no guest rooms
Telephone: emergency use only
Outdoor Night Lighting: CBA
Outdoor Cooking Facilities: BBQ CBA
Cleanup: provided
View: cityscape, river, park, fountain, landscaped grounds, garden patio

RESTRICTIONS:

Alcohol: provided, or BYO with corkage fee
Smoking: outdoors only
Music: amplified OK with restrictions

Wheelchair Access: yes
Insurance: not required

Overwhelmed? Use the search criteria on www.HereComesTheGuide.com to narrow down your choices.

303

The Pavilion Event Center at Boulder Ridge

Event Center

1000 Old Quarry Road, San Jose
408/323-9900 X125
www.boulderridgegolfclub.com
events@boulderridgegolfclub.com

● Rehearsal Dinners	● Corp. Events/Mtgs.
● Ceremonies	● Private Parties
● Wedding Receptions	Accommodations

At the top of a picturesque road that starts at Almaden Lake and heads up into the Santa Theresa Hills, there's a wedding venue that's sure to entice you with its spectacular, unobstructed views in virtually all directions.

Perched high on a plateau overlooking Boulder Ridge golf course, The Pavilion Event Center was named for the dramatic sandstone rock formations that dot the hillside fairways. These striking boulders, which were part of land that was once home to the Ohlone Indians, now contribute to this location's unique landscape.

The Pavilion's rough-hewn stone and earth-colored exterior blends organically with the natural tones of the Santa Cruz Mountains in the distance. Spreading out in front of the building is a verdant lawn, adorned with several Craftsman-style arbors, each framing a different vista. The Welcome Arbor, with its nearby fountain, faces north, presenting arriving guests with a bird's-eye view of downtown San Jose's skyline. The Bridal Arbor, which you can enhance with your choice of flowers, garlands, crystals, or other decorations, becomes the focal point when everyone takes their seats and turns to watch the bride begin her walk down the aisle. Vows are exchanged at the Gazebo, facing west towards the Almaden Valley, allowing the setting sun to form the perfect, glowing backdrop for the ceremony.

After the "I do"s, invite everyone to enjoy cocktails and hors d'oeuvres on the adjoining Terrace, where a large granite-topped bar is a great place to get the party started. Since there's something interesting to catch your eye no matter where you look, it may be hard to tear your friends and family away from the scenery, but even after they sit down to dinner in the Pavilion they're never far from the natural beauty and twinkling lights outside.

Wraparound windows framed in hand-stained sustainable wood cover two sides of the dining room and a floor-to-ceiling fireplace with stone hearth dominates the fourth. Chandeliers with mottled glass shades and California *plein air* paintings reinforce the indoor/outdoor motif of the open, airy space.

An on-site coordinator will help you choreograph your event from start to finish, but she's also happy to work with your own wedding planner. And when it comes to food, the chef can customize your menu, including ethnic specialties.

Before your shuttle or limo whisks you away to your new life, take a quiet stroll under the stars with your beloved—a truly romantic end to a memorable celebration.

CEREMONY CAPACITY: The facility holds 300 seated guests indoors or outdoors.

EVENT/RECEPTION CAPACITY: The site can accommodate 225 seated guests indoors with a dance floor and 300 seated outdoors.

MEETING CAPACITY: Meeting spaces hold 200 seated guests.

FEES & DEPOSITS: A $2,000 deposit is required to reserve your date and the balance is due 30 days prior to the event. Full wedding packages start at $150/person and include the site rental fee, parking shuttle, ceremony and banquet chairs, hors d'oeuvres, entrée, champagne toast, house wine, beer, soft drinks, wedding cake, service charge and sales tax.

AVAILABILITY: Year-round, daily, 7am–midnight. Site visits are by appointment only. Please call 408/323-9900 x125.

SERVICES/AMENITIES:

Catering: provided
Kitchen Facilities: n/a
Tables & Chairs: provided
Linens, Silver, etc.: provided
Restrooms: wheelchair accessible
Dance Floor: (15' x 15') provided
Bride's Dressing Area: yes
Meeting Equipment: CBA
Other: spa services, A/V equipment, parking shuttle, event coordination

Parking: large lot
Accommodations: no guest rooms
Telephone: emergency use only
Outdoor Night Lighting: provided
Outdoor Cooking Facilities: none
Cleanup: provided
View: fairways, landscaped grounds, panorama of mountains, hills and valley

RESTRICTIONS:

Alcohol: provided or BYO wine with $20 corkage fee; no outside liquor or beer
Smoking: outdoors only
Music: amplified OK with restrictions

Wheelchair Access: yes
Insurance: recommended

San Jose Woman's Club

75 South Eleventh Street, San Jose
408/772-6667

sjwomansclub.org
rentals@sjwomansclub.org

Historic Woman's Club

- Rehearsal Dinners
- Ceremonies
- Wedding Receptions
- Corp. Events/Mtgs.
- Private Parties
- Accommodations

With its façade of tall arched windows and imposing entryway, the San Jose Woman's Club building makes a graceful impression. Completed in 1929, the Spanish-style structure has hosted a wide variety of events over the years, and many couples continue to be married here.

The foyer, with its fireplace niche and tiled stairway, is often used for small ceremonies; the stairs serve as both an entrance for the bride and a convenient spot for photos. It's also a relaxed space for sipping champagne and mingling.

The Ballroom, however, is the building's *pièce de résistance*. A high, slightly vaulted ceiling spans the enormous room, and light from a wall of tall arched windows brings out the shine on the maple floor. The floor itself is unusual in that it has a special "spring" construction to enhance dancing. Up above, the beams crisscrossing the ceiling are all hand-stenciled, and the ornate parchment-and-wrought-iron chandeliers glow amber when lit. You can exchange vows on the curtained stage, while your favorite tune is played on the Steinway baby grand piano.

The Ballroom has plenty of space for a large reception, but if you need additional seating, the adjacent Tea Room comes in very handy. Separated from the Ballroom by two sliding glass pocket doors, it has easy access to the kitchen via a pass-through counter at one end. Like the Ballroom, its pastel unadorned walls make a neutral backdrop for potted plants and flowers. The club offers a great deal of flexibility, not only for weddings, but for private parties, seminars, concerts or lectures—and its fees are very affordable.

CEREMONY CAPACITY: The club holds 400 seated theater-style.

EVENT/RECEPTION CAPACITY: The Ballroom holds 350 seated and the Tea Room holds 100 seated guests, banquet-style.

MEETING CAPACITY: The Ballroom holds 400 seated theater-style and the Tea Room holds 125 seated theater-style. The Fireside Room holds 25 seated conference-style.

FEES & DEPOSITS: A refundable security deposit is required to hold your date, and is returned 21 days after the event if the site is left in good condition and all the rules are followed. For weekday events, Monday–Thursday, the rental is $1,750; Friday or Sunday $2,250; and Saturday $2,850. The rental fee is payable 90 days prior to the event. These prices cover a 5-hour event, each additional hour runs $250. Smaller rooms may be available, call for pricing. Security personnel are required at $46.50/officer: 1 off-duty police officer for up to 150 guests, 2 for over 150 guests.

For weekday business functions or meetings, the rental rate varies depending on guest count and event duration. Call for specifics.

AVAILABILITY: Year-round.

SERVICES/AMENITIES:

Catering: select from preferred list or BYO, extra fee
Kitchen Facilities: prep only
Tables & Chairs: provided
Linens, Silver, etc.: BYO
Restrooms: wheelchair accessible
Dance Floor: in Ballroom
Bride's Dressing Area: yes
Meeting Equipment: lighted podium, stage with lights and sound system

Parking: adjacent lot, on-street
Accommodations: no guest rooms
Telephone: no
Outdoor Night Lighting: yes
Outdoor Cooking Facilities: BYO
Cleanup: renter
View: no

RESTRICTIONS:

Alcohol: provided or BYO, licensed server
Smoking: outside only
Music: amplified OK with restrictions; amplification not required in many cases, acoustics are superb

Wheelchair Access: yes
Insurance: certificate required; special event insurance available
Other: no rice, birdseed or confetti; no tacks or tape on walls

Silicon Valley Capital Club

Private Club

50 West San Fernando, 17th Floor, San Jose
408/971-9300

www.sanjoseclub.com
jenna.torres@ourclub.com

● Rehearsal Dinners	● Corp. Events/Mtgs.	
● Ceremonies	● Private Parties	
● Wedding Receptions	Accommodations	

Occupying the penthouse floor of the Knight Ridder Building in the heart of downtown, the Silicon Valley Capital Club has always enjoyed some of the most spectacular views to be found anywhere in San Jose. But since its recent multimillion-dollar renovation, this private club has also become one of the hottest event sites in the South Bay.

Those stunning 360-degree panoramas are just the beginning: A winning combination of indoor and outdoor spaces can be used together to create a fabulous flow during your celebration.

Festivities begin the moment your guests arrive at the top floor. The elevator doors open to the Vertex Lounge, a terrific, visually striking place to host the cocktail hour. Weathered barn wood recycled from local wineries and farms has been incorporated into the walls, lending a rustic warmth. But all eyes are drawn to the centerpiece of the room—the bar, which is lit from end to end by a stunning "chandelier" comprised of dozens of illuminated glass cylinders that drop from the ceiling. The lounge happens to have its own outdoor aerie, the Sky Terrace, which is outfitted with casual seating and firepits. From here you can watch the sun set and the city come alive, as night falls and a glittering carpet of lights spreads out below.

When it's time for dinner, everyone moves into the main ballroom, a contemporary and elegant space with two walls of floor-to-ceiling glass overlooking the city. Designed in neutral shades of gray, the décor is compatible with just about any color scheme. Unusual amber-tinted glass chandeliers make the room sparkle, and you can modulate the mood even more with additional uplighting. The view is visible from every seat in the house, as is the wedding cake, which is gloriously showcased in a windowed alcove against the backdrop of the city. The ballroom's South Terrace gives you even more options: This al fresco deck can be set up with cocktail tables for mingling before and after the reception, and also serves as a lofty spot for guests to take a break from dining and dancing.

If you're hosting an intimate affair or rehearsal dinner, you might want to reserve one of the Capital Club's six smaller event rooms. They all provide sweeping vistas, and some have private balconies.

At such an elevated place you'd expect equally high-level cuisine and the Capital Club does not disappoint. Their Michelin-Star chef uses locally sourced seafood and "Farm to Table" produce, prime grass-fed beef, and other fresh ingredients in a wide range of dishes, from classic comfort food with a twist to more innovative choices based on cutting-edge cooking techniques. He's happy to develop a menu specifically for your occasion.

Experienced planners will assist with all the details ensuring that your event comes off perfectly, so whether you're hosting a wedding, a private party or a corporate gala, you and your guests will feel like you're on top of the world.

CEREMONY CAPACITY: The South Terrace holds 150 seated or standing.

EVENT/RECEPTION CAPACITY: The club accommodates 200 seated guests indoors, 300 with indoor and outdoor seating.

MEETING CAPACITY: Meeting rooms accommodate 2–180 seated guests.

FEES & DEPOSITS: A $5,000 nonrefundable deposit is required to book the club. Food and beverage service is provided; meals run $25–110/person. Half of the estimated catering total is due 90 days prior to event and the balance 96 hours prior. Alcohol, tax and a 22% service charge are additional, as are ceremony setup fees.

AVAILABILITY: Year-round, daily. Closed most major holidays.

SERVICES/AMENITIES:

Catering: provided, no BYO
Kitchen Facilities: n/a
Tables & Chairs: provided
Linens, Silver, etc.: provided
Restrooms: wheelchair accessible
Dance Floor: portable, extra fee
Bride's & Groom's Dressing Areas: yes
Meeting Equipment: A/V equipment

Parking: garage with validation
Accommodations: no guest rooms
Telephone: house phones
Outdoor Night Lighting: yes
Outdoor Cooking Facilities: n/a
Cleanup: provided
View: panorama of Silicon Valley
Other: coordination

RESTRICTIONS:

Alcohol: provided, no BYO
Smoking: outside only
Music: amplified OK

Wheelchair Access: yes, elevator
Insurance: not required
Other: no rice, birdseed or confetti

The professionals in the back of this book are the best in the business. How do we know? Read page 637.

Silver Creek Valley Country Club

Country Club

5460 Country Club Parkway, San Jose
408/239-5888
www.scvcc.com
catering@scvcc.com

● Rehearsal Dinners	● Corp. Events/Mtgs.
● Ceremonies	● Private Parties
● Wedding Receptions	○ Accommodations

Whoever invented the phrase "storybook wedding" must have attended one at Silver Creek Valley Country Club (SCVCC). Every last detail at this upscale facility has been carefully thought out to ensure the most memorable experience possible for all guests.

Driving into the club, you pass through a master-planned gated community. Here, swaying palms keep watch over sprawling houses that echo the earth tones of nearby Mount Hamilton and the adjoining foothills. At the end of a long, curving driveway stands the main clubhouse, a golden-hued edifice reminiscent of an Italian villa. Inside, every visitor experiences stunning grandeur and personalized service.

As you make your way through the expansive foyer, you immediately take note of the marble flooring and large columns. However, what really commands your attention is the imposing and ornate rotunda. Encircled by gold-tipped wrought iron and capped by a vast domed skylight, it soars over dual curving staircases that descend to the floor below. (Note that photographers love to pose the wedding party on the landing halfway down the stairs. Flooded with light, it's a prime spot for photos.)

French doors off the foyer lead to the Yerba Buena Ballroom, Silver Creek's main event space. Like the rest of the building's valley-facing side, this unusual crescent-shaped room features a back wall made entirely of glass. Every guest enjoys spectacular views of the championship golf course and the evergreen valley beyond, and at night thousands of twinkling lights from the surrounding homes yield a panorama that's even more dramatic.

The Ballroom's décor creates a seamless visual connection with the outdoor scenery: Pale green carpets and drapes and beige walls reflect the palette of the surrounding hills and foliage. Overhead, three Mediterranean-modern chandeliers cast a warm glow, while a cream-colored marble floor in the center invites everyone to dance.

If you have a smaller-sized gathering, or you'd like to serve cocktails and hors d'oeuvres while pictures are being taken, consider the adjoining Chaboya Lounge. This L-shaped space boasts a wood-paneled, granite-topped bar, cozy fireplace, and a terracotta patio that shares the club's sweeping vistas.

Have you always dreamed of saying your vows in an exotic South Sea setting? Silver Creek Valley Country Club can save you the plane fare. It's just a short pleasant walk from the clubhouse to a majestic waterfall, where couples exchange vows on a raised flagstone Ceremony Landing at the base of this triple-level water feature. Or get married in front of the Cypress Dome with your guests seated on a rolling expanse of lawn. The site itself is certainly photogenic, but photographers also like to snap pictures of the bride and bridesmaids arriving via golf cart (the SCVCC mode of transport), as well as the just-marrieds departing for the reception in the same fashion.

From the custom-designed china to the tasteful furnishings and friendly, accommodating staff, Silver Creek Valley Country Club offers still more amenities that will make planning your wedding easy and enjoyable. Put yourself in the hands of the club's on-site event coordinators, and prepare for a "storybook wedding" that has the happiest of endings.

CEREMONY CAPACITY: The outdoor ceremony area holds up to 300 seated guests.

EVENT/RECEPTION CAPACITY: The club accommodates 300 seated or 500 standing guests indoors.

MEETING CAPACITY: Meeting rooms accommodate up to 250 seated guests.

FEES & DEPOSITS: Rental fees for weddings and events range $5,000–10,000 depending on event date. Rental fees for meetings start at $250. Meals range $34–128/person. Tax, alcohol and a 20% service charge are additional. Valet parking service is available upon request.

AVAILABILITY: Year-round, daily, 8am–midnight.

SERVICES/AMENITIES:

Catering: provided; outside ethnic cuisine caterers ok upon approval
Kitchen Facilities: n/a
Tables & Chairs: provided
Linens, Silver, etc.: provided
Restrooms: wheelchair accessible
Dance Floor: provided
Bride's & Groom's Dressing Areas: yes
Meeting Equipment: CBA, extra charge

Parking: self-parking or valet, extra charge
Accommodations: no guest rooms
Telephone: house phones
Outdoor Night Lighting: yes
Outdoor Cooking Facilities: n/a
Cleanup: provided
View: panorama of valley and hills
Other: event coordination

RESTRICTIONS:

Alcohol: provided, no BYO
Smoking: outdoors only
Music: amplified OK indoors and outdoors

Wheelchair Access: yes
Insurance: required for outside ethnic cuisine caterer
Other: no rice, birdseed or glitter

The Tech Museum of Innovation

Museum

201 South Market Street, San Jose
408/795-6221
www.thetech.org
maureenl@thetech.org

● Rehearsal Dinners	● Corp. Events/Mtgs.
● Ceremonies	● Private Parties
● Wedding Receptions	Accommodations

All you people who yawn at the prospect of going to a museum listen up: The Tech is not just a museum, it's an adventure. In fact, The Tech may be the most exciting thing to happen to the South Bay in years.

Located in downtown San Jose, facing Plaza de Cesar Chavez and just across from the Fairmont Hotel, this bright mango building houses 300 high-tech interactive exhibits that will energize the most jaded visitor. And wonder of wonders!—if you host an event here, the exhibits are available for your guests' enjoyment.

Events are held in the museum lobby, the exhibit galleries, and the Hackworth IMAX Dome Theater. You can reserve any combination of spaces or rent the entire museum. The lobby is a fantastic place for a large party. It's a three-level atrium with a 45-foot cylindrical tower rising up through it and, when used in conjunction with the adjacent New Venture Hall, it can accommodate 500 for a sit-down dinner.

The galleries lend themselves to standing receptions. They're thoroughly modern, displaying a mix of steel, glass and plastic, with walls and ceilings painted in jewel shades of purple, yellow and blue. Each gallery has a different theme. *The Silicon Valley Innovation Gallery* shows how Silicon Valley technologies are revolutionizing human thought, creativity and communication. At *Reface,* you can combine your image with that of other visitors in ways that are often funny and sometimes strange, or experiment with a revolutionary electronic musical instrument that lets you create music from different cultures using cubes and pucks. *The Exploration Gallery* gives you the opportunity to go places you've only been able to imagine: Step onto the Shake Platform to experience an earthquake, or feel just like an astronaut on the Jet Pack Chair. In *The Tech Energy Gallery,* you can harness sun, wind and water power to make the Power Tower glow, while *View From Space* lets you watch hurricanes form or see the spread of an El Niño event over a globe almost six feet in diameter.

In addition to these extraordinary galleries, The Tech has one more cutting-edge gem that will dazzle you and your guests: the Hackworth IMAX Dome Theater. The only one of its kind in Northern California, it features a giant hemispherical screen whose image dwarfs that of a conventional theater and puts the audience in the center of the action. Outfitted with state-of-the-art audiovisual equipment, the theater can be reserved exclusively for a performance or presentation, but we recommend you also use it for viewing an IMAX film. Experience rafting down the world's deadliest river, traveling to the Red Planet, a spellbinding climb up sheer vertical walls to the summit of Everest or the adventure, drama and emotion of some of your favorite Hollywood movies.

The Tech aims to inspire the innovator in everyone; yet, even if you don't come away wanting to be a scientist when you grow up, you'll have to admit that this place makes traditional meeting rooms and party themes feel obsolete. Part of the next generation of museums, The Tech triumphs at making science, math and technology not only accessible, but positively fun.

CEREMONY CAPACITY: The New Venture Hall can accommodate up to 300 seated indoors, and the Rooftop Terrace holds 150 seated outdoors.

EVENT/RECEPTION CAPACITY: The Tech can accommodate 500 seated guests or 2,500 standing.

MEETING CAPACITY: The Large Group Meeting Room holds up to 65 seated guests, and the New Venture Hall, 400 seated guests. The Noyce Center for Learning holds a maximum of 125 seated guests and can be divided into three separate meeting rooms.

FEES & DEPOSITS: 50% of the rental fee is the deposit required to secure your date, along with a $1,000–2,500 security/cleaning deposit. The rental fee ranges $500–12,500 depending on the space(s) used. Exclusive use of the Hackworth IMAX Dome Theater can be arranged at an additional cost. Fees are based on a 4-hour time period. An additional 30% per hour will be charged after the first 4 hours. Meals start at $20/person. Tax, alcohol and service charge are additional.

AVAILABILITY: Year-round, daily, 6pm–midnight. Closed Christmas Day.

SERVICES/AMENITIES:

Catering: provided, or select from list
Kitchen Facilities: prep only
Tables & Chairs: BYO or through caterer
Linens, Silver, etc.: through caterer
Restrooms: wheelchair accessible
Dance Floor: CBA
Meeting Equipment: CBA, extra charge
Other: on-site coordinator

Parking: Convention Center garage, nearby lots
Accommodations: no guest rooms
Telephone: pay phone
Outdoor Night Lighting: no
Outdoor Cooking Facilities: no
Cleanup: through caterer
View: no

RESTRICTIONS:

Alcohol: provided
Smoking: outdoors only
Music: amplified OK

Wheelchair Access: yes
Insurance: certificate required

The Villages Golf and Country Club

Golf & Country Club

5000 Cribari Lane, San Jose
408/223-4687

www.thevillagesgcc.com
theclubhouse@the-villages.com

● Rehearsal Dinners	● Corp. Events/Mtgs.
● Ceremonies	● Private Parties
● Wedding Receptions	○ Accommodations

We've heard the sad tale before: You'd love to have a country club wedding, but there's one tiny little problem—you don't belong to a country club. Lucky for you, membership isn't required at The Villages Golf and Country Club. Perched in the hills above southeastern San Jose, this facility has everything you're looking for: a handsome Spanish Mission-style clubhouse; lovely banquet rooms; well-tended gardens, and a verdant, meticulously groomed golf course. You get all this, plus a variety of wedding packages, at a price that won't make you dip into your honeymoon fund.

In the clubhouse, you'll find three special event rooms that can be used separately or in combination. Though all three have a versatile cream-and-tan color scheme and frosted-glass-and-brass chandeliers, each one has its own distinct design elements: The Oak Room features a gleaming hardwood oak dance floor; the Sunset Room has a large window that takes advantage of the view of the Santa Clara Valley; and the elegant Fairway Room boasts panoramic golf course views. Adjacent to this trio of rooms is a foyer area with a grand piano. The Oak and Fairway Rooms are particularly lovely when used together, but no matter what configuration of these areas you choose, they're all brimming with sophisticated country club ambiance.

So, now that we've introduced you to the Villages Golf and Country Club, you won't have to give up your dream of a country club wedding. And if there's no wedding in your future, but you'd still like to book your event here, go right ahead—the flexible, competent staff can help you with whatever type of gathering you've got in mind. The price is right, the setting is fabulous, and they'll be happy to see you even if you don't have a membership card.

CEREMONY CAPACITY: Limited indoor ceremony space available. Contact facility for more information.

EVENT/RECEPTION & MEETING CAPACITY: The clubhouse holds up to 250 seated or 600 standing guests. This space can be divided into smaller reception areas.

FEES & DEPOSITS: A $2,100 room rental deposit is required to reserve your date. The estimated event total is due 7 working days prior to the event. Meals range $38–68/person. Tax, alcohol and an 18% service charge are additional. One or more security officers are required (depending on guest count) at the rate of $100/officer.

AVAILABILITY: Year-round, Tuesday–Sunday, 6am–11pm.

SERVICES/AMENITIES:

Catering: provided, no BYO

Kitchen Facilities: n/a

Tables & Chairs: provided

Linens, Silver, etc.: provided

Restrooms: wheelchair accessible

Dance Floor: hardwood floor

Meeting Equipment: projection screen

Other: on-site coordinator, PA system

Parking: large lot

Accommodations: no guest rooms

Telephone: pay phone

Outdoor Night Lighting: yes

Outdoor Cooking Facilities: no

Cleanup: provided

View: golf course, Santa Clara Valley, city lights

RESTRICTIONS:

Alcohol: provided, or wine corkage $10/bottle

Smoking: outdoors only

Music: amplified OK indoors only

Wheelchair Access: yes

Insurance: not required

Other: no rice or open flames

Want to know WHAT TO ASK a potential location or vendor? Check out our Questions to Ask starting on page 17.

David's Restaurant & Banquet Facility

Restaurant and Event Facility

5151 Stars & Stripes Drive, Santa Clara
408/986-1666 x21

www.davidsbanquetfacility.com
jean@davids-restaurant.com
jeandavidsrestaurant@gmail.com

- Rehearsal Dinners
- Ceremonies
- Wedding Receptions
- Corp. Events/Mtgs.
- Private Parties
- Accommodations

For many couples, nothing says romance like a golf course, and for them there's David's Restaurant and Banquet Facility, two neighboring venues on the Santa Clara Golf Course that share the same beautiful panorama of velvety green fairways.

With its sharply steepled roof, wood beamed ceiling and huge windows overlooking the greens, the restaurant feels like a cathedral—especially at night by candlelight. During cold weather, the natural stone fireplace makes a beautiful backdrop for an indoor ceremony, but on a sunny day you might prefer to get married outside on the adjacent patio.

Just steps away is David's Banquet Facility, which has five rooms facing the fairways. Clean and modern, with baffled wood ceilings, stylish chandeliers, wood trim, and large picture windows, the rooms can be opened up into one grand space with a fireplace at either end, or partitioned into smaller spaces for a more intimate event. Stage your ceremony on the grassy landscaped area next to the fairway, or in front of one of the granite-faced fireplaces. A long foyer with a high ceiling provides plenty of room for pre-banquet cocktails.

David's can arrange any type of affair, from an informal barbecue to an elegant sit-down dinner, with equal ease. They specialize in Continental cuisine, offering a choice of 44 hors d'oeuvres, from petit beef Wellington suxcllcs to sushi. Feast on entrées as elaborate as chicken Voldostano with proscuitto and gruyère cheese, or as simple and delicious as broiled salmon filet. For vegetarians, there is an array of choices, like stuffed red bell pepper and charbroiled polenta with fresh seasonal squash.

Other options include international custom menus and a variety of buffets, from Mexican or Italian-style to the Grand Buffet with a wide selection of hors d'oeuvres, salads, pastas and entrées. Buffet desserts, such as chocolate-dipped strawberries, double lemon cake and mini éclairs, are an irresistible finale to a great meal.

Its golf course location lends David's an open, breezy, out-in-the-country feeling; yet it's right in the heart of Silicon Valley, within walking distance to major hotels. David's has over 35 years of restaurant and banquet experience and can handle every detail of your event. If you want to make planning your celebration easier, put yourself in their capable hands.

CEREMONY, EVENT/RECEPTION & MEETING CAPACITY: The location holds up to 500 seated or 600 standing guests, indoors or outdoors.

FEES & DEPOSITS: A $1,000 deposit is required to reserve your date. The balance is due 7 days prior to the event. Rental fees range $0–1,000 depending on the space, day and time rented. Meals range $30–45/person. Tax, alcohol and a 19% service charge are additional.

AVAILABILITY: Year-round, daily, 7am–midnight or later.

SERVICES/AMENITIES:

Catering: provided
Kitchen Facilities: n/a
Tables & Chairs: provided
Linens, Silver, etc.: provided
Restrooms: not wheelchair accessible
Dance Floor: provided
Bride's & Groom's Dressing Areas: yes
Meeting Equipment: provided

Parking: large lot
Accommodations: no guest rooms
Telephone: pay and house phones
Outdoor Night Lighting: yes
Outdoor Cooking Facilities: BBQ
Cleanup: provided
View: park, garden, landscaped grounds
Other: event coordination, on-site florals, chair covers

RESTRICTIONS:

Alcohol: provided
Smoking: outside only
Music: amplified OK

Wheelchair Access: yes
Insurance: not required

Freedom Hall and Gardens

Gardens and Event Facility

Address withheld to ensure privacy. Santa Clara
408/379-FREE (3733)
www.freedomhall.com
info@freedomhall.com

Rehearsal Dinners	Corp. Events/Mtgs.
● Ceremonies	Private Parties
● Wedding Receptions	Accommodations

You would never in a million years guess that it was there. It's woodsy and flowery, with splashing fountains—perfect for taking the most idyllic of wedding photos. Yet the recently remodeled Freedom Hall and Gardens is right in the middle of Silicon Valley's high-tech empire in Santa Clara. What could be more convenient?

On weekends, this little oasis is as private and quiet as a desert island. Tucked away amid the silent office buildings, it's practically invisible to anyone passing by. But oh what this place has to offer: a fountain-pond surrounded by carpets of colorful flowers; natural stone formations; towering redwoods and weeping willows; and butterflies flitting across the pond by the rocky waterfall.

Ceremonies here are lovely. Picture your guests seated on the lawn at one end of the pond. You glide across the bridge spanning the water in front of them, and down the grassy aisle to stand in front of the fountain with your husband-to-be. Your music plays (via the professional outdoor sound system) as clouds drift through the blue sky overhead.

After exchanging vows, you and the wedding party walk the few yards to Freedom Hall, whose floor-to-ceiling windows command a panorama of the gardens. While the guests assemble, you wait in the Bride's Room, decorated with glass cases displaying a collection of wedding favors commemorating every wedding at Freedom Hall since the first one in 1995. You make your grand entrance through the bridal arch into the hall.

Dinner is served in the completely transformed Hall, which now features a gleaming hardwood floor, a granite bar, and Tuscan-inspired wrought-iron chandeliers. But the facility's most beautiful "decoration" is its view of the gardens. Guests are free to stroll outside, champagne glasses in hand, and meander along the winding brick paths through the redwoods.

Although the setting is quite appealing, what you don't see is the well-coordinated operation behind the event. Freedom Hall and Gardens hosts 170 weddings a year, and they know their stuff. The venue is Diamond-certified, which means that brides and grooms who were married here have been interviewed by an independent organization to determine the rate of customer satisfaction. Freedom Hall has consistently achieved a near-perfect score. It's not surprising that Freedom Hall and Gardens was voted "Best Wedding Reception Facility" by *The Knot* magazine from 2007 through 2012.

The cuisine features classic American dishes such as a chef's carving station with New York roast steak, chicken Madeira, rice pilaf, pasta marinara, steamed vegetables and fresh-baked breads. There's a selection of passed hors d'oeuvres such as jumbo prawns, stuffed mushrooms and blue cheese pastries. As for dessert, any menu you choose includes complimentary chocolate-dipped strawberries as a sweet surprise before the wedding cake.

If you yearn for a ceremony in the redwoods, but your practical side requires a central location, Freedom Hall and Gardens offers both. You and your guests get the charm of a forest sanctuary, while being within walking distance of the Santa Clara Marriott and Great America. This place has everything you need.

CEREMONY & EVENT/RECEPTION CAPACITY: The site holds up to 250 guests indoors or outdoors, maximum.

MEETING CAPACITY: Meetings do not take place at this location.

FEES & DEPOSITS: A $1,500 deposit is required. The balance is due 10 days prior to the event. There are no separate rental fees. Price per person, including the meal and alcohol starts at $79. There is a 100 person minimum charge. Tax and an 18% service charge are additional.

AVAILABILITY: Year-round, Friday 6:30pm–midnight, Saturday and Sunday 10am–midnight. Weekdays by special arrangment.

SERVICES/AMENITIES:

Catering: provided
Kitchen Facilities: n/a
Tables & Chairs: provided
Linens, Silver, etc.: provided
Restrooms: wheelchair accessible
Dance Floor: provided
Bride's Dressing Area: yes
Meeting Equipment: n/a

Parking: large lot
Accommodations: no guest rooms
Telephone: office phone
Outdoor Night Lighting: yes
Outdoor Cooking Facilities: no
Cleanup: provided
View: garden, pond, fountain, grounds
Other: event coordination, on-site wedding cake, professional DJ

RESTRICTIONS:

Alcohol: provided with package
Smoking: designated areas only
Music: amplified OK

Wheelchair Access: yes
Insurance: not required

Hilton Santa Clara

Hotel

4949 Great America Parkway, Santa Clara
408/562-6703

www.hiltonsantaclara.com
info@hiltonsantaclara.com

- Rehearsal Dinners
- Ceremonies
- Wedding Receptions
- Corp. Events/Mtgs.
- Private Parties
- Accommodations

The Silicon Valley isn't the first place most people think of when planning a wedding or social gathering, and that's a shame. It means they're missing out on one of the nicest hotels in the area—the Hilton Santa Clara. Given its location, it's been a popular place for high-tech industry meetings, but it also has a number of features that make it an excellent choice for a special occasion.

The Hilton Santa Clara's exterior has the sleek, modern good looks you'd expect a large upscale hotel to have, but when you enter the lobby, you'd swear you were in an exclusive boutique hotel. Utilizing Classical, Art Nouveau and modern design elements, the lobby has an enticing air of relaxed, understated luxury. The neutral color scheme is anything but bland, while marble floors, wall panels and blond wood molding add natural luster to the room. Wall sconces, standard lamps and light fixtures, all made of sinuously curving wrought iron and frosted glass, make a stunning visual statement. Wherever you look, there is something to captivate your eye: two life-sized sculptures that could have been done by Rodin or Degas, richly colored and textured upholstery, framed prints and paintings.

All of the function areas in the Hilton Santa Clara reflect the imaginative style and attention to detail displayed in the lobby. There are two large ballrooms available for weddings and events: the 2,800-square-foot Sierra and the 1,500-square-foot Coastal. Each ballroom can be divided into three smaller rooms if desired. Another option for smaller, more casual get-togethers is La Fontana Lounge, just off the lobby. Softly lit by fixtures hanging from the coffered ceiling and enlivened by modern paintings, it's made-to-order for cocktail parties, receptions and "welcome" parties. By special arrangement, and depending on availability, you can rent the Concierge Room, a sort of super-deluxe "den" where guests watch TV, play games or just sit and chat over drinks. It's the perfect place for family and friends to relax after the reception.

In our opinion, the Hilton Santa Clara needs no more to recommend it than what we've already described, but we can't help mentioning just a few more benefits. They have a superb staff that can assist you in everything from menu selections to room rentals for your guests. The bridal package includes a complimentary suite for the bride and groom with chocolate-covered strawberries and a bottle of champagne. And the Hilton Santa Clara's location can't be beat—California Great America theme park is literally steps away, and the VTA lightrail stops right outside the hotel, giving you access to all the attractions of downtown San Jose. Should you wish to venture further afield, major freeways leading to the Monterey Peninsula or San Francisco are within easy reach. With all it has to offer, this Hilton qualifies as one of the South Bay's undiscovered treasures.

CEREMONY CAPACITY: The Coastal Ballroom holds 115, and the Sierra Ballroom 250.

EVENT/RECEPTION CAPACITY: The Coastal Ballroom accommodates 60–100 seated or 200 standing, and the Sierra Ballroom 150–200 seated or 250–300 standing guests.

FEES & DEPOSITS: For weddings, a $2,000 nonrefundable deposit is required when the contract is signed. The event balance and a final guest count are due 1 week prior to the event.

There are a variety of packages from which to choose. Prices range $66–80/person. Tax and a 20% service charge are additional. All packages include hors d'oeuvres, butler-passed champagne and sparking cider during the cocktail hour, champagne toast, 2 bottles of house wine per table, elegant floor-length linens, 2-course dinner and complimentary cake-cutting service. Complimentary wedding-night accommodations are provided for the bride and groom.

AVAILABILITY: Year-round, daily, 6am–midnight, including holidays.

SERVICES/AMENITIES:

Catering: provided
Kitchen Facilities: n/a
Tables & Chairs: provided
Linens, Silver, etc.: provided
Restrooms: wheelchair accessible
Dance Floor: yes
Bride's & Groom's Dressing Areas: guest room
Meeting Equipment: CBA

Parking: complimentary
Accommodations: 280 guest rooms
Telephone: pay and guest phone, internet
Outdoor Night Lighting: access only
Outdoor Cooking Facilities: no
Cleanup: provided
View: Great America amusement park
Other: on-site wedding coordinator

RESTRICTIONS:

Alcohol: provided, or wine corkage $15/bottle
Smoking: outside only
Music: amplified OK, volume limits after 11pm

Wheelchair Access: yes
Insurance: not required
Other: no open flames or fog machines; decorations need approval

Want to find more venues and services? Check out our informative website, www.HereComesTheGuide.com.

321

Hakone Estate and Gardens

Japanese Gardens

21000 Big Basin Way, Saratoga
408/741-4994 X103
www.hakone.us
events@hakone.com

- Rehearsal Dinners
- Ceremonies
- Wedding Receptions
- Corp. Events/Mtgs.
- Private Parties
- Accommodations

We all have our own idea of the perfect getaway, a place to escape to when the world is too much for us. For some, it's a little grass hut on a tropical island; for others it's a villa on the Riviera. For Oliver and Isabel Stine, however, it was a Japanese garden.

Inspired by exhibits they saw at the 1915 Panama-Pacific Exposition, the Stines purchased 16 acres near Saratoga on which to build Hakone Gardens, their summer home. In 1932, the property was bought by a financier, who owned it until 1960 when six families bought it. Then the City of Saratoga purchased the gardens in 1966, and hired a Japanese landscape gardener to restore them to their former splendor. The gardens are now maintained under the watchful eye of the nonprofit Hakone Foundation.

Because Hakone is open to the public seven days a week until 5pm, outdoor events must be held after 5. If you're an early bird, you can also schedule your event in the morning before the facility opens. During these times you have the entire gardens to yourself. Larger weddings often take place in the gravel area near the Koi Pond (the garden area) while truly intimate ceremonies of 15 or fewer are held in the Wisteria Pavilion, a charming wooden structure perched on the banks of the pond and entwined with wisteria. Afterwards, guests can walk the short distance to the Madrone Mound, a gravel-topped rise shaded by an arching oak tree and bamboos, which is equally fine for a seated or standing reception.

Those wishing to tie the knot during more conventional hours are welcome to do so—indoors. Hakone features two meticulously detailed and authentic Japanese structures that are available for four-hour or all-day rentals. The Lower House has redwood walls in the reception area, a tea ceremony room (not available to the public, unless you're going to have a tea ceremony there) and a shoe-removal rock near the entrance. The Cultural Exchange Center is a replica of a 19th-century Kyoto tea merchant's shop and living quarters. Built in 1991, the building was assembled in Japan using traditional methods and materials, then set up on its present site by Japanese carpenters. Display cases containing various Japanese artifacts line the walls of the reception area, and elsewhere in the building there is a traditional tatamied tea ceremony room. The Cultural Exchange Deck, overlooking the Santa Clara Valley, is perfect for a breathtaking ceremony, formal seated dinner or a more relaxed cocktail reception.

Weddings are popular at Hakone Gardens, and on moonlit summer nights they're nothing short of enchanting. Business functions also benefit from the quiet and peaceful atmosphere. In fact, the way we see it, any type of event—whether indoors or out—will be enhanced by these beautiful surroundings.

CEREMONY CAPACITY: The Garden Area or the Madrone Mound holds 150 seated or standing guests; the Cultural Exchange Center (CEC) holds 80 seated theater-style; the Lower House 60 seated theater-style.

RECEPTION CAPACITY: The Cultural Exchange Center accommodates 60 seated or standing indoors, with an additional 40 guests seated on the adjacent deck. The Madrone Mound holds 150 seated or standing outdoors. The Lower House holds 40 seated guests.

MEETING CAPACITY: The Cultural Exchange Center accommodates 80 seated theater-style or 35–40 seated conference-style. The Lower House holds 60 guests seated theater-style or 20 seated conference-style.

FEES & DEPOSITS: To secure your date, a $600 refundable deposit plus half the rental fee is required; the balance is due 90 days prior to the event. For weddings and special events taking place between May and October, use fees range $1,050–6,600 depending on space(s) rented. Overtime is $400–600/hour, not to go past 10pm. Off-season rates available.

For business meetings, use fees range $120–200/hour depending on space(s) rented.

AVAILABILITY: For weddings and receptions, the Garden Area and Madrone Mound are available 8am–11am or 5pm–9pm (or 10pm with overtime fee); the Lower House and Cultural Exchange Center 9am–9pm (or 10pm with overtime fee). For business functions, year-round, daily, 8am–5pm, except Christmas Day and New Year's Day.

SERVICES/AMENITIES:

Catering: preferred list
Kitchen Facilities: prep only
Tables & Chairs: provided
Linens, Silver, etc.: through caterer
Restrooms: limited wheelchair accessibility
Dance Floor: yes
Bride's Dressing Area: yes
Meeting Equipment: DVD player, LCD projector/screen, white boards, easels, wireless internet

Parking: large lot, free parking for guests
Accommodations: no guest rooms
Telephone: emergency use only for meetings
Outdoor Night Lighting: yes
Outdoor Cooking Facilities: no
Cleanup: renter or caterer
View: Santa Clara Valley, Japanese gardens, cascading waterfalls and koi pond
Other: gift shop, picnic tables, access to gardens, trails and paths, tea ceremony & guided tours

RESTRICTIONS:

Alcohol: wine, beer and champagne only, through caterer or BYO
Smoking: parking lot only
Music: amplified OK indoors with volume limits

Wheelchair Access: limited
Insurance: not required
Other: no rice, decorations restricted

The Mountain Winery

14831 Pierce Road, Saratoga
408/913-7125

www.mountainwinery.com
weddings@mountainwinery.com

Historic Winery and Event Venue

● Rehearsal Dinners	● Corp. Events/Mtgs.
● Ceremonies	● Private Parties
● Wedding Receptions	Accommodations

Set high up in the Saratoga foothills, this historic winery has wonderful sweeping views of the entire Silicon Valley. Amazingly, it only takes 15 minutes to drive here from the valley, and once you arrive, you'll be delighted with everything you see on the mountaintop.

The two main buildings on the property, the Historic Winery Building and the Chateau, were constructed in 1905 by French winemaker Paul Masson. Both are fashioned of stone masonry, and represent fine examples of French country architecture. Masson lived in the Chateau, where he often entertained guests like John Steinbeck, Charlie Chaplin and Ansel Adams, who took many of the black & white photos on display. Host your own event here, and you'll understand why this place has always attracted such prestigious visitors.

If you're planning a large indoor event, like a fundraising gala, wedding reception or casino night, reserve the ivy-covered Winery Building. Its stone walls and fragrant oak casks give the space a delicious, Old World ambiance. Outdoor ceremonies, champagne receptions and wine tastings are held in the Vista Point area, a tranquil slate patio bordered by trees and lush landscaping.

Expecting a crowd? The perfect spot is the Chateau Deck, an expansive terrace at the edge of the crest. Flanked by oak trees, it provides a view of the valley that will take your breath away. If you need a theater setting for your event, the Amphitheater is seasonally available. It has a stage with a striking backdrop: the stone portal of a San Jose cathedral that crumbled in the 1906 quake.

This venue is so versatile you're bound to find an area that fits your needs. In addition, corporations looking for team building programs will appreciate the innovative packages available, including gourmet cooking, historical tours and wine classes.

The Mountain Winery has expanded its scope since its early days as a family winery, but still offers the same beauty and serenity that enchanted Paul Masson when he first came here over a century ago.

CEREMONY & EVENT/RECEPTION CAPACITY: The winery can accommodate 20–200 seated or 25–300 standing indoors, and 20–2,500 seated or 20–5,000+ standing outdoors.

MEETING CAPACITY: There are 3 different indoor meeting rooms that can accommodate 10–250 seated, and multiple outdoor areas that can hold upwards of 2,500 people.

FEES & DEPOSITS: The rental fee, contract and estimated guest count are required when the facility is reserved. The final balance is due 1 week prior to the event. Site fees range $3,000–12,000 depending on guest count. Meals start at $50/person, plus tax and a 20% service charge.

The rental fee includes use of the site, setup, cleanup and staff.

AVAILABILITY: Year-round, daily, 8am–midnight.

SERVICES/AMENITIES:

Catering: provided

Kitchen Facilities: n/a

Tables & Chairs: provided

Linens, Silver, etc.: provided

Restrooms: wheelchair accessible

Dance Floor: provided

Bride's Dressing Area: yes

Meeting Equipment: flipcharts, screen, projector

Parking: large lot

Accommodations: no guest rooms

Telephone: house phone

Outdoor Night Lighting: yes

Outdoor Cooking Facilities: limited

Cleanup: provided

View: panorama of the valley floor and coastal hills

RESTRICTIONS:

Alcohol: provided

Smoking: outside only

Music: amplified OK with volume limits

Wheelchair Access: yes

Insurance: liability required

Saratoga Country Club

Country Club

21990 Prospect Road, Saratoga
408/253-0340

www.saratogacc.com
lthibeault@saratogacc.com

● Rehearsal Dinners	● Corp. Events/Mtgs.
● Ceremonies	● Private Parties
● Wedding Receptions	Accommodations

Perched high in the wooded hills above the Santa Clara Valley, the Saratoga Country Club offers everything you need for a superb wedding or festive gathering: beautiful surroundings, a romantic ceremony spot, a casually elegant clubhouse and fabulous food. And best of all, you don't have to be a member to host your event here.

The ceremony site, on top of a gentle hill, is one reason couples gravitate to the club. Drenched in sunlight and surrounded by panoramic hillside views, it's as pretty as a wedding bouquet. The centerpiece is a majestic, one-of-a-kind, 15-foot-high white wrought-iron domed gazebo, set on cobblestones. Encircled by a large lawn and enclosed by a decorative fence, it's a private haven for family and friends to witness your exchange of vows. After the ceremony, it's just a short walk to the clubhouse reception by way of a spectacular lighted staircase with white railings, flanked by pines and oleanders.

The contemporary clubhouse is a well-appointed two-story structure painted in soft beige that harmonizes with the encompassing hillsides. An imposing portico and pergola-shaded walkway add drama to the building's entrance, where the exquisitely crafted cherrywood and cut-glass double doors are reminiscent of the work of Frank Lloyd Wright. In the Main Dining Room, the cream-colored walls are awash in sunlight, thanks to plenty of large windows interspersed with stately columns. French doors lead to spacious decks overlooking the verdant golf course below and the Santa Clara Valley in the distance. There's also a dance floor and stage area, and the soft, neutral beige-and-white color scheme of the dining room allows you to dress it up or down to your taste. Needless to say, this facility is not limited to wedding receptions; in fact, when we viewed it, it was set up for a graduation party with bright colored napkins, star-garlanded centerpieces and displays of yearbook photos and other school-related decorations. The dining room is also available on a limited basis during the week for business functions.

Are all these great features beginning to intrigue you? Well, let us sweeten the pot just a little bit more. When you book your event at the Saratoga Country Club, you also get the services of events manager extraordinaire, Linda Thibeault. Her assistance is invaluable, especially for weddings. Every year, she updates a minutely detailed wedding guide outlining everything you need to know to plan your wedding, from a reception schedule to a list of preferred vendors. She's a calming influence for brides and a welcome resource for advice. Linda even provides a detailed map to send out with your invitations, in case some of your guests are directionally impaired (the country club's secluded location is just minutes from highways I-280, SR-85 and I-880). So, schedule a trip to the Saratoga Country Club. Even if you're not a member, you'll be given VIP treatment!

CEREMONY CAPACITY: The Lawn Area holds up to 250 seated guests.

EVENT/RECEPTION & MEETING CAPACITY: The Dining Room accommodates 250 seated guests. Conference rooms are available for smaller groups.

FEES & DEPOSITS: A nonrefundable deposit, based on a percentage of the room rental fee and/or catering costs, is required when the contract is signed. The balance may be paid in installments, depending on the amount of time remaining between the signing of the contract and the date of the event, with the final payment due 10 days prior to the event. Any additional balance accrued is due at the end of the event. Room rental fees range $360–2,600 depending on the space(s) rented. (Be sure to ask about any special offers!) Banquet and buffet meals are available and start at $58/person. Tax, alcohol and a 20% service charge are extra.

AVAILABILITY: Year-round, daily, 7am–1am.

SERVICES/AMENITIES:

Catering: provided, no BYO
Kitchen Facilities: n/a
Tables & Chairs: provided
Linens, Silver, etc.: provided
Restrooms: wheelchair accessible
Dance Floor: yes
Bride's Dressing Area: yes
Meeting Equipment: CBA, extra fee

Parking: ample on site
Accommodations: no guest rooms
Telephone: house phone
Outdoor Night Lighting: no
Outdoor Cooking Facilities: no
Cleanup: provided
View: golf course and Santa Clara Valley
Other: event coordination

RESTRICTIONS:

Alcohol: provided, no BYO
Smoking: outdoors only
Music: amplified OK with restrictions

Wheelchair Access: yes
Insurance: not required
Other: no rice or birdseed

This is important! Tell locations you're reading HERE COMES THE GUIDE and ask if our information is still current.

327

Saratoga Foothill Club

20399 Park Place, Saratoga
408/867-3428
www.saratogafoothillclub.com
lbeesley@msn.com

Historic Women's Club

- Rehearsal Dinners
- Ceremonies
- Wedding Receptions
- Corp. Events/Mtgs.
- Private Parties
- Accommodations

On a quiet residential street near the crossroads of Big Basin and Sunnyvale/Saratoga Roads lies the Saratoga Foothill Club, a 1915 Arts and Crafts-style landmark. Designed by Julia Morgan as a women's club, it houses the oldest social organization in Saratoga. With a brown-shingled façade, sloping roof and decorative windows, it's one of the most distinguished small redwood structures in California: In 1978, the club received the distinction of being listed in the National Register of Historic Landmarks.

Equally noteworthy is the club's adjoining paved courtyard, dubbed the neighborhood's "Secret Garden." The cozy enclave is dotted with Japanese maples, whose summer-to-autumn crimson foliage provides a burnished backdrop for wedding ceremonies. On one side, a long wooden arbor is adorned with mature wisteria vines whose graceful lavender blooms debut in early spring. Beneath the arbor, a bench formed by twisted branches is an eye-catching place to gather the bridal party for photographs. Lush Japanese privets hedge the courtyard, lending privacy and a peaceful vision of greenery to the scene.

The club's interior further enhances the venue's appeal. A formal redwood foyer ushers guests into a hall that's ideal for a buffet reception or sit-down dining. The hardwood floor, half-timbered walls and 30-foot-high vaulted ceiling convey a quaint, chapel-like charm. (In fact, this room is sometimes used for ceremonies during the cooler months.) A bank of striking multipaned windows frames a view of the leafy courtyard, while just above, sunlight streams down from an elaborate circular window, setting the entire space aglow. The wedding cake looks picture-perfect in front of the windows, which highlight the newlyweds during the cake cutting. The room also has a raised platform stage that can hold musicians, a DJ, or even a decorated head table. Glass-transomed wooden doors open to an anteroom with a brick fireplace, a convenient spot to put a buffet table. Here and there authentic period fixtures—like rich wood paneling or eye-catching lamps—add vintage flair.

With its beautiful architectural details and overall feeling of comfort and warmth, the Saratoga Foothill Club offers a unique and intimate environment for celebrations.

CEREMONY CAPACITY: The outdoor patio holds 150 seated, and the club's interior holds 200 seated.

EVENT/RECEPTION CAPACITY: The site accommodates 150 seated banquet-style or 200 seated theater-style indoors, and 150 seated or 300 standing guests outdoors.

MEETING CAPACITY: The Main Room holds 200 seated theater-style.

FEES & DEPOSITS: A $500 refundable security deposit is required when reservations are made. The rental fee ranges $600–2,100. There is only one event per day. Wedding packages (based on 100 guests) start at $4,995 and include buffet, service, china, linens, cake, DJ and beverage package.

AVAILABILITY: Year-round, daily, 9:30am–10pm.

SERVICES/AMENITIES:

Catering: provided by *Panetta's Catering*
Kitchen Facilities: moderate
Tables & Chairs: provided
Linens, Silver, etc.: through caterer
Restrooms: wheelchair accessible
Dance Floor: yes
Bride's Dressing Area: yes
Meeting Equipment: BYO

Parking: call for details
Accommodations: no guest rooms
Telephone: house phone
Outdoor Night Lighting: yes
Outdoor Cooking Facilities: no
Cleanup: caterer or renter
View: of coastal hills and courtyard
Other: new air conditioning, baby grand piano available

RESTRICTIONS:

Alcohol: BYO wine, champagne and beer in bottles or cans; no kegs
Smoking: on patio only
Music: amplified OK with volume limits

Wheelchair Access: yes
Insurance: certificate required

Saratoga Springs

Resort

22801 Big Basin Way, Saratoga
408/867-3016 x51

saratoga-springs.com/CA/weddings-events
jennifer@saratoga-springs.com

- Rehearsal Dinners
- Ceremonies
- Wedding Receptions
- Corp. Events/Mtgs.
- Private Parties
- Accommodations

Imagine celebrating the best day of your life in a veritable forest, with the ambient sounds of birds in the trees and leaves rustling in a cool afternoon breeze. Then, as night falls, a thousand stars twinkle overhead as you glide around a dance floor set into a rocky hillside. For many brides, a natural environment like this is far more stirring than any ballroom adorned with crystal chandeliers. And best of all, it can be found just minutes from San Jose.

The drive to Saratoga Springs takes you right through the upscale, horse-loving community of Saratoga, a tourist favorite. Just three blocks long, the village is known for one-of-a-kind boutiques, wide pedestrian sidewalks and three country inns, which come in handy for any friends and relatives who may want to make a weekend of it.

Leaving town, the road winds around and crosses a spring-fed stream as it heads towards the tree-studded foothills and Saratoga Springs itself, the oldest privately owned picnic grounds in the area. Once a booming logging center, these bucolic woodlands later became a stopping point for travelers making the arduous journey by wagon to the beach. Nowadays, the fifth generation of the Giannini family has updated the site's amenities, yet kept the woodsy ambiance for hosting affordable weddings and special events. Although there are several unique locales on the 125-acre preserve, two in particular offer the kind of awe-inspiring vistas that led Sierra Club founder John Muir to call the great outdoors "God's big show."

Cathedral Grove, named for the spectacular way the majestic redwoods and towering box elders lean towards each other—their branches form an arch like the ceiling of a Gothic church—is both private and very quiet. This lush hideaway provides lots of shade with a hint of dappled light filtering through the leafy canopy above. Soothing sounds of water are all around, coming from a brook in the gorge and two nearby creeks. In fact, you'll cross one of them as you make your entrance over a bridge to exchange vows with your groom in front of a dramatic rock cliff.

The grove, which can accommodate 200 guests, has ample room for dancing, a DJ setup, and ceremony or reception seating at either long, family-style tables or more formal, round ones, where your guests will enjoy the venue's signature barbecue buffet. Although many couples like the rustic setting just as it is, you can easily glam it up if you want. The on-site wedding planner can arrange to hang Japanese lanterns or flickering candles and have the trees and bridge spangled with pinpoint lights.

Speaking of bridges, one of the area's most recognizable landmarks, Longbridge, frames another choice wedding venue. This graceful stone span, built in 1904 on one of the highest elevations on the property, creates a stunning visual backdrop for either your ceremony or reception. From this site, the panoramic views are fantastic. Plus, the hillside dancing area to the right is surrounded by nature in all its glory.

Saratoga Springs is blessed with lots of wonderful photo spots, but the place where you can best capture the spirit of your day may be the romantic islet in Redwood Grove where two creeks, rather fittingly, join together as one.

CEREMONY CAPACITY: The facility holds 650 seated guests outdoors.

EVENT/RECEPTION & MEETING CAPACITY: The site accommodates 1,000 guests outdoors, seated or standing.

FEES & DEPOSITS: 50% of the total event cost is required to reserve your date and the balance is due 1 week prior to the event. Rental fees range $0–3,000 depending on the day and time of the event, the space rented, and whether minimum catering requirements are met. Meals range $40–45/person. Tax and service charges are additional.

AVAILABILITY: Year-round, daily, 8am–11pm.

SERVICES/AMENITIES:

Catering: provided
Kitchen Facilities: n/a
Tables & Chairs: some provided
Linens, Silver, etc.: CBA
Restrooms: wheelchair accessible
Dance Floor: CBA
Bride's Dressing Area: CBA
Meeting Equipment: BYO
Other: picnic area, event coordination

Parking: large lot
Accommodations: no guest rooms
Telephone: emergency use only
Outdoor Night Lighting: provided
Outdoor Cooking Facilities: BBQ on site
Cleanup: provided
View: creek, forest, hills, landscaped grounds meadow, and park

RESTRICTIONS:

Alcohol: provided, or BYO with corkage fee
Smoking: outdoors only
Music: amplified OK with restrictions

Wheelchair Access: yes
Insurance: not required

Villa Montalvo at Montalvo Arts Center

Historic Mansion & Grounds

15400 Montalvo Road, Saratoga
408/961-5856
www.montalvoarts.org/rentals
kkirkpatrick@montalvoarts.org

- Rehearsal Dinners
- Ceremonies
- Wedding Receptions
- Corp. Events/Mtgs.
- Private Parties
- Accommodations

Nestled against a wooded slope in the private and secluded Saratoga hills is Montalvo Arts Center, a lovely complex with a variety of venues for concerts, weddings, corporate events and private parties. For weddings, the focal point of this estate is its beautiful Mediterranean-style mansion, Villa Montalvo. Built in 1912 as the private summer residence of Senator James Duval Phelan, this National Register Historic Landmark is now home to an arboretum and a nonprofit center for the arts.

An inviting one-way road leads up to Villa Montalvo. As you round the last turn, you get your first glimpse of the estate's expansive manicured lawns and colorful gardens, as well as the mansion's terracotta-tile roof, light stucco walls and wide veranda. To your left, you'll also see the Love Temple, one of two ceremony sites on the grounds; it's an open-air, white-columned pavilion set at the end of a wide, rose-lined brick path featuring historic marble statues. Couples get married on its steps, with a view of the surrounding Mediterranean garden and the Villa and woods in the background.

Directly behind the Villa, the Oval Garden offers a lush garden setting complete with classical statues and wisteria-covered pergolas. This open-air courtyard is an intimate and delightful place for a ceremony; a brick pathway serves as the center aisle, and a column-supported arcade is the backdrop for taking vows.

The Villa's first floor and outdoor verandas are available for receptions. Guests can sip champagne and sample hors d'oeuvres in the Spanish courtyard, and dine on the veranda while enjoying splendid views of the estate's lawns and gardens. Reserve well in advance. The Montalvo Arts Center is an extraordinary site for an elegant and sophisticated wedding.

CEREMONY CAPACITY: The Oval Garden accommodates 250 seated. The Side Veranda seats 130 in case of inclement weather. The Love Temple capacity is 160.

EVENT/RECEPTION CAPACITY: The Villa's indoor capacity is 190 seated or 200 standing; outdoors, it's 300 seated or 1,000 standing. The Love Temple accommodates 160 seated. Events with over 300 guests may incur an additional cost, and require special arrangements with the Events Manager.

MEETING CAPACITY: Meeting venues accommodate groups of 4–300 people; the Villa's main floor holds up to 100. The Carriage House Theatre can accommodate up to 300 people seated theater-style. The outdoor Garden Theatre accommodates 1,200 guests. The upper Villa has 3 large rooms for staff meetings or dressing rooms. The Cottage accommodates up to 14 guests.

FEES & DEPOSITS: For weddings, the rental fee for 9 hours' use ranges $9,000–15,000. Half the total fee is required as a nonrefundable deposit when the site is booked; the balance is payable 6 months prior to the event along with a refundable $1,000 damage deposit and a certificate of insurance. For a Love Temple or Oval Garden ceremony only, the rental fee is $4,500. Call for details and for weekday and winter rates. Special rates may apply for last-minute events.

For other special events and business functions, the Villa can accommodate groups of 4–3,000. For fees and details, call the Event Manager at 408/961-5856.

AVAILABILITY: Ceremonies are held year-round, and take place 10am–1pm. Ceremony/receptions are held year-round, 2pm–11pm in 9-hour blocks. All-day rentals also available. For other special and business functions, contact the Events Manager.

SERVICES/AMENITIES:

Catering: select from preferred list
Kitchen Facilities: ample
Tables & Chairs: provided
Linens, Silver, etc.: caterer
Restrooms: wheelchair accessible
Dance Floor: yes
Bride's & Groom's Dressing Areas: yes
Meeting Equipment: full range CBA, extra fee

Parking: valet may be required for over 200 guests, carpooling encouraged
Accommodations: no guest rooms, hotel partners
Telephone: house phone
Outdoor Night Lighting: yes
Outdoor Cooking Facilities: BYO
Cleanup: caterer
View: manicured lawns, formal gardens, historic sculptures and Santa Clara Valley vista

RESTRICTIONS:

Alcohol: through caterer
Smoking: outdoors only, designated area
Music: amplified OK with restrictions until 10pm

Wheelchair Access: yes
Insurance: certificate required

Overwhelmed? Use the search criteria on www.HereComesTheGuide.com to narrow down your choices.

333

The Historic Del Monte Building

Banquet & Event Facility

100 South Murphy Avenue, Sunnyvale
408/735-7680
www.thehistoricdelmonte.com
maria@delvillas.com

Rehearsal Dinners	● Corp. Events/Mtgs.
● Ceremonies	● Private Parties
● Wedding Receptions	Accommodations

Built in 1904 and originally used for drying and packing the Valley's apricots, peaches and prunes, the three-story Del Monte Building had been long neglected when a local developer decided to save and restore it. The process wasn't easy. First they had to hire three trucks to carefully move the wooden structure from its location beside railroad tracks to a breezy corner across the street. Then they spent a year rebuilding it from the outside in. Their hard work has paid off, and the beautifully refurbished Historic Del Monte Building is now a terrific place for wedding receptions or corporate meetings—right in the heart of Sunnyvale's vibrant downtown.

The main entrance is on a lovely treelined street. Take the wide carpeted staircase (or the elevator at the rear entrance) to the second and third floors where the fully equipped banquet facilities are located. When you step into the Grand Ballroom, everything you see is totally inviting, from the golden Wilshire chandeliers set against a stark white ceiling to the warm mahogany wainscoting. A gleaming hardwood dance floor dominates the room's center. During the day, light filters into the room through white-framed windows and French doors. Set back into another wall is a handcrafted bar fashioned out of mahogany and beveled glass mirrors.

The third floor houses the Del Monte Room, a smaller space with a cathedral ceiling supported by five white fluted columns. At night, a dozen gold-plaited faux candle chandeliers glow overhead, while during the day natural light flows in through windows along two sides. Like the Ballroom, the Del Monte Room has a built-in bar, and it also has a spacious outdoor terrace.

When you gaze up at the Del Monte Building, fronted by tall sycamore trees and illuminated by old-fashioned lamp posts, it's hard to believe that it was the first commercial structure erected in the city, that it led such a rugged prior existence and that it almost disappeared. By breathing new life into it, the developer not only preserved a little bit of Sunnyvale's past, but created a delightful place to celebrate.

CEREMONY CAPACITY: The building can accommodate up to 225 seated guests.

EVENT/RECEPTION CAPACITY: The Del Monte Room holds 170 seated with dancing or 350 standing; the Grand Ballroom, 280 seated with dancing or 500 standing guests.

MEETING CAPACITY: The Grand Ballroom holds 500 seated theater-style or 180 seated classroom-style. The Del Monte Room holds 275 theater-style or 100 seated classroom-style.

FEES & DEPOSITS: For wedding receptions, a $2,000 deposit is required when the site is booked; a second deposit is due 2 months prior to the event, with the remaining balances due 1 week prior to the event. Wedding packages start at $66/person, and can include meals, wedding cake, flowers and DJ. Beverage packages and tax are additional. December pricing may vary; call for specific information. Call for specific details.

AVAILABILITY: Year-round, Monday–Thursday, 7am–11pm; Friday and Saturday, 7am–midnight or Sundays until 9pm. Ceremonies take place Friday evenings, 6:30pm–7:30pm or Sundays, noon–4pm.

SERVICES/AMENITIES:

Catering: provided

Kitchen Facilities: n/a

Tables & Chairs: provided

Linens, Silver, etc.: provided

Restrooms: wheelchair accessible

Dance Floor: provided

Bride's Dressing Area: no

Meeting Equipment: full range

Parking: lots, on street and valet

Accommodations: no guest rooms

Telephone: pay phone

Outdoor Night Lighting: deck only

Outdoor Cooking Facilities: no

Cleanup: provided

View: downtown Sunnyvale

Other: full event coordination

RESTRICTIONS:

Alcohol: provided, no BYO

Smoking: deck only

Music: amplified OK indoors

Wheelchair Access: yes

Insurance: not required

Orchard Pavilion
at the Sunnyvale Community Center

550 East Remington Drive, Sunnyvale
408/730-7751
weddings.insunnyvale.com
rcotter@ci.sunnyvale.ca.us

Banquet & Community Facility

- Rehearsal Dinners
- Ceremonies
- Wedding Receptions
- Corp. Events/Mtgs.
- Private Parties
- Accommodations

Gazing out the towering windows at the lush, rolling grounds, the lake with dancing fountains, and the sun-drenched patio area, you'd swear you'd landed at an exclusive country club. You'd be absolutely wrong. This lovely locale—the Orchard Pavilion at the Sunnyvale Community Center—is one of the most reasonably priced, yet visually appealing, venues in the South Bay.

The Pavilion is actually located in the complex's new Senior Center, which opened its doors in July of 2003. But banish any visions of cramped, gloomy rooms full of endless bingo games. Instead, prepare to experience 32-foot ceilings, bleached parquet floors, and graceful curving architecture that affords sweeping views of the 11-acre gardens and grounds.

Accented by several extraordinary glass and bronze sculptures, the center's design has already received several awards. Wander past the reception area and down a vast, whitewashed hallway that's open to the second story, and you'll find almost limitless options for events both large and small.

The centerpiece of the facility is undisputedly the Orchard Pavilion. An airy room of nearly 5,000 square feet, it can be used in its entirety or divided into three smaller spaces. Skylit cupolas top each section, allowing a natural brightness to wash over the light-colored floors and walls. All three sections also feature south-facing, floor-to-ceiling windows and doors that open to the 4,000-square-foot patio and uninterrupted views of the lake and fountains just beyond.

Specifically designed with events in mind, the Pavilion comes with a separate service entrance that provides easy access to the industrial-sized kitchen, as well as unobtrusive deliveries to the banquet rooms. Behind a full-length curtain on one wall is a raised stage area that's perfect for either the band or the wedding party.

Couples who prefer to say their vows in the open air often choose the patio for the ceremony. Afterwards, everyone drifts inside for the reception and dancing, or the entire event can be staged al fresco. Low-slung granite seats along the patio's border invite guests to relax and enjoy the meticulously groomed gardens, which are adorned with flowers year-round.

If you have a more intimate event in mind, the Center's Oak Lounge is ideally suited with its dark-oak floors, comfy leather couches and chairs, and scattering of tables that encourage conversation. You might also use this space for a pre-ceremony cocktail party or the receiving line.

The Community Center houses still more alternatives for the cost-conscious. A ballroom in an adjoining building has a dark wood parquet floor and ample space for dining and dancing. With its floor-to-ceiling windows and a pass-through bar revealing a patio bedecked with clay tubs full of flowers, the room encourages guests to stroll outside and take in the views. Here, a small pond with cubist-style concrete fountains makes the perfect backdrop for a sunlit ceremony.

There's no shortage of smaller rooms that may be used as the bridal party's changing spaces, for gift display, or anything else your wedding requires. One visit and you'll agree: This stunning facility is much more "Ritz" than Rec Center.

CEREMONY, EVENT/RECEPTION & MEETING CAPACITY: The facility holds up to 300 guests, seated or standing.

FEES & DEPOSITS: A deposit ranging $500–1,000 is required to reserve your date. The balance is due 30 days before event. Rental fees range $60–300/hour depending on space rented.

AVAILABILITY: Year-round. Events must conclude no later than midnight (including cleanup time).

SERVICES/AMENITIES:

Catering: BYO, licensed and insured
Kitchen Facilities: fully equipped
Tables & Chairs: provided
Linens, Silver, etc.: through caterer
Restrooms: wheelchair accessible
Dance Floor: yes
Bride's Dressing Area: CBA
Meeting Equipment: provided, may be extra charge

Parking: public lot
Accommodations: no guest rooms
Telephone: pay phone
Outdoor Night Lighting: yes
Outdoor Cooking Facilities: BYO
Cleanup: caterer or renter
View: pond, fountain, landscaped grounds
Other: sound system

RESTRICTIONS:

Alcohol: BYO with licensed server
Smoking: designated areas
Music: amplified OK indoors

Wheelchair Access: yes
Insurance: liability required

Tarragon

140 South Murphy Avenue, Sunnyvale
408/737-8003

www.dinetarragon.com
info@dinetarragon.com

Restaurant & Banquet Facility

●	Rehearsal Dinners	●	Corp. Events/Mtgs.
●	Ceremonies	●	Private Parties
●	Wedding Receptions		Accommodations

Two years into a long engagement, Dottia Bilic pushed her fiancé for an answer: When were they going to get married? Tony, who was in the midst of building a restaurant from the ground up, asked her to wait until it was finished so they could have their wedding there, making it special. Well, she did wait, they did get married and "Tarragon" is indeed special.

This popular restaurant is located in downtown Sunnyvale on lively, historic Murphy Street. Even among the plethora of eating establishments here, Tarragon is a standout. Its earthy, soft peach façade and sun-dappled sidewalk dining area contribute to a welcoming entrance that beckons you inside.

Indoors, the chic décor creates a warm and inviting ambiance. To your right is a gorgeous inlaid wood bar, while to the left are curved leather booths trimmed with dark, rich wood set against a brick wall. Modern copper wall sconces and art-glass lamps cast a soft glow throughout the entire L-shaped room. But it's towards the back where the magic happens—an open kitchen bustling with energy prepares a mouth-watering array of California-American dishes with gourmet flair. This is not frou-frou cuisine, but rather the kind of meal, beautifully presented, that you can heartily enjoy while savoring every bite. And for brides who think that the food is as important as the setting, Tarragon is an excellent choice.

You can host your cocktail and/or dinner reception in the restaurant itself (depending on day and time), or opt for the second-story Banquet Room. This private event space, which runs the full length of the building, has windows at one end and a wall of retractable glass doors at the other that open to a delightful terrace. Slate floors, a wraparound stone wall capped with flowering plants, and treetop views of Murphy Street make this sweet al fresco spot a charming ceremony site. It's also perfect for hosting your cocktail hour.

Back inside, the Banquet Room is ideal for larger groups or can be sectioned off for more intimate parties. The part closest to the terrace has a high, angled ceiling, polished wood dance floor and framed French posters. In the center of the room is a stylish wooden bar, and on the opposite wall there's a flat screen TV for playing home movies of the happy couple. A coffered ceiling, chandeliers of copper and glass, and textured walls in a peachy Tuscan tone complete the look of this expansive space. Of course, you can add any accoutrements you like, and Dottia and her staff will happily bring in a design and lighting team to help you realize your own unique backdrop. In fact, they pride themselves on going that extra mile with personalized service that includes customizing the menu to incorporate your favorite dishes—and even creating ethnic specialties if you desire.

The owners of Tarragon firmly believe that celebrating your marriage with great food in a romantic place is a recipe for success. It certainly worked for them!

CEREMONY CAPACITY: The patio holds 25 seated guests outdoors and the Banquet Room holds 200 seated indoors. A wall of sliding doors between them can be opened so that the indoor and outdoor spaces can be used in combination.

EVENT/RECEPTION CAPACITY: The Banquet Room can accommodate 200 seated or 300 standing indoors.

MEETING CAPACITY: The site holds 175 guests seated classroom-style or theater-style.

FEES & DEPOSITS: A $500 deposit is required to reserve your date and the balance is due 2 weeks prior to the event. Rental fees range $500–1,000 depending on the day of the event. Meals range $35–65/person. Tax, alcohol and a 20% service charge are additional.

AVAILABILITY: Year-round, daily.

SERVICES/AMENITIES:

Catering: provided
Kitchen Facilities: n/a
Tables & Chairs: provided
Linens, Silver, etc.: provided
Restrooms: not wheelchair accessible
Dance Floor: provided
Bride's Dressing Area: no
Meeting Equipment: provided, A/V equipment

Parking: large lot, limited, garage nearby
Accommodations: no guest rooms
Telephone: office phone
Outdoor Night Lighting: provided
Outdoor Cooking Facilities: no
Cleanup: provided
View: no
Other: event coordination

RESTRICTIONS:

Alcohol: provided
Smoking: outside only
Music: amplified OK indoors

Wheelchair Access: yes, restaurant level only
Insurance: not required

The professionals in the back of this book are the best in the business. How do we know? Read page 637.

339

Tri-Valley and Livermore Wine Country

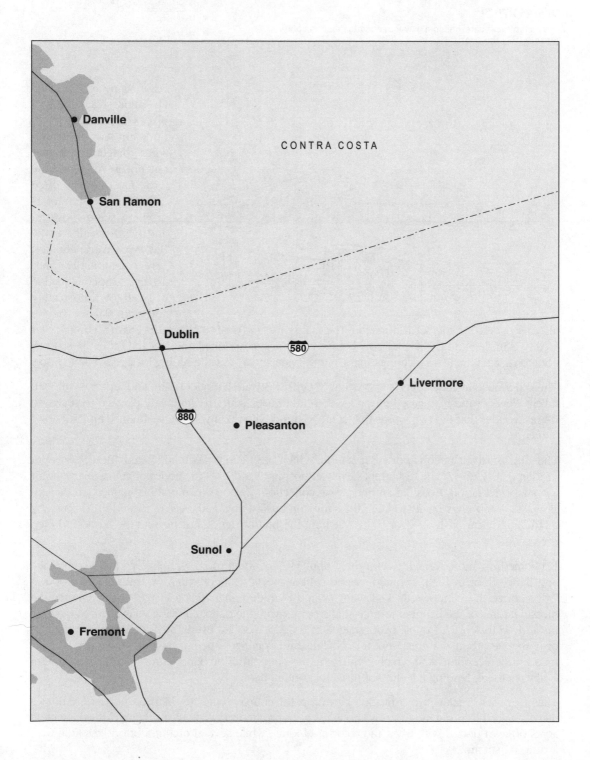

The Clubhouse at Las Positas

Golf Course and Clubhouse

915 Clubhouse Drive, Livermore
925/455-7070
www.clubhousecatering.com, www.beebsatlaspositas.com
jensolaro@yahoo.com

- Rehearsal Dinners
- Ceremonies
- Wedding Receptions
- Corp. Events/Mtgs.
- Private Parties
- Accommodations

Used to be a town like Livermore was simply a place you passed through on your way to somewhere bigger and better; but not anymore. These days, Livermore is often called "Little Napa" for its growing wine industry, and folks from all over the Bay Area routinely stop here to sample the wines and enjoy the combination of small-town hospitality and rural flavor. They've also discovered another local attraction: The Clubhouse and Golf Course at Las Positas. This popular facility is in demand not just for golf, but for weddings, corporate banquets and other special celebrations. What makes it so appealing? Great service and a versatile setting for a reasonable price.

The Clubhouse includes Beeb's Sports Bar & Grill, a private banquet room, and a patio—all with lovely views of the manicured grounds. The enthusiastic staff are genuinely pleased to serve, so it's no wonder that the two words that come to mind when you visit the Clubhouse are "friendly" and "fun."

The "fun" starts at Beeb's Sports Bar & Grill, which has been consistently voted "Best Sports Bar in Alameda County." The restaurant's lively atmosphere and built-in service area are just right for a casual celebration. Boasting an impressive collection of sports memorabilia, games, and television sets, Beeb's has plenty to keep the sports enthusiast engaged. Seated guests can even enjoy a little golf (vicariously, of course) by watching the putting action just beyond the bank of dining room windows.

For something more formal, opt for the Clubhouse's banquet room with its own private entrance and dance floor. A high, pyramid-shaped ceiling meets walls of windows trimmed in wood; a ledge above the windows decked with ivy and twinkle lights adds a festive touch. One of the nicest features of the banquet room is that it opens onto the patio, allowing your event to become instantly al fresco. The ample patio, shaded by a deep, wooden overhang, is delightful for a buffet or barbecue. It's also a great spot for cocktails and appetizers before inviting your guests inside for a buffet reception. And whether you're on the patio or in the banquet room, the pastoral vista is always there, lending a feeling of peaceful contentment.

That view also makes a picturesque backdrop for couples who get married here. Ceremonies usually take place out on the private lawn under an archway. The surrounding hillsides cradle acres of lawn dotted with trees and colorful blooms, while several quaint foot-bridges arch over a running stream.

As you can see, you don't need to be a sports aficionado to fully appreciate the Clubhouse at Las Positas. However, if you would like to make sports an integral part of your event, it's very easy to do: The banquet room has TV monitors ready and waiting. Show an instructional video to improve your group's golf game, or entertain guests with "athletic" home movies. One group of partying skydivers played tapes of their most spectacular jumps! Brides and grooms have even made use of the A/V equipment to show a retrospective of them growing up. And don't forget golf—a tournament can be incorporated into any event—including a wedding!

Wherever inspiration takes you, the clubhouse staff will follow. As the folks here are fond of saying, "If we don't have it, we will find it and provide it for you." Now, that's the kind of attitude that has made Las Positas not just a local favorite, but a bona fide Bay Area destination.

CEREMONY CAPACITY: The ceremony site holds 270 seated guests; the clubhouse, 130 seated guests.

EVENT/RECEPTION CAPACITY: The banquet room can accommodate 130 seated or 150 standing guests; the patio holds 140 seated or 220 standing guests.

MEETING CAPACITY: Event spaces accommodate 30–150 seated guests.

FEES & DEPOSITS: For weddings and social functions, a $1,000 deposit is required to reserve your date; the balance is due 10 days prior to the event. Room rental fees range $800–1,400. Buffets run $30–36/person. Wedding packages are available starting at $36/person and include appetizers, champagne toast and dinner. Beverage packages start at $15/person. Custom menus are available. Tax, alcohol and a 20% service charge are additional. A $400 ceremony setup fee is extra.

For business functions, a $100–500 deposit is required to reserve your date. The balance is due the day of the event. Room rental fees range $200–500 depending on space rented. Meals run $6–19/person; tax, alcohol and a 20% service charge are additional.

AVAILABILITY: Year-round, daily, 6am–1am. Site tours are by appointment only.

SERVICES/AMENITIES:

Catering: provided
Kitchen Facilities: n/a
Tables & Chairs: provided
Linens, Silver, etc.: provided
Restrooms: wheelchair accessible
Dance Floor: provided
Bride's Dressing Area: yes
Meeting Equipment: some provided, more CBA

Parking: large lot
Accommodations: no guest rooms
Telephone: emergency use only
Outdoor Night Lighting: yes
Outdoor Cooking Facilities: BBQ CBA
Cleanup: provided
View: 22-acre landscaped park
Other: event coordination, big screen TV, projector screen

RESTRICTIONS:

Alcohol: provided, or BYO wine and champagne *with corkage fee*
Smoking: outside only
Music: amplified OK

Wheelchair Access: yes
Insurance: not required
Other: no birdseed or rice

Crooked Vine and Stony Ridge Winery

Winery

4948 Tesla Road, Livermore
925/449-0458

www.crookedvine.com
events@crookedvine.com

● Rehearsal Dinners	● Corp. Events/Mtgs.
● Ceremonies	● Private Parties
● Wedding Receptions	○ Accommodations

The Livermore Valley, one of the country's oldest winemaking regions, is less than an hour from San Francisco and so picturesque that at some point you start fantasizing about owning a vineyard…or having a friend who does. Fortunately, within minutes of entering Crooked Vine and Stony Ridge Winery, you feel you are among friends because their passion, commitment and *joie de vivre* are contagious.

Owned by the Corbett family, this boutique winery has produced a dazzling array of varietals from century-old grapevines. At the same time, they've created a charming setting where you can celebrate your wedding in style—and have the entire property to yourselves.

As your guests arrive, they're ushered down a treelined pathway to a pair of tall redwood gates, emblazoned with an iron-forged version of the "crooked vine" logo. Inside those gates is a self-contained event site with three separate areas. To the left is the Barrel Room, with its stone-pillared façade and latticework arbor at the entry. To the right is the spacious Garden Courtyard, a shaded, stone-floored reception patio. And directly ahead is the manicured Ceremony Lawn, where friends and family await your walk down the aisle to a raised, Craftsman-style gazebo bordered by fragrant lavender and silvery shrubs.

Once vows have been sealed with a kiss, it's time to raise a toast with a flute of the venue's signature sparkling wine. Cocktails and appetizers can be served al fresco, but most brides opt for the climate-controlled Barrel Room. High ceilings, concrete floors and rows of stacked barrels bedecked with romantic tea lights set the scene. A black granite bar runs the length of one wall and framed paintings of colorful vineyards hang above it. At the center of the room, oak barrels are set up as cocktail tables. A dramatic focal point—and a popular backdrop for photos—are the two massive, antique, hand-carved barrels depicting joyful nymphs and cherubs at play among the vines.

If you can slip away, you and your groom will also want to take advantage of some other cool photo ops, by taking a walk through neat rows of cabernet vines in front of the tasting room, or posing with the winery's mint condition 1930s car and early 1940s pickup truck.

Then rejoin everyone for dinner in the Garden Courtyard beneath the twinkling lights strung overhead. Your menu will be expertly paired with wine selections from their much-lauded reds and whites.

As night falls, take the party back inside where the great acoustics of the Barrel Room will get everybody dancing. And for those out-of-towners who want to explore the Livermore/Dublin area the next day (but not too early), the folks at Crooked Vine will be happy to help them choose from among the region's many points of interest.

CEREMONY & EVENT/RECEPTION CAPACITY: The facility can accommodate 100 seated or 200 standing indoors and 200 seated or standing outdoors.

MEETING CAPACITY: Meeting spaces hold 100 seated guests.

FEES & DEPOSITS: 50% of the rental fee and a refundable damage deposit is required to reserve your date. The balance is due 30 days prior to the event. Rental fees start at $2,900 for Friday events, $3,800 for Saturday, and $2,500 for Sunday; and vary depending on the time of the event, guest count and the space rented.

AVAILABILITY: Year-round, daily, 11am–10pm.

SERVICES/AMENITIES:

Catering: select from preferred list
Kitchen Facilities: none
Tables & Chairs: provided
Linens, Silver, etc.: through caterer
Restrooms: wheelchair accessible
Dance Floor: available
Bride's Dressing Area: yes
Meeting Equipment: some provided
Other: picnic area

Parking: large lot
Accommodations: no guest rooms
Telephone: emergency use only
Outdoor Night Lighting: provided
Outdoor Cooking Facilities: no
Cleanup: provided
View: garden courtyard, landscaped grounds, hills, vineyards

RESTRICTIONS:

Alcohol: provided
Smoking: designated areas only
Music: amplified OK with restrictions

Wheelchair Access: yes
Insurance: liability required

Garré Vineyard & Winery
and Martinelli Event Center

Vineyard & Winery

7986 Tesla Road, Livermore
925/371-8200

www.garrewinery.com
garre@garrewinery.com

● Rehearsal Dinners	● Corp. Events/Mtgs.
● Ceremonies	● Private Parties
● Wedding Receptions	Accommodations

Garré Vineyard & Winery is a bit like a small village—a charming one surrounded by grapevines. One of the Livermore Valley's original wineries, this gem, with its Italian Wine Country style, has always drawn a crowd. Maybe it's because of the café on the premises, the park-like setting, the Tasting Room or the jazz they serve up with the food and the bocce ball.

That popularity has increased even more with Garré's Martinelli Event Center, a private facility located just a short drive up the hill from the winery. Set on an elevated vineyard, it's a grand Hacienda-style venue with wrought-iron gates, a bell tower, and palm trees at the entrance. The ballroom, which has been designed for both beauty and versatility, features a vaulted beamed ceiling, wood wainscoting and accents, high windows, and contemporary chandeliers. There are three built-in, remote-controlled projection screens (for that slide show of the bride and groom), as well as wireless microphones for the toasts. The building's stone-paved inner courtyard with fireplace and fountain is ideal for a bar setup and appetizers, or for a reception under the stars. A nearby ceremony site is not only surrounded by vines, but also offers views of vineyard-laced rolling hills. The entire facility—including an enormous patio and lawn, an exquisite bridal suite, and a comfortable groom's dressing area—is laid out in a way that allows for seamless transitions from ceremony to hors d'oeuvres to dining and dancing.

Back down the hill on the winery property is the Grand Pavilion and Oak Staging Area, another gorgeous wedding site. Old-fashioned 19th-century streetlamps line the paths and illuminate the area at night. One walkway leads up to a small stage beneath the property's centuries-old oak tree. Bordered by flowerbeds and Italian cypress and backed by rows of Cabernet vines, this is a dignified spot for a ceremony. Across the grass, an elegant white pavilion provides 6,000 square feet of banquet and dance space for large parties. During the summer, the walls of the "big white tent" can come down, revealing the surrounding vineyards and gardens and connecting the ceremony area with the reception site. It's an incredibly festive environment and a marvelous place to sample the masterful pairings of food and wine recommended and prepared by our Executive Chef and highly trained culinary staff. Try a Garré Vineyard Cabernet Sauvignon with pan-seared fillet mignon wrapped in bacon with wild mushroom demi-glaze and freshly grated horseradish mashed potatoes. Or, indulge in a Cabernet Franc with Dijon-herb encrusted rack of lamb with truffled white bean ragout and Cabernet Franc reduction. Two full-size bocce ball courts that are lit at night offer a before- and after-dinner diversion, adding to the Old World ambiance.

Tours of Garré Winery's event sites are by appointment only. We suggest that to really experience what Garré is like, make a reservation for lunch or dinner, too. That way you'll be able to stroll the grounds, take in the views, and taste their award-winning food and wine.

CEREMONY CAPACITY: The Martinelli Event Center holds up to 200, and the Pavilion up to 300 seated guests.

EVENT/RECEPTION CAPACITY: The Café holds up to 50 seated guests, the Café Courtyard up to 100, the Martinelli Center up to 250, and the Pavilion up to 300.

MEETING CAPACITY: Spaces are available for 12–200 guests. Facilities include conference capabilities.

FEES & DEPOSITS: A $1,200 nonrefundable deposit is required to reserve your date, and the balance is due 2 weeks prior to the event. Rental fees range $400–4,000 depending on the venue, day and guest count. Meals range $35–75/person. Tax, alcohol and a 20% service charge are additional.

AVAILABILITY: Year-round, daily, anytime.

SERVICES/AMENITIES:

Catering: provided
Kitchen Facilities: n/a
Tables & Chairs: provided, *Chiaviari* chairs at Event Ctr.
Linens, Silver, etc.: provided
Restrooms: wheelchair accessible
Dance Floor: yes
Bride's Dressing Area: yes
Meeting Equipment: available only in the Martinelli Center: video projectors, DVD/VCR, amplifier, electronically operated projection screen, program speakers, wireless microphone, wireless connections

Parking: ample on site
Accommodations: no guest rooms
Telephone: emergency use only
Outdoor Night Lighting: yes
Outdoor Cooking Facilities: no
Cleanup: provided
View: vineyards, valley, mountains, meadow, fountain, gardens

RESTRICTIONS:

Alcohol: provided, wine, beer or champagne only
Smoking: outdoors only
Music: amplified OK

Wheelchair Access: yes
Insurance: liability required

Want to know WHAT TO ASK a potential location or vendor? Check out our Questions to Ask starting on page 17.

Murrieta's Well

Wine Estate

3005 Mines Road, Livermore
925/456-2425
www.murrietaswell.com
catering@wentevineyards.com

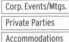

● Rehearsal Dinners	● Corp. Events/Mtgs.
● Ceremonies	● Private Parties
● Wedding Receptions	Accommodations

An almost operatic love for romance might seize you when you first set eyes upon this lovely little wine estate, tucked away in a pastoral fold of picturesque Livermore Valley. Named for the artesian well where Joaquin Murrieta, the notorious Robin Hood of El Dorado, and his band of desperados purportedly watered their horses, this history-rich property is just the place for an event worth singing about for decades.

Your celebration can begin on the graceful Vineyard Patio. The enchanting 100-year-old winery building with its huge double doors and second-story balcony provides an elegant backdrop to every party played out here. Artistically and fragrantly framed in bright bursts of crimson—red roses, geraniums, wispy bottlebrush and a delicate Japanese maple—and by the 92-acre vineyard that yields the grapes for the property's handcrafted blends of Meritage, Zarzuela and Zinfandel wines, this attractive outdoor space is ideal for a wedding ceremony, a reception, or any other affair set—California style—under a canopy of brilliant blue or starry-night skies.

For show-stopping entrances and tasteful transitions use the terracotta stairway accented with antique Spanish tiles that winds its way, via a gentle, lushly planted slope, from the patio to the quiet Upper Terrace. A red-carpet-caliber stop for photo ops, it looks out over the small adobe fountain that caps the well of legend and lore. Guests can stroll up this stairway after the ceremony to cocktails, passed hors d'oeuvres and gorgeous views that stretch from the chestnut mares whinnying in a lower pasture to a skyline of oaks and palms.

Dinner and dancing are served up in style in the wonderful old winery building. In its appropriately named Barrel Room, located on the ground floor, heavy wood beams and pillars, high ceilings, rustic stone walls and ancient wine barrels create a dramatic ambiance. The twinkling lights and twining vines that climb the broad wooden columns add a theatrical touch designed to transport your guests to another place and time. Any little additions—white-clad tables, glassware and cutlery, simple arrangements of flowers—look remarkable in this room. It's an interior rich with the flavor of tradition and good living that typifies the wine country experience, one that's sure to enhance the sparkle of your event.

At the back of the Barrel Room a wooden staircase leads upstairs to the broad tasting room foyer, where a trellised breezeway offers guests a private place to take a breather from all the excitement. At the foot of the stairway, an enormous gilt mirror doubles the pleasure of admiring your wedding cake. And throughout your reception, Wente Vineyards' award-winning restaurant and catering staff (set up out of sight on the second floor) whisks upstairs and down with their mouthwatering pairings of fabulous food and fine Murrieta's Well and Wente Vineyards wines.

CEREMONY CAPACITY: Outdoor spaces are available, seating up to 110 guests.

EVENT/RECEPTION & MEETING CAPACITY: Indoor and outdoor spaces are available, holding up to 110 seated or 150 standing guests.

FEES & DEPOSITS: A $500–3,000 deposit is required to reserve your date. An estimated 50% of the final balance is due 6 months prior to the event. The anticipated balance is payable 2 weeks prior to the event; all incurred expenses are due the day of the event. Rental fees range $500–3,000 depending on the day and season of the event. *Wente Catering* provides sit-down dinners and buffets, including a custom-designed wedding cake. These range $50–75/person. Tax, beverages, rentals and a 20% service charge are additional.

AVAILABILITY: Year-round, daily, 6pm–11pm, indoors.

SERVICES/AMENITIES:

Catering: provided
Kitchen Facilities: n/a
Tables & Chairs: provided
Linens, Silver, etc.: provided
Restrooms: wheelchair accessible
Dance Floor: CBA
Bride's & Groom's Dressing Areas: no
Meeting Equipment: CBA

Parking: large lot
Accommodations: no guest rooms
Telephone: emergency use only
Outdoor Night Lighting: yes
Outdoor Cooking Facilities: no
Cleanup: provided
View: vineyards, garden, hills
Other: event coordination, custom-designed wedding cake

RESTRICTIONS:

Alcohol: provided
Smoking: outside only
Music: amplified OK until 10pm

Wheelchair Access: yes
Insurance: liability required

Poppy Ridge Golf Course
Rees Jones Scottish Heathland Course

Golf Course and Clubhouse

4280 Greenville Road, Livermore
925/447-6779
www.poppyridgegolf.com/weddings
bgarza@poppyridgegolf.com

- Rehearsal Dinners
- Ceremonies
- Wedding Receptions
- Corp. Events/Mtgs.
- Private Parties
- Accommodations

Grapevines line a narrow private road that winds through gently sloping hills to a graceful hacienda-style clubhouse. Set on a hill, the spacious tile-roofed building overlooks the pristine fairways and greens of the Poppy Ridge Golf Course, one of the Northern California Golf Association's two premier golf facilities. First opened for play in 1996, the 27-hole course and clubhouse is the sister facility of top-ranked Poppy Hills Golf Course in Pebble Beach and, like the flower it's named for, it epitomizes the sunny charm of the Golden State.

Rustic-style double doors open to a peaceful lobby, a perfect ambiance for conjuring up heartfelt messages for the guest book. A few steps further, sunlight cascades through skylights, an appropriate introduction to the airy restaurant that adjoins the far side of the lobby. The high-ceilinged Porter's Restaurant is a picturesque place for weddings, company parties, tournament banquets and more. It comes with a full walk-up bar, and two walls of floor-to-ceiling windows that showcase breathtaking views. The north window boasts a particularly commanding vista of the Chardonnay and Zinfandel courses, as well as a wraparound deck.

In addition to its enviable panorama, the restaurant has also earned high marks from repeat clientele for excellent food: The mouthwatering menus for hors d'oeuvres, sit-down dinners and buffets include tempting entrées that incorporate fresh, local ingredients and are accompanied by zesty sauces. The Executive Chef selects the menu for each event with the upmost care and consideration. Equal attention is paid to the other aspects of your celebration: The site fee—an incredible value—includes an event planner and on-site coordinator, a bartender, and all the props for the right presentation. And, of course, the staff is expert at helping you personalize your occasion and executing every detail.

If you'd prefer to entertain outdoors, reserve one of the building's wide, sun-splashed terraces with their unobscured backdrops of glistening lakes and lush greens. There's plenty of room for a ceremony on the inviting East Terrace, set with a beautiful white arbor and chairs for your guests. Crystal and flatware sparkle in the natural light on the partially covered North Terrace, with its Spanish-style tower and sweeping, flower-lined stairway. Whatever the occasion, this is a glorious setting for making merry. Lean out over the balustrade to admire the scenic surround, retire to a shady spot for an appreciative pause, or raise a toast in the archway of the tower. Then, grab colleagues, family and friends for a photo shoot on the property—with such lovely environs, your photographer will have no trouble creating romantic portraits to add to your album of memories.

CEREMONY CAPACITY: Poppy Ridge holds up to 200 seated guests, indoors or outdoors.

EVENT/RECEPTION CAPACITY: Indoors, Poppy Ridge holds up to 170 seated or 300 standing guests; outdoors, up to 175 seated or 200 standing guests.

MEETING CAPACITY: Spaces are available which hold up to 150 guests.

FEES & DEPOSITS: The rental fee is required to reserve your date. The balance is due 14 days prior to the event. Rental fees range $300–3,000 depending on the type of event. Some of the services and amenities included in the rental fee are listed below. Meals range $41–50/person. Tax, alcohol and service charge are additional.

AVAILABILITY: Year-round, daily, 6am–midnight. Site tours by appointment.

SERVICES/AMENITIES:

Catering: provided, no BYO
Kitchen Facilities: full kitchen
Tables & Chairs: included
Linens, Silver, etc.: included
Restrooms: wheelchair accessible
Dance Floor: included
Bride's Dressing Area: yes
Meeting Equipment: CBA, extra charge
Other: event coordination, patio heaters, umbrellas, chargers and garden arch included in rental fee

Parking: for up to 300 cars
Accommodations: partner hotels nearby
Telephone: emergency use only
Outdoor Night Lighting: yes
Outdoor Cooking Facilities: yes
Cleanup: provided
View: vineyards, fairways, hills, pond Livermore valley, landscaped grounds

RESTRICTIONS:

Alcohol: beer, champagne and spirits provided or BYO wine and champagne with corkage fee
Smoking: outdoors only
Music: amplified OK

Wheelchair Access: yes
Insurance: liability required

Shrine Event Center

Banquet Facility

170 Lindbergh Avenue, Livermore
925/373-4880

www.shrineeventcenter.com
sales@shrineeventcenter.com

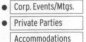

- Rehearsal Dinners
- Ceremonies
- Wedding Receptions
- Corp. Events/Mtgs.
- Private Parties
- Accommodations

Towering palms and graceful willow trees flank the Shrine Event Center, whose spacious interior has hosted many wonderful celebrations. The grand ballroom is larger than most event facilities in the area, and it can take on any theme you have in mind.

Events often begin in the Lounge, where two built-in bars with mirrored backsplashes make serving cocktails both attractive and easy. Matching nearby counters can hold the appetizer or dessert display. The Lounge is also a fun retreat for after-dinner cordials.

The Lounge leads directly into the Lindbergh Ballroom, the centerpiece of the venue. Open, airy and contemporary, the ballroom features a dramatic vaulted ceiling with polished wooden beams. Rows of fabric swags overhead lend a soft, elegant look. At one end of the ballroom, an east-facing stage is perfect for your band or DJ, while risers are available for elevating the head table just below.

One of the best things about the Shrine Event Center is its adaptability. The ballroom accommodates a wide range of events, from a corporate seminar to a beautiful wedding. For a sophisticated gala, deck the space out in white linen and crystal. If you're planning something more informal, like a luau-style banquet, the room easily transforms into a Caribbean paradise with vibrant colors and tropical décor. Add tulle, flowers, or twinkle lights as the spirit moves you. Track lighting on dimmers allows you to adjust the mood throughout your party. There's also a retractable screen for showing a photo or video montage, and even a disco ball in case you want to turn it up a notch when the dancing gets going. The on-site coordinator will work with you to design your event, and can recommend vendors to help you bring your ideas to life.

If you like, host both your ceremony and reception in the ballroom, where movable room dividers let you create separate areas if desired. Large conferences or banquets can combine adjacent breakout rooms with the ballroom, and seat up to 950 guests theater-style. The center's state-of-the-art sound system is another plus, especially for corporate events.

The Shrine Event Center is easily accessible by freeway I-580 and close to the Livermore Municipal Airport, local hotels (one within walking distance), restaurants and nightclubs—something you'll appreciate if you're inviting out-of-town guests. Plus, there are plenty of nearby wineries, hiking trails and other attractions to keep your family and friends happily occupied before and after your event.

Flexibility, convenience, affordability, complimentary on-site parking—and you can bring your own caterer and alcohol! With so much to offer, it's no wonder this venue is in demand!

CEREMONY CAPACITY: Ceremonies take place upon request.

EVENT/RECEPTION CAPACITY: The main ballroom accommodates 450 seated for dining and dancing. Adjoining side rooms each seat 50 guests.

MEETING CAPACITY: The facility holds up to 950 guests seated theater-style.

FEES & DEPOSITS: A nonrefundable deposit is required to hold your event date. The rental fee, which includes a 5-hour event plus 2 hours for setup and 1 hour post-event for cleanup, ranges $1,000–3,600 depending on the date and number of guests attending the event. Overtime starts at $124/hour and may increase depending on the number of security guards required. A refundable $1,000-minimum security deposit is also required.

AVAILABILITY: Year-round, daily.

SERVICES/AMENITIES:

Catering: BYO licensed and pre-approved or select from list
Kitchen Facilities: fully equipped
Tables & Chairs: provided
Linens: available, or BYO
Silver, China etc.: through caterer or BYO
Restrooms: wheelchair accessible
Dance Floor: yes
Bride's Dressing Area: yes
Meeting Equipment: A/V equipment CBA, extra charge

Parking: large complimentary lot
Accommodations: hotels nearby
Telephone: emergency use only
Outdoor Night Lighting: yes
Outdoor Cooking Facilities: yes
Cleanup: caterer, renter and some provided
View: East Bay foothills

RESTRICTIONS:

Alcohol: through caterer or BYO licensed server
Smoking: outside only
Music: amplified OK

Wheelchair Access: yes
Insurance: certificate required

Want to find more venues and services? Check out our informative website, www.HereComesTheGuide.com.

353

Wente Vineyards
Event Center, Golf Course & Vineyard Lawn

Restaurant & Golf Course

5050 Arroyo Road, Livermore
925/456-2425
www.wentevineyards.com
catering@wentevineyards.com

- Rehearsal Dinners
- Ceremonies
- Wedding Receptions
- Corp. Events/Mtgs.
- Private Parties
- Accommodations

Situated in a picturesque canyon at the southern end of the Livermore Valley, Wente Vineyards Restaurant, Event Center and Golf Course is surrounded by grapevines, sycamore groves and rolling hills. The site, with its beautifully landscaped grounds, is a versatile setting for corporate retreats, special events, and of course, Tri-Valley Wine Country weddings!

Founded 125 years ago, Wente Vineyards is the country's oldest continuously operated family-owned winery. It's no wonder, then, that the architecture reflects a sense of California history. White Spanish-style stucco buildings are accented with tile roofs and floors, and terracotta pots full of flowering plants set a cheery tone. The event center includes the Cresta Blanca Room, where indoor receptions are held, and the adjacent Terrace Lawn, a pretty spot for a garden wedding ceremony. There's space here, too, for an elegantly tented reception. Or use an open-sided tent for dancing, and set up tables and chairs outside to enjoy the view, which includes the changing seasonal colors of the sycamore trees.

Speaking of views: One of the best can be had on the new Vineyard Lawn near a pond at the golf course's 18th hole. Ceremonies and receptions on this green expanse can accommodate up to 1,000 of your nearest and dearest; in the background, lush vineyards and the golden Sandstone Hills cast a romantic spell.

Wente's award-winning restaurant casts a spell of its own. Three private dining rooms and terraces with vineyard views accommodate intimate receptions, rehearsal dinners, bridal showers or any other celebration. Wente, which has been Green Certified by Alameda County, has earned much critical acclaim for its cuisine, wine and sustainability. (They're among the first wineries in the state to be recognized by the recently established Certified California Sustainable Winegrowing Alliance.) Menus focus on simple foods with complex flavors, and incorporate the freshest locally grown and organic ingredients. Experienced staff will assist you with menu choices and wine selection, as well as recommendations for event services such as photography, floral design and overnight accommodations.

Wente also offers private wine tastings in their wine caves (a superb idea for your rehearsal dinner) and customized wine labeling for wedding favors. Sometimes event hosts organize a round of golf on Wente's Greg Norman-designed course, located just a chip shot away from the Conference Center. In keeping with their environmental sensitivity, the course was recently designated a "Certified Audubon Cooperative Sanctuary" by the Audubon International Program.

With its first-rate facilities, acres of vineyards and warm, Mediterranean ambiance, Wente is an extremely popular event site. They book up quickly, so don't wait too long to pay this East Bay oasis a visit.

CEREMONY CAPACITY: The Lawn and Garden can accommodate 350 seated; the Charles Wetmore and Cresta Blanca Rooms each hold 60–150 seated guests.

EVENT/RECEPTION CAPACITY: The site holds 15–150 seated indoors, and 20–1,000 seated outdoors.

MEETING CAPACITY: Event spaces hold 16–100 seated guests.

FEES & DEPOSITS: For weddings, a $500–5,000 nonrefundable deposit is required to reserve your date. An estimated 50% is due 6 months prior, and the estimated event balance is payable 2 weeks prior to the event; all incurred expenses are due on the day of the event. Facility rental fees range $500–5,000 depending upon day and season. Catering is provided: Buffets, luncheons and dinners, including a custom-designed wedding cake, range $50–75/person. Tax, beverages, rentals and a 20% service charge are additional.

For business functions, social events and meetings, facility rental fees range $150–5,000 depending on the spaces rented. Food is provided; prices will vary depending on menus and services selected. Call the sales department for specific rates.

AVAILABILITY: Year-round, daily, 7am–11pm, indoors. The Vineyard Lawn is available until 10pm.

SERVICES/AMENITIES:

Catering: provided
Kitchen Facilities: n/a
Tables & Chairs: provided
Linens, Silver, etc.: provided
Restrooms: wheelchair accessible
Dance Floor: available
Bride's Dressing Area: yes, in Event Center only
Meeting Equipment: full range, extra charge

Parking: large lot with parking attendants
Accommodations: no guest rooms
Outdoor Night Lighting: yes
Outdoor Cooking Facilities: no
Telephone: pay phones
Cleanup: provided
View: vineyards surrounded by rolling hills
Other: event coordination

RESTRICTIONS:

Alcohol: beer, champagne, spirits
and Wente wine provided
Smoking: outside only
Music: amplified OK

Wheelchair Access: yes
Insurance: liability required
Other: no birdseed, rice or petals

Casa Real at Ruby Hill Winery

Winery, Garden & Ballroom

410 Vineyard Avenue, Pleasanton
925/931-0200

www.casarealevents.com
info@casarealevents.com

● Rehearsal Dinners	● Corp. Events/Mtgs.
● Ceremonies	● Private Parties
● Wedding Receptions	Accommodations

The name, Casa Real, means House of Royalty, and we have no doubt that you and your guests will feel to the manor born when you arrive at this dramatic property set in the heart of the Livermore Valley Wine Country.

Acres upon acres of vineyards frame the 20,000-square-foot villa. The beautiful Mediterranean-style fountain surrounded by roses is a paparazzi-pleasing backdrop for red carpet arrivals and departures. Enormous hand-carved mahogany doors with wrought-iron hinges open into the jaw-dropping Entrance Hall with its 32-foot ceiling, Italian tile floor and white limestone trim. Three huge chandeliers; artisan-crafted limestone niches, rosettes and medallions; and clerestory-style windows set high in the walls lend the space a classical, yet romantic, feel. It's a gallery fit for rows of marble statues or shining suits of antique armor, but you might be perfectly happy with a roomful of celebrants and a beautiful floral arrangement atop the round mahogany table that sits at its center.

From this hall, five additional sets of massive mahogany doors lead in other directions. To the east, the similarly trimmed Amber Room with its honey and cocoa accents embraces you in an atmosphere of luxury and intimacy. Large enough for a sizeable indoor ceremony or sit-down gathering, its focal point is a 12-foot hand-carved limestone fireplace before which vows, performances and spirited toasts are surely in order. The Entrance Hall's north doors lead to the 9,000-square-foot Grand Salon, ideal for magnificent fêtes and feasts, with its soaring ceiling, mahogany bar and expansive windows. Twenty massive half-moon chandeliers, star-like pin lights, and sconces around the room's perimeter vary the mood; the champagne-colored Italian tile floor invites dancing; and handsome mahogany king's tables suggest banqueting in grand style.

No detail goes unattended in this regal oasis. In addition to the spacious, elegantly appointed restrooms, a posh chamber the size of a small condo (with couch, credenza, standing mirror, private bathroom and a granite-topped vanity that seats up to four) serves as a corporate closing room, a lounge for the bride and attendants or a peaceful semiprivate retreat.

For outdoor ceremonies, cocktails and other activities, the Sun Garden's terrace, walkways, limestone fountains and plants provide an idyllic setting. Views of the vineyards and the rolling East Bay hills abound, and a canopy of blue sky caps its protective walls. Within them Valencia orange trees, lavender, white tree roses and other beautiful blooms share space with 12 lovely magnolia trees that border the garden's central lawn. And don't forget the historic Ruby Hill Winery right next door; it's a great spot for a rehearsal dinner or optional wine-tasting activities.

CEREMONY CAPACITY: The facility holds 300 seated guests indoors and 450 seated outdoors.

EVENT/RECEPTION CAPACITY: The site can accommodate 500 seated with a dance floor or 600 seated without.

MEETING CAPACITY: The site holds 600 seated guests.

FEES & DEPOSITS: A deposit equal to the rental fee or a minimum of $2,500, whichever is greater, is required to reserve your date. 50% of the estimated event costs is due 6 months prior to the event. The balance is due 10 days before the event. Rental fees range $800–5,000 depending on the day and time of the event.. Meals range $40–70/person. Tax, alcohol and a 20% service charge are additional. A $550 ceremony setup fee is additional.

AVAILABILITY: Year-round, Sunday–Thursday, 9am–10pm; Friday and Saturday (and Sundays before a national holiday), 9am–11pm.

SERVICES/AMENITIES:

Catering: provided
Kitchen Facilities: n/a
Tables & Chairs: provided
Linens, Silver, etc.: provided
Restrooms: wheelchair accessible
Dance Floor: yes
Bride's Dressing Area: yes
Meeting Equipment: CBA
Other: event coordination

Parking: large lot; directed or valet parking required for over 250 guests
Accommodations: no guest rooms
Telephone: emergency use only
Outdoor Night Lighting: provided
Outdoor Cooking Facilities: n/a
Cleanup: provided
View: fountains, landscaped grounds, garden, courtyard, hills, valley and vineyards

RESTRICTIONS:

Alcohol: provided
Smoking: outside only
Music: amplified OK with restrictions

Wheelchair Access: yes
Insurance: liability required

Castlewood Country Club

Golf Club

707 Country Club Circle, Pleasanton
925/485-2237

www.castlewoodcc.org
kamestoy@castlewoodcc.org

● Rehearsal Dinners	● Corp. Events/Mtgs.
● Ceremonies	● Private Parties
● Wedding Receptions	○ Accommodations

Once the site of the fabulous "La Hacienda Del Pozo de Verona" and the former estate of Phoebe Apperson Hearst, California's beloved hostess and first lady of philanthropy, the Castlewood Country Club still retains the aura of elegance and grace that were the hallmarks of its famous resident. The drive up Pleasanton Ridge, which overlooks the Amador Valley and is flanked by green fairways and gated estates, continues to generate a feeling of opulence and success. Giant palms line the Clubhouse approach, while the country club pool, built by Mrs. Hearst, sparkles like a huge aquamarine amid emerald lawns.

The princely porte-cochère that marks the entrance to the Clubhouse is reminiscent of the palatial 53-room California Mission-style mansion that once crowned the rise. This red carpet-style entrée through a beautiful colonnade is a fitting introduction to the spaces within.

Guests can gather in the handsomely furnished Grand Lobby with its soaring ceiling and majestic fireplace. Gleaming terracotta-colored floors reflect light in a way that adds warmth and splendor. The lobby leads to the Del Pozo Lounge, a 2,000-square-foot private prefunction space of castle-like splendor. A magnificent granite-and-marble bar in the back of the room draws guests in to relax with a cocktail in hand before stepping into the 6,000-square-foot Grand Ballroom. The room's 12-foot-high windows let in breathtaking valley and golf course views, and 10 massive Spanish-style chandeliers combine with other ambient lighting to halo festivities in just the right light. Event menus are customized by Castlewood's award-winning chef, and served up by a staff experienced in fine dining and topnotch service.

Let a waltz across the polished hardwood floors lead to the Del Pozo Terrace, where 1,600 additional square feet of function space and more stunning valley and woodland vistas expand the party possibilities. Perfect for pre-dinner or après-dinner drinks and tête-à-têtes, it's also an excellent ceremony space. For brides and grooms who wish to tie the knot on Castlewood's Oak Tree Lawn, the property's ancient oak tree, whose branches spread overhead like a lacy fan, is a spectacular natural backdrop for the wedding couple.

If the bride and her attendants need to freshen up, they can do so in quarters fit for a queen. Entrance is through the Ladies Card Room, where rich carpeting, card tables, wingback chairs and golf course views create an inviting vibe. The bathrooms feature vanities and wraparound counters with upholstered cream-and-bronze-colored seating. The groom and his groomsmen also have their own space, but we're betting they'll spend little time there. After all, how often can you celebrate like a Spanish grandee in a 21st-century castle?

CEREMONY CAPACITY: The facility holds 200 seated guests indoors and 300 seated outdoors.

EVENT/RECEPTION CAPACITY: The site can accommodate 350 seated or 500 standing indoors.

MEETING CAPACITY: The site holds 400 seated guests.

FEES & DEPOSITS: A $2,500 deposit is required to reserve your date. Rental fees range $500–3,500 depending on the day and time of the event and the space rented. Meals range $36–60/person. Tax, alcohol and a 20% service charge are additional.

AVAILABILITY: Year-round.

SERVICES/AMENITIES:

Catering: provided or BYO
Kitchen Facilities: fully equipped
Tables & Chairs: provided
Linens, Silver, etc.: provided
Restrooms: wheelchair accessible
Dance Floor: provided
Bride's Dressing Area: yes
Meeting Equipment: some provided
Other: A/V equipment

Parking: large lot
Accommodations: no guest rooms
Telephone: emergency use only
Outdoor Night Lighting: CBA
Outdoor Cooking Facilities: BBQ CBA
Cleanup: caterer or renter
View: fairways, landscaped grounds, pool area; panorama of hills and valley

RESTRICTIONS:

Alcohol: provided
Smoking: designated areas only
Music: amplified OK with restrictions

Wheelchair Access: limited
Insurance: not required

This is important! Tell locations you're reading HERE COMES THE GUIDE and ask if our information is still current.

Palm Event Center in the Vineyard

Winery, Garden & Ballroom

1184 Vineyard Avenue, Pleasanton
925/426-8666

www.palmeventcenter.com
info@palmeventcenter.com

- Rehearsal Dinners
- Ceremonies
- Wedding Receptions
- Corp. Events/Mtgs.
- Private Parties
- Accommodations

The ambiance here is purely palatial or maybe "palazzo," since the feeling you'll get is that you've stepped into the Italian countryside. Set on a 110-acre winery estate and fashioned in a size, scale and simplicity that emphasize the beauty and character of its vineyard setting, the Palm Event Center is certainly a magnificent place for a party.

The facilities are surrounded by vineyards and enjoy views of Mt. Hamilton and Ruby Hill. Guests arrive via a graceful palm-lined approach to find themselves in front of an imposing winery with its roots in the past. The atmosphere is one of privacy and refinement. Celebrations take place in the adjacent Palm Event Center, which has been built using antique brick recycled from an old historic winery. Carefully designed in a manner that blends wine country and Romanesque styles, it's a majestic edifice that bespeaks both taste and means.

The enchantment continues when you step into the Ballroom through the Palm's massive redwood doors. They're made from wine barrels that were aged over 50 years, and constructed by a master carpenter. Inside, a 24-foot-high ceiling and honey-colored Italian-tile floor define the grand scale of this spacious room. High Roman windows connect you with the outdoors: Look through them and you can see the tops of the palms. Weddings, fancy fundraisers, high-end dinner dances and corporate galas will all look impossibly posh in this sumptuous interior. Larger-than-life appointments include French oak barrels and two 800-pound king's tables ideal for presenting cakes, registration, buffets or banquets in royal style. Handsome portable screens can partition off any area, including the sleek tan-and-black granite bar. And the magnificent catering kitchen enables an all-star staff to turn out delicious contemporary cuisine, guaranteed to dazzle your palate. The sky is the limit on lighting, but even better than the stars, this heaven of dual pin spots is on adjustable dimmers. Even the seating is exquisite: Italian designer chairs are ultra-comfy and welcoming after a mad whirl (or two or three) around the ballroom.

On the eastern wall, huge floor-to-ceiling windows and glass doors open onto a sizeable, two-tiered patio, which can also be accessed from a trellis- and trumpet-vine-bordered walkway on the side of the building. Floored in tasteful gray stone and attractively lit, it's perfect for cocktails and hors d'oeuvres or for after-dinner drinks under the stars. The well-manicured lawn is another lovely gathering place, perhaps for a ceremony beneath a gorgeous redwood trellis, or for a convivial chat.

The cavernous Estate Room, lined with wine barrels and glittering tea lights, provides more space and is a beautiful setting for an indoor ceremony. This room can also host extra activities and sideshow attractions like an auction, or double as a swanky lounge or casino room. Clean, crisp and cool, it's full of wine-cave romance and the fragrance of ripening vintages.

CEREMONY CAPACITY: The facility holds 300 seated guests indoors and 400 seated outdoors.

EVENT/RECEPTION CAPACITY: The Palm accommodates 400 seated with a dance floor, or 500 seated without.

MEETING CAPACITY: The site seats 600 guests.

FEES & DEPOSITS: A deposit equal to the rental fee or a minimum of $2,500, whichever is greater, is required to reserve your date. 50% of the estimated event total is due 6 months prior to the event. The balance is due 10 days before the event. Rental fees range $800–5,000 depending on day and time of the event. Meals range $40–60/person. Tax, alcohol and a 20% service charge are additional. A $550 ceremony setup fee is additional.

AVAILABILITY: Year-round, daily, 8am–11pm.

SERVICES/AMENITIES:

Catering: provided
Kitchen Facilities: n/a
Tables & Chairs: provided
Linens, Silver, etc.: provided
Restrooms: wheelchair accessible
Dance Floor: yes
Bride's Dressing Area: yes
Meeting Equipment: CBA, extra charge
Other: event coordination

Parking: large lot; directed or valet parking required for over 275 guests
Accommodations: no guest rooms
Telephone: emergency use only
Outdoor Night Lighting: yes
Outdoor Cooking Facilities: n/a
Cleanup: provided
View: vineyards, garden, hills, landscaped grounds, fountain

RESTRICTIONS:

Alcohol: provided
Smoking: outside only
Music: amplified OK with restrictions

Wheelchair Access: yes
Insurance: certificate required

Palm Pavilion

Event Center

4501 Pleasanton Avenue, Pleasanton
925/426-7600

www.alamedacountyfair.com
fcater@alamedacountyfair.com

●	Rehearsal Dinners	●	Corp. Events/Mtgs.
●	Ceremonies	●	Private Parties
●	Wedding Receptions		Accommodations

Set on 267 beautifully land-scaped acres in the heart of downtown Pleasanton, the Palm Pavilion is home to many events year-round, including weddings, private parties and corporate affairs.

Surrounded by its name-sake trees, the versatile facility enables you to celebrate indoors and out. Inside, the golden oak bar, pale terracotta tiles and cream walls lend the space an inviting warmth, while a variety of lighting options make this large (5,000-square-foot) space feel surprisingly intimate. Generous windows on three sides showcase views of the golf course and main lawn area. Three adjoining patios—two open and one covered—let you and your guests revel in the balmy Pleasanton weather. In addition, the building is fully air-conditioned, and boasts up-to-date audiovisual technology.

Just a few steps away is the Wine Garden where ceremonies are held. Couples exchange vows on a raised platform near a burbling fountain, against a lush backdrop of flowers, ferns and other greenery. The stucco wall enclosing the garden ensures privacy.

If you're a bride on a budget, you won't find a better venue than the Palm Pavilion. The experienced staff will give you as much (or as little) assistance as you want, and they can handle everything from an upscale wedding to a quinceañera. Plus, they provide services and amenities you won't find at smaller facilities, such as an on-site plant nursery, acres of nearby parking, security, and plenty of privacy.

And because the Pavilion is part of the nonprofit Alameda County Fairgrounds, the revenue they generate goes back into maintaining and improving the property, ensuring that the grounds and buildings are always in tip-top shape.

With so much to offer, the Palm Pavilion could be the surprise perfect place for your special event!

CEREMONY CAPACITY: Various outdoor locations hold in excess of 2,000 guests; the Palm Pavilion up to 275 seated guests.

EVENT/RECEPTION CAPACITY: Indoor spaces accommodate 225 seated or 275 standing guests. The Garden holds up to 200 seated or 250 standing guests.

MEETING CAPACITY: Spaces are available which hold up to 3,000 guests.

FEES & DEPOSITS: 50% of the estimated event total is required to reserve your date. The balance is due 30 days prior to the event. The rental fee is $800 Sunday–Thursday and $1,400 Friday and Saturday. Meals start at $27/person. A 22% service charge and sales tax are additional.

AVAILABILITY: Year-round, daily, 8am–midnight.

SERVICES/AMENITIES:

Catering: provided, no BYO
Kitchen Facilities: n/a
Tables & Chairs: provided
Linens, Silver, etc.: provided
Restrooms: wheelchair accessible
Dance Floor: yes, permanent
Bride's Dressing Area: CBA
Meeting Equipment: some provided, more CBA

Parking: large lots
Accommodations: partner hotels nearby
Telephone: emergency use only
Outdoor Night Lighting: yes
Outdoor Cooking Facilities: BBQ
Cleanup: provided
View: golf course, garden, park, grounds
Other: coordination available for fee; on-site florals, picnic area, A/V equipment

RESTRICTIONS:

Alcohol: provided
Smoking: outside only
Music: amplified OK with restrictions

Wheelchair Access: yes
Insurance: not required

Ruby Hill Golf Club

Private Golf Club

3400 West Ruby Hill Drive, Pleasanton
925/461-3504
www.rubyhill.com
mjohnson@rubyhill.com

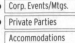

● Rehearsal Dinners	● Corp. Events/Mtgs.
● Ceremonies	● Private Parties
● Wedding Receptions	Accommodations

Judging by its beautiful entrance, with a Tuscan-style gatehouse, trellised driveway and meticulous landscaping, Ruby Hill is no ordinary golf club. In fact, what lies beyond the impressive gates is not just a golf course, but an exclusive private community surrounded by vineyards and spread over acres of open land. It's so exclusive that in order to take a peek at this lovely facility you have to make an appointment.

The clubhouse and fairways are a short drive up the hill, and as you make your way to the top, you pass dozens of spectacular homes whose graceful architecture defines the development. Most of these houses are reminiscent of Italian villas, and when you finally reach the clubhouse, you're hardly surprised to find that it's the largest and most striking "villa" of them all.

Step through the arched front door into the Fireside Room and you're more than a little awestruck by the grand scale and inviting ambiance. The vast marble floor gleams softly, bathed in natural light from a stunning domed skylight overhead. Elegant conversational seating is arranged beneath the skylight and in front of a large stone fireplace. You can't help but notice rich details, like the crown molding, wall sconces and window trim, all seemingly fashioned from stone, and the eclectic antiques and art, which add a personal touch.

From the Fireside Room, walk down the regal staircase into the Main Dining Room, where indoor receptions and special events are held. The sheer grandeur of the space makes you want to sit down to fully appreciate the soaring 40-foot ceiling, giant potted palms and abundant light streaming in through a multitude of high windows and glass doors. Walls are painted a warm Tuscan wheat accented with creamy white trim, and the Florentine motif in the custom carpet swirls beneath your feet in muted earth tones.

To one side of the Main Dining Room is a similarly appointed small private dining room for rehearsal dinners or meetings. On the other side is the Lounge, a clubby space with dark maple woodwork, a marble fireplace and granite-topped bar that's well suited for cocktails. All three rooms open out onto an expansive arcaded patio that overlooks a formal garden and emerald lawn, as well as views of the golf course, the Livermore hills and Mt. Diablo.

The patio also overlooks a stunning oval terrace that's custom-made for al fresco ceremonies and receptions. Paved with smooth Napa Valley stone and enclosed by two wisteria-covered trellises, the terrace feels intimate despite the fact that it's completely open to the sky, the breeze and panoramic vistas.

The effort that has gone into making Ruby Hill Golf Club a showplace is evident in unexpected places, too. The women's lounge (and carpeted "locker room") is practically palatial, not only in size but in amenities such as elaborately tiled bathrooms with gorgeous granite counters, plush seating and mirrors everywhere. Even the telephone booths are refined private nooks with their own doors, granite counters and art on the wall!

This is a glorious spot for any upscale affair or holiday party. And if you're interested in a corporate golf tournament, Ruby Hill Golf Club has the first Jack Nicklaus-designed golf course in Northern California. The clubhouse was built to exacting standards so you'd feel right at home. We're quite sure you will.

CEREMONY CAPACITY: The Fireside Room holds 200 seated, and the Terrace 250 seated.

EVENT/RECEPTION CAPACITY: The Main Dining Room accommodates 200 seated or 350 standing. The Main Dining Room in conjunction with the adjoining outdoor patio can accommodate 300 seated. The Terrace holds 250 seated or 300 standing guests.

MEETING CAPACITY: Several spaces accommodate 8–45 seated guests.

FEES & DEPOSITS: A $3,000 nonrefundable deposit is required to reserve your date. The estimated food and beverage total is due 1 month prior to the event. Meals range $40–50/person; tax, alcohol and a 20% service charge are additional. Customized menus available.

AVAILABILITY: Year-round.

SERVICES/AMENITIES:

Catering: provided, no BYO
Kitchen Facilities: n/a
Tables & Chairs: provided
Linens, Silver, etc.: provided
Restrooms: wheelchair accessible
Dance Floor: yes
Bride's & Groom's Dressing Rooms: yes
Meeting Equipment: CBA, extra charge
Other: full event and day-of coordination

Parking: large lot and valet
Accommodations: no guest rooms; hotels nearby with complimentary shuttle service
Telephone: emergency use only
Outdoor Night Lighting: yes
Outdoor Cooking Facilities: yes
Cleanup: provided
View: vineyards, Jack Nicklaus Golf Course

RESTRICTIONS:

Alcohol: provided, or corkage $15/bottle
Smoking: outside only
Music: amplified OK with restrictions

Wheelchair Access: yes
Insurance: not required
Other: no rice, birdseed or glitter

Overwhelmed? Use the search criteria on www.HereComesTheGuide.com to narrow down your choices.

365

Elliston Vineyards

Winery

463 Kilkare Road, Sunol
925/862-2377
www.elliston.com
info@elliston.com

● Rehearsal Dinners	● Corp. Events/Mtgs.
● Ceremonies	● Private Parties
● Wedding Receptions	Accommodations

When gold rush pioneer Henry Ellis carved out an estate for himself in 1890, he picked a prime setting: a sheltered canyon tucked between two tree-covered ridges. Here he set up house in a three-story mansion constructed of thick sandstone from nearby Niles Canyon, and went about enjoying life in the country. Today his lovely homestead, now surrounded by vineyards, has become a prime setting for hosting weddings, receptions and private parties.

Garden-style ceremonies are held outdoors alongside the historic mansion, in a garden brimming with native flora and including an expansive lawn and arbor. Stage your photos here, and you'll have some striking options for a backdrop—the century-old stone house, vibrant displays of azaleas and camellias and sprawling vineyards. But if you'd like to search for more photographic possibilities, go right ahead—there are plenty of photo opportunities at Elliston.

A short walkway takes you from the garden to the Terrace Room, a secluded 2,000-square-foot banquet room set into the hillside. Its vaulted ceiling and glass walls add to the feeling of spaciousness, while the surrounding deck gives guests a chance to dine al fresco at umbrella-shaded tables. A Victorian gazebo next to the deck is large enough for a bridal table or a quartet of musicians to serenade partygoers. The entire site is sheltered by oak, eucalyptus and olive trees, creating an ideal venue for you and your guests to celebrate.

Whether you're a bride planning your wedding or a wine aficionado, Elliston Vineyards is a destination worth seeking. Centrally located, with access from several East Bay freeways, you're close to civilization but you'd never know it—the quiet country atmosphere will give you the delicious feeling of being a million miles away.

CEREMONY CAPACITY: Outdoors, the South Lawn holds 225 seated; indoors the Terrace Room can accommodate 125 seated guests.

EVENT/RECEPTION CAPACITY: The Terrace Room and adjoining deck seat 225 guests, with 125 guests seated indoors and 100 guests seated outdoors.

MEETING CAPACITY: The facility accommodates up to 150 seated guests.

FEES & DEPOSITS: A nonrefundable $2,000 deposit is required when reservations are confirmed. 50% of the estimated event total is due 6 months prior to your function, with additional 25% payment due 2 months prior to the event. The remaining balance, with a confirmed guest count, is due 2 weeks prior to the event. Event minimums may apply. Minimums include meals, beverages, facility fees, service charge and tax. The actual cost will depend on the menu and beverage package selected, and guest count. Three-course luncheon and dinner menus, including hors d'oeuvres, start at $42/person; buffets start at $39/person and require a 50-person minimum.

For meetings and conferences, a nonrefundable $500 deposit is required when reservations are confirmed. Room fees range $500–750. Minimums may apply. Continental breakfast, full lunch and afternoon snack run $44/person.

AVAILABILITY: Year-round, daily.

SERVICES/AMENITIES:

Catering: provided
Kitchen Facilities: n/a
Tables & Chairs: provided
Linens, Silver, etc.: provided
Restrooms: wheelchair accessible
Dance Floor: yes
Bride's Dressing Area: yes
Meeting Equipment: A/V, overhead projector, screen, flip charts, podium, DVD/VCR and monitor, extra charge

Parking: large lot, parking attendants
Accommodations: no guest rooms
Telephone: office phone
Outdoor Night Lighting: yes
Outdoor Cooking Facilities: no
Cleanup: provided
View: vineyards and hills
Other: event planning and day-of coordination

RESTRICTIONS:

Alcohol: wine, beer or champagne provided, no BYO
Smoking: outside only
Music: amplified OK inside only

Wheelchair Access: yes
Insurance: not required
Other: no rice, birdseed or confetti

Sunol Valley Golf Club

Golf Club

6900 Mission Road, Sunol
925/862-2408

www.sunolvalley.com
catering@sunolvalley.com

- Rehearsal Dinners
- Ceremonies
- Wedding Receptions
- Corp. Events/Mtgs.
- Private Parties
- Accommodations

Set against a sun-drenched backdrop of rolling hills and a wide-open sky, the Sunol Valley Golf Club displays an abundance of beauty and style that discerning brides will love. Outstanding vistas, which blend artful landscaping with the area's natural rural charm, distinguish the property. It's as private and pristine as an island paradise—only this island paradise has topnotch amenities and it's perfectly groomed.

Couples usually exchange vows on a lawn next to the golf course. Graceful palm trees preside over the ceremony, and the palm-dotted fairways spread all the way to the distant hills, making you and your guests feel like you're in the middle of an oasis.

Afterwards, host a reception in your choice of banquet rooms, all of which convey an easy, country-club elegance. The attractively appointed Coronado Room, with its built-in bar, corner stage and chandeliers, comfortably seats around 220 and boasts one of the largest permanent dance floors in the valley. Sunlight streams in through windowed walls that open onto a deck that looks out over the surrounding hills. Larger parties spill into the Pavilion Room, with more floor-to-ceiling windows, balconies and a breathtaking view of the velvety greens, ponds and palms of the links. This captivating setting also works well for an indoor ceremony, and a private bride's changing room is provided.

Just outside the Pavilion Room, the Mediterranean Room, with its lobby-like length and appeal, is a welcoming prefunction space and a super spot for guests to mingle and meet over drinks, buffet service or passed hors d'oeuvres.

The Mission Room, though smaller than the Coronado and Pavilion Rooms, has the same clubby feel. Floored in slate and a tasteful taupe-colored carpet, it's dominated by a handsome granite bar and a spectacular outlook onto the course. The beamed ceiling, illuminated by chandeliers, enhances any nighttime event.

If low-key and lovely is a mood you prefer, the Garden Room downstairs is a cheerful enclave with private patio access, a large dance floor and a built-in bar. And if the golf course beckons, there's no need to resist. Book a tee time or ask the staff to coordinate a photo shoot out where the grass is perpetually greener.

CEREMONY CAPACITY: Indoors, the club holds up to 500 seated guests. Outdoors, the lawn area holds up to 250 seated guests.

EVENT/RECEPTION CAPACITY: The club accommodates up to 500 seated or 800 standing guests.

MEETING CAPACITY: The facility accommodates up to 500 seated guests.

FEES & DEPOSITS: A $1,000–3,000 deposit is required to reserve your date, and the balance is due 14 days prior to the event. Rental fees range $250–1,500 depending on space rented. Meals range $31–41/person. Tax, alcohol and a 20% service charge are additional.

AVAILABILITY: Year-round, daily, 7am–midnight.

SERVICES/AMENITIES:

Catering: provided
Kitchen Facilities: n/a
Tables & Chairs: provided
Linens, Silver, etc.: provided
Restrooms: wheelchair accessible
Dance Floor: yes
Bride's Dressing Area: yes
Meeting Equipment: CBA, extra charge

Parking: large lot
Accommodations: no guest rooms
Telephone: house phone
Outdoor Night Lighting: access only
Outdoor Cooking Facilities: no
Cleanup: provided
View: garden, fairways and hills
Other: event coordination

RESTRICTIONS:

Alcohol: provided
Smoking: outside only
Music: amplified OK indoors

Wheelchair Access: yes
Insurance: not required
Other: no rice, birdseed or confetti

East Bay

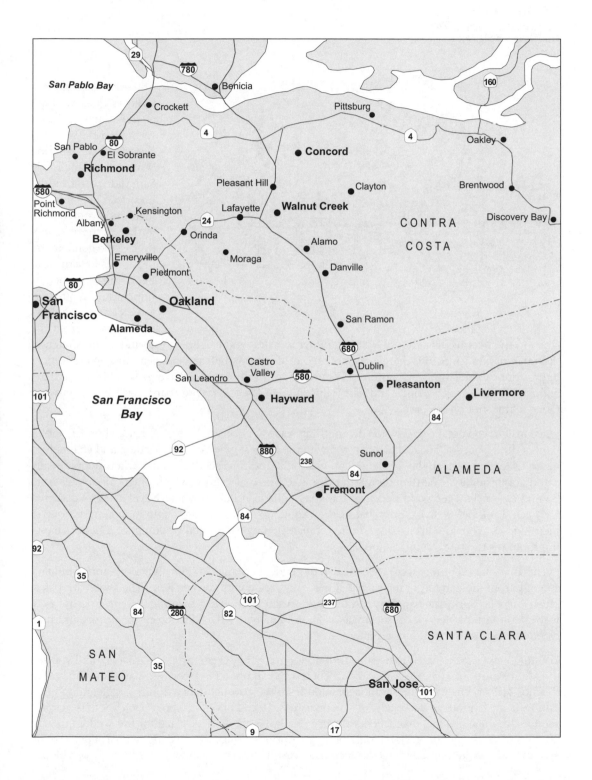

Albert H. DeWitt Officers' Club

Historic Officers' Club

641 West Red Line, Alameda
510/747-7529
www.cityofalamedaca.gov
arpd@ci.alameda.ca.us

- Rehearsal Dinners
- Corp. Events/Mtgs.
- Ceremonies
- Private Parties
- Wedding Receptions
- Accommodations

The Albert H. DeWitt Officers' Club was built at the Alameda Naval Air Station in 1941 when America was entering World War II, and Uncle Sam didn't stint on the luxuries. The military men and women who gathered here got a taste of the gentleman's life, and so can you. Even the entrance is imposing: A 40-foot-long canopy shelters the walkway from the street to the massive front doors. Walking under it makes you feel like a VIP, and it's no stretch of the imagination to picture the glamorous arrival of famous military, political and entertainment figures during the club's heyday. John F. Kennedy, for example, attended a gala in his honor here, and Lucille Ball, Henry Fonda and Van Johnson were fêted at a wrap party for *Yours, Mine and Ours,* a film shot on the base.

Once inside, you get the impression that nothing was too good for the Navy's elite. There are tables handcrafted from solid oak, chairs covered with the highest grade calfskin leather, and chandeliers made of leaded crystal; the Officers' Club was built and furnished in an era when people really cared about quality. And then there's the palpable sense of history, which practically oozes from behind every dark redwood panel. In the cozy Squadron Room, where Naval aviators gathered for a last drink before flying off to battle, their squadron insignia stare down in mute testimony to their heroics. You couldn't ask for a more intimate setting for a small wedding, or a better changing room for the bride at a large one.

Events that shaped history were conceived in the Trident Room next door. Officers planned military strategy from the comfort of the same leather wingback chairs you see here. The stately fireplace, plush carpets, dark oak paneling and antique crystal chandeliers give the Trident Room a rich, warm, comfortable feel—acoustically as well as visually. It's the ideal room for drinks and hors d'oeuvres before the wedding ceremony.

You might even be tempted to use the Trident Room for the ceremony itself—that is, until you see the Main Ballroom, which echoes the Trident Room's sumptuous décor, and has some innovative touches of its own. Along one wall, separated from the parquet dance floor by a gleaming brass railing, is a two-foot elevated platform with overstuffed leather booths. Above each booth is a crystal sconce that matches the chandeliers in every detail. It's the perfect place for the wedding party, family and guests of honor. To the right of the platform is a stage for the band, with a superb sound system and a large pull-down movie screen, in case you want to show slides, movies or videos.

If you're planning a smaller wedding and don't need the space of the Main Ballroom or the Trident Room, the Terrace Room, with its hand-painted floral motifs and green lattice work, provides a serene atmosphere. Or on sunny days, you can move outdoors into the lovely Terrace Garden for a ceremony al fresco.

The Officers' Club was built to provide rest and relaxation for America's fighting men and women. But now that times have changed, it's proving to be a much better place for love than it ever was for war.

CEREMONY CAPACITY: Outdoors, the Main Patio holds 300 or the Terrace Garden 200 seated; indoors, the Trident Room holds 225 seated.

EVENT/RECEPTION & MEETING CAPACITY: Individual spaces at the center can accommodate 30–250 seated or 50–450 standing indoors, and up to 200 seated or 400 standing outdoors. The entire facility holds 500 seated or 1,100 standing guests.

FEES & DEPOSITS: A $500 refundable cleaning and security deposit is required when reservations are made. For an outdoor ceremony, the setup fee is $150. Rental fees range $30–175/hour depending on the day of the week and room selected. The rental balance is payable 14 days prior to the event.

AVAILABILITY: Year-round, daily, except major holidays, 9am–midnight.

SERVICES/AMENITIES:

Catering: BYO caterer; contract and insurance required
Kitchen Facilities: n/a
Tables & Chairs: provided
Linens, Silver, etc.: BYO or caterer
Restrooms: wheelchair accessible
Dance Floor: parquet floor, portable and patio
Bride's & Groom's Dressing Areas: yes
Meeting Equipment: CBA, extra charge

Parking: large lots; complimentary parking
Accommodations: no guest rooms, CBA
Telephone: emergency use only
Outdoor Night Lighting: yes
Outdoor Cooking Facilities: no
Cleanup: renter or caterer
View: landscaped garden

RESTRICTIONS:

Alcohol: BYO; insurance required
Smoking: outside only
Music: amplified OK with volume limits; curfew 11pm weekdays, midnight Fri and Sat

Wheelchair Access: yes
Insurance: extra liability may be required
Other: no rice or confetti; decorations require approval

The professionals in the back of this book are the best in the business. How do we know? Read page 637.

Grandview Pavilion

Banquet & Special Event Center

300 Island Drive, Alameda
510/865-5322

www.grandviewpavilion.com
info@grandviewpavilion.com

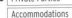

- Rehearsal Dinners
- Ceremonies
- Wedding Receptions
- Corp. Events/Mtgs.
- Private Parties
- Accommodations

Fairy tales begin in places like this. Set in the tranquil community of Harbor Bay on historic Bay Farm Island in Alameda, the perfectly picturesque Grandview Pavilion does seem almost too good to be true. The lovely ivy-covered Mediterranean-style building sits just at the edge of the championship 36-hole Chuck Corica Golf Course, far enough away from the main complex to maintain an aura of seclusion without sacrificing the lush tree-dotted green and fairway views.

There is a soft sheen to the handsome Spanish-style doors that open onto the elegantly tiled foyer and spacious Ballroom. Full-size French windows cover the facing wall, creating a backdrop of eucalyptus, pine trees and meticulously manicured lawns. The Edenic surroundings find their way inside in the luxuriant garden feel of the carpet's pale floral tones and the sunlit brilliance of the cream-colored walls and white crown moldings and trim. Coppered chandeliers hang from the airy coffered ceilings, and the built-in granite, copper and mahogany bar and service area has back-to-back access from either room.

It's a magnificent stage for any high-end social or corporate event, but weddings are truly exceptional here. In the Ballroom, enormous mirrors overlook the polished, hand-laid cherrywood dance floor, amplifying the area and the energy. There's even a professional DJ booth seamlessly tucked away behind one retractable mirror for clutter-free entertaining. If dancing isn't on the agenda, the dance floor is an ideal place to set up a dramatic serpentine table showcasing an exquisite food presentation.

Did we mention that all the food for this venue is provided by one of the Bay Area's top caterers? *Grand Catering* has been wowing clients with excellent service and delectable dining experiences for decades. Their offerings look and taste like works of art. Whether your plans are simple (French bistro, BBQ, California cuisine) or extravagant (Asian fusion, luau with full roast pig, mashed potato bar with martini glass service), the eats will be outstanding—a true feast for the eyes and palate.

As if this weren't enough, the facility has recently added a spectacular tri-peaked tent pavilion. When the weather's warm, its clear "walls" are opened to let in balmy breezes. During cooler months or for evening events, the pavilion can be enclosed and heated for guests' comfort. But no matter what the season, this venue provides a garden experience with views of the surrounding flowers, plants and golf course. If you have your ceremony in the Garden Tent Pavilion, a white trellis at one end serves as an arch. Two indoor fountains create their own soothing music, while chandeliers and twinkle lights add an enchanting sparkle.

There's even a beautiful room for the bride and her attendants with pink champagne walls, soft moss-colored carpeting and private restrooms with peach marble accents, but our guess is the ladies will spend little time there.

CEREMONY CAPACITY: The Garden Tent Pavilion holds up to 200 seated guests.

EVENT/RECEPTION & MEETING CAPACITY: The Ballroom holds up to 275 seated guests with a dance floor or 450 standing. The total seated capacity for a reception is 420. The Garden Tent Pavilion can accommodate up to 120 seated guests.

FEES & DEPOSITS: For weddings, the rental fee is required to reserve your date; the estimated event total is due 30 days prior to the event. Room rental fees range $1,600–3,800. Wedding reception food and beverage minumum is $35/person. Tax and a 20% service charge are additional.

For corporate meetings, room rental fees start at $200. Breakfast starts at $10/person, lunch at $18/person.

AVAILABILITY: Year-round, daily.

SERVICES/AMENITIES:

Catering: provided, no BYO
Kitchen Facilities: n/a
Tables & Chairs: provided
Linens, Silver, etc.: provided
Restrooms: wheelchair accessible
Dance Floor: yes
Bride's Dressing Area: provided
Meeting Equipment: full sound system, wireless mics, 2 LCD projectors, 2 built-in projection screens

Parking: large lot
Accommodations: no guest rooms
Telephone: emergency use only
Outdoor Night Lighting: yes
Outdoor Cooking Facilities: CBA
Cleanup: provided
View: golf course
Other: event coordination

RESTRICTIONS:

Alcohol: provided
Smoking: outdoors only
Music: amplified music indoors only, acoustic music outdoors OK

Wheelchair Access: yes
Insurance: not required

Oakland Yacht Club

Yacht Club

1101 Pacific Marina, Alameda
510/522-6868

www.oaklandyachtclub.com
emendes@oaklandyachtclub.com

● Rehearsal Dinners	● Corp. Events/Mtgs.
● Ceremonies	● Private Parties
● Wedding Receptions	Accommodations

Jack London would not recognize the place! The famous author-adventurer was a member of the Oakland Yacht Club in 1913, when access was by dinghy only and members tied up at wood pilings driven into the mud. Today, many decades and moves later, the organization's airy, well-appointed clubhouse occupies a quiet, park-like setting in a treelined Alameda neighborhood with a private 220-slip marina and views of the Oakland skyline and the Oakland/Alameda Estuary. There's no stress here. The atmosphere is relaxed, and the friendly staff will bend over backwards to make certain every aspect of your affair is shipshape.

Your guests will have plenty of parking and easy access to the two-story facility. Event spaces include the Regatta Room downstairs, with a built-in wet bar, big windows, a sheltered patio and excellent views of the marina and estuary where kayaks and sailboats drift by at eye level. It's perfect for small meetings and gatherings. Adjacent restrooms have showers, dressing areas and patio access.

For the main event, the Commodore's Hall upstairs is a gorgeous room with a view. Its pale blue hue mirrors the water and sky and fills the space with a pleasant sense of peace and possibility. Brightly colored burgees—the flags from yacht clubs with reciprocating privileges—festoon the walls near the entrance, where an ample vestibule houses a cloakroom that can double as gift storage.

Like the waters it rests beside, the room has a natural flow and a nautical feel. The floor-to-ceiling windows on its north side open onto a series of individual balconies, set with tables and chairs, that look down on the boats berthed in the marina below and out toward the East Bay hills and the dramatic Oakland skyline. On the far end of the hall, a built-in oak dance floor can serve as an indoor ceremony space, a stage, or a place to move to the music. A circular oak bar occupies the opposite end of the room. Sizable celebrations of every kind can be easily accommodated in the area in between and serviced from the club kitchen where a well-trained staff expertly prepares fine party fare. Add a podium for speakers and a pull-down screen and you have a room fit for any occasion. There's even a windowed alcove with city and sea vistas just right for framing the couple's first bite of cake.

The peaceful city park, situated between a tranquil lagoon and the picturesque marina, is an outdoor option for exchanging your wedding vows. OYC staff adds guest seating, flowers, an arch, chairs for your harpist or string quartet—whatever you want to personalize your special ritual. Nature provides the rest: live oaks, willow, birdsong and, of course, the spectacular estuary view.

Next door to the clubhouse, an attractive hotel makes visiting attendees' accommodation easy and offers additional venues for rehearsal dinners, brunches and other pre- and post-function mixers. Those with a boat may want to make use of the club's guest dock—it might be just the spot to park that getaway launch and set sail for the future.

CEREMONY CAPACITY: The facility holds 200 seated guests outdoors.

EVENT/RECEPTION CAPACITY: Indoors, the club can accommodate 200 seated without a dance floor, 170 with a dance floor, or 225 standing guests.

MEETING CAPACITY: The club holds 200 seated.

FEES & DEPOSITS: The rental fee is required to reserve your date. 90% of the estimated event total is due 10 days prior to the event, the balance is due on the day of the event. Rental fees range $150–500 depending on the space and time rented. Meals range $7.50–40/person. Tax, alcohol and a 20% service charge are additional.

AVAILABILITY: Year-round, Tuesday–Sunday, 9am–11pm. Times vary depending on already scheduled member events.

SERVICES/AMENITIES:
Catering: provided
Kitchen Facilities: n/a
Tables & Chairs: provided
Linens, Silver, etc.: provided
Restrooms: wheelchair accessible
Dance Floor: provided
Bride's Dressing Area: yes
Meeting Equipment: some provided
Other: grand piano, picnic area, A/V equipment, event coordination

Parking: large lot
Accommodations: no guest rooms
Telephone: emergency use only
Outdoor Night Lighting: CBA
Outdoor Cooking Facilities: no
Cleanup: provided
View: panorama of ocean/bay and coastline

RESTRICTIONS:
Alcohol: provided, or BYO wine with corkage fee
Smoking: not allowed
Music: amplified OK with restrictions

Wheelchair Access: yes
Insurance: liability required

Round Hill Country Club

Country Club

3169 Round Hill Road, Alamo
925/934-8211

www.rhcountryclub.com
heathera@roundhillcc.org
rachelj@roundhillcc.org

● Rehearsal Dinners	● Corp. Events/Mtgs.
● Ceremonies	● Private Parties
● Wedding Receptions	Accommodations

Set atop a gentle rise, the clubhouse at Round Hill Country Club presides over a sun-dappled golf course amidst the rolling hills of the exclusive community of Alamo. Conveniently located and secluded, the venue has been a favorite site for social and corporate events for decades. And although this is a private club, its beautiful facilities are available to nonmembers.

With four distinctly different interior event areas, an expansive patio and a Wedding Terrace, Round Hill offers many options for choreographing your celebration. Another plus are their in-house Event Directors, who will help you organize all the details. Flexibility is key at the club, and they rarely say "no" to requests.

Couples usually exchange vows outdoors on the Wedding Terrace, an intimate space that seems to embrace everyone in it. Umbrellas can be provided to shade guests from the sun, but they'll still have a clear view of the postcard-perfect backdrop: the 18th green and the picturesque Alamo hills.

Formal affairs are often held in the Vista Ballroom, adorned with mirrors that enhance the feeling of spaciousness. A series of arched windows look out onto the Breezeway, a light-filled prefunction space that extends the entire length of the ballroom. As friends and family mingle over cocktails here, they have a view of the outdoor pool area. In the adjoining Living Room, guests can take a break from the festivities by relaxing on comfortable sofas in a homey atmosphere. These three areas work extremely well together, and create a wonderful flow to an event.

For something less formal but equally appealing, consider the casual elegance of the Fairway Grill & Lounge. Dining is hosted in the Grill, designed with an exceptionally high, open-beamed ceiling outfitted with polished brass chandeliers. On one side of the room, a fire blazing in the cast stone fireplace lends a cozy warmth, while on the other side floor-to-ceiling windows overlook manicured golf greens and the Fairway Patio. The Lounge, with its built-in bar, is also where the dance floor is set up. Guests appreciate the easy access from the Grill & Lounge to the patio, which serves as a lovely spot for dining overflow or al fresco cocktails.

The President's Room is ideal for small events and is often used in combination with the Ballroom and/or the Grill & Lounge. It's popular for rehearsal dinners and anniversary parties—some groups have even used it for a casino games evening! When the weather turns cool, it also doubles as an indoor ceremony site.

Hosting your event at Round Hill is like inviting guests to enjoy your own private villa. For the day at least, they can indulge in the privileges and amenities of this prestigious country club.

CEREMONY CAPACITY: The President's Room holds 200 seated guests. The outdoor wedding site accommodates 200 guests

EVENT/RECEPTION CAPACITY: The Vista Ballroom accommodates 300 seated or 400 standing guests, and the Fairway Grill 160 seated or 200 standing. The President's Room holds up to 100 seated or 120 standing guests, and can be divided into 2 smaller spaces that each hold 50 seated or 60 standing guests.

MEETING CAPACITY: The Vista Ballroom holds 400 guests seated theater-style or 150 classroom-style; the President's Room 200 guests seated theater-style or 64 classroom-style.

FEES & DEPOSITS: A $2,000 deposit is required to reserve your date; the balance is due 14 days prior to the event. Room rental fees range $200–2,000 depending on space rented. Luncheons range $15–25/person, dinners $35–50/person. Tax, alcohol and a 20% service charge are additional. A $600–1,000 ceremony setup fee is extra.

AVAILABILITY: Year-round, daily, 6am–1am.

SERVICES/AMENITIES:

Catering: provided, no BYO

Kitchen Facilities: n/a

Tables & Chairs: provided

Linens, Silver, etc.: provided

Restrooms: wheelchair accessible

Dance Floor: parquet floor

Bride's & Groom's Dressing Areas: CBA

Meeting Equipment: CBA, extra charge

Parking: valet required, extra charge

Accommodations: no guest rooms

Telephone: emergency use only

Outdoor Night Lighting: yes

Outdoor Cooking Facilities: CBA

Cleanup: provided

View: pool, rolling hills, trees, golf course

Other: event coordination

RESTRICTIONS:

Alcohol: provided or wine and champagne corkage $15/bottle

Smoking: outside only

Music: amplified OK indoors

Wheelchair Access: yes

Insurance: not required

Other: no rice, confetti or birdseed

Want to know WHAT TO ASK a potential location or vendor? Check out our Questions to Ask starting on page 17.

Bancroft Hotel

2680 Bancroft Way, Berkeley
510/549-0113
www.bancrofthotel.com
kelly@bancrofthotel.com

Boutique Hotel

● Rehearsal Dinners	● Corp. Events/Mtgs.
● Ceremonies	● Private Parties
● Wedding Receptions	● Accommodations

Housed in a historic landmark building across the street from the University of California and next door to the Berkeley Art Museum, the Bancroft Hotel has become one of the premier hotels in the East Bay. Originally built in 1928 as the home of the College Women's Club, it was designed by Walter T. Steilberg, an associate of architect Julia Morgan (of Hearst Castle fame).

After a complete renovation of the property, the Bancroft Hotel had its much-acclaimed grand opening in 1994. Guests admired the handsome public spaces, graced with antiques, vintage-style furniture and period reproductions; furnishings in the Bancroft's 22 beautifully appointed guest rooms were reproduced from Walter Steilberg's original drawings, and many of the rooms are enhanced with balconies and views of the bay. There's an ambiance of timeless elegance, and whether you're dreaming of a celebration with an air of romantic nostalgia or quiet refinement, the Bancroft Hotel is an absolute must-see.

Most receptions unfold in the Great Hall, a glamorous event space inspired by the turn-of-the-century Arts and Crafts movement. This one-of-a-kind 4,000-square-foot room is lavished with floor-to-ceiling woodwork, period fixtures and stained-glass transoms. Gleaming hardwood floors and lofty ceilings add to the sense of tradition and grandeur, and two giant fireplaces provide warmth and atmosphere. The Hall actually has three distinct sections, which can be used for different aspects of your event. The raised hardwood stage at one end can hold musicians, a dance floor or the head table, while the recessed middle section can be transformed into an intimate dining space. Use the other end for additional reception seating, or for a buffet and bar setup. The Great Hall is not only spacious, but also extremely flexible—you could arrange your party in a variety of ways and still have it work fabulously.

The light and bright Steilberg Conference Room is distinguished by pale, gently curving walls and a magnificent fireplace trimmed in tile and rich mahogany. Windows at one end frame a pleasing view of the city and a slice of the San Francisco Bay in the distance. Another way to savor the vista is to sneak away to the Rooftop Terrace and share a champagne toast with your sweetie.

The Bancroft Hotel does have comfortable and attractive accommodations for your out-of-town relatives and friends—but why not reserve the entire boutique hotel exclusively for you and your guests for a destination weekend? A complete buyout gets you all the event spaces, guest rooms—even the parking lot! In fact, *Bancroft Catering* can customize all your meals to your liking throughout your stay, so you never really have to leave the hotel at all.

If you plan on "going green" for your wedding, then you'll appreciate the Bancroft's environmentally safe cleaning products, luxurious bamboo towels, organic linens and other "green" amenities. Eco-weddings are a specialty, and the in-house culinary team offers earth-friendly tableware alternatives and organic menus. In 2011 all the guest rooms were renovated, and the lobby was redone, too. Check out its new look, featuring custom-designed, recycled tile and American clay walls.

Whether you're hosting a large bash or a cozy gathering, the Bancroft Hotel is a distinctive indoor wedding site with a conveniently located, yet very serene environment.

CEREMONY CAPACITY: Indoors, up to 250 seated guests. Three tiered sections in the Great Hall available for smaller groups to have more intimate gatherings.

EVENT/RECEPTION CAPACITY: The facility holds 175–250 seated guests (depending on whether or not a dance floor is required), or 300 for a standing reception.

MEETING CAPACITY: The hotel accommodates 250 seated theater-style.

FEES & DEPOSITS: To secure your date, the entire rental fee is required as a deposit when you sign your contract. The rental fee runs $800–2,000 and varies depending on the season and day of week. The entire hotel is available for a buyout. Luncheons start at $19/person, dinners at $36/person. Tax, alcohol and service charge are additional.

AVAILABILITY: Year-round, daily, anytime.

SERVICES/AMENITIES:

Catering: provided
Kitchen Facilities: n/a
Tables & Chairs: provided
Linens, Silver, etc.: CBA, extra charge
Restrooms: wheelchair accessible
Dance Floor: provided
Bride's Dressing Area: CBA
Meeting Equipment: banquet tables, flip charts, extra fee for TV/VCR and overhead projector

Parking: adjacent lot or valet CBA
Accommodations: 22 guest rooms
Telephone: emergency use only
Outdoor Night Lighting: CBA
Outdoor Cooking Facilities: no
Cleanup: provided
View: SF Bay and Berkeley hills
Other: event coordination available

RESTRICTIONS:

Alcohol: provided
Smoking: not allowed
Music: amplified OK until 10:30pm unless all guest rooms are booked by client

Wheelchair Access: event space only
Insurance: not required

Berkeley City Club

2315 Durant Avenue, Berkeley
510/280-1532

www.berkeleycityclub.com
events@berkeleycityclub.com

Historic Hotel and Social Club

● Rehearsal Dinners	● Corp. Events/Mtgs.
● Ceremonies	● Private Parties
● Wedding Receptions	Accommodations

The Berkeley City Club, located just one block from the UC Berkeley campus, is a sensational landmark building and a proud member of Historic Hotels of America®. Although it's long been a private member social club, its hotel and event facilities welcome the public.

Designed in 1929 by famed architect Julia Morgan, the popular venue is like a miniature Hearst Castle. The Moorish Gothic-style building features landscaped inner courtyards and fountains, plus a wealth of graceful arches, domed ceilings, pillars, leaded-glass windows and doors, and art. Together they create a gorgeous backdrop for your wedding—and your photos!

The detailing and craftsmanship are impressive throughout. The Drawing Room and Members' Lounge are large and gracious, with beamed ceilings, pianos, fireplaces, wall tapestries, tiled floors, Oriental carpets and sizable leaded-glass windows. The Ballroom, which has a stage, parquet floor, concert grand piano, and its own leaded-glass windows overlooking the courtyard, also has plenty of room for dancing along with your reception. For an outdoor affair, the sheltered, ivy-covered Terrace is a wonderful spot on a warm day or evening. Many of these event spaces are connected to one another, and can be used individually or in combination.

The Camelia Courtyard is perfect for an intimate ceremony or cocktail reception. Filled with greenery and framed by the building's arches, it's evocative of a Mediterranean garden. A smaller, lushly planted fountain courtyard on the opposite side of the club lends itself to a cozy luncheon or rehearsal dinner. Even if you don't host an event in one of these courtyards, you'll definitely want to take advantage of their photogenic qualities for your wedding album.

Many couples like to host both their ceremony and reception here: The club's soaring architecture and private, contemplative areas provide a spiritual atmosphere for exchanging vows; at the same time, the versatile reception facilities and experienced staff ensure a flawless event.

Speaking of flawless, the club's hair salon and esthetician services make it easy for you and your bridesmaids to look and feel your best for the wedding. Whether you arrive the day before or the day of, you'll be able to relax while the on-site professionals take you from stressed to beautiful.

The Berkeley City Club is a tranquil oasis in this bustling college town. Family and friends who stay overnight will appreciate the newly renovated guest rooms, all of which offer outstanding views of the San Francisco Bay or Berkeley hills. Hotel guests also have special privileges: They can take a dip in the magnificent swimming pool, enjoy the Dining Room's outstanding cuisine, and sample premier wines in the Venetian Room. From this conveniently located getaway, exploring Berkeley couldn't be easier: Famed Telegraph Avenue, museums, restaurants, the Theater District and public transit are all close by.

CEREMONY, EVENT/RECEPTION CAPACITY: Event spaces hold 14–260 seated guests. The Venetian Ballrooom holds up to 350 standing guests.

MEETING CAPACITY: The Berkeley City Club has 5 meeting rooms that accommodate up to 280 seated theater-style or 125 seated classroom-style.

FEES & DEPOSITS: A $1,200 nonrefundable rental deposit is required when the reservation is confirmed; the balance and a final guest count are due prior to the function. Rental fees range $500–3,000 depending on space or day selected. For a separate bar setup, a bartender fee will apply. On weekdays, luncheons begin at $28/person, and dinners at $45/person. Menus and event details can be arranged with the event coordinator. If your group would like to stay overnight, bed and breakfast rates will apply. Call for more information.

AVAILABILITY: Year-round, Tuesday–Friday, 8am–11pm; Saturday–Sunday, 9am–11pm. Closed Thanksgiving, Christmas and New Year's Day.

SERVICES/AMENITIES:

Catering: provided, no BYO
Kitchen Facilities: n/a
Tables & Chairs: provided
Linens, Silver, etc.: provided
Restrooms: wheelchair accessible
Dance Floor: yes
Bride's Dressing Area: yes
Meeting Equipment: full range CBA

Parking: small lot, valet or prepaid CBA
Accommodations: 35 guest rooms
Telephone: pay and guest phones
Outdoor Night Lighting: yes
Outdoor Cooking Facilities: BBQ CBA
Cleanup: provided
View: indoor courtyards
Other: event coordinator, candelabras, fireplaces, pianos; complimentary amenities for overnight guests include a hot breakfast buffet

RESTRICTIONS:

Alcohol: provided, no BYO
Smoking: not allowed
Music: amplified OK until 11pm

Wheelchair Access: yes
Insurance: sometimes required
Other: security sometimes required

Brazilian Room

Historic Banquet Facility

Tilden Park, Berkeley (operated by East Bay Regional Parks)
510/544-3164
www.brazilianroom.org
brazil@ebparks.org

- Rehearsal Dinners   • Corp. Events/Mtgs.
- Ceremonies   • Private Parties
- Wedding Receptions   Accommodations

High in the hills of North Berkeley lies Tilden Park, popularly considered "the Jewel of the East Bay." Hiking trails with names like Seaview or Skyline wind past creeks, mineral springs, and sylvan meadows, up to the sweeping panorama offered at Inspiration Point. Just about every vista in Tilden Park is inspirational. Encompassing the Tilden Nature Area, most of the park's 2,077 acres serve as tranquil shelters for native plants and wildlife. Rangers here are serious about preserving this magnificent habitat—they even close one of their roads seasonally to protect migrating newts—and the result is a cornucopia of natural beauty. Visitors also enjoy the abundance of recreational activities, including steam trains, a golf course, and an antique merry-go-round. For generations of Bay Area residents, outings to Tilden Park have been part of a happy tradition, beginning with a youngster's first pony ride and perhaps culminating in a wedding ceremony at the historic Brazilian Room.

Once part of the 1939 Golden Gate Exposition on Treasure Island, the Brazilian Room was presented as a gift to the East Bay Regional Park District by the country of Brazil. The original interior hardwood paneling was kept intact, while a new exterior of local rock and timber was constructed by the Works Project Administration to permanently house the room.

To reach the Brazilian Room, follow Grizzly Peak Boulevard to Wildcat Canyon Road, and behold a cascading glen dotted with thick stands of fragrant pine, oak, and eucalyptus. Add to this scene a building of remarkable architectural achievement with its own beautiful garden, and you have a striking location for any celebration.

Wedding ceremonies are extremely popular on the flagstone patio, with its dramatic panorama of sloping lawn and tree-studded hillsides. After toasting the newlyweds, guests can sip their champagne among the colorful mix of lavender, foxglove, breath of heaven, and other flowers that make up the small garden adjoining the patio, or sample hors d'oeuvres under the cherry tree, abloom in April with perfumey-pink blossoms.

The setting at the Brazilian Room is just as lovely indoors as out. The building's Old English-style façade is defined by a trio of leaded-glass doors, each with dormer-style threshold. When guests move inside for the reception, they'll find that floor-to-ceiling leaded-glass windows that run along both sides of the hall. The rear windows offer a close-up look at the forest, evoking the romance of a light-filled mountain cabin. Dark wooden beams create a novel pattern on the ceiling, and polished wood flooring and a huge stone fireplace give the space additional rustic charm.

The serene pastoral surroundings at the Brazilian Room offer an environment free from noise and distraction, where nature's gifts are honored and preserved and the modern world is in harmony with the building's heritage. It's a place you'll want to make part of your own family tradition.

CEREMONY CAPACITY: The patio holds 180 seated; the main room, up to 150 seated or 225 standing guests.

EVENT/RECEPTION CAPACITY: The main room holds 225 standing guests or 150 seated.

MEETING CAPACITY: The main room accommodates 150 seated conference-style or 225 seated theater-style.

FEES & DEPOSITS: A $300 deposit is required to secure your date. If cancelled more than 120 days prior to the event, $100 of this deposit is refundable. For a 12-hour block, a $600 deposit is required. $200 is refundable if cancellation is made more than 120 days prior to the event. Signed contracts are required 2 weeks after the initial deposit, the fee balance and cleaning & damage deposits are due 120 days prior to the event date. For events reserved fewer than 120 days away, the entire rental balance and all deposits are due when the contract is signed.

Weekend rates for Friday night, Saturday, Sunday and holidays (min. 7 hours) range $1,900–3,800 depending on the day and time frame reserved. Weekday rates range $300–750 depending on day and length of time rented. The seasonal Sunday rate November through March is $1,900 for a 7-hour block, 9am–midnight; each additional hour is $250. For nonresidents of Alameda and Contra Costa counties, there is a surcharge that equals 20% of the room rental fee. Optional services are available at an extra charge. NOTE: This fee information is for 2012. For current prices visit www.brazilianroom.org.

AVAILABILITY: Saturday, Sunday and holidays 9am–4pm or 5pm–midnight; Friday evening 5pm–midnight; Friday day 8am–4pm; Monday, Wednesday, Thursday 8am–midnight; Sunday, November through March 9am–midnight.

SERVICES/AMENITIES:

Catering: select from preferred list
Kitchen Facilities: ample
Tables & Chairs: provided
Linens, Silver, etc.: BYO
Restrooms: wheelchair accessible
Dance Floor: yes
Bride's Dressing Area: yes
Meeting Equipment: PA, projector and screen, microphones, extra fee

Parking: in lot, no fees
Accommodations: no guest rooms
Telephone: pay phone
Outdoor Night Lighting: yes
Outdoor Cooking Facilities: yes
Cleanup: caterer
View: great views of Tilden Park with lots of trees and relative privacy
Other: fireplace available, extra fee

RESTRICTIONS:

Alcohol: BYO; wine, beer or champagne only, kegs of beer restricted to patio and kitchen
Smoking: outside only
Music: amplified OK indoors, outdoors with restrictions

Wheelchair Access: yes
Insurance: extra liability is required
Other: decorations restricted

Want to find more venues and services? Check out our informative website, www.HereComesTheGuide.com.

385

Claremont Hotel Club and Spa

Landmark Hotel

41 Tunnel Road, Berkeley
510/549-8591
www.claremont-hotel.com
catering@claremont-hotel.com

● Rehearsal Dinners	● Corp. Events/Mtgs.	
● Ceremonies	● Private Parties	
● Wedding Receptions	● Accommodations	

The brilliant white, castle-like Claremont Hotel Club & Spa has been a Bay Area landmark since 1915 when it debuted. Spread over 22 acres, the hotel is set high in the Berkeley Hills and commands one of the best views in the Bay Area. Along with its panoramic vista, the hotel's grand design, fragrant rose gardens and luxurious amenities have made it a perennial favorite, drawing admirers from around the globe. A long list of presidents, Hollywood stars and other famous guests have stayed here. Among them was architect Frank Lloyd Wright, who proclaimed the Claremont "one of the few hotels in the world with warmth, character and charm." We tend to agree. After all, could the esteemed Mr. Wright be wrong?

The Claremont's assets have also made it a sought-after locale for weddings. Couples can host their entire event here, from a rehearsal dinner at the Meritage at the Claremont to a sublime honeymoon in a grand suite. A variety of ballrooms—each one with its own distinctive ambiance—accommodate groups of every size, from an intimate gathering to a gala reception. In the Horizon Room, warm tones and vintage crystal chandeliers create a delicate, timeless elegance—and the panoramic view from the wall of west-facing windows encompasses both bridges and the San Francisco skyline. The adjacent Lanai Room is a lovely indoor ceremony space and comes complete with an outdoor balcony for great photo opportunities.

The Claremont also boasts a 20,000-square-foot fitness center, Pilates studio, and lap pool. You'll definitely want to spend some time being pampered at Spa Claremont, which offers wedding packages that include facials, hairstyling, manicures, pedicures and makeup application, ensuring that you'll be picture-perfect on your wedding day.

Planning your event here is stress-free, thanks to a team of wedding experts who will guide you through every decision and take care of all the details. And when you're ready to wind down after the festivities, you'll find an atmosphere of relaxation in the Claremont's guest rooms. All feature plush bathrobes and slippers, cable TV, video-game consoles and high-speed internet access. Many also provide exceptional views of San Francisco Bay.

Conceived as an English estate, this historic hotel and grounds have surrounded guests with elegance, sophistication and charm for nearly a century. So, whether you come here to get married in style or simply enjoy a delectable dinner for two, the Claremont is a peaceful and romantic retreat from the world.

CEREMONY CAPACITY: Indoor spaces hold 20–300 seated; outdoor spaces up to 150 seated guests.

EVENT/RECEPTION CAPACITY: The largest ballroom accommodates 300 seated with dancing, 360 seated without, or 500 standing for a cocktail reception. Capacities for the 20 other rooms range 10–350 seated guests.

MEETING CAPACITY: There are 20 rooms that hold 20–400 seated theater-style, 30–275 classroom-style, or 8–60 conference-style.

FEES & DEPOSITS: For special events and weddings, a $2,500 nonrefundable deposit is required to hold your date. Half of the total estimated bill is due 4 months prior to the event; the balance is due 7 days prior to the event.

Wedding packages are available starting at $160/person, and include champagne reception, dinner served with dinner wines, wedding cake, tax and service charges. Any menu or package can be customized. There is a $1,500–2,000 ballroom or outdoor ceremony rental fee. Facilities are also available for rehearsal, day-after wedding brunch, and the hotel offers reduced pricing for overnight guest rooms.

Fees for business functions and meetings vary depending on room(s) and services selected. Corporate day meeting packages are available; call for specific pricing.

AVAILABILITY: Year-round, daily, 6am–midnight.

SERVICES/AMENITIES:

Catering: provided, no BYO
Kitchen Facilities: n/a
Tables & Chairs: provided
Linens, Silver, etc.: provided
Restrooms: wheelchair accessible
Dance Floor: provided
Bride's & Groom's Dressing Areas: CBA
Meeting Equipment: full range A/V
Other: event coordination, spa, fitness center

Parking: self-parking and valet
Accommodations: 279 guest rooms
Telephone: guest phones
Outdoor Night Lighting: access only
Outdoor Cooking Facilities: BBQ
Cleanup: provided
View: entire East Bay and San Francisco Bay plus San Francisco skyline

RESTRICTIONS:

Alcohol: provided, or corkage $25/bottle
Smoking: outdoors only
Music: amplified OK indoors only

Wheelchair Access: yes
Insurance: required

The Faculty Club

University of California at Berkeley
510/643-0834
www.berkeleyfacultyclub.com
info@berkeleyfacultyclub.com

Historic Campus Club

● Rehearsal Dinners	● Corp. Events/Mtgs.
● Ceremonies	● Private Parties
● Wedding Receptions	● Accommodations

UC Berkeley has many picturesque settings, but the loveliest one may well be that of the Faculty Club. Located in the heart of campus, it's quietly ensconced in a grove of redwoods, oaks and maples next to meandering Strawberry Creek. Built in 1902 by the renowned architect Bernard Maybeck in traditional Arts and Crafts style, it's designed to create a cozy, intimate feeling.

The crowning glory of the club is the three-story Great Hall. With its vaulted ceiling, massive stone fireplace, and stained-glass windows featuring heraldic crests of the great universities of the world, it's reminiscent of many a European cathedral. Light from the floor-to-ceiling windows warms the redwood paneling and suffuses the Hall in a golden glow.

Two charming smaller spaces are also available for functions. The Heyns and Seaborg rooms (named respectively after a chancellor and a distinguished University Nobel Laureate) both have French doors leading to a private outdoor area with a garden view. The Seaborg Room is especially striking, with its open-beamed A-frame ceiling and wisteria-framed windows overlooking the peaceful Faculty Glade Lawn.

The Faculty Club has long been a favorite site for meetings, bar and bat mitzvahs, anniversary parties, class reunions, retreats and retirement dinners. But it really comes into its own during weddings. Many couples like to have the ceremony right outside on the Faculty Glade Lawn, then move into the Great Hall for the wedding feast. (The Heyns and Seaborg Rooms also have private terraces for al fresco ceremonies.) Aside from the building itself, the staff is the Faculty Club's greatest asset. They've been producing events since 1902, and they're experienced at accommodating a wide range of special requests. Do any of your guests have particular dietary needs? The Faculty Club can provide gluten-free, vegetarian or vegan dishes. For the ultimate in convenience, your family and friends are welcome to stay overnight in the club's hotel bedrooms (which are often reserved for visiting scholars). From these comfortable lodgings, it's just a quick walk down the stairs to the ceremony. Also, if the bride needs a room for changing, or for storing flowers or gifts, the club will provide one.

The Faculty Club's full catering service handles all the food and beverages—including the bar—and they offer menus for every type of event, from a brunch buffet to a formal sit-down dinner. Their catering staff hails from all over the world, and can create authentic cuisine from many countries including India, Mexico, Peru, Greece and Spain. The Faculty Club has been serving its members and guests for over 100 years, and will do everything possible to make your event successful and enjoyable.

CEREMONY CAPACITY: The Faculty Glade holds 250 seated guests; indoor spaces hold up to 200 seated.

EVENT/RECEPTION CAPACITY: The Great Hall holds 200 seated or 300 standing for a cocktail party.

MEETING CAPACITY: The club can accommodate 300 guests seated theater-style.

FEES & DEPOSITS: The room rental fee is required as a nonrefundable deposit to secure your date; the event balance is due 14 days prior to the event. Catering is provided; meal prices range $18–65/person; beverages, alcohol, tax and a 20% service charge are additional.

AVAILABILITY: Year-round, daily, anytime (except days on which there is a Cal home football game).

SERVICES/AMENITIES:
Catering: provided
Kitchen Facilities: n/a
Tables & Chairs: provided
Linens, Silver, etc.: provided
Restrooms: wheelchair accessible
Dance Floor: yes
Bride's & Groom's Dressing Areas: yes
Meeting Equipment: BYO or CBA, extra charge
Other: event coordination, baby grand and upright pianos, wireless internet connection in hotel and banquet rooms

Parking: pay parking on campus evenings and weekends; reserved/hosted parking is available, restrictions may apply
Accommodations: 23 guest rooms
Telephone: pay and house phones
Outdoor Night Lighting: yes
Outdoor Cooking Facilities: no
Cleanup: provided
View: lawn, creek and garden

RESTRICTIONS:
Alcohol: provided or BYO wine, corkage $18/bottle
Smoking: not allowed
Music: amplified OK until 11pm

Wheelchair Access: except to Seaborg Room
Insurance: not required
Other: no rice or glitter; no nails, staples or tacks on walls

Hotel Durant

2600 Durant Street, Berkeley
510/845-8981

www.hoteldurant.com
durantsales@jdvhotels.com

Hotel

- Rehearsal Dinners
- Ceremonies
- Wedding Receptions
- Corp. Events/Mtgs.
- Private Parties
- Accommodations

A Berkeley landmark with strong ties to the UC campus, this historic Spanish Mediterranean-style establishment has charmed visitors from around the world since 1928. Hotel Durant's location in the heart of Berkeley is as good as it gets: just a block from the university, minutes from Tilden Park and the famous Gourmet Ghetto, and close to the San Francisco and Oakland airports. Plus, it's just a short drive over the Bay Bridge to The City.

Arriving guests immediately experience the hotel's hospitality, which begins in the high-ceilinged lobby with its unique appointments, friendly staff and comfortable seating. A blue-and-gold color scheme echoes the University's colors and gives a respectful nod to the nearby campus.

Just off the lobby are three popular yet completely different options for events. The first two are in the hotel's restaurant, Henry's, where delectable breakfast, luncheon, appetizer and dinner combinations are created for your guests. The Main Dining Room, filled with natural light from grand, double-paned bay windows overlooking Durant Avenue, is ideal for upscale gatherings and every type of private function. More casual get-togethers are held in the dashing and congenial pub. The third option is the Board Room, an intimate space that can be booked on its own or in conjunction with some of the other rooms in the hotel.

Upstairs is the California Room, a favorite of the scholarly crowd. Its four large windows have showered light on plenty of parties over the years, from sedate sit-down dinners to boisterous mixers to high-powered meetings and corporate functions. Off Durant Avenue by way of a private entrance, the University Room provides yet another very flexible event space. Its neutral décor is brightened by skylights and double-paned windows that afford more Durant Avenue views.

Having too much fun at the party to leave? You can take the elevator home to one of Hotel Durant's 143 rooms. Better yet, consider reserving the entire Executive Level for your wedding party or close friends. This floor offers an exclusive lounge with complimentary continental breakfast and a wine hour in the afternoon, making it a wonderful gathering spot for your nearest and dearest. All guest rooms feature a 37" or 42" flat screen TV, high-speed wireless internet access, an honor bar, refrigerator, in-room safe and iPod docking station. And for the business person's convenience, there's a business center in the lobby.

Nearby attractions like the Lawrence Hall of Science, Zellerbach Hall, the UC Art Museum across the street, Julia Morgan Center, the Botanical Gardens and, of course, dynamic Telegraph Avenue undoubtedly add to the appeal of this much-loved Berkeley hotel. Book early—this one sells out.

CEREMONY CAPACITY: The hotel accommodates up to 75 seated guests indoors.

EVENT/RECEPTION & MEETING CAPACITY: Hotel Durant holds up to 60 seated and 90 standing indoors.

FEES & DEPOSITS: A nonrefundable deposit is required to reserve your date. The balance is due 10 days prior to the event. Rental fees range $300–900. Luncheons start at $25/person, dinners at $45/person. Tax, alcohol and a 22% service charge are additional.

AVAILABILITY: Year-round, daily, 7am–midnight.

SERVICES/AMENITIES:

Catering: provided
Kitchen Facilities: n/a
Tables & Chairs: provided
Linens, Silver, etc.: provided
Restrooms: wheelchair accessible
Dance Floor: CBA
Bride's & Groom's Dressing Areas: CBA
Meeting Equipment: some provided

Parking: limited on site, nearby lots
Accommodations: 143 guest rooms
Telephone: house phone
Outdoor Night Lighting: access only
Outdoor Cooking Facilities: no
Cleanup: provided
View: no

RESTRICTIONS:

Alcohol: provided, or BYO with corkage fee
Smoking: outside only
Music: amplified OK indoors with restrictions

Wheelchair Access: yes
Insurance: not required

This is important! Tell locations you're reading HERE COMES THE GUIDE and ask if our information is still current.

391

UC Botanical Garden

Botanical Garden

200 Centennial Drive, Berkeley
510/642-3352
botanicalgarden.berkeley.edu/rentals/facilities.shtml
mdrich@berkeley.edu

- Rehearsal Dinners
- Ceremonies
- Wedding Receptions
- Corp. Events/Mtgs.
- Private Parties
- Accommodations

In the hills above UC Berkeley resides a garden of earthly delights: a spectacular 34-acre site nestled in Strawberry Canyon and overlooking the San Francisco Bay. The Botanical Garden is home to over 12,000 different kinds of plants, including many rare and endangered species. The garden feels like a horticultural wonderland, with plants grouped by geographical region, showcasing the world's rich botanical diversity. A stroll through these varied environments takes you from a cloud forest to a New World Desert, past a Japanese pool with waterfalls, and a Chinese Medicinal Herb Garden—there's even an orchid and carnivorous plant house! First established in 1890, the Garden's mission is research, education and conservation. The Botanical Garden is more than just a place with pretty flowers—it's a living museum. Amidst this natural splendor are several lovely sites to celebrate life's momentous occasions.

Imagine pledging your love in a grove of majestic redwood trees. Your guests are seated in a demi-amphitheater, atop benches built into the very earth itself. Expectant yet relaxed, they catch teasing glimpses of flowing white as you make your way up a forest path between majestic trees stretching their branches heavenward. The air is crisp, fresh, tinged with the scent of moist bark and leaves, and you're filled with the enormity of the moment. At last you reach the amphitheater, and your groom takes your hand as the ceremony begins.

Or perhaps you had something more intimate in mind? Then make your way to the Garden of Old Roses, a storybook bower high on the garden's eastern slope with all the visual allure of Monet's garden at Giverny. Rough-hewn steps climb down a terraced knoll, resplendent with a mix of lavender, blooming annuals and antique roses. The steps lead to a site where your family and friends wait. Opposite, masses of climbing roses cascade over the beams of a quaint wooden pergola. Completing the romantic vignette, a panorama of the bay unfolds beyond acres of sprawling foliage, like a blue ribbon edging a flowery chintz gown.

Still another option is to wed and have your reception at the Conference Center, set in the middle of the Palm and Cycad Garden above lush Strawberry Creek. Surrounded by luxuriant palms, rare cycads and tree ferns, the center's broad tiled Terrace makes a sunny place for a ceremony, with the palms defining a natural aisle. Or put a bar and food stations on the Terrace where guests can enjoy pre-reception mingling. Meanwhile, you and your photographer can take advantage of the many scenic backdrops. One particularly appealing spot is just beyond the Terrace: a footbridge poised between the lushly green banks of the creek. Here in the forest's dewy coolness, brightly colored dragonflies dart from delicate ferns to lily pads, and the silhouette of you and your groom is faintly mirrored in the water below.

Inside the Conference Center are two adjoining rooms, the Mirov and the smaller Ornduff. Each has greenhouse windows that let the sunshine in, as well as showcase the surrounding greenery. You might host your banquet in the Mirov, then do the cake cutting in the Ornduff and dance on the Terrace. Or during the cooler months, begin in the Ornduff for cocktails, then move into Mirov for your reception.

Whichever sites you choose at the Botanical Garden, you can be sure of one thing: You're taking the concept of "a simple garden wedding" to a whole new level!

CEREMONY CAPACITY: Outdoor garden spaces seat up to 100 guests; indoors the site accommodates up to 60–100 seated guests.

EVENT/RECEPTION CAPACITY: Outdoor spaces hold up to 40–60 guests; indoors, the site accommodates up to 100 seated or standing guests.

MEETING CAPACITY: Two spaces hold 10–70 guests seated theater-style or at tables.

FEES & DEPOSITS: Rental fees range from $75–400/hour depending on site(s) chosen, number of hours rented and day of event.

AVAILABILITY: Various UC Botanical Garden sites are available year-round, 9am–midnight.

SERVICES/AMENITIES:

Catering: select from list
Kitchen Facilities: kitchenette
Tables & Chairs: yes
Linens, Silver, etc.: BYO or through caterer
Restrooms: wheelchair accessible
Dance Floor: CBA, extra fee
Bride's Dressing Area: yes
Meeting Equipment: internet access, more equipment CBA

Parking: University lot, fees paid in advance
Accommodations: no guest rooms
Telephone: house phone/local and card calls
Outdoor Night Lighting: yes
Outdoor Cooking Facilities: no
Cleanup: caterer or renter
View: botanical garden, creek, SF Bay, city, Golden Gate Bridge

RESTRICTIONS:

Alcohol: BYO, permit required
Smoking: not allowed
Music: amplified OK with restrictions

Wheelchair Access: limited
Insurance: liability required

Trilogy at The Vineyards - Club Los Meganos

Private Club

1700 Trilogy Parkway, Brentwood
925/809-7180
www.vineyardsweddings.com
marc.valone@trilogyresortliving.com

- Rehearsal Dinners
- Ceremonies
- Wedding Receptions
- Corp. Events/Mtgs.
- Private Parties
- Accommodations

Club Los Meganos at Trilogy at The Vineyards, which debuted in the summer of 2010, is, quite simply, spectacular. Even the drive up to the venue is a pleasure, as you pass olive groves, stately Italian cypress trees and a profusion of white roses and bright flowers. When you arrive at the club, situated just above a series of gentle hills neatly planted with grapevines, you sense that this place is something special.

The 34,000-square-foot club devotes an entire wing specifically to events: the Mount Diablo Events Center, named for the well-known peak visible from almost everywhere on the property. Interior spaces throughout are beautifully designed and incorporate rich woods, natural stone and sweeping expanses of glass in a way that's reminiscent of Frank Lloyd Wright. Outdoors, there's a nod to Mediterranean influences like the circular stone plaza, the tiered terracotta fountain and, of course, the surrounding landscape itself.

Ceremonies are held on the Event Promenade, a sprawling, lush lawn that features unobstructed views of the nearby hills in the foreground and Mount Diablo in the distance.

Serve cocktails and hors d'oeuvres on the Promenade, or indoors in the Reception Foyer. Here, as throughout the club, there's a masterful blend of contemporary design with an underlying homage to the Miwok tribe who once called this area home. A display case with Native American artifacts sits on one wall of this bright, airy space, while a modern painting of an Indian and vibrant turquoise pottery also capture your attention. Glass "NanaWalls," which reveal a spacious patio overlooking the gardens and water features, quickly fold away creating seamless access to the outdoors.

Dinner and dancing take place in the event center's versatile ballroom. Designed with a high, coffered ceiling and decorated in soothing shades of cocoa, cream and muted sky blue, the room has a sophisticated look. There's a view of Mount Diablo through more folding glass doors that open to the Promenade, creating a wonderful indoor-outdoor flow. A state-of-the-art A/V system with drop-down screens and a gleaming wooden dance floor set the stage for a lively party.

For a unique rehearsal dinner or bridal shower, check out the Culinary Studio, a dream kitchen/dining room where you have an opportunity to observe the chef in action, perhaps whipping up a special menu using ingredients from local orchards. Or, you can relax outside on the adjoining private patio/herb garden with a glass of vino from the on-site wine cellar.

As if all this weren't enticing enough, both the bride and groom get to prepare for the day in the Hii/Kome Room, outfitted with full-length mirrors, a poker table, Wii games and movies.

CEREMONY CAPACITY: The Event Promenade can accommodate up to 250 seated outdoors.

EVENT/RECEPTION CAPACITY: The facility holds 200 seated indoors and 250 seated outdoors.

MEETING CAPACITY: Meeting spaces hold 200 seated guests.

FEES & DEPOSITS: A $1,000 deposit is required to reserve your date and the balance of the estimated event total is due 30 days prior to the event. Rental fees range $750–7,000 depending on the guest count, time of year and day of the week. Meals start at $34/person. Tax, alcohol and service charge are additional.

AVAILABILITY: Year-round, daily, afternoons and evenings, only one event per day and only 25 weddings per year.

SERVICES/AMENITIES:

Catering: provided
Kitchen Facilities: n/a
Tables & Chairs: provided
Linens, Silver, etc.: provided
Restrooms: wheelchair accessible
Dance Floor: provided
Bride's Dressing Area: yes
Meeting Equipment: provided

Parking: large lot
Accommodations: no guest rooms
Telephone: office and guest phones
Outdoor Night Lighting: provided
Outdoor Cooking Facilities: BBQ CBA
Cleanup: provided
View: garden, meadow, mountains, vineyards
Other: baby grand piano, spa services, A/V equipment, event coordination

RESTRICTIONS:

Alcohol: provided
Smoking: outdoors only
Music: amplified OK

Wheelchair Access: yes
Insurance: liability required

Wedgewood Wedding and Banquet Center
at Brentwood Golf Club

Golf Club

100 Summerset Drive, Brentwood
866/966-3009

www.wedgewoodbanquet.com/brentwood
sales@wedgewoodbanquet.com

- Rehearsal Dinners
- Ceremonies
- Wedding Receptions
- Corp. Events/Mtgs.
- Private Parties
- Accommodations

First impressions mean a lot, and the lovely drive up to the Brentwood Golf Club along a wide concourse lined with stately royal palms really sets a grand tone. The clubhouse itself, with its sloping, shingle roof and mix of pale earth tones and natural stone, has the look of a relaxed, upscale country retreat surrounded by acres and acres of lushly landscaped grounds.

Private events have their own entrance via a shaded pathway that leads around the side of the building. Follow it and you come to the Ceremony Pavilion Patio, overlooking the first tee of the golf course. Front and center is the pavilion itself, a classical Italian-style rotunda with six white columns topped with an ornate wrought-iron dome. It's an elegant stage for exchanging vows, backed by a dense screen of graceful olive and Japanese maple trees mixed with vivid red and white oleanders.

Just around the corner, behind the clubhouse, is the trellised Terrace where guests can raise a congratulatory glass of bubbly and mingle during the cocktail reception. Dappled sunlight filters through the overhead beams, which create a natural awning above a row of stone pillars. This peaceful spot enjoys views of the fairway, a pond that overflows into a rushing waterfall, and a nearby bridge spanning a profusion of pastel flowers. Naturally all of these scenes make very picturesque backdrops for your wedding photos.

The Ballroom, decorated in soothing hues of sandstone and adobe, has tall windows along two walls that look out over the ceremony site and terrace to the verdant vistas beyond. As the sun sets and everyone is seated for dinner, create just the right mood by dimming the wrought-iron chandeliers and spotlights. Large enough to seat 200 with a permanent dance floor, this high-ceilinged space can accommodate an additional 150 by simply removing a dividing wall and expanding into the adjoining club restaurant. This also gives you access to the restaurant's large bar and the four LCD flat screens behind it to display home movies, photos or even a real-time video of the wedding itself.

The Wedgewood Banquet Center chain, which oversees special events at numerous locations throughout California, prides itself on service. With their experienced staff you can count on guidance, flexibility and attention to your specific needs. Customization is welcome, so if there's something special you'd like, just ask. You'll have a dedicated wedding planner who will work with you throughout the entire process, from the first consultation until the last guest says good-bye. They've designed a whole array of packages, many of which are all-inclusive and cover not only the menu, linens and setup, but everything from invitations and flowers to photographer and band. This is a boon for all you busy brides who just want to relax and enjoy your own wedding.

CEREMONY CAPACITY: The site holds 350 seated guests outside.

EVENT/RECEPTION & MEETING CAPACITY: The facility can accommodate 350 seated or 500 standing outdoors.

FEES & DEPOSITS: 25% of the estimated event total is required to reserve your date and the balance is due 10 days prior to the event. All-inclusive wedding packages start at $40/person. Tax, alcohol and a 20% service charge are additional.

AVAILABILITY: Year-round, daily, in 5-hour time blocks depending on the day.

SERVICES/AMENITIES:
Catering: provided
Kitchen Facilities: n/a
Tables & Chairs: provided
Linens, Silver, etc.: provided
Restrooms: wheelchair accessible
Dance Floor: provided
Bride's Dressing Area: yes
Meeting Equipment: provided
Other: picnic area, event coordination

Parking: large lot
Accommodations: no guest rooms
Telephone: emergency use only
Outdoor Night Lighting: access only
Outdoor Cooking Facilities: no
Cleanup: caterer or renter
View: fountain, fairways, landscaped grounds, mountains

RESTRICTIONS:
Alcohol: provided
Smoking: outdoors only
Music: amplified OK

Wheelchair Access: yes
Insurance: not required

Overwhelmed? Use the search criteria on www.HereComesTheGuide.com to narrow down your choices.

Oakhurst Country Club

Country Club

1001 Peacock Creek Drive, Clayton
925/672-9737 X217
www.countryclubreceptions.com
events@oakhurstcc.com

- Rehearsal Dinners
- Ceremonies
- Wedding Receptions
- Corp. Events/Mtgs.
- Private Parties
- Accommodations

Located on a bench of land just above Ygnacio Valley and the growing city of Clayton, Oakhurst Country Club sits near the base of Mt. Diablo's steep and wild eastern rampart.

The vistas from its two event spaces, the west-facing Heritage and Diablo View rooms, are impressive. The larger Heritage Room takes in a sweeping panorama of the Diablo Valley, from Pleasant Hill to the Carquinez Strait. The smaller Diablo View Room scans the vividly chiseled profiles of Mt. Diablo's precipitous lesser-known side. A wide terrace that zigzags across the clubhouse's west side connects both rooms from the outside and is a highly popular feature with wedding parties. Besides its unfettered view of distant landscapes, the terrace provides a closer-in look at the club's azure-watered swimming pool, putting green and golf course.

Because it's surrounded by a visually arresting landscape, it's no surprise that Oakhurst hosts many outdoor wedding ceremonies. But exchanging vows outside also gets a boost from the club's attractive appearance. The clubhouse is fronted by a majestic porte-cochère, whose twin support pillars are clad in large flagstones and whose steeply angled roof rests atop big, bold wooden trusses. Couples often enjoy getting married next to this structure, which provides a dramatic architectural backdrop to the club's landscaped front.

When celebrants move indoors to the banquet rooms, they pass through an airy window-lined lobby that opens out to a 40-foot-high atrium. Those striking trusses you first see under the porte-cochère continue inside, adding yet another eye-catching element to the clubhouse's design.

Over the past decade Oakhurst has assembled an unflappable, well-organized, people-oriented staff, and developed a wide range of packages. Naturally, the many brides who've enjoyed worry-free weddings here have generated enthusiastic word of mouth about this site. To them, Oakhurst seems blessed with everything in just the right proportion: a savvy wedding team, plenty of options and flexibility, a memorable setting and fine architecture. That's a pretty nice combination to bring to your wedding day.

CEREMONY CAPACITY: Indoors, this location seats up to 100 guests; outdoors, up to 150 seated guests.

EVENT/RECEPTION & MEETING CAPACITY: Indoors, the Diablo View Room seats up to 68 guests with additional open terrace seating for 50. Heritage Room seats up to 190 with a covered terrace that seats up to an aditional 72 guests.

FEES & DEPOSITS: A nonrefundable deposit, which is applied to your food and beverage total, is required to reserve your date. The amount of the deposit is equal to 25% of the event minimum. 50% is due 6 months prior, and 100% of the final estimated balance is due 10 days prior to the event date. Rental fees range $200–1,000 depending on the space reserved and day rented. Wedding packages, including room rental, start at $50/person. Meals range $23–45/person. Tax, alcohol and a 20% service charge are additional.

AVAILABILITY: Year-round, daily, 6am–11pm.

SERVICES/AMENITIES:

Catering: provided
Kitchen Facilities: n/a
Tables & Chairs: provided
Linens, Silver, etc.: provided
Restrooms: wheelchair accessible
Dance Floor: CBA, extra fee
Bride's Dressing Area: yes
Meeting Equipment: CBA or BYO

Parking: large lot
Accommodations: no guest rooms
Telephone: emergency use only
Outdoor Night Lighting: CBA
Outdoor Cooking Facilities: BBQ CBA
Cleanup: provided
View: mountains, hills, fairways

RESTRICTIONS:

Alcohol: provided, or BYO with corkage fee
Smoking: outdoors only
Music: amplified OK

Wheelchair Access: yes
Insurance: not required
Other: no rice, birdseed or glitter

Blackhawk Museum

Museum

3700 Blackhawk Plaza Circle, Danville
925/648-1434
www.blackhawkmuseum.org
bjbarnette@scottswc.com

- Rehearsal Dinners
- Ceremonies
- Wedding Receptions
- Corp. Events/Mtgs.
- Private Parties
- Accommodations

The Blackhawk Museum is an exciting place for private events. Overlooking Blackhawk Plaza, the building is a study in glass, granite and stainless steel—a multi-million-dollar facility that showcases rare classic automobiles and automotive fine art and artifacts in elegant, sumptuous surroundings. The foyer is awe-inspiring with its soaring skylights and dusty rose Italian granite floors and walls. The juxtaposition of metal and stone with soft rich colors creates a vivid impression. As the sun sets through the tinted glass façade, the entire space is bathed in a warm glow.

The dining area presents a striking contrast—black from its granite floor to unadorned ceiling. Beautiful vintage cars border the dining area and are highlighted by a network of computerized lights. Here guests are dazzled by colorful fender curves, gleaming surfaces and sparkling brass and chrome.

And what's particularly nice about this 65,000-square-foot facility is that you have so many options from which to choose. The facility's numerous event spaces include the automobile galleries, lobbies, mezzanine, terraces, classroom, executive room, outdoor plaza with fountain, and more. If you're seeking a smashing venue in the East Bay for a personal celebration or a company soirée, this is the place to have an unforgettable event.

CEREMONY/EVENT & RECEPTION CAPACITY: The site holds 40–500 seated or 75–1,000+ standing guests indoors, and 40–400 seated or 70–600 standing outdoors.

MEETING CAPACITY: Event spaces hold 22–500 seated guests.

FEES & DEPOSITS: The Museum is rented through *Scott's Catering* of Walnut Creek. Rental fees start at $500 and vary depending on the day of week, date of the event, and the time of day. Per person prices are flexible and menus are customizable for almost any budget. Meals start at $27/person and range depending on your event needs. For information contact *Scott's Catering* at the Blackhawk Museum 925/648-1434 or bjbarnette@scottswc.com or heatherp@scottswc.com.

AVAILABILITY: Year-round, except Thanksgiving and Christmas Days. During operating hours (Wednesday–Sunday, 10am–5pm), functions with catered meals may be scheduled in the event areas 7:30am–5pm, and the entire facility is available from 5:30pm–11:30pm. On Mondays and Tuesdays, when the museum is closed to the public, the entire facility is available for events 7:30am–11:30pm.

SERVICES/AMENITIES:

Catering: provided
Kitchen Facilities: n/a
Tables & Chairs: provided
Linens, Silver, etc.: provided
Restrooms: wheelchair accessible
Dance Floor: provided
Bride's Dressing Area: yes
Meeting Equipment: microphone, podium, portable and adjustable stage, screen, zoned speaker system

Parking: large lots
Accommodations: no guest rooms
Telephone: no
Outdoor Night Lighting: access only
Outdoor Cooking Facilities: no
Cleanup: provided
View: East Bay hills; Blackhawk Plaza's ponds, fountains and waterfalls
Other: piano

RESTRICTIONS:

Alcohol: provided, service until 11:30pm
Smoking: outside only
Music: amplified limited, must end by 11:30pm

Wheelchair Access: yes
Insurance: liability required

Crow Canyon Country Club

Country Club

711 Silver Lake Drive, Danville
925/735-5700

www.crow-canyon.com
sandy.merlo@ourclub.com
sharon.cox@ourclub.com

- Rehearsal Dinners
- Ceremonies
- Wedding Receptions
- Corp. Events/Mtgs.
- Private Parties

Accommodations

Nestled against the foothills of Mt. Diablo and overlooking a championship 18-hole golf course, Crow Canyon Country Club offers a versatile combination of indoor and outdoor spaces for rehearsal dinners, wedding receptions, parties and business functions.

As you step into the club's impressive lobby, your eyes are drawn upward to the soaring ceiling with its glittering crystal chandelier. It's the ideal spot for mingling in conjunction with the adjacent lounge, which features a large granite bar, fireplace and big screen TV. Not surprisingly, the lounge is a popular hangout for grooms and their guys, who enjoy a little downtime relaxation here during the event.

Both the lobby and the lounge adjoin the Grand Ballroom, Crow Canyon's main reception area. Divisible into three sections, it can be configured to suit the size of your event. Natural light flows in through a wall of windows, and no matter where you're seated you have a fantastic view of the redwood-studded golf course and Mt. Diablo in the distance. Fifteen crystal-and-bronze chandeliers supply plenty of sparkle, and dimmers allow you to set the mood. The room's neutral palette is compatible with any color scheme, so by incorporating your choice of linens, flowers and other décor you can easily bring the look you envision to life. For added flexibility, a stage (great for the head table, a band or DJ) and hardwood dance floor are permanently set up in the center of the room.

The ballroom opens onto three patios, expanding your options even further. Use one or all of them for al fresco cocktails, additional seating, or simply as a place where guests can go for a little fresh air and a close-up view of the fairways and hills. The beauty of the club's layout is that all of these spaces are connected to each other, creating a wonderful indoor-outdoor flow.

In addition to the patios, Crow Canyon has several smaller rooms that lend themselves to intimate private parties, corporate luncheons or meetings, and indoor ceremonies. Speaking of ceremonies, couples often tie the knot on the golf course surrounded by mature redwoods and the wide blue sky.

Crow Canyon's Events Director and Coordinator like to say "Yes!" to requests and are dedicated to making your wedding day the best one possible. They'll recommend preferred vendors or you can choose your own, and either way they'll work closely with them to ensure that your setup is perfect and everything runs smoothly. A variety of reception packages are available, and the club's catering team will customize your menu—including any dietary or cultural needs. You can even bring in an outside caterer with approval.

Among Danville's handful of special event venues, Crow Canyon Country Club stands out for its appealing spaces, wide range of services and attention to detail. Whether you have an informal affair or a sophisticated soirée in mind, this is one facility that can handle it from start to finish.

CEREMONY CAPACITY: The Club holds up to 300 guests outdoors and up to 330 guests indoors. Many options are available, including larger capacities. Call for details.

EVENT/RECEPTION & MEETING CAPACITY: The club can accommodate 10–330 seated or 15–500 standing guests indoors; outdoor patios adjoining almost every room provide additional event space.

FEES & DEPOSITS: Room rental fees range $300–1,800 and food and beverage minimums range $350–13,000 depending on the day and time of the event, and space rented. Food service is provided; catered events require 7 days advance confirmation of guest count. Approximate per person rates: breakfast $15–24, luncheon $16–28, dinner $28–49, with a variety of fun food reception stations. Customized menus are available. Alcohol, tax and a 20% service charge are additional.

AVAILABILITY: Year-round, daily, 6am–midnight. Extra hours may be added for an additional fee.

SERVICES/AMENITIES:

Catering: provided
Kitchen Facilities: n/a
Tables & Chairs: provided
Linens, Silver, etc.: provided
Restrooms: wheelchair accessible
Dance Floor: yes
Bride's Dressing Room: yes
Meeting Equipment: overhead screen, VCR and monitor, LCD and slide projectors, phone lines, flip charts, wireless internet; all equipment extra charge

Parking: large lot, valet available
Accommodations: no guest rooms
Telephone: emergency use only
Outdoor Night Lighting: yes
Outdoor Cooking Facilities: BBQ
Cleanup: provided
View: Mt. Diablo and golf course
Other: baby grand and upright pianos

RESTRICTIONS:

Alcohol: provided; wine corkage $15/bottle
Smoking: outdoors only
Music: amplified OK indoors

Wheelchair Access: yes
Insurance: not required

The professionals in the back of this book are the best in the business. How do we know? Read page 637.

403

Discovery Bay Golf and Country Club

Golf and Country Club

1475 Clubhouse Drive, Discovery Bay
925/634-0700
www.dbgcc.com
banquets@dbgcc.com

● Rehearsal Dinners	● Corp. Events/Mtgs.
● Ceremonies	● Private Parties
● Wedding Receptions	Accommodations

Down the long and winding road that leads through the tawny East Bay hills to where rivers gather to form the Sacramento Delta, you'll find a little Eden in the newly minted township of Discovery Bay. Set like an emerald at the heart of this gated community, the Discovery Bay Country Club offers a perfect slice of paradise at a highly affordable price.

Broad lawns, clouds of colorful flowers, and grand old pepper, willow, poplar, and ash trees greet guests as they approach the handsome clubhouse. Ceremonies and gatherings are often held on the exquisitely manicured front lawn, where a gentle slope provides a natural dais. Events held on the west patio enjoy a stunning view of Mt. Diablo. Serene and sophisticated, surrounded by shade trees and tickled by breezes and birdsong, the lawn, patio and clubhouse are brilliant environments for any affair.

Inside the bisque-colored Mediterranean-style building, sunlight waterfalls through the skylights and down the tall white columns of the property's atrium-style lobby. Just ahead, the spacious lounge with its broad bar, floor-to-ceiling windows and elegant baby grand Disklavier (it's like having a concert pianist on call!) offers gorgeous golf course views and comfortable seating. This is a spectacular place to greet guests or to entertain them with cocktails and hors d'oeuvres. The lounge also has its own stone patio screened by tall hedges and trees where partygoers can step into the sunshine. The facility's on-site coordinator and well-trained staff will ensure that everyone feels quite at home.

But the lawns, lobby and lounge are merely an introduction. The welcome extends to the property's beautiful dining room. You won't need to bring anything into this glamorous setting, with its softly colored carpets and walls, classic furnishings, and breathtaking views of the rolling fairways and lakes. Multiple levels of indoor lighting, including chandeliers, spots and recessed illumination in the handsomely coved ceiling will spotlight your event to perfection. Or you can shower your guests in sunlight on the outdoor veranda. Framed by the country club's verdant, meticulously groomed gardens and greens, this is a picturesque place for a wedding ceremony or *plein air* gathering or reception. The north- and west-facing panorama takes in Mt. Diablo and rarely fades to black without an extravagant sunset and its finale of twinkling stars.

Two smaller dining rooms make excellent choices for more intimate events—for showers and pre- or post-wedding celebrations—and there is a Bridal Suite Meeting Room that can be reserved for the bride and her entourage. Also available off the lobby, down a wide, mirrored hall, are the club's carpeted, spa-quality locker rooms equipped with personal lockers, showers, hair dryers and toiletries, all of which allow the bridal party to relax and enjoy in the midst of the wedding day whirl.

CEREMONY & EVENT/RECEPTION CAPACITY: The site holds a maximum of 200 guests, seated or standing, indoors or outdoors.

MEETING CAPACITY: Conference room holds 20 seated guests.

FEES & DEPOSITS: A $1,000 deposit is required to reserve your date. Rental fees range $0–500 depending on your guest count. Wedding prices range $45–55/person. Tax, alcohol and an 18% service charge are additional.

AVAILABILITY: Year-round. Weddings take place on Fridays, Saturdays and Sundays.

SERVICES/AMENITIES:

Catering: provided
Kitchen Facilities: n/a
Tables & Chairs: provided
Linens, Silver, etc.: provided
Restrooms: wheelchair accessible
Dance Floor: provided
Bride's & Groom's Dressing Areas: yes
Meeting Equipment: some provided

Parking: large lot, valet optional
Accommodations: no guestrooms
Telephone: office phone
Outdoor Night Lighting: CBA
Outdoor Cooking Facilities: BBQ CBA
Cleanup: provided
View: golf course, mountains, lake, garden
Other: event coordination, bridal suite

RESTRICTIONS:

Alcohol: provided or BYO wine with corkage fee
Smoking: outdoors only
Music: amplified OK indoors only

Wheelchair Access: yes
Insurance: not required

Palmdale Estates

Historic Estate

159 Washington Boulevard, Fremont
925/462-1783

www.palmdaleestates.com
veenaatpalmdale@mac.com

- Rehearsal Dinners
- Ceremonies
- Wedding Receptions
- Corp. Events/Mtgs.
- Private Parties

Accommodations

Originally part of the Old Mission San Jose garden, Palmdale Estates is a beautifully landscaped site, featuring dozens of stately palms and native California trees, verdant lawns, gardens and a pond. In the midst of this lovely setting is Best House, a Tudor-style mansion whose delightful interior and grounds create a storybook backdrop for weddings any time of year.

Built in 1915, the house reflects much of the elegant and ornate detailing of the period: graceful arched doorways, bas-relief ceiling moldings, crystal chandeliers, hand-painted murals and gleaming hardwood floors. Moiré silk draperies add a rich, old-fashioned quality to the décor. The Ballroom, though the largest space in the house, still has an intimate feeling with its cream-colored walls, oversize decorative marble fireplace and huge leaded-glass window overlooking the garden. At one end of the Ballroom, a few steps take you up to the Music Room, a glitzy alcove with gold leaf walls and a colorful stained-glass window. At the other end are the formal Dining Room and Solarium, two light and airy rooms with an abundance of leaded-glass windows and views of the "backyard."

When you get married here, you have exclusive use of the main floor of the house as well as the adjacent lawns, and can orchestrate your wedding any way you like. During warm months, most couples tie the knot in the white gazebo on the rear lawn, which is bordered by pines and redwoods and dotted with palms and fruit trees. They have their reception outdoors as well, setting up tables on the grassy expanse next to the gazebo. Afterwards, guests are invited inside for dancing and cake cutting. In winter, receptions are generally held in the Ballroom, with the other spaces used according to the couple's preferences; a fluid floor plan offers plenty of flexibility. (The Starr Garden, behind the adjacent Peach Mansion, is also available for ceremonies and receptions.)

Indian weddings are quite popular at this location: There are two permanent Mandaps on the property and the on-site caterer specializes in North Indian, South Indian and Gujarati cuisine.

Whether you celebrate under the magnificent palms or in the gracious surroundings of Best House, you can't help but enjoy the quiet beauty of Palmdale Estates.

CEREMONY CAPACITY: The Best House Garden with gazebo accommodates 500 seated; the Starr Garden, 200 seated guests.

EVENT/RECEPTION CAPACITY: Best House holds 200 seated indoors and, combined with outdoor spaces, up to 500 guests. Starr Garden holds 200 seated guests.

MEETING CAPACITY: The Ballroom holds 100 seated conference-style or 75 theater-style.

FEES & DEPOSITS: To rent the mansion and garden, a $1,600 security deposit is required when the rental agreement is submitted. The rental balance is payable 9 months prior to the event. The facility provides catering; however, during certain time periods, you can make arrangements for your own caterer; call to get specific dates. Rental fees range $500–3,500 depending on space selected and date and time rented. Meals start at $27/person. Tax, alcohol and service charge are additional.

AVAILABILITY: Year-round, daily, except Thanksgiving and Christmas Days.

SERVICES/AMENITIES:

Catering: provided or BYO (call for specifics)
Kitchen Facilities: minimal
Tables & Chairs: provided for 200 guests
Linens, Silver, etc.: provided with catering
Restrooms: wheelchair accessible
Dance Floor: Ballroom or Solarium
Bride's Dressing Area: yes
Meeting Equipment: PA system, flip charts, VCR, and overhead projector

Parking: large lot
Accommodations: no guest rooms
Telephone: lounge phone
Outdoor Night Lighting: CBA
Outdoor Cooking Facilities: no
Cleanup: caterer or CBA
View: East Bay hills
Other: event coordination

RESTRICTIONS:

Alcohol: BYO
Smoking: outside only
Music: amplified OK within limits

Wheelchair Access: yes
Insurance: not required

Lafayette Park Hotel & Spa

Boutique Hotel

3287 Mount Diablo Boulevard, Lafayette
925/283-3700, 800/368-2468
www.lafayetteparkhotel.com
lwong@lafayetteparkhotel.com

● Rehearsal Dinners	● Corp. Events/Mtgs.
● Ceremonies	● Private Parties
● Wedding Receptions	● Accommodations

Few hotels are given any kind of special recognition, so the fact that the Lafayette Park Hotel & Spa is one of the few in the East Bay to have received a Four Diamond Award should tell you something: Namely, that they maintain an impeccable standard of comfort, ambiance and service. With its distinctive architecture—dormers, shuttered French windows, and peaked roofline—this local landmark looks like a French chateau. Behind its high walls, European charm abounds in lovely courtyards, a variety of event spaces, and a luxurious full-service health spa.

Just by walking around the hotel, you're struck by how its design and décor make you feel welcome. In the atrium-like lobby, sunlight streams in through windows 60 feet overhead, illuminating the sweeping oak staircase and white marble floor. On cool days, the couches in front of the oversize fireplace are the obvious place to relax. The warmth of wood is everywhere—even in the intricate inlaid floors in front of the elevators.

Step outside into the sunny Fountain Courtyard, and you quickly realize how idyllic this spot is for a ceremony or champagne reception. Enclosed by the golden walls of the hotel, the space becomes an Old World plaza with a trickling limestone fountain in its center, ringed by potted rose bushes, manicured trees and flowers.

From the Fountain Courtyard, it's a short walk inside to the Independence Ballroom where larger receptions and parties are held. The coffered ceiling is outfitted with handmade crystal chandeliers and spot lighting, which can be adjusted to create any mood.

Smaller ceremonies take place upstairs in the Wishing Well Courtyard. Named for the rose-entwined stone wishing well in its center, this petite patio is also embraced by the hotel's walls. As you gaze up at the shuttered windows, wrought-iron balconies and clinging ivy, you once again feel like you're in the middle of a French countryside inn. That European flavor carries over into the nearby George Washington Room, a more intimate reception space. Here, the Early American/French décor features gilt-framed mirrors, marble-topped consoles and a deep green carpet set off by fleur de lis border designs.

The Diderot Library, with its oak paneling, 18th-century marble fireplace mantel and hardwood floor, is custom-made for rehearsal dinners, bridal showers, brunches and executive meetings.

A wonderful Lafayette Park amenity is their European Day Spa. In addition to providing an appealing selection of face and body treatments, the Spa features a fitness pavilion, a pool and poolside café, an outdoor fireplace and a spa. The bride and her attendants will not be able to pass up an opportunity to indulge here before and even after (why not!) the Big Day. Everyone staying overnight will appreciate the nicely appointed rooms, many of which have their own wood-burning fireplaces. The hotel also offers a complimentary premium room for the honeymoon couple, and special rates for wedding guests.

Melding European elegance with California comfort, the Lafayette Park Hotel is indisputably one of the East Bay's favorite locations for weddings and special events.

CEREMONY CAPACITY: For seated groups, the Fountain Courtyard accommodates 160, the Wishing Well Courtyard 64, and the George Washington Room accommodates 130.

EVENT/RECEPTION CAPACITY: The hotel can accommodate 24–150 seated or 30–200 standing guests indoors, and 60–220 seated or 50–230 standing outdoors. The Independence Ballroom and Courtyard combined hold 300 seated or 350 standing guests.

MEETING CAPACITY: A variety of spaces accommodate 15–200 theater-style, or 8–45 conference-style.

FEES & DEPOSITS: A $2,000 nonrefundable, nontransferable deposit is required to reserve your date. The hotel's wedding packages include butler service hors d'oeuvres, beverages, linens, champagne toast, candle centerpieces and a premium guest room. The rental fees start at $1,000 and vary depending on spaces rented. Wedding packages start at $88/person. Tax and service charges are additional. Fees for business functions vary depending on overnight rooms, services and menus selected.

AVAILABILITY: Year-round, daily. Business functions, 8am–5pm or 6pm–11pm; weddings, 11am–4pm or 6pm–11pm.

SERVICES/AMENITIES:

Catering: provided
Kitchen Facilities: n/a
Tables & Chairs: provided
Linens, Silver, etc.: provided
Restrooms: wheelchair accessible
Dance Floor: yes
Bride's Dressing Area: CBA
Meeting Equipment: full range, A/V company
Other: event coordination

Parking: complimentary self-parking, valet available
Accommodations: 138 guest rooms
Telephone: guest rooms
Outdoor Night Lighting: yes
Outdoor Cooking Facilities: CBA
Cleanup: provided
View: courtyard and pool

RESTRICTIONS:

Alcohol: provided, no corkage fee
Smoking: outdoors only
Music: amplified within limits

Wheelchair Access: yes
Insurance: not required

Want to know WHAT TO ASK a potential location or vendor? Check out our Questions to Ask starting on page 17.

Wildwood Acres

1055 Hunsaker Canyon Road, Lafayette
925/283-2600
www.wildwoodacres.com
events@wildwoodacres.com

●	Rehearsal Dinners	●	Corp. Events/Mtgs.
●	Ceremonies	●	Private Parties
●	Wedding Receptions		Accommodations

It's hard to believe, as you drive through the suburban sprawl that makes up most of Contra Costa County, that a rustic jewel like Wildwood Acres could exist here. Nestled in a wooded canyon only five miles from downtown Lafayette, it's suitable for a wide variety of events. Whether you're planning a country-style reception, family reunion, or frothy Victorian wedding with picture hats and parasols, Wildwood Acres can magically transform itself into the ideal venue.

The indoor facility is a 2,000-square-foot lodge with warm decorative flooring and a 60-foot garden mural. Open-beamed ceilings, Oriental rugs, and a stone fireplace with benches on either side make the room cozy. And, there's even a full-service bar. This would be an especially nice area for a Christmas party, an intimate wedding or other winter event.

The outdoor facilities, however, are what make Wildwood Acres so special. If you're getting married here, there's a lovely ceremony site up on a hill in a fern grotto, deep in a grove of towering bay trees and bigleaf maples. Exchange vows on a stone platform in one corner while your guests, seated in the adjacent open area, savor their surroundings. Afterwards, have your reception on two terraces, shaded by a natural canopy of alder and maple trees. A redwood gazebo houses the band, and there's plenty of room to kick up your heels on the sunken dance floor. All around, pottery urns overflowing with impatiens and ferns add spots of color, and winding paths lead to shady nooks containing wrought-iron or wooden benches.

CEREMONY, EVENT/RECEPTION & MEETING CAPACITY: The Lodge holds 165 seated or 250 standing guests; the Outdoor Area holds up to 400 guests seated or standing.

FEES & DEPOSITS: To reserve your date, a $500 deposit is required. The site rental fee ranges $80–600/hour depending on the day of the week and time of year. Complete catering packages, which include food, beverages and setup, start at $49/person. Tax and an 18% service charge are additional.

Midweek business functions start at $36/person and include breakfast, lunch and nonalcoholic beverages. Tax and an 18% service charge are additional.

AVAILABILITY: Year-round, daily, 7:30am–midnight.

SERVICES/AMENITIES:

Catering: provided
Kitchen Facilities: n/a
Tables & Chairs: provided
Linens, Silver, etc.: provided
Restrooms: wheelchair accessible
Dance Floor: indoor and outdoor provided
Bride's & Groom's Dressing Areas: yes
Meeting Equipment: full range

Parking: ample
Accommodations: no guest rooms
Telephone: calling cards OK
Outdoor Night Lighting: yes
Outdoor Cooking Facilities: n/a
Cleanup: provided
View: canyon, gardens
Other: event coordination

RESTRICTIONS:

Alcohol: provided, no BYO
Smoking: designated areas only
Music: amplified OK

Wheelchair Access: yes
Insurance: not required

Hacienda de las Flores

Historic Home & Garden

2100 Donald Drive, Moraga
925/888-7045
www.moragahacienda.com
rents@moraga.ca.us

- Rehearsal Dinners
- Ceremonies
- Wedding Receptions
- Corp. Events/Mtgs.
- Private Parties
- Accommodations

An authentic Spanish-style mansion, the Hacienda de las Flores sits on land that was once the hunting ground for Miwok Indians. The historic town-owned structure is painted white with blue trim, and is surrounded by well-maintained park grounds. Inside the Hacienda, hardwood floors, beamed ceilings and a fireplace create a warm and inviting setting. Outdoors, a large lawn spreads out behind the building, enhanced by blue atlas cedar trees, pines, willows, palms and flowers. A circular flowerbed and fountain in the middle of the patio serve as the focal point for large parties or wedding receptions.

From the upper Hacienda lawn, flagstone stairs lead down to the Pavilion, a semicircular building with huge Corinthian columns overlooking a walled garden with lawn and patio. A set of large wrought-iron gates leads guests into the enclosure, where small seated functions or ceremonies can take place. Tranquil and secluded, the Hacienda offers one of the prettiest garden environments for special events in the East Bay.

CEREMONY CAPACITY: The Hacienda holds 50 seated or 75 standing guests indoors, and the adjacent lawn up to 200 seated or standing. The Pavilion holds 50 seated or 60 standing indoors, and the Pavilion lawn 150 seated or standing.

EVENT/RECEPTION CAPACITY: The Hacienda accommodates 200 guests outdoors or 100 for a seated meal indoors, throughout a few rooms. The Pavilion seats 50 inside and has an outdoor capacity of 150.

MEETING CAPACITY: There are 9 rooms that can accommodate 12–60 seated guests.

FEES & DEPOSITS: Event rental fees range $935–4,500 depending on the space selected, time of year and residency. To reserve your date, half of the rental fee, a $750 refundable security deposit and a $250 nonrefundable application fee are required. Remaining fees are due 6 months prior to the event. A deposit is required if you plan to use a non-preferred caterer or musicians. The damage deposit will be refunded within 60 days after the event provided all conditions have been met.

For weekday business meetings, fees vary depending on room(s) selected, and include room setup. There is an additional fee for use of the Hacienda kitchen.

AVAILABILITY: For special events, Friday (2pm–10pm) and Saturday and Sunday (8 consecutive hours between 9am–10pm); additional hours are available for the front end of events only. For weekday business meetings, the facility is available 8am–9pm.

SERVICES/AMENITIES:

Catering: select from preferred list

Kitchen Facilities: ample

Tables & Chairs: provided

Linens, Silver, etc.: through caterer

Restrooms: wheelchair accessible

Dance Floor: yes

Bride's Dressing Area: yes

Meeting Equipment: no

Parking: lot and on street

Accommodations: no guest rooms

Telephone: no

Outdoor Night Lighting: access only

Outdoor Cooking Facilities: no

Cleanup: provided

View: fountain, lawns, flowerbeds and trees

RESTRICTIONS:

Alcohol: BYO wine, beer or champagne only

Smoking: outside only

Music: amplified OK with restrictions
on speaker location

Wheelchair Access: yes

Insurance: included in fees

Other: decorations restricted; no birdseed, rice, confetti, flower petals, small feathers, loose glitter or mylar balloons

California Ballroom

1736 Franklin Street, Oakland
510/834-7761

www.californiaballroom.com
info@californiaballroom.com

- Rehearsal Dinners
- Ceremonies
- Wedding Receptions
- Corp. Events/Mtgs.
- Private Parties
- Accommodations

During the Roaring Twenties, everyone loved a party. These were the days when folks dressed to the nines for "dinner and dancing." If you lived in the East Bay during those rollicking times, the highlight of your night on the town would probably have been doing the Charleston at the Leamington Hotel's elegant grand ballroom. Though the Leamington is no longer in business, its Ballroom is still going strong, rechristened as the California Ballroom. Thanks to a loving renovation, an invitation to this impressive landmark—just a few blocks from picturesque Lake Merritt—is still an occasion to look forward to.

When you arrive at the Ballroom, pass through a pair of wrought-iron gates that open to a walkway shaded by a burgundy awning. Once inside, stand back and take in the authentic Art Deco styling of this appealing space. The cream-colored walls contrast nicely with carpeting the color of fine claret, which gives way to a 700-square-foot hardwood dance floor polished to a high gloss. In fact, the Ballroom is quite spacious, and even if you leave plenty of room for dancing, you can still comfortably seat 250 guests for dinner. Have more guests than that? Put tables on the dance floor, and have them cleared when folks are ready to kick up their heels.

The Ballroom feels even more expansive thanks to the lofty ceiling, which also sports a classic balcony reminiscent of a vintage playhouse. The ceiling itself is an art piece, lined with gold-leaf cornices and boasting gold-leaf panels in traditional Art Deco style. Ornate chandeliers bear complementary detailing, echoed throughout the décor. For example, along the walls you'll find several beveled-glass mirrors topped with elaborate gold carvings of heraldic emblems and cherubim. The more time you spend in the Ballroom, the more grace notes you discover, such as the antique-style light sconces that help set the mood with their subtle glow. Potted greenery illumined with twinkle lights accents the walls, and there's even a built-in bar in one corner, with a mirrored backsplash for a jazzy touch.

Perhaps the fanciest ornamentation is reserved for the proscenium of the large stage, which focuses all eyes up front towards its intricate design. A polished wood apron extends beyond burgundy velvet curtains and a scalloped valance. Many couples are so taken with the stage's innate drama that they hold their wedding ceremonies here, with guests seated below. Afterwards, the crowd heads for the bar and the dance floor is quickly cleared or set with more tables. You may decide to put the head table on the stage so everyone can admire the happy couple; alternatively, you might let your band or DJ be front and center, so they can best assist in coordinating each phase of your event.

The Ballroom includes a coat room (don't you wish more places offered this old-fashioned amenity?), as well as ample parking. There's an on-site kitchen, and you can bring in the caterer of your choice to serve the latest haute cuisine, or some retro favorites (think Veal Oscar and Cherries Jubilee). Completely private and reasonably priced, the California Ballroom brings a nostalgic glamour to your wedding or other momentous celebration.

CEREMONY, EVENT/RECEPTION & MEETING CAPACITY: The Ballroom holds 200 seated classroom-style, 300 seated at round tables, 350 seated theater-style or 600 standing guests.

FEES & DEPOSITS: Half of the rental fee (as a nonrefundable deposit) is required to reserve your date. The balance is due 90 days prior to the event. A cleaning deposit, along with security and other fees are due 30 days prior to the event. Rental fees range $1,000–2,500 depending on the day and time rented and the type of event. A $75/hour rehearsal charge is additional.

There is a discount for 501(c)(3) nonprofit groups on weekdays. For weekday business meetings and functions, fees vary depending on the day and time of the event; call for specific rates.

AVAILABILITY: Year-round, daily, until midnight on weekdays and until 2am on weekends.

SERVICES/AMENITIES:

Catering: BYO

Kitchen Facilities: moderately equipped

Tables & Chairs: provided

Linens, Silver, etc.: CBA, BYO or through caterer

Restrooms: wheelchair accessible

Dance Floor: hardwood floor

Bride's Dressing Area: yes

Meeting Equipment: CBA, extra charge

Parking: on-site lot and on-street

Accommodations: no guest rooms

Telephone: no

Outdoor Night Lighting: access only

Outdoor Cooking Facilities: no

Cleanup: renter or caterer

View: no

Other: stage, wetbar, event coordination CBA

RESTRICTIONS:

Alcohol: BYO, must have controlled bar

Smoking: outdoors only

Music: amplified OK indoors

Wheelchair Access: yes

Insurance: certificate required

Other: no tape, tacks or nails; no open flames; no rice or birdseed

---

Want to find more venues and services? Check out our informative website, www.HereComesTheGuide.com.

415

Camron-Stanford House

Lakeside Victorian Mansion

1418 Lakeside Drive, Oakland
510/444-1876, Special Events
www.cshouse.org
rentals@cshouse.org

● Rehearsal Dinners	● Corp. Events/Mtgs.
● Ceremonies	● Private Parties
● Wedding Receptions	Accommodations

Gracing the shore of Lake Merritt, the Camron-Stanford House is the last of the grand Victorian homes that once ringed the lake. Constructed in 1876, it derives its name from the Camrons, who were the first residents, and the Stanfords, who occupied it for the longest period. When the building was scheduled for demolition in the late 1960s, concerned citizens formed the Camron-Stanford House Preservation Association and spent the intervening years raising funds to return the home to its former splendor.

Elaborate molding and authentic wallpaper patterns and fabrics have all been used to match the originals as closely as possible. Rooms filled with period artifacts, antiques and photos take you back to the late 1800s. The only operational gas chandelier in Northern California is located here. Outside, a large rear veranda overlooks Lake Merritt. Receptions can take place in the house, on the veranda or on the expansive lawn that extends to the lake. An iron fence enclosing the site ensures privacy, while allowing guests to appreciate the colorful tapestry of boats, birds and joggers that surrounds them.

CEREMONY CAPACITY: The Veranda alone holds up to 90 seated guests; the veranda and lawn combined (facing the lake) hold 250 seated.

EVENT/RECEPTION & MEETING CAPACITY: The facility accommodates 50 guests inside or 200 outside.

FEES & DEPOSITS: Half the rental fee and a refundable $500 cleaning deposit are required when the facility is booked. Base rental fees range $300–1,200 for up to 200 guests and include staffing. Fees vary depending on space(s) selected and length of time rented. Additional hours are available at the rate of $175/hour.

AVAILABILITY: Year-round, weekdays until 10pm; Saturdays until 11pm.

SERVICES/AMENITIES:

Catering: BYO licensed
Kitchen Facilities: moderate
Tables & Chairs: BYO
Linens, Silver, etc.: BYO
Restroom: wheelchair accessible (ground level only)
Dance Floor: CBA
Bride's Dressing Area: CBA
Meeting Equipment: BYO

Parking: on-street, lot
Accommodations: no guest rooms
Telephone: emergencies only
Outdoor Night Lighting: BYO
Outdoor Cooking Facilities: BYO
Cleanup: caterer
View: Lake Merritt and Oakland city skyline

RESTRICTIONS:

Alcohol: BYO
Smoking: not allowed
Music: amplified OK outside only

Wheelchair Access: limited
Insurance: proof required
Other: no tacks or tape; no candles, no flame-heated chafing dishes; no confetti or rice

Chabot Space & Science Center

Space and Science Center

10000 Skyline Boulevard, Oakland
510/336-7421
www.chabotspace.org
rentals@chabotspace.org

● Rehearsal Dinners	● Corp. Events/Mtgs.
● Ceremonies	● Private Parties
● Wedding Receptions	Accommodations

Looking for an out-of-this-world location to celebrate your wedding? Let the stars smile on you at Chabot Space and Science Center. In the evenings, this state-of-the-art science education center perched high in the Oakland hills makes a unique setting for private events.

The center is surrounded by 13 wooded acres in Joaquin Miller Park, and its architecture takes full advantage of that fact: Numerous floor-to-ceiling windows, a glass skyway, and a catwalk-like loggia hugging the exterior really make you feel like you're up in the trees. The two main buildings, the Spees and Dellums Buildings, are linked at the second floor by the skyway, and at ground level by an amphitheater and a courtyard with gardens. Exposed ceilings, black floors, and architectural details in green glass, aluminum and blond wood create a smart, polished look throughout the center.

Event spaces in the Spees Building include the Tien MegaDome Theater, where you can project your own slides, DVD, VHS, or PowerPoint presentations; a café, which provides a handy reception site; and a surround-sound planetarium featuring one of the world's most advanced immersive visualization systems. This allows them to take their audience on real-time journeys to the edge of the known universe and back again. We were particularly taken with the idea of a celestial ceremony in the planetarium: Imagine getting married on a spot-lit stage beneath a 70-foot dome of gorgeous night sky thick with stars, while your guests sit spellbound in comfortable tiered seats. If you want to go all out, you can even make arrangements with the projectionist to create a sky that changes throughout the event.

Another appealing ceremony option—and one that will give every guest a great vantage point—is the semicircular amphitheater surrounded by trees. This is a particularly appropriate place to mark an important moment in time, as the amphitheater also functions as a nifty clock. At the top level of the amphitheater, the Pleiades Courtyard stretches back to the Spees Building café. Together, the two spaces make a convenient indoor/outdoor spot for serving post-ceremony refreshments. After dining, guests will enjoy strolling through the adjacent EnviroGarden, designed to showcase native plants.

You'll also want to consider serving cocktails in the sleek open spaces of the Spees Building. Although the Spees is a two-story structure, there are several areas where you can stand on the ground floor and gaze up unobstructedly to the top of the building. The most striking of these is the Rotunda, an atrium-like space capped by a huge octagonal skylight. During the day, light flowing in from the skylight illuminates a decorative green glass compass inlaid on the first floor.

If you set up musicians or a DJ on the Rotunda's circular "balcony," the music floats down to your guests mingling below.

Indoor receptions can take place in the exhibit spaces of the three-level Dellums Building, but the size and configuration of your event will depend on the current exhibits. The top floor of the Dellums opens to the outdoor plaza of the observatory complex. This is the highest point of the center, and from here the sweeping bay views over the treetops are sure to wow your guests. The three domes house telescopes named "Leah," "Rachel" and "Nellie." You can arrange for access to the domes, and can actually hold a small sit-down dinner inside the larger of the two.

Chabot Space and Science Center is a stellar (sorry, we couldn't resist) location, not just for weddings, but for private and corporate events, too. And even if you aren't an astronomy buff, you'll delight in the sunset over the bay and the dazzling nighttime panorama of city lights twinkling below.

CEREMONY CAPACITY: The Obsevatory Complex and the Amphitheater each seat 150 guests, the Ask Jeeves Planetarium holds up to 241 seated guests and the Dellums Building accommodates up to 200 guests.

EVENT/RECEPTION CAPACITY: The facility can accommodate 150–500 seated or 200–1,000 standing guests indoors, and 100–150 seated outdoors.

MEETING CAPACITY: Galileo, Kepler and Copernicus can each hold up to 45 seated guests. The Ask Jeeves Planetarium holds up to 241 guests seated theater-style, and the Tien MegaDome holds up to 205 guests seated theater-style.

FEES & DEPOSITS: 50% of the rental fee is required to reserve your date. A $1,000 refundable cleaning deposit, along with the balance of the rental fee, is due 30 days prior to the event. Rental fees range $1,500–15,000 depending on space rented. There is a discount for 501(c)(3) nonprofit groups.

AVAILABILITY: Year-round, Mondays and Tuesdays, 6am–midnight, or Wednesday–Sundays, 5pm–midnight. Some seasonal restrictions apply, call for details.

SERVICES/AMENITIES:

Catering: select from preferred list
Kitchen Facilities: full kitchen
Tables & Chairs: BYO
Linens, Silver, etc.: BYO
Restrooms: wheelchair accessible
Dance Floor: built in or BYO
Bride's Dressing Area: no
Meeting Equipment: some provided

Parking: ample free parking on site
Accommodations: no guest rooms
Telephone: emergency use only
Outdoor Night Lighting: yes
Outdoor Cooking Facilities: no
Cleanup: some provided
View: panoramic and bay views
Other: use of exhibits, some event coordination provided

RESTRICTIONS:

Alcohol: BYO
Smoking: not allowed
Music: amplified OK

Wheelchair Access: yes
Insurance: extra liability required
Other: no balloons or confetti

Highlands Country Club

Country Club

110 Hiller Drive, Oakland
510/849-0743
highlandscc@aol.com

● Rehearsal Dinners	● Corp. Events/Mtgs.
● Ceremonies	● Private Parties
● Wedding Receptions	Accommodations

Suppose you wanted a place for your event that had a genuine "country club" ambiance, but you only had a limited budget. Where could you go? Well, you might want to take a little drive over to the Highlands Country Club.

Embraced by a sloping green sweep of lawn, and overlooking tennis courts and crystal-blue swimming pools, this architectural phoenix has literally risen from its ashes (the original club was destroyed in the 1991 Berkeley-Oakland Hills fire). The community surrounding the club has also been rebuilt, and few, if any, traces of the previous devastation are visible from the club itself.

What is visible from the club's Fireside Room is a panoramic view of the San Francisco Bay and adjacent communities that is so spectacular it almost makes additional decoration redundant. Hardwood floors, a neutral color scheme and large windows showcase the magnificent vista, while the soaring stone fireplace and antique brass chandeliers add a touch of friendly rusticity. There's even a small balcony that affords you the luxury of watching the sun set over the Golden Gate or the fog pour over the Berkeley hills as you sip champagne and enjoy the breeze. In front of the clubhouse, a sunny patio surrounded by verdant lawns and small trees is available for outdoor receptions. Although it's high up on a hill, this country club is fresh, unpretentious and quite down-to-earth.

CEREMONY CAPACITY: The Fireside Room, patio or gazebo accommodate up to 100 guests, maximum.

EVENT/RECEPTION CAPACITY: The Fireside Room and Patio, combined, hold up to 100 guests.

MEETING CAPACITY: The club holds 100 guests, maximum.

FEES & DEPOSITS: The rental fee is $1,200, and includes use of the Fireside Room, deck and patio areas for 4 hours; extra hours can be arranged. To secure your date, all of the nonrefundable rental fee plus a refundable $1,200 security deposit are required.

AVAILABILITY: Year-round, daily, 8am–11pm. Use of the deck and patio is seasonal. Only 1 event is booked per day.

SERVICES/AMENITIES:

Catering: BYO
Kitchen Facilities: moderately equipped
Tables & Chairs: provided
Linens, Silver, etc.: CBA or BYO
Restrooms: wheelchair accessible
Dance Floor: dining room or patio
Bride's Dressing Area: no
Meeting Equipment: microphones, screen

Parking: on-street
Accommodations: no guest rooms
Telephone: pay phones
Outdoor Night Lighting: access only
Outdoor Cooking Facilities: BBQ
Cleanup: caterer or renter
View: East Bay hills and San Francisco Bay
Other: bar

RESTRICTIONS:

Alcohol: BYO
Smoking: outdoors only
Music: amplified OK indoors with volume limits

Wheelchair Access: yes
Insurance: certificate required
Other: no rice, birdseed, petals or glitter

This is important! Tell locations you're reading HERE COMES THE GUIDE and ask if our information is still current.

Lake Temescal Beach House

Lakefront Event Facility

Temescal Regional Recreation Area, Oakland
510/544-3164
www.brazilianroom.org
brazil@ebparks.org

● Rehearsal Dinners	● Corp. Events/Mtgs.
● Ceremonies	● Private Parties
● Wedding Receptions	○ Accommodations

A beach in the middle of Oakland? With water and sand and everything? Yes! And so much more, thanks to the East Bay Regional Park District, who developed this scenic gem as one of its first three parks back in 1938. Today, the 48-acre property is a neighborhood oasis where busy urbanites can experience nature's rejuvenating powers. Lake Temescal can even become your own private getaway when you rent the handsome Beach House for your wedding or special event.

It's a leisurely stroll from the parking area down to the Beach House, picnic lawns and lake, and your guests will find it a rewarding nature walk. The East Shore Trail gently curves through stands of oak and willow, revealing sensory surprises: A flicker of ginger turns out to be a red squirrel; native songbirds warble from the treetops; the air is scented with the spicy aroma of bay laurel. Water lilies grace the shoreline, while butterflies flit amongst the cattails.

As the path slopes downward, the trees part to reveal the Beach House set against a forested knoll, overlooking a sweep of sandy shore. The two-story building has a cut-stone foundation accented with a trio of arches on the lower floor. The upper story (which is the rental space) is all windows, promising a spectacular view. Constructed in 1940, the historic Beach House has the quality craftsmanship and relaxed, unpretentious style typical of the era. Two wide flights of stone steps lead you to the rear of the building, where a terraced garden provides a lush backdrop to a charming flagstone patio. Fragrant roses in creamy white, lipstick pink and deep scarlet bloom from spring to fall, a romantic addition to any wedding ceremony. The sound of rushing water beckons you to a nearby footbridge spanning a waterfall that cascades down to the lake. Boughs of oak, fern and colorful rhododendron encircle a small clearing just beyond the bridge. A stone bench invites you to survey the waterscape below, where snowy egrets and cormorants cavort in the lake, and majestic blue herons pose regally on the mossy bank.

As the evening grows cool, your guests can still enjoy the lakeside panorama as they retreat inside the Beach House, thanks to the long row of picture windows in the Lakeview Room and adjoining Fireside Room. Both spaces evoke an Americana theme, with gleaming hardwood floors, log cabin walls awash in an oh-so-pale mint green, and polished copper wall sconces. The Fireside Room also boasts a high ceiling with dark, rough-hewn open beams. A grand flagstone hearth at the far end crackles and glows with a gas-burning fire, keeping everyone toasty. Double French doors give a glimpse of the garden, and admit more natural light. Leave these doors open during your event, and you'll let in the soothing harmony of the waterfall and the songbirds.

The Beach House and its peaceful surroundings capture the gentle simplicity of the past, and when you come here for a visit you might find yourself daydreaming about the possibilities...*an intimate garden fête, complete with breezy broad-brimmed hats and elegant china...the nostalgic warmth of a holiday gathering around the fireplace...a picnic on the patio, while lake trout jump for dragonflies in the lazy summer twilight...or stealing a kiss from your sweetheart on the shore of the moonlit lake.* Be creative—whatever celebration you imagine, Lake Temescal Beach House will make it wonderful.

CEREMONY CAPACITY: The Patio holds up to 130 seated guests.

EVENT/RECEPTION & MEETING CAPACITY: This location holds up to 80 seated guests.

FEES & DEPOSITS: A $100 deposit is required to secure your date. If cancelled more than 120 days prior to the event, $50 of this deposit is refundable. Signed contracts are required 2 weeks after the initial deposit to the Reservations Office at the East Bay Regional Park District Office in Oakland.

Weekend rates for Friday night, Saturday, Sunday, and holidays (min. 8 hours) range $1,050–1,500 depending on the day and time frame reserved. Each additional hour is $150. Weekday rates range $250–675 depending on day and length of time rented. If you opt to bring your own food without a caterer, there is an additional fee. Evening non-catered events are prohibited. For nonresidents of Alameda and Contra Costa counties, there is a surcharge that equals 20% of the room rental fee. Fees as of 2012 season, visit their website at www.brazilianroom.org for current prices.

AVAILABILITY: Year-round, daily; Monday–Thursday, 8am–10pm; Friday, 8am–midnight; Saturday, 10am–midnight; Sunday, 10am–10pm.

SERVICES/AMENITIES:

Catering: select from preferred list
Kitchen Facilities: prep only
Tables & Chairs: provided
Linens, Silver, etc.: BYO
Restrooms: wheelchair accessible
Dance Floor: yes
Bride's Dressing Room: yes
Meeting Equipment: BYO

Parking: large lot, fee charged April–Sept.
Accommodations: no guest rooms
Telephone: pay phone by beach
Outdoor Night Lighting: patio only
Outdoor Cooking Facilities: no
Cleanup: through caterer
View: hills, lake, park
Other: fireplace available, extra fee

RESTRICTIONS:

Alcohol: BYO wine, beer or champagne
Smoking: outside only
Music: amplified OK indoors, outdoors with restrictions

Wheelchair Access: yes
Insurance: extra liability is required

Oakland Marriott City Center

Hotel

1001 Broadway, Oakland
510/466-6455
www.oaklandmarriott.com
sales@oaklandmarriott.com

- Rehearsal Dinners
- Ceremonies
- Wedding Receptions
- Corp. Events/Mtgs.
- Private Parties
- Accommodations

There are quite a few reasons why the Oakland Marriott City Center has become a popular choice for a destination wedding or special event. One of the most important is its incredibly convenient location. Situated between historic Old Oakland and Uptown (Oakland's Arts and Entertainment District), it's close to the trendy new restaurants, businesses and residential spaces that are adding an amazing vitality to the city. The Paramount and Fox Theaters, the Oakland Museum, Chinatown, and the Housewives Market are mere blocks away, as is Jack London Square, Oakland's colorful waterfront district, and picturesque Lake Merritt. And both the Oakland and SF Airports are just a short drive from here.

The Marriott's jazzy interior also gets the thumbs up from guests. From the entryway and lobby to the event spaces, restaurants and guest rooms, the hotel's sophisticated design features contemporary décor accented by natural elements including wood, glass and metal. A warm autumn color palette is used throughout, ranging from shades of gold and sunset orange to light tan and rich, deep brown.

But if you're hosting a celebration here, what's best about this party-perfect site can be found inside its event spaces and accommodations. There are two huge ballrooms; a presidential suite (great for the wedding night!); a stunning 21st-floor banquet room with drop-dead views of the Bay, San Francisco, and the Oakland Hills; 489 stylish, well-appointed guest rooms and suites… plus much more.

Hold your gala in the 10,000-square-foot Grand Ballroom on the ground floor. It's adjacent to the sleek lobby, an impressive entrance for your affair, be it a romantic wedding, fundraising blowout or stylish corporate gathering. This ballroom can be divided into as many as seven chambers if your requirements aren't quite as lavish, or you can book the somewhat smaller Junior Ballroom on the second floor, which can be partitioned into three salons. Both ballrooms have high ceilings, mood lighting, audiovisual capabilities and graceful prefunction foyers that are ideal for everything from registration and intermission to pre-event mixers with cocktails and passed hors d'oeuvres.

More intimate affairs of up to 150 can be held in the Skyline Room, the hotel's rooftop ballroom where a spectacular bird's-eye view of the bridges, San Francisco and the surrounding cities will make spirits soar.

Food for all events is prepared by the hotel's caring and experienced banquet staff, and whether you're planning a small affair or inviting a large crowd, you'll receive the same award-winning Marriott service.

Our guess is that you and your guests will love this location. The Twelve Bars Lounge and LEVEL TWO Restaurant, with their dramatic atrium views, are congenial places for family and friends to mingle. Additional amenities—like the fitness facilities, business center and pool—might tempt them to stay put, but there's a lot to entice them beyond the hotel, too. Trains, planes, buses, and rental cars are all readily available, so it's easy to explore the many attractions the region has to offer.

CEREMONY CAPACITY: The hotel seats 900 guests indoors.

RECEPTION CAPACITY: The hotel can accommodate 600 seated or 1,000 standing indoors.

MEETING CAPACITY: The Convention Center holds 3,500 seated guests.

FEES & DEPOSITS: 30% of the total event cost is required to reserve your date. A portion is due 90 days prior to the event and the balance is due 30 days prior. Rental fees range $500–1,500 depending on the space rented. Meals range $49–69/person. Tax, alcohol and a 21% service charge are additional.

AVAILABILITY: Year-round, daily, anytime.

SERVICES/AMENITIES:

Catering: provided
Kitchen Facilities: n/a
Tables & Chairs: provided
Linens, Silver, etc.: provided
Restrooms: wheelchair accessible
Dance Floor: portable provided
Bride's & Groom's Dressing Areas: yes
Meeting Equipment: provided
Other: grand piano, A/V equipment

Parking: large lot, valet available
Accommodations: 489 guest rooms
Telephone: pay or guest phones
Outdoor Night Lighting: access only
Outdoor Cooking Facilities: no
Cleanup: provided
View: panorama of hills and San Francisco Bay, Lake Merritt, pool area

RESTRICTIONS:

Alcohol: provided or BYO with corkage fee
Smoking: not allowed
Music: amplified OK indoors

Wheelchair Access: yes
Insurance: liability required

Oakland Museum of California

Art, History and Natural Science Museum

1000 Oak Street, Oakland
510/318-8505
www.museumca.org/rent-museum
weddings@museumca.org

- Rehearsal Dinners
- Ceremonies
- Wedding Receptions
- Corp. Events/Mtgs.
- Private Parties
- Accommodations

The Oakland Museum of California is not just one of the city's most distinctive landmarks—it's also an oasis of serenity and beauty. In contrast to its modern, concrete exterior, OMCA's multi-tiered layout, open-air settings and views of Lake Merritt make it an amazing place for weddings and other special events.

The museum is built on three levels, with stairs and walkways leading the visitor through the site's intriguing variety of courtyards, terraces and gardens. A koi pond full of water lilies and papyrus plants graces the first level, and sculptures and artifacts are installed throughout the grounds. The Great Court Garden, a spacious lawn shaded by deodar cedars, sweet gum and alder trees, is lovely for a wedding, reception, corporate picnic or similar event. Concrete pillars topped by planters form two sides of the courtyard; creeping-fig-covered walls form the other two sides. The air is perfumed by swags of Japanese honeysuckle interspersed with mounds of blue cape plumbago and purple lantana.

Other outdoor venues include the Terraces, which look out on the gardens, and the Patio, which houses the OMCA Pavilion, a tented area that overlooks the koi pond. Another terrace has a view of Lake Merritt and the Oakland hills. If you happen to be wandering around the museum grounds and see a perfect spot but don't find it listed for rent, ask about it. OMCA will let you reserve almost any of its outside spaces.

For indoor functions, consider the museum's dining area, which forms a "bridge" over one of the main stairways. Two floor-to-ceiling windows allow you to view the koi pond from one side and the bustling museum from the other. The James Moore Theater is used for a multitude of events, such as concerts, theatrical performances and movie screenings. Both the theater and the Lecture Hall are suitable for business meetings and seminars. Additionally, the California Room is ideal for board meetings and small retreats of up to 40 people.

At OMCA, you really can have a garden wedding: Exchange vows under a shady tree canopy surrounded by blooming flowers, and dine al fresco on a terrace with Lake Merritt vistas. The lake also makes a wonderful backdrop for photos, especially at sunset when the sky is painted with color.

OMCA's location is great for your out-of-town guests, too. It's close to hotels, restaurants and local attractions—plus San Francisco is just a short drive over the Bay Bridge. As you can see, the Oakland Museum of California offers all sorts of unexpected possibilities.

CEREMONY CAPACITY: The Great Court Gardens accommodate up to 750 seated or 2,000 standing guests. The Terrace holds 60 seated or 100 standing, and the Patios—including the OMCA Pavilion—hold 150 seated or 250 standing.

EVENT/RECEPTION CAPACITY: For the Gardens, Terrace and Patio areas, see figures above. The museum café holds 150 seated guests, or 120 with a dance floor and small stage.

MEETING CAPACITY: The James Moore Theater accommodates 275 seated theater-style; the Lecture Hall holds 100; and the California Room seats up to 40.

FEES & DEPOSITS: A refundable deposit is required at the time of booking. 50% of the facility rental fee is payable 180 days prior to the event. The balance is due 30 days prior to the event. Rental fees for a 6-hour block start at $450 for a meeting space and vary depending on the area(s) rented. Contact the Events Services Department for the rental rates of specific areas. Security and other services are an additional charge. The OMCA garage, with a 170-car capacity, can be rented after regular museum hours.

AVAILABILITY: Year-round, daily, 8am–11pm. The museum café is available all day Monday and Tuesday, and after 5pm on Wednesday–Sunday. The outdoor Terraces and Garden are seasonal areas, available May–October as weather permits.

SERVICES/AMENITIES:

Catering: select from preferred list
Kitchen Facilities: fully equipped
Tables & Chairs: provided, up to 250 guests
Linens, Silver, etc.: through caterer
Restrooms: wheelchair accessible
Dance Floor: CBA, extra fee
Bride's Dressing Area: CBA
Meeting Equipment: full range
Other: some event coordination provided

Parking: museum garage, extra fee
Accommodations: no guest rooms
Telephone: emergency use only
Outdoor Night Lighting: CBA or BYO in gardens
Outdoor Cooking Facilities: no
Cleanup: provided or caterer
View: Lake Merritt from upper level

RESTRICTIONS:

Alcohol: provided, no BYO
Smoking: not allowed
Music: amplified OK

Wheelchair Access: yes
Insurance: required
Other: no rice, birdseed or confetti

Overwhelmed? Use the search criteria on www.HereComesTheGuide.com to narrow down your choices.

427

Preservation Park

Victorian Homes

1233 Preservation Park Way, Oakland
510/874-7580
www.preservationpark.com
events@preservationpark.com

- Rehearsal Dinners
- Ceremonies
- Wedding Receptions
- Corp. Events/Mtgs.
- Private Parties
- Accommodations

Occupying two blocks just a heartbeat away from Oakland's City Center, Preservation Park is an eye-catching re-creation of a Victorian neighborhood. Sixteen Victorian homes have been beautifully restored and colorfully painted. The setting has been further enhanced with period park benches, ornate wrought-iron fences, old-fashioned street lamps and a bronze fountain from Paris.

The park's social center is the Pavilion, a graceful bandstand where ceremonies usually take place. While the bride and groom exchange vows on stage, their guests, seated on the lawn just below them, can appreciate the lovely landscaping and vintage architecture that surrounds them. Outdoor receptions are held in the adjacent Fountain Circle, a circular plaza with a large two-tiered fountain topped by the moon goddess Diana at its center. There's plenty of room for a band, or you could have an outdoor buffet on either side of the Pavilion.

If you're planning an indoor reception, two houses just off the Fountain Circle are available. The Ginn House, circa 1890, features two delightful light and airy parlors reminiscent of those in an English country home. Nile Hall, circa 1911, is a craftsman-style building with a sensational space for a grand and elegant party. It has a 30-foot-high ceiling, skylights, multiple windows, a stage and a theatrical lighting and sound system. This room is well designed, with soft colors, nice detailing and attractive appointments—and enough space to accommodate an extensive guest list. You can reserve one or both houses, as they're connected by a spacious interior hallway.

The park is not only popular for weddings, it's hosted a wide range of events. When you reserve the outdoor spaces, the entrance gates are closed to cars so you and your guests can savor the feeling of having this charming "town" all to yourselves. For a remarkable glimpse of old-time Oakland, pay a visit to Preservation Park—it's well worth the trip.

CEREMONY CEREMONY CAPACITY: Ginn House holds 80 seated, Nile Hall 200 seated and the Pavilion Area 150–300 seated or 300–500 standing guests.

RECEPTION & MEETING CAPACITY: Various rooms hold 10–150 seated or 20–200 standing guests indoors. The Pavilion Area accommodates up to 300 seated and 500 standing.

FEES & DEPOSITS: A $500 deposit is required to secure your date. The rental fee is payable 120 days prior to the event. The fee for Nile Hall is $1,325; for Nile Hall plus the Ginn House, the fee is $2,100. The rental fee for the outdoor Pavilion Area is $1,100–2,450 without setup. If you rent the Pavilion Area in conjunction with Ginn House and Nile Hall, the fee is $775 without setup.

AVAILABILITY: Year-round, daily, 8am–11pm. The outdoor Pavilion, May to mid-October.

SERVICES/AMENITIES:

Catering: select from preferred list, or BYO-licensed, extra charge
Kitchen Facilities: sctup only
Tables & Chairs: provided, extra fee outdoors
Linens, Silver, etc.: provided by caterer
Restrooms: wheelchair accessible
Dance Floor: CBA
Bride's Dressing Area: CBA
Meeting Equipment: sound equipment, DVD, WiFi, microphones, flip charts

Parking: on-street or City garage nearby
Accommodations: no guest rooms
Telephone: no
Outdoor Night Lighting: yes
Outdoor Cooking Facilities: no
Cleanup: caterer
View: gardens and fountain

RESTRICTIONS:

Alcohol: provided, no BYO
Smoking: outside only
Music: amplified OK

Wheelchair Access: yes
Insurance: may be required

Scott's Seafood Restaurant

Waterfront Restaurant

2 Broadway, Jack London Square, Oakland
510/444-5969
www.scottseastbay.com
tiffanyc@scottsjls.com

● Rehearsal Dinners	● Corp. Events/Mtgs.
● Ceremonies	● Private Parties
● Wedding Receptions	Accommodations

One of Jack London Square's most recognizable landmarks, Scott's Seafood has long been a popular destination for fine dining. But what many people don't know is that this waterfront restaurant is also a versatile event location with seven private banquet rooms. Diners enjoy terrific views of passing ships and the San Francisco skyline, and out-of-town guests appreciate the convenience of nearby hotels, plenty of parking, and ferry service for day excursions.

Each banquet room is individually decorated and has its own unique ambiance. The newly remodeled Pavilion is the largest venue, accommodating up to 350 seated or 600 for a cocktail reception. Brides find this space irresistible thanks to a combination of appealing features: During the day, natural light flows in through tall windows, and interior trees create a garden atmosphere. In the evening, tea lanterns suspended from the high, vaulted ceiling cast a soft light over the festivities. Persian rugs and mahogany Chiavari chairs add sophisticated touches. The Pavilion's front doors open to the adjacent patio, making it easy for guests to take in some fresh air, the boardwalk scene and the wonderful view.

The Harborview Rooms are warm and inviting, with large windows overlooking the picturesque wooden boardwalk. Designed with faux-painted ceilings, modern chandeliers, leather chairs, and a copper-and-granite bar, they convey a feeling that's both classical and contemporary. Smaller celebrations can be held in the charming waterfront Terrace, the Port of Oakland Room or the intimate Jack London Rooms, all of which are ideal for engagement parties, bridal showers, rehearsal dinners and day-after gatherings.

Scott's Seafood, Jack London Square offers amenities you don't normally find in standard banquet rooms, such as elegant full-length table linens, ivory overlays, charger plates, hurricane table lanterns and personalized menu cards to commemorate the occasion. In-house bakery and floral services are also available.

Scott's has an extensive menu selection, and all dishes are prepared on site. Customer favorites include Stuffed Tuscan Chicken Breast, Peppercorn Crusted Filet Mignon and Layered Polenta Tower. Fresh seafood is delivered daily and presented in both modern and traditional ways. Salmon Alla Bella, Shiitake Crusted Tuna, Dungeness Crab Stuffed Halibut and Seafood Chiopino Pasta are just a few of your choices. The catering staff is happy to customize your menu, and can accommodate kosher, vegetarian, vegan, gluten-free and other special dietary requests.

With 27 years in business and a seasoned staff, Scott's also provides off-site catering to many Bay Area banquet venues, homes and offices. No event is too big or too small, and they're experts at handling everything from hors d'oeuvre station receptions and carryout platters to full-service plated meals. Their high level of personal service ensures you'll have the event you envisioned and, like so many of their satisfied clients, you'll doubtless be back for other celebrations for years to come.

CEREMONY CAPACITY: Scott's Waterfront Pavilion holds 350 seated or 800 standing; the Harbor View Rooms accommodate 220 seated or 450 standing guests.

EVENT/RECEPTION CAPACITY: Various interior rooms accommodate 12–220 seated or 20–450 standing guests. The Waterfront Pavilion holds 350 seated or 800 standing.

MEETING CAPACITY: Several spaces accommodate 10–350 seated guests.

FEES & DEPOSITS: A $500 deposit is required to secure your date. The food and beverage estimate is payable 7 days prior, with the remaining balance due the day of the event. Seated meals and buffets start at $30/person; hors d'oeuvres start at $20/person. Tax and a 20% service charge are additional.

AVAILABILITY: Year-round, daily, 7am–midnight.

SERVICES/AMENITIES:
Catering: provided, including kosher
Kitchen Facilities: n/a
Tables & Chairs: provided
Linens, Silver, etc.: provided
Restrooms: wheelchair accessible
Dance Floor: yes, extra charge
Bride's Dressing Area: no
Meeting Equipment: full range
Other: in-house bakery and florist, event coordination

Parking: valet or parking lot, discounted validation available
Accommodations: no guest rooms
Telephone: emergency use only
Outdoor Night Lighting: yes
Outdoor Cooking Facilities: none
Cleanup: provided
View: SF skyline and bay, Alameda Harbor

RESTRICTIONS:
Alcohol: provided
Smoking: designated areas
Music: amplified OK

Wheelchair Access: yes
Insurance: not required

Skyline Community Church

Church

12540 Skyline Boulevard, Oakland
510/531-8212
www.skylineucc.org
office@skylineucc.org

Rehearsal Dinners	● Corp. Events/Mtgs.
● Ceremonies	● Private Parties
● Wedding Receptions	Accommodations

High in the Oakland hills, past handsome hillside residences, woodsy Joaquin Miller Park and the Chabot Space & Science Center, you'll find a pleasant surprise just off Skyline Boulevard. When you see the sign for Skyline Community Church, turn into the drive. Let it lead you up past the two lower parking lots on a sun-splashed, flower-flanked climb to the white wooden bell tower that signals your arrival at the church. Set on the crest of a hill that borders the East Bay Regional Park District, this quiet sanctuary sits under an expanse of blue sky and sunlight. Birds sing in the treetops. Gentle breezes stir the pines. Noise and commotion seem far, far away.

It's a charming venue for a wedding, retreat, or any other event where an open and affirming environment fits the bill. Couples of any faith or sexual orientation, are welcome, which makes it the perfect place for interfaith marriages and same-sex unions. You're also free to invite your own priest, rabbi, or other spiritual leader to officiate.

Receptions are generally held in the picturesque circular courtyard, outfitted with teak benches flanked by urns overflowing with succulents. The courtyard provides plenty of space for your DJ or band and dance floor, and can be set up with tenting, umbrella-shaded tables or whatever suits your celebration.

On one side of the courtyard, a little path that winds through the well-kept lawn ends in a heart-shaped pattern just in front of an old-fashioned gazebo with a peaked roof and weathervane that spins with the cooling winds. From here you can look down on a hillside lovingly planted and tended, like the other nicely landscaped parts of the property, by church members. The gazebo is an attractive spot to tie the knot, but you might want to save it for the cake cutting and photos and opt instead for a ceremony in the chapel on the opposite side of the courtyard.

Accessed by four large doors, the fan-shaped sanctuary has a beamed ceiling, parquet floor and a stunning wall of glass behind the altar that frames uninterrupted views of regional parkland and the hills that roll toward Mt. Diablo. Acoustics in this hall are ethereal, making solo, a cappella, string or pipe organ (yes, this church has one!) performances sublime. Sea-blue carpeting leads down the stairs to the Meditation Room. It's a great spot for the groom and his guys to dress and meet with the pastor. The groom can then shake off any pre-wedding jitters in the serene labyrinth garden, which is also a beautiful site for photos. It even works perfectly for a tea ceremony prior to the wedding ceremony!

The bride and her attendants can get ready in the Friendship Room off the courtyard. Often used for fellowship and community gatherings, it features big windows, a compact adjacent kitchen, and double-mirrored cabinets with stage lighting that encourage plenty of primping.

Safe, private, relaxed and family-friendly, Skyline Community Church has much to offer children, too. Kids are encouraged to ring the church bell as the newlyweds leave the grounds. It's all so sweet and embracing...you and your guests will feel like you've found your own little piece of heaven.

CEREMONY CAPACITY: The Chapel holds 250 seated guests; the Courtyard, 300 seated guests.

EVENT/RECEPTION & MEETING CAPACITY: The Courtyard holds up to 300 seated guests.

FEES & DEPOSITS: A $500 deposit is required to reserve your date. The balance is due 4 weeks prior to the event. Rental fees range $950–2,600 depending on the space rented.

AVAILABILITY: Year-round, Monday through Saturday 9am–11pm; Sunday 1pm–11pm.

SERVICES/AMENITIES:
Catering: BYO
Kitchen Facilities: limited
Tables & Chairs: through caterer
Linens, Silver, etc.: through caterer
Restrooms: wheelchair accessible CBA
Dance Floor: through caterer
Bride's & Groom's Dressing Areas: yes
Meeting Equipment: digital projector and motorized screen with remote; WiFi

Parking: large lot, on-street
Accommodations: no guest rooms
Telephone: emergency phone available
Outdoor Night Lighting: yes
Outdoor Cooking Facilities: BBQ on site
Cleanup: caterer or renter
View: forest, mountains, valley, garden
Other: event coordination

RESTRICTIONS:
Alcohol: BYO wine, beer or champagne through licensed & insured caterer
Smoking: outside only at gazebo trellis
Music: amplified OK with restrictions

Wheelchair Access: limited
Insurance: liability required

The professionals in the back of this book are the best in the business. How do we know? Read page 637.

The Terrace Room
at the Lake Merritt Hotel

1800 Madison Street at Lakeside, Oakland
510/903-3580, Catering Department

www.theterraceroom.com
elizabeth@theterraceroom.com

Hotel and Conference Facility

● Rehearsal Dinners	● Corp. Events/Mtgs.
● Ceremonies	● Private Parties
● Wedding Receptions	Accommodations

Time has been good to the Lake Merritt Hotel. After three renovations in ten years, this classic 1927 Art Deco landmark is now filled with furnishings and accessories that enhance the building's striking architectural features.

The décor includes plush axminster carpeting, the design of which was inspired by a vintage fabric containing both a geometric pattern and exotic flowers in chestnut, gold, red and green; walls painted in a rich terracotta color; wrought-iron chandeliers; overstuffed Art Deco furniture covered in jewel-tone mohair fabric; and Lloyd Loom wicker chairs and cocktail tables.

The restoration extends to The Terrace Room, the hotel's restaurant and one of Oakland's premier entertainment sites. Twenty-foot, floor-to-ceiling windows along the entire front of this grand space offer an enchanting panorama of Lake Merritt, Lakeside Park and the Oakland hills. During the day the multilevel restaurant is bathed in light. At night, it has an intimate, almost cabaret feeling, and the view of the lake is spectacular: The dark surface of the water perfectly reflects the glittering Necklace of Lights gracing its perimeter.

The Terrace Room features a semicircular hardwood dance floor, and a sizable mural along one wall depicting Lake Merritt as it appeared over 40 years ago. A shiny black grand piano and Art Deco fixtures are nice finishing touches. In addition to its great location along Lake Merritt, the hotel provides a wide range of services, many of which can be specifically tailored to your special event.

CEREMONY CAPACITY: The Terrace Room holds 160 standing and/or seated guests.

EVENT/RECEPTION CAPACITY: The Terrace Room accommodates 200 seated or 350 standing guests.

MEETING CAPACITY: The Terrace Room holds 200 seated.

FEES & DEPOSITS: A $1,500 nonrefundable security deposit is required to reserve your date. An estimated 50% payment is required 2 months prior and the balance is due 1 month prior to your event. Full seated service, including food and beverage, starts at $30/person. Tax and a 20% service charge are additional. Any menu can be customized.

AVAILABILITY: For special events, year-round, Saturdays and Sundays 4pm–1am (call for details). Note that The Terrace Room and Lounge are also open to the public for dining: The Terrace Room hours are Monday–Friday, 11am–2pm for lunch and 5–8pm for dinner (9:30pm on Thursday and Friday). Additionally, The Terrace Room serves brunch on Saturday and Sunday.

SERVICES/AMENITIES:
Catering: provided, no BYO
Kitchen Facilities: n/a
Tables & Chairs: provided
Linens, Silver, etc.: provided
Restrooms: wheelchair accessible
Dance Floor: yes
Bride's Dressing Area: no
Meeting Equipment: podium and microphone available

Parking: on-street
Accommodations: no guest rooms
Telephone: emergency only
Outdoor Night Lighting: access only
Outdoor Cooking Facilities: no
Cleanup: provided
View: Lake Merritt, Oakland hills, cityscape
Other: event coordinator on site

RESTRICTIONS:
Alcohol: provided, or BYO wine and champagne only with corkage fee
Music: amplified OK with volume limits
Smoking: outdoors only

Wheelchair Access: yes
Insurance: required for vendors
Other: no food or beverages in lobby; no rice or confetti

Wedgewood Wedding & Banquet Center
at Metropolitan Golf Links

Golf Course Clubhouse

10051 Doolittle Drive, Oakland
866/966-3009

www.wedgewoodbanquet.com/metropolitan
sales@wedgewoodbanquet.com

● Rehearsal Dinners	● Corp. Events/Mtgs.
● Ceremonies	● Private Parties
● Wedding Receptions	Accommodations

For red carpet treatment alongside the greens and fairways of a beautiful 18-hole golf course—just minutes from downtown Oakland and the Oakland Airport—book your special event at the Wedgewood Banquet Center at the Metropolitan Golf Links. This great value and year-round course (designed by American Society of Golf Course Architects member Fred Bliss and long-time Bay Area resident and World Golf Hall of Famer Johnny Miller) is a terrific venue for weddings, golf events, corporate or other social functions and holiday parties. It was also awarded sanctuary status by Audubon International. Its spacious feel, plus long views to the Oakland hills, the bay, downtown Oakland and San Francisco lend it an uplifting outlook and unhurried charm.

To better accommodate weddings and special events, this facility has undergone an extensive renovation that includes a major banquet room expansion, additional ceremony space alongside the golf course, and attractive landscaping around the new event areas. The sizeable banquet room, with its two windowed walls, now opens onto a matching, 3,000-square-foot tent with amenities such as a built-in bar, state-of-the-art sound system, permanent dance floor, carpeting and cooling Casablanca fans. Also new is an expansive lawn, complete with gazebo and rose garden, that's custom-made for ceremonies. Guests reach the banquet center via a breezeway that leads to the patio of the golf course's Sweet Spot Café. The patio can also be used as additional space for large celebrations, and features uninterrupted views of the course and the bayside surroundings.

Of course, one of the most reassuring aspects of booking an event at this appealing East Bay location is the professionalism and service you'll experience at the hands of the expert planning staff. Five lavish wedding packages include invitations, flowers, cake and music, as well as the DJ, minister and menu—all of which are carefully sampled, screened and priced to ensure top quality, affordability and maximum satisfaction. Menu options are varied and generous with room for customization.

Will you choose the cream-white dendrobium orchids and bar grass in tall cylinder vases or the big bowls of floating roses, gerberas or gardenias? The stacked whipped cream cake with fresh flowers or the white-chocolate cake shaped like a gift box with a cascading ribbon? We can't list all of your options, but we can promise you this: You won't have to do any legwork, you'll know just what you're getting—and you won't lose track of the cost. Your only worry will be what to do after the party is over.

CEREMONY CAPACITY: The center accommodates 350 indoors or outdoors.

EVENT/RECEPTION CAPACITY: The center holds 300 seated and 350 standing indoors or outdoors.

MEETING CAPACITY: Wedgewood accommodates 200 seated.

FEES & DEPOSITS: A 25% deposit is required to reserve your date. The next 25% is due 90 days prior and the balance is due 10 days prior to the event. All-inclusive wedding packages start at $30/person. Tax, alcohol and a 20% service charge are additional.

AVAILABILITY: Year-round, daily, 6am–midnight.

SERVICES/AMENITIES:

Catering: provided
Kitchen Facilities: n/a
Tables & Chairs: provided
Linens, Silver, etc.: provided
Restrooms: wheelchair accessible
Dance Floor: provided
Bride's & Groom's Dressing Areas: CBA
Meeting Equipment: full range CBA, extra charge

Parking: large lot
Accommodations: no guest rooms
Telephone: emergency only
Outdoor Night Lighting: access only
Outdoor Cooking Facilities: no
Cleanup: provided
View: fairways, landscaped grounds, SF skyline
Other: event coordination

RESTRICTIONS:

Alcohol: provided
Smoking: outside only
Music: amplified OK

Wheelchair Access: yes
Insurance: not required
Other: no rice, confetti or glitter; no open flames

Orinda Country Club

Country Club

315 Camino Sobrante, Orinda
925/254-4313
www.orindacc.org
catering@orindacc.org

● Rehearsal Dinners	● Corp. Events/Mtgs.
● Ceremonies	● Private Parties
● Wedding Receptions	Accommodations

In the early 1920s, Orinda pioneer E.I. deLaveaga had a grand idea: to build a luxurious subdivision, centered around a country club that would provide its residents with "…family recreation, wholesome, happy country life…and something for every member of the family to do—golf, swimming, tennis, dancing…." He hired the finest architects, engineers and landscapers, and in 1925 the Orinda Country Club first opened its doors, bringing deLaveaga's joyful vision to life. Now, almost a century later, this spectacular club continues to offer its members and guests a host of recreational and social activities, all in a setting of unparalled natural beauty.

Designed by noted San Francisco architect Hamilton Murdock, the Orinda Country Club is a classic example of the the Spanish Mediterranean style that reached its pinnacle in the 1920s and '30s. Design elements such as a red-tile roof, balconies, archways, and a textured stucco exterior create a building that is in complete harmony with its woodland environment. Though it has been renovated many times since its opening, the clubhouse still evokes the glamour of those bygone days. You wouldn't be at all surprised to see Katherine Hepburn strolling off the tennis court or Clark Gable teeing up on the golf course (and that isn't just a fantasy—Bing Crosby, Bob Hope, Joe DiMaggio and Jack Benny are among the celebrities who have played golf here).

The clubhouse's interior reflects the handsome Spanish influence of its exterior. The main event space is the Grand Ballroom, which lives up to its name in every way. Upon entering, your eye travels upwards, past ornate metal chandeliers to the arched balcony supported by spiral columns, finally taking in the coffered ceiling and elaborately painted molding edged with copper. Large mirrors reflect the soft gold of the walls and the shining hardwood floors, and plush area rugs add touches of color. Fireplaces at both ends of the room can be lit in cool weather, heightening the room's warm, sumptuous ambiance.

Arched French doors lead from the ballroom to the Terrace Room. Here, one wall of windows opens onto fabulous views of the golf course and surrounding hillsides, so thickly covered in oaks, bays and alders that it must look much the same as when E.I. deLaveaga first set eyes on the property. A balcony runs the length of the terrace, perfect for contemplating the wooded vistas surrounding you. Large parties can use the terrace and the Grand Ballroom. There's even a "semiprivate" room just off the terrace that's popular with anyone looking for a place to relax and enjoy the festivities without feeling overwhelmed.

As befits such an exclusive, upscale establishment, the service here is "above par." The expert staff can assist you in every detail of your event, from choosing linen colors to selecting wines that will complement your customized menu. Everything is included in the price: bartenders, servers, insurance, and an on-site coordinator. And since only one event is scheduled per day, you and your guests can relax and savor every moment you spend at this unique facility. When you book your event at the Orinda Country Club, you're not just a customer, but a "member in spirit," participating in a tradition of gracious hospitality that's sure to continue for another 100 years.

CEREMONY CAPACITY: The Grand Ballroom accommodates 144 seated guests.

EVENT/RECEPTION CAPACITY: The Grand Ballroom holds up to 350 seated or 600 standing guests.

MEETING CAPACITY: Meetings do take place at this location. Call the Sales Department for details.

FEES & DEPOSITS: A $2,000 deposit is required to reserve your date. 50% of the estimated charges are due 3 months prior and the balance is due 7 days prior to the event. Rental fees range $250–3,000 depending on type of event and space rented. Meals range $32–52/person. Tax, alcohol and a 20% service charge are additional.

AVAILABILITY: Tuesday–Sunday, 7am–midnight.

SERVICES/AMENITIES:

Catering: provided
Kitchen Facilities: n/a
Tables & Chairs: provided
Linens, Silver, etc.: provided
Restrooms: wheelchair accessible
Dance Floor: provided
Bride's Dressing Area: CBA
Meeting Equipment: some provided, more CBA

Parking: large lot, valet optional
Accommodations: no guest rooms
Telephone: house phone
Outdoor Night Lighting: yes
Outdoor Cooking Facilities: no
Cleanup: provided
View: golf course, hills, forest, canyon
Other: event coordination, grand piano, on-site florals, A/V equipment

RESTRICTIONS:

Alcohol: provided
Smoking: outside only
Music: amplified OK

Wheelchair Access: yes
Insurance: not required

Want to know WHAT TO ASK a potential location or vendor? Check out our Questions to Ask starting on page 17.

Guild Hall at Piedmont Community Church

Community Hall

400 Highland Avenue, Piedmont
510/547-5700
www.piedmontchurch.org
jean@piedmontchurch.org

● Rehearsal Dinners	Corp. Events/Mtgs.
● Ceremonies	● Private Parties
● Wedding Receptions	Accommodations

You'll see the landmark bell tower of the beautiful Piedmont Community Church long before you arrive. Gleaming in the sunlight, the ivory-colored Mission-style building looks a bit like a wedding cake, set atop an ivy- and flower-covered rise overlooking the prosperous community that gives the venue its name.

An extensive renovation prior to the church's 100th-year anniversary added numerous features, making the facilities here even more guest-friendly. You can enter through a number of private and public stairways, ramps and drives, all of which lead to an expansive, landscaped inner courtyard that radiates around a colorful central fountain. This is, of course, the perfect place for an outdoor ceremony roofed in blue sky and skirted in blossoms. But you might want to use this area and the upper courtyard that surrounds it for music and cocktails, and instead get married in the church itself.

Nothing will prepare those attending for the regal ambiance within. Plush royal-blue carpet, dark pews cushioned in velvet, a lustrous, carved-beam ceiling, and two walls of stained-glass windows with floral motifs in brilliant, jewel colors evoke an Old World opulence. Couples tie the knot at an altar fit for a king and queen, beneath a rotunda brightened with lofty stained-glass windows. The church comes with a fabulous pipe organ hidden behind one altar wall, an organist, and acoustics that will naturally amplify even a whispered "I do." There are also separate spaces for the couple to get ready: the lounge-like Altar Guild Room for the groom; and a comfortable salon with mirrors, bathroom, vanity, private entrance and more for the bride and her retinue.

Across the courtyard, the welcoming Guild Hall provides a perfectly grand setting for a celebration of any kind. The beamed ceiling soars overhead, hardwood floors gleam golden, and pale sage-colored walls exude an embracing calm. Enormous windows can be left open on sunny days, and there's a generous stage for musicians. Another plus: a spacious commercial-quality kitchen that will surely please your caterer. Like the other structures on the property, Guild Hall has a private entrance, landscaped outdoor seating areas, and is flanked by graceful colonnades.

If your party is very large or very small, you may want to use the Clara Barton and Doris Murdock Rooms. Both open to the upper courtyard and provide parlor-like space for a guest lounge, additional buffet tables or a quieter, more intimate gathering. Panel doors separate the two rooms so that they can be used individually or together.

Sound heavenly? It is—especially when glasses are raised, toasts are made and the church bells chime for you.

CEREMONY CAPACITY: The sanctuary holds 300 seated guests. The outdoor area holds 100 seated.

EVENT/RECEPTION CAPACITY: Guild Hall can accommodate up to 200 seated guests.

MEETING CAPACITY: Meetings do not take place at this facility.

FEES & DEPOSITS: A deposit is required to reserve your date. The balance is due 30 days prior. Rental fees range $1,750–3,950 depending on the space rented, the length of your rental, and whether or not you are a Piedmont Community Church member. Fees include clergy on staff, organist, complimentary event coordination for the rehearsal and ceremony, fireplace, grand piano, tables and chairs.

AVAILABILITY: Year-round, daily, call for details.

SERVICES/AMENITIES:

Catering: BYO
Kitchen Facilities: fully equipped
Tables & Chairs: provided
Linens, Silver, etc.: CBA or through caterer
Restrooms: wheelchair accessible
Dance Floor: provided
Bride's Dressing Area: yes
Meeting Equipment: n/a

Parking: on street
Accommodations: no guest rooms
Telephone: house phone
Outdoor Night Lighting: provided
Outdoor Cooking Facilities: none
Cleanup: provided
View: fountain, garden, landscaped grounds
Other: grand piano, clergy on staff, complimentary event coordination

RESTRICTIONS:

Alcohol: BYO
Smoking: not allowed anywhere on the premises
Music: amplified OK indoors with restrictions

Wheelchair Access: yes
Insurance: liability required

Piedmont Community Hall

711 Highland Avenue, Piedmont
510/420-3081, 510/420-3075
probb@ci.piedmont.ca.us

Community Park Building

● Rehearsal Dinners	● Corp. Events/Mtgs.
● Ceremonies	● Private Parties
● Wedding Receptions	○ Accommodations

This facility is one of the most popular event venues in Northern California—and for good reason. The building is not only very attractive inside and out, but it has the added benefit of being situated in a lovely park setting.

Azaleas and camellias provide splashes of color near the circular landscaped plaza in front of the hall. Redwoods and flowering cherry trees shade portions of the plaza, and behind the building a stream and more trees complete the circle of greenery.

The garden is home to another structure, a Japanese Tea House which was relocated here after it was donated to the City of Piedmont. Couples can have a small ceremony in the Tea House, or brides can spend some quiet time here before the wedding or use it as a private place to dress and get ready for the big event. Two side walls of the Tea House are removable, so when the weather is mild, it's a terrific spot for an extra bar or hors d'oeuvres station.

Receptions take place in the Piedmont Community Hall, a splendid structure, Mediterranean in style with light taupe walls and terracotta tile roof. The hall's interior looks so chic you'd never believe this is a city-owned facility. The main event space is a great party room, with a high, beamed ceiling, shining herringbone hardwood floors and chandeliers. Floor-to-ceiling windows allow lots of natural light and ensure that the "outdoor" feeling of the adjacent park carries over to your reception. This is a refined, nicely designed space, suitable for an elegant wedding, company party or corporate retreat. As we said, it's a popular spot, so remember to reserve early.

CEREMONY CAPACITY: The site holds up to 200 seated or standing guests indoors or outdoors.

EVENT/RECEPTION & MEETING CAPACITY: The site maximum is 200 guests. The hall accommodates 200 standing or 120 seated guests. The patio area holds 150–200 guests.

FEES & DEPOSITS: For events on Friday, Saturday, Sunday or holidays, a $1,000 security deposit is due 2 weeks after booking and is refundable 6 weeks after the event. May–October weekend rates range $2,200–3,700 for an 8-hour block Friday–Sunday. Piedmont residents receive a discounted rate. Additional hours available at $250/hour. Payment is due 90 days prior to the event. For Monday–Friday and off-season rates, please call for specifics.

Weekday rates for business functions vary depending on event duration; call for more information.

AVAILABILITY: Year-round, daily, 8am–midnight (1 event per day). Call early—the summer months are booked quickly.

SERVICES/AMENITIES:

Catering: BYO

Kitchen Facilities: fully equipped

Tables & Chairs: provided

Linens, Silver, etc.: BYO

Restrooms: wheelchair accessible

Dance Floor: hardwood floor

Bride's and Groom's Dressing Area: restrooms

Meeting Equipment: screen, TV, VCR, microphones, PA system

Parking: on- and off-street

Accommodations: no guest rooms

Telephone: pay phone

Outdoor Night Lighting: yes

Outdoor Cooking Facilities: BYO

Cleanup: caterer or renter

View: park setting

RESTRICTIONS:

Alcohol: BYO, must have controlled bar

Smoking: not allowed

Music: amplified OK

Wheelchair Access: yes

Insurance: included in weekend rates; for weekday use, BYO or purchase from Hall

Wedgewood Wedding & Banquet Center
at Delta View Golf Course

Event Center at Golf Club

2222 Golf Club Road, Pittsburg
866/966-3009
www.wedgewoodbanquet.com/delta-view
sales@wedgewoodbanquet.com

- Rehearsal Dinners
- Ceremonies
- Wedding Receptions
- Corp. Events/Mtgs.
- Private Parties
- Accommodations

The staff at Wedgewood Wedding and Banquet Center at Delta View Golf Course knows just what to do to make your event a huge success. Whether the party unfolds indoors or out, this rambling Mission-style clubhouse set amid handsomely sculpted fairways overlooking the Sacramento River Delta provides grounds for a wonderful celebration.

When they arrive, guests will naturally congregate on one of the broad, sunlit patios where tables and chairs can either be appealingly arranged or whisked away in welcome. Double glass doors open to the tastefully carpeted bar and receiving area, where your partygoers can meet one another, mingle and munch, or sip on champagne and signature drinks at a delightful salutary reception. The bar opens onto a spacious vestibule with plenty of room for a guest book, gift table, and additional socializing.

The grass is always green on the manicured lawn just beyond the patio, where a white gazebo surrounded by snow-white tree roses and other cloud-colored blossoms is fringed by a curtain of willow. You can tie the knot in this favorite spot or have your ceremony indoors in the Delta View Room, an airy hall with a subtly Mediterranean style. Thirteen sets of windowed double doors framed with gauzy curtains flood the room with natural light. Recessed lighting keeps the mood calm and congenial at night. The built-in wooden dance floor invites diners to step lively when the music begins—that is, if the fine food and dining companions don't hold them entranced at their tables. The Board Room next door also entices with its intimate dimensions and relaxing ambiance. It's an excellent space for after-dinner drinks, cake cutting and toasts, as well as smaller dinners, meetings and gatherings.

Other very special spaces on this premier property include a well-appointed bride's changing room with an elegant white couch, full-length mirror, vanity table and plenty of room for hanging elaborate gowns. It opens onto a semiprivate breezeway and small patio garden with views of the final green. The Mountain View Room, by the pub and grill, features its own built-in dance floor and could serve as a great place for dancing and drinks with a clubbier feel or a playroom for the kids in attendance. You can even use the pub and grill after hours.

Remember, this is a Wedgewood Wedding and Banquet Center, which means that everything from invitations, response cards and thank-you notes, to toasting goblets, photographers, customized cakes, flowers, music and menu selections is available in carefully designed packages executed according to your wishes and to the most exacting standards. After all, they have their trademark reputation to uphold and marvelous memories to create.

CEREMONY CAPACITY: The site holds 250 seated guests indoors or outdoors.

EVENT/RECEPTION CAPACITY: The facility can accommodate 250 seated or 300 standing indoors.

MEETING CAPACITY: The site holds 250 seated.

FEES & DEPOSITS: 25% of the estimated total is required to reserve your date. The balance is due 10 days prior to the event. There are no rental fees as long as certain food and beverage minimums are met. All-inclusive weding packages start at $30/person. Tax, alcohol and a 20% service charge are additional.

AVAILABILITY: Year-round, daily, anytime.

SERVICES/AMENITIES:

Catering: provided
Kitchen Facilities: n/a
Tables & Chairs: provided
Linens, Silver, etc.: provided
Restrooms: wheelchair accessible
Dance Floor: provided
Bride's Dressing Area: yes
Meeting Equipment: CBA
Other: event coordination

Parking: large lot
Accommodations: no guest rooms
Telephone: emergency use only
Outdoor Night Lighting: provided
Outdoor Cooking Facilities: no
Cleanup: provided
View: fairways, hills, Sacramento River Delta, landscaped grounds

RESTRICTIONS:

Alcohol: provided
Smoking: not allowed
Music: amplified OK

Wheelchair Access: yes
Insurance: liability required

Want to find more venues and services? Check out our informative website, www.HereComesTheGuide.com.

445

Rockefeller Lodge

Historic Lodge

Address withheld to ensure privacy. San Pablo
510/235-7344, Deborah, Event Coordinators
www.rockefellerlodge.com
rocklodge1@gmail.com

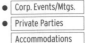

● Rehearsal Dinners	● Corp. Events/Mtgs.
● Ceremonies	● Private Parties
● Wedding Receptions	Accommodations

Have you always wanted to do something a bit different? Maybe have a Victorian theme in one room and French lace and balloons in another? Or perhaps treat your guests to milk and cookies baked on the spot? Whatever your fantasy, the lodge's proprietors would love the challenge of making your special event a reality.

Tucked within a quiet, treelined San Pablo neighborhood, the historic, two-acre garden lodge is named for famed industrialist John D. Rockefeller who purchased the property around the turn of the century and turned it into his private hunting lodge. The brown-shingled building and its spacious interior retain a rustic dignity, thanks to hardwood floors, hand-hewn ceiling beams and a noteworthy fireplace: Rockefeller had it constructed of burnt bricks recovered from the 1906 earthquake. These days, receptions and company parties enjoy the rooms' cozy comfort all year round.

During its illustrious past, the property had once been a Japanese Buddhist temple and the current owners, the Marshall family, have retained the retreat's fragrant, woodsy serenity. Indeed, it's the lush grounds that attract most wedding couples. Winding brick paths and wisteria-covered arbors invite leisurely strolls, and splashing fountains lull guests into relaxed contentment. Wedding ceremonies are held on a red-bricked patio, with the couple saying their vows in a gazebo framed by redwoods. A tented patio area can host the reception, or during warmer months why not dine in the twinkle-lit gardens beneath a moonlit sky?

With its diverse past, versatile rooms and enchanting grounds, the lodge can accommodate a wide range of creativity. As it turns out, the Marshalls also run *Party Time Caterers,* so they're just the folks to help you pull it all together, no matter what you envision.

CEREMONY & EVENT/RECEPTION CAPACITY: The lodge and grounds accommodate 410 seated guests; the lodge alone holds 150 seated. The entire site holds 410 for a reception.

MEETING CAPACITY: The lodge holds up to 150 seated guests.

FEES & DEPOSITS: A $600 security deposit is required to secure your date. The facility rental fee is complimentary for a 5-hour block Monday–Friday; it's $1,200 on Saturday and Sunday (day or evening). A 1-hour rehearsal can be arranged on Thursday evenings for $100. For events taking place November–March, except holidays, the rental fee is reduced by $600. Additional hours are $200/hour.

Buffets for over 100 guests range $13–29/person. Catering for 50 people, minimum, starts at $17/person; tax and an 18% service charge are additional. Full payment is required 14 days prior to the event. There is a $4.50/person beverage service charge which includes labor, glasses and nonalcoholic beverages. Any menu can be customized.

AVAILABILITY: Year-round, daily, 10am–4pm or 5pm–11pm. Available for any 6-hour block of time on Sunday.

SERVICES/AMENITIES:

Catering: provided, no BYO

Kitchen Facilities: n/a

Tables & Chairs: provided

Linens, Silver, etc.: provided

Restrooms: wheelchair accessible

Dance Floor: yes

Bride's Dressing Area: yes

Meeting Equipment: BYO

Parking: 2 lots

Accommodations: no guest rooms

Telephone: emergency use only

Outdoor Night Lighting: yes

Outdoor Cooking Facilities: no

Cleanup: provided

View: landscaped grounds and waterfalls

Other: full event planning

RESTRICTIONS:

Alcohol: BYO, service fee required

Smoking: outside only

Music: amplified OK inside only, 4-piece band limit

Wheelchair Access: yes

Insurance: certificate required

Other: no rice or birdseed

Alcosta Senior and Community Center
Park and Gardens

Community Center

9300 Alcosta Boulevard, San Ramon
925/973-3250

www.sanramon.ca.gov/parks/parks_facilities/rental.htm
pcstechniciansfacilities@sanramon.ca.gov

- Rehearsal Dinners
- Ceremonies
- Wedding Receptions
- Corp. Events/Mtgs.
- Private Parties
- Accommodations

The Alcosta Senior and Community Center not only has something for everyone, it offers a number of wonderful features you don't always find in a community center.

We love the fact that this venue has both indoor and outdoor event spaces, and comes with a fully equipped commercial kitchen. The center's banquet facility, the upscale Vista Grande Room, is well suited for wedding receptions, large meetings and other special events. The walls are painted a pleasant dusky peach, and the light oak floor is great for dancing. A high vaulted ceiling and windows with views of rolling hills add to its charm.

Sophisticated lighting and sound systems let you create the mood and music you want: Use lighting to highlight an area in a festive or sultry way; plug in your iPod (or any audio device) to listen to your own playlist.

Multiple doors open to an adjoining terrace, which extends your seating—and your celebration—outside. Shaded by a vine-covered arbor, the terrace is a lovely spot for dining, socializing and simply enjoying the fresh air and view of the hills. When the weather is warm, leave the Vista Grande Room doors open so that guests can flow easily between the two spaces.

Ceremonies here are held in the Gazebo, a Victorian-style confection with a white picket railing and peaked shake roof. Standing in the middle of a park-like setting, it's encircled by flowering trees and overlooks a broad lawn where family and friends are seated.

Throughout your event, the "park" provides a relaxing place for guests to stroll along brick paths, have a quiet conversation under a tree and even play bocce ball. As you sit on a bench soaking up the sun, you can't help but appreciate the unexpected beauty and serenity of this private little haven.

We think the Alcosta Senior and Community Center is a real find, and for those on a budget, very easy on the pocketbook.

CEREMONY CAPACITY: The Vista Grande Room seats 115 banquet-style or 200 seated theater-style.

EVENT/RECEPTION CAPACITY: The facility can accommodate up to 115 seated banquet-style.

MEETING CAPACITY: Several spaces accommodate 20–200 seated guests.

FEES & DEPOSITS: A $50–200 security deposit is due when you book the facility (depending on spaces rented). The rental fee ranges $45–165/hour on weekends (6pm Friday to 6pm Sunday) and $20–90/hour weekdays (6pm Sunday to 6pm Friday) and is due 90 days prior to the event. If the booking occurs less than 90 days prior to the event, the rental fee is due at the time of the booking along with the security deposit. San Ramon residents receive a discounted rate. The Vista Grande Room can be partitioned in half, and may be rented as a half space. There is an additional fee for use of the kitchen.

AVAILABILITY: Year-round. Monday–Thursday, 5pm–10pm; Friday, 5pm–1am; Saturday, 8:30am–1am; and Sunday, 8:30am–10pm.

SERVICES/AMENITIES:

Catering: pre-approved list or BYO with approval
Kitchen Facilities: fully equipped, extra fee
Tables & Chairs: provided
Linens, Silver, etc.: BYO
Restrooms: wheelchair accessible
Dance Floor: yes
Bride's Dressing Area: CBA, extra fee
Meeting Equipment: CBA, extra fee
Other: piano, extra fee

Parking: ample lot
Accommodations: no guest rooms
Telephone: emergency use only
Outdoor Night Lighting: yes
Outdoor Cooking Facilities: BBQ
Cleanup: renter or caterer
View: Las Trampas Regional Park hills, landscaped surroundings

RESTRICTIONS:

Alcohol: BYO, insurance required
Smoking: outside only
Music: amplified OK inside only

Wheelchair Access: yes
Insurance: sometimes required
Other: decorating restrictions; no birdseed, candles, confetti, rice, glitter, petals or bubbles; red wine and punch discouraged

The Bridges Golf Club

Golf Club

9000 South Gale Ridge Road, San Ramon
925/735-4253, Special Events

www.thebridgesgolf.com
abaker@kempersports.com

- Rehearsal Dinners
- Ceremonies
- Wedding Receptions
- Corp. Events/Mtgs.
- Private Parties
- Accommodations

Perched on a gentle rise in the foothills of Mt. Diablo, the Bridges Golf Clubhouse looks every bit the Mediterranean villa, with its tiled roof, white walls and Moorish turrets. The interior has the feel of an exclusive country club, and from almost every window the view is a vision in green: acres of velvety fairways, rolling away into the distance. The setting is so lovely, you might easily forget that this place was built primarily for golf.

When you enter the clubhouse lobby, a pair of elaborate wrought-iron gates to your left opens into a swanky bar inside one of those exotic towers you noticed out front. The magnificent double-high coved ceiling boasts a massive chandelier that would seem at home in a Medici castle! The bar adjoins the Golfer's Patio, where guests can quaff cocktails under the shade of a sycamore while surveying the players on the links.

French doors and windows make up one wall of The Bridges' main dining area, appropriately christened the "View Room." Wall sconces and an antique-style chandelier produce a romantic candelabra effect, and together with the sunlight enhance the warm glow of the room's earth tones. A crosshatch of wooden ceiling beams harmonizes with the wood trim of the richly upholstered chairs and oak tables.

A veranda runs along the greens-side of the club, accessed by both the View Room and the adjacent Fireplace Room. Used separately, these two spaces are divided by a tasteful partition of wooden shutters topped with glass cutaways; to combine the rooms for a larger event, the partition is simply folded away. The ambiance of richness and comfort in the View Room also pervades the Fireside Room, a cozy space for a rehearsal dinner. Your focus here is drawn to a grand stone hearth with a novel design: The fireplace is actually double-sided, and doors lead to a curved patio that surrounds the hearth's outdoor face. They call this the "Back Fireplace," and if there's a chill in the evening air, simply snuggle up by the hearth and behold the picturesque panorama.

The club's most dramatic room is the Garden Pavilion, just a few steps from the clubhouse. It's a grand space, with a 25-foot ceiling, antique wrought-iron chandeliers and a wall of huge archways overlooking the fairways. Guests love to step through the center arch onto the "Looking Terrace," where they have a panoramic view of the greens, Mt. Diablo and the color-streaked sky as the sun sets behind the hills. The archways have tall French doors and windows, and the facility is climate controlled for year-round comfort. When the weather is perfect, however, you are still able to open the windows and let in the afternoon breeze. Set for an elegant reception, the Pavilion is breathtaking: Tables are covered with linens, flowers and votive candles; silver and crystal sparkle in the candlelight, and the whole room is filled with a warm glow. If you'd like a more informal ambiance, however, the Pavilion's flexibility can accommodate your creativity. Some couples have brought in lion or dragon dancers for entertainment, and one even hosted a luau with hula dancers. During the holiday season, Bridges transforms the Pavilion with festive decorations, but if you have a different look in mind the club's event coordinators will be happy to help you achieve it.

The Bridges Golf Club encourages "proper etiquette and the highest standards" on the golf course. This emphasis on quality and tradition is also reflected in the clubhouse and Pavilion, so whether you host a customized golf tournament, a conference or the most sophisticated wedding reception, your event will be first class all the way.

CEREMONY CAPACITY: The outdoor ceremony site on the First Fairway holds up to 300 seated guests. Indoors, the facility seats up to 100. Ceremonies only take place at The Bridges in combination with a reception.

EVENT/RECEPTION CAPACITY: The clubhouse accommodates 120 seated or 150 standing guests. The Garden Pavilion holds up to 300 seated or 400 standing guests.

MEETING CAPACITY: The Fireside and the View Rooms, combined, hold 80 guests seated theater-style. The Garden Pavilion holds 300 guests seated theater-style.

FEES & DEPOSITS: A $2,000 nonrefundable deposit is required to secure your date. 50% of the food and beverage minimum is due 6 months prior to the event, and the balance is due 2 weeks prior to the event. Room rental fees range $300–3,000 depending on space rented. Packages range $47–67/person; tax, alcohol and a 20% service charge are additional. Food and beverage minimums apply and range $750–20,000 depending on space and time rented. Specials are available for Friday and Sunday bookings.

AVAILABILITY: Year-round, daily, 7am–2am.

SERVICES/AMENITIES:

Catering: provided, or BYO
Kitchen Facilities: n/a
Tables & Chairs: provided up to 300 guests
Linens, Silver, etc.: provided
Restrooms: wheelchair accessible
Dance Floor: yes
Bride's Dressing Area: CBA
Meeting Equipment: CBA, extra fee

Parking: large lot
Accommodations: no guest rooms
Telephone: emergency use only
Outdoor Night Lighting: yes
Outdoor Cooking Facilities: CBA
Cleanup: provided
View: fairways, East Bay Hills, Mt. Diablo
Other: event coordination

RESTRICTIONS:

Alcohol: provided, or corkage $14/bottle
Smoking: outside only
Music: amplified OK

Wheelchair Access: yes
Insurance: not required

This is important! Tell locations you're reading HERE COMES THE GUIDE and ask if our information is still current.

451

The Ranch at Little Hills

Ranch

18013 Bollinger Canyon Road, San Ramon
925/426-3066

www.theranchatlittlehills.com
weddings@theranchatlittlehills.com

- Rehearsal Dinners
- Ceremonies
- Wedding Receptions
- Corp. Events/Mtgs.
- Private Parties
- Accommodations

For a joyous celebration in the great outdoors few places can top The Ranch at Little Hills. This 25-acre oasis nestled in the East Bay hills next to the vast Las Trampas Regional Wilderness is mere minutes from the freeway, but you and your guests will feel like you've managed to get completely away from it all.

The well-equipped property, part of the East Bay Regional Parks system, is perfect for anything from a corporate gathering or family fun to a wedding on the grass—all framed in oaks and canopied by the sky. Events here are run by *The California Parks Company,* which has successfully catered to over a million guests in their two decades of operation.

A secluded path leads from the parking lot to the Pergola Deck, where wedding parties of all sizes can witness a romantic ceremony. Afterwards, it's just a few steps to Oak Knoll for the reception. Here, a natural wood fence and enormous live oaks seclude the large white pavilion and patio. Twinkle lights, lanterns, uplights and spots can augment moonlight and stars when night falls. There's a pretty little bride's room close at hand with vanity and mirrors, white wicker furniture and a closet for gowns and accessories. Another plus: an on-site coordinator to take care of all the details.

If Oak Knoll is too formal, kick back in Moonshine Heaven or Buckeye Flat, where picnic tables amid parkland trees set the scene for relaxed al fresco dining. Host a fabulous high-end picnic or a quaint wedding in the woods, and feel free to bring in hay bales and live musicians to add flair to your ranch-style affair. The venue's outdoor concession stand serves as a beverage and snack bar for these spots and for High Falutin' Hill on the opposite side of the rise.

No matter where your wedding takes place, you'll find a plethora of photo opportunities throughout the park. There are also numerous places where you and your new spouse can take a break from the festivities and steal a few moments alone.

More than likely if you've opted for a natural environment, outdoor activities will be part of the mix. The Ranch at Little Hills has a wealth of options. You can party poolside near the Pergola Deck and lawn, or take your celebration over to Lowlander's Holler and entertain guests in a shady pavilion surrounded by two softball fields, basketball hoops, a rock climbing area, dunk tank, trout pond and more.

From corporate and school groups to wedding celebrants, everyone seems to enjoy themselves here. So why not prolong the party? Out-of-towners who wish to extend their stay in the sunny East Bay will find a wide range of accommodations nearby, as well as a variety of great things to see and do.

CEREMONY, EVENT/RECEPTION & MEETING CAPACITY: The facility holds 250 seated or standing guests outdoors.

FEES & DEPOSITS: The rental fee is required to reserve your date, and the balance is due 2 weeks prior to the event. The rental fee ranges $1,850–2,850. Catering packages range $24–40/person and beverage packages range $10–22/person.

AVAILABILITY: May–October, flexible hours.

SERVICES/AMENITIES:

Catering: provided
Kitchen Facilities: n/a
Tables & Chairs: provided
Linens, Silver, etc.: provided
Restrooms: wheelchair accessible
Dance Area: provided
Bride's Dressing Area: yes
Meeting Equipment: provided

Parking: large lot
Accommodations: no guest rooms
Telephone: emergency use only
Outdoor Night Lighting: provided
Outdoor Cooking Facilities: BBQ on site
Cleanup: provided
View: canyon, hills, landscaped grounds
Other: picnic area, event coordination

RESTRICTIONS:

Alcohol: provided
Smoking: designated areas only
Music: amplified OK outdoors with restrictions

Wheelchair Access: yes
Insurance: not required

San Ramon Community Center

Community Center

12501 Alcosta Boulevard, San Ramon
925/973-3200
www.sanramon.ca.gov/parks/parks_facilities/rental.htm
pcstechniciansfacilities@sanramon.ca.gov

● Rehearsal Dinners	● Corp. Events/Mtgs.
● Ceremonies	● Private Parties
● Wedding Receptions	Accommodations

We'd like to introduce you to a sophisticated facility whose spaces can compete with those of the best event sites. There's even a rose garden and an amphitheater for ceremonies! Would you believe that this beautifully designed venue is a community center?

Built in 1989, this outstanding rose-colored granite-and-glass structure features pools, fountains and lush landscaping. Inside, the Fountain Room is the most popular area for receptions. Curved laminated beams radiate from a center point, creating a domed ceiling 40 feet high. This sizable room, decorated in subtle plums and lavenders, is equally suitable for black-tie affairs, casual parties and large meetings.

For smaller events we like the cool, gray Terrace Room, which is perfect for intimate dinners or cocktail mixers. Guests are welcomed into the space through a wonderful gallery that features different works of art each month. Warmed by light filtering through a 40-foot wall of windows, it also overlooks the center's fountain courtyard.

If you're interested in a site in this area, come take a look. We think that the San Ramon Community Center is a real find—the price and the ambiance are both sure to please.

CEREMONY CAPACITY: Outdoors, the Rose Garden holds 75 seated guests and the Amphitheater seats 250. Indoors, the Fountain Room seats 250 banquet-style or 300 theater-style; the Terrace Room seats 80 banquet-style or 110 theater-style.

EVENT/RECEPTION CAPACITY: The Fountain Room holds 250 seated guests. The Terrace Room accommodates 80 seated or 140 for a standing reception. Outdoors, the Rose Garden holds 120 seated or 175 standing guests, and the Amphitheater seats 250.

MEETING CAPACITY: Several spaces accommodate 20–250 seated guests.

FEES & DEPOSITS: A $100–1,000 security deposit (depending on the room rented) is required when you book the facility. The rental fee is due 90 days prior to the event. If the booking occurs less than 90 days prior, the rental fees are due at the time of the booking along with the security deposit. Rental fees range $45–320/hour depending on the day and spaces rented. Sunday evening events as well as San Ramon residents will receive a discounted rate. A 4-hour minimum is required for the Fountain and Terrace Rooms.

AVAILABILITY: Year-round, daily: Sunday–Thursday, 8:30am–10pm; Friday and Saturday, 8:30am–1am.

SERVICES/AMENITIES:

Catering: preapproved list, BYO with approval
Kitchen Facilities: fully equipped, extra fee
Tables & Chairs: provided
Linens, Silver, etc.: BYO
Restrooms: wheelchair accessible
Dance Floor: yes, extra fee
Bride's Dressing Area: CBA, extra fee
Meeting Equipment: full range, extra charge

Parking: ample lot
Accommodations: no guest rooms
Telephone: emergency use only
Outdoor Night Lighting: yes
Outdoor Cooking Facilities: no
Cleanup: renter or caterer
View: San Ramon Valley hills, landscaped gardens, fountains

RESTRICTIONS:

Alcohol: BYO, insurance required
Smoking: outside only
Music: amplified OK inside only

Wheelchair Access: yes
Insurance: sometimes required
Other: decorating restrictions; no candles, birdseed, confetti, glitter, rice, petals or bubbles; red wine and punch discouraged

Wedgewood Wedding & Banquet Center
at the San Ramon Golf Club

Golf Club and Banquet Facility

- Rehearsal Dinners
- Ceremonies
- Wedding Receptions
- Corp. Events/Mtgs.
- Private Parties
- Accommodations

9430 Fircrest Lane, San Ramon
866/966-3009
www.wedgewoodbanquet.com/san-ramon
sales@wedgewoodbanquet.com

Waterfowl often swim with their offspring in the small lake between the wedding gazebo and the 9th-island green. A 50-year-old weeping willow growing at the water's edge frames the tranquil scene. At San Ramon Golf Club, romantic settings like this are as much a part of the landscape as the fairways and surrounding foothills.

Over the years the ranch-style clubhouse has transformed into a popular banquet and wedding facility. A recent renovation has given this property a fresh look, with new paint and décor throughout, recessed lighting and a completely refurbished bar. Of special interest to brides are the floor-to-ceiling mirrors in what the club boasts is "the largest bridal dressing room in Contra Costa County." Cherubic angels adorn the vanity and an antique French armoire, while potted plants and a Goddess of Love water fountain add to the charming atmosphere of the space.

Almost all wedding ceremonies at the club take place on the lawn outside the reception hall. On a sunny day the weeping willow casts a cooling shadow across the grass, providing plenty of shade for your guests. Evening affairs are even more enchanting, with the lights from the white gazebo reflecting off the lake. When the ceremony begins, the bride appears at the French double doors of the Wedgewood Room and then walks along the curving path to her groom. Because weddings are held year-round, the club is always ready with an alternative indoor site. Should rain clouds appear at the last minute, the staff will open a room adjoining the reception hall. With a fire crackling in the brick fireplace the setting becomes quite cozy.

Receptions take place in the Wedgewood Room, brightened by a bank of windows overlooking the lake and golf course. The tinted windows afford complete privacy while allowing everyone to enjoy the view. The patio between the building and lawn is a lovely spot to serve appetizers—guests can sit at umbrella-shaded tables or stroll along the bank to watch the swans, herons, turtles and other wildlife.

Wedgewood Wedding and Banquet Center operates many facilities throughout the state, and is known for their all-inclusive wedding packages. When you book your wedding here almost everything can be covered: food, beverages, DJ, cake, flowers and invitations. The folks at Wedgewood focus on delivering value and service, and pride themselves on taking care of all your needs. The club also offers conveniences you might not expect to find at a privately owned facility, such as an 18-hole golf course open to the public, plenty of parking, and an entire building reserved just for your event. And, with 25 years of wedding planning experience, the Wedgewood Banquet Center staff will help make your celebration one you'll always remember.

CEREMONY CAPACITY: Outdoors, the lawn area holds 400 seated guests. Indoors, the Wedgewood Room holds 400 seated guests.

EVENT/RECEPTION CAPACITY: The Wedgewood Room holds 400 seated guests or 500 for a cocktail reception. The lawn area accommodates 500 seated or 700 for a standing reception.

MEETING CAPACITY: Several spaces accommodate 50–300 seated guests.

FEES & DEPOSITS: 25% of the estimated event total is required to reserve your date, another 25% is due 90 days prior and the balance is due 10 days prior to the event. All-inclusive wedding packages start at $40/person. Tax, alcohol and a 20% service charge are additional. There are no room rental fees as long as certain food and beverage minimums are met.

AVAILABILITY: Year-round, daily, 6am–midnight.

SERVICES/AMENITIES:

Catering: provided
Kitchen Facilities: n/a
Tables & Chairs: provided
Linens, Silver, etc.: provided
Restrooms: wheelchair accessible
Dance Floor: yes
Bride's Dressing Area: yes
Meeting Equipment: full range, extra charge
Other: event coordination

Parking: ample lot
Accommodations: no guest rooms
Telephone: emergency use only
Outdoor Night Lighting: yes
Outdoor Cooking Facilities: no
Cleanup: provided
View: lake, hills, fairways, waterfall, swans and ducks

RESTRICTIONS:

Alcohol: provided
Smoking: outside only
Music: amplified OK

Wheelchair Access: yes
Insurance: not required
Other: no rice, confetti or glitter; no open flames

Overwhelmed? Use the search criteria on www.HereComesTheGuide.com to narrow down your choices.

Civic Park Community Center

Community Center

1375 Civic Drive, Walnut Creek
925/256-3575
www.walnut-creek.org/rentals
rentals@walnut-creek.org

● Rehearsal Dinners	● Corp. Events/Mtgs.
● Ceremonies	● Private Parties
● Wedding Receptions	○ Accommodations

Romance is in the air at Civic Park Community Center. It blossoms in the rose gardens and flutters about the shade trees growing in this tranquil urban hideaway. It also resides in the Center's wedding gazebo, an inspiration not only for ceremonies, but for marriage proposals as well. Recently, a young man was so taken with the pretty structure he hung twinkle lights around it and hired a caterer to serve dinner for two beneath its canopy. Then, after he and his girlfriend toasted their love for each other with glasses of champagne, he popped the question—and she accepted!

Located at the edge of Walnut Creek's busy downtown, the park and buildings that make up the community center feel surprisingly secluded. Mature sycamores and redwoods help screen out the sights and sounds of passing traffic. In many places the trees are so tall and thick you can barely see their tops. As you walk beneath their wide boughs or perhaps picnic on the lawn in their long, cool shadows, you have the pleasant impression you've stepped through the looking glass into the countryside.

Weddings have become so popular here they often have to be scheduled a year in advance. Along with the ceremony and reception sites, you can also reserve the center's Social Hall or Conference Room for a casual rehearsal dinner. These two small, unadorned rooms in the main building can be decorated in any style that suits you, and both of them open to a large commercial kitchen available for your use. On the day of the wedding, the carpeted lounge in the back of the building can be rented as a changing room for the bridal party. A big plus for many brides is the fact that all of the important wedding areas are just steps apart, making the transition from the changing room to the ceremony in the gazebo to the reception in the Assembly Hall easy and convenient.

Another plus is the simple architecture of the spacious Assembly Hall. The building's uncomplicated interior is a blank canvas awaiting your personal vision. The six-foot banquet tables and metal-and-resin chairs provided by the center can be set up in any arrangement you choose. Many couples like to dress them up by renting special chair covers, tablecloths and table settings. The neutral tones of the well-lit room blend easily with almost any décor, and the overhead lights can be dimmed or brightened to accent the changing mood of the occasion. A full Bose sound system, with speakers on all the overhead trestle beams, will have your guests swaying to the music wherever you place the dance floor.

With the exception of a fog machine or nails in the wall, the transformation of the Assembly Hall is only limited by your imagination. One bride and groom expanded their reception outside the building by opening the room's 10-foot sliding glass door that leads to a small patio and the park beyond. Connecting the nearby trees with colorful ribbons they created a large grassy "courtyard." Another couple arrived early to reserve the first-come-first-served picnic tables and barbecue grills beside the hall for their guests to enjoy during the reception.

However you celebrate at the center, you'll love the flexibility of the spaces, and the park setting is sure to provide a beautiful backdrop.

CEREMONY, EVENT/RECEPTION & MEETING CAPACITY: Various indoor areas hold up to 250 seated banquet-style or 250 theater-style. Smaller events can also be accommodated. The gazebo and park area holds up to 300 guests seated or standing. (Chairs not provided outdoors.)

FEES & DEPOSITS: A $500 nonrefundable deposit is required to reserve your date. The balance and security deposit are due in full 90 days prior to your event. Rental fees range $50–170/hour depending on the day and the room rented. An additional $75 fee is charged if alcohol is served.

AVAILABILITY: Year-round: Monday–Thursday, 8am–10pm; Friday and Saturday, 8am–1am; Sunday, 8am–midnight.

Weekend reservations may be made up to 1 year in advance. Weekday evenings may be scheduled on a limited basis depending on availability. Rental hours must include setup and cleanup time.

SERVICES/AMENITIES:

Catering: BYO
Kitchen Facilities: large, commercial kitchen
Tables & Chairs: provided for indoor use
Linens, Silver, etc.: BYO or through caterer
Restrooms: wheelchair accessible
Dance Floor: yes
Bride's & Groom's Dressing Areas: may be available, extra fee
Meeting Equipment: BYO

Parking: limited on site
Accommodations: no guest rooms
Telephone: emergency use only
Outdoor Night Lighting: yes
Outdoor Cooking Facilities: BYO BBQ
Cleanup: caterer or renter
View: park, garden, landscaped grounds
Other: WiFi available (except Assembly Hall)

RESTRICTIONS:

Alcohol: BYO wine and beer only, permits required; not allowed at youth events
Smoking: outdoors only
Music: amplified OK indoors with restrictions

Wheelchair Access: yes
Insurance: not required
Other: no birdseed, confetti, rice, rose petals, aerosol streamers, hay, sand or glitter; security required at all youth events

The Clubhouse at Boundary Oak

Banquet & Event Facility

3800 Valley Vista Road, Walnut Creek
925/934-3600 x21
www.playboundaryoak.com
egaines@playboundaryoak.com

● Rehearsal Dinners   ● Corp. Events/Mtgs.
● Ceremonies   ● Private Parties
● Wedding Receptions   Accommodations

Nature abounds at this premier Walnut Creek venue, known for its wonderful views. Sitting on acres of manicured greens, it's bordered by open space and ringed by an extensive network of rustic, ridgeline trails.

The Clubhouse at Boundary Oak, named for a particularly majestic and artfully gnarled 350-year-old tree on the grounds, is just moments from town yet feels worlds away. From its hilltop perch it offers a front row seat to the location's expansive vistas.

Perhaps the best way to start off your momentous day in this city/country setting is to opt for an outdoor ceremony at one of two terrific sites. For peaceful panoramas that include the surrounding fairways, a towering stand of eucalyptus trees and a glimpse of Concord in the distance, exchange vows at the Lake View, set on a knoll beside the 9th-hole water feature and its impressive center fountain. If you prefer a more intimate alternative, get married on the Patio, which overlooks the putting green with the lake and fountain in the background.

You may be tempted to enjoy hors d'oeuvres and a glass of bubbly al fresco as well, but there are also several inviting spots inside the clubhouse. For example, the multilevel Mira Room adjoining the Patio has a long bar, wooden floors and great sunset views. Then, when you're ready for dinner, just step through the arched entryway into the Vista Room. This architecturally interesting space is cantilevered above the walkway below with three walls of windows that angle outwards, making the outdoors feel like part of the room. A pyramid-style ceiling completes the whole "mid-century modernist" feel.

If, however, your dream reception (or the size of your guest list) calls for something larger, take a short stroll through the Main Entrance Foyer—which doubles as a gallery displaying works by local artists—and start your festivities in the Atrium. In this bright space, anchored by a large permanent bar and rows of slanted skylights running the length of the ceiling, friends and family can mingle over cocktails. At dinnertime, three sets of double doors open to reveal the beautifully decorated Celebration Ballroom, which easily hosts 250 for dinner and dancing.

Before the day is over, the bride and groom may also want to have their photographer snap a picture of them standing beneath the spreading branches of the great oak. They'll have a classic photo that's not only representative of this lovely venue, but will provide a memorable addition to their wedding album.

CEREMONY CAPACITY: The site accommodates 275 seated outdoors and 250 seated indoors.

EVENT/RECEPTION CAPACITY: The clubhouse holds 250 seated or 400 standing guests indoors.

MEETING CAPACITY: Meeting rooms hold 250 seated guests.

FEES & DEPOSITS: 25% of the estimated event total is required to confirm your date. The event balance and final guest count is due 14 business days prior to the event. All events must meet a food and beverage minimum that varies depending on the date and time booked. Flexible wedding packages start at $46/person. Tax, alcohol and service charge are additional.

AVAILABILITY: Year-round, daily.

SERVICES/AMENITIES:

Catering: provided
Kitchen Facilities: n/a
Tables & Chairs: provided
Linens, Silver, etc.: provided
Restrooms: wheelchair accessible
Dance Floor: yes
Bride's Dressing Area: yes
Meeting Equipment: CBA

Parking: large lot
Accommodations: partner hotels nearby
Telephone: house phone, extra fee
Outdoor Night Lighting: access only
Outdoor Cooking Facilities: BBQ CBA
Cleanup: provided
View: garden, landscaped grounds, fountain, fairways, hills, lagoon, lake, mountains, valley

RESTRICTIONS:

Alcohol: provided
Smoking: outdoors only
Music: amplified OK indoors with restrictions

Wheelchair Access: yes
Insurance: may be required

The Gardens at Heather Farm

Garden Education Center

1540 Marchbanks Drive, Walnut Creek
925/947-1678
www.gardenshf.org
rentals@gardenshf.org

● Rehearsal Dinners	● Corp. Events/Mtgs.
● Ceremonies	● Private Parties
● Wedding Receptions	Accommodations

Something is always in bloom at this nonprofit garden education center. Covering six landscaped acres, it features a series of paved footpaths that wind their way through a colorful variety of flowerbeds, herb and rock gardens and water features. Off in the distance there's a pond with two fountains, and beyond that a view of Mt. Diablo.

Anyone who equates romance with roses will want to tie the knot beneath the fragrant, rose-covered gazebo, surrounded by rose bushes that bloom continuously from spring through fall. Afterwards you and your guests can stroll through the gardens, admiring the wide range of floral and herbal displays on your way to the patio. This large terrace, like the rest of the garden center, offers an abundance of olfactory and visual treats. Concrete-and-tile planters border the patio and are filled with a horticultural riot of textures, scents and hues. A caterer-friendly pavilion—complete with sink, electrical outlets, lighting and a beautiful granite countertop—is great for a buffet setup or as a serving station for a cocktail party.

Receptions are usually held upstairs in the Camellia Room. Light and airy, it has a high beamed ceiling and floor-to-ceiling windows that afford a commanding view of Mt. Diablo and the gardens. With its neutral walls and light-colored floor, this pleasant space is easy to decorate.

A spacious wraparound deck gives guests access to the outdoors; to explore the gardens they simply take the ramp or stairs from the deck to the patio and pavilion below. The nearby Meadow Garden, with its expansive lawn, is also available for outdoor receptions.

Since they were first established in 1968, the Gardens at Heather Farm have become one of Walnut Creek's most popular venues. When you have your event here, you not only get to enjoy this delightful (and educational!) garden setting, you're supporting a living museum and wildlife habitat.

CEREMONY CAPACITY: The site holds 150 seated guests indoors or outdoors.

EVENT/RECEPTION & MEETING CAPACITY: The facility accommodates 150 seated guests for dining or 300 standing indoors, and 300 seated or standing outdoors on the patio or in the garden.

They offer customized floor plans that include dining, dancing and auditorium styles as well as standing formats for cocktail receptions, special events or company mixers. Some larger groups may be accommodated with custom floor plans utilizing their outdoor areas and wraparound deck.

FEES & DEPOSITS: A nonrefundable deposit of 50% of the rental fee is required to reserve your date; a $500–800 security deposit and the balance of the rental fee are due 6 months prior to the event. A garden ceremony setup is an additional $300 charge; use of the pavilion and patio is an additional $250 charge. Weekday rental fees, Monday 9am–Friday 2pm, range $75–200/hour with a 2-hour minimum. Rental fees Friday 2pm–Sunday 10pm and holidays range $800–2,300 depending on the space rented and time of year. Extra hours are available.

AVAILABILITY: Year-round, daily. Weekdays, 9am–10pm; weekend times vary.

SERVICES/AMENITIES:

Catering: select from list, additional fee for off-list catering, by approval
Kitchen Facilities: moderately equipped
Tables & Chairs: provided, including chairs for a gazebo ceremony
Linens, Silver, etc.: BYO
Restrooms: wheelchair accessible
Dance Floor: yes
Bride's Dressing Area: yes
Meeting Equipment: podium, PA, projection screen

Parking: lot and on-street
Accommodations: no guest rooms
Telephone: emergency use only
Outdoor Night Lighting: yes
Outdoor Cooking Facilities: BYO BBQ
Cleanup: caterer or renter
View: gardens, Mt. Diablo and pond

RESTRICTIONS:

Alcohol: BYO
Smoking: outside only
Music: amplified OK indoors only

Wheelchair Access: yes
Insurance: proof of liability insurance required
Other: no confetti, rice, birdseed, flower petals, butterfly or balloon releases

---

The professionals in the back of this book are the best in the business. How do we know? Read page 637.

463

Heather Farm Community Center

Community Center

301 North San Carlos Drive, Walnut Creek

925/256-3575

www.walnut-creek.org/rentals
rentals@walnut-creek.org

- Rehearsal Dinners
- Ceremonies
- Wedding Receptions
- Corp. Events/Mtgs.
- Private Parties
- Accommodations

Clark Gable was on the brink of becoming a major movie star when he came to Heather Farm in 1931 to make the motion picture *Sporting Blood*. Of course that was during the park's former life as a horse ranch and racetrack. The actor was so taken with the place he stabled his thoroughbreds there. Today Heather Farm shows little evidence of its equestrian past, but it retains a country-like atmosphere that draws visitors from all around the East Bay.

Tucked behind a hill on the outskirts of Walnut Creek, the 102-acre park is an oasis of shade trees, green grass and flower gardens. Meandering paths connect the picnic and nature areas with the swim center, tennis courts and athletic fields. With groves of trees and meadows separating the facilities from one another, it's almost as if each site is a park unto itself. And nestled in one of the most picturesque of these spots is Heather Farm Community Center.

Wedding receptions at the center are held in the Lakeside Room overlooking a large pond. One of our favorite features of this venue is its wraparound deck, which extends over the water. Guests who stroll out here are treated to an unobstructed view of ducks and geese swimming between the two large fountains that aerate the man-made lagoon. On the opposite shore, sycamores, oaks and pepper trees shade the extensive lawns and create a protective screen around the center. Some couples are so charmed by the scenery they hold their wedding ceremony on the deck followed by the reception inside.

The pond and fountains are also visible from the Lakeside Room through the wide windows along two walls. Although the hall is spacious, the dark wood interior and coffered ceiling add a coziness to the ambiance. More warmth comes from the fireplace nook, where friends and family can gather to toast the bride and groom. Pretty and unpretentious, the room requires very little decorating for those who want to keep their reception simple. Banquet and round tables, along with folding chairs, are provided with the reservation—the atmosphere, be it casual or elegant, is totally up to you.

And you won't have to worry about keeping your reception private in the middle of a park. Tall bushes and trees mask the entrance to the Lakeside Room from the rest of the park and the community center is closed to the public while you celebrate the day or night away.

CEREMONY CAPACITY: The Deck accommodates up to 140; the Lakeside Room holds up to 200 guests.

EVENT/RECEPTION & MEETING CAPACITY: The Lakeside Room accommodates 200 guests.

FEES & DEPOSITS: A $500 nonrefundable deposit is required to reserve your date. The balance and security deposit are due in full 90 days prior to your event. Rental fees range $50–170/hour depending on room, day and time rented. An additional $75 fee is charged if alcohol is served.

AVAILABILITY: Year-round: Monday–Thursday, 8am–10pm; Friday and Saturday, 8am–1am; Sunday, 8am–midnight.

Weekend reservations may be made up to 1 year in advance. Weekday evenings may be scheduled on a limited basis depending on availability. Rental hours must include setup and cleanup time.

SERVICES/AMENITIES:
Catering: BYO
Kitchen Facilities: moderately equipped
Tables & Chairs: provided
Linens, Silver: through caterer
Restrooms: wheelchair accessible
Dance Floor: yes
Bride's Dressing Area: may be available, extra fee
Meeting Equipment: BYO

Parking: ample on site
Accommodations: no guest rooms
Telephone: emergency use only
Outdoor Night Lighting: yes
Outdoor Cooking Facilities: BYO BBQ
Cleanup: caterer or renter
View: pond, trees, garden, park, fountains
Other: WiFi

RESTRICTIONS:
Alcohol: BYO wine and beer only, permits required, not allowed at youth events
Smoking: outside only
Music: amplified OK indoors only

Wheelchair Access: yes
Insurance: not required
Other: no confetti, rice, birdseed, rose petals, acrosol streamers, hay, sand or glitter; security required at all youth events; fountains cannot be guaranteed to function at all times

Scott's Gardens

Restaurant & Gardens

1333 North California Boulevard, Walnut Creek
925/934-0598

www.scottseastbay.com
jenniferf@scottswc.com

●	Rehearsal Dinners	●	Corp. Events/Mtgs.
●	Ceremonies	●	Private Parties
●	Wedding Receptions		Accommodations

Take note! If you're looking for an exceptional East Bay outdoor wedding spot, you must see this facility. Scott's Gardens is a site that could be aptly described as an urban oasis. Situated in the heart of Walnut Creek's retail district, Scott's has spared no expense to transform a small hillside into a brick-walled, multi-terraced courtyard garden with a conservatory cover. If you're worried about the weather, don't fret—during November through April, the garden is totally glass-enclosed and heated to keep your guests comfortable.

Under the broad canopy of a 400-year-old oak tree (the site's centerpiece) you'll find amenities such as designer wood benches and sizable free-standing umbrellas, in addition to lush landscaping. Of special interest are a green lattice aviary, several fountains and an antique water wheel. Observe the details here. All of the terraces are paved with slate, and even the outdoor bar and indoor dressing room feature marble counters. The latter is one of the best bride's dressing rooms we've seen, with floor-to-ceiling mirrors and a well-lit makeup area. At the topmost terrace, you'll find a back stairway leading to Scott's Restaurant, where there's another outdoor patio for evening rehearsal dinners and small weekend receptions. Inside the restaurant, additional private and semiprivate rooms are available for parties.

CEREMONY CAPACITY: The Garden holds up to 200 seated or standing guests.

EVENT/RECEPTION CAPACITY: The Garden accommodates a maximum of 140 seated guests, or 300 for a standing reception.

MEETING CAPACITY: Several spaces hold 32–120 seated guests.

FEES & DEPOSITS: A deposit is required to secure your date and the balance is due prior to the event. The rental fee on Saturday ranges $500–1,000; Sunday and Friday rates range $350–500. There is an additional ceremony fee of $250 for the outdoor terrace or $500 for the indoor garden. Rental includes tables, Chiavari chairs, linens and serviceware. Menu offerings start at $33/person with additional costs for hors d'oeuvres and cake. Alcohol, tax and service fees are additional.

AVAILABILITY: Year-round, daily, 8am–4pm or 6pm–midnight.

SERVICES/AMENITIES:

Catering: provided, no BYO
Kitchen Facilities: n/a
Tables & Chairs: provided
Linens, Silver, etc.: provided
Restrooms: wheelchair accessible
Dance Floor: yes
Bride's Dressing Area: yes
Meeting Equipment: full range audiovisual

Parking: complimentary valet
Accommodations: no guest rooms
Telephone: no
Outdoor Night Lighting: yes
Outdoor Cooking Facilities: CBA
Cleanup: provided
View: landscaped garden
Other: event coordination, flowers, wedding cakes, invitations, music, transportation, favors

RESTRICTIONS:

Alcohol: provided, no BYO
Smoking: outside only
Music: DJ or small combos only

Wheelchair Access: yes
Insurance: not required

Shadelands Arts Center

Arts and Education Center

111 North Wiget Lane, Walnut Creek
925/256-3575

www.walnut-creek.org/rentals
rentals@walnut-creek.org

● Rehearsal Dinners	● Corp. Events/Mtgs.	
● Ceremonies	● Private Parties	
● Wedding Receptions	☐ Accommodations	

There are quite a few reasons why Shadelands Arts Center has become a local favorite. Not only is it a great value for those looking for an affordable event venue, it's also one of the largest facilities in the East Bay (accommodating up to 300!) where you can bring the caterer of your choice.

Another plus is the building itself, which is easy to work with thanks to its neutral décor. The white interior is amenable to virtually any kind of decorating, and the high, open-beamed ceiling—often draped for weddings—gives the space a lofty feeling.

State-of-the-art sound and lighting systems (and an A/V staff person on site during your event) enable you to create whatever ambiance you like. Whether you're having a live band or planning to listen to your own playlist through your iPod, the music will sound great because the room was designed for music or theater performances and the acoustics are excellent. You can also entertain your guests with a slideshow or video on the large projection screen. Use lighting in a variety of colors to create a particular mood or to highlight the ceiling or dance floor. Custom gobos with your initials or scenes that you've selected can be projected on the walls. Add to all these features a gleaming hardwood floor and a full catering kitchen and you have an event site that will satisfy all your needs.

Shadelands is perfectly suited for large weddings, because the entire event can be held in the main hall. If you require more space, the hall opens onto an expansive, enclosed patio that can be used for a ceremony, cocktail party or additional reception seating. It works well as a place for supervised activities for children, too.

For corporate functions, Shadelands supplies most of the equipment required for presentations: an LCD projector (extra fee), large projection screen, sound and lighting equipment—and complimentary Wi-Fi.

The venue is also popular for fundraisers, as it provides different rooms for a silent auction and banking.

The center's staff are very accommodating, going out of their way to help you create the event you want while staying within your budget. And access to the fully equipped professional kitchen—with the option of bringing in your own caterer—are real benefits for couples planning a casual wedding or rehearsal dinner.

With its flexibility, ample parking and reasonable prices, Shadelands Arts Center is in demand. Its convenient location is also appreciated by guests coming from all over the Bay Area. If you want to host a wedding, private party or corporate event that's very much your own, this is definitely a location to consider.

CEREMONY CAPACITY: The Banquet Room holds 350 seated guests.

EVENT/RECEPTION CAPACITY: The Banquet Room can accommodate 300 seated at round tables.

MEETING CAPACITY: The Banquet Room holds 350 seated theater-style or 150 guests seated conference-style.

FEES & DEPOSITS: A $500 nonrefundable deposit is required to secure your date. The balance and security deposit are due 90 days prior to the function. An additional $75 fee is charged if alcohol is served. Rental fees range $70–195/hour depending on the time frame of the event.

AVAILABILITY: Year-round, daily until 1am. The venue may be booked up to 1 year in advance.

SERVICES/AMENITIES:

Catering: BYO
Kitchen Facilities: fully equipped, commercial
Tables & Chairs: provided
Linens, Silver, etc.: BYO or caterer
Restrooms: wheelchair accessible
Dance Floor: provided
Bride's & Groom's Dressing Areas: CBA, extra fee
Meeting Equipment: full range

Parking: large lots, ample parking
Accommodations: no guest rooms
Telephone: emergency use only
Outdoor Night Lighting: yes
Outdoor Cooking Facilities: BYO
Cleanup: renter or caterer
View: no
Other: WiFi available

RESTRICTIONS:

Alcohol: BYO, permits required; not allowed at youth events
Smoking: outside only
Music: amplified OK, indoors only

Wheelchair Access: yes
Insurance: not required
Other: security required at all youth events; no rice, birdseed, confetti, glitter, fog machines, bubbles, hay, sand, rose petals or aerosol streamers

Want to know WHAT TO ASK a potential location or vendor? Check out our Questions to Ask starting on page 17.

469

Shadelands Ranch Museum

Museum

2660 Ygnacio Valley Road, Walnut Creek
925/935-7871
www.walnutcreekhistory.info
wcshadelands@sbcglobal.net

Rehearsal Dinners	● Corp. Events/Mtgs.
● Ceremonies	● Private Parties
● Wedding Receptions	Accommodations

Stately shade trees tower above the lawn, gardens and terrace surrounding the former Penniman home at Shadelands Ranch Museum. From its curved glass bay windows to its classical white columns and wraparound veranda, the 1903 Colonial Revival house reflects the refinement and elegance of a bygone era when the handsome two-story home was the heart of a large fruit ranch in the Ygnacio Valley.

Today Shadelands is lovingly maintained by the Walnut Creek Historical Society and the City of Walnut Creek. Citrus, pomegranate, walnut and quince still grow among the sycamores and redwoods shading the aptly named property. The fruit trees, along with the herb and vegetable gardens planted on the site, also serve as a reminder of Shadelands' rural past. While strolling the paths leading toward the patio and garden at the back of the house, it's easy to imagine the gracious hospitality that was once extended to guests of the ranch over 100 years ago. These days, events at Shadelands are held outdoors with the carefully restored house providing a charming backdrop.

On the spacious lawn at the back of the house, couples exchange vows in a gazebo encircled by roses. The garden setting is lovely on its own, or can be easily decorated to suit your taste. For an evening wedding, tiny lights can be woven through the trees, adding an enchanting ambiance to the occasion.

After the ceremony, the celebration continues on the adjoining patio. The terrace is large enough to accommodate tables for the reception and a DJ. Or, in keeping with the turn-of-the-(last)-century atmosphere, you might want to hire a band to play in the gazebo and have your guests dance on the patio.

Access to the inside of the house is limited to the kitchen, which is available as a bridal changing room or as a preparation site for the caterer. As committed as Shadelands is to keeping the ranch authentic to its early 20th-century style, the "old-fashioned" kitchen comes with a new gas range masquerading as a black wood-burning stove and a refrigerator camouflaged with wood paneling. Modern restrooms are adjacent to the new barn, just behind the circa 1902 water tank house and worker's cabin that border the garden.

Of the many reasons to hold your wedding and reception at the nonprofit Shadelands Ranch Museum, the most satisfying may be that the money you spend here goes toward preserving the history of Walnut Creek for future generations. Of course, at the same time, you and your betrothed will be making a little history of your own.

CEREMONY CAPACITY: The lawn area holds 250 seated guests.

EVENT/RECEPTION CAPACITY: The lawn area accommodates 250 seated or 400 standing guests.

MEETING CAPACITY: The location holds up to 250 seated guests for outdoor parties and meetings.

FEES & DEPOSITS: A $300 nonrefundable deposit is required to secure your date, and is applied toward the rental fee. An additional $500 refundable damage deposit is also required, and due 30 days before your event. Rental fees range $175–275/hour depending on the day of the week and the number of hours rented.

AVAILABILITY: April–October.

SERVICES/AMENITIES:
Catering: BYO
Kitchen Facilities: fully equipped
Tables & Chairs: up to 250 chairs and 55 tables provided
Linens, Silver, etc.: BYO or caterer
Restrooms: wheelchair accessible
Dance Floor: patio available
Bride's Dressing Area: yes, in kitchen
Meeting Equipment: tables and chairs

Parking: ample
Accommodations: no guest rooms
Telephone: use cell phones
Outdoor Night Lighting: yes
Outdoor Cooking Facilities: BYO or caterer
Cleanup: renter or caterer, trashcans provided
View: landscaped grounds, garden, gazebo

RESTRICTIONS:
Alcohol: BYO, beer and wine only
Smoking: outside only
Music: amplified OK with volume limits, no amplifiers after 11pm

Wheelchair Access: yes
Insurance: proof of liability insurance required
Other: no rice, birdseed, confetti or nails

Solano County

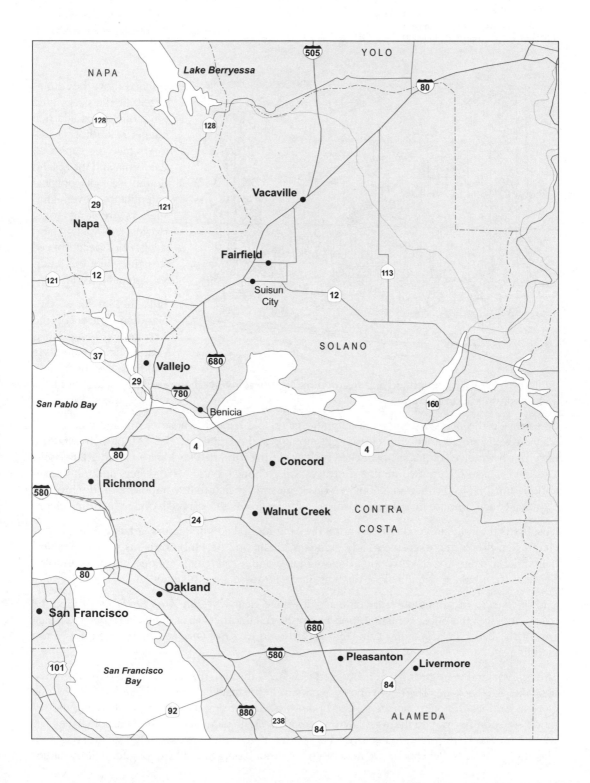

Jefferson Street Mansion

1063 Jefferson Street, Benicia
707/746-0684
www.jeffersonstreetmansion.com
info@jeffersonstreetmansion.com

Historic Mansion

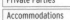

● Rehearsal Dinners	● Corp. Events/Mtgs.
● Ceremonies	● Private Parties
● Wedding Receptions	Accommodations

Perched above the Carquinez Strait, the sleepy little town of Benicia is a rich nugget of California history. Once the capitol of California and the Solano County seat, its political and military movers-and-shakers are long gone. However, they left behind a legacy of beautiful old structures like the Jefferson Street Mansion.

Built in 1861 for a commanding officer of the Arsenal, this classical Federal Italianate-style building has been meticulously renovated, retrofitted and restored by its current owner, giving it a new lease on life as a fabulous special event venue.

Once inside the mansion, enter the magnificent double parlors, whose cream-and-pale green-washed walls are adorned with custom gilt molding and medallions. The 12-foot-high windows have plush wine velvet drapes, bedecked with gold fringe and tied back with plump gold tassels. The parlors also feature two marble fireplaces, oil paintings, crystal chandeliers and gilt-framed antique mirrors. In the elegant Salon, nervous brides can regain their composure on the brocade "fainting couch" or pose for whimsical photos with the groom in a carved wooden "courting chair."

Upstairs is the fully air-conditioned bride's dressing room. Like the parlors, it has gilt molding, a chandelier, fireplace and custom-made drapes in cream and peach brocade, as well as practical items like a white-and-gold wooden dressing table and a full-length antique mirrored armoire. There's also a balcony on this floor that's available for tossing the bouquet.

With its wealth of sumptuous appointments, it's quite clear why *Bay Area Backroads* called the mansion one of the "Most Romantic Spots in Northern California," the California Heritage Council gave it the 2004 "Preservation of the Year Award" and CBS *Eye On The Bay* featured it as a top wedding site.

Though you and your guests are encouraged to wander through the mansion, the primary festivities take place outside. The new Veranda works well for smaller events and ceremonies anytime of year. And it's the perfect place for the bride to begin her grand entrance, descending the veranda steps on her way to the west lawn where a classical colonnaded wisteria arbor shades her waiting guests. Here, vows are exchanged beneath a 15-foot-high trellised "arch" guarded by two majestic palm trees. Receptions are held on the mansion's opposite side among fountains, statues and flowerbeds, or in the elegant fabric-draped Grand Pavilions (each with its own chandeliers). The buffet is set up in front of two exquisite antique back-bars, fashioned with intricate carving and spoolwork.

No matter how beautiful the surroundings, your event isn't going to be much of a success without a competent staff working behind the scenes, and that's exactly what you'll get at the Jefferson Street Mansion. A concierge captain/coordinator, provided at no charge, considers it her personal mission to keep each bride calm, elegant and relaxed. Another plus: The "one event per day" policy means you can celebrate as long (and as enthusiastically) as you want. And although we've described the mansion in terms of weddings, the entertainment possibilities at this topnotch facility are practically endless. So if you're seeking a venue with the romance of the past and the convenience of the present, take a trip to Benicia and the Jefferson Street Mansion. Your event is sure to be a day you and your guests will never forget.

CEREMONY CAPACITY: West Lawn holds 275 seated guests. The East Tent holds 275 seated guests.

EVENT/RECEPTION CAPACITY: The East Patio accommodates 250 seated or 350 standing. The mansion holds 50 seated or 100 standing.

MEETING CAPACITY: The mansion holds up to 40 guests seated theater-style.

FEES & DEPOSITS: A $2,500 deposit is required to reserve your Saturday date, or a $1,500 deposit to reserve your Friday or Sunday date. The balance is due 2 weeks prior to the event. Rental fees range $1,750–3,000 depending on guest count. For weddings, meals start at $48/person and include all service staff, equipment, gold band china, linens, 2 entrées, salad, starch, vegetable, signature fruit platters and breads.

For business functions, see their website for fee information.

AVAILABILITY: Year-round, daily, 7am–midnight.

SERVICES/AMENITIES:
Catering: provided, or BYO extra fee
Kitchen Facilities: use fee required
Tables & Chairs: provided
Linens, Silver, etc.: provided
Restrooms: wheelchair accessible
Dance Floor: yes
Bride's Dressing Area: yes
Meeting Equipment: some provided, other CBA, extra fee

Parking: large lot
Accommodations: no guest rooms
Telephone: house phone
Outdoor Night Lighting: yes
Outdoor Cooking Facilities: no
Cleanup: provided
View: panorama of SF Bay, Carquinez Strait, rolling hills
Other: full range of decorations and florals

RESTRICTIONS:
Alcohol: provided, or corkage $10/bottle
Smoking: outside only
Music: amplified OK

Wheelchair Access: yes
Insurance: liability required

Admiral's Mansions at Mare Island
and St. Peter's Chapel & the Mare Island Museum

Walnut Avenue, Mare Island, Vallejo
707/643-1711 Catering, 707/557-1538 Chapel/Mansions
www.alexscatering.com
info@alexscatering.com

Mansions, Historic Chapel & Park

● Rehearsal Dinners	● Corp. Events/Mtgs.
● Ceremonies	● Private Parties
● Wedding Receptions	Accommodations

With the 1996 closure of Mare Island Naval Installation, four landmark buildings are now available for special events. These venues are operated by the Mare Island Historic Park Foundation, so you no longer need military connections. And since they're located in the island's quaint historic district (which dates back to the mid 1800s), you feel like you have an entire small town all to yourself.

Set in its own grassy park with a eucalyptus grove, St. Peter's is a picturesque interdenominational chapel. Built in 1901, it's the oldest naval chapel in the United States. A classic example of Victorian Gothic architecture, this tidy brown shingle with cream-colored trim, steep pitched roof and a soaring octagonal spire, has as much charm and history inside as out. The largest collection of Tiffany glass under one roof is displayed in the chapel's 29 exquisite stained-glass windows, and they fill the intimate interior with a soft rosy light. One window depicts Sir Galahad who, when illuminated, becomes the ultimate knight in shining armor. Rich wood paneling complements the creamy plaster walls, and open beams accentuate the vaulted ceiling. The chapel also displays a collection of memorial plaques. Some are set into the ceiling and others (one dates back to the Civil War), hang on the walls, making intriguing reading.

Naturally there's a pipe organ (it's the original one from 1926!) to fill the sanctuary with strains of "Here Comes The Bride." After the ceremony, take advantage of the lovely setting for formal photos while your guests make the short trip back down Walnut Avenue to Officer's Row.

Receptions and business retreats are held in the Admiral's and the Captain's former quarters, 2 of the 13 white Colonial Revival mansions lining Officer's Row. As you enter the Admiral's Quarters, it's easy to imagine the social galas of a century ago. The brass nautical lamps that lit the entryway then still hang on either side of the massive oak front door; the wide front veranda graced with Corinthian columns still invites guests to stroll outside for a leisurely chat. The gracious feel of the place continues inside in the vestibule, a large U-shaped entry hall complete with an inviting fireplace and built-in seating. Your guests can enjoy cocktails and hors d'oeuvres in here and as they explore the first- and second-floor rooms, all furnished in period pieces. The Captain's

Quarters, similar in style to the Admiral's, are often reserved for smaller functions. The 1855 Mare Island Museum building also has several spacious rooms available.

For an al fresco treat, set up a buffet and umbrella-shaded tables in the Victorian gardens adjacent to both of these mansions: It's an acre of lawns interspersed with low hedges, flowerbeds, and a variety of trees brought back from the far corners of the world by sea captains.

If you really want to make a splash, depart via ferry or yacht—the ferry terminal and marina are just a short distance from the island. But no matter which mode of transportation you choose, an event here is a trip back in time and a chance to relive a little of the grace and gentility of another era.

CEREMONY CAPACITY: The Chapel holds 200 seated guests. The Admiral's Mansion seats up to 100 guests using all available rooms. The Captain's Mansion holds up to 100 guests. The Garden area is about 1 acre and holds up to 800 seated guests. The Main Hall in the Museum will seat up to 500 guests.

EVENT/RECEPTION CAPACITY: The facility can accommodate 125–700 seated or 200–1,000 standing guests indoors, and 800 seated or 2,000 standing outdoors.

MEETING CAPACITY: The Admiral's Mansion seats 150–160 using all rooms, with 40 maximum in any one room. The Museum Main Room holds 325 seated or 550 standing guests. The Musuem can seat 60 to 300 depending on which room is selected.

FEES & DEPOSITS: For weddings, a nonrefundable 50% rental deposit plus a $200 refundable security deposit are required to secure your date. Reception rental fees range $850–1,400 depending on the space selected. Ceremony rental fees range $200–700 depending on space rented. Organ in Chapel is available for $75 and use of the pianos is $35/event. Catering is provided by *Alex's Catering*. Meals range $50–75/person. Tax, alcohol and an 18% service charge are additional.

Fees for business meetings vary; call for more information.

AVAILABILITY: Year-round, daily, 8am–10pm.

SERVICES/AMENITIES:

Catering: provided or BYO upon approval
Kitchen Facilities: moderately equipped
Tables & Chairs: BYO
Linens, Silver, etc.: caterer
Restrooms: wheelchair access CBA
Dance Floor: patio, or CBA, extra charge
Bride's & Groom's Dressing Areas: yes
Meeting Equipment: video player and projector

Parking: large lot and private street parking
Accommodations: no guest rooms
Telephone: emergency use only
Outdoor Night Lighting: CBA
Outdoor Cooking Facilities: through caterer
Cleanup: caterer, renter or CBA, extra fee
View: historic Alden Park
Other: grand piano, event coordination, tours of Mare Island's historic locations

RESTRICTIONS:

Alcohol: CBA or BYO, licensed and insured server
Smoking: designated outdoor areas
Music: amplified OK with volume limits
Other: no rice, food or alcohol in Chapel

Wheelchair Access: Chapel and Mansions have ramps, gardens have full access
Insurance: certificate required

Hiddenbrooke Golf Club

Golf Club

1095 Hiddenbrooke Parkway, Vallejo
707/558-1153 Catering
www.hiddenbrookegolf.com
contact@hiddenbrookegolf.com

- Rehearsal Dinners
- Ceremonies
- Wedding Receptions
- Corp. Events/Mtgs.
- Private Parties
- Accommodations

Most people who take the American Canyon exit off Interstate 80 in the rolling hills between Vallejo and Fairfield head west toward Napa. Few ever venture into the beautiful valley that lies hidden east of the turnoff, just half a mile over a ridge. Those who do find themselves on a graceful two-mile drive that dips, sweeps and curves through rolling hills down to Hiddenbrooke Golf Club, the centerpiece of a master-planned development minutes from the freeway in time, but a world away in feel.

Arriving guests are let off in a porte-cochère area dominated by four massive flagstone-faced pillars. A flower-lined arcade leads from there directly to the clubhouse banquet room. This room is posh, with high-quality materials and finishes that make it a perfect venue for weddings or meetings that run from semi- to pull-out-all-the-stops-formal.

The entrance is through tall twin dark wood doors, inset with top-to-bottom rows of square glass panels. The foyer's floor is a gleaming expanse of marble tiles. On the immediate left there is a large cloak room. Further on the right, a hallway lined with paintings, lamp tables, delicate little sconces and a mirror leads to two wood-and-tile-lined bathrooms. The far end of the entryway culminates in a floor-to-ceiling stone-faced fireplace, with a window occupying the top third of its back wall. Guests can sit in front of the fireplace and peer through the window at golfers on the 18th hole.

A glossy baby grand piano sits to one side of the fireplace and marks the entrance to an area of the clubhouse that can be set up to accommodate smaller parties. This section has several dining tables and looks out south and west through large windows. The dark-wood-paneled bar in the corner conveys an inviting feeling—exactly the ambiance you'd expect at a fine golf club. French doors open out to a large, sun-splashed patio and bar terrace. These areas are often available for use in conjunction with weddings. Be sure to ask about them when booking.

The clubhouse is dominated by high windows that look out over the golf course and to the ridges beyond. Its walls are finished in creamy white and accentuated with white wainscoting. The countertops are capped with red granite and the curtains are colored a subtle powdered rose. There are large potted plants throughout the room, and warm paintings of farmlands and buildings evoke Tuscany and Napa. The room's effect is a complete one: "Since the room is so elegantly designed, decorations are often unnecessary," says Carmen Juarez, Hiddenbrooke's marketing director.

An on-site wedding sales manager provides full, four-star service, from catering and menus to recommendations for transportation and entertainment. Ceremonies take place outdoors on the

Ceremony Green, which overlooks the lush green hillsides, or in the enclosed Pavilion. A separate conference or banquet room in an adjacent building is ideal for business meetings and weddings.

Hiddenbrooke is an elegant refuge, the kind of place that inspires visitors to think they have stumbled onto some wonderful secret, and later to realize that for a few precious hours they were happily taken away from the cares and worries of the world.

CEREMONY CAPACITY: The Pavilion and Ceremony Green each hold up to 250 guests.

EVENT/RECEPTION & MEETING CAPACITY: The Clubhouse holds 80, the Brookside Room 50, and the Pavilion 250 seated guests. For meetings, the Boardroom seats 16 guests conference-style.

FEES & DEPOSITS: A $1,000 deposit is required to reserve your date. Inclusive packages start at $50/person. Tax, alcohol and service charge are additional.

AVAILABILITY: Year-round, daily, 7am–11pm Sunday through Friday; til midnight on Saturday.

SERVICES/AMENITIES:

Catering: provided, no BYO
Kitchen Facilities: n/a
Tables & Chairs: provided
Linens, Silver, etc.: provided
Restrooms: wheelchair accessible
Dance Floor: CBA, extra charge
Bride's Dressing Area: yes
Meeting Equipment: CBA, extra charge

Parking: large lot
Accommodations: no guest rooms
Telephone: emergency only
Outdoor Night Lighting: CBA, extra charge
Outdoor Cooking Facilities: n/a
Cleanup: provided
View: 18-hole golf course
Other: event planning, baby grand player piano, golf tournaments

RESTRICTIONS:

Alcohol: provided, or BYO wine with corkage fee
Smoking: outside only
Music: call for details

Wheelchair Access: yes
Insurance: not required
Other: no rice, confetti or birdseed

Kenyon Estate

Private Estate

Address withheld to ensure privacy. Vallejo

707/745-3812

www.kenyonestate.com
info@kenyonestate.com

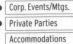

- Rehearsal Dinners
- Ceremonies
- Wedding Receptions
- Corp. Events/Mtgs.
- Private Parties
- Accommodations

If there was ever a fairy-tale setting, it would be Kenyon Estate, a beautiful villa on the crest of a hill with views of rivers, rooftops and three famous peaks—Mount Diablo, Mount Tamalpais, and Mount Saint Helena. The magnificent handcrafted, wrought-iron gates will open for your guests alone, and the private drive will lead them to the cobbled courtyard (you can actually land a helicopter here), where a red carpet stretches beneath the long entry trellis to the massive arched doors that open into the Mission-style mansion.

Greet your guests inside the fabulous foyer, with its 24-foot ceiling and tumbled travertine marble floor. An enormous and resplendent Spanish-style chandelier showers the vestibule in a flattering light, making it a glorious place to welcome friends and family or pile gifts high on a table designed to showcase them handsomely. Next, escort everyone outside to the columned breezeway that looks out over the grounds.

Cocktails and passed hors d'oeuvres are superbly served up in and around the elegant colonnade or on the adjacent lawn and spectacular Sunset Terrace. Scatter outdoor furnishings to create a relaxing milieu surrounded by flowerbeds and hillside plantings of hibiscus, lavender, redwoods, palms, and ornamental plum trees—celebrants will be surprised by the patterned walkways, lovely fountains and commanding views of the palatial terrace. A premier outdoor entertainment or ceremony space, it's canopied in blue sky by day and dazzlingly lit by lampposts and perimeter landscape lighting at night. On one end, a circular platform backed by a half-moon-shaped trellis perched on white Greco-Roman columns provides a heavenly spot to exchange vows. And, if sunset and starlight don't provide enough drama, the structure can be washed in colored uplights after dark.

Of course all of this is visible from the Great Room, a banquet hall of regal dimensions where you and your guests can dine. The granite, working fireplace and tumbled travertine floor add Old World opulence, as do the Mediterranean-style sconces, amber glass, and wrought-iron-and-gold accents. Nine arched, glass double doors lead out onto the breezeway and terrace, and the double-recessed ceilings with crown moldings house mood-setting lights. Designed with weddings and large gatherings in mind, this is a luxurious, yet flexible, space and a graceful frame for any type of event, from executive luncheon to dinner-dance gala.

The attention to detail continues throughout the villa, which is laid out like a sumptuous private home. In the Italian Renaissance-style restroom, you'll find a custom Mona Lisa washbasin among other unique and well-chosen accoutrements. Adjacent to the Great Room, the plushly carpeted, 12-seat Executive Theater—featuring leather chairs and dark chocolate walls—is the perfect place for the groom and his men to repair to. Naturally, the bride and her attendants also have their own inviting hideaway, too: They can sequester themselves in a Bride's Room with a sitting area, full bath and a paparazzi-proof private entrance.

CEREMONY, EVENT/RECEPTION & MEETING CAPACITY: The site accommodates 150 seated guests, indoors or outdoors.

FEES & DEPOSITS: A $2,000 deposit is required to reserve your date, and the payment schedule is customized to suit your needs. Packages start at $12,600 for 100 guests, and include exclusive use of the Courtyard, New Sunset Terrace and Great Room for 5 hours; parking attendants; day-of wedding coordinator; Chiavari chairs; basic floor-length linens in choice of colors; tableware; passed hors d'oeuvres; carving station with formal buffet; service and tax. No corkage on beer and wine. Custom packages are also available. Their select list of caterers can provide any type of cuisine: Indian, Chinese banquet, Wine Country buffet, plated, family style, stations, etc.

AVAILABILITY: Year-round, daily.

SERVICES/AMENITIES:

Catering: provided or BYO
Kitchen Facilities: limited
Tables & Chairs: provided
Linens, Silver, etc.: through caterer
Restrooms: wheelchair accessible
Dance Floor: provided
Bride's Dressing Area: yes
Meeting Equipment: A/V equipment, more CBA
Other: day-of wedding coordination included

Parking: large lot, valet optional
Accommodations: no guest rooms
Telephone: emergency use only
Outdoor Night Lighting: provided
Outdoor Cooking Facilities: BBQ CBA
Cleanup: provided
View: fountain; panorama of meadow, hills, river and bay

RESTRICTIONS:

Alcohol: provided or BYO
Smoking: designated areas only
Music: amplified OK

Wheelchair Access: yes
Insurance: liability required

Sacramento, Central Valley and Chico

Orland

Chico

SIERR

BUTTE

Willows

Oroville

NN

Live Oak

NEVADA

LUSA

SUTTER

Yuba City

Linda YUBA

Colfax

Sacramento R.

Foresth

Arbuckle

5

Auburn

Newcastle

80

EL

YOLO

Knights Landing

Rocklin

Placerv

5

Roseville

50

Lake Berryessa

Woodland

Citrus
Heights

Folsom

505

Arden-Arcade

Carmichael

Winters

★ Sacramento

80

Clarksburg

SACRAMENTO

AMADOR

Napa

Fairfield

5

Galt

Ryde

SOLANO

Lodi

Vallejo

CAL

Stockton

Canyon Oaks Country Club

Golf Club

999 Yosemite Drive, Chico
530/343-2582
www.countryclubreceptions.com
catering@canyonoakscc.com

- Rehearsal Dinners
- Ceremonies
- Wedding Receptions
- Corp. Events/Mtgs.
- Private Parties

Accommodations

The Sierra Nevada foothills provide some of Northern California's most beautiful outdoor scenery, including Chico's Bidwell Park, a nearly 4,000-acre state treasure. The Upper Park, highly prized for its rugged canyon terrain, hiking trails and abundant wildlife, is an ode to nature in the wild. It's also the next door neighbor of Canyon Oaks Country Club, whose rolling hills and profuse greenery provide a tamer version of nature and a lovely setting for your wedding.

To reach this lush property, located in the upscale community of Canyon Oaks, you drive through a wrought-iron gate past pine and oak trees to the clean-lined, contemporary clubhouse. The surrounding golf course is one of the most prestigious in Northern California, and is the key factor in an enticing incentive to hold your festivities here: a complimentary golf package. As part of your rehearsal day, four lucky members of your group can enjoy a full round of pre-wedding play or, for an additional fee, you can have a tournament arranged for all your guests. Even if you're not a golfer, you'll appreciate the verdant, well-maintained landscaping that often draws visiting quail, rabbits and even the occasional deer.

Canyon Oaks prides itself on anticipating your every need, and their staff will help guide you through your event. When it's time to get ready, you and your bridesmaids can retreat to the spacious, fully mirrored Bridal Room while the groom and his attendants relax in their own space—complete with TV and poker table. From here it's just a short walk to the picture-perfect gazebo, bordered by flowers. Set between the 1st and 18th fairways, this outdoor ceremony site affords fantastic, unobstructed golf course views. You can heighten the drama of your entrance by arriving in a golf cart or, as one recent bride did, in a horse-drawn carriage.

After tying the knot, you and your photographer can take full advantage of several nearby scenic backdrops, including romantic bridges and a waterfall made of natural rock. Meanwhile, your friends and family start the festivities with a lovely al fresco cocktail hour by sampling an array of hors d'oeuvres to the accompaniment of live music or a DJ.

For the main reception, move inside to the second-story Vista Room, so named for the banks of large windows that frame those expansive exterior views. Muted earth tones, wainscoted walls, a large stone fireplace and crystal chandeliers help set a tone of low-key elegance. A variety of menu options, ranging from tri-tip to sushi, are available for your menu. After dining, some guests will gravitate to the central dance floor while others might drift out to the large private terrace. Here they can bask in the night air, gaze up at the stars, and take a quiet moment to savor nature's gifts one more time.

CEREMONY CAPACITY: The facility holds 200 seated guests outdoors.

EVENT/RECEPTION CAPACITY: The club can accommodate 175 seated or 225 standing guests indoors.

MEETING CAPACITY: Meeting spaces hold up to 150 seated guests.

FEES & DEPOSITS: A nonrefundable deposit, which is applied to your food and beverage total, is required to reserve your date. The amount of the deposit is equal to 25% of the estimated event total. 50% is due 6 months prior, and 100% of the final estimated balance is due 10 days prior to the event date. Rental fees range $400–2,000 depending on the day of the event and the space rented. Meals range $32–68/person. Tax, alcohol and a 20% service charge are additional.

AVAILABILITY: Year-around, daily, 7am–midnight.

SERVICES/AMENITIES:

Catering: provided
Kitchen Facilities: n/a
Tables & Chairs: provided
Linens, Silver, etc.: provided
Restrooms: wheelchair accessible
Dance Floor: portable provided
Bride's & Groom's Dressing Areas: yes
Meeting Equipment: some provided, CBA
Other: event coordination

Parking: large lot
Accommodations: no guest rooms
Telephone: house phone
Outdoor Night Lighting: CBA
Outdoor Cooking Facilities: BBQ on site
Cleanup: provided
View: fairways, hills, lagoon, fountain, landscaped grounds

RESTRICTIONS:

Alcohol: provided
Smoking: not allowed
Music: amplified OK

Wheelchair Access: yes
Insurance: not required

This is important! Tell locations you're reading HERE COMES THE GUIDE and ask if our information is still current.

DoubleTree By Hilton Sacramento

Hotel

2001 Point West Way, Sacramento
916/924-4900
www.sacramento.doubletree.com
rlsa_ds@hilton.com

- Rehearsal Dinners
- Ceremonies
- Wedding Receptions
- Corp. Events/Mtgs.
- Private Parties
- Accommodations

Fresh-baked chocolate chip cookies offer a warm welcome when you check in at the DoubleTree by Hilton Sacramento, but it's the friendly staff and newly renovated ballrooms that truly make this venue an excellent choice for a destination wedding or special event.

The hotel can accommodate almost any size group or function: Each of its three ballrooms—which were beautifully upgraded in 2012—has a unique style, as well as its own entrance, foyer and convenient parking for easy access.

If you're planning an outdoor wedding ceremony, the Capital Patio is an ideal spot. Adjoining the Capital Ballroom, it's bordered by a gentle creek and overlooks a lush garden and rolling lawn. The bride makes her grand entrance through the garden and across a quaint footbridge that spans the creek. A petal-strewn aisle leads to the patio, and a wooden arbor where vows are exchanged in the shade of sheltering trees. Both the bridge and arbor can be decorated with flowers, fabric or garlands coordinated with your color scheme to give it a personal touch. In the evening, twinkle lights add a magical quality to the setting.

A favorite option for intimate receptions or rehearsal dinners is the tented Event Pavilion and patio. In spring and summer the pavilion is normally left open-sided, but even during cooler weather when its "walls" are drawn down, you still feel warm, comfortable and connected to the surrounding greenery through clear acrylic windows. Couples hosting their reception in the pavilion can tie the knot just a few steps away beneath a delicate wrought-iron gazebo.

Seasoned event professionals will help orchestrate your celebration, from offering vendor recommendations to day-of coordination. Several wedding packages as well as customized menus are available. Certain ethnic cuisines, including Indian and Middle Eastern, may be prepared and brought in by a licensed caterer.

The hotel has 448 oversized guest rooms with balconies, which means all your friends and family can stay in one place. And whether they're lounging by the hotel pool, shopping in the nearby mall or taking in the historic attractions of Old Sacramento, your guests will enjoy their free time almost as much as attending your wedding.

CEREMONY CAPACITY: The site holds 1,300 seated guests indoors and 200 seated outdoors.

EVENT/RECEPTION CAPACITY: The facility can accommodate 830 seated or 1,500 standing indoors and 150 seated or 250 standing outdoors.

MEETING CAPACITY: Meeting spaces hold 1,300 seated guests.

FEES & DEPOSITS: 25% of the estimated total event cost is required to reserve your date, with the balance due 10 days prior to the event. Rental fees range $100–5,000 depending on the space(s) rented. Meals range $30–57/person. Tax, alcohol and a 21% service charge are additional.

AVAILABILITY: Year-round, daily.

SERVICES/AMENITIES:

Catering: provided, or BYO (ethnic cuisine only)
Kitchen Facilities: limited
Tables & Chairs: provided
Linens, Silver, etc.: provided
Restrooms: wheelchair accessible
Dance Floor: provided, portable CBA
Bride's Dressing Area: CBA
Meeting Equipment: CBA
Other: grand piano, A/V equipment, event coordination

Parking: large lot, valet/self-parking
Accommodations: 448 guest rooms
Telephone: house phone
Outdoor Night Lighting: provided
Outdoor Cooking Facilities: BBQ CBA
Cleanup: provided
View: fountain, garden, landscaped grounds, pool area, waterfall

RESTRICTIONS:

Alcohol: provided, or BYO with corkage fee
Smoking: outside only
Music: amplified OK with restrictions

Wheelchair Access: yes
Insurance: liability required

The Firehouse

1112 Second Street, Old Sacramento
916/442-4772
www.firehouseoldsac.com
melinda@harvego.com

Historic Restaurant

● Rehearsal Dinners	● Corp. Events/Mtgs.
● Ceremonies	● Private Parties
● Wedding Receptions	Accommodations

When those scorching Valley days begin—along about May—everyone heads for a favorite oasis. None is cooler, greener, or leafier than the sprawling brick patio at the back of The Firehouse, the Gold Rush era landmark restaurant where Sacramentans have dined, politicked and gotten married for over 50 years.

Built in 1853, it's located in the heart of the old riverfront historic district and really did house Engine Company No. 3, which stabled its horses in what is now the wine cellar. The Firehouse opened as a restaurant in 1960, with the owners scouring the Central Valley and Sierra foothills for antique furnishings. It offers seven cool Gilded Era dining and reception areas with 12-foot ceilings, mahogany wainscoting, ornate mirrors, and massive paintings of grande dames and friskier ladies.

Most popular for weddings is the Courtyard, the al fresco dining area that's won local awards for "best special occasion" and "best outdoor" dining. Enter through the narrow 19th-century alley at the back of The Firehouse and you really do feel transported to another place and time: The wrought-iron balconies, ivy-covered brick walls, fountains, and canopy of mulberry and Chinese elm trees feel more like New Orleans than Sacramento. With lights laced through the overhanging branches, it's magic on summer nights.

Guests seated in the Courtyard dine on California nouveau continental cuisine accompanied by selections from the 25,000-bottle wine cellars, the largest in the Valley. Decoration here is simple—perhaps just some flowers. "If you didn't add anything extra, it'd still be spectacular," says Mario Ortiz, General Manager, Sommelier and 41-year employee of The Firehouse, though he recalls one outside event planner who created a "Wedding in Paris" theme with a canvas Eiffel Tower. Bring in a band, orchestra or DJ, and you can dance out here, too.

Larger wedding parties spill over into the adjacent Courtyard Grill, a garden-like room under a Tiffany-style glass dome with a long bar, floor-to-ceiling windows, and a massive fireplace used on cool harvest nights. This space can also be used by itself for small events.

Some weddings and the ubiquitous Capitol fundraisers, receptions and banquets are held in the Golden Eagle Room and adjoining Salon. Or, guests can thread their way past an iron grille door and down a narrow staircase into a pair of small, immaculate banquet rooms known as Wine Cellars I and II.

The Firehouse has long been a draw for politicos and celebrities, with Ronald Reagan holding both of his inaugural dinners here, and Mayor Kevin Johnson a recent guest. It's become a pilgrimage site for tourists who wander through with cameras, trying to capture the rich mélange of Gold Rush memorabilia, rococo chandeliers, bare brick walls and long, gleaming bars.

Out-of-town visitors will enjoy the ambiance of the building itself, as well as the bustling boardwalks and horse-drawn carriages out front. And its location in the heart of downtown Sacramento makes it easy for everyone to find. So if you want to combine Old World elegance with a rambunctious history lesson and a magical walled garden, The Firehouse has it all.

CEREMONY CAPACITY: The Courtyard holds up to 300 seated guests. Indoors, The Firehouse holds up to 120 seated guests.

EVENT/RECEPTION CAPACITY: The Courtyard holds up to 300 seated or 500 standing guests. Indoors, 7 banquet rooms hold up to 120 seated or 175 standing guests. Several configurations are available; call for details.

MEETING CAPACITY: The Firehouse can accommodate up to 200 guests seated theater-style.

FEES & DEPOSITS: A $750–1,500 deposit is required to reserve your date. A second payment of 50% of the food and beverage minimum is due 90 days prior to the event date, and the remaining 50% is due 30 days prior. The balance is due upon completion of the event. Rental fees range $0–1,500 depending on room rented and day and time rented. Meals range $22–56/person for the dinner menu and weekend day events. Tax, alcohol and a 20% service charge are additional. Check with the Special Events department for possible lower rates on Fridays and Sundays.

AVAILABILITY: Year-round, daily. Weekend hours for courtyard use only are 11am–4pm and 6:30pm–midnight.

SERVICES/AMENITIES:

Catering: provided, no BYO
Kitchen Facilities: n/a
Tables & Chairs: provided
Linens, Silver, etc.: provided
Restrooms: wheelchair accessible
Dance Floor: CBA
Bride's Dressing Area: CBA
Meeting Equipment: CBA, extra charge

Parking: large lots, valet CBA
Accommodations: no guest rooms
Telephone: no
Outdoor Night Lighting: yes
Outdoor Cooking Facilities: BBQ CBA
Cleanup: provided
View: fountain, garden, landscaped grounds
Other: event coordination

RESTRICTIONS:

Alcohol: provided
Smoking: outside only
Music: amplified OK with restrictions

Wheelchair Access: yes
Insurance: not required

The Reserve at Spanos Park

Golf Course and Clubhouse

6301 West Eight Mile Road, Stockton
209/477-4653
www.countryclubreceptions.com
catering@reserveatspanospark.com

● Rehearsal Dinners	● Corp. Events/Mtgs.	
● Ceremonies	● Private Parties	
● Wedding Receptions	Accommodations	

Bordered by the maze of rivers and tributaries that make up California's Delta and positioned amid the rapidly developing region between North Stockton and Lodi, The Reserve at Spanos Park is a golfer's sanctuary. Designed to blend in with the surrounding environment, the Reserve's tranquility lies in its offering of wide-open space and stunning sunset views of Mt. Diablo. Golfers are not the only ones seeking asylum at this "reserve." Blue herons and egrets make occasional appearances among the 18 holes and eight lakes of its 7,000-yard championship course. And although the Reserve has the look and feel of an exclusive country club, fear not—this semiprivate club is affordably priced and does not require membership for facilities usage.

The main event space, the Mount Diablo Room, opened its doors in September of 2004. This versatile 3,200-square-foot venue can accommodate large receptions, rehearsal dinners, bar/bat mitzvahs or corporate events. Whatever celebration you're planning, you can be assured of eating well: The skilled catering team's creations feature the region's bounty of fruits, vegetables (Stockton is home to the Asparagus Festival) and Lodi Appelation wines. Beyond the tiled foyer lies the spacious banquet area, brightened by a wall of windows and a large skylight. The interior is attractively designed with a high ceiling, earth-toned tile and carpet, granite countertops and brick wainscoting. Glass doors open to the western-facing terrace, an ideal place for saying your vows or hosting a rehearsal dinner. Couples also have the option of holding their ceremony on the first tee, overlooking a small lake.

At the adjacent clubhouse, a porte-cochère offers arriving guests shelter from the heat or rain. Inside, two meeting rooms are available as dressing areas for the bride, groom and wedding parties. The relaxed atmosphere at the Clubhouse Bar makes it a perfect spot for friends and family to unwind before or after the ceremony. Out back, a wraparound patio overlooks the fairways and can be used for smaller weddings or informal dinners.

Easy to find and conveniently located, The Reserve at Spanos Park is a little more than a mile west of Interstate 5 between Stockton and Sacramento. Lodging is just minutes away, and shopping is close by for those last minute gifts.

While you don't have to be a golfer to hold your event at The Reserve, golf enthusiasts will certainly appreciate their state-of-the-art indoor learning center, first-rate practice facility, and complete short game area. Whether you choose to link up at the first tee or incorporate a round of golf into your next event, the experienced staff at The Reserve will provide superb customer service and assist you in every aspect of your special celebration.

CEREMONY, EVENT/RECEPTION & MEETING CAPACITY: The Reserve holds up to 200 seated or 250 standing guests, both indoors and outdoors.

FEES & DEPOSITS: A nonrefundable deposit, which is applied to your food and beverage total, is required to reserve your date. The amount of the deposit is equal to 25% of the estimated event total. 50% is due 6 months prior, and 100% of the final estimated balance is due 10 days prior to the event date. Rental fees range $50–1,200 depending on space rented, day and time of the event and guest count. Meals range $20–70/person. Tax, alcohol and a 20% service charge are additional.

AVAILABILITY: Year-round, daily, 6am–1am.

SERVICES/AMENITIES:

Catering: provided, no BYO

Kitchen Facilities: n/a

Tables & Chairs: provided

Linens, Silver, etc.: provided

Restrooms: wheelchair accessible

Dance Floor: yes

Bride's & Groom's Dressing Areas: CBA

Meeting Equipment: CBA, extra fee

Parking: medium-sized lot

Accommodations: hotels nearby

Telephone: pay phone

Outdoor Night Lighting: yes

Outdoor Cooking Facilities: BBQ CBA

Cleanup: provided

View: fairways, lake, mountains, meadow

RESTRICTIONS:

Alcohol: provided or BYO wine with corkage fee

Smoking: outdoors only

Music: amplified OK

Wheelchair Access: yes

Insurance: not required

Overwhelmed? Use the search criteria on www.HereComesTheGuide.com to narrow down your choices.

491

Bear Flag Farm

Winery, Organic Farm & Private Estate

Address withheld to ensure privacy. Winters

530/753-9494

www.bearflagfarm.com
info@bearflagfarm.com

Rehearsal Dinners	● Corp. Events/Mtgs.
● Ceremonies	● Private Parties
● Wedding Receptions	Accommodations

Just an hour from San Francisco and 20 minutes from Sacramento lies an exquisite organic farm and winery. Surrounded by peach and apricot orchards, lavender fields, grapevines and seasonal row crops, Bear Flag Farm looks as if it was plucked straight from the French countryside. The winery, main house, guest cottage and barn are like a tiny village, with orange tile roofs and golden stucco walls that seem to glow in the sunlight.

As guests arrive, they drive onto the farm past a wrought-iron gate that opens onto a winding driveway divided by a row of flowering crepe myrtles. At the end of the drive, their cars are whisked away by a valet to a parking area hidden from view.

The farm offers several wonderful ceremony and receptions sites, so the couple can pick the ones that suit them best. Some brides like to glide through the French doors of the cottage onto a small terrace, and then walk down the steps to exchange vows on the soft lawn below. Or, the couple might say "I do" on the 3,000-square-foot lavender lawn, nestled in the lavender field. Yet another option is a ceremony next to the vineyard, where guests are seated after being treated to fresh lemonade or minty iced tea and a stroll through the almond orchard.

Formal dinners, buffets, champagne receptions, cake-cutting ceremonies and dancing can be staged on the grand terrace, in the grassy amphitheater guarded by sycamore trees, or under a sprawling tent shading the vineyard lawn. Parasols are available for daytime events, and as the sun sets, silk lanterns or even chandeliers can be used to cast a romantic glow over the evening's festivities.

Bear Flag Farm provides a tremendous amount of flexibility for its guests. Since only one daylong event is allowed per weekend, couples have the time and space to fully prepare for their celebration. The preferred list of caterers includes some of the best Bay Area and Sacramento chefs, and early in the year Bear Flag Farm works with each chef to select specific crops that will be harvested fresh from the farm for seasonal menus. In this way, Bear Flag Farm's goal of providing a true field-to-table experience is fulfilled, and guests reap the rewards of flavors only available to those who come to the farm. Live music is not only allowed, but encouraged—the one restriction being that it has to end at a reasonable hour out of consideration for neighboring farmers.

In addition to weddings, Bear Flag Farm hosts other events such as private and corporate parties. Part of Bear Flag Farm's mission is to expand people's awareness of organic and sustainable farming. That shouldn't be hard—its benefits and delights are easy for anyone to appreciate as they linger amid this abundance of fruit trees, grapevines and rows of lavender.

CEREMONY, EVENT/RECEPTION & MEETING CAPACITY: The location accommodates up to 200 seated guests outdoors.

FEES & DEPOSITS: The rental fee for exclusive use of the farm starts at $15,000.

AVAILABILITY: The regular season begins in May and ends in October. All events must end by 10pm.

SERVICES/AMENITIES:

Catering: select from list
Kitchen Facilities: prep only
Tables & Chairs: through facility or planner
Linens, Silver, etc.: through facility or planner
Restrooms: wheelchair accessible
Dance Floor: provided
Bride's Dressing Area: yes
Meeting Equipment: BYO

Parking: valet provided
Accommodations: no guest rooms
Telephone: emergency use only
Outdoor Night Lighting: yes
Outdoor Cooking Facilities: BBQ on site
Cleanup: through caterer
View: vineyards, mountains, meadows, garden, lavender fields

RESTRICTIONS:

Alcohol: through caterer
Smoking: designated area only
Music: amplified OK with time & volume restrictions

Wheelchair Access: limited
Insurance: liability required

Wine Country

Hans Fahden Vineyards

Winery

4855 Petrified Forest Road, Calistoga
707/942-6760
www.hansfahden.com
mary@hansfahden.com

- Rehearsal Dinners
- Ceremonies
- Wedding Receptions

- Corp. Events/Mtgs.
- Private Parties
- Accommodations

High in the mountains between Santa Rosa and Calistoga, the Hans Fahden family has created an incredible place with outdoor sites elegant enough for satin gowns and tuxedos, and a marvelous indoor facility with some of the most extraordinary features we've ever seen.

Even at first glance, the winery's gardens and event facilities are quite lovely, but like a Fabergé egg, their outward beauty is only a prelude to a wealth of creativity, craftsmanship and aesthetic richness within.

Your special event may start in the Teahouse, a quaint wooden structure covered with wisteria, grapevines and red climbing roses. Small gatherings can use the Teahouse for ceremonies or receptions, but larger groups mingle there before descending into the gardens below. The gardens are an exquisite combination of French country style and wildlife habitat, and if they remind you of an Impressionist painting, it's no coincidence. Winery owners and landscapers Antone and Lyall Fahden relied heavily on Monet's paintings of the gardens at Giverny when they designed their own. As you travel the path down to the pond, your senses are tantalized by the sights and smells of roses, irises, petunias, pansies, cornflowers, poppies, ornamental grasses and native shrubs. The garden has been cleverly planted so that something different blooms each month, creating one wave of color after another. In late spring, roses take center stage; other floral "coming attractions" include matilija poppies, oleander, zinnias, sunflowers and blue pitcher sage. Midway between the Teahouse and pond, a terraced lawn bordered by a volcanic-ash rock wall and beds of pink evening primroses, lavender, roses and California poppies serves as a ceremony site for large weddings. The covered bridge spanning the lily pond can also be used for weddings, and brings you close to a variety of wildlife—thanks to the ducks, egrets, quail and mourning doves that call the gardens home.

After exchanging vows, join your guests in the winery building, a long graceful structure whose mellow wood exterior and peaked, sage-green roof blend with the rugged mountainside behind it. Inside, a gray slate floor, high beamed ceiling of grooved pine and redwood, and cream walls give the room a simple beauty that complements the glory of the gardens viewed through French doors. In one corner, a grand piano provides background music as your guests nibble appetizers and sip champagne. Just when everyone thinks that their eyes simply couldn't take in any more beauty, the 400-pound Douglas fir doors at one end of the room are thrown open to reveal a wine cave containing candlelit tables set for dinner. This amazing cave is like the jewel within a Fabergé egg: gorgeous, surprising and utterly unique. Formed of volcanic ash rock, the T-shaped cave's walls are lined with wine barrels; metal fixtures with grape-leaf cutouts and twinkle-light-wrapped poles provide subtle lighting. At the T's apex, two wine barrels support a massive arrangement of fresh flowers; above, gold candle sconces in floral designs await lighting. When these sconces are lit, along with the candelabras on the tables and the twinkle lights, Ali Baba's cave itself could not be more enchanting. Magical doesn't even begin to describe an event here—as you sit down to dinner, surrounded by flowers, flickering shadows and the piquant smell of aging wine, you'll feel as if you're part of a breathtaking fairy tale. And, unlike limestone caves, this cave's volcanic-ash rock adjusts to body temperature when occupied, so you can wear the most daring *décolleté* gown and never have to throw a jacket over your shoulders.

If you're thinking that Hans Fahden sounds like a wonderful place, but you're not planning to get married anytime soon, keep in mind that the winery can accommodate all types of events, from a gala celebration to a business seminar. But we can't help feeling that the site's stunning visual appeal may be most appreciated at a wedding. So, brides, if your fantasy includes a vision of you in a magnificent Vera Wang gown against a backdrop of pristine natural beauty, you owe yourself a visit to Hans Fahden Winery. They can make your dream wedding a beautiful reality!

CEREMONY CAPACITY: The Teahouse holds up to 50 guests; the Amphitheater 120 guests.

EVENT/RECEPTION CAPACITY: The Main Hall holds 120 seated guests; the Wine Cave holds 120 seated guests. The facility accommodates up to 100 guests December–March, or 120 guests outdoors, May–October.

MEETING CAPACITY: The Main Hall holds 120 seated theater-style; the Wine Cave 120 guests.

FEES & DEPOSITS: For events, a $2,500 deposit is required to reserve your date; the balance is due 10 days prior to the event. The rental fee is $4,500 on weekdays including Friday, $5,500 on Sunday, and $6,500 on Saturday.

AVAILABILITY: Year-round, daily, 10am–10pm.

SERVICES/AMENITIES:

Catering: select from preferred list
Kitchen Facilities: prep only
Tables & Chairs: provided
Linens, Silver, etc.: BYO
Restrooms: wheelchair accessible
Dance Floor: textured cement floor
Bride's & Groom's Dressing Areas: yes
Meeting Equipment: BYO
Other: day-of coordinator, baby grand piano, rentals valuing $5,000+ included with rental fee

Parking: on-site lot
Accommodations: no guest rooms, Calistoga is 5 minutes away
Telephone: emergency use only
Outdoor Night Lighting: yes
Outdoor Cooking Facilities: BBQ
Cleanup: caterer
View: vineyards, Mayacamas mountains

RESTRICTIONS:

Alcohol: full bar available, wine provided or BYO, no corkage fee with 1 case minimum purchase
Smoking: outdoors only
Music: amplified OK until 1/2 hour before departure

Wheelchair Access: limited
Insurance: certificate required
Other: no rice, birdseed, confetti, sparklers or butterfly releases

The Geyserville Inn
& Hoffman House Restaurant

21714 Geyserville Avenue, Geyserville
877/857-4343

www.geyservilleinn.com
catering@geyservilleinn.com

Inn & Restaurant

- Rehearsal Dinners
- Ceremonies
- Wedding Receptions
- Corp. Events/Mtgs.
- Private Parties
- Accommodations

This wine country destination is a rare "triple threat" venue that offers a lovely outdoor wedding site, full-scale dinner and reception facilities, and inviting accommodations for family and guests. The inn provides all of this at a terrific price point—and that's even before you add in other amenities, such as an excellent restaurant, the Hoffman House right next door (where many newlyweds eat their first breakfast together as a married couple), a swimming pool and plenty of parking. Catering is done on site by the Hoffman House, and the kitchen uses ingredients from all over Sonoma County's great breadbasket, an agricultural wonderland that consistently produces many of the country's finest vegetables, meats and dairy products. This award-winning restaurant has won six gold medals for its food at the regional Harvest Fair.

The inn offers a pair of lawns for ceremonies and receptions. Each is partially covered by shade cloth so that tents aren't needed during summer months. The smaller lawn is bordered by low hedges and ornamental trees. The larger one is a long, wide expanse of beautifully tended grass that sidles right up to a vineyard on two sides. Bordered by three white wooden arbors, it looks lovely when set with tables for an afternoon or evening meal. The main arbor, which is surrounded by wild roses and decorated with iron railings and Japanese-style lamps, is a superb spot for a head table or exchanging vows. A ceremonial gateway at the opposite end of the lawn lends an element of drama—brides often use it to make their entrance, then begin a stately march the length of the lawn. And we can't overlook the view from here: a green panorama of the tree-covered Mayacamas Hills in the distance.

We doubt you'll need any additional enticements to stay at the inn, but there is one more: a choice of three luxury suites for the bridal couple, set apart from the main building and next to the lawns. All of them feature a private entrance and patio or deck, along with sweeping views of the vineyards. Each also has HDTV and a Jacuzzi, and two have a fireplace and wetbar. The main building also offers junior suites with patios or decks.

Geyserville Inn is the only facility in the area that can easily combine so many services and conveniences under one roof. But the inn's attractive amenities are not the only reason to come here; there's also the powerful appeal of the wine country itself, with its earthy, romantic cachet.

The small town of Geyserville adds considerably to the allure: It has a rural look and feel, with no cookie-cutter homes, large developments or chain stores. Slick hasn't arrived here yet, and the locals are proud that so many out-of-towners feel drawn to this rustic setting.

Geyserville Inn is the kind of place you look for when you want a simple, no-hassle wedding. All of its components work so well together that it's easy to imagine settling in and letting capable hands take care of you, from your rehearsal dinner to that wonderful first bite of post-wedding brunch.

Note: This property is owned by the Christensen Family.

CEREMONY, EVENT/RECEPTION & MEETING CAPACITY: Indoor spaces hold up to 50 seated or 65 standing guests. The Lawns hold up to 250 seatedguests.

FEES & DEPOSITS: 50% of the rental fee is required to reserve your date. The balance is due 30 days prior to the event. Rental fees range $100–5,500 depending on the space selected. Dinner banquet prices range $40–60/person. Tax, alcohol and an 19.5% service charge are additional.

AVAILABILITY: Year-round, daily until 10pm for events. The Hoffman House Restaurant is also open daily from 7:30am for breakfast and lunch.

SERVICES/AMENITIES:
Catering: provided
Kitchen Facilities: fully equipped
Tables & Chairs: provided
Linens, Silver, etc.: provided
Restrooms: wheelchair accessible
Dance Floor: CBA
Bride's Dressing Area: CBA
Meeting Equipment: CBA, extra fee
Other: event coordination, wedding suites, picnic area, Hoffman House Restaurant next door

Parking: large lot or on street
Accommodations: 41 guest rooms including 5 suites
Telephone: guest phone
Outdoor Night Lighting: yes
Outdoor Cooking Facilities: no
Cleanup: provided
View: panorama of vineyards, mountains

RESTRICTIONS:
Alcohol: provided or BYO wine, beer or champagne with $15 corkage fee
Smoking: outdoors only
Music: amplified OK with restrictions

Wheelchair Access: yes
Insurance: liability required

The professionals in the back of this book are the best in the business. How do we know? Read page 637.

499

Trentadue Winery

Winery

19170 Geyserville Avenue, Geyserville
707/433-3294
www.trentadue.com
events@trentadue.com

- Rehearsal Dinners
- Ceremonies
- Wedding Receptions
- Corp. Events/Mtgs.
- Private Parties
- Accommodations

Italians are famous for their warm hospitality and zest for living. They may not have invented *la dolce vita* ("the sweet life"), but they perfected the recipe for it: good friends, good food and good wine, plus a generous splash of lively music. If this sounds like your idea of a good time, you'll be happy to know that Trentadue Winery can provide all the ingredients for a really smashing special event.

The winery entrance is marked by stone pillars topped with crouching lions; from here it's a short drive through the vineyards to the tasting room and event facilities. A bubbling lion-head fountain marks the entrance to the Garden Area, which consists of a quaint lattice arbor with stage, dance floor, room for tables, and a sunny lawn area. At one end of the lawn, a smaller Tuscan-style arbor, its columns and trellis wrapped in leafy vines, makes a romantic spot for exchanging vows. Along the west side of the entire space, a windbreak of sweet gum and redwood trees casts a shade as cool and refreshing as a drink of spring water on a hot afternoon. Standing here in the sun, it's hard to imagine anything lovelier, but at night, with twinkle lights covering fences, trees and both arbors, everything sparkles like a miniature Milky Way. Additional lighting, thoughtfully equipped with dimmers, means your guests will be able to see the festivities without being blinded.

A second, more dramatic, ceremony site is the vast North Lawn on the opposite side of the Vineyard Pavilion. Getting married here is like getting married in a vineyard: There are grapevines all around you with views of redwoods and mountains beyond.

But what if your event is planned for the cooler months? Never fear—the Trentadue family has built an indoor facility, the Sala del Leone ("Hall of the Lion"). This expansive space has a white, peaked, beamed ceiling, hand-sponged golden walls, and intriguing glass and wrought-iron light fixtures and sconces. Plenty of arched French doors all around the building allow your guests to feel connected to the natural beauty that surrounds them, yet protected from the elements. Potted olive trees (yes, they are strung with twinkle lights) create a "Mediterranean" look, but this versatile room blends with any décor. Recently, a corporate event featured a Morrocan theme, draping the walls to resemble a Bedouin tent. Should your guests wish to wander over to the arbor area, they are free to do so, because when you host your event at Trentadue, all the facilities are included in the rental price. And though the panoramic views of spreading vineyards and distant wooded mountains may make you think you're far from the madding crowd, the bustling town of Santa Rosa is a mere 20 minutes away!

So if you like to party "Italian style," the folks at Trentadue Winery would be happy to help you out. They can provide everything from award-winning wines to topnotch coordination services. All you need to do is add friends and stir!

CEREMONY, EVENT/RECEPTION & MEETING CAPACITY: The Sala del Leone Vineyard Pavilion holds 250 seated. The lawn and garden areas can accommodate up to 500 guests, seated or standing.

FEES & DEPOSITS: A $4,000 partially refundable rental deposit and signed contract are required to reserve your date. The remaining rental fee plus a $750 refundable security deposit are required 30 days before the event. Fees are based on guest count and time of year. Overtime is available at $1,000/hour and extra setup time runs $100/hour. Rental fees range $6,500–10,000 depending on guest count and date of event. There are discounts available for events taking place on weekdays and Sundays.

AVAILABILITY: Year-round, daily, 11am–10pm, excluding holidays.

SERVICES/AMENITIES:

Catering: select from approved list
Kitchen Facilities: ample
Tables & Chairs: provided
Linens, Silver, etc.: through caterer
Restrooms: wheelchair accessible
Dance Floor: indoor provided
Bride's & Groom's Dressing Areas: yes
Meeting Equipment: BYO
Other: event coordination

Parking: ample on site
Accommodations: no guest rooms
Telephone: emergency use only
Outdoor Night Lighting: garden arbors
and lawn
Outdoor Cooking Facilities: BBQ, extra fee
Cleanup: provided
View: mountains and vineyards

RESTRICTIONS:

Alcohol: provided
Smoking: outdoors only
Music: amplified OK with volume restrictions, music until 10pm

Wheelchair Access: yes
Insurance: extra liability required
Other: no confetti, rice, birdseed or glitter; no tacks or nails; children must be supervised

Beltane Ranch

Private Estate and Ranch

11775 Sonoma Highway, Glen Ellen

707/833-4233

www.beltaneranch.com
anne@beltaneranch.com

Rehearsal Dinners	●	Corp. Events/Mtgs.	
●	Ceremonies		Private Parties
●	Wedding Receptions	●	Accommodations

The story goes that in 1892, Mary Ellen Pleasant, a black woman from New Orleans, built this house in Sonoma's fabled Valley of the Moon. It was both a refuge from and celebration of the great business success she had enjoyed in San Francisco. She created a wooden confection, graced with delicate lathed railings and Victorian-style wood trim, as well as grand verandas strewn with wicker furnishings. The handsome new home was called "Beltane," a likely reference to the ancient Celtic festival of spring and Thomas Bell, her long-time big-city business partner.

It's easy to see what drew her to erect this two-story, five-room structure on this spot. Beltane nestles beneath venerable oaks atop a gentle slope that rises from the valley's main highway. To reach it, you turn onto a narrow drive flanked by old trees, vineyards, grassy fields and beautiful hand-built stone walls. The front of the house is bordered by a flower garden that's enclosed by a classic white picket fence.

Next to the house are two lawns used for ceremonies. The larger one is edged with flowerbeds, low stone walls and towering oaks. A stage for the DJ in one corner is festooned with strings of lights that create a festive glow, day or night. The smaller lawn right behind the house is a bit more intimate. It's especially appealing when a musician, positioned in one corner of the adjacent upstairs veranda, provides soft music during the ceremony. Another lawn near the trellised entrance to the main house often hosts small receptions.

When brides who've wed here talk about what they liked, the first thing they cite is Beltane's authenticity. A still-working ranch that raises cattle and grows grapes and olives, Beltane evokes Old Sonoma from the days before the county became an upscale destination. The lovingly maintained old house has nothing slick about it. Its vibrant gardens have evolved over the years and seem part of the landscape, not something designed on a drafting table. Bridal party members often enjoy breakfast fruit harvested from raspberry bushes planted decades ago by the owner's grand aunt. Another attractive feature is the stand-alone cottage, a Berber-carpeted hideaway that has a firebox, sitting area, private bath, and a small garden and deck overlooking the main lawn.

Brides also like Beltane's seasoned staff, many of whom have been on site at least 15 years. One dividend of the ranch's reputation for great service is that quite a few newlyweds return for their anniversaries. (The ranch has even welcomed the children of couples who have been married here.)

Beltane remains one of the most beautiful old ranch houses in California. Owned by the same family since the 1930s, and surrounded by 1,000 acres of open-space preserve, the ranch's 100 acres are the place to hold a true Sonoma County country wedding. Everything here—site and surroundings—blends seamlessly to create a perfect pastoral stage.

CEREMONY, EVENT/RECEPTION & MEETING CAPACITY: Beltane Ranch can accommodate up to 150 guests, seated or standing outdoors; and 14 seated or standing indoors.

FEES & DEPOSITS: One third of the rental fee is required to reserve your date. The next third is due 3 months prior to the event and the final third is due 2 weeks prior. Event packages include 5 bed & breakfast rooms and a garden cottage, exclusive use of the ranch, and a full breakfast for all B&B guests. The rental fee for a Saturday wedding with up to 75 guests is $12,500, and includes B&B accommodations on Friday and Saturday night. For each additional guest up to 150, there is an $80/person charge (cap at $16,000). One or two-night packages for intimate weddings and special events of up to 30 people are available starting at $3,775.

AVAILABILITY: Outdoor events held from the first weekend in June through the first weekend in October. Intimate weddings and events available year-round. Events may be held from 4pm–10pm.

SERVICES/AMENITIES:

Catering: select from list
Kitchen Facilities: prep only
Tables & Chairs: provided
Linens, Silver, etc.: through caterer
Restrooms: not wheelchair accessible
Dance Floor: provided
Bride's Dressing Area: yes
Meeting Equipment: CBA

Parking: large lot
Accommodations: 6 guest rooms
Telephone: office phone
Outdoor Night Lighting: garden arbors and lawn
Outdoor Cooking Facilities: caterers only
Cleanup: provided
View: mountains, vineyards, forest, garden

RESTRICTIONS:

Alcohol: BYO
Smoking: outdoors only
Music: amplified OK outdoors with restrictions

Wheelchair Access: limited
Insurance: extra liability required

B.R. Cohn Winery

Winery

15000 Sonoma Highway, Glen Ellen
707/931-7930, 800/330-4064 x130
www.brcohn.com/weddings
vallerie@brcohn.com

- Rehearsal Dinners
- Ceremonies
- Wedding Receptions
- Corp. Events/Mtgs.
- Private Parties
- Accommodations

Just 45 minutes north of the Golden Gate Bridge in the heart of Sonoma Valley, B.R. Cohn Winery offers a multitude of possibilities in a romantic Wine Country atmosphere. Olive trees, whose graceful branches shade the road leading up to the winery, are a fitting introduction to this pastoral location.

From the top of the hill, it's a short walk down to the outdoor Amphitheater, a spectacular ceremony site with a large stage and terraced lawn. Couples exchange vows on the stage beneath an enormous oak tree. Behind them is a stunning natural backdrop: acres of lush Cabernet vineyards and a full view of the Sonoma Mountains. Guests seated on the stage or lawn have the perfect vantage from which to enjoy the lovely panorama.

Nearby is another gorgeous venue to tie the knot: Oak Hill. Set in the middle of a vineyard, this rustic spot is shaded by 300-year-old oaks and manzanita trees and so private that all you hear is the occasional chirping of birds. Guests have a 360-degree view of the surrounding grapevines, and on hot days a soft breeze keeps them comfortable. Nature provides ample "decoration" so you don't need to add anything—except perhaps some rose petals for the aisle.

A third choice is the Poolside Arbor. Ideal for smaller ceremonies and cocktail receptions, it features landscaped gardens and fruit trees and has a view of the olive grove, vineyards and mountains in the distance.

When it's time to dine, most couples invite their guests to the Olive Grove for an al fresco celebration. This expansive lawn is shaded by more than a dozen 140-year-old French Picholine olive trees. Flowers make a colorful border, while tiny lights woven throughout every other tree create nighttime sparkle. Although this grove is usually used for receptions, it's equally beautiful for ceremonies.

A new indoor ceremony/reception option, due to be completed in 2013, is the Barrel Room. Lined with wooden wine casks, it will provide a cool alternative during those hot summer months, and a wonderful venue in winter, too. The aroma of aging wine, soft lighting and flickering candles will make dinners here both fragrant and romantic.

In addition to its numerous event spaces, B.R. Cohn provides a charming cottage for the bride, her entourage and her family. Outfitted with an antique vanity, full-length mirror and couches, it's a cozy place to primp and relax.

Nestled between the Mayacamas and Sonoma Mountains, B.R. Cohn Winery's 90 acres possess a wealth of beauty, tranquility and options. Add to that fine wines and a friendly, experienced event coordinator and you have everything you need for an outstanding event.

CEREMONY & EVENT/RECEPTION CAPACITY: The winery holds up to 250 seated or standing guests outdoors. Indoor capacity is a tented terrace area that holds up to 50 seated or 75 standing guests.

MEETING CAPACITY: Meeting spaces accommodate 50 seated guests.

FEES & DEPOSITS: A deposit in the amount of 50% of the site fee is required to secure your date; the balance is due 6 months prior to the event. Site fees range $4,500–9,000 depending on the day of your event and the guest count. Fees include use of the site for ceremony and reception, site coordinator services, and time necessary for ceremony rehearsal.

AVAILABILITY: Year-round, daily, flexible hours. Outdoor spaces available April–November, weather permitting.

SERVICES/AMENITIES:

Catering: select from list or BYO with approval
Kitchen Facilities: prep area only
Tables & Chairs: BYO or through caterer
Linens, Silver, etc.: BYO or through caterer
Restrooms: wheelchair accessible
Dance Floor: CBA, extra fee
Bride's Dressing Area: yes
Meeting Equipment: BYO
Other: event coordination

Parking: ample, complimentary; shuttles or valet for over 150 guests
Accommodations: no guest rooms
Telephone: office phone
Outdoor Night Lighting: yes
Outdoor Cooking Facilities: no
Cleanup: caterer
View: vineyards, olive trees, Sonoma Mountains, landscaped grounds

RESTRICTIONS:

Alcohol: wine provided; BYO BC, no hard alcohol
Smoking: designated areas
Music: amplified OK outdoors until 10pm

Wheelchair Access: yes
Insurance: certificate of liability required

Want to know WHAT TO ASK a potential location or vendor? Check out our Questions to Ask starting on page 17.

Jack London Lodge

Lodge, Restaurant & Historic Tavern

13740 Arnold Drive, Glen Ellen
707/938-8510

www.jacklondonlodge.com
info@jacklondonlodge.com

●	Rehearsal Dinners	●	Corp. Events/Mtgs.
●	Ceremonies	●	Private Parties
●	Wedding Receptions	●	Accommodations

Located in the quaint village of Glen Ellen, the Jack London Lodge is a perennial favorite for Wine Country celebrations. Named for the famous writer who lived nearby until his death, the venue includes the historic 1905 brick building that houses the saloon, the adjoining Wolf House Dining Room and Creekside Patio where special events are held, and a 22-unit lodge.

Couples getting married here have a number of choices. For more traditional ceremonies, there are several churches just minutes away, including a historic church within walking distance of the lodge. But many brides and grooms prefer to exchange vows outdoors on the lodge's Creekside Lawn, a lovely grass area adjacent to the patio, pool and the treelined Sonoma Creek. The bride and groom can stand next to the creek with a tapestry of trees as a backdrop, or under a rose-covered arbor at the entrance to the patio.

Wedding receptions, rehearsal dinners and other special events are hosted on the Creekside Patio, which is shaded by the branches of towering trees and overlooks Sonoma Creek. With its bubbling stone fountain and outdoor serving bar, it's an al fresco setting adaptable for all types of gatherings, from casual barbecues to candlelit suppers. Flowerbeds filled with perennials provide an abundance of color, eliminating the need for any additional decoration.

The Patio connects to the Saloon, which is also a great place for socializing. Your guests can wander in for a change of scene during or after your event. Its period décor, Jack London memorabilia, Tiffany lamps and antique oak bar will give them a taste of another era.

For smaller gatherings, the elegant Wolf House Dining Room offers a warm and intimate ambiance, with its honey-gold walls, rustic brick fireplace, and beautiful view of the creek along with two creekside decks. This space is a perfect year-round option for rehearsal dinners, receptions and parties for all occasions.

One reason the Jack London Lodge is so popular is that it's one of the few facilities in the Wine Country where you can have your event and house many of your out-of-town guests all at the same location. The lodge's 22 spacious guest rooms feature charming vintage furniture and are set off in a secluded area that has a swimming pool and in-ground spa. Colorful seasonal flowers surround the pool and grace the front of the lodge, affording guests a garden experience. A very private three-bedroom, three-bath house just a few minutes from the Lodge is a convenient retreat for wedding parties. The woodsy setting, full of oak and pine trees, makes this a tranquil place for brides who need their own dressing room or a quiet getaway. It's also wonderful for families who want to spend some quality time together.

The garden setting, historic atmosphere and excellent food and lodging attract celebrants from all over the country. And the location is ideal: just minutes from the City of Sonoma, Jack London State Park, wineries, golf, horseback riding, balloon rides and a long list of other activities. So if this Valley of the Moon facility is the right place for you, we suggest you reserve it as early as possible. Your family and friends will be extremely grateful.

CEREMONY CAPACITY: Ceremonies can be arranged on the patio or lawn for up to 150 guests.

EVENT/RECEPTION CAPACITY: The Creekside Patio holds 40–150 guests. The Wolf House dining room holds 20–60 seated or 20–80 standing guests

FEES & DEPOSITS: Fees and deposits vary depending on the type of event and will be quoted accordingly. Meals start at $25/person for lunch, $41/per person for dinner. Alcohol, tax and a 20% service charge are additional.

AVAILABILITY: Daily, 10am–10pm. The Wolf House Dining Room is available year-round, and the Creekside Patio May–October.

SERVICES/AMENITIES:

Catering: provided by *Wolf House Restaurant*
Kitchen Facilities: n/a
Tables & Chairs: some provided
Linens, Silver, etc.: provided
Restrooms: wheelchair accessible
Dance Floor: deck or patio
Bride's Dressing Area: guest room CBA
Meeting Equipment: no

Parking: on-street and lot
Accommodations: 22 guest rooms
Telephone: no
Outdoor Night Lighting: yes
Outdoor Cooking Facilities: no
Cleanup: provided
View: treelined Sonoma Creek

RESTRICTIONS:

Alcohol: provided, wine and champagne corkage $13/bottle
Smoking: outdoors only
Music: OK with restrictions

Wheelchair Access: yes
Insurance: not required
Other: no rice, birdseed, confetti, tape or staples

Vineyard Ranch & Barn

Private Ranch Estate

Address withheld to ensure privacy. Glen Ellen

www.julieatwoodevents.com
info@julieatwoodevents.com

● Rehearsal Dinners | ● Corp. Events/Mtgs.
● Ceremonies | ● Private Parties
● Wedding Receptions | Accommodations

Cabernet grapes hang heavy on rows of vines disappearing towards the eastern mountains, and a long view of Sonoma Valley stretches before you. This is only one of the lovely scenes you see as you survey Vineyard Ranch's idyllic surroundings and consider all the possibilities.

The 140-year-old ranch is spread out over 70 acres, with horses roaming the property amidst olive trees, vineyards and organic gardens. Numerous areas on the estate lend themselves to events, especially the contemporary barn and gardens. Included with this stunning setting are the services of one of the Bay Area's most elite planners, Julie Atwood Events (JAE). Their team offers complete wedding planning from start to finish, as well as site tours of other exclusive properties for rehearsal parties, brunches, and other events.

By handling the coordination, design and staging for all events at this private estate, JAE ensures that every wedding has a distinctive, totally personal feeling. To help you realize your vision, they'll provide you with a select cadre of Wine Country resources, including florists, musicians, lighting designers and lodging. They'll also assist you in choosing a caterer from their exclusive list who will create a menu just for you using only the freshest and best regional foods, highlighted by seasonal vegetables, herbs and olive oil from the ranch's own garden. Your feast will be paired with wines that you have chosen from fabulous Sonoma County wineries.

Couples married here usually exchange vows in the barn or garden, or on an expansive lawn, with vineyards and the Sonoma Mountains as a backdrop. From their ceremony site, a path spilling over with roses and lavender guides them to the oak-shaded flagstone patio where the festivities begin.

Cocktails may be served on the patio in the dappled shade of an oak canopy. Dinner and dancing follow in the Vineyard Pavilion or in the barn, depending on the size of your group. After dinner, the barn becomes the uber-Wine Country lounge. It can completely change its look to suit your event: Considering an Old California atmosphere? Bring in handmade textiles and a Latin orchestra. Rich metallics and a state-of-the-art DJ turn the space into an edgy SOMA loft. Or, to create a classic, romantic backdrop for a swinging Big Band, just add chandeliers, crystal and silk.

And so…newlyweds, friends, family and barn swallows party into the night. Barn swallows? You bet! Bluebirds, owls and other creatures of nature are what keep the ranch fly- and chemical-free. This is an estate that supports sustainable farming and artisan producers, and all the vendors who work here share the same philosophy. The venue and the in-house planner also contribute to local charities.

In addition to weddings, the ranch specializes in out-of-the-box corporate events, ranging from winemaker dinners and fly-fishing seminars to horse-drawn wagon rides to the vineyard for al fresco cocktails. Whatever your celebration at Vineyard Ranch, you can be assured of several things: You'll see beauty everywhere you look; you're going to enjoy yourself immensely; and every detail will be handled for you.

CEREMONY CAPACITY: The Meadow holds up to 200 seated guests and the Garden up to 100 seated guests. The Vineyard Lawn holds up to 200 seated guests.

EVENT/RECEPTION CAPACITY: The Barn holds up to 175 seated or 250 standing guests and the patio up to 150 standing guests. The Vineyard Pavilion seats up to 250 for dining.

MEETING CAPACITY: The barn holds up to 100 seated, classroom-style.

FEES & DEPOSITS: A 50% deposit is required to reserve your date. The balance is due 30 days prior to the event. Site fees range $5,000–9,000 for barn parties* up to 200 guests, and $12,500–16,500 for full ranch parties up to 250 guests, depending on guest count, site usage and event type. Co-ordination fees vary depending on scope for events at Atwood Ranch, and start at $8,500 for other SF and North Bay locations. Complete "one-stop-shopping" packages for Atwood Ranch weddings are available through Julie Atwood Events.

Meals range $90–250/person. Alcohol is additional. Liability insurance, equipment rentals and parking/shuttle services are required and additional to the fee. The fee includes vendor access to site for 2 days and day of event, client access for up to 10 hour day-of plus 3 hours for rehearsal, site staffing and vendor supervision.

*Barn capacity for seated dinner/dances, maximum 160; for standing receptions or dinners without dancing, maximum 250.

AVAILABILITY: Year-round, daily, 9am–11pm. One event per weekend. The maximum guest count is 250 guests, June–October; 100, November–May.

SERVICES/AMENITIES:

Catering: select from preferred list only
Kitchen Facilities: through coordinator
Tables & Chairs: through coordinator
Linens, Silver, etc.: through coordinator
Restrooms: not wheelchair accessible, portables
Dance Floor: provided, extra fee
Bride's Dressing Area: yes
Meeting Equipment: CBA

Parking: shuttle required, extra charge
Accommodations: no guest rooms
Telephone: available
Outdoor Night Lighting: yes, minimal
Outdoor Cooking Facilities: CBA
Cleanup: caterer
View: vineyards, pond, hills, gardens
Other: event coordination and management included

RESTRICTIONS:

Alcohol: BYO wine, liquor by licensed provider
Smoking: very restricted
Music: OK with restrictions

Wheelchair Access: limited
Insurance: liability required
Other: no rice, birdseed, confetti, sparklers or fireworks

Healdsburg Country Gardens

Private Country Estate & Vineyards

Address withheld to ensure privacy. Healdsburg

707/431-8630

www.hcgweddings.com
info@hcgweddings.com

Rehearsal Dinners	Corp. Events/Mtgs.
● Ceremonies	Private Parties
● Wedding Receptions	● Accommodations

As you walk through the "tunnel" of rose-covered arches at the entrance of Healdsburg Country Gardens, you're completely enveloped by its fragrant beauty. And when you emerge from this magical walkway, the scenery only gets better.

What greets you is a lush rose garden, dotted with flowers, ancient oaks and towering redwoods. Walkways wind through lawns bordered by beds of vibrant lavender, lilacs, roses and wisteria, past a bubbling fountain and two aviaries filled with colorful birds. Framing this gorgeous tableau are sweeping views of estate vineyards, which are visible from almost everywhere in the garden.

Four spacious event areas flow together seamlessly, so guests can easily mix and mingle. The site's focal point is the historic four-story redwood barn. Built in 1902, it has huge doors on two sides that open to vistas of the gardens and vineyards. Walls are decorated with bouquets of dried flowers, and a grapevine-covered terrace wraps around the building. At night, tiny white lights in the arbor and soft lighting inside the barn and throughout the gardens add a romantic glow while your friends and family dine, dance or just stroll through the grounds. The barn's perfect acoustics will also enhance the music your band or DJ is playing.

Some of the best photo opportunities are in front of the 1920s cottage, which faces the barn from the other side of the garden. This adorable little house is the epitome of charming: Constructed in the wood-slat fashion of the time and enclosed by a picket fence, it beckons you to sit on the covered front porch and watch the grapes grow. Flowering vines creep up the support posts, while a colorful array of blossoms peek through the railings. The side deck and arbor offer yet more views of vineyards and garden. Brides use the interior of the cottage as a dressing room.

Couples get married under a majestic oak, while guests seated on a large shady lawn admire the vineyards in the background. Following the ceremony, champagne and hors d'oeuvres are served near the oak tree or on the barn's wraparound terrace. The party then moves to a large adjoining lawn, where guests dine at tables beneath market umbrellas. Afterwards, everyone has an opportunity to dance in the barn, stroll through the gardens, and simply enjoy the irresistible setting of this Wine Country estate.

Owners Barbara and Walt Gruber specialize in just one kind of event: beautiful Wine Country weddings. So come and walk through the tunnel of roses; what you'll find on the other side is a private haven that can be exclusively yours for a day and it's only one and a half miles from Healdsburg Plaza!

Shown by appointment only. Not open to the public.

CEREMONY CAPACITY: The large lawn with the oak tree holds 150 seated guests.

EVENT/RECEPTION CAPACITY: The terrace, lawns and garden can accommodate 150 seated.

FEES & DEPOSITS: For weddings, half the rental fee is the deposit that holds your date. Rental fees for up to 150 guests are $13,500 for Saturdays ($12,500 for other days). The rental balance and a $500 refundable cleaning/security deposit are payable 90 days prior to the event. The fee covers a 6-hour block plus guest arrival, setup and cleanup times.

AVAILABILITY: May–October, 11am–9pm.

SERVICES/AMENITIES:

Catering: BYO, licensed and insured
Kitchen Facilities: prep only
Tables & Chairs: provided; plus market umbrellas
Linens, Silver, etc.: BYO
Restrooms: wheelchair accessible
Dance Floor: on terrace, or barn's cement floor
Bride's & Groom's Dressing Areas: yes
Meeting Equipment: n/a

Parking: ample lot, attendants provided
Accommodations: cottage for 2, guesthouse for 6
Telephone: emergency use only
Outdoor Night Lighting: yes
Outdoor Cooking Facilities: yes
Cleanup: caterer and renter
View: panorama of vineyards, rolling hills and gorgeous gardens

RESTRICTIONS:

Alcohol: caterer or BYO
Smoking: designated area only
Music: amplified OK until 9pm

Wheelchair Access: yes
Insurance: extra insurance required
Other: no pets, children must be supervised, decorations are restricted

Want to find more venues and services? Check out our informative website, www.HereComesTheGuide.com.

511

Madrona Manor

Historic Inn

1001 Westside Road, Healdsburg
707/433-1542 X111

www.madronamanor.com
kacie@madronamanor.com

● Rehearsal Dinners	● Corp. Events/Mtgs.
● Ceremonies	● Private Parties
● Wedding Receptions	○ Accommodations

"Madrona Manor"…the very name sounds like something out of a romantic novel, and if romance is what you're looking for, you've come to the right place. Built in 1881 by Sonoma County businessman John Paxton as a family residence, it became an inn during the 1980s and earned a spot in the National Register of Historic Places. Current owners Bill and Trudi Konrad worked diligently to restore this landmark to its former splendor, and they've succeeded admirably.

This elegant boutique hotel is a classic example of Victorian architecture with period scrollwork, a mansard roof, dormer windows and columned verandas. The property occupies eight acres of prime Sonoma County real estate, whose tangled woodlands have been lovingly coaxed into a garden showplace with fountains, rolling lawns, herb gardens, a citrus grove and a rainbow of seasonal flowers.

The manor's interior shows the same attention to detail and eye for authenticity as the grounds. The first-floor rooms all have fireplaces, crystal chandeliers, carved sideboards and turn-of-the-century art. The Palm Terrace is a large covered veranda, whose wicker furniture, potted palms and cheerful upholstery make it reminiscent of a Victorian conservatory.

Madrona Manor offers four types of wedding packages, and each one makes ample use of the manor's felicitous environs. The favored ceremony site is the capacious Wedding Lawn, bordered by masses of flowers and towering sycamores.

The Victorians were known for their elaborate multicourse repasts, and Madrona Manor is as authentic in this as it is in everything else. Thanks to Chef Jesse Mallgren, the venue has a prestigious one-star Michelin rating. Chef Mallgren's considerable talents and renowned seasonal menus are at your disposal. Another talented staff member is director of special events Emily Rowan, who is adept at creating breathtakingly romantic destination weddings.

Madrona Manor is also available during the week and in the off-season. Of course, nonwedding events such as celebratory dinners or corporate functions are also welcome. If your love life could use a jump-start, you don't have to wait for Valentine's Day—just take a trip to Madrona Manor, where romance is in the air all year round.

CEREMONY & EVENT/RECEPTION CAPACITY: The facility can accommodate 150 guests.

MEETING CAPACITY: The manor has various rooms which can hold 15–28 seated conference-style or theater-style.

FEES & DEPOSITS: For weddings, 50% of the facility fee is required upon booking to reserve your date. The facility fee ranges $1,500–12,000. Meals range $52–65/person. Tax, alcohol and a 20% service charge are additional.

AVAILABILITY: Year-round.

SERVICES/AMENITIES:

Catering: provided, no BYO
Kitchen Facilities: n/a
Tables & Chairs: provided
Linens, Silver, etc.: provided
Restrooms: wheelchair accessible
Dance Floor: Amber Room and Rose Room
Bride's Dressing Area: yes, during the day
Meeting Equipment: projector, screen, conference phone and broadband

Parking: complimentary
Accommodations: 22 guest rooms
Telephone: guest or house phones
Outdoor Night Lighting: yes
Outdoor Cooking Facilities: no
Cleanup: provided
View: estate gardens, Dry Creek Valley
Other: personal coordinator provided

RESTRICTIONS:

Alcohol: provided
Smoking: designated areas outside
Music: amplified OK indoors only

Wheelchair Access: yes
Insurance: not required
Other: no rice, birdseed, confetti or bubbles

Villa Chanticleer

Historic Lodge

1248 North Fitch Mountain Road, Healdsburg
707/431-3303
www.villachanticleer.com
prreservations@ci.healdsburg.ca.us

● Rehearsal Dinners	● Corp. Events/Mtgs.	
● Ceremonies	● Private Parties	
● Wedding Receptions	Accommodations	

Among the trees and manicured lawns of a 17-acre park owned by the City of Healdsburg you'll find Villa Chanticleer, a charming venue that will put you in mind of a gentler, more graceful time.

Built in 1910 as a country resort, the villa has a rich history of hosting weddings, receptions, parties and community events. And thanks to functional upgrades over the years, guests appreciate not only the peace and beauty of the lovely surroundings, but the facility's modern amenities as well.

When you arrive on the villa grounds, take a moment to enjoy the many large trees, the fresh air and the birdsong. As you cross the stone steps to enter the Villa Main Building, notice the wide veranda shaded by a handsome, wisteria-draped arbor. Inside, you're welcomed by an open, gracious lobby. The bar area directly ahead is conveniently U-shaped and surrounded by eight large booths, perfect for a quiet drink or conversation.

The doors to your right lead to the Dining Room; those on your left open to the Ballroom. Each 3,000-square-foot room features redwood paneling, light-toned hardwood floors and bucolic views. In the Dining Room, generous picture windows frame panoramic vistas of the Alexander Valley below and Geyser Peak in the distance. From the Ballroom, you can see the veranda, the lawn, and the hillside covered in oaks, maples and bay laurel trees. A centrally located, modern commercial kitchen is easily accessible from both spaces, adding to their versatility.

A short walk from the villa is the casual yet elegant Wedding Garden. Wrought-iron gates invite you into the two-level secluded lawn bordered by terraced flowerbeds and redwood trees. A quaint gazebo may serve as either a backdrop or the focal point for your ceremony.

The Annex and the Picnic/Barbecue area are available for more informal events.

This multifaceted facility provides a memorable setting for large or intimate gatherings, and the price is quite attractive. No wonder Villa Chanticleer has been a favorite of wedding couples and their guests for generations.

CEREMONY CAPACITY: The Ballroom and Dining Room each accommodate 300 seated guests; the Wedding Garden holds up to 250 guests.

EVENT/RECEPTION CAPACITY: The Dining Room and Ballroom each hold 300 seated banquet-style, 250 seated at 60-inch round tables, or 300 standing guests. The Annex (which is a smaller building located next to the Main Villa) accommodates 150 seated guests or 200 for a standing reception. Outdoor picnic facilities hold 200 people and the bar area up to 100 guests.

MEETING CAPACITY: For corporate functions, the entire building holds up to 600 seated guests.

FEES & DEPOSITS: The villa's 12-hour rental fee ranges $795–4,995 depending on day of the event. Fees for the Wedding Garden range $875–1,200 depending on day of the week. The rental fee for the Villa Annex is approximately half that of the villa. An hourly rate is also available for both buildings; call for details. Rental fees are due when reservations are confirmed. A security/damage deposit is required: $1,000 for the Wedding Garden, or the villa and $600 for the Annex. These are due 60 days prior to your event and will be refunded 30 days after the event. There is a rental fee for use of the picnic area; a $200 security/damage deposit is required.

AVAILABILITY: Year-round, daily, including some holidays.

SERVICES/AMENITIES:

Catering: BYO licensed caterer
Kitchen Facilities: commercial
Tables & Chairs: provided
Linens, Silver, etc.: silver provided, BYO linens
Restrooms: wheelchair accessible
Dance Floor: yes
Bride's Dressing Area: yes
Meeting Equipment: PA, easels, screen, podium, stage

Parking: large lot, 185 spaces
Accommodations: no guest rooms
Telephone: pay phone
Outdoor Night Lighting: no
Outdoor Cooking Facilities: BBQ
Cleanup: caterer or provided, extra fee
View: nearby mountain range

RESTRICTIONS:

Alcohol: service only through the American Legion
Smoking: outdoors only
Music: amplified OK indoors only

Wheelchair Access: yes
Insurance: extra required
Other: no rice, birdseed, metallic balloons, streamers or confetti

The Carneros Inn

Inn and Spa

4048 Sonoma Highway, Napa
707/299-4967, Wedding Department

www.thecarnerosinn.com
bbaglietto@thecarnerosinn.com

- Rehearsal Dinners
- Ceremonies
- Wedding Receptions
- Corp. Events/Mtgs.
- Private Parties
- Accommodations

The Carneros Inn, 4:00 Thursday afternoon:

The in-laws have landed, your adoring fans arrive tomorrow for the rehearsal dinner, and the wedding whirlwind is about to begin, but you two are already having the time of your lives....

After a leisurely morning you brunched al fresco at the Hilltop Restaurant, had a full-body massage at The Spa, and then melted away any remaining tension in the poolside hot tub, which has one of the best vineyard views in Napa. Tonight you're going to play "spot the celeb," while sipping a cult Cabernet by one of the inn's fireplaces, followed by dinner at Farm Restaurant, where the cuisine celebrates the bounty of Carneros and its neighboring farmers and ranches. As the sun sets behind lavender hills, you'll be able to relax knowing that everything will be expertly taken care of.

The Carneros Inn is the area's only resort, nestled among 27 acres of rolling hills, grapevines, unspoiled farmland, and scenic apple orchards. Its architectural style is based on cues from the local countryside—barns, silos and ranchers' cottages—but rendered with a shot of industrial soul. The resulting look has a clean, modernist aesthetic softened by a hip, "farm-shui" vibe—true luxury without any pretense.

Beautifully landscaped walking paths meander from the apple orchard—their premier ceremony location—through flowering gardens with fountains to all the facilities on the property. A wide range of inspiring event locations can accommodate the size and style of almost any celebration. The Napa and Sonoma Ballrooms showcase the resort's rustic-luxe design with their soaring peaked roofs, hand-crafted barn-board walls, and state-of-the-art lighting and sound. Both light-filled ballrooms are divisible into smaller sections for more intimate events, and each opens onto the Carneros Courtyard through multiple sets of French doors.

The trellised Carneros Courtyard is custom-made for outdoor gatherings. Along with its spacious lawn, apple trees and stone wood-burning fireplace, it's wired for sound and has festival lighting. It's a dream setting for an open-air cocktail reception or post-dinner cigars and cognac by a roaring fire.

For rehearsal dinners or smaller weddings and private events, reserve the Hilltop Restaurant. Its patios flank the signature infinity-edged pool, and whether you're entertaining inside the restaurant or out, you'll enjoy a breathtaking view of the hills and surrounding vineyards.

Wine tasting is a favorite pastime in the valley, but the resort offers a long list of other tempting activities. Get the blood moving with a yoga class, a round of bocce ball or a swim in the "infinity" lap pool (which is lined with cabanas, outfitted with phone and internet). The Fitness Barn (overlooking the pool) provides plenty of equipment, and features retractable walls to take advantage of the Napa weather.

At the end of a thoroughly satisfying day, your own little hideaway awaits. Indulge in an outdoor shower for two on your private patio with a view of bucolic vineyards and rolling hills. Then luxuriate in the heated slate floors, 800-thread-count sheets, and a match-ready fireplace. Although The Carneros Inn is only an hour from San Francisco, you'll feel like you've traveled to another world, a place where beauty and serenity reign and every one of your sophisticated desires is catered to.

CEREMONY, EVENT/RECEPTION & MEETING CAPACITY: The Inn holds up to 175 guests, indoor or outdoor, seated or standing.

FEES & DEPOSITS: 50% of the estimated event total is required to reserve your date. 50% is due 6 months prior and any remaining balance is due 14 days prior to the event. Rental fees range $8,000–12,000 depending on the space rented. Food and beverage minimums for dinner begin at $175/person. Tax and a 20% service charge are additional.

AVAILABILITY: Year-round, daily, anytime.

SERVICES/AMENITIES:

Catering: provided
Kitchen Facilities: n/a
Tables & Chairs: provided
Linens, Silver, etc.: provided
Restrooms: wheelchair accessible
Dance Floor: provided
Bride's Dressing Area: CBA
Meeting Equipment: CBA
Other: spa services, A/V equipment

Parking: large lot
Accommodations: 86 cottages and private homes
Telephone: office and house phones
Outdoor Night Lighting: yes
Outdoor Cooking Facilities: BBQ CBA
Cleanup: provided
View: garden, meadow, mountains, vineyards, hills, pool

RESTRICTIONS:

Alcohol: provided
Smoking: outdoors only
Music: amplified OK indoors; outdoors, acoustic only with volume restrictions

Wheelchair Access: yes
Insurance: not required

This is important! Tell locations you're reading HERE COMES THE GUIDE and ask if our information is still current.

517

Chardonnay Golf Club

Golf Club

2555 Jameson Canyon Road, Napa
707/252-5984

www.chardonnaygolfclub.com
nmendoza@chardonnaygolfclub.com

- Rehearsal Dinners
- Ceremonies
- Wedding Receptions
- Corp. Events/Mtgs.
- Private Parties
- Accommodations

Set among vineyards in Napa's Jameson Canyon, Chardonnay Golf Club is immersed in a quintessential Wine Country landscape: Rows of Merlot, Syrah and Chardonnay grapevines stretch away to oak-tufted hills, and the view west from the club's first hole extends for miles toward distant peaks.

Being in the country, this place has a very easy-going feel to it. That includes the low-key approach Chardonnay takes to weddings. Their staff is open to what it calls "building a budget," which means working with you to create an event that fits not only your vision, but your pocketbook, too. Ninety percent of the weddings at the club are custom packages, and 60% of all weddings here come from referrals. In other words, Chardonnay makes a lot of couples happy, and their flexibility has earned them good word-of-mouth.

Much of the club's confidence in meeting brides' needs is based on the talents of a seasoned staff. All of its members have worked in Napa Valley for years, and possess catering and fine-dining experience. Of special note is executive chef Adolfo Garcia, who was executive chef of the wildly popular Napa Valley Wine Train for several years. His food, served by an impeccably trained wait staff, is why wedding meals here have a luxe feel to them, from appetizers to dessert.

Chardonnay's two outdoor wedding sites are distinctively different, yet both have powerful appeal. The first is beneath a 200-year-old tree, which club members call simply "The Oak Tree." Its dramatic silhouette, against a backdrop of golf greens and vineyards, has made it the preferred spot for scores of ceremonies under its great branches.

The second is the Moonlight Grove, a simple rose-decked arbor at one end of a lawn whose grass is as thick and fine as a bowling green's. The lawn fans out from an enormous, shimmering white tent where receptions are held. Inside, the venue is all graceful billows and folds (you feel like you're dining inside a cloud!). This is an ideal site, removed from the club's main buildings and activities, while providing country vistas and an effortless blending of indoors and out. The tent is set up around a permanent brick floor, and you can have the numerous side panels opened or closed as you like. Just steps from the tent are plenty of photo opportunities: a small lake, a wooden bridge, under The Oak Tree or by the garden-flanked arbor at the Moonlight Grove.

Smaller receptions often use the Clubhouse, which has a 30-foot sloping ceiling and a massive sandstone fireplace. Large picture windows frame an extensive view of the golf course and hill-tops beyond. The Clubhouse also has a porch with an awning for shade, and added seating in the adjacent Banquet Room.

Chardonnay has all the ingredients you need to experience the classic Napa Valley wedding you've always wanted.

CEREMONY CAPACITY: Indoors, the Clubhouse and Banquet Room hold up to 200 seated guests. Outdoors, The Oak Tree accommodates up to 250 seated guests and the Moonlight Grove holds up to 400 seated.

EVENT/RECEPTION CAPACITY: Indoors, the Clubhouse and Banquet Room hold up to 200 seated or 300 standing guests; The Moonlight Grove holds up to 450 seated or 600 standing guests.

MEETING CAPACITY: Event spaces accommodate up to 350 guests seated at tables.

FEES & DEPOSITS: A $2,500 deposit is required to reserve your date. The balance is due 10 days prior to the event. Rental fees range $2,500–5,500 depending on the space rented. Meals range $25–85/person. Tax, alcohol and a 20% service charge are additional.

AVAILABILITY: Year-round, daily, anytime.

SERVICES/AMENITIES:

Catering: provided
Kitchen Facilities: yes
Tables & Chairs: provided
Linens, Silver, etc.: provided
Restrooms: wheelchair accessible
Dance Floor: provided
Bride's Dressing Area: yes
Meeting Equipment: some provided, more CBA
Other: event coordination, on-site wedding cake, picnic area, A/V equipment

Parking: large lot
Accommodations: no guest rooms
Telephone: office phone
Outdoor Night Lighting: yes
Outdoor Cooking Facilities: BBQ on site
Cleanup: provided
View: fairways, hills, pond, forest, valley, vineyards

RESTRICTIONS:

Alcohol: provided
Smoking: outdoors only
Music: amplified OK

Wheelchair Access: yes
Insurance: not required

The Meritage Resort and Spa

Resort and Spa

875 Bordeaux Way, Napa
707/251-1900

www.themeritageresort.com
sthomas@themeritageresort.com

● Rehearsal Dinners	● Corp. Events/Mtgs.
● Ceremonies	● Private Parties
● Wedding Receptions	● Accommodations

Opened in 2006 with an expansion in 2012, this elegant three-story complex has the look of an opulent Tuscan villa thanks to sienna- and umber-colored buildings, a dazzling cedar loggia and a flagstone-faced porte-cochère. Yet The Meritage Resort and Spa is unlike any other venue in Northern California. With its innovative approach to luxury and epicurean delights, the resort may be the quintessential embodiment of the Wine Country lifestyle.

The buzz in Napa is all about The Meritage's Estate Cave, a manmade marvel carved 128 feet into a hillside. Situated beneath The Meritage's vineyards and gardens, the vast 22,000-square-foot cave is home to Spa Terra, the world's only underground four-star spa. Lavished with natural stone and copper water features, this gently lit haven offers a long list of indulgences including nurturing couples' treatments and bridal beauty services. The Estate Cave also boasts the Trinitas Cellars Tasting Room and a novel reception area that evokes the warm glow and dramatic ambiance of Old World Florentine wine caves.

The grounds of The Meritage Resort and Spa are equally alluring. Laced with walking paths, the hilltop's lush landscape provides the perfect backdrop for slow, romantic strolls. Weddings take full advantage of the stunning scenery on the Vineyard Terrace, which overlooks nine acres of grapevines and a cabana-lined pool. Large ceremonies can be held on the Piazza, a sun-splashed courtyard. If you prefer an intimate indoor option, then tie the knot at one of Napa's only private chapels, Our Lady of the Grapes. With a soaring wood-beamed ceiling and stained-glass windows that let in natural light, the chapel casts an ethereal radiance over the proceedings.

Receptions unfold in the Meritage Grand Salon or the Carneros Ballroom, the two largest ballrooms in Napa Valley (each divisible into up to 10 sections). With dark wood trim and imposing chandeliers decorated with stylized grapes, they have an appealing Italian flair. The ballrooms are bracketed by long loggias that bathe them in soft northern natural light, and prefunction areas that face out onto the resort's inner courtyards. All of these adjoining spaces are lovely for mingling and wine tasting.

Superior hospitality and plush accommodations are other keys to The Meritage's success. Many of the guest rooms have private balconies and vineyard views, and you can reserve a private wing of accommodations for the wedding party and family members. As the VIP couple, why not stay in one of nine sumptuous suites? They're decked out with marble baths, granite counters and a chef's kitchen where meals can be prepared and served just for the two of you.

Speaking of food, The Meritage's award-winning restaurant, Siena, has a stellar wine list and Tuscan-influenced menus that are available for your event. Artfully incorporating ingredients from local organic farms, the rustic and naturally flavorful cuisine promises to be as inspiring as the setting. Guests can also sample a gourmet coffee or gelato at the resort's Blend Café, and top off an evening in Crush Ultra Lounge with its six bowling lanes and upscale American cuisine.

If it all sounds a little overwhelming, don't worry. The Meritage's accomplished wedding coordinator will personally arrange all the details, so you'll be free to enjoy every moment of your celebration. This is a deluxe, one-stop resort where guests are utterly pampered. Mission accomplished.

CEREMONY CAPACITY: The outdoor space holds up to 200 seated guests, the Chapel holds up to 60 seated, and the Estate Cave holds up to 230 seated.

EVENT/RECEPTION CAPACITY: The Ballroom holds up to 770 seated banquet-style, 600 seated with a dance floor or 1,100 standing guests. Outdoor spaces hold up to 200 seated or 300 standing guests.

MEETNG CAPACITY: Event spaces accommodate 10–1,000 seated guests indoors.

FEES & DEPOSITS: Rental fees range $3,000–12,000 depending on season and space rented. Meals range $45–85/person. Tax, alcohol and a 21% service charge are additional.

AVAILABILITY: Year-round, daily, call for details.

SERVICES/AMENITIES:

Catering: provided
Kitchen Facilities: n/a
Tables & Chairs: provided
Linens, Silver, etc.: provided
Restrooms: wheelchair accessible
Dance Floor: yes
Bride's Dressing Area: yes
Meeting Equipment: CBA

Parking: large lot, valet optional
Accommodations: 322 guest rooms & suites
Telephone: house phone, guest room phones
Outdoor Night Lighting: yes
Outdoor Cooking Facilities: no
Cleanup: provided
View: vineyards, valley, garden, hills
Other: event coordination, spa services

RESTRICTIONS:

Alcohol: BYO wine only with corkage fee
Smoking: outside only
Music: amplified OK indoors and outdoors

Wheelchair Access: yes
Insurance: not required

The Westin Verasa Napa

Resort Hotel

1314 McKinstry Street, Napa
707/257-5153
www.westinnapa.com/weddings
jperkins@westinnapa.com

- Rehearsal Dinners
- Ceremonies
- Wedding Receptions
- Corp. Events/Mtgs.
- Private Parties
- Accommodations

Located at the nexus of foodie heaven, premium vineyards and small-town charm, The Westin Verasa Napa is the epitome of relaxed luxury, offering beautiful surroundings and exceptional service. Add in crème de la crème dining created by one of the country's most prominent—and Michelin-starred—chefs and you'll elevate your wedding celebration to a sublime experience.

Designed like a rambling, Craftsman-style lodge, the hotel makes generous use of natural rock, pale woods and lots of glass. Its open, airy lobby keeps things low-key and sophisticated with an emphasis on quality materials like slate floors, thick rugs and soft leather sofas arranged near a polished stone fireplace. A four-sided bar in front of a wall of windows is a magnet for mingling, while the outdoor Fireside Plaza and its fountain topped with flames makes a fun setting for an inspired wine & tapas reception.

Each of The Westin's two ceremony areas has a distinctive flavor. Garden lovers will gravitate to the Oval Lawn, a grassy expanse hugged on three sides by the hotel. You'll exchange vows beneath a billowing canopy framed by towering palms, while overlooking the lush banks of the Napa River with the Mayacama Mountains in the distance. Enjoy cocktails on the adjacent bocce ball courts before taking a short country stroll along the river to your reception site.

For larger groups, there's the Solera Courtyard, a spacious plaza next to the Amphora Ballroom. It's a captivating locale with stone flooring, rock-and-wood pillars, flower-filled ceramic urns and border landscaping that mixes bamboo, red maple and a host of native plants to great effect. This is especially true at the semicircular end of the courtyard, where a curved wall set off by abundant greenery make an ideal backdrop for tying the knot. Savor some chilled bubbly and mouth-watering appetizers under strands of starry twinkle lights before moving inside to one of the reception rooms, each with a wine-related name like Barrique, Cepage, Domaine and Amphora. Muted, neutral tones will appeal to the most discerning brides, as will the coffered ceilings and shirred fabric light fixtures.

But no description of this destination resort would be complete without emphasizing the glorious food that is a highlight of any event here. Under the guidance of Chef Ken Frank, all ingredients are locally sourced and combined to perfection. The presentation is spectacular, but awakening your taste buds is the raison d'être of the menu (which can be completely customized). For the ultimate gourmet affair, book the La Toque Terrace, an intimate private dining room adjoining Frank's much-lauded restaurant.

In one of literature's most famous lines of poetry, Omar Khayyam suggested that "A jug of wine, a loaf of bread and thou" is all you need to be happy. But if he were alive today—and planning a wedding—he'd probably add The Westin Verasa Napa to the list. Their gorgeous rooms, friendly staff, gustatory delights and proximity to all the region's attractions will make you very, very happy indeed.

CEREMONY CAPACITY: The hotel holds 180 seated indoors and 250 seated outdoors.

EVENT/RECEPTION CAPACITY: The resort accommodates up to 180 seated or 230 standing guests indoors, and up to 250 seated or 350 standing outdoors.

MEETING CAPACITY: Meeting space hold up to 200 seated guests.

FEES & DEPOSITS: 50% of the food, beverage and setup cost is required to reserve your date and the balance is due 30 days prior to the event. Rental fees range $500–5,000 depending on space, day and time rented. Morning meals range $26–42/person, noon meals range $38–48/person, and evening meals range $75–190/person. Tax, alcohol and a 21% service charge are additional.

AVAILABILITY: Year-round, daily.

SERVICES/AMENITIES:

Catering: provided
Kitchen Facilities: n/a
Tables & Chairs: provided
Linens, Silver, etc.: provided
Restrooms: wheelchair accessible
Dance Floor: portable provided
Bride's Dressing Area: yes
Meeting Equipment: provided, A/V equipment, business center

Parking: valet required
Accommodations: 180 guest rooms
Telephone: guest phone
Outdoor Night Lighting: provided
Outdoor Cooking Facilities: no
Cleanup: provided
View: mountains, river, garden courtyard, landscaped grounds, pool area
Other: event coordination, in-house wedding cake, in-house florals, in-room spa services, Jacuzzi, workout room

RESTRICTIONS:

Alcohol: provided
Smoking: not allowed
Music: amplified OK with restrictions

Wheelchair Access: yes
Insurance: liability required
Other: no confetti, rice or birdseed; wedding coordinator required for ceremonies

---

Overwhelmed? Use the search criteria on www.HereComesTheGuide.com to narrow down your choices.

523

Wedgewood Wedding & Banquet Center
at Foxtail Golf Club

Event Center at Golf Club

100 Golf Course Drive, Rohnert Park
866/966-3009

www.wedgewoodbanquet.com/foxtail
sales@wedgewoodbanquet.com

● Rehearsal Dinners	● Corp. Events/Mtgs.
● Ceremonies	● Private Parties
● Wedding Receptions	Accommodations

The Wedgewood at Foxtail Golf Club is one of the Wine Country's newest wedding locations, offering both class and outstanding value. The 36-hole municipal golf course sits in the middle of Rohnert Park, a friendly community just south of Santa Rosa and an hour north of San Francisco. With trees blocking out most of the surrounding suburbs, all you see from the 125 feet of floor-to-ceiling windows in the Banquet Center are velvety greens, the occasional golfer, and a duck or two heading for the pond just off the 9th hole.

Yes, only a short stroll from the center lies a calm green pond looking newly transplanted from the English countryside. Complete with weeping willows, waterfowl and a lacy white gazebo bordered by roses, it's an idyllic setting for exchanging vows. In addition to being very pretty, this waterside spot accommodates 300 seated guests, all comfortably facing away from the sun.

Weddings are held year-round in either an afternoon or an evening time slot, but they never overlap. In winter, couples get married inside before an arch and floral displays the facility sets up. During the warmer months, the bride changes in a room off the Banquet Center, then comes out through double doors along a curving walkway to the gazebo for the service. While the couple poses for pictures afterwards, guests walk up a red carpet into the center, a 3,300-square-foot, airy white hall filled with natural light from the expanse of windows. Everyone enjoys appetizers and drinks in the bar area until the newlyweds are announced and take their place at the head table. Since there are no noise restrictions, you can party until midnight.

With five all-inclusive packages available, your only concern is transportation and, of course, the dress. Catering runs the gamut from a buffet with BBQ chicken and a no-host bar to a sit-down dinner with "duet" entrées like filet mignon and salmon bearnaise accompanied by a hosted full bar. You can add extras like a cappuccino bar with petit fours and chocolate-covered strawberries, but all packages include a DJ and music, a dance floor, invitations, a choice of linen colors and help with planning the affair. In some cases, a wedding night room at a premium local hotel is part of the package.

"We take the headache out of parties," says Bill Zaruka, whose family operates Wedgewood Foxtail and several other venues in California that collectively oversee some 700 weddings a year. "We know what we're doing—and we do it right," he promises. Part of doing it right is being flexible, and Zaruka assures us that they are happy to customize their all-inclusive packages to suit the particular needs of their clients. Thus, a Russian couple enjoyed borscht at their reception, and a Vietnamese pair held a tea ceremony. Some couples have released butterflies during the ceremony, while one even rolled their Harley out to the gazebo for photos.

Although Wedgewood Foxtail is popular for weddings, it also hosts golf tournaments, fundraisers, retirement parties and civic luncheons. "We're unpretentious," Bill notes. "But the food is always hot, presented well, and our filet mignon is cooked to perfection!"

CEREMONY CAPACITY: The ceremony area accommodates up to 300 guests; indoors, the center holds up to 300 seated guests.

EVENT/RECEPTION CAPACITY: The center holds up to 300 seated or 400 standing guests.

MEETING CAPACITY: The center accommodates up to 200 guests seated theater-style.

FEES & DEPOSITS: 25% of the estimated event total is required to reserve your date. The next 25% is due 90 days prior to the event and the balance is due 10 days prior. All-inclusive packages start at $26/person. Tax, alcohol and a 20% service charge are additional.

AVAILABILITY: Year-round, daily, anytime.

SERVICES/AMENITIES:

Catering: provided, no BYO
Kitchen Facilities: n/a
Tables & Chairs: provided
Linens, Silver, etc.: provided
Restrooms: wheelchair accessible
Dance Floor: yes
Bride's Dressing Area: yes
Meeting Equipment: full range CBA, extra charge

Parking: ample on site
Accommodations: hotels nearby
Telephone: emergency use only
Outdoor Night Lighting: yes
Outdoor Cooking Facilities: no
Cleanup: provided
View: fairways, pond, mountains
Other: event coordination

RESTRICTIONS:

Alcohol: provided
Smoking: outdoors only
Music: amplified OK

Wheelchair Access: yes
Insurance: not required
Other: no rice, confetti or glitter; no open flames

Auberge du Soleil

180 Rutherford Hill Road, Rutherford
707/963-1211

www.aubergedusoleil.com
brittany.payton@aubergeresorts.com

Luxury Inn & Restaurant

- Rehearsal Dinners
- Ceremonies
- Wedding Receptions
- Corp. Events/Mtgs.
- Private Parties
- Accommodations

On a Napa hillside, near the Silverado Trail, you'll find the lovely and highly acclaimed Auberge du Soleil. The Mediterranean-style building welcomes guests through a simple, yet refined, garden courtyard, shaded by a canopy of gray olive trees. The beautifully appointed, understated lobby is refreshing in warm earth tones, and gives you a sense of what's to come.

The inn's private dining rooms are at the base of a curved staircase that descends from the lobby. The Cedar Room is the smaller of the two. It's circular, and right in its center, seemingly supporting the ceiling, is a cedar tree trunk which acts as the room's focal point. Light sand-colored walls frame the many French doors and windows that overlook the valley below; original artwork and cozy furnishings lend a fresh contemporary flavor to the room. The wood ceiling and a large stone fireplace make this a very comfortable spot, one where guests can chat or just curl up in front of the fire. The Cedar Room is terrific for smaller gatherings and dinners, and also serves as a cocktail area or bridal suite.

The adjacent Vista Rooms offer valley view dining for larger groups. Everything here is designed to be soothing to the eye: An olive-hued carpet inscribed with an olive branch pattern, stone wall sconces, natural cedar ceiling and soft sand-colored walls combine to make an inviting environment. No matter where you sit, you'll be able to take in glorious panoramic views of the Napa Valley. One mirrored wall is strategically placed to reflect acres of vineyards into the room, and multiple French doors invite diners to amble outside onto the adjacent decks.

The Terrace and ceremony deck have unparalleled vistas, and on warm days or evenings can be set up for outdoor receptions with tables and umbrellas. A stone-sculpted fountain is set off to one side of the Terrace, and terracotta pots filled with brilliantly colored annuals are placed around its periphery. The Terrace offers guests a sheltered spot where they can enjoy hors d'oeuvres and watch a sunset or wedding ceremony. The ceremony deck, which extends out from the Terrace, offers the bride and groom a special spot to take their vows while their lucky guests get to see them, framed by the panorama beyond.

The ambiance here is both warm and *très chic*. For an upscale California-style wedding, the Auberge has few peers.

CEREMONY CAPACITY: The Terrace and Ceremony Deck hold 120 guests.

EVENT/RECEPTION CAPACITY: The Cedar Room holds up to 40 seated guests or 75 standing; the Vista Room I and II, combined, hold 120 seated or standing.

MEETING CAPACITY: There are 4 rooms which hold 10–60 seated guests.

FEES & DEPOSITS: A deposit of 25% of the estimated event total along with a signed contract & policies are required to confirm your date. An additional 50% of the estimated total is due 60 days prior to the event; the estimated balance is due 7 days prior, with any remaining balance payable upon departure. The facility fee ranges $500–5,000 based on date, time of event and room(s) selected. There is a $500 ceremony fee. Luncheons start at $60/person and dinners at $98/person. Beverages, tax and a 20% service charge are additional.

For business meetings or conferences, a $15/person conference fee applies, which includes coffee and tea service.

AVAILABILITY: Year-round, daily, 6am–midnight. Weddings take place 10am–3pm or 5pm–11pm.

SERVICES/AMENITIES:
Catering: provided, no BYO
Kitchen Facilities: n/a
Tables & Chairs: provided
Linens, Silver, etc.: provided
Restrooms: wheelchair accessible
Dance Floor: yes
Bride's & Groom's Dressing Areas: CBA
Meeting Equipment: CBA

Parking: valet
Accommodations: 52 guest rooms and suites
Telephone: emergency only
Outdoor Night Lighting: yes
Outdoor Cooking Facilities: no
Cleanup: provided
View: panorama of Napa Valley and vineyards

RESTRICTIONS:
Alcohol: provided, no BYO
Smoking: area CBA
Music: amplified OK with approval

Wheelchair Access: elevator
Insurance: not required

Hilton Sonoma Wine Country

Hotel

3555 Round Barn Boulevard, Santa Rosa
707/569-5529
www.hiltonsonomahotel.com
salesadmin@hiltonsonoma.com

- Rehearsal Dinners
- Ceremonies
- Wedding Receptions
- Corp. Events/Mtgs.
- Private Parties
- Accommodations

Set on a knoll above Santa Rosa, this hotel has the best view in town. The vista takes in the city's landmark red Round Barn, as well as much of Santa Rosa to the south and the high hills that form its eastern limits. Although it's a 250-room facility with several wings, the Hilton's architecture successfully evokes a more intimate feeling. The low-key design of wooden buildings, spread out over a series of terraces and connected by staircases and arcades, creates a casual, resort-like ambiance.

Because the hotel is also centrally located in the Wine Country—only minutes away from Dry Creek's famous zinfandels and the Russian River's sparkling champagnes—it's a great place for an extended stay with family and friends. Rooms have either king or double-queen beds and charming bay windows. When your guests aren't off wine tasting or sightseeing, they'll probably spend most of their time at the large swimming pool, surrounded by lawns and shade trees. (Also, the bar here is very sleek and sophisticated, and is often itself a destination for Santa Rosans out for a night on the town.)

As you would expect, the Hilton offers a variety of event spaces, including three ballrooms: the 3,000-square-foot Golden Gate; the 2,600-square-foot Nagasawa (which has a lobby); and the Sonoma, easily the most popular with its steeply sloping ceiling of dark knotty pine and adjoining terrace.

The terrace, sheltered under an elaborate trellis of crisscrossing fir beams, is available year-round thanks to outdoor heaters and windshields. A multitude of chairs and curtained couches encourages socializing, and the indoor/outdoor combination of terrace and ballroom creates an easy flow. Right next to the terrace is a lawn that can host a small wedding and looks out over the hotel's sweeping city view. A second al fresco ceremony site is on a sloping lawn near the swimming pool.

The Hilton's pricing is very competitive, so the high caliber of their food comes as a nice surprise. Couples who have their reception here are invariably impressed with the cuisine and the service, and give both excellent reviews. Some brides have reported that their guests raved about their dining experience for months after the wedding.

With 13 acres of redwood and eucalyptus-dotted grounds, the Hilton Sonoma has created an oasis-like setting. You and your guests will appreciate the refreshing feeling of being a bit above and away from it all, even in the midst of Wine Country's biggest city.

CEREMONY & EVENT/RECEPTION CAPACITY: Both indoor and outdoor spaces hold up to 250 seated or 350 standing guests in one area.

MEETING CAPACITY: Several spaces are available which hold 20–250 seated guests.

FEES & DEPOSITS: A $1,500 deposit is required to reserve your date. The balance is due 10 working days prior to the event. Rental fees range $250–2,500 depending on day, time and season of the event. Meals range $25–85/person. Tax, alcohol and a 21% service charge are additional.

AVAILABILITY: Year-round, daily, anytime.

SERVICES/AMENITIES:

Catering: provided
Kitchen Facilities: n/a
Tables & Chairs: provided
Linens, Silver, etc.: provided
Restrooms: wheelchair accessible
Dance Floor: yes
Bride's Dressing Area: yes
Meeting Equipment: provided

Parking: large lot, complimentary self-parking
Accommodations: 250 guest rooms
Telephone: house phone
Outdoor Night Lighting: CBA
Outdoor Cooking Facilities: BBQ CBA
Cleanup: provided
View: hills, forest, cityscape, grounds
Other: event coordination, A/V equipment, assistance with rentals

RESTRICTIONS:

Alcohol: provided
Smoking: outdoors only
Music: amplified OK

Wheelchair Access: yes
Insurance: required

The professionals in the back of this book are the best in the business. How do we know? Read page 637.

529

Mayacama

Private Golf Club

1240 Mayacama Club Drive, Santa Rosa
707/569-2951
www.mayacama.com
ldarling@mayacama.com

- Rehearsal Dinners
- Ceremonies
- Wedding Receptions
- Corp. Events/Mtgs.
- Private Parties
- Accommodations

Your Mayacama experience begins the moment you pass through the gated entry to the exclusive private residence resort where the golf club resides. From here it's a leisurely two-mile drive to your destination—just enough time to leave the rest of the world behind, soak up the serenity of a native landscape dotted with discreet luxury villas, and prepare to be wowed when you arrive at the clubhouse.

The sprawling Mediterranean-style compound at the top of the hill is truly special. Fronted by a circular drive, it boasts a dramatic domed entryway with arched iron gates that open into the sublime Courtyard Terrace. Shady, colonnaded walkways hug the perimeter and a soaring Mission-style tower rises like a citadel against the back wall. This bold, al fresco locale offers an inviting welcome for your guests and will later serve as the setting for your dinner reception.

But first, there's the all-important wedding ceremony and Mayacama has a wonderful spot for it: a sunkissed patio extending out from the hillside just below the clubhouse. While the couple says "I do," guests enjoy an added pleasure—a sweeping view of the rolling fairways, forested hills, and deep blue lake of the Jack Nicklaus-designed golf course spread out before them. After vows are exchanged, everyone walks to the back of the patio and steps through a pair of ivy-framed wooden doors that mark the entrance to "The Cave." Built into the hill, this elegant underground wine cellar is a cool, stone-floored space that's perfect for champagne toasts. A staircase inside the cellar leads back up to the clubhouse where the festivities continue.

Guests gather at the rear of the clubhouse for a cocktail reception on the multi-tiered Back Terrace. Breathtaking, 270-degree panoramic views include manicured fairways in front, the Mayacama foothills to the left and the occasional hawk circling above. It would be tempting to spend your entire celebration right here, but then you'd miss dining in that romantic Courtyard Terrace you saw upon arrival.

And romantic it is: Candlelit tables are arranged amidst ancient olive trees beneath the night sky, and more candles flicker along the edge of the central fountain. While your family and friends are reveling in this heavenly place, they'll feast on inspired California cuisine and local wines. Mayacama's seasonal and customizable menus center on fresh organic fruits and vegetables, locally raised meats and poultry, and fresh herbs from their own gardens. Sonoma's bounty of artisan cheeses and olive oils are key ingredients, too.

When dessert is finished, dancing commences in the adjoining Living Room, where a high, crossbeam ceiling, lots of glass and comfy sofas near a fireplace make this space both open and intimate. And since it also flanks the Back Terrace, guests can easily step outside, get cozy next to the blazing fire pit, and savor a cognac under the stars.

Tally up the commanding vistas, striking architecture, impeccable décor—and some pre-wedding pampering at their top-of-the-line spa—and it's obvious to anyone why Mayacama is a winning choice for a memorable event.

CEREMONY CAPACITY: The site accommodates 300 seated guests outdoors.

EVENT/RECEPTION CAPACITY: The facility holds 85 seated or 150 standing and 300 seated or 450 standing.

MEETING CAPACITY: Meeting spaces seat up to 40 guests.

FEES & DEPOSITS: 25% of the total event cost is the nonrefundable deposit required to reserve your date and the balance is due 10 days prior to the event. The site fee starts at $7,500, and varies depending on the day and time of the event, the guest count, and the spaces rented. Meals start at $75/person. Tax, alcohol and a 20% service charge are additional.

AVAILABILITY: Year-round, daily.

SERVICES/AMENITIES:

Catering: provided
Kitchen Facilities: n/a
Tables & Chairs: some provided, CBA
Linens, Silver, etc.: some provided, CBA
Restrooms: wheelchair accessible
Dance Floor: provided
Bride's Dressing Area: yes
Meeting Equipment: some provided, CBA
Other: in-house wedding cake, spa services, complimentary event coordination

Parking: valet required
Accommodations: 27 guest rooms
Telephone: guest phone
Outdoor Night Lighting: CBA
Outdoor Cooking Facilities: BBQ on site
Cleanup: provided
View: forest, pond, garden, fountain, lake; panorama of mountains, fairways and valley

RESTRICTIONS:

Alcohol: provided
Smoking: designated areas only
Music: amplified OK

Wheelchair Access: yes
Insurance: liability required

Oakmont Golf Club

Golf Course and Clubhouse

7035 Oakmont Drive, Santa Rosa
707/537-3671
www.weddingsinsonoma.com
tina@oakmontgc.com

● Rehearsal Dinners	● Corp. Events/Mtgs.	
● Ceremonies	● Private Parties	
● Wedding Receptions	Accommodations	

Located in the heart of the Wine Country, the Oakmont Golf Club is just one hour north of San Francisco and 10 minutes from downtown Santa Rosa. Nestled under weeping willows and majestic oaks, it offers panoramic views of the Mayacama Mountains and the entire Sonoma Valley.

This restaurant and banquet facility has developed a dedicated clientele that appreciates not just the lovely setting, but the event spaces and affordable cuisine as well. The large, brightly lit banquet room can be used in its entirety or divided into a series of smaller rooms. Floor-to-ceiling windows frame expansive views of Oakmont's award-winning golf course and the surrounding mountains. Just outside, a spacious terrace overlooking the 18th green is a refreshing spot for a summer cocktail reception.

The venue's two ceremony sites take advantage of the beautiful scenery. The first is the banquet room terrace, which is accessed by three double doors. On a sunny day you can sit beneath umbrellas and just enjoy the view of Hood Mountain and the Mayacamas Mountains, as well as the golf course's groves of mature firs, sycamores, maples and redwoods.

The second option is a tree-and-grass-fringed pond about 250 yards from the clubhouse. Guests are seated under shade trees facing the pond and waterfall, which serve as a marvelous backdrop during the ceremony. A storybook bridge beneath a canopy of tall willows spans the pond and invites post-ceremony photos.

The club's impressive bar is right down the hallway from the banquet room, and rewards with huge picture windows that look out onto the fairways and peaks.

Oakmont is easy to get to, easy on the eyes, and easy on the budget—plus their staff have years of experience in dealing ably and amiably with people's expectations. All these assets have made it a local favorite, and it's certain to be a favorite with you, too.

CEREMONY & MEETING CAPACITY: The site accommodates 300 guests indoors or outdoors.

EVENT/RECEPTION CAPACITY: The site holds up to 250 seated or 300 standing guests indoors or outdoors.

FEES & DEPOSITS: A $1,500 deposit is required to reserve your date. Rental fees start at $350, and vary depending on the day and time of year. Meals range $32–50/person. Tax and a 20% service charge are additional.

AVAILABILITY: Year-round, daily, 6am–midnight (or later with special arrangements).

SERVICES/AMENITIES:

Catering: provided
Kitchen Facilities: n/a
Tables & Chairs: provided
Linens, Silver, etc.: provided
Restrooms: wheelchair accessible
Dance Floor: yes
Bride's Dressing Area: yes
Meeting Equipment: some provided, more CBA

Parking: ample on site
Accommodations: no guest rooms
Telephone: guest phone
Outdoor Night Lighting: yes
Outdoor Cooking Facilities: BBQ on site
Cleanup: provided
View: mountains, fairways, hills, fountain, lake
Other: wedding coordination for rehearsal and day of event

RESTRICTIONS:

Alcohol: provided or BYO with corkage fee
Smoking: outdoors only
Music: amplified OK with volume restrictions

Wheelchair Access: yes
Insurance: not required

Paradise Ridge Winery

4545 Thomas Lake Harris Drive, Santa Rosa
707/528-9463
www.prwinery.com
events@prwinery.com

Winery

- Rehearsal Dinners
- Ceremonies
- Wedding Receptions
- Corp. Events/Mtgs.
- Private Parties
- Accommodations

So sweeping is the view from the western veranda at the Paradise Ridge Winery that a bride can get an inkling of what it's like to be an eagle, suspended above hillside vineyards and oak groves, gazing for miles over the Russian River Valley. Yet the winery is just minutes from downtown Santa Rosa in the heart of Sonoma County wine country. Its proximity to the city, as well as its spectacular scenery, draws locals who flock here for sunset wine tasting on the veranda. Wedding parties come to the 156-acre family-run estate, too, and not just for the view. Owners Walter Byck and the late Marijke Byck-Hoenselaars combined the European traditions of Marijke's Dutch homeland with their own artistic tastes to create a unique setting for celebrations.

The centerpiece of the winery is a spacious, newly remodeled two-story building whose stucco walls, loggia, and mahogany veranda echo early California architecture. Built for special events, it houses the Vineroom (the estate's tasting room), the Champagne Cellar, and a professional caterering kitchen. Guests drive up to the winery through pastures, vineyards, and the unique four-acre "Marijke's Grove" of artwork set among the oaks (also a potential ceremony site). They then gather on the covered veranda before being seated for the ceremony on the Poetry Terrace, a terracotta patio with two bridal stages—and a spectacular wine country vista.

A separate deluxe changing room is reserved for the bride and her entourage, so they can relax and sip champagne before the big moment. The bride makes her grand entry through the Vineroom's double doors onto the veranda, and then descends eight steps to the Poetry Terrace, which is shaded by colorful crepe myrtle trees. The groom makes his own entrance from the loggia, because the owners feel it's his special day, too.

After the ceremony, guests mingle on the Poetry Terrace and enjoy estate-bottled wines, champagne and hors d'oeuvres. As dusk descends, twinkle lights add a romantic touch. When it's time for the reception, the doors to the Vineroom are thrown open. An oversized wood-burning fireplace and dramatic Italian chandeliers evoke Old World charm, and floor-to-ceiling windows capture magnificent sunsets over a vineyard panorama. At night, ambient lighting casts a honeyed glow over the room. If you're hosting a large gala, additional tables can be placed on the wraparound veranda, which shares an indoor/outdoor bar with the Vineroom. Wedding parties usually dance on the Vineroom's oak floor, but you can also set up a band on the Poetry Terrace. With the city lights winking in the distance and the moon cresting over the hillside, it's absolutely glorious.

While most couples prefer a sunset wedding during the warmer months, winter weddings here are also lovely. The Champagne Cellar is a novel option for an intimate ceremony in front of the grand, wood-burning fireplace. Your caterer, selected from the winery's preferred list, will help you create delicious pairings from the estate's vintages.

At the close of the festivities, friends and family gather in the winery's European-style courtyard for a traditional send-off of the newlyweds, whose marriage has been magnificently launched at this sophisticated venue.

CEREMONY CAPACITY: The Poetry Terrace holds 250 seated; the Champagne Cellar, 175.

EVENT/RECEPTION CAPACITY: The winery holds 250 seated or 250 standing guests indoors, and 110–250 seated or 250 standing outdoors.

MEETING CAPACITY: Several spaces accommodate 40–250 seated guests.

FEES & DEPOSITS: Half of the rental fee is required to confirm your date. The rental balance is due 4 months prior to the event; a beverage deposit and a refundable $500 security deposit are due 30 days prior. The rental fee ranges $3,500–9,500 depending on guest count, day of the week and time of year. Wine, champagne and beer are charged on consumption, with the estimated total payable 30 days in advance. In January, February and March the winery offers 50% off the facility fee. For business meetings or seminars on other days, the rental fee varies depending on guest count, day of week and time of day. Weekday minimums start at $700, call for details.

AVAILABILITY: Year-round, daily. Special events and business functions, 8am–1am.

SERVICES/AMENITIES:

Catering: select from list
Kitchen Facilities: fully equipped
Tables & Chairs: provided
Linens, Silver, etc.: through caterer and winery
Restrooms: wheelchair accessible
Dance Floor: wood floor/terrace
Bride's Dressing Area: yes
Meeting Equipment: podium, microphone, audio system, screen

Parking: ample on site, complimentary
Accommodations: no guest rooms
Telephone: courtesy phone
Outdoor Night Lighting: yes
Outdoor Cooking Facilities: no
Cleanup: caterer and facility
View: vineyards and Russian River Valley, panoramic west-facing sunset views

RESTRICTIONS:

Alcohol: wine, beer and champagne provided
Smoking: designated area outdoors
Music: amplified OK with volume limits, outside until 10:30pm

Wheelchair Access: yes
Insurance: additional liability required
Other: no confetti, glitter, rice, birdseed, fresh flower petals or bubbles; children must be supervised

---

Want to know WHAT TO ASK a potential location or vendor? Check out our Questions to Ask starting on page 17.

Vintners Inn

Restaurant and Hotel

4350 Barnes Road, Santa Rosa
707/566-2607
www.vintnersinn.com
weddings@vintnersinn.com

- Rehearsal Dinners
- Ceremonies
- Wedding Receptions
- Corp. Events/Mtgs.
- Private Parties
- Accommodations

Stepping onto the grounds of this 92-acre estate is a little like going through the proverbial looking glass—you're just a few minutes north of bustling Santa Rosa, but you appear to have entered a small village in Tuscany. Suddenly you're enveloped by vineyards, flowerbeds, courtyards, and fountains in a tranquil setting artfully designed to enhance peace of mind.

A grand bell tower and French fountain mark the entrance to Vintners Inn Event Center, created especially with weddings in mind. The interior features a beautifully detailed ceiling, an abundance of windows, wood and stone surfaces, vibrant wall coverings and rich fabric furnishings. Outdoor terraces are surrounded by rows of grapevines, gardens, orchards and a multitude of flowers. An expansive prefunction area doubles as a wedding chapel for indoor ceremonies. Mirrored stone alcoves on either side of the room are filled with candles and flowers, adding warmth and beauty to the space. When the weather is balmy, however, most couples prefer to tie the knot under the Wedding Pavilion or the Wedding Gazebo, gorgeous ceremony spots at the edge of a vineyard. A simple structure of four tall white columns topped by a wooden trellis frames the leafy vineyard backdrop and provides shade as you say your vows. Guests enjoy this quintessential Wine Country tableau from their seats on the adjacent lawn.

The *pièce de résistance* of the center is the Rose Ballroom, a 3,200-square-foot space with walls of windows overlooking the gardens. The richly decorated room features a 15-foot ceiling, impressive iron chandeliers and plush Axminster carpeting thoughout. It's also equipped with state-of-the-art audiovisual systems, including theater-sized screens that automatically drop down for a DVD or video presentation. The Ballroom opens onto a trellised veranda and stone fireplace, flanked by gardens and lawn.

The estate is also home to the nationally renowned restaurant, John Ash & Co., and the deluxe, Four-Diamond Vintners Inn, a 44-room boutique hotel housed in three separate villas. A short stroll across manicured lawns and tile pathways takes you from restaurant to hotel, and gives you a sense of just how close you are to some of the most important things in life: good food and wine, a soft (and elegant) place to lay your head at night, and a tangible connection to nature. Walk out of your guest room and in one minute you can be standing in the vineyards or sitting on the restaurant's wisteria-draped rear terrace, touching the tendrils of grapevines just inches away.

The restaurant, which receives the *Wine Spectator's* Best of Award of Excellence year after year, showcases California cuisine. Its menu changes seasonally to take advantage of fresh, locally grown foods, and dishes are paired with an award-winning wine list featuring some 500 wines. Because the cuisine is such an integral part of this venue's appeal, bridal couples work with the chef to select a multicourse menu and design their own wedding cake. Hors d'oeuvre choices might include Ahi Tuna Sashimi on Wonton Chips with Avocado Tartar or Lamb and Rosemary Meatballs, while entrées range from Pan Seared Salmon with White Bean Purée to Grilled Pork Chops with Cheddar Cheese Grits, Braised Cabbage and Madeira Sauce.

Many guests want to fully experience the Wine Country, and plan an overnight stay at the inn. Nearby attractions include more than 200 Sonoma County wineries, hot-air balloon tours, golf, tennis, fishing, and even whale-watching and kayaking on the coast.

CEREMONY & EVENT/RECEPTION CAPACITY: The Event Center holds up to 250 seated or 500 standing guests, indoors or outdoors.

MEETING CAPACITY: The Event Center holds up to 240 guests, seated conference-style.

FEES & DEPOSITS: 50% of the estimated event total is required to reserve your date. The balance is due 120 days prior to the event. Any remaining balance is due at the conclusion of the event. Rental fees range $3,500–10,000 depending on space rented and guest count. Multiple-course meals start at $65/person. Wedding cake, tax, alcohol and a 20% service charge are additional.

AVAILABILITY: Year-round, daily, 9am–midnight.

SERVICES/AMENITIES:

Catering: provided
Kitchen Facilities: full kitchen
Tables & Chairs: provided
Linens, Silver, etc.: provided
Restrooms: wheelchair accessible
Dance Floor: CBA
Bride's Dressing Area: yes
Meeting Equipment: full range CBA

Parking: large lot, valet available
Accommodations: 44 guest rooms
Telephone: house phone
Outdoor Night Lighting: yes
Outdoor Cooking Facilities: BBQ CBA
Cleanup: provided
View: vineyards, gardens, landscaped grounds
Other: bocce ball court, jogging trail through the vineyards, working vegetable gardens, dining terraces

RESTRICTIONS:

Alcohol: provided or BYO wine with corkage fee
Smoking: outdoors only (restricted by County ordinance)
Music: amplified OK with restrictions

Wheelchair Access: yes
Insurance: not required

Vine Hill House

3601 Vine Hill Road. Sebastopol
888/889-0929

www.vinehillhouse.com
info@vinehillhouse.com

Private Guest House and Gardens

- Rehearsal Dinners
- Ceremonies
- Wedding Receptions
- Corp. Events/Mtgs.
- Private Parties
- Accommodations

It takes practically no time at all for Vine Hill House to rejuvenate the flagging spirit and lower the blood pressure of anyone beleaguered by city stresses. As you head through the Russian River Valley on a picturesque two-lane, country highway, and up the hill through apple orchards and vineyards, you can't help but wonder what awaits you. By the time you've reached the guest house and gardens, the fragrant air and country quiet have already begun to smooth your rough edges.

Enter through a small gate to the left of the guest house and into the garden, and any remaining tenseness melts away. What you see before you is a landscape of uncommon beauty. Set on a slight rise, the garden has an almost 360-degree view of the surrounding hills, covered with apple orchards and row upon perfect row of premium-quality grapevines. You can see distant Mount St. Helena to the north and the coastal mountain range stretching south.

Fortunately for you, this breathtaking setting can be the backdrop for your celebration. You won't need much in the way of decoration, since nature's already done such a great job. And what nature hasn't done, owners Dan and Jan O'Connell have. The handsomely landscaped grounds are tidy and well-groomed: One part of the garden is covered with plush lawns bordered by flowerbeds, densely planted with brightly-hued blooms; another section is planted with a small grove of firs, redwoods, oaks and madrones.

Weddings in this little bit of heaven are particularly sweet. The bride makes her entrance either from the guest house or through the entry gate, and walks along the garden path to a peaceful ceremonial lawn. Seated guests have the dual pleasure of watching the ceremony and taking in the spectacular view. For receptions, the manicured lawn is turned into an al fresco dining room, filled with linen-clad tables shaded by market umbrellas. No matter where you sit, you're treated to an eyeful of rolling hills, vineyards and endless sky. Later on, dance under stars and stately oak trees, where there's ample room for a band or DJ. And if the weather becomes uncooperative, tents or canopies are provided so that you don't have to worry about the elements.

Vine Hill House sits in the center of the gardens, and is a real charmer. Built in the late 1800s, the house was originally a two-story stagecoach stop, located further down the hill. Restored as a classic single-story, 1920s-style cottage around 80 years ago, it was relocated up the hill in 1957 to its present-day setting. The updated, fully furnished house is perfect for overnight stays, with a large sunny kitchen, living room, and two bedrooms with private bathrooms. Each sunlit room has windows overlooking gardens, vineyards or orchards. For those who really want to unwind, there's even an outdoor spa. During events the bridal party has exclusive use of the guest house to get ready, or to just relax. The house and gardens are also great for corporate meetings, picnics, nonprofit events, company seminars or retreats.

This is a place where you and your guests can slow down, relax and take in the changing landscape: blossoming apple trees and fields of mustard flowers in the spring; warm breezes and the sounds of frogs and crickets in summer; a blaze of color and the excitement of the annual harvest and crush in the fall. The beauty here is compelling, and we think you'll be more than a little tempted to stay overnight to prolong your experience.

CEREMONY, EVENT/RECEPTION & MEETING CAPACITY: Outdoors, the site accommodates up to 225 guests; indoors, 20 guests.

FEES & DEPOSITS: A nonrefundable deposit of $2,800 and the signed contract are required to reserve your date. The balance is required 3 months prior to the event. For a 6-hour wedding, fees range $4,495–9,995 April–November. Overtime is $700/hour. Overnight stays in the guest house run $340–385/night. Elopement, intimate and complete event packages are available; call for more detailed information.

For meetings and nonprofit events, call for more detailed information.

AVAILABILITY: Outdoor events, April 1–November 30, 10am–10pm.

SERVICES/AMENITIES:

Catering: select from list
Kitchen Facilities: fully equipped and prep area
Tables & Chairs: provided, plus market umbrellas
Linens, Silver, etc.: CBA, extra charge
Restrooms: wheelchair accessible
Dance Floor: yes
Bride's Dressing Area: yes
Meeting Equipment: provided

Parking: ample on site
Accommodations: guest house, sleeps 6
Telephone: house phone, internet access
Outdoor Night Lighting: yes
Outdoor Cooking Facilities: BBQ, caterer's kitchen facility
Cleanup: caterer
View: vineyards, apple orchards, Sonoma hills
Other: tents/canopies can be arranged; heaters provided

RESTRICTIONS:

Alcohol: BYO, no corkage fees
Smoking: outdoors, designated areas only
Music: amplified OK with volume restrictions

Wheelchair Access: yes
Insurance: certificate required

Gloria Ferrer Caves & Vineyards

Winery

23555 Highway 121, Sonoma
707/996-7256 x1999
www.gloriaferrer.com
special.events@gloriaferrer.com

● Rehearsal Dinners	● Corp. Events/Mtgs.
● Ceremonies	● Private Parties
● Wedding Receptions	☐ Accommodations

You can find this winery atop a gentle slope in the Sonoma Carneros area by driving up the long private entry road through picturesque rolling hills dotted with vineyards. At the crest, you'll spy Gloria Ferrer Caves & Vineyards, a Spanish-style hacienda offering Old World hospitality. When you host your ceremony and reception here, you have exclusive use of all indoor and outdoor spaces, and the flexibility to choreograph your event any way you like.

A sublime spot for saying "I do" is beneath a long arbor in front of the stairs at the winery entrance. Imposing Mediterranean-inspired columns support a wooden trellis entwined with Pinot Noir grapevines. The couple weds at one end of the arbor with the cultivated hills and fields in the background, while guests lounge comfortably beneath the arbor's dappled shade. Alternatively, dress up the arbor with banquet tables laden with hearty local fare and Gloria Ferrer bubbly, and enjoy a delightful al fresco luncheon.

Dinner is usually served in the Main Cave. Available year-round except during the fall crush, it's one of the Wine Country's most unique venues. This subterranean world, lined with rows of bottles and barrels of wine, lends an authentic Wine Country atmosphere to your celebration. Flickering candelabras on tables and dramatic uplighting along the stone walls create an irresistibly romantic ambiance.

The party continues with dancing in the Visitor Center, called the Sala de Catadores. This warm and inviting space is highlighted by an attractive mahogany bar and fireplace of matching wood and tile. Adjoining the Sala is the aptly named Vista Terrace, a serene patio that takes full advantage of the panoramic view of Sonoma Valley and the Gloria Ferrer vineyards below. Refreshed by balmy breezes, it's a lovely place to take a break from the festivities for some conversation and a glass of wine.

If you're planning a smaller meeting, luncheon or shower, two more options are available in the off-season. The Executive Dining Room features rich mahogany accents and windows that look out onto a colorfully landscaped promenade. The slightly larger Conference Room is filled with natural light flowing in through multiple French doors. They open onto a deck, which overlooks the hillside and can be used as additional dining space or as a breakout area for a meeting.

Elopement alert: Those of you who only want to tie the knot at Gloria Ferrer can reserve just the Arbor for a ceremony. This special package comes with setup and rehearsal time, a bridal changing room with bathroom, champagne flutes for up to 100, and more.

The Gloria Ferrer portfolio has been praised by many, including *Wine Spectator* magazine who called their sparkling wines "some of California's best." Having an opportunity to sample this renowned bubbly is just one more benefit of getting married here. With winemaking traditions that stretch back to 18th-century Spain, the Ferrer family expanded their offerings in 1991 to include premium quality estate Pinot Noir and Chardonnay varietal wines. The knowledgeable staff will guide you in selecting just the right pairings for your private function.

This winery is an off-the-beaten-path, very secluded getaway that provides a beautiful backdrop for any event.

CEREMONY CAPACITY: The Vista Terrace or Grapevine Arbor can accommodate up to 120 seated or standing guests.

EVENT/RECEPTION CAPACITY: The Visitor Center, Main Cave, and Grapevine Arbor hold up to 120 for a reception.

MEETING CAPACITY: The Conference Room seats up to 60 guests for lunch or meetings and the outdoor Arbor and indoor Main Cave seat up to 120.

FEES & DEPOSITS: 50% of the rental fee is required as a nonrefundable deposit to reserve your date; the balance is due 60 days prior to the event. Wine fees are payable the day of the event. Rental fees range $3,000–6,000 depending on guest count. The wine fee is a required 1–4-case minimum purchase (based on guest count). Additional wine may be purchased by the bottle; call for current prices. Tax is additional.

AVAILABILITY: Year-round, daily. Weddings held in the evenings. Private parties held both daytime and evenings.

SERVICES/AMENITIES:

Catering: select from preferred list
Kitchen Facilities: ample
Tables & Chairs: up to 120 provided
Linens, Silver, etc.: through caterer
Restrooms: wheelchair accessible
Dance Floor: provided
Bride's Dressing Area: yes
Meeting Equipment: CBA

Parking: large lot
Accommodations: no guest rooms
Telephone: house phone
Outdoor Night Lighting: limited
Outdoor Cooking Facilities: no
Cleanup: caterer
View: vineyards and surrounding foothills
Other: event coordinator

RESTRICTIONS:

Alcohol: wine and champagne provided
Smoking: designated outdoor areas only
Music: amplified OK inside only

Wheelchair Access: yes
Insurance: liability certificate required

Want to find more venues and services? Check out our informative website, www.HereComesTheGuide.com.

541

Viansa Winery & Vineyards

Winery

25200 Arnold Drive, Sonoma
707/935-5744
www.viansa.com
events@viansa.com

- Rehearsal Dinners
- Ceremonies
- Wedding Receptions
- Corp. Events/Mtgs.
- Private Parties
- Accommodations

If you've ever gone wine tasting in Sonoma, you probably noticed Viansa as you drove into the county, or maybe you caught a glimpse of it on your way back home. If, however, you actually stopped to visit the winery, chances are you didn't get much further. This place is so wonderful, it's easy to spend hours here—sampling the wines, having lunch, shopping in the Italian Marketplace and just strolling the grounds. Set atop a hill overlooking the Valley of the Moon and resembling a Tuscan Villa, Viansa embraces you with Italian hospitality and satisfies all your senses.

The Villa (aka the winery building), with its tiled roof, terracotta walls and shuttered windows is your first taste of Tuscany. A series of French doors along the left wing opens onto a circular courtyard, flanked by olive trees and grapevines; colorful flowerpots encircle the fountain in the center and mark the perimeter.

To the right of the Villa a stone-walled staircase takes you past the thriving grapevines on either side up to a huge bronze door at the top. As you pass through the doorway, you enter a thoroughly enchanting hilltop "village." To one side is an intimate fountain courtyard, enclosed by ivy-clad walls and shaded by silvery olive trees; to the other is Le Mura, the fully enclosed, tented reception pavilion. A few steps further is the expansive Main Lawn, a picnic area beneath a trellis laced with grapevines, and the Italian Marketplace. Everywhere you look you'll see bright red geraniums spilling out of planters, wrought-iron benches and, of course, the delicate presence of olive trees shimmering in the sun.

Once the winery closes to the public, Viansa is yours to enjoy. Get married in the circular courtyard or candlelit wine cellar. If you like the festive ambiance of the Marketplace, serve sparkling wine here while your guests mingle amongst vibrant displays of wines, mustards, olive oils, pestos and other gourmet delicacies. For a gorgeous finale, hold your reception in Le Mura: Linen-draped tables set with crystal and flowers are an elegant complement to the flagstone floor and soaring white canopy overhead. If you like, you can add candelabras festooned with flowers for a romantic glow.

Before the sun sets completely, take a walk up to Alto Piano, the highest point of the property. From the edge of the plateau you have a fantastic view of Viansa's 91 acres of restored wetlands far below. This seasonal home to one million ducks, shorebirds and golden eagles also attracts avid bird watchers during peak migrations every spring.

The people at Viansa have long felt that Americans should be able to enjoy wine and food together, just as Italians have done for centuries. Guests who dine here appreciate the extraordinary amount of care that goes into the cuisine and service, and they have responded with their patronage: 80% of the winery's event business is word of mouth. At Viansa, they've not only created an exquisite environment for celebrating, they've made it possible for each guest to have an unforgettably delicious Italian experience.

CEREMONY CAPACITY: The Courtyard and the Lawn accommodate up to 200 seated guests.

EVENT/RECEPTION & MEETING CAPACITY: Le Mura, the tented pavilion, holds 200 seated guests. Outside, the facility holds 200 standing.

FEES & DEPOSITS: A nonrefundable deposit is required to reserve your date; the final balance is due 2 weeks prior to the event. Facility rental fees, including rehearsal time, start at $4,000 and can range up to $10,000 depending on the date selected for your event. Meals start at $80/person; tax, alcohol and a 20% service charge are additional.

AVAILABILITY: The winery is open year-round. Weddings take place May–October in the evenings only; call for details.

SERVICES/AMENITIES:

Catering: provided, no BYO
Kitchen Facilities: n/a
Tables & Chairs: provided
Linens, Silver, etc.: provided
Restrooms: wheelchair accessible
Dance Floor: area provided
Bride's Dressing Area: yes
Meeting Equipment: CBA, extra fee
Other: event coordination

Parking: large lot
Accommodations: no guest rooms
Telephone: pay phones
Outdoor Night Lighting: yes
Outdoor Cooking Facilities: no
Cleanup: provided
View: Sonoma Valley, mountains, vineyards, wetlands preserve

RESTRICTIONS:

Alcohol: wine and beer only provided, no BYO
Smoking: outside only
Music: amplified OK

Wheelchair Access: yes
Insurance: certificate required
Other: no rice or birdseed

Harvest Inn

Hotel

One Main Street, St. Helena
707/963-9463, 800/950-8466
www.harvestinn.com
weddings@harvestinn.com

- Rehearsal Dinners
- Ceremonies
- Wedding Receptions
- Corp. Events/Mtgs.
- Private Parties
- Accommodations

If an elegant, classic wedding is what you have your heart set on, well, we've found a place that every bride should put on her A-list. Whether your dream is a Wine Country wedding, a sophisticated black-tie affair, or an intimate ceremony amid roses and grapevines, the fabulous Harvest Inn can make your vision a reality.

Stroll along the inn's curving brick pathways to the Manor House Lawn. Encircled by mature redwoods, birches and flowerbeds, this sunny verdant expanse is perfect for large events. Behind you the Manor House, with its spiral chimney, dormer windows and distinctive architecture, is a majestic backdrop for your festivities.

From the house it's a short walk via a quaint stone Wishing Bridge to the Vineyard Terrace, where you'll exchange vows, fanned by breezes redolent of ripening grapes. Guests can admire the terrace's fountain, fragrant plantings of roses and lavender, and panoramic vineyard and mountain views. (By the way, Harvest Inn is one of the few venues in the Napa Valley where you can get married right next to a vineyard.)

Afterwards, everyone walks back to the Manor House lawn for photos and California sparkling wine while the terrace is set for the reception. When dinner is over, guests simply step into the adjacent Vineyard View Room for dancing and cocktails. In keeping with the Inn's beautiful architecture, this space boasts white walls, exposed wood beams, plenty of windows and a massive stone fireplace. Though we saw the Vineyard View Room in the summer, it would be equally lovely for winter events, with a crackling fire casting a warm glow. For more intimate weddings, the Vin Rose Lawn, with its rose border and shady trees, is a delightful spot.

Within Harvest Inn's eight acres of landscaped grounds, several guest cottages are hidden among trees, flowers, lawns, fountains, ponds and statues—a combination that creates a secluded, romantic ambiance. The structures all display appealing architectural design elements: exposed beams, plaster walls, dormer windows, stained glass and unique arched or spiral chimneys. Inside, the guest rooms feature such deluxe amenities as fireplaces, down featherbeds and comforters, and private terraces.

St. Helena, with its shops, restaurants and Napa Valley charm, is only a short drive away. And, if you're a wine aficionado, there are dozens of nearby wineries where you can sample the fruit of the vine to your heart's content. Whether you're a garden lover or just looking for a place that will have your guests marveling at your party-planning prowess, Harvest Inn is likely to be the perfect choice. And if your beloved is reluctant to pop the question, why not book a weekend at Harvest Inn? The romantic atmosphere (helped along by a glass of premium Napa Valley wine) will have him proposing in no time at all!

CEREMONY CAPACITY: The Vin Rose Lawn holds 50 seated guests and the Vineyard View Terrace holds 120 seated guests. Indoors, the Fountain View Room holds 120 seated and the Vineyard View Room each hold 60 seated guests.

EVENT/RECEPTION & MEETING CAPACITY: The inn's rooms each hold 60–120 seated or 80–150 standing guests indoors; outdoors the lawn and terrace accommodate 50–120 seated or 120–150 standing.

FEES & DEPOSITS: 50% of the site rental fee is the nonrefundable deposit that reserves your date. Site fees range $2,500–17,000 depending on venue selected. The estimated event balance is due 60 days prior to the event. The site fee includes guest rooms (which are required), as well as all sales and occupancy taxes; call for details. For weddings, a professional event or wedding coordinator is required to be on site on the day of the event.

AVAILABILITY: Year-round, daily, 11am–11pm.

SERVICES/AMENITIES:

Catering: select from preferred list
Kitchen Facilities: prep only
Tables & Chairs: provided
Linens, Silver, etc.: provided
Restrooms: wheelchair accessible
Dance Floor: yes
Bride's Dressing Area: CBA, extra charge
Meeting Equipment: CBA, extra charge

Parking: some on site; valet required
Accommodations: 74 guest rooms
Telephone: guest phones
Outdoor Night Lighting: CBA, extra charge
Outdoor Cooking Facilities: CBA
Cleanup: caterer and facility
View: vineyards, mountains, gardens

RESTRICTIONS:

Alcohol: Wine or beer provided, or BYO through licensed caterer, with corkage fee
Smoking: outside only
Music: amplified OK indoors only

Wheelchair Access: yes
Insurance: required for all vendors
Other: no rice, confetti, rose petals or birdseed

Meadowood Napa Valley

Resort

900 Meadowood Lane, St. Helena
707/967-1223
www.meadowood.com
lbates@meadowood.com

- Rehearsal Dinners
- Ceremonies
- Wedding Receptions
- Corp. Events/Mtgs.
- Private Parties
- Accommodations

Driving into the exclusive Meadowood Napa Valley property is indeed a pleasure. You follow a narrow tree-shaded lane, flanked by forested hillsides, to the sophisticated estate, which includes a wine education program, executive conference center and first-rate recreational facilities. The superbly designed buildings are reminiscent of New England during the early 1900s, with white balconies, gabled roofs and gray clapboard siding. All is secluded on 250 acres of densely wooded Napa Valley countryside.

The sprawling, multi-tiered clubhouse accommodates private parties. It's set high, overlooking lush green fairways and manicured lawns. The large Vintners' Room and Woodside Room are available for indoor meetings or receptions. The Vintners' Room is fabulous, with high ceilings and a stone fireplace, decks with umbrella-shaded tables and outstanding views.

For outdoor celebrations, Meadowood arranges tables and tents on the lawns next to the Vintners' Room. There is something very special about this facility. It provides award-winning cuisine, deluxe accommodations and an environment to match. It ranks high on our list of special event locations.

CEREMONY CAPACITY: The resort can accommodate 20–250 seated or 80–400 standing guests outdoors.

EVENT/RECEPTION CAPACITY: The Vintners' Room seats 120 guests indoors, and with the lawn area, up to 250 seated guests. The Woodside Room seats 60 guests, 80 in conjunction with an adjacent lawn area.

MEETING CAPACITY: There are several rooms which hold 12–140 seated guests.

FEES & DEPOSITS: For weddings, the $750–7,500 facility fee also serves as the deposit required to secure your date. The facility fee includes ceremony coordination, rehearsal and setup, a white aisle runner, china, glassware and floor-length white table linens with overlays and napkins. Votive candles and moon lanterns are provided for evening events. Catering services are provided: lunch buffets and barbecues start at $73/person, 3-course luncheons start at $60/person, and 4-course dinners start at $127/person. Tax and a 20% service charge are applied to the final total.

For business functions or other events, fees vary depending on room(s) selected and services required; call for more specific information.

AVAILABILITY: For weddings, special events and business functions, year-round, daily, anytime. Call for details.

SERVICES/AMENITIES:

Catering: provided, no BYO
Kitchen Facilities: n/a
Tables & Chairs: provided
Linens, Silver, etc.: provided
Restrooms: wheelchair accessible
Dance Floor: CBA in Vintners & Woodside rooms
Bride's Dressing Area: CBA
Meeting Equipment: CBA

Parking: multiple lots, valet CBA
Accommodations: 99 guest rooms and suites
Telephone: guest phones
Outdoor Night Lighting: yes
Outdoor Cooking Facilities: provided
Cleanup: provided
View: fairways, Napa hills
Other: spa and fitness facilities, golf, croquet, tennis, wine education

RESTRICTIONS:

Alcohol: provided, or BYO wine with $35 corkage fee
Smoking: outside only
Music: amplified OK indoors, outdoors with restrictions

Wheelchair Access: yes
Insurance: not required

This is important! Tell locations you're reading HERE COMES THE GUIDE and ask if our information is still current.

547

Brix

7377 St. Helena Highway, Yountville
707/944-2547
www.brix.com
matt@brix.com

● Rehearsal Dinners	● Corp. Events/Mtgs.
● Ceremonies	● Private Parties
● Wedding Receptions	Accommodations

Brix may sit right on Napa Valley's main highway, but once you're inside you're in some sort of Wine Country Dreamtime, where nothing matters but good food, good wine and the sharing of both with family and friends. (By the way, "Brix" is a term used by wine growers that refers to the percentage of sugar in ripening grapes.)

Brix is surrounded by vineyards, but behind the restaurant is a huge kitchen garden, formally laid out in the European style. Many of the fruits, vegetables and herbs used in Brix's cuisine are grown here—you frequently see a white-garbed sous-chef in the garden, gathering ingredients for an order. Here, too, you can hold a ceremony amid the flowers and fruit, with a vista of the vineyards stretching out across the valley to the foot of the western mountains.

Intimate receptions often take place in the Oakville Room, which succeeds in being both elegant and informal. Sunflower-yellow walls and an abundance of wood details create a warm, deliciously inviting atmosphere. At the far end, a *trompe l'oeil* mural makes you think you're looking out a large picture window at a quintessential Wine Country landscape. Along one side of the room, a grand mirror reflects the lovely scene on the opposite side: tall windows framing a serene view of the adjacent tree-filled patio.

The largest reception site is the Flower Garden Dining Area. Set around a fountain and bordered by an ever-changing mix of flowers, plantings and grasses that reflect the colors of the season, this al fresco space enjoys sweeping views of nearby vineyards and the Mayacamas Mountains beyond. Here you're seated on Chiavari chairs at tables regally set with Riedel stemware, St. Andrea silverware and Villeroy & Boch bone china. The food, the service and the ambiance will make you feel totally pampered.

Smaller events find a cozy nest in the (literally!) rose-covered Cottage, which has its own private patio. Inside, pale wainscoting rises up to meet mellow ochre walls, with glass sconces providing soft illumination. The western wall, which is almost all glass, overlooks the covered patio with its garden view. As your gaze rests on the long dining table, it's easy to visualize the toasts, the laughter, and the easy conviviality of an intimate reception or rehearsal dinner in this cheerful room.

In addition to growing a significant percentage of the produce used in the restaurant, Brix bakes their own bread and smokes its own salmon. Other ingredients are procured in season, and as fresh as possible. The wine list is graced by some of Napa's most prestigious vintages—it annually wins the *Wine Spectator* Best of Award of Excellence and the International Restaurant & Hospitality Diamond Award. (Really, if their wine list were a movie, it would star Denzel Washington, Julia Roberts and 52 others of the same star caliber.)

Warm, relaxed and intimate: if these words describe the wedding your heart desires, Brix awaits you.

CEREMONY CAPACITY: 150 outdoors at the vineyard site.

EVENT/RECEPTION CAPACITY: The Flower Garden Dining Area holds up to 150 guests. Indoors, the Oakville Room holds up to 60 guests, the Cottage holds up to 30 and the Reserve Cellar up to 12 guests.

MEETING CAPACITY: The Oakville Room holds up to 80 guests seated conference-style.

FEES & DEPOSITS: A $50/person deposit is required to reserve your date. 50% of site fees due at booking, the balance is due at the close of your event. Meals range $38–68/person. Tax, alcohol, and a 20% service charge are additional.

AVAILABILITY: Year-round, during lunch and dinner Monday–Saturday and brunch and dinner on Sunday.

SERVICES/AMENITIES:

Catering: provided
Kitchen Facilities: n/a
Tables & Chairs: provided
Linens, Silver, etc.: provided
Restrooms: wheelchair accessible
Dance Floor: patio or CBA
Bride's Dressing Area: yes
Meeting Equipment: BYO

Parking: shuttle required for groups over 60
Accommodations: no guest rooms
Telephone: emergency use only
Outdoor Night Lighting: terrace
Outdoor Cooking Facilities: yes
Cleanup: provided
View: vineyards, garden, mountains

RESTRICTIONS:

Alcohol: provided
Smoking: outside only
Music: amplified OK

Wheelchair Access: yes
Insurance: not required

Santa Cruz Area

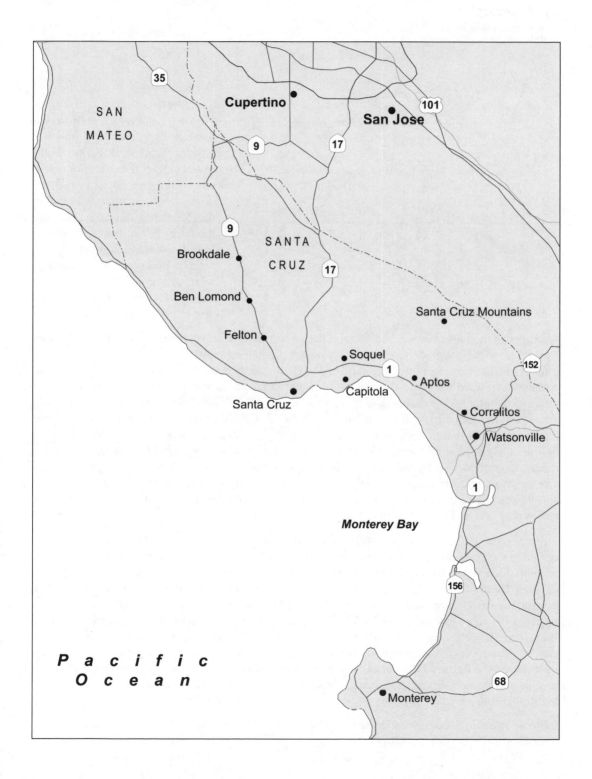

Historic Sand Rock Farm

Historic Country Inn

Address withheld to ensure privacy. Aptos
831/688-8005
www.sandrockfarm.com
weddings@sandrockfarm.com

- Rehearsal Dinners
- Ceremonies
- Wedding Receptions
- Corp. Events/Mtgs.
- Private Parties
- Accommodations

Tucked into a rural valley in the pretty seaside community of Aptos, a former stagecoach route leads to a forested haven— Historic Sand Rock Farm. Established in 1885, the estate flourished as a working ranch, farm, and one of the original family wineries in the Monterey Bay Area through the early 1900s. But by 1999, the farm had fallen into disuse. Enter veteran innkeeper Kris Sheehan, who transformed the historic estate into a vintage boutique inn and celebration venue.

Though just minutes from the beach, Sand Rock Farm rests within 10 acres of sun-dappled woodlands. The focal point of the estate is a wonderful shingled mansion surrounded by meadows, trails, twisting oaks and towering redwoods. Thoughtfully restored, the elegant inn retains an authentic Arts and Crafts aesthetic. Rich redwood details and period light fixtures enhance the interiors, while rocking chairs, garden benches and trickling fountains inspire outdoor relaxation. Zen-like tranquility can be found in any of Sand Rock Farm's lovely gardens, where tiered stone fountains delight hummingbirds and visitors alike. Enjoy a fragrant ramble in Eva's Garden among heirloom roses, or stroll the Spiral Garden, where vintage lilacs adorn hidden nooks inviting romantic interludes. Equally romantic are the five beautifully appointed guest rooms, which convey a warm, nostalgic ambiance. Amenities include two-person Jacuzzi tubs, hand-printed wallpaper and flower-filled views. Luxurious furnishings like a French hand-carved armoire and an antique half-poster bed make you feel like the Lady of the Manor!

This exclusive country estate also offers an array of wonderful event sites. Elaborate ceremonies unfold in the spacious Redwood Grove, where couples pledge their love among mature redwoods, accompanied by the melodious splashing of a wine-barrel fountain. Across the Grove is the rustic Carriage Barn, boasting high whitewashed ceilings and exposed beams. Down a tree-shaded path beyond the barn lies the versatile Winery Meadow, 5,000 square feet of level field ringed with soaring trees. The meadow includes the Heart Redwood Pavilion with a wisteria-covered trellis and the Wine Terrace Workshop, which has rough-hewn stone walls and a garden setting. These spaces can be dressed up with linens and elaborate floral centerpieces, or styled California-casual. And then there's the Barrel Aging Cellar, Sand Rock Farm's signature site. An arched, ivy-clad doorway reveals an open-air dining or dancing space sheltered by the farm's original sand rock walls. At night, this sultry enclave is aglow with moonlight and white silk lanterns.

Intimate gatherings often feature the reception rooms of the inn itself. The central redwood staircase affords the bride a graceful entrance into the parlor for an old-fashioned wedding ceremony.

Afterwards, French doors swing open onto the expansive dining decks where guests enjoy champagne and delicious appetizers overlooking a lush shade garden.

Sand Rock Farm, officially a "Green Hotel," works closely with caterers who partner with neighboring organic farmers and winemakers to create tantalizing cuisine.

Considering avoiding the wedding hoopla altogether? Sand Rock Farm's Elopement Package makes it easy. So whether you're planning a lavish gala, a spontaneous getaway or a honeymoon to remember, let Historic Sand Rock Farm treat you to its legendary hospitality.

CEREMONY, EVENT/RECEPTION & MEETING CAPACITY: Indoors, Sand Rock Farm holds up to 150 seated guests; outdoors, up to 250 seated. Five exclusive sites on the property to choose from; please contact for details.

FEES & DEPOSITS: A $750–2,500 nonrefundable deposit is required to reserve your date. 50% of the balance is due 60 days prior to your event and the balance is due 15 days prior to your event. Wedding packages range $100–150/person. Tax, beverage package and service charge are additional.

AVAILABILITY: Year-round, daily, 9am–9pm. Weddings take place in 5 hour blocks.

SERVICES/AMENITIES:

Catering: select from list
Kitchen Facilities: moderate
Tables & Chairs: included in package
Linens, Silver, etc.: included in package
Restrooms: wheelchair accessible
Dance Floor: CBA
Bride's & Groom's Dressing Areas: CBA
Meeting Equipment: CBA, extra charge

Parking: limited, more CBA off site
Accommodations: 5 guest rooms
Telephone: emergency use only
Outdoor Night Lighting: CBA
Outdoor Cooking Facilities: no
Cleanup: included in package
View: garden, grounds, fountains, hills, forest
Other: event coordination required

RESTRICTIONS:

Alcohol: beverage package available, or BYO with corkage fee
Smoking: outdoors only with restrictions
Music: amplified OK with restrictions

Wheelchair Access: yes
Insurance: liability required

Seascape Beach Resort

Oceanfront Resort

1 Seascape Resort Drive, Aptos
800/929-7727

www.seascaperesort.com
weddings@seascaperesort.com

● Rehearsal Dinners	● Corp. Events/Mtgs.
● Ceremonies	● Private Parties
● Wedding Receptions	● Accommodations

Spread out along the bluffs overlooking Monterey Bay, this resort definitely lives up to its name. From almost any vantage point, inside or out, you have sweeping ocean vistas, and if you're one of those people who comes alive in the sea air (and who isn't?), you'll find the surroundings here quite rejuvenating.

Take the ceremony spot, for example: It's an expanse of lawn on top of a bluff, set against a postcard-beautiful backdrop of cypress trees and shimmering sea. The miniforest at the edge of the property is a favorite place for the bride and groom to have their pictures taken, and a short path leads down to the beach for a walk along the sand.

Receptions are held indoors in a variety of banquet rooms. The largest, the Seascape Room, has a light, airy feel and fabulous ocean views. Smaller weddings take place in the Riviera Room, which has one wall of windows that face the bay and another that overlooks the treetops. A skylight adds to the natural light in the space. Probably the most popular room for intimate gatherings is the Bayview Room. It not only faces the ocean, but has its own terrace. For a very small party or rehearsal dinner, reserve the Peninsula Room. It, too, benefits from an abundance of windows as well as views of the bay and tree-studded bluff.

All of these spaces, along with additional rooms, are also available for meetings. Each one has state-of-the-art audio, video, computer, high-speed internet and modem connections. Another huge benefit are the in-house professional meeting, wedding and special event planners who will assist you with the planning and execution of your event.

Whether you're getting married or hosting a meeting, conference or retreat here, Seascape is a great place to bring your guests for an extended stay. All of the accommodations (from suites to two-bedroom beach villas) have decks or patios, kitchenettes and fireplaces, and many have direct ocean views. You can go for a dip in one of three heated pools and hot spas, or take advantage of the tennis courts, gym and Olympic-size pool at the Seascape Sports Club. Sanderlings, the on-site restaurant, offers dining with sweeping ocean vistas. Nearby there are award-winning golf courses, and, of course, the Santa Cruz/Monterey/Carmel coastline is one of the most spectacular stretches of coast in the country. So, if you're tempted to turn your event into a vacation, go ahead—Seascape makes it easy.

CEREMONY CAPACITY: The Wedding Bluff accommodates 250 seated guests.

EVENT/RECEPTION & MEETING CAPACITY: The resort holds 50–250 seated indoors.

MEETING CAPACITY: 8 rooms accommodate 35–400 guests.

FEES & DEPOSITS: For weddings or special events, a nonrefundable $2,000 deposit is required to reserve your date. Ceremony site fees start at $600. Wedding packages start at $85/person including catering and room rental. Seated meals for non-wedding special events or business functions start at $30/person; alcohol, tax and a 20% service charge are additional.

For special events or day meetings, the banquet room rental fees range $400–800/day, with catering à la carte. Meeting packages are available which include meals, refreshment breaks, banquet/meeting room rentals and basic audiovisual.

AVAILABILITY: Year-round, daily, 7am–11pm. Wedding receptions are held on Saturdays and Sundays in the Seascape Room, 4pm–9:30pm; or in the Riviera or Bayview Rooms, 1pm–6:30pm. For meetings or conferences, please call the sales department.

SERVICES/AMENITIES:

Catering: provided, no BYO
Kitchen Facilities: n/a
Tables & Chairs: provided
Linens, Silver, etc.: provided
Restrooms: wheelchair accessible
Dance Floor: provided
Bride's & Groom's Dressing Areas: rentable suites
Meeting Equipment: fully equipped

Parking: on site for 500 guests
Accommodations: 285 suites and villas
Telephone: pay phones
Outdoor Night Lighting: yes
Outdoor Cooking Facilities: no
Cleanup: provided
View: Pacific Ocean panorama
Other: coordination, theme and beach events

RESTRICTIONS:

Alcohol: provided, no BYO
Smoking: outdoors only
Music: amplified OK with limits

Wheelchair Access: yes
Insurance: not required
Other: no rice, confetti, birdseed or uncontained candles

Overwhelmed? Use the search criteria on www.HereComesTheGuide.com to narrow down your choices.

555

Seascape Golf Club

Golf Club

610 Clubhouse Drive, Aptos
831/688-3213 x217
www.countryclubreceptions.com
sales@seascapegc.com

- Rehearsal Dinners
- Ceremonies
- Wedding Receptions
- Corp. Events/Mtgs.
- Private Parties
- Accommodations

Santa Cruz and its environs have long been renowned for spectacular scenery. Clusters of forested hillsides hug a shoreline that teems with marine life and rainbow-hued flora, and the favorite pastime of locals seems to be watching for that twilight moment when the setting sun kisses the blue surf. Santa Cruz's quaint suburbs boast small-town charm aplenty, attracting artisans, tourists and nature-seekers by the thousands. Yet, like the monarch butterflies that flutter among the region's many eucalyptus groves, Santa Cruz has undergone a transformation during the last decade or so, shedding its Bohemian persona in favor of a laid-back sophistication. You'll want to take advantage of the area's attributes for your special celebration, and one of the nicest spots to do this lies in the beachside village of Aptos.

From Highway 1, head shoreward into a quiet residential neighborhood tucked away in the coastal highlands. Here you'll find the appropriately named Seascape Golf Club, perched on a bluff facing the Pacific. The cream-colored building has an arched colonnade running along the front, accented with flowering herbs and shrubs; a towering pine stands at one end, while a willow spills its languid boughs over the other, contributing to Seascape's lush allure.

Seascape is known for its "Weddings on the Green," ceremonies on the manicured grass of the 10th tee. To reach this magic spot from the parking lot, follow a flight of mariner-style stairs with ropes for banisters down to a delightful garden hollow. Landscaped slopes dotted with cheery surprises of color cradle a swath of lawn, ample enough for an enchanting ceremony for 240 guests. Set an archway, gazebo or columns just so, and your friends and family will enjoy a sweeping vista of the redwood-studded fairways. Then, while you newlyweds pose for scenic wedding photos, guests enjoy an open-air cocktail hour on an adjacent lawn, set up with umbrella-shaded tables.

For the dinner and dancing phase of your event, Seascape brings the party inside to the Monarch Room. This breezy, sun-washed space comes with a high ceiling and clerestory windows; ornate bronze chandeliers lend a dash of formality. The airy mood is enhanced by a neutral palette and a ribbon of windows that wraps around the room's outer edge, embracing a view that extends over swaying treetops and gently rolling fairways. Those reluctant to forsake the outdoors simply walk out to the terrace where garden benches invite a quiet respite, the better to watch the stars illuminate the sky.

A short walkway connects the Monarch Room to the Clubhouse, another attractive space for smaller events (or as a foul-weather backup for the ceremony and cocktail hour). The Clubhouse's natural wood ceiling and a cool-blue color scheme convey a relaxed-yet-refined quality. Windows frame the pretty golf course panorama, with the blue expanse of the Pacific just beyond. Set café tables and chairs on the Clubhouse's adjoining terrace, and guests can delight in the salty tang of the sea air.

Also delightful are Seascape's "package deals," which let you mix and match your event options. Seascape even offers "A Little Tyke's Reception," which provides a party room, buffet and entertainment for the kids—all you bring is the babysitter.

CEREMONY, EVENT/RECEPTION & MEETING CAPACITY: The club hosts up to 240 seated or 300 standing guests.

FEES & DEPOSITS: A nonrefundable deposit, which is applied to your food and beverage total, is required to reserve your date. The amount of the deposit is equal to 25% of the estimated event total. 50% is due 6 months prior, and 100% of the final estimated balance is due 10 days prior to the event date. Rental fees range $150–1,200 depending on space rented. Meals range $10–46/person. Tax, alcohol and a 20% service charge are additional.

AVAILABILITY: Year-round, daily, 6am–midnight.

SERVICES/AMENITIES:

Catering: provided, no BYO

Kitchen Facilities: n/a

Tables & Chairs: provided

Linens, Silver, etc.: provided

Restrooms: wheelchair accessible

Dance Floor: yes

Bride's & Groom's Dressing Areas: yes

Meeting Equipment: CBA, extra charge

Parking: large lot

Accommodations: no guest rooms

Telephone: emergency use only

Outdoor Night Lighting: yes

Outdoor Cooking Facilities: no

Cleanup: provided

View: Pacific Ocean, fairways

Other: event coordination

RESTRICTIONS:

Alcohol: provided, or BYO wine with corkage fee

Smoking: outdoors only

Music: amplified OK

Wheelchair Access: yes

Insurance: not required

Monarch Cove Inn

Inn

620 El Salto Drive, Capitola
831/464-1295
www.monarch-cove-inn.com
monarchcoveinn1@gmail.com

- Rehearsal Dinners
- Ceremonies
- Wedding Receptions
- Corp. Events/Mtgs.
- Private Parties
- Accommodations

We're going to ask you to participate in a guided meditation: Relax, breathe deep, and envision your private sanctuary...a place of perfect beauty, peace, and contentment.... Did you conjure up an image of the seashore? Then slow your breathing to the rhythm of the waves.... Or perhaps you see yourself in a pretty garden, filled with butterflies, songbirds and delicate blossoms? Then let the sweetly fragrant air fill your senses.... Now, imagine combining these two idyllic havens into one spectacular seaside garden venue.... Can you picture a romantic wedding at such a divine spot? Wake up! Your dream has come true—at the Monarch Cove Inn.

Poised on an ocean bluff, the Monarch Cove Inn looks out onto a breathtaking curve of forested shoreline, home to flocks of pelicans and the bright butterflies that inspired the inn's name. Yet the enviable location of this dove-colored Victorian is only part of its allure. The delightfully understated architecture has just enough period features—gabled roof, angled bay windows—to evoke the grace of the past, yet is not so ornate as to make modernists uncomfortable. Originally built in 1883 as a private retreat for two wealthy British families, in the '20s the property passed to an oil magnate who added quaint cottages for his celebrity visitors, like silent film star Mary Pickford (it is even rumored that Al Capone once spent the night!). Today, the Monarch Cove Inn offers a variety of genial accommodations—as well as an enchanting site for an oceanview wedding.

The inn's vintage façade is framed against a backdrop of swaying treetops and flowering greenery. Listen closely and you can hear the rush of the tide just beyond. Off to one side, a serpentine path meanders through an informal English garden, where a parade of fluffy hydrangeas, wild lavender and California poppies charms the eye. Here, a winsome statue peeks out from behind a hedge; there, a canopy of climbing heirloom roses makes an inviting hideaway. Finally, the path comes to a large clearing, and you find yourself face to face with the sea; when the sun dispels the morning mist, the breathtaking azure panorama stretches all the way to Monterey.

The clearing comprises a carpet of green lawn that sweeps along the cliffs, and an expansive wooden deck that takes center stage. Couples say their vows on the deck or the lawn, with the splashing surf just below. A hidden path leads down to an area called The Terrace (really a swath of grass perched below the gardens) where guests sip cocktails and savor the refreshing sea breeze.

Next, everyone moves to the deck for the reception. Whether styled elegant, casual or somewhere in between, the picture-postcard setting will have everyone wearing an "I'm-in-Heaven" smile.

The wedding party usually takes over the inn for the weekend, and though continental breakfast is brought to each room, you can arrange for an al fresco brunch the next morning out on the deck. To experience the inn's nighttime ambiance, host a rehearsal dinner beginning with a blazing sunset, followed by a candlelight soirée. Lodging includes spacious suites and private cottages, some with Jacuzzi and fireplace, all with dynamic views. One thing is certain: Whatever room is yours for the night, the Inn will make you feel at home.

CEREMONY, EVENT/RECEPTION CAPACITY: The site holds 150 guests outdoors.

MEETING CAPACITY: The inn accommodates up to 25 guests seated theater-style.

FEES & DEPOSITS: A $2,500 deposit is required to reserve your date. The balance is due 60 days prior to the event. Rental fees range $4,000–10,000 depending on the date of the event. Catering packages start at $65/person with a 100 guest minimum. Tax and service charge is included.

AVAILABILITY: Year-round, daily, 10am–6pm.

SERVICES/AMENITIES:

Catering: provided
Kitchen Facilities: prep only
Tables & Chairs: provided
Linens, Silver, etc.: provided
Restrooms: wheelchair accessible
Dance Floor: on deck
Bride's Dressing Area: CBA
Meeting Equipment: BYO
Other: wedding planner/coordinator available

Parking: limited on site; off-site lot provided, shuttle recommended
Accommodations: 11 guest rooms
Telephone: emergency use only
Outdoor Night Lighting: access only, BYO
Outdoor Cooking Facilities: BYO
Cleanup: caterer or renter
View: ocean panorama, garden, hills

RESTRICTIONS:

Alcohol: BYO
Smoking: outside only
Music: amplified OK outside with volume restrictions

Wheelchair Access: limited
Insurance: not required

Shadowbrook

Restaurant & Gardens

1750 Wharf Road, Capitola
831/475-1222
www.shadowbrook-capitola.com
office@shadowbrook-capitola.com
banquets@shadowbrook-capitola.com

- Rehearsal Dinners
- Ceremonies
- Wedding Receptions
- Corp. Events/Mtgs.
- Private Parties
- Accommodations

Shadowbrook is unlike any place we've ever seen and, truth be told, you can't really see it until you're actually in it. Almost completely hidden at the base of a steep, beautifully landscaped hillside, the site has a tantalizing aura of mystery and romance. We were intrigued. Instead of descending via the cable car, we walked down one of the winding garden paths through a riot of palms, ferns, colorful flowers, waterfalls and koi-filled ponds.

When we finally reached the restaurant, it proved to be quite remarkable. The building—originally built in the 1920s as a log cabin summer home—now consists of seven distinctly different rooms and three patios in tiers above Soquel Creek. Shadowbrook continues to be named "Most Romantic Restaurant" by various Bay Area publications year after year, and it's easy to see why. The garden theme, so meticulously executed outside, is carried throughout the interior. Greenery is visible everywhere, from vines clinging to the ceilings in the Main Dining Room to the almost-100-year-old cypress growing through the ceiling of the Garden Room. And then there's your choice of views: gardens, woods, the quietly flowing creek or all of the above.

Weddings have been held at Shadowbrook since the early 1950s, and the recently remodeled Rock Room Lounge is a sublime spot for a ceremony. While its massive wooden beams, impressive stone fireplace and stone walls convey a comforting sense of history, it's the partially glass ceiling and wall that make ceremonies here truly magical. Through the glass everyone can watch the bride's entrance as she walks down a garden path, framed by the gorgeous landscape. Outdoor ceremonies on the private Creekside Patio are also blessed by nature: Held at the water's edge, they're enveloped in a lush mix of ferns, flowers and coastal redwoods. At dusk, the surrounding treescape comes alive with twinkle lights that mirror the stars in the evening sky.

Every room at Shadowbrook has its own individual charms. The Fireside Room dates back to 1947, and the original stone fireplace, redwood walls, and Craftsman-style lighting fixtures preserve its rustic feel. A lovely choice for an intimate event is the Redwood Room, featuring redwood beams and wainscoting, and a sun-drenched brick patio next to the chef's herb garden. The Owner's Private Reserve Room will make you feel like you have the restaurant all to yourself, as a fire blazes in the river rock fireplace. Larger groups who still want a sense of privacy will appreciate the Wine Cellar Room, a redwood and brick room with a brick fireplace and a collection of fine wines on display. Last, but certainly not least, is the Greenhouse Room, which delights the senses with an abundance of plants and light. Windows along the entire length of the room afford a view of the creek, and open to let in fresh coastal breezes.

For decades people have been drawn to Shadowbrook for its incomparable ambiance, and now they have another reason to come: the food. Chef de Cuisine Ashley Hosmer utilizes regional products, organics and hormone-free meats to provide diners with consistently high-quality cuisine. Each menu is tailored to your tastes, and thanks to a talented on-site pastry chef, Robyn Wood, you can even order custom wedding and celebration cakes. It's clear to us that the restaurant's popularity has only increased its emphasis on customer service. As the Banquet and Events Manager says, "We're more interested in having you tell us what you want, rather than us telling you what you can have."

CEREMONY CAPACITY: The Creekside Patio and the Rock Room Lounge each accommodate up to 100 guests.

EVENT/RECEPTION & MEETING CAPACITY: For large events, wedding receptions or personal preference, you may reserve the entire restaurant (which accommodates up to 225 seated guests) when it is not open to the public. For rehearsal dinners and smaller social or business functions, you may reserve private areas or rooms within the restaurant. The Greenhouse Room holds 60 guests, the Wine Cellar Room 46, the Redwood Room 26, and the Owner's Private Reserve Room 18.

FEES & DEPOSITS: For weddings and larger events, there is a facility fee of $2,500 for exclusive use and $500–1,250 for semiprivate use. For smaller social or business events during regular operating hours, private room rental fees range $100–200 depending upon the size of the room. The deposit required to book most events is equal to the food and beverage minimum or the facility fee/room rental fee, whichever is higher. Three-course meals start at $35/person. Alcohol, tax and service charges are additional.

AVAILABILITY: Daily, 9am–10pm. Earlier hours for business meetings can be arranged.

SERVICES/AMENITIES:

Catering: provided, no BYO (except for cake)
Kitchen Facilities: n/a
Tables & Chairs: provided
Linens, Silver, etc.: provided
Restrooms: wheelchair accessible
Dance Floor: in lounge area
Bride's & Groom's Dressing Areas: yes
Meeting Equipment: PA, microphones, projection screen, other CBA for a fee

Parking: ample, complimentary
Accommodations: no guest rooms
Telephone: complimentary
Outdoor Night Lighting: on patio and paths
Outdoor Cooking Facilities: no
Cleanup: provided
View: Soquel Creek and gardens

RESTRICTIONS:

Alcohol: provided, or BYO with corkage fee
Smoking: patio only
Music: amplified OK indoors with volume limits; outdoors, acoustic only

Wheelchair Access: yes
Insurance: not required
Other: no rice or birdseed

The professionals in the back of this book are the best in the business. How do we know? Read page 637.

561

Chaminade Resort & Spa

Resort & Spa

One Chaminade Lane, Santa Cruz
831/475-5600
www.chaminade.com
snorfleet@benchmarkmanagement.com

- Rehearsal Dinners
- Ceremonies
- Wedding Receptions
- Corp. Events/Mtgs.
- Private Parties
- Accommodations

Set high on a mountain bluff overlooking forested hills, Chaminade Resort & Spa is a sublime Mediterranean-style retreat blessed with a stunning view of Monterey Bay and the Santa Cruz Mountains. A recent $11 million renovation has added a refreshing, contemporary flair to this historic estate, mingling the best of Old World elegance and modern luxury. The original Mission-style buildings, constructed in the 1930s, have been expanded into a gracious resort set in the midst of meticulously tended gardens and embraced by 300 acres of native oak, redwood and madrone.

Naturally, such romantic surroundings make Chaminade a prime spot for weddings. Have your ceremony on the Courtyard Terrace, an intimate setting reminiscent of a Spanish plaza thanks to planter walls brimming with flowers and the tranquil splashing of a tiered fountain. Couples recite their vows atop a slightly elevated stage, canopied by an arbor laced with climbing roses and seasonal wisteria. In the background, a sweeping vista of native woodland and the brilliant blue bay accents the photo-worthy moment. Another pretty possibility is the Sunset Patio, which guests enter through an archway of bougainvillea. Ornamental grasses, lavender and blooming perennials create a fragrant garden atmosphere, and as the bride and groom recite their vows they're framed by a dramatic panorama of rolling hills and the Pacific on the horizon.

Large receptions are held in the Santa Cruz Ballroom. A high, soffited ceiling arches overhead, while windows on three sides overlook the wooded valley and the sea in the distance. The ballroom has a generous dance floor and access to its own balcony. Smaller celebrations gather in the Sunset Room, with arched floor-to-ceiling windows that bring the outside in; another choice is the Seascape Room, which adjoins the Fireside Patio and shares the same spectacular views of the forest and ocean.

Lavish and varied wedding packages offer a number of bride-pleasing amenities, such as complimentary valet parking for all your guests and custom wedding cakes.

After the festivities wind down, you and your guests will discover that the accommodations here are as enticing as the scenery. Guest rooms have been stylishly updated with granite counters, Spanish-inspired dark wood furnishings and a bold color palette that reflects the rich beauty of the California coast. Newlyweds will also appreciate the lush views from their private patio, and dreamy featherbeds that invite late-morning lingering.

Another feel-good feature: Chaminade Resort is a certified "Green Business." This commitment extends to their spa, which has a holistic approach to relaxation and rejuvenation, and only uses natural products. Throw a private spa party for your bachelorette gathering, or choose the "Time for Two Package" and indulge in some pampering for you and your groom; the spa also has special bridal options, including makeup consultation and application.

With an on-site pool, tennis courts and, of course, miles of beautiful hiking trails, there's plenty to keep everyone entertained. And let's not forget dinner in the Sunset Restaurant, the resort's award-winning fine dining establishment. Off property, you can stroll on a beach, go wine tasting, rock climb or board a yacht for a sunset cruise.

You'll be able to relax and truly enjoy yourself, knowing you've entrusted your celebration to experienced professionals, dedicated to providing world-class hospitality down to the tiniest detail. Along with the outstanding facilities and gorgeous location, a "dream come true" wedding at Chaminade Resort & Spa is virtually a sure thing.

CEREMONY CAPACITY: The Courtyard Terrace holds 250 seated and the Sunset Patio up to 200 seated guests.

EVENT/RECEPTION & MEETING CAPACITY: The facility can accommodate 250 seated or 300 standing, indoors or outdoors.

FEES & DEPOSITS: For weddings, a $1,000–5,000 nonrefundable deposit is required (based on guest count); the estimated balance is due 5 working days prior to the event. For Saturday evening Ballroom events, there is a guest minimum. Other spaces also have guest minimums, call for details.

Wedding packages are available that include site rentals, setup, cleanup, all furniture and linens, professional event coordination, generous hors d'oeuvres, buffet or sit-down meal, deluxe wedding cake, discounted guest rooms and complimentary valet parking. Packages range $94–154/person; beverages, tax and service charges are additional. Wedding package price varies depending on day of week and time of year. Special rates are available for overnight accommodations for the wedding couple, call for details.

For other types of events, call for details.

AVAILABILITY: Year-round, weekends. Saturday wedding reception luncheons 11am–4pm, dinners 5pm–midnight. Friday and Sunday events, please call for hours of availability.

SERVICES/AMENITIES:

Catering: provided, no BYO
Kitchen Facilities: n/a
Tables & Chairs: provided
Linens, Silver, etc.: provided
Restrooms: wheelchair accessible
Dance Floor: included in package
Bride's Dressing Area: yes
Meeting Equipment: provided
Other: on-site wedding cake, spa services, tennis courts, A/V equipment, hiking trails, event coordination

Parking: complimentary valet
Accommodations: 156 guest rooms
Telephone: house phone
Outdoor Night Lighting: provided
Outdoor Cooking Facilities: BBQ CBA
Cleanup: provided
View: garden patio, pool area, fountain, landscaped grounds; panorama of forest, valley, Pacific Ocean and rolling hills

RESTRICTIONS:

Alcohol: provided, no BYO
Smoking: outdoors only
Music: amplified OK indoors, acoustic only outdoors

Wheelchair Access: yes
Insurance: not required
Other: no rice or birdseed

Hilton Santa Cruz/Scotts Valley

Hotel

6001 La Madrona Drive, Santa Cruz
831/440-1000
www.santacruzscottsvalley.hilton.com
sjcsv-salesadm@hilton.com

● Rehearsal Dinners	● Corp. Events/Mtgs.
● Ceremonies	● Private Parties
● Wedding Receptions	● Accommodations

Tucked against the redwood-forested foothills of the Santa Cruz Mountains, the Hilton Santa Cruz/Scotts Valley presides over its serene and picturesque surroundings. Its striking architectural design, featuring a lavish cut-stone façade and rounded turrets, evokes a fairy-tale castle. Inside the magnificent wood-trimmed lobby, the gentle refrain of a three-story waterfall provides a soothing welcome to this sophisticated mountain retreat. A huge cathedral window and filigreed copper chandeliers cast soft illumination, and a dramatic staircase sweeps down from a second-story mezzanine.

The hotel is spread over the hillside, offering diverse locales and views for each part of your celebration. A hallway on the second floor leads to the Veranda, a favorite place to exchange vows that overlooks a wild meadow. Dappled shade plays across this spacious patio, which is covered by a redwood-slat canopy entwined with twinkle lights. Most brides also add other imaginative décor like garlands, ivy or paper lanterns.

Social hours are held on the light-filled mezzanine; in the hotel's restaurant lounge; or out on the top-floor pool deck, set at the edge of a bluff that embraces a peaceful panorama of treetops and sky. Meanwhile, the bridal party escapes to the Wedding Garden, an idyllic spot for photographs. This sheltered terrace is landscaped with flowering shrubs and lush greenery, and gazes out to the tree-cloaked hills. At one end of the garden, a petite redwood pergola atop a raised stone stage is the perfect backdrop for romantic portraits. Some couples can't resist the Wedding Garden's charms, and hold an intimate ceremony here followed by cocktails on the Veranda.

When it's time for the reception, open the French doors from the Veranda right into the Forest Ballroom where your guests are treated to creative California cuisine and the hotel's award-winning service. As nighttime falls, step out onto the Veranda and breathe in the pure mountain air beneath a star-filled sky.

The Hilton Santa Cruz/Scotts Valley experience goes beyond the wedding: Their event experts can organize the entire weekend, and also coordinate your rehearsal dinner and day-after brunch. In fact, your special event easily becomes a minivacation for your guests (or a honeymoon for you!). The on-site restaurant has a great selection of local wines and craft brews. Comfortable, smartly decorated accommodations are outfitted with thoughtful amenities—like a microwave and refrigerator—to see everyone through the weekend. Newlyweds should opt for one of the luxury two-room suites, all of which come with a marble-clad whirlpool tub—a few also include a balcony or a fireplace. And if you want your pooch to be part of the wedding, feel free to bring him/her along—the hotel is pet-friendly, too!

The Hilton's location is another plus. San Jose airport and bustling Silicon Valley are just 30 minutes away, while it's only a scenic five-mile drive to the Santa Cruz beaches and boardwalk. With the Hilton as base camp, your group is perfectly situated to explore the region's 40 boutique wineries. In fact, you're sure to score genius points with your friends and family for selecting such a versatile and hospitable destination wedding venue.

CEREMONY CAPACITY: The site holds 250 seated indoors and 200 seated outdoors.

EVENT/RECEPTION CAPACITY: The hotel can accommodate 250 seated or 300 standing indoors and 200 seated or 250 standing guests outdoors.

MEETING CAPACITY: Meeting spaces seat 250.

FEES & DEPOSITS: A $1,000 deposit is required to reserve your date and the balance is due 5 days prior to the event. Rental fees range $0–1,900 depending on the day and time of the event, guest count and the spaces rented. Meals start at $23/person. Tax, alcohol and a 20% service charge are additional.

AVAILABILITY: Year-round, daily.

SERVICES/AMENITIES:

Catering: provided or BYO licensed caterer
Kitchen Facilities: prep only
Tables & Chairs: provided
Linens, Silver, etc.: provided
Restrooms: wheelchair accessible
Dance Floor: provided
Bride's Dressing Area: yes
Meeting Equipment: provided
Other: spa services

Parking: large lot, complimentary self and valet
Accommodations: 174 guest rooms including 19 one-bedroom suites
Telephone: house and guest phones
Outdoor Night Lighting: provided
Outdoor Cooking Facilities: none
Cleanup: provided
View: garden patio, pool area, landscaped grounds; panorama of canyon, forest, fields valley, mountains and rolling hills

RESTRICTIONS:

Alcohol: provided, or BYO with corkage fee
Smoking: designated areas only
Music: amplified OK with restrictions

Wheelchair Access: yes
Insurance: not required

Hollins House at Pasatiempo

Banquet Facility

20 Clubhouse Road, Santa Cruz

831/431-3231

www.thehollinshouse.com
mseifert@pasatiempo.com

- Rehearsal Dinners
- Ceremonies
- Wedding Receptions
- Corp. Events/Mtgs.
- Private Parties
- Accommodations

The Hollins House, built in 1929 by championship golfer Marion Hollins, is located above the Pasatiempo Golf Club in the Santa Cruz Mountains, not far from Highway 17. Approached through acres of green fairways, the house is situated atop a knoll and offers panoramic views of Monterey Bay. You can reserve either the entire facility or just the Hollins Room and Patio.

The Main Dining Room is very long, with high ceilings, big mirrors and picture windows with views of the garden and ocean beyond. There's also a fireplace and hardwood parquet dance floor. The Tap Room is a more informal space, a cocktail lounge with a long brass bar, fireplace and windows overlooking garden and ocean. The adjacent garden is narrow, with a lawn bordered by profusely blooming impatiens. A medium-sized patio, surrounded by wisteria and situated next to the Hollins Room, is a picturesque place for an outdoor reception. The Hollins Room is an intimate private dining room with a big mirror, fireplace, chandelier, rounded bay windows with bench seat and a vista of the Pacific Ocean framed by nearby oak trees. The banquet coordinator will assist you with all of your event arrangements, from flowers to specialized menus.

CEREMONY CAPACITY: The Garden with gazebo holds 200 seated guests.

EVENT/RECEPTION CAPACITY: The entire facility accommodates 80–250 seated or standing guests in the summer and fall and 175 guests during cooler months. The Hollins Room and Patio, combined, hold 30 seated guests.

MEETING CAPACITY: The Hollins Room accommodates 10–30 seated conference-style; the Main Dining Room holds 50 seated conference- or theater-style.

FEES & DEPOSITS: A nonrefundable $2,500 deposit for the entire Hollins House or $500 deposit for the Hollins Room is required to secure your date. The total balance is due 7 days prior to the event, along with the final guest count. The facility fee for the entire Hollins House ranges $3,500–5,500. For the Hollins Room and Patio, it's $500. The ceremony setup fee is $900.

Hors d'oeuvres/buffets run approximately $40/person and seated meals for up to 100 guests run $40–53/person. You may customize your menu with help from the chef and in-house event coordinator. For parties of 50 or more, a $300 security guard is required. Alcohol, tax and a 20% service charge are additional. There's also a $2/person cake-cutting charge.

For meetings, Hollins House offers customized packages that may include continental breakfast, full lunch and dinner, plus tee times when available.

AVAILABILITY: For weddings, the entire Hollins House is available Saturday 11am–4pm and 4pm–11pm with a buyout, or Sunday 4pm–9pm. For the Main Dining Room and Patio only, 6pm–11pm Saturday. Meeting availability is 8am–4pm Monday–Friday, and Tuesday–Saturday evenings from 6pm–11pm.

SERVICES/AMENITIES:

Catering: provided, no BYO
Kitchen Facilities: n/a
Tables & Chairs: provided
Linens, Silver, etc.: provided
Restrooms: wheelchair accessible
Dance Floor: yes
Bride's Dressing Area: yes
Meeting Equipment: A/V, extra charge
Other: meetings with golf

Parking: large lots
Accommodations: no guest rooms
Telephone: emergency use only
Outdoor Night Lighting: yes
Outdoor Cooking Facilities: BBQ CBA
Cleanup: provided
View: Monterey Bay and Pasatiempo Golf Course

RESTRICTIONS:

Alcohol: provided
Smoking: outside only
Music: amplified OK

Wheelchair Access: yes, ramp
Insurance: not required

Want to know WHAT TO ASK a potential location or vendor? Check out our Questions to Ask starting on page 17.

Amphitheatre of the Redwoods
at Pema Osel Ling

2013 Eureka Canyon Road, Santa Cruz Mountains
831/761-6270
www.polmountainretreat.com
info@polmountainretreat.com

●	Rehearsal Dinners	●	Corp. Events/Mtgs.
●	Ceremonies	●	Private Parties
●	Wedding Receptions	●	Accommodations

The Amphitheatre of the Redwoods is part of the Pema Osel Ling Retreat Center, a name that means "Lotus Land of Clear Light." The phrase conjures up images of a mystical mountain paradise, and it's an apt vision: Sequestered on over 102 acres of redwood forests, open meadows and gardens, this natural haven provides a sense of tranquility that's often missing from the frenzy surrounding a wedding. That peaceful easy feeling begins as you start the drive up Eureka Canyon into the wilds of the Santa Cruz Mountains. Dense woods with mist-shrouded treetops, fern grottoes and an occasional deer prepare you for the center's rustic yet welcoming ambiance.

With a variety of on-site accommodations ranging from large family homes to cozy cabins and campsites, you will want to take over the entire center for your own destination wedding weekend. Guests often meet up first at the Orchard House, a two-story lodge with a fireplace and a towering redwood growing right up through the front deck. Greet everyone with the center's signature mint iced tea, hand out maps and itineraries, and let the fun begin.

The retreat center has two extraordinary locations for ceremonies. The Amphitheatre of the Redwoods is a real-life "fairy ring"—a circle of redwoods born from one "grandmother" tree that survived a storm. Underground, all the trees' roots intertwine for added strength—just as you and your groom will support each other during your marriage. As you exchange vows, the wind whistles through the branches and the cry of blue jays and chattering squirrels makes you feel like you're in the middle of nowhere. A soaring canopy of magnificent redwoods stretches heavenward, the boughs weaving patterns against the blue sky. What an inspired place to say "I do"! For a more spacious ceremony site, get married at the Bayview Meadow and Terrace. With guests seated on the treelined meadow, bride and groom wed on a redwood deck at the edge of a hillside. Behind them, green thickets soften the view, while the distant blue waters of Monterey Bay wink in the sunlight.

Receptions are celebrated in the Gallery Meadow, which overlooks an Asian fountain courtyard. Choose the configuration of canopies and extras you want, and the center's event pros will make it happen. The Celebration Hall, a ranch-style A-frame that opens to a lawn and plaza, offers an indoor/outdoor option. Several more benefits are worth noting. One is the knowledgeable staff, who'll assist you in structuring your agenda to include yoga, massage, hikes, bonfires, pool parties or whatever you can dream up. Then there's the award-winning gourmet catering. From vegan to prime rib, the on-site culinary team will not only whip up a delicious wedding feast, but will handle brunches, rehearsal dinners and barbecues, too.

There is no curfew here so you can party as late as you like, and there's no corkage fee so you can bring your own libations. What there is at this retreat is beautiful scenery, friendly banquet staff and a refuge of freedom and renewal to call your own.

The Pema Ling Osel Retreat Center is a nonprofit run by the Vajrayana Foundation that preserves the spiritual, cultural and artistic traditions of Tibetan Buddhism. Couples who choose Amphitheatre of the Redwoods or any other of the retreat center's event venues have the added pleasure of supporting the foundation's mission to cultivate the Buddhist ideals of peace and compassion in the world.

CEREMONY CAPACITY: The center holds 150 seated guests indoors and 400 seated outdoors.

EVENT/RECEPTION CAPACITY: The center accommodates 120 seated or standing indoors and 400 seated or standing outdoors.

MEETING CAPACITY: Meeting spaces hold 120 seated guests indoors and 400 seated outdoors.

FEES & DEPOSITS: A $1,000 deposit is required to reserve your date. 40% of the estimated event total is due within 2 weeks of the initial deposit, and the balance is due upon check-in. Rental fees range $1,950–5,950 depending on the day of the event, the length of your stay and the time of year, among other factors. Meals range $20–88/person. Tax and a 20% service charge are additional.

AVAILABILITY: Year-round, daily, anytime.

SERVICES/AMENITIES:

Catering: provided
Kitchen Facilities: fully equipped
Tables & Chairs: some provided, CBA
Linens, Silver, etc.: some provided, CBA
Restrooms: wheelchair accessible
Dance Floor: portable provided, CBA
Bride's Dressing Area: yes
Meeting Equipment: some provided, CBA
Other: event coordination, pool, fire pit

Parking: large lot
Accommodations: 56 beds in various cabins and houses, camping space for 200 tents
Telephone: house phones (local only); calling cards required for long distance
Outdoor Night Lighting: provided
Outdoor Cooking Facilities: BBQ on site
Cleanup: provided
View: courtyard, landscaped grounds, fountain, garden, pond, forest, valley, canyon; panorama of hills, coastline and ocean

RESTRICTIONS:

Alcohol: BYO
Smoking: in designated areas only
Music: amplified OK

Wheelchair Access: yes
Insurance: liability required

Kennolyn
Hilltop Hacienda & Stone Creek Village

Address withheld to ensure privacy. Soquel

831/479-6700

www.kennolyn.com
events@kennolyn.com

Special Event & Retreat Center

● Rehearsal Dinners	● Corp. Events/Mtgs.
● Ceremonies	● Private Parties
● Wedding Receptions	○ Accommodations

The first event venue in Santa Cruz County to earn the prestigious Diamond Certified Award, Kennolyn offers a variety of facilities with their own personality, unique features and considerable charm. The Hilltop Hacienda, set literally on top of one of the Santa Cruz Mountains, overlooks redwood forests and Monterey Bay. It not only has a fabulous view, but it's so quiet up here you can truly hear yourself think (or not think, as the case may be). You enter this Spanish-style building through a sun-drenched courtyard, with a four-tiered fountain bubbling in its center and pots of vibrant flowers all around. Step into the banquet room and you'll find it equally welcoming. Spacious and unpretentious in design, it has a wood-beamed ceiling with wrought-iron chandeliers that convey elegant simplicity. At one end of the room, a lofty fireplace mantel of rich chocolate brown provides a striking contrast to the light tan walls. Sets of white French doors along two sides open onto either the courtyard or a heavenly patio that faces the bay. When the sun goes down, you can extend the day's warmth by lighting a fire in the fireplace. As you might imagine, weddings here are delightful, and for corporate seminars or retreats you'd be hard pressed to find a more restful spot.

Located in another part of this 300-acre redwood paradise is Stone Creek Village, a miniature "town" reminiscent of a bygone era when logging and mining were going concerns. It contains a terrific lodge, sports facilities and Kennolyn's overnight accommodations. While this area is most often used for weekend reunions and retreats, it has become very popular for wedding weekends. This is a wonderful arrangement, where over the course of a weekend, the bridal families and wedding party spend quality time together in the Village, and join their extended family and friends at the Hilltop Hacienda for the wedding reception itself. Some couples and their overnight guests start off the wedding day with a ropes course, then join the rest of the wedding guests for a ceremony on the Hacienda lawn followed by the reception. Afterwards, they can all go back to Stone Creek Village and relax.

The old-fashioned Lodge, with its great river rock fireplace, is Stone Creek Village's main space. Your guests can stay in cabin cottages appointed with antiques, down comforters and old-fashioned stoves.

Kennolyn's gorgeous surroundings will bring beauty and serenity to any event.

CEREMONY CAPACITY: The site holds up to 50 seated indoors or 300 seated outdoors.

EVENT/RECEPTION CAPACITY: The site can accommodate 120 seated or standing indoors and 300 seated or standing outdoors.

MEETING CAPACITY: Meeting spaces hold up to 100 seated guests.

FEES & DEPOSITS: To reserve your date, 25% of your anticipated event total is required as a non-refundable deposit. Another 25% payment is required 90 days prior to the event date. The balance plus a refundable $500 damage deposit are payable 10 days prior to the event. Wedding packages start at $56/person and include a private consultation with Kennolyn's professional wedding coordinator, event coordination on the wedding day, hors d'oeuvres, buffet or plated meal, setup and cleanup, tables, chairs and linens, plus an invitation to Kennolyn's Wedding Day Overview. Beverages, facility fee, tax and a 20% service charge are additional.

AVAILABILITY: May–October, Friday–Sunday or by arrangement.

SERVICES/AMENITIES:

Catering: provided, no BYO
Kitchen Facilities: n/a
Tables & Chairs: provided
Linens, Silver, etc.: provided
Restrooms: wheelchair accessible
Dance Floor: courtyard or CBA, extra fee
Bride's & Groom's Dressing Areas: yes
Meeting Equipment: CBA

Parking: ample, several lots
Accommodations: 30 cabin cottages and suites
Telephone: house phones
Outdoor Night Lighting: yes
Outdoor Cooking Facilities: BBQ
Cleanup: provided, renter cleans decorations
View: vistas of Monterey Bay and Santa Cruz
Other: event coordination, carriage rides, full range of sports activities

RESTRICTIONS:

Alcohol: provided, no BYO
Smoking: courtyard or patio only
Music: amplified OK until 9:30pm

Wheelchair Access: most areas, not all
Insurance: not required
Other: no pets, glitter, rice or birdseed; decorations with approval

Monterey and Carmel

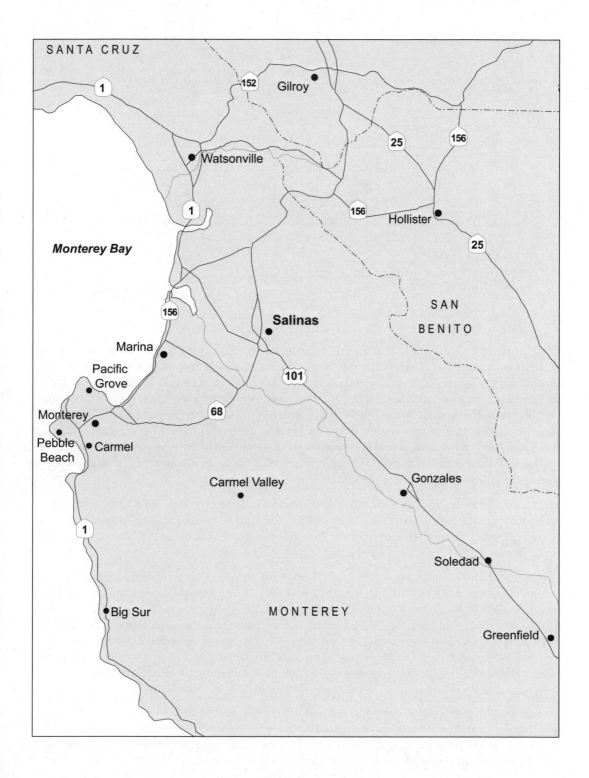

SANTA CRUZ

1

152 Gilroy

1

Watsonville

25   **156**

Monterey Bay

156 Hollister

25

156

SAN BENITO

156

Salinas

Marina

Pacific Grove

101

Monterey

68

Pebble Beach   Carmel

Carmel Valley

Gonzales

1

Soledad

Big Sur   MONTEREY

Greenfield

Carmel Valley Ranch

Resort

One Old Ranch Road, Carmel
831/620-6490

www.carmelvalleyranch.com
rschanding@carmelvalleyranch.com

- Rehearsal Dinners
- Ceremonies
- Wedding Receptions
- Corp. Events/Mtgs.
- Private Parties
- Accommodations

As we drive through the gate of Carmel Valley Ranch, a large black-tailed deer nonchalantly saunters in front of our car. It's a perfect welcome to this exclusive country hideaway, whose nearly 500 acres of rolling foothills are a breathtaking embodiment of the valley's timeless allure. Neon-colored wildflowers pop from green meadows, rare California condors glide overhead, and countless oak trees play host to warbling sparrows and Steller's jays. Just beyond, the tawny Santa Lucia Mountains take on a rosy-mauve glow as the sun dips below the horizon. So careful were the designers to maintain ecological harmony that the resort buildings seem almost sculpted into the pastoral surroundings by Mother Nature herself. The golf course is accredited by the Audubon Society, and native wildlife wanders undisturbed throughout the grounds.

The ranch's fresh design puts a playful spin on Carmel's signature style: The décor is a warm expression of natural textures and earth tones, punctuated by the occasional rich, fruit-inspired hue or contemporary pattern. An extra layer of luxe has been added, making this already impressive venue keenly desirable for any celebration.

The ranch's hub is the Lodge, where open lobby and reception areas flow into the view-filled lounge and restaurant: Walls of picture windows look out to a turquoise pool and deck, framed by landscaped hillsides and a stand of oaks dripping with Spanish moss. Two sophisticated ballrooms, which adjoin a partially covered wraparound terrace, face the oak canopy. A tall stacked-stone fountain splashes water into a rectangular pool, turning the terrace into a refreshing place for cocktail mixers. Social hours can also convene beneath an adjacent pavilion. For an exciting rehearsal dinner, invite your guests into the Adventure Kitchen for a live cooking demo.

One of the resort's multiple ceremony sites is the River Lawn, a sweep of grass crowned by a froth of seashell-pink climbing roses and flanked by 100-year-old sycamore trees. A backdrop of forested hills completes the pretty tableau. And since we're in the heart of Carmel Valley Wine Country, why not wed on the resort's signature Vineyard Lawn—it's bordered by acres of grapevines and enjoys views of the Santa Lucia Mountains and a lovely water feature.

For a reception with an indoor-outdoor flow, reserve the Golf Clubhouse. It boasts its own terrace next to the Valley Lawn (another ceremony site with lush mountain and canyon views). A charming spot for an intimate al fresco dinner is the Organic Garden. Fragrant year-round with the scent of herbs, it's surrounded by lavender fields and overlooks the Santa Lucia Mountains. Wherever you celebrate on the property, you'll appreciate the staff's personalized, unobtrusive service and expertise in organizing your destination event weekend.

After the festivities, savor some alone time in your spacious luxury suite; actually, ALL the accommodations are suites with cathedral ceilings, cozy fireplaces and balconies for soaking up the valley vista. Though the rooms convey a soothing understated elegance, they include up-to-the-minute amenities embodying the latest technological advances.

If this isn't enough pampering, the resort's Spa Aiyana, a 10,000-square-foot facility, offers an exhilarating menu of services and includes a salon, fireplace suites and treetop fitness center. Ahhh, what a sublime way to round out your extraordinary Carmel Valley Ranch experience!

CEREMONY CAPACITY: The resort accommodates up to 250 seated guests indoors and 400 outdoors.

EVENT/RECEPTION CAPACITY: The resort holds 220 seated indoors and 300 outdoors; 300 standing indoors and 400 outdoors.

MEETING CAPACITY: The resort accommodates 250 seated guests.

FEES & DEPOSITS: A deposit equal to the site fee plus 10% of the estimated food and beverage cost is required to reserve your date. The balance is due according to your customized deposit schedule as agreed upon in your contract. Site fees start at $2,500, depending on venue selection. Dinners start at $90/person. Tax, alcohol and a 21% service charge are additional.

AVAILABILITY: Year-round, daily, 6am-11pm.

SERVICES/AMENITIES:

Catering: provided
Kitchen Facilities: yes
Tables & Chairs: provided
Linens, Silver, etc.: provided
Restrooms: wheelchair accessible
Dance Floor: provided, portable CBA
Bride's & Groom's Dressing Areas: CBA
Meeting Equipment: provided
Other: spa services, A/V equipment

Parking: large lot, self-parking, valet parking
Accommodations: 139 guest suites
Telephone: house and office phones
Outdoor Night Lighting: CBA
Outdoor Cooking Facilities: BBQ CBA
Cleanup: provided
View: landscaped grounds, garden, forest, mountains, golf course, vineyards

RESTRICTIONS:

Alcohol: provided
Smoking: outside only
Music: amplified OK with restrictions

Wheelchair Access: yes
Insurance: not required

Want to find more venues and services? Check out our informative website, www.HereComesTheGuide.com.

575

Hyatt Carmel Highlands

Oceanside Inn

120 Highlands Drive, Carmel
831/622-5457
www.carmelhighlands.hyatt.com
weddinghigph@hyatt.com

- Rehearsal Dinners
- Ceremonies
- Wedding Receptions
- Corp. Events/Mtgs.
- Private Parties
- Accommodations

Built in 1916 in the Carmel Highlands just south of Carmel, this particular Hyatt Hotel is one of the most sought-after event locations in California. Noted for its panoramic views and extraordinary cliffside setting, the hotel provides an idyllic environment for a special celebration.

After its multi-million-dollar award-winning renovation, this venue is more stunning than ever. Commanding one of the world's most spectacular vistas, with exploding waves crashing 200 feet below, the hotel offers a variety of first-class facilities for either business functions or weddings. For outdoor ceremonies, a redwood deck complete with contemporary gazebo is perched just above the rocky cliffs overlooking the Pacific.

After the ceremony guests are escorted into a variety of reception areas—each is elegant, with comfortable furnishings and outstanding views. The hotel's chefs are renowned for culinary excellence, and the extensive wine and champagne list frequently garners the Grand Award from *Wine Spectator*. The staff can organize a traditional party or a more creative event for the adventuresome. If you're looking for a very special place for one of life's great moments, the incomparable Hyatt Carmel Highlands should be high on your list.

CEREMONY CAPACITY: The outdoor gazebo accommodates 100 seated guests. If the weather is uncooperative, the Fireside Room can be used.

EVENT/RECEPTION CAPACITY: The inn can accommodate 12–120 seated guests indoors. The gazebo and deck hold up to 100 seated outdoors.

FEES & DEPOSITS: Site fees range $1,000–5,000. Luncheons start at $85/person, dinners at $105/person; alcohol, tax and an 18% service charge are additional. Half the estimated total is due 4 weeks prior to the event, and the balance is due 10 working days prior. A final confirmed guest count is required 3 working days in advance of the event.

AVAILABILITY: Year-round, daily, anytime.

SERVICES/AMENITIES:

Catering: provided, no BYO
Kitchen Facilities: n/a
Tables & Chairs: provided
Linens, Silver, etc.: provided
Restrooms: wheelchair accessible
Dance Floor: CBA, extra charge
Bride's Dressing Area: CBA
Meeting Equipment: full range CBA, extra fee
Other: off-premise catering also available

Parking: complimentary valet
Accommodations: 48 guest rooms
Telephone: house, guest room or pay phone
Outdoor Night Lighting: limited
Outdoor Cooking Facilities: n/a
Cleanup: provided
View: coastline panorama at the gateway
to Big Sur

RESTRICTIONS:

Alcohol: provided
Smoking: outdoors only
Music: amplified restricted

Wheelchair Access: limited
Insurance: may be required

La Playa Hotel

Historic Hotel

Camino Real and 8th Street, Carmel
800/582-8900, 831/293-6107

www.laplayahotel.com
info@laplayahotel.com

- Rehearsal Dinners
- Ceremonies
- Wedding Receptions
- Corp. Events/Mtgs.
- Private Parties
- Accommodations

Occupying several acres in the heart of residential Carmel, just two blocks from the beach, La Playa remains one of the most beautiful and inviting places we've had the pleasure to write about.

Originally built in 1904 as a private residence, La Playa was expanded and converted into a hotel in 1916. Standing in front of the building, you feel a bit like you've been transported to Europe. Its distinctly Mediterranean style, with earthy terracotta-tile roofs, soft pastel walls and a bright green formal garden, are reminiscent of Italy. Even though there's a lovely patina about La Playa, make no mistake—this newly renovated boutique resort hotel offers contemporary freshness along with its romantic Old World appeal.

Outdoor celebrations are held in the Courtyard, surrounded by lush gardens with a fountain, technicolor annuals, manicured lawns and climbing bougainvillea. The entire setting, which also enjoys peeks of Carmel Bay, is gorgeous and private.

Inside the hotel, rooms of various sizes host a wide range events, and most have amazing views of the garden and Pacific Ocean.

La Playa Hotel is a sublime destination for a personal or business retreat—here tasteful furnishings, French doors and magnificent views are standard amenities. We can't help but love this place, and if you share our sentiments feel free to stay overnight or have your honeymoon here, too!

CEREMONY CAPACITY: The courtyard area seats 150 guests.

EVENT/RECEPTION CAPACITY: The hotel can accommodate 12–150 seated guests.

MEETING CAPACITY: There are several rooms which hold 12–120 seated guests.

FEES & DEPOSITS: For weddings, a $1,900 nonrefundable deposit is required to confirm your date and banquet space. Half the estimated event total is due 3 months prior to the function; the remaining balance is due 1 month prior to the event. Rental fees range $450–3,000 depending upon the space rented. Reception buffets and plated meals range $34–87/person. Room rental fees, beverages, tax and a 20% gratuity are additional. For meeting or corporate event information, contact the sales and catering department.

AVAILABILITY: Year-round, daily.

SERVICES/AMENITIES:

Catering: provided, no BYO

Kitchen Facilities: n/a

Tables & Chairs: provided

Linens, Silver, etc.: provided

Restrooms: wheelchair accessible

Dance Floor: portable

Bride's Dressing Area: CBA, extra fee

Meeting Equipment: CBA, extra fee

Parking: on-street, valet

Accommodations: 75 guest rooms

Telephone: guest phones

Outdoor Night Lighting: limited

Outdoor Cooking Facilities: no

Cleanup: provided

View: ocean and gardens

RESTRICTIONS:

Alcohol: provided, no BYO

Smoking: not allowed

Music: amplified OK until 10pm with restrictions

Wheelchair Access: yes

Insurance: not required

Mission Ranch

Historic Retreat

26270 Dolores Street, Carmel
831/624-3824
www.missionranchcarmel.com
banquet@missionranchcarmel.com

- Rehearsal Dinners
- Ceremonies
- Wedding Receptions
- Corp. Events/Mtgs.
- Private Parties
- Accommodations

Mission Ranch has been a Carmel tradition for over 50 years. Once a working dairy, the Ranch is a delightful and rustic retreat, extensively renovated in 1992. Situated on the grounds are a turn-of-the-century farmhouse, a bunkhouse, hotel rooms and triplex cottages with spectacular views of Carmel Beach and rugged Point Lobos. These historic buildings, surrounded by 100-year-old cypress trees and natural landscaping, offer the kind of quiet and peaceful ambiance not found in nearby bustling downtown Carmel.

Outdoor celebrations and ceremonies are often held on the brick patio of the Patio Barn or on the 4-plex lawn adjoining the meadow. The Patio Barn is known for its friendly bar and great dance floor, and it features a stage for live music. It has a wall of full-length glass doors opening onto a brick patio with a restful view of meadows and wetlands rolling down to Carmel River Beach. The Large Barn is also used as an adjunct to the Patio Barn for larger parties with its lofty three-story-high ceiling. The Catering Department prides itself on the uncompromising quality of its food and creative menus for any occasion. If you're looking for a place to hold a relaxed event in a classic country setting, this is it.

CEREMONY CAPACITY: The Patio accommodates 96 seated guests, the 4-Plex Lawn accommodates 168 seated guests.

EVENT/RECEPTION CAPACITY: The Patio Barn can accommodate up to 96 seated guests and the Large Barn up to 168 seated guests. There is a 50-guest minimum for rental of the barns.

MEETING CAPACITY: There are 3 different facilities which hold 12–168 seated guests.

FEES & DEPOSITS: The rental fee is required to reserve a date. A deposit in the amount of 60% of all estimated services is due 60 days prior to the event, with the remaining estimated balance due 10 days prior. The rental fee is $3,500–4,000 on Saturday and $2,500–3,500 on Friday or Sunday. The rental fees cover a 5-hour maximum period. Entrée prices start at $48/person. Alcohol, tax, and an 18% gratuity are additional. Call for meeting room rates.

AVAILABILITY: Year-round, daily, 8am–10pm.

SERVICES/AMENITIES:

Catering: provided, no BYO
Kitchen Facilities: n/a
Tables & Chairs: provided
Linens, Silver, etc.: provided
Restrooms: wheelchair accessible
Dance Floor: yes
Bride's Dressing Area: no
Meeting Equipment: BYO

Parking: large lot
Accommodations: 31 guest rooms
Telephone: guest phones
Outdoor Night Lighting: CBA
Outdoor Cooking Facilities: CBA
Cleanup: provided
View: meadow with sheep, Pt. Lobos & ocean
Other: full event planning services

RESTRICTIONS:

Alcohol: provided, no BYO
Smoking: not allowed in barns
Music: volume restrictions; no amplified outdoors

Wheelchair Access: yes
Insurance: required for entertainment

This is important! Tell locations you're reading HERE COMES THE GUIDE and ask if our information is still current.

Wedgewood Wedding & Banquet Center
at Rancho Cañada Golf Course

Public Golf Club

4860 Carmel Valley Road, Carmel
866/966-3009

www.wedgewoodbanquet.com/carmel
sales@wedgewoodbanquet.com

● Rehearsal Dinners	● Corp. Events/Mtgs.
● Ceremonies	● Private Parties
● Wedding Receptions	Accommodations

The lovely green fairways and Spanish Colonial buildings of Wedgewood at Rancho Cañada Golf Course are spread out on a spacious plateau in sun-splashed Carmel Valley. At this serene country club, you won't find any pretensions—just friendly professional service and appealing event spaces. Resting on land that was once part of a Spanish rancho, the historic facility pays homage to its heritage with classic Iberian architecture and décor that hints at the romantic days of Spanish grandees and exotic beauties in lace mantillas. The buildings sport red-tile roofs, dark wood trim and arched doorways; tall oaks and fragrant pine trees, manicured hedges and flowerpots provide color.

The nicely landscaped grounds include a small pond fringed with bamboo and golden poppies, silhouetted against forested hillsides. Such a picturesque spot makes a dreamy backdrop for wedding ceremonies. But if you prefer, Wedgewood can also arrange a beach wedding just a short drive away on Carmel's Monastery Beach. Here the staff sets up chairs and an archway right on the sand. Afterward, the celebration continues back at the club.

Social hours are usually held in the Fountain Courtyard, accented by garden beds brimming with cheerful scarlet, yellow and magenta blooms. A splashing fountain in the center of the plaza provides a tranquil vision and hacienda flair. Guests take the shade beneath a covered patio with wooden beams, ginger-hued wall tiles and a stone wood-burning fireplace. They can also mingle in the tastefully appointed foyer just inside before retiring to one of the adjacent banquet rooms for the reception.

The Fiesta Ballroom is a commodious event space with a wood-beam ceiling and skylights contributing to an open, airy quality. Elaborate Mission-style chandeliers convey Old World elegance, and expansive picture windows make it seem as if your reception is set among oak groves and camellia bushes, with everything cradled by the hilly vistas. Smaller gatherings enjoy the Merienda Room. It also features a vaulted, open-beam ceiling and rustic fixtures. Creative accents include an alcove that showcases a framed watercolor and stone sculpture, and a series of beveled mirrors that add sparkle to a corner of the room. A wall of picture windows captures the cascading green fairways, adorned with clusters of trees and flowers and surrounded by the majestic hills. You can admire the view up close on the Merienda's outdoor patio, which is also suitable for cocktails or even a wedding ceremony.

The scenic setting is not this venue's only inviting attribute—so is the very reasonable price tag. Wedgewood Wedding and Banquet Centers are known for offering a range of all-inclusive event packages that take you from champagne toast to after-dinner coffee for a modest charge and a lot of extras. And if you want to make golf part of your weekend, you'll get discounted rates for that as well.

Though this facility is open to the public, the welcoming ambiance and quality service is on par with that of an exclusive country club. And the prestigious Carmel Valley location, just a few minutes from the fabled Carmel Mission, world-class shops and legendary beaches, will make your guests feel even more privileged to attend your special event.

CEREMONY CAPACITY: The Merienda Patio holds up to 95 seated guests, and the Clubhouse Lawn up to 400 seated guests.

EVENT/RECEPTION & MEETING CAPACITY: The Fiesta Ballroom accommodates up to 400 seated or 550 standing guests, and the Merienda Ballroom up to 200 seated or 300 standing. These spaces can be divided into smaller sections for meetings or intimate events.

FEES & DEPOSITS: 25% of the total estimated event cost is required to reserve your date. Another 25% is due 90 days prior, and the final payment along with the final guest count is due 10 days prior to the event. All-inclusive wedding packages start at $40 per guest. Tax, alcohol and service charge are additional.

AVAILABILITY: Year-round, daily, 7am–midnight.

SERVICES/AMENITIES:

Catering: provided, no BYO
Kitchen Facilities: n/a
Tables & Chairs: provided
Linens, Silver, etc.: provided
Restrooms: wheelchair accessible
Dance Floor: yes
Bride's Dressing Area: yes
Meeting Equipment: some

Parking: large lot
Accommodations: no guest rooms
Telephone: pay phones
Outdoor Night Lighting: limited
Outdoor Cooking Facilities: CBA
Cleanup: provided
View: golf fairways, valley, mountains
Other: event coordination

RESTRICTIONS:

Alcohol: provided
Smoking: outside only
Music: amplified OK

Wheelchair Access: yes
Insurance: not required

Bernardus Lodge

415 W. Carmel Valley Road, Carmel Valley
831/658-3504
www.bernardus.com
kclayton@bernardus.com

Lodge & Resort

● Rehearsal Dinners	● Corp. Events/Mtgs.
● Ceremonies	● Private Parties
● Wedding Receptions	● Accommodations

You have to love a resort where the Concierge greets you by name and hands you a glass of fine wine as soon as you cross the threshold. This is just the beginning of the personalized services you'll receive at Bernardus Lodge.

Serenity and natural beauty are hallmarks of Carmel Valley, and the lodge's tasteful Old World-meets-Monterey styling harmonizes with the surrounding wilderness. The young resort has already garnered a collection of prestigious accolades, and may soon surpass the fame of the winery for which it was named. Bernardus vintages strive to "transcend the ordinary," and this idyllic retreat accomplishes the feat superbly.

The warm and inviting lobby has a pastoral European flavor with rich woods and textures softened by fresh-cut flowers and the glow from a stone hearth. A vaulted ceiling crowns the expansive space, and a glass door at the far end offers a tantalizing glimpse of what lies beyond. Set along a terraced hillside, the boutique resort's 57 sumptuous suites occupy several adobe buildings, spread out among acres of gardens, stately oak and pine trees, and a working vineyard.

The centerpiece of the grounds is the Croquet Lawn, a carpet of manicured grass. Overlooking the green is Wicket's Terrace, a delightful patio with a limestone fireplace and a trellis to shelter your intimate al fresco gathering. Adjoining the terrace is Wicket's Proper, a casual bistro with a built-in bar, hardwood floors, and plenty of windows facing the terrace. Small rehearsal dinners feel right at home in Marinus, the lodge's award-winning and decidedly sophisticated gourmet restaurant. A stunning 12-foot-wide limestone fireplace with a raised hearth lends distinction, and a sweep of windows brings in a magnificent mountain vista. Marinus also opens onto a peaceful terrace, complete with a meditation pool and water garden.

Lavish receptions come alive in the Meritage Ballroom, a discreetly elegant banquet space with 22-foot vaulted ceilings and wrought-iron chandeliers. Arched windows above French doors are hugged by velvet draperies, pulled back to capture a lush garden view. Several more cozy rooms at the lodge offer their own unique charms.

Perhaps what makes most brides fall in love with Bernardus is the spectacular Wedding Garden, a vast cornucopia of floral and herbal delights. A splashing fountain encircled with fragrant rosebushes welcomes the wedding guests, who take their seats on the lawn facing an elevated flagstone pavilion.

With the bridal party posed on the pavilion's broad steps, the bride and groom exchange vows under a classic stone pergola adorned with flowering vines. If you get married as evening falls, the setting sun paints a luminous panorama of cotton-candy pink and dusky orange over the Santa Lucia Mountains.

The romance continues in private guest suites that define sensual splendor: a complimentary wine grotto, limestone fireplace, two-person tub, and a featherbed dressed in imported linens that enfold you in a dreamy embrace. For more pampering, the on-site spa offers a tempting array of signature treatments, and the salon attends to all your styling needs. With its outstanding amenities and superb cuisine, Bernardus Lodge is an epicurean paradise that alternately nurtures and titillates the senses. Any event here is sure to be sensational.

CEREMONY CAPACITY: The Wedding Garden accommodates up to 150 seated guests.

EVENT/RECEPTION CAPACITY: The resort can accommodate 12–150 seated or 12–200 standing guests indoors.

MEETING CAPACITY: Meeting spaces hold up to 150 seated guests.

FEES & DEPOSITS: For special events, a deposit equal to the event space rental fee and 10% of the estimated food & beverage total is required to reserve your date. Half of the remaining estimated event total is payable 60 days prior, and the balance 30 days prior to the event. In-house catering is provided: Luncheons start at $48/person, dinners at $88/person. Alcohol, tax and a 20% service charge are additional. The rental fee is $1,500 for the Wedding Garden, $2,500 for the Meritage Ballroom and $750 for the Harvest Room. The rental fee for the outdoor cocktail reception area (prior to dinner) is complimentary with the confirmation of the Meritage Ballroom or the Harvest Room.

AVAILABILITY: Year-round, daily until 11pm, including holidays.

SERVICES/AMENITIES:

Catering: provided, no BYO
Kitchen Facilities: n/a
Tables & Chairs: provided
Linens, Silver, etc.: provided
Restrooms: wheelchair accessible
Dance Floor: portable floor
Bride's Dressing Area: guest room CBA
Meeting Equipment: full range, extra fee

Parking: complimentary valet and self-parking
Accommodations: 57 guest rooms
Telephone: in guest rooms
Outdoor Night Lighting: access only
Outdoor Cooking Facilities: no
Cleanup: provided
View: Santa Lucia Mountains, vineyard
Other: spa package, croquet and bocce ball, tennis, lap pool, lawn, wedding cakes

RESTRICTIONS:

Alcohol: provided
Smoking: not allowed
Music: amplified OK indoors, curfew 11pm, acoustic only outdoors

Wheelchair Access: yes
Insurance: not required
Other: no confetti

The Holly Farm

Private Estate & Garden

9200 Carmel Valley Road, Carmel Valley
831/625-1926

www.hollyfarm.com
info@hollyfarm.com

- Rehearsal Dinners
- Ceremonies
- Wedding Receptions
- Corp. Events/Mtgs.
- Private Parties
- Accommodations

Here's a gem of a location that offers something rare—not only exclusive use, but the option to house up to 24 of your event guests for two to six days. Doyle and Mary Moses, The Holly Farm's owners, have fashioned their chic tropical hideaway in Carmel with destination weddings, special events and corporate retreats in mind, so you can treat your closest friends and family to a fun-filled getaway in a lush fantasy world of comfort and ease.

First established over 100 years ago, The Holly Farm is a private six-and-a-half-acre estate located in a sunny inland valley only five miles from the coast. The property contains the last holly "farm" in the state: 49 enormous holly trees that flank both sides of the entrance drive to the property. Doyle, himself a noted artist, expanded the original 4-bedroom, 3-bath adobe hacienda, and now it could easily grace the pages of *Architectural Digest*. Inside you'll find a pleasing mix of California-style architecture and contemporary furnishings; walls are a warm apricot, floors are oak and Mexican tile. Guests can mingle in front of the fireplace in the spacious, fully stocked kitchen, and then sit down for a rehearsal dinner or other intimate gathering in the sun-filled sunken dining room. The living room is kept cozy by a second fireplace, and there's a beautiful view of the Santa Lucia Mountains beyond the private fountain patio.

At the end of a nearby tropical garden path lies the Banana Cabana. This whimsical redwood bungalow features "island wild" décor, with bamboo curtains, futons, murals, eclectic artifacts and a wraparound redwood deck. Meanwhile, the newlyweds can play "Tarzan and Jane" in the Paraiso Suite, sheltered from the rest of the grounds by a low vine-covered adobe wall. This exotic getaway has a rustic service area for champagne and strawberries, a private bath and dressing room with potted orchids, and a Carmel flagstone fireplace.

Outdoors, the romance continues in the picturesque and colorful landscape. The Holly Farm's immaculately tended tropical gardens are complemented by hundreds of sweet-scented blossoms spilling over flowerbeds and pots; a small pond and sparkling waterfall next to a majestic oak tree make a lovely setting for wedding photos and ceremonies of up to 200 guests. A sweeping lawn with a classic farm windmill is perfect for larger weddings, while al fresco receptions in the Carriage House enjoy an impressive stone bar and an entertainment space for cocktails and dancing.

To top it all off, The Holly Farm also has a versatile chef who insists on using only the finest ingredients, including organic produce. The Moses family is passionate about food, and loves to create artfully presented dishes inspired by your personal favorites—whether they're gourmet vegan or hearty barbecue fare.

Up to 24 guests can actually lodge at The Holly Farm, but others staying nearby can still attend the wedding, the reception, Sunday Garden Brunch or an afternoon game of bocce ball. Past guests have dubbed this unique experience a "Wedding-Moon," so relaaax, and turn over all the details to The Holly Farm's expert and devoted care. We've sampled their hospitality firsthand, and can't decide what we enjoyed most—the delicious offerings the chef brought to our doorstep or being lulled to sleep by the tranquil melody of splashing fountains.

The staff here will lavish you with personal attention, and can arrange for the cream of local vendors to assist at your event. Their reputation for quiet efficiency and fine taste has earned them the patronage of an elite clientele. You too can join the privileged, when you "slow down and settle in" at the delightful Holly Farm.

CEREMONY CAPACITY: The Waterfall Pond Area holds up to 200 seated or standing guests; the Windmill Lawn Area accommodates up to 250 seated guests.

EVENT/RECEPTION & MEETING CAPACITY: The Carriage House seats 70 comfortably; the Banquet Lawn Area holds 250 seated guests. The Adobe Hacienda's Dining Room holds 32 seated guests.

FEES & DEPOSITS: The Holly Farm offers various wedding packages that start at $26,000. The fees include exclusive use of the estate and all its facilities, sleeping accommodations for up to 24 people, daily maid service, assisted parking and event planning guidance. A $5,000 deposit plus a refundable $500 security deposit are required when reservations are confirmed. Catered meals are not included in the package, and start at $43/person. Alcohol, tax and a 15% service charge (on food only) are additional.

Fees for corporate retreats or business meetings vary; call for more information.

AVAILABILITY: Larger weddings, late April–November. Smaller, off-season weddings can be arranged. Corporate retreats or business meetings, daily, year-round.

SERVICES/AMENITIES:

Catering: provided, no BYO
Kitchen Facilities: available in guest cottages
Tables & Chairs: provided
Linens, Silver, etc.: provided
Restrooms: most are wheelchair accessible
Dance Floor: in Carriage House
Bride's & Groom's Dressing Areas: yes
Meeting Equipment: microphone, screen

Parking: on site, with attendant
Accommodations: up to 24 guests
Telephone: yes
Outdoor Night Lighting: yes
Outdoor Cooking Facilities: BBQs
Cleanup: provided
View: Carmel hills, valley and Santa Lucia Mtns.
Other: wireless internet, ping pong, darts, volleyball, bocce ball, croquet; massage, ceremonial music, bride's hair/makeup/nails

RESTRICTIONS:

Alcohol: BYO, no corkage fees
Smoking: outside only
Music: provided or BYO, amplified OK, with volume restrictions

Wheelchair Access: yes
Insurance: certificate required

Overwhelmed? Use the search criteria on www.HereComesTheGuide.com to narrow down your choices.

Holman Ranch, Vineyard & Winery

Historic Private Estate

Address withheld to ensure privacy. Carmel Valley
831/659-2640
www.holmanranch.com
info@holmanranch.com

- Rehearsal Dinners
- Ceremonies
- Wedding Receptions
- Corp. Events/Mtgs.
- Private Parties
- Accommodations

High atop the sunny hills of Carmel Valley rests Holman Ranch and Vineyard, a historic private estate available for your one-of-a-kind event. Blessed with a treasure chest of scenic jewels, the ranch has a rich legacy of hosting society's elite. In 1928, the secluded location became a favorite gentlemen's retreat for Hollywood celebrities like Charlie Chaplin. When the Holmans purchased the property in 1943, their improvements helped make the ranch the center of the Carmel Valley social scene. Recently, the 400-acre spread was adopted by the Lowder family, who've completed a loving restoration that retains the ranch's Old World character while adding up-to-the-minute luxuries and sleek winery caves. This 21st-century renaissance features enhanced interiors and lavish outdoor spaces that make the most of the spectacular view-filled grounds.

A private road climbs to the ranch's pond and stables, where guests park and are shuttled to the hilltop entrance. Arriving at the Main Plaza, visitors get a captivating first impression: a mélange of red-tile roofs, landscaped walkways, shade trees and glimpses of grapevines against a mountainous panorama. Finally eyes rest on the Hacienda itself, an architectural gem crafted of Carmel stone and oak, with tile and metal details. This easy blend of grand Spanish style and relaxed Western attitude evokes an aura of rustic elegance.

Both varied and flexible, Holman Ranch holds a myriad of possibilities…so why not stage each phase of your event in a different spot? Ceremonies are gorgeous on the Hacienda Lawn, which sweeps to the edge of a hillside studded with Pinot Noir grapevines. Wedding guests have an endless view of the Carmel Valley, alive with chaparral, oak trees and hawks soaring overhead. As the sunset burnishes the Santa Lucia Mountains, the scene becomes even more postcard-perfect. Against this breathtaking backdrop, couples say their vows atop the Ceremony Veranda, a demilune stone platform that seems suspended above the valley floor.

Afterwards, serve cocktails on the nearby Stone Terrace, which is ringed with olive trees. Or serve appetizers along with a special tasting of Holman Ranch's unique estate-produced olive oils and wines—oenophiles will especially appreciate that the vintages maintain the grape's integrity from vine to bottle. Everyone is free to relax in the adjoining Great Room, where a vaulted ceiling, fireplace and player piano contribute to a comfortable, homey ambiance.

Receptions bask in the warm valley twilight out on the Rose Patio, dressed with rose bushes and potted citrus trees. Family-style rehearsal dinners might prefer the Arbor, a magnificent wooden promenade at the Plaza's center, where olive trees and young grapevines lend a Mediterranean flair. Then, move the party to the barn-style Carriage House, where an explosion of twinkle lights along whitewashed rafters creates the illusion of dancing beneath a star-filled sky.

When it's time to cut the wedding cake, gather friends and loved ones in the Hacienda's Inner Courtyard. Here high stone walls surround an enclave built of moss-fringed tiles and graced with an old oak tree at the center. Some couples hang paper lanterns or fairy lights from its spreading boughs, while the cake is showcased beneath a white gauze canopy.

And let yourself think outside the wedding: Host a casual welcome dinner or barbecue that includes bocce ball or horseshoes so the families can get acquainted before the main event. You can even throw a pool party, complete with umbrella drinks and beach balls. Weekend event packages include use of 10 recently restored guest rooms, including a 2-bedroom/2-bath private house with its own cozy kitchen. Altogether, the ranch can accommodate up to 38 overnight guests. The inviting home-away-from-home experience comes with a deluxe Continental-plus breakfast and the ranch's recreation facilities. From refined entertainment to laid-back fun, Holman Ranch Vineyard & Winery can arrange it all, and oh so well.

Holman Ranch is shown by appointment only. Please call to schedule a visit.

CEREMONY CAPACITY: The site can accommodate 200+ seated guests.

EVENT/RECEPTION CAPACITY: Outdoors, the Rose Patio holds 200 seated and the Main Plaza holds 200+ seated. Indoors, the Carriage House holds 150 seated guests.

MEETING CAPACITY: The Conference Room holds 10 seated around a boardroom table with executive chairs, the Carriage House holds 200 seated.

FEES & DEPOSITS: A nonrefundable deposit of one third of the site and room rental fees is required to reserve your date. A second nonrefundable deposit totaling 50% of the balance is due 6 months before the event. The remaining balance is due 1 month prior. The site rental fee ranges $1,000–30,000 depending on the time of year, day of the week and hours of usage. Rental of the 10 guest rooms, which is required for weekend events during high season (April 15–November 15), starts at $7,500 plus tax for a 3-day/2-night package and includes daily breakfast and access to the pool and fitness center

AVAILABILITY: Year-round, anytime. Off-season rates apply November 15–April 15.

SERVICES/AMENITIES:

Catering: select from preferred list or BYO, licensed
Kitchen Facilities: prep only for caterer use, full kitchen for overnight guests
Tables & Chairs: provided for up to 150 guests
Linens, Silver, etc.: through caterer
Restrooms: 5 are wheelchair accessible, 6 total
Dance Floor: provided
Bride's Dressing Area: yes
Meeting Equipment: some provided

Parking: large lot, limited to 100 cars
Accommodations: 10 guest rooms
Telephone: in guest & conference rooms
Outdoor Night Lighting: provided
Outdoor Cooking Facilities: caterer or rental
Cleanup: caterer and renter
View: vineyards, panoramic views of Carmel Valley and the Santa Lucia Mountains
Other: player piano, A/V equipment, pool, vineyard tours, heaters and market umbrellas; estate-grown wine and olive oil available

RESTRICTIONS:

Alcohol: BYO, served through licensed caterer or bartending service
Smoking: designated areas only
Music: amplified OK with restrictions

Wheelchair Access: yes
Insurance: required

Scheid Vineyards Estate Winery

Winery

1972 Hobson Avenue, Greenfield
831/455-9990
www.scheidvineyards.com
stefani@scheidvineyards.com

● Rehearsal Dinners	● Corp. Events/Mtgs.	
● Ceremonies	● Private Parties	
● Wedding Receptions	Accommodations	

For many brides, the venue hunt goes something like this: Your heart is set on a winery or vineyard wedding, but a tour of Napa, Sonoma, and Paso Robles Wine Country leaves you with sticker shock. The affordable options? Some are so remote that guests might need a GPS and 4-wheel drive to get there. Still others are a bit pretentious, and you wouldn't be surprised if a concierge with a French accent attempted to screen your guests from behind a red velvet rope. Disappointed, you're ready to give up on your winery wedding dream. Don't. Instead, head to the Salinas Valley and visit Scheid Vineyards Estate Winery, a congenial, versatile and scenic event site that's also easy on the wallet.

The Salinas Valley, you ask? Yes, that fertile, unspoiled *arroyo* an hour south of Monterey that inspired the famous novels of Steinbeck and Kerouac. The picturesque terrain between the rugged Santa Lucia Mountains to the west and the chaparral-cloaked Gabilan range to the east boasts a temperate climate that's ideal for growing grapes. The pace slows down in this viticulture Eden, and you get a sense that a celebration here would capture the rustic simplicity you've been searching for.

You're right. Scheid is situated in Greenfield's rural environs, just two easy minutes from a highway exit. Surrounded by fields and mountains, the Tasting Room is in a renovated 100-year-old barn painted cornflower blue. Wedding ceremonies are held in a spacious backyard garden. One section sports raised beds brimming with herbs and ripening vegetables; the demonstration vineyard flourishes at the center; and on the north side, a ribbon of rose bushes lines the first fragrant stretch of the wedding aisle. Guests look on from a pair of lawns edged with grapevines, while the couple shares their vows atop a raised stage. Afterwards, the newlyweds pose for photos in the vineyard, or beneath a long arbor canopied with fruit-laden grapevines on an adjacent deck.

Guests, meanwhile, enjoy the social hour strolling through the kitchen garden, playing bocce ball, or relaxing at cocktail tables on the nearby Vineyard Patio. When it's time to dine, it's just steps to the Vineyard Pavilion, a red brick courtyard accented with wine barrels and market lights. Dancing is divine beneath the glittering evening stars, which are especially abundant out here in the country.

For something different, why not set up pre-dinner mingling in the Barrel Reserve? Guests get a behind-the-scenes peek at wine production, and the piquant aroma of fermenting grapes lends an air of romance to the festivities. Rehearsal dinners or receptions in front of gigantic stainless steel wine vats or stacks of oak wine barrels are exciting and memorable. Your experienced site coordinator will help out with lots of clever ideas, as well as assist with wine and meal pairings—Scheid's handcrafted, multiple-award-winning vintages are sure to please. Another bonus: Rental includes the Vineyard Guest House, a roomy and smartly outfitted retreat where the bride and her attendants prepare in privacy, style and comfort.

So there you have it—a charming venue that's far from city stress yet easy to find, all at a friendly price point. *Eureka!*

CEREMONY, EVENT/RECEPTION & MEETING CAPACITY: The site holds 50 seated indoors and 200 seated outdoors.

FEES & DEPOSITS: 50% of the site fee is required to reserve your date and the balance is due 30 days prior to the event. Rental fees range $500–2,000 depending on whether the booking is for ceremony only, or ceremony and reception.

AVAILABILITY: Year-round, daily, noon–midnight.

SERVICES/AMENITIES:

Catering: select from preferred list or BYO
Kitchen Facilities: fully equipped
Tables & Chairs: provided
Linens, Silver, etc.: through caterer
Restrooms: wheelchair accessible
Dance Floor: provided
Bride's Dressing Area: yes
Meeting Equipment: CBA
Other: picnic area, umbrellas, heaters, event coordination

Parking: large lot
Accommodations: no guest rooms
Telephone: office phone
Outdoor Night Lighting: provided
Outdoor Cooking Facilities: BBQ CBA
Cleanup: provided
View: garden patio, landscaped grounds; panorama of hills, fields and vineyards

RESTRICTIONS:

Alcohol: provided
Smoking: outdoors only
Music: amplified OK

Wheelchair Access: yes
Insurance: liability required

Beach Resort Monterey

Waterfront Hotel

2600 Sand Dunes Drive, Monterey

831/655-7650

www.montereybeachresort.com
mbrweddings@montereybeachresort.com

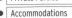

- Rehearsal Dinners
- Ceremonies
- Wedding Receptions
- Corp. Events/Mtgs.
- Private Parties
- Accommodations

For the couple who dream of exchanging vows in full view of rolling waves, an endless blue horizon, and the dynamic Monterey skyline, this is your place. It also has the delightful distinction of being the only resort in the area that's located directly on the beach and can accommodate beach wedding ceremonies. Miles of pristine white sand stretch in either direction; during the day sailboats dot the white-capped waters of the bay, and at night the lights of Monterey glitter on the far shore.

Of course, it takes more than a beautiful beach to make a first-class event facility, and Beach Resort Monterey has a variety of unique venues. A wedding reception, corporate event, or any type of large gathering can be held in one of two ballrooms on the fourth floor. The Points Ballroom has plenty of windows with a sweeping vista of Monterey Bay. The La Grande Room is smaller than the Points Ballroom, but virtually identical to it in all other respects, including the panoramic view.

With all this stunning scenery, you'd expect outdoor events at Beach Resort Monterey to be popular and they are. Adventurous couples can tie the knot on the resort's beach or the South Terrace, both of which take advantage of the spectacular view. If you'd like an al fresco ceremony but prefer a more intimate setting, opt for the Ocean Deck or Wedding Garden.

As evening descends, retire indoors to one of the elegant ballrooms for dinner and dancing. The resort's catering professionals can even customize your package with specialty menu items to enhance your wedding theme. Then keep the festivities going with an after party in the aptly named Bayview Room.

For a rehearsal dinner or post-wedding brunch, the Captain's Table on the hotel's top floor serves up panoramic views of the ocean and Monterey skyline along with its California coastal cuisine.

The resort is a great place for a destination wedding, because in addition to its flexible event spaces it boasts upgraded guestrooms that make staying here a pleasure. Amenities include 42″ flat panel HD TVs, iHome docking stations, complimentary WiFi and garden or ocean views.

At the Beach Resort Monterey you and your guests not only have access to your very own "backyard" beach, you can take a little vacation and enjoy all that this famous coastal region has to offer.

CEREMONY CAPACITY: The resort can accommodate 10–300 seated or standing, indoors or outdoors.

EVENT/RECEPTION CAPACITY: The resort accommodates 10–300 seated or standing guests.

MEETING CAPACITY: Several banquet rooms hold 5–400 seated guests.

FEES & DEPOSITS: For weddings, 25% of the estimated total is required to reserve your date. Wedding packages range $77–107/person excluding beverages. Reception-only packages are also available.

AVAILABILITY: Year-round, daily, 7am–10pm on the South Terrace, Ocean Deck and in the Wedding Garden. Beach ceremonies available May–October. All events must conclude at 10pm. An after-party location is available from 10pm–2am at an additional cost.

SERVICES/AMENITIES:

Catering: provided
Kitchen Facilities: n/a
Tables & Chairs: provided
Linens, Silver, etc.: provided
Restrooms: wheelchair accessible
Dance Floor: provided
Bride's & Groom's Dressing Areas: CBA
Meeting Equipment: CBA, extra charge

Parking: self-parking; valet CBA
Accommodations: 196 guest rooms
Telephone: emergency use only
Outdoor Night Lighting: yes, more CBA
Outdoor Cooking Facilities: n/a
Cleanup: provided
View: Pacific Ocean and Monterey coastline
Other: event coordination, decorations

RESTRICTIONS:

Alcohol: provided
Smoking: designated areas
Music: amplified OK until 10pm

Wheelchair Access: yes, except to beach
Insurance: required for vendors
Other: no rice, birdseed or glitter; rose petals must be real outdoors and artificial indoors; only preferred vendors may be used

The professionals in the back of this book are the best in the business. How do we know? Read page 637.

593

Club Del Monte
at Monterey's Naval Postgraduate School

1 University Circle, Monterey
831/656-1049
www.mwrtoday.com/monterey/dining/catering
mwrcatering@nps.edu

Historic Landmark

- Rehearsal Dinners
- Ceremonies
- Wedding Receptions
- Corp. Events/Mtgs.
- Private Parties
- Accommodations

Club Del Monte is an Art Deco jewel set amongst 25 acres of sprawling lawns dotted with oak, cypress, and pine. Originally built in 1880 as the grand Hotel del Monte, it was destroyed twice by fire and rebuilt. The present imposing structure (which is the 1926 incarnation) resembles a Spanish-Moorish fortress. It remained an elegant hotel until 1951, when it was acquired by the Navy for its Naval Postgraduate School. As you can see, this facility's history is long and illustrious.

Your guests will step back in time and feel like royalty, when welcomed with cocktails in the Quarterdeck Lounge. This majestic lobby was built on the scale of a castle foyer, with soaring 30-foot ceilings which are crosshatched with hand-painted wooden beams. Two stately rows of stone columns grace both sides of the room, framing a towering floor-to-ceiling window that overlooks the estate-like grounds.

Proceed to the Ballroom for a formal dinner-dance; you'll be transported back to the era when Jean Harlow, Clark Gable and Carole Lombard danced here, and when water cascaded down the room's main attraction: an ornately tiled fountain that dominates one wall. The fountain and the elaborate tilework bordering the floor-to-ceiling arched windows at either end of the room bring the Moorish influence inside, and give the space a spicy, exotic ambiance. Other Art Deco details include the lacy plasterwork ceiling, huge wrought-iron chandeliers, and matching wall sconces. French doors opening onto the terrace and overlooking the European-style rose gardens are the finishing touch.

For a buffet luncheon or catered business meeting, La Novia Room, with plaster walls and rich wood trim, offers the elegance of the ballroom but on a more intimate scale. It opens onto La Novia Terrace, an atrium with a rustic brick fireplace, window benches and a brick floor. There are outdoor settings, too. The lawn works well for a romantic Victorian wedding. Club Del Monte offers a treasure-trove of site options, and as you'd expect from a naval facility, everything here is top rank.

CEREMONY CAPACITY: The facility accommodates up to 400 seated or standing guests on the lawn.

EVENT/RECEPTION CAPACITY: Indoors, several rooms hold 25–600 seated or 25–1,000 standing guests.

MEETING CAPACITY: The Ballroom holds 600 seated in rounds of 10, 500 seated theater-style; the La Novia Room holds 90 in rounds of 10, 75 theater-style.

FEES & DEPOSITS: For weddings and receptions, a $550–1,600 nonrefundable deposit, depending on the room reserved, is required to book the facility. 75% of the estimated event total is payable 4 weeks prior to the function, and the balance is due 1 week prior.

Catering is provided starting at $30/person, with a $3/person cake-cutting fee. Wine, champagne and a 15% service charge are additional.

Weekday meeting fees vary depending on catering services required.

AVAILABILITY: Year-round, daily. Weddings can be booked 11am–4pm or 6pm–11pm; conferences or other special events, 7am–4pm or 6pm–11pm. Extra hours are available for an additional charge.

SERVICES/AMENITIES:

Catering: provided, no BYO
Kitchen Facilities: n/a
Tables & Chairs: provided
Linens, Silver, etc.: provided
Restrooms: wheelchair accessible
Dance Floor: yes
Bride's Dressing Area: yes, additional fee
Meeting Equipment: CBA

Parking: on-base lot; weekday carpooling recommended for large events
Accommodations: military or Department of Defense cardholders only
Telephone: no
Outdoor Night Lighting: no
Outdoor Cooking Facilities: no
Cleanup: provided
View: of lawns and gardens

RESTRICTIONS:

Alcohol: provided, no BYO
Smoking: outside only, 20 feet away from building
Music: amplified OK

Wheelchair Access: yes
Insurance: not required
Other: no rice, birdseed, glitter, confetti, bubbles or wall decorations

InterContinental The Clement Monterey

Waterfront Hotel

750 Cannery Row, Monterey
831/375-4500
www.ictheclementmonterey.com
ggrammatico@pahotel.com

- Rehearsal Dinners
- Ceremonies
- Wedding Receptions
- Corp. Events/Mtgs.
- Private Parties
- Accommodations

Throughout the years, Monterey's timeless natural beauty has been the inspiration for artists, poets and novelists alike. Recently, a downtown renaissance has put a glamorous polish on historic districts like Cannery Row, and author John Steinbeck would be amazed to see these formerly rough-and-tumble dockside streets dramatically transformed into a thoroughly modern boulevard. Today's Cannery Row is alive with fashionable boutiques, delectable eateries, upscale galleries and a vibrant street scene that attracts visitors from all over the world. And right next door, at the heart of the action, sits the celebrated Monterey Bay Aquarium.

Can this quaint yet oh-so-now slice of paradise get any better? Yes, it can. InterContinental The Clement Monterey was designed as a serene coastal retreat for personal rejuvenation and spectacular private celebrations.

Wedding ceremonies are staged on an expansive landscaped courtyard facing the sapphire-blue waters of the bay. Two fire pits provide an ambient glow, particularly romantic at sunset. Couples say their vows with the bay in the background, while seabirds trace graceful curves on the horizon, and otters and sea lions perch atop the rocky shore.

With such a picturesque setting, have your social hour out in the fresh ocean air as well. While the bridal party poses for pictures, guests enjoy the hotel's boardwalk and pier, which extends out over the bay. Cut-outs along the wooden pier reveal tantalizing peeks directly down at the teeming underwater world of the Monterey Bay Sanctuary.

As twilight descends, retire indoors to admire the vista from another perspective. The Pacific Ballroom is a refined setting for a bayside gala, replete with picture windows that capture a panorama of the moonlit ocean and the star-filled heavens. Bring the sparkle indoors by decorating with luminarias and fairy lights—the banquet staff can customize your event according to your wishes. The view will be even more impressive from the Ocean Terrace Ballroom, located upstairs. It's an intimate space that boasts a huge bayview terrace.

The resort's equally impressive public spaces are tranquil and welcoming, thanks to the stylish use of wood and other natural materials, along with décor in soothing shades of green and blue, evocative of the sea and sky. One of the most notable spaces is the Reading Room, warmed by a contemporary stone-faced fireplace. Adjacent to the Reading Room, the Library serves as a private dining salon that's perfect for formal rehearsal dinners.

One of the benefits of a destination event at InterContinental The Clement Monterey is that friends and family can have a minivacation, because there's simply no end to the area's fun-filled activities. Hotel accommodations feature up-to-the-minute amenities, and many have fireplaces, ocean views and balconies. Their on-site spa pampers with the latest in beautification and wellness treatments.

The hotel's VIP Kid's Club provides entertaining and innovative recreational programs for kids from 4 to 13 years old. VIP babysitting is also available for younger children, enabling parents to enjoy the wedding celebration.

Rich with promise, this magnificent hotel opened in May 2008. Reserve your event space now to take advantage of Monterey's legendary allure.

CEREMONY CAPACITY: The resort holds 220 seated indoors or outdoors.

EVENT/RECEPTION & MEETING CAPACITY: The facility accommodates 220 seated or 350 standing indoors or outdoors.

FEES & DEPOSITS: A nonrefundable deposit of 25% of the estimated food and beverage total and 100% of the facility fee is required to confirm your event, and is due within 14 days of contract signing. 25% of the estimated remaining balance is due 120 days prior, and the balance is due 14 days prior to the event. Facility fees range $2,000–5,000 depending on the space(s) rented. Wedding packages range $89–145/person. Tax and a 20% service charge are additional.

AVAILABILITY: Year-round, daily, 6am–midnight.

SERVICES/AMENITIES:

Catering: provided
Kitchen Facilities: n/a
Tables & Chairs: provided
Linens, Silver, etc.: provided
Restrooms: wheelchair accessible
Dance Floor: provided
Bride's Dressing Area: yes
Meeting Equipment: provided

Parking: valet and self-parking
Accommodations: 208 guest rooms
Telephone: house phone
Outdoor Night Lighting: provided
Outdoor Cooking Facilities: BBQ CBA
Cleanup: provided
View: ocean
Other: spa, 24-hour fitness center, pool, Jacuzzi, babysitting, kid's club

RESTRICTIONS:

Alcohol: provided
Smoking: designated areas only
Music: amplified OK with restrictions

Wheelchair Access: yes
Insurance: not required

Monterey Beach Party
at Del Monte Beach House

285 Figueroa Street, Monterey
831/648-7240
www.montereybeachparty.com
info@montereybeachparty.com

Historic Beach House

- Rehearsal Dinners
- Ceremonies
- Wedding Receptions
- Corp. Events/Mtgs.
- Private Parties
- Accommodations

If you love the sea, you've probably fantasized about spending time at a private beach house with the sand right outside your door and seals and pelicans as your only neighbors. You've pictured yourself admiring ocean views and spectacular sunsets from your front porch, and gathering friends and family around an evening bonfire, with the sublime setting putting everyone in a summertime state of mind no matter what the time of year.

Well, the event professionals at Monterey Beach Party (MBP) can cheerfully make your fantasy a reality, at least for your wedding day. They've been arranging festivities-to-remember for years, and many of the most memorable have happened at the historic Del Monte Beach House.

Located next to a waterfront park and wharf, and within walking distance to Monterey hotels and activities, the beach house is a simple cloud-colored building trimmed in sailor blue. Steps from its broad front deck descend onto the sand, and since Monterey Beach Party lays claim to its own stretch of this pristine shoreline, they'll set up your event right at the water's edge.

Ceremonies are accompanied by a palm tree-lined wedding aisle, white padded chairs, a classic wooden wedding arch and the blue Pacific. Drinks and appetizers are served on the deck, and while the bridal party poses for scenic photos the staff sets up the outdoor reception. The usual motif includes tiki torches, a bonfire and colorful beach chairs, and the beach site can accommodate up to 1,000 guests. Want fire and hula dancers? Ask, and Monterey Beach Party will make it happen. This is also one of the only local beaches that allow cocktails—so bring on the paper umbrellas!

Inside the beach house, social hours and receptions are anything but dull thanks to a myriad of novelty attractions: Ping pong, pool, shuffleboard and a "surf's up" photo backdrop are all sure-fire icebreakers. If you prefer a more elegant ambiance, the staff will remove the games and have everything looking fancy as you please. The newly renovated interior features light, faux-finished floors, open-beamed ceilings and pillars clad in bamboo. Most couples like to play up the beachy theme by choosing tropical colors from a wide array of linens and other vibrant décor. Just ask the staff for help and ideas!

A stage at one end of the room is outfitted with a rear projection screen and a state-of-the-art lighting and sound system. Amp up the entertainment by booking the house DJ or band, who will "wow" your guests with cool tunes and a light show.

MBP also takes care of the food, which is both hearty and delicious: Entrées are grilled fresh during your event, and whether you opt for the Luau Feast, Lobster Bash or Clam Bake, your guests are sure to be satisfied.

And here's a thought: If you're planning a formal affair at another Monterey venue, why not change things up by reserving the Del Monte Beach House for your rehearsal dinner? Their inclusive event packages and high-caliber service are not only a tremendous value, they practically guarantee good times. Lots of venues can host a wedding...but if you want a party, then this is the place.

CEREMONY & MEETING CAPACITY: The site holds 100 seated guests indoors and 300+ seated outdoors.

EVENT/RECEPTION CAPACITY: The facility can accommodate 250 seated or 500 standing indoors and 400+ seated or 600+ standing outdoors.

FEES & DEPOSITS: A $1,500 nonrefundable deposit is due at the time of booking. 100% of the estimated total is due 30 days prior to the event, and any remaining balance is due on the business day following the event.

Their all-inclusive wedding package is $100/person and includes the site fee, beach ceremony, beach party reception, choice of 4 menu options, cake-cutting fee, assorted beverages and bar setup and more, plus tax and service charge. Alcohol is additional.

AVAILABILITY: Year-round, daily, 11am–4pm or 6pm–11pm.

SERVICES/AMENITIES:

Catering: provided
Kitchen Facilities: on site
Tables & Chairs: provided
Linens, Silver, etc.: provided or CBA
Restrooms: wheelchair accessible
Dance Floor: provided
Bride's Dressing Area: CBA
Meeting Equipment: some provided

Parking: city lot ($1.50/hour fee)
Accommodations: no guest rooms
Telephone: emergency use only
Outdoor Night Lighting: provided
Outdoor Cooking Facilities: BBQ on site
Cleanup: provided
View: ocean/bay
Other: clergy on staff, A/V equipment, event coordination

RESTRICTIONS:

Alcohol: provided, or BYO with corkage fee
Smoking: outdoors only
Music: amplified OK with restrictions

Wheelchair Access: yes
Insurance: not required
Other: no rice, birdseed or fake petals on beach

Want to know WHAT TO ASK a potential location or vendor? Check out our Questions to Ask starting on page 17.

Monterey Museum of Art—La Mirada

Historic Estate, Museum & Gardens

720 Via Mirada, Monterey
831/372-3689
www.montereyart.org
events@montereyart.org

- Rehearsal Dinners
- Ceremonies
- Wedding Receptions
- Corp. Events/Mtgs.
- Private Parties
- Accommodations

The Monterey Museum of Art—La Mirada is one part historic home, one part gardens, and one part art gallery...all adding up to one incredible and unique event location!

Resting on a picturesque mesa above Monterey Bay, La Mirada, as the museum is most commonly known, began as a Mexican adobe that once housed pioneer John C. Fremont. At the dawn of the Jazz Age, new owner Gouverneur Morris, a silent movie mogul, embarked on a dizzying era of expansion and lavish decoration: Artists created hand-painted murals, and Hollywood designers transformed the estate into a graceful retreat, suitable for distinguished luminaries like Rudolf Valentino and Charlie Chaplin. In 1936, Morris sold La Mirada to the Work family, and doyenne Maud Porter Work renovated the Rose Garden, which still bears her name. In 1983 Frank Work donated the entire estate—including the priceless art and furnishings—to the Monterey Museum of Art so that the public might enjoy its grounds and eclectic treasures. More recently, the museum added the Dart Wing, which encompasses four modern galleries with views of the gardens.

Today, visitors enter the museum via a cozy courtyard that recalls La Mirada's Early California heritage. Colorful European tiles embellish thick adobe walls, and potted citrus trees give a cheerful greeting. Through the lobby is the bi-level Rose Garden and Patio, a sweet site for wedding ceremonies. An Art Deco tiled fountain is the focal point of the upper patio, which overlooks the showy blossoms just below. A pair of bay and fig trees stretch their boughs wide, as if embracing the wedding couple as they say their vows. A brick path descends to the garden, where more than 125 species of flora are ablaze in vibrant springtime hues. A view out to neighboring Estero Lake with a slice of the bay in the distance completes the idyllic milieu.

Prefer a modern twist? Then hold your social hour on the Drawing Room Patio, where an avant-garde fountain, a large bronze horse, and a Buddha statue peeking out from lush landscaping are conversational ice-breakers. Tall glass doors slide open to the Drawing Room, a glamorous scene of retro opulence. At one end stands a 17th-century lacquered panel, a relic of China's Forbidden City; in the window casement, a pair of brass peacocks catches the sunlight. Crystal chandeliers, gilded mirrors, a grand piano and intriguing objets d'art let you party in the lap of luxury.

La Mirada has several other options to make your day memorable: For a culture-filled social hour, invite guests to tour the latest exhibitions. Meanwhile, bride and groom pose for photos in the estate's former living quarters, still festooned with extravagant trappings of the past—silk wallpaper and antique rarities that convey a timeless air of romance. Another photogenic environment is the Rhododendron Garden, a sheltered dell awash with violet-hued blooms flourishing beneath flowering trees.

Whether your wedding vision is nostalgic or fashion-forward, quaint or bold, Gatsbyesque or exotic, La Mirada can make it happen with grace and style.

CEREMONY, EVENT/RECEPTION & MEETING CAPACITY: The museum holds 100 seated or 150 standing guests indoors, and 150 seated or 300 standing outdoors.

FEES & DEPOSITS: A nonrefundable deposit of 50% of the total event cost is required to reserve your date. The balance is due 30 days prior to the event. There are two wedding packages priced at $2,500 and $5,000.

AVAILABILITY: Year-round, daily, call for details.

SERVICES/AMENITIES:

Catering: select from approved list
Kitchen Facilities: fully equipped
Tables & Chairs: some provided, CBA or through caterer
Linens, Silver, etc.: CBA or through caterer
Restrooms: wheelchair accessible
Dance Floor: CBA
Bride's Dressing Area: yes
Meeting Equipment: some provided, CBA
Other: grand piano, picnic area, docent tours, galleries open for guests, event coordination, A/V equipment, wireless internet, stereo/CD

Parking: valet or shuttle required for groups of 70 or more
Accommodations: no guest rooms
Telephone: office phone
Outdoor Night Lighting: provided
Outdoor Cooking Facilities: CBA
Cleanup: provided
View: courtyard, garden, cityscape, ocean/bay, forest, lake, fountain, landscaped grounds

RESTRICTIONS:

Alcohol: BYO
Smoking: not allowed
Music: amplified OK with restrictions

Wheelchair Access: yes
Insurance: liability required

Monterey Plaza Hotel & Spa

Oceanfront Resort

400 Cannery Row, Monterey
831/646-1700

www.montereyplazahotel.com
weddings@montereyplazahotel.com

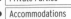

● Rehearsal Dinners	● Corp. Events/Mtgs.
● Ceremonies	● Private Parties
● Wedding Receptions	● Accommodations

There's something about being next to the ocean that most of us find irresistible. Maybe it's the bracing aroma of sea air, or the way the light glints off the waves. Whatever it is, you experience that special "something" here at the Monterey Plaza Hotel & Spa. Built right at the water's edge, the Plaza takes advantage of a spectacular bayside setting that's just a heartbeat away from the world-renowned Monterey Bay Aquarium and Cannery Row.

The plaza's 17,000 square feet of event space encompasses an array of sophisticated banquet rooms enhanced by Mediterranean-inspired furnishings. A recent $3 million renovation has brought fresh polish to the décor, and ensured that all the amenities are state-of-the-art—including advanced audiovisual and wireless capabilities. Aesthetic upgrades, like decorative crown moldings and Villeroy & Boch plateware and silver, add extra elegance to your affair.

Ceremonies at the resort are held on either of two sun-splashed terraces, both embracing panoramic vistas of the Pacific. On the Lower Terrace, the bride captures every eye as she descends the main staircase to a broad, tiled deck; on the sprawling Upper Plaza, the wedding processional walks beneath a white trellis, set off by terracotta planters brimming with flowers. Then vows are exchanged under a simple arch with the ocean and sky as a blue-on-blue backdrop.

Afterwards, most receptions take place in the Monterey Bay Room or the Dolphins Room. The latter is so close to the water you can see otters floating by and hear the gentle lapping of the waves. Both rooms mirror the earthy palette of the coastal milieu—deep marine blues and greens, terracotta reds, and warm, sun-kissed golds. Scenic artwork adorns the walls, complementing the gorgeous floor-to-ceiling bay view. For a more formal gala, the Cypress Ballroom has teakwood paneling, new custom chandeliers and its own terrace overlooking the seascape.

Rich with history and diverse activities, Monterey is a sightseer's paradise; and with the plaza's exceptional hospitality, your guests will appreciate the fact that you've chosen it as their home base—especially when they experience the hotel's rooftop spa! This is the place to relax before the big celebration (or unwind after), by indulging in a massage, facial, or one of the spa's signature treatments. The spa even boasts an outdoor sundeck complete with fireplace and whirlpool tubs, where you can enjoy a light lunch along with the invigorating salt-laced breezes.

Newlyweds often opt to stay in a spacious luxury suite, featuring a fireplace and oceanview deck. The accommodating staff can even transform your suite into a celebratory setting for a cocktail party or a post-wedding brunch. However, we highly recommend a romantic candlelight dinner for two on your private deck, where you can raise your glasses to the glorious sunset coloring the horizon, the boundless sea, and each other.

CEREMONY CAPACITY: The Lower Terrace accommodates 120 guests seated in rows and a few more standing guests; the Upper Plaza holds 250 guests seated in rows.

EVENT/RECEPTION CAPACITY: Various rooms seat 30–250 with dancing.

MEETING CAPACITY: There are 11 conference rooms (17,000 square feet of meeting space), which accommodate up to 250 guests.

FEES & DEPOSITS: The rental fee for a 5-hour event ranges $850–2,500, depending on the banquet room reserved. It is payable, along with the $2,000–2,500 ceremony site fee (if applicable), when reservations are confirmed. The event balance (based on the estimated food and beverage total) is due 10 working days prior to the function. Meals start at $65/person. Additional evening hours may be purchased at $500/hour. Wedding cake, alcohol, tax and a 19% service charge are additional. Note that overnight accommodations for the bride and groom can be arranged at a special rate for up to two nights.

AVAILABILITY: Year-round, daily, until 10pm.

SERVICES/AMENITIES:

Catering: provided, no BYO
Kitchen Facilities: n/a
Tables & Chairs: provided
Linens, Silver, etc.: provided
Restrooms: wheelchair accessible
Dance Floor: provided
Bride's & Groom's Dressing Areas: CBA
Meeting Equipment: some provided, other CBA extra fee

Parking: valet, extra fee
Accommodations: 290 guest rooms
Telephone: emergency use only
Outdoor Night Lighting: additional CBA
Outdoor Cooking Facilities: CBA
Cleanup: provided
View: Monterey Bay and Pacific Ocean

RESTRICTIONS:

Alcohol: provided, no BYO
Smoking: outside only
Music: amplified OK with volume restrictions

Wheelchair Access: yes
Insurance: required for outside vendors only
Other: no glitter, birdseed or rice

The Perry House

201 Van Buren Street, Monterey
831/647-0114

www.perryhousemonterey.com
debbie@eventsbyclassic.com

Bayview Event Facility

● Rehearsal Dinners	● Corp. Events/Mtgs.	
● Ceremonies	● Private Parties	
● Wedding Receptions	Accommodations	

Pocketed in a leafy residential neighborhood overlooking Monterey Bay, the historic Perry House, an eye-catching Queen Anne-style Victorian in a pleasing buttercup shade, is just right for an elegant yet homey celebration.

Originally built in 1860 by ship captain Manuel Perry, this local landmark housed generations of the Perry family up until the 1960s. The property's Carriage House then served alternatively as an art gallery, tearoom, flower shop and even a costume museum. Embracing a fresh vision of the site's potential, Events by Classic purchased the Perry House in 2010, and their stunning renovation has re-imagined the vintage home as a dynamic wedding venue.

Ceremonies are held in the garden courtyard, a manicured lawn flanked by the Main House and the Carriage House. A stately white pergola anchors the seaward side, framing the wedding couple as they say "I do" amidst flowery landscaping and a filtered backdrop of sea and sky.

After the vows, the social hour kicks off in the Carriage House, a convivial spot complete with cocktail seating, a fireplace and a state-of-the-art audiovisual system. One wall of windows gazes into a quiet, shade-dappled corner of the garden; another wall displays sepia-toned photos of Monterey's bygone days. The highlight of the space, however, is a breathtaking dome ceiling of amber-and-pistachio-hued stained glass evoking the room's Art Deco heritage as well as a sense of occasion.

Just outside, a rustic stone and brick oven produces delicious wood-fired pizzas. In fact, all event cuisine is grilled or cooked to order, creating a savory aroma that melds with the salty tang of the ocean air. Equally inviting are dreamy panoramas of sailboat-filled harbors and wooded heights, which are best viewed from the cascade of balconied stairways of the Main House. As twilight descends, a sigh-inducing sunset gives way to a glittering skyscape of stars and city lights.

The Perry House becomes even more enchanting at night, when a profusion of fairy lights sparks across porch railings, tree trunks and rooflines. This is when the action usually shifts to the Captain's Room on the lower floor of the Main House, where receptions flow freely from bay windowed nooks out onto the terrace.

Yet another intriguing gathering place is the second-story Harbor View Lounge, a virtual sanctuary of 18th-century opulence that's also used for the bridal party's pre-wedding prep. This spacious salon has a luxurious sitting area and an adjoining boudoir with a sumptuous bed worthy of royalty. Newlyweds often retreat to the Lounge to survey the revels unfolding below, or to share some private time.

Like its sister property, Gatherings, the Perry House is an all-inclusive venue. The experts at *Events by Classic* are known for going out of their way to produce personalized events with five-star catering and superb service. Their specialty is innovative roaming receptions, where food stations are strategically placed throughout the property to encourage a lively atmosphere and maximum mingling.

Blessed with enduring charm, the Perry House overflows with character, warmth and thoughtful touches, and is well on its way to creating a romantic, new legacy.

CEREMONY CAPACITY: The site accommodates 80 guests seated indoors and 120 seated outdoors.

EVENT/RECEPTION CAPACITY: The facility holds 80 seated or 100 standing indoors and 140 seated or standing outdoors.

MEETING CAPACITY: Meeting spaces hold 60 seated guests.

FEES & DEPOSITS: A $2,500 deposit is required to reserve your date. 50% of the event total is due 90 days prior and the balance is due 7 days prior to the event. Rental fees range $2,490–5,490 depending on the day of the event and whether or not you book a ceremony with your reception. Meals range $78–98/person. Tax, alcohol and an 18% service charge are additional.

AVAILABILITY: Year-round, daily; Friday & Saturday until 10pm; Sunday–Thursday until 9pm.

SERVICES/AMENITIES:

Catering: provided
Kitchen Facilities: n/a
Tables & Chairs: provided
Linens, Silver, etc.: provided
Restrooms: wheelchair accessible
Dance Floor: provided
Bride's Dressing Area: yes
Meeting Equipment: some provided, A/V equipment
Other: outdoor pizza oven and fire pit, speakers throughout the property, complimentary event coordination

Parking: garage nearby
Accommodations: no guest rooms
Telephone: emergency use only
Outdoor Night Lighting: provided
Outdoor Cooking Facilities: BBQ on site
Cleanup: provided
View: fountain, garden, landscaped grounds; panorama of cityscape and bay

RESTRICTIONS:

Alcohol: provided, or BYO with corkage fee
Smoking: designated areas only
Music: amplified OK indoors

Wheelchair Access: yes
Insurance: liability required

Want to find more venues and services? Check out our informative website, www.HereComesTheGuide.com.

605

Tarpy's Roadhouse & Monterey Stone Chapel
Restaurant and Chapel

2999 Monterey-Salinas Highway, Monterey
831/655-2999
www.tarpys.com
banquet@tarpys.com

- Rehearsal Dinners
- Ceremonies
- Wedding Receptions
- Corp. Events/Mtgs.
- Private Parties
- Accommodations

We know what you're thinking: How appealing can a place be with the word "roadhouse" in its name? Well, in this case, very appealing indeed. Though this historic stone building and its five landscaped acres boast a slightly raffish past (it's the site where Matt Tarpy was lynched for the murder of his neighbor in 1873), it's now known for delicious food, eclectic atmosphere and an enticing array of both indoor and outdoor event spaces.

The most popular spot for a garden ceremony is on the Chapel Lawn, a velvety carpet of green surrounded by redwoods, pines and blossoming greenery. While guests look on from white chairs, couples say "I do" in front of an old-fashioned white gazebo. Continue to savor this scenic milieu during your cocktail hour, and invite your guests to meander onto an adjoining lawn, where a pond with a spouting fountain provides a mini-ecosystem for turtles and all sorts of fish.

For a quaint, intimate ceremony, who can resist the Monterey Stone Marriage Chapel? A picture window looks out to the garden, and whisper-pink walls, white-lace curtains and angel-themed décor lend an air of ethereal romance. Guest chairs are arranged facing a stone fireplace, whose mantel is embellished with candles, floral wreaths and garlands. Against this pretty backdrop, the bride and groom declare their love. During evening weddings, luminarias cast a dreamy glow over the charming tableau. The Chapel comes with a private changing room and sound system, as well as three on-site nondenominational ministers, should you choose to have one of them conduct your ceremony.

A sunset gathering or reception dinner lit by Craftsman-style lanterns and twinkling stars is nothing short of sensational in the courtyard. A vine-covered stone arch leads to an enchanting enclave with a honeysuckle-draped grotto and a stone-and-wood arbor laced with passionflower vines. The walls of the restaurant building rise on two sides, sporting more flowering vines, as well as a bronze frieze of dancing figures. Wooden tables and metal chairs are complemented by market umbrellas and heat lamps for all-weather comfort.

The restaurant itself has a variety of pleasing rooms for receptions and rehearsal dinners. In the Shell Room, soft cream walls and crisp white linens impart a relaxed elegance, while a fireplace constructed entirely of seashells provides a whimsical counterpoint. The Vintner's Room displays award-winning local wines, contemporary art and views of the restaurant's lush gardens. Upstairs, the Library is a spacious, private room with a large hearth, chandeliers and distinctive metal-and-leather chairs. Adjoining the Library is a private patio, where the bold hues of fuchsias and nasturtiums vie for attention. One side of the patio is a wall, ingeniously built into the hillside, with nooks and crannies abloom with flowers and aromatic herbs. A delightful mélange of textures, colors and scents, this terracotta-paved terrace is a lovely option for pre-dinner cocktails or post-dinner dancing.

Whatever your special occasion, Tarpy's is sure to fill the bill. And don't worry, you won't find any shady characters drinking bathtub gin at this roadhouse—just delighted diners enjoying the congenial ambiance.

CEREMONY CAPACITY: The site seats 50 indoors and 70 outdoors.

EVENT/RECEPTION CAPACITY: Tarpy's accommodates 80 seated and 110 standing indoors; 110 seated or standing, outdoors.

MEETING CAPACITY: The facility seats 80 guests.

FEES & DEPOSITS: A $50 minimum deposit is required to reserve your date; deposit rates vary depending on the size of the event. The balance is due on the day of the event. Rental fees may apply depending on event specifications. Meals start at $14/person. Tax, alcohol and a 20% service charge are additional.

AVAILABILITY: Year-round, daily, 8:30am–midnight.

SERVICES/AMENITIES:

Catering: provided, no BYO
Kitchen Facilities: n/a
Tables & Chairs: provided
Linens, Silver, etc.: provided
Restrooms: wheelchair accessible
Dance Floor: CBA
Bride's & Groom's Dressing Areas: CBA
Meeting Equipment: some provided

Parking: large lot
Accommodations: no guest rooms
Telephone: emergency use only
Outdoor Night Lighting: yes
Outdoor Cooking Facilities: BBQ CBA
Cleanup: provided
View: forest, garden, pond
Other: clergy on staff; A/V equipment

RESTRICTIONS:

Alcohol: provided, or BYO with corkage fee
Smoking: outside only
Music: amplified OK with volume restrictions

Wheelchair Access: yes
Insurance: not required
Other: no glitter, birdseed or rice

Gatherings, a Private Venue
and Monterey Beach Weddings

157 15th Street, Pacific Grove
831/647-0114
www.montereyweddingsites.com
debbie@eventsbyclassic.com

Private Wedding Venue

- Rehearsal Dinners
- Ceremonies
- Wedding Receptions
- Corp. Events/Mtgs.
- Private Parties
- Accommodations

Gatherings is an all-inclusive event venue that offers the perfect wedding trifecta: a homey, vintage-style setting; superb, made-to-order cuisine; and beach wedding ceremonies. This clever combo is the brainchild of *Events by Classic,* a family-run culinary team that's been pleasing local palates for years. The venue itself is a fetching Victorian in Pacific Grove, a historic Monterey suburb known for its simple charm. When we first drove up the treelined street to Gatherings, a mother goose and her fuzzy goslings were waddling along the roadside, an appropriately quaint welcome to this cozy home.

Built in 1907, the recently restored moss-colored house now has modern amenities, but still retains its original Art Deco flair. The home makes the most of its petite size, with votives and fresh flowers spread throughout the rooms. Events here are warm, relaxed affairs, and doors are left open so that there's a natural flow from one area to the next. The foyer introduces Gatherings' inviting aesthetic: cherry and gold brocade wallpaper, Art Deco fixtures, and soft impressionist masterpieces that convey the elegance of a bygone era.

The three adjoining event rooms are similarly arrayed. In the Parlor, period furnishings are clustered around a fireplace; a plasma TV above a rose marble mantle often plays a photographic montage of the wedding couple. A leaded-glass transom frames the passageway to the Dining Room, whose gleaming wood floors make a perfect dance floor. Ceiling speakers and adjustable lights let you set the desired mood, and a bay window showcases the wedding cake. Finally, the Music Room boasts a player piano that can also be played by hand. A viewing window peers into a state-of-the-art chef's kitchen, and guests are welcome to wander in and check out the culinary action up close.

Mingling also extends to the home's wooden deck, part of which is tented, twinkle-lit and dotted with cocktail tables; the rest is open to the refreshing sea air, and comes with a wood bar and an outdoor fireplace. As evening descends, firelight, candlelight and moonlight create a romantic glow.

And if your romantic vision includes a beach wedding ceremony, then Gatherings will stage yours on one of the local beaches. Lover's Point, a lovely coastal enclave, is just a couple of blocks away, so afterwards it's easy to return to Gatherings for the reception.

In keeping with the personable theme, Gatherings offers butlered receptions that allow friends and family to roam freely. Committed to five-star service, the impeccably turned-out staff is both friendly and well trained. All food is cooked or grilled during the event—which is not only tastier, but more fun, too. Gatherings has several event packages that offer terrific value. All of them allow you to bring your own alcohol, for example, and they'll provide the bartender at no extra cost.

Events by Classic recently acquired The Perry House, a historic property that's divine for garden weddings with a view of the Monterey Bay—and capacity for up to 150. So if your celebration won't quite fit at Gatherings, then check out The Perry House! At either venue, the congenial proprietors will give their all to exceed your expectations.

CEREMONY CAPACITY: The site holds 75 seated guests outdoors.

EVENT/RECEPTION & MEETING CAPACITY: The venue can accommodate 75 seated or standing indoors and outdoors.

FEES & DEPOSITS: A $1,500 deposit is required to reserve your date and the balance is due 2 weeks prior to the event. Wedding packages range $3,785–8,190 depending on the day of the week, the number of guests and the menu selection.

AVAILABILITY: Year-round, daily, until 10pm.

SERVICES/AMENITIES:

Catering: provided
Kitchen Facilities: n/a
Tables & Chairs: provided
Linens, Silver, etc.: provided
Restrooms: wheelchair accessible
Dance Floor: provided
Bride's Dressing Area: no
Meeting Equipment: CBA

Parking: on street, valet included
Accommodations: no guest rooms
Telephone: emergency use only
Outdoor Night Lighting: provided
Outdoor Cooking Facilities: no
Cleanup: provided
View: garden courtyard
Other: grand piano, on-site florals, A/V equipment, complimentary event coordination

RESTRICTIONS:

Alcohol: BYO
Smoking: outdoors only
Music: iPod station available, acoustic OK

Wheelchair Access: yes
Insurance: not required

Gold Country and Yosemite

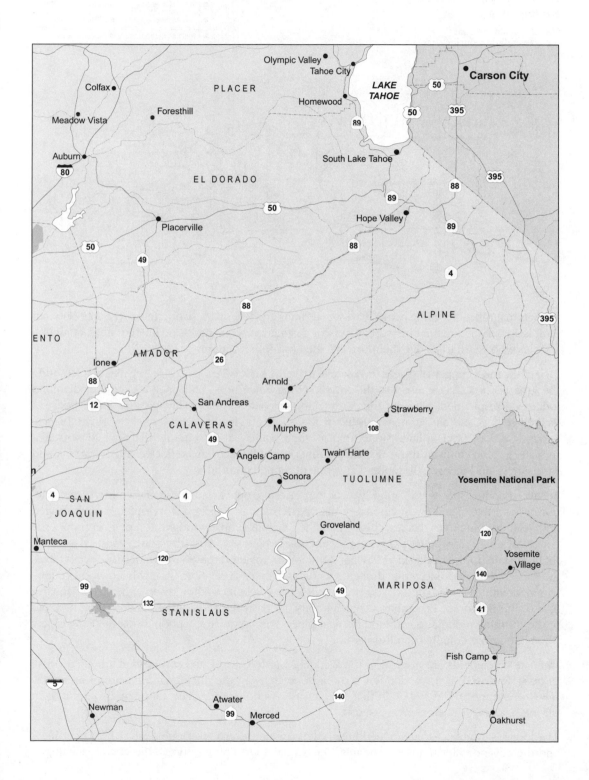

Tenaya Lodge at Yosemite

Mountain Resort

1122 Highway 41, Fish Camp
877/247-9249
www.tenayalodge.com
tenayaweddings@dncinc.com

- Rehearsal Dinners
- Ceremonies
- Wedding Receptions
- Corp. Events/Mtgs.
- Private Parties
- Accommodations

With its magnificent soaring peaks, backwoods trails and legendary panoramas, Yosemite National Park is a cherished natural treasure. It's also a destination wedding locale like no other, attracting couples who yearn to pledge their love enfolded by Mother Nature.

One of the most congenial places in Yosemite to tie the knot is Tenaya Lodge, the first hotel to bring the luxuries of a classic resort to this awe-inspiring wilderness. Built in 1990, the four-diamond lodge is a resplendent blend of the earthy and the contemporary. The spacious lobby boasts a vaulted ceiling, and natural materials like wood, stone and leather create a rich, warm ambiance. A cut-slate floor holds a huge stone fireplace, and whimsical mountain artifacts (a snowshoe, a miniature cabin) enliven the walls. Native American influences are reflected in the carpets and furnishings, and the overall impression is one of refined comfort.

Tenaya's banquet spaces also embody rustic elegance, and put Yosemite's scenic wonders on display during your fête. The newest ceremony site, the Terrace, is a second-story outdoor deck fringed with feathery pine trees that are close enough to touch. A simple wrought-iron pergola frames the couple against this verdant expanse and an endless blue sky. After the vows, guests descend a flight of stairs to the open-sided Pavilion for another angle on the lovely scenery. Cocktail tables are clustered on one side, while dinner is served beneath the Pavilion's honey-hued wood ceiling, trimmed with twinkle lights. If you prefer an indoor celebration, then reserve the 10,000-square-foot Grand Ballroom. Tasteful and contemporary, it boasts floor-to-ceiling windows that look out to the stunning mountains carpeted in sugar pines. For a smaller reception, book the Forest View Room, affording equally beautiful vistas.

Intimate ceremonies are magical in the Wedding Garden, a private lawn nestled among a copse of trees. Enclosed by a wooden fence and a stone archway, the quaint garden features an artistic metal sculpture of a leafy bough that doubles as a wedding arch. The staff can also arrange an off-the-beaten-path ceremony—just ask.

The lodge is a haven for green weddings—the banquet rooms are Double Silver LEED-certified, and the cuisine is local and sustainable. Tenaya has four dining options: the casual Jackalope's

Bar and Grill for fun after-parties; the family-friendly Timberloft Pizzeria; the Sierra Restaurant, which includes an outdoor patio with fire pit; and the upscale Embers for romantic fireside dining and exquisite organic seasonal menus. Any of these can be reserved for your rehearsal dinner, depending on your desired atmosphere.

Yosemite's rugged grandeur, made famous by photographer Ansel Adams' indelible images, will enhance your own wedding photos, too. Tenaya's knowledgeable event planning professionals can point out the best backdrops, as well as arrange activities for your guests. Nature lovers can feed their souls with spectacular sunsets and scintillating starscapes. The more adventurous might like to golf, bike, ice skate, ride horses or hike to a waterfall. Meanwhile, the bride will probably want to unwind at Ascent Spa. Bridal spa packages, along with 12 treatment rooms, steam rooms and a sauna, offer a wealth of pampering so that when it's time for the bride to make her grand entrance, she'll be as serene as the surrounding landscape.

Well-appointed accommodations include spa suites, but we recommend the newlyweds cuddle up in one of the secluded cottage-style rooms with fireplaces for quality alone-time. Think of Tenaya Lodge at Yosemite as "Happiness in the High Sierras!"

CEREMONY CAPACITY: The site holds 400 seated guests indoors and 350 seated outdoors.

EVENT/RECEPTION CAPACITY: The facility can accommodate 850 seated or 1,000 standing indoors and 275 seated or 350 standing outdoors.

MEETING CAPACITY: Meeting spaces hold up to 1,200 seated guests.

FEES & DEPOSITS: A $2,500 deposit is required to reserve your date and the balance is due 30 days prior to the event. Rental fees range $700–2,500 depending on the day and time of the event and the space rented. Meals range $50–75/person. Tax, alcohol and a 20% service charge are additional.

AVAILABILITY: Year-round, daily, 10am–midnight.

SERVICES/AMENITIES:
Catering: provided
Kitchen Facilities: n/a
Tables & Chairs: provided
Linens, Silver, etc.: provided
Restrooms: wheelchair accessible
Dance Floor: portable provided
Bride's Dressing Area: yes
Meeting Equipment: some provided
Other: grand piano, spa services, A/V equipment, event coordination

Parking: large lot, complimentary valet
Accommodations: 297 guest rooms, suites and cottages
Telephone: house phone
Outdoor Night Lighting: yes
Outdoor Cooking Facilities: none
Cleanup: provided
View: garden, landscaped grounds, panorama of forest and mountains

RESTRICTIONS:
Alcohol: provided or BYO wine or champagne with corkage fee
Smoking: designated areas only
Music: amplified OK with restrictions

Wheelchair Access: yes
Insurance: not required

This is important! Tell locations you're reading HERE COMES THE GUIDE and ask if our information is still current.

613

Monte Verde Inn

18841 Foresthill Road, Foresthill
530/888-8123
www.monteverdeinn.net
monteverde@foothill.net

Inn & Garden

● Rehearsal Dinners	● Corp. Events/Mtgs.
● Ceremonies	● Private Parties
● Wedding Receptions	● Accommodations

If you're looking for a very special place, it's in Foresthill, a small hamlet about 40 minutes northeast of Sacramento. Here you'll find the historic Monte Verde Inn, which is, in a word, wonderful.

The property was originally a gathering spot for Native Americans, and after gold was discovered in 1849, it became a toll station and respite for travelers. A private residence was built on the site in 1936, and today this stately Georgian-style manor is a gracious reminder of the past. A glassed-in sun porch covers the front of the manor house, and makes a sparkling backdrop for photos of the bridal party.

The landscaped grounds have the feel of an English country estate: A long entry drive, lined with flowering plum trees, draws you back in time. Manicured lawns, 100-year-old quince trees and a veritable tapestry of flowers (changed seasonally according to the whim of the owners) invite you to celebrate amid a garden of earthly delights. For ceremonies try the patios—they're surrounded by tall cedars that form an informal outdoor cathedral. At night, "fairy lights" and turn-of-the-century streetlights create a glittering halo around dancing couples.

Guests can also enjoy the inn's inviting interior, whose large open rooms feature an array of architectural embellishments and antiques. Spacious, newly refurbished guest rooms occupy the second floor. They're prettily decorated and have high ceilings, hardwood floors and Oriental carpets. The inn offers a wedding package that accommodates up to 16 overnight guests, and includes champagne and snacks, plus a full breakfast. For a nominal charge, you can invite other friends or family staying nearby to join you for this "morning after" get-together.

Your congenial proprietors, Douglas and Kelly Dalisa, have a very personal connection to the Monte Verde Inn. They fell in love with the beautiful inn and gardens and were actually married here. Someday, they thought, they would like to own and operate this place…. Years passed and at last their dream came true: In early 2006, they purchased the inn and have already made substantial upgrades. Thrilled by their new venture, Doug and Kelly go out of their way to ensure that your event will be all you imagined and more.

As innkeepers, your hosts are eminently qualified. Doug, a professional chef and graduate of the California Culinary Academy, personally prepares all the inn's meals using only the freshest, highest-quality ingredients. With his extensive knowledge of wines, he is more than happy to suggest perfect pairings for your bright California menu. The warm and friendly Kelly has a bachelor's degree in Hotel & Restaurant Management. She's worked in the catering industry for years, and was even an award-winning instructor in Culinary Arts and Hospitality Management! Now she lavishes her expertise upon the inn's lucky guests.

All these elements combined—the enchanting grounds, delicious cuisine, quaint accommodations, and enthusiastic service—create the Monte Verde Inn's successful mix of country charm and elegance.

CEREMONY CAPACITY: The patio accommodates 225 seated or standing guests; indoors, the inn holds 100.

EVENT/RECEPTION CAPACITY: Inside, 100 guests maximum; outdoors, up to 225 seated.

MEETING CAPACITY: The inn holds up to 100 seated guests.

FEES & DEPOSITS: A $1,000 deposit is required to secure your date. Rates start at $84/person, which includes rental of the Inn for 5 hours, rehearsal, all setups for ceremony and reception, color-coordinated, fresh floral centerpieces for all tables, wedding cake, hors d'oeuvres, full buffet and nonalcoholic beverages. Note that all food is prepared from fresh ingredients on the premises. Alcoholic beverages, tax and a 21% service charge are additional.

AVAILABILITY: Year-round, daily.

SERVICES/AMENITIES:

Catering: provided, no BYO
Kitchen Facilities: n/a
Tables & Chairs: provided
Linens, Silver, etc.: provided
Restrooms: wheelchair accessible
Dance Floor: patio
Bride's Dressing Area: yes; also CBA for bridal party
Meeting Equipment: BYO

Parking: 2 large lots
Accommodations: 6 guest rooms
Telephone: house phone
Outdoor Night Lighting: yes
Outdoor Cooking Facilities: no
Cleanup: provided
View: garden and forests
Other: event coordination included

RESTRICTIONS:

Alcohol: provided; wine, beer and champagne only
Smoking: outside only
Music: amplified OK

Wheelchair Access: outdoor access only, limited indoor access
Insurance: not required

Winchester Country Club

Private Golf Club

3030 Legends Drive, Meadow Vista
530/878-3015
www.winchestercountryclub.com
dcarrier@winchestercountryclub.com

- Rehearsal Dinners
- Ceremonies
- Wedding Receptions
- Corp. Events/Mtgs.
- Private Parties
- Accommodations

As you make the scenic drive towards Meadow Vista, less than an hour north of Sacramento, you're invigorated by the crisp, clean air of the Sierra Nevadas. Your destination, the Winchester Country Club, lies at the top of a majestic ascent lined with towering evergreens. This meticulously maintained venue boasts a rustic-meets-modern aesthetic, evoking both the homey warmth of the country and contemporary elegance.

The award-winning Clubhouse is situated on its own promontory, and at 32,000 square feet is spacious and impressive. Fashioned of dark wood and cut stone, its exterior resembles a forest lodge; yet, within you'll find a sophisticated lobby, decked in marble and intricate wood inlays that echo the forested environs. Constructed in 2004 with large events in mind, Winchester offers a view-filled ceremony site and three reception options. At the rear of the Clubhouse, a broad stone deck features a ramp that sweeps down onto a velvety lawn called the Ceremony Green. Guests seated in white chairs can easily follow your graceful descent as you make your grand entrance. They'll be even more captivated as they witness your exchange of vows against a breathtaking panorama of nature: thickets of pine trees and rolling hills silhouetted against a vast blue sky.

After the ceremony, explore the grounds for memorable photo ops while your guests retreat inside to the Clubhouse Lounge for the cocktail hour. Traditional wood paneling and a stately bar lend a sense of occasion, and the views—fit for a coffee-table book—put everyone at ease. The Lounge adjoins the beautiful Main Dining Room, where a wall of windows takes in the treelined fairways and the stunning Sierra Foothills. Patios on either side of the Dining Room invite guests to mingle in the mountain air and watch the stars as they fill the evening sky.

If you're looking to imprint your own style on a space, opt for the Upstairs Banquet Room. Here, coffered ceilings and a neutral palette will harmonize with whatever décor you choose. For an ethereal, romantic effect, simply drape tulle and fairy lights across the high ceilings. Lofty multi-paned windows look out across feathery treetops, adding to the banquet room's allure.

Prefer to party in the great outdoors? Celebrate on the Clubhouse Deck overlooking the picturesque Ceremony Green. It'll accommodate up to 400 of your nearest and dearest, and all or part of the deck can be elegantly tented, complete with chandeliers and canopy-style ceiling swags. A short path leads to a sheltered dance floor patio that's visible from the deck so guests can watch the dancing without leaving their seats.

Winchester is the kind of place that encourages you to indulge your wedding fantasies: As a grand finale, one adventurous couple led their surprised guests to the driving range and made their getaway by helicopter!

This facility's event professionals take pride in their wedding packages, which include separate dressing suites for the bride and groom, the ceremony site, and complimentary amenities like the cake cutting and champagne toast. The on-site coordinator will also gladly assist with vendor referrals and your day-of needs.

Truly a diamond in the rough, Winchester Country Club is a Gold Country bridal bonanza!

CEREMONY CAPACITY: The site holds 200 seated guests indoors, and 400 seated outdoors.

EVENT/RECEPTION & MEETING CAPACITY: The facility accomodates 150 seated or 200 standing indoors and 375 seated or 500 standing outdoors.

FEES & DEPOSITS: 25% of the estimated event cost is required to reserve your date, and the balance is due 10 days prior to the event. Customizable packages start at $102/person and include the facility fee, tax and service charge.

AVAILABILITY: Year-round, 8am–11pm, Mondays, Wednesdays–Sundays.

SERVICES/AMENITIES:

Catering: provided
Kitchen Facilities: n/a
Tables & Chairs: provided
Linens, Silver, etc.: provided
Restrooms: wheelchair accessible
Dance Floor: provided
Bride's Dressing Area: yes
Meeting Equipment: provided
Other: A/V equipment, event coordination

Parking: large lot
Accommodations: no guest rooms
Telephone: emergency use only
Outdoor Night Lighting: provided
Outdoor Cooking Facilities: BBQ CBA
Cleanup: provided
View: landscaped grounds; panorama of fairways, cityscape, mountains, and valley

RESTRICTIONS:

Alcohol: provided
Smoking: designated areas only
Music: OK with restrictions

Wheelchair Access: yes
Insurance: not required

Wedgewood Wedding & Banquet Center
at Sequoia Mansion

Historic Mansion

643 Bee Street, Placerville
866/966-3009

www.wedgewoodbanquet.com/sequoia-mansion
sales@wedgewoodbanquet.com

- Rehearsal Dinners
- Ceremonies
- Wedding Receptions
- Corp. Events/Mtgs.
- Private Parties
- Accommodations

This wonderful old Victorian mansion, formerly known as the Bee-Bennett House, can't help but catch the eye of even the most modern bride. From its perch atop a knoll, it immediately captures your attention with its multi-gabled roof, wraparound porch and beautiful period details. Built in 1853 (by a business tycoon whose fortune was partly amassed from the Pony Express), it's held court here ever since, mainly as a private residence. In 2002, it was restored and turned into a popular restaurant by current owners Nello and Danica Olivo, and today this outstanding example of "gold rush era" elegance continues to glitter in its latest incarnation—an utterly charming special event venue managed by Wedgewood Wedding & Banquet Centers.

Getting married at the mansion is like being the heroine of a historic novel. The experience begins in the upstairs Bridal Room, decorated in rich red velvet. As you look out the window, you can watch your guests take their seats near a lily pond beneath the shade of a majestic Sequoia. When you're ready, step outside and descend the graceful dual staircase to The Lawn, a sweeping grass and garden area where vows are exchanged. For an even more dramatic entrance, arrive at Sequoia's circular drive via a horse-drawn carriage.

Smaller ceremonies can also be held on The Patio, an intimate flagstone terrace around the side of the building that's planted with lush greenery and another towering Sequoia next to the altar. There's plenty of room to arrange tables for cocktails or dinner afterwards.

Several indoor ceremony and reception choices are available as well, starting with Victoria Hall, a chapel-like space when lit with stately candelabras, and the glass-enclosed, light-filled Veranda, which overlooks the lawn and evokes a bygone era.

The Dining Room, with its comfortable couches and an adjoining bar, is ideal for serving cocktails, but if you're a wine lover Sequoia offers a unique option: a wine tasting hosted in the stone cellar with selections from the owners' private NelloOlivo Vineyards.

The magnificent Empire Room is the perfect setting for a regal reception. Eight glass-and-brass Victorian-style chandeliers drop from the soaring, open-beamed cathedral ceiling, casting a warm glow over elegantly decked tables and a hardwood dance floor. Off to one side, there's a draped stage for a band, DJ or sweetheart table. If you like, you can use the adjoining Veranda for a buffet setup or additional seating.

Of course, photo ops abound throughout the mansion, with gilded mirrors, arched windows and a curved staircase serving as memorable backdrops. And whether it's adding your own personal touches to the décor or creating your menu, the staff will do its best to help you realize your dream wedding. Wedgwood Wedding & Banquet Centers offer all-inclusive packages that are customizable and affordable, ensuring that you'll enjoy both great service and exceptional value.

CEREMONY CAPACITY: The site holds 300 seated guests, indoors or outdoors.

EVENT/RECEPTION CAPACITY: The facility accommodates 300 seated or 600 standing indoors and 300 seated or standing guests outdoors.

MEETING CAPACITY: Meeting spaces hold up to 250 seated guests.

FEES & DEPOSITS: 25% of the estimated event total is required to reserve your date and the balance is due 10 days prior to the event. Meals range $24–31/person. Tax, alcohol and a 21% service charge are additional.

AVAILABILITY: Year-round, daily, 7am–midnight.

SERVICES/AMENITIES:

Catering: provided
Kitchen Facilities: n/a
Tables &Chairs: provided
Linens, Silver, etc.: provided
Restrooms: wheelchair accessible
Dance Floor: yes
Bride's & Groom's Dressing Areas: yes
Meeting Equipment: some provided, A/V equipment

Parking: large lot, limited
Accommodations: no guest rooms
Telephone: house phone
Outdoor Night Lighting: CBA
Outdoor Cooking Facilities: no
Cleanup: provided
View: forest
Other: in-house wedding cake, in-house florals, clergy on staff, event coordination

RESTRICTIONS:

Alcohol: provided
Smoking: outdoors only
Music: acoustic only

Wheelchair Access: yes
Insurance: not required

Overwhelmed? Use the search criteria on www.HereComesTheGuide.com to narrow down your choices.

619

Tahoe Area

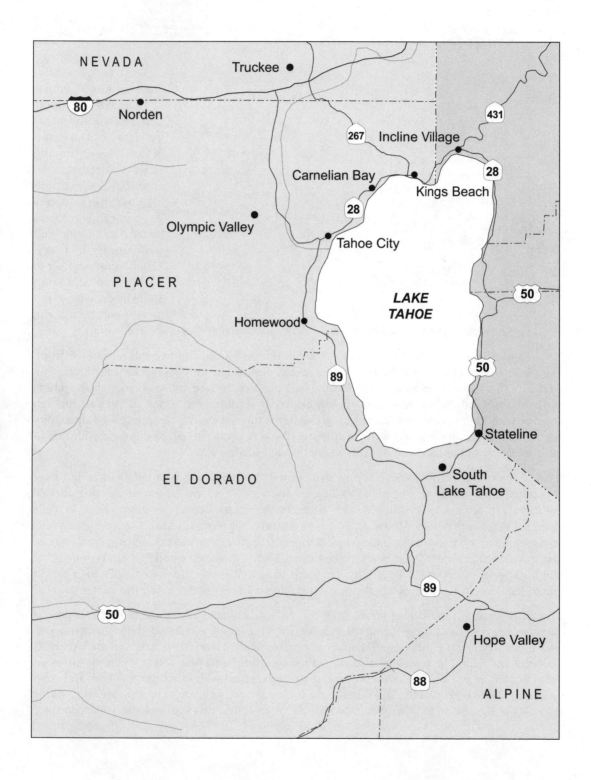

Big Water Grille

Lakeview Restaurant

341 Ski Way, Incline Village
775/833-0606

www.bigwatergrille.com
john@bigwatergrille.com

● Rehearsal Dinners		● Corp. Events/Mtgs.	
● Ceremonies		● Private Parties	
● Wedding Receptions		Accommodations	

Catching just a glimpse of Lake Tahoe, with its brilliant color and amazing clarity, can take your breath away. But big views of Big Blue, as the country's only alpine lake is affectionately known, can sometimes be hard to find for your wedding day festivities. That is, until you get to Big Water Grille, a North Shore mecca where your nearest and dearest can revel for hours in what are arguably the area's most spectacular and unobstructed vistas.

Located just a quarter mile from Diamond Peak in Incline Village and two miles from the Hyatt, Big Water Grille masterfully balances being a special destination with being a favorite dining spot of the locals. Clad in river rock, the residential building is on a slope just steep enough and jutting just far enough off the shoreline that you feel like you're getting away from it all. A clean, modern interior with high ceilings and recessed lighting gives the restaurant's three levels an open, airy feel. The striking artwork by top local artists is fabulous, but it's tough to compete with that irresistible view of the lake, visible everywhere through soaring glass walls.

There's enormous flexibility in planning how to use the facility for your celebration, but most wedding parties are drawn first to the inviting outside deck. Here, you can exchange vows, framed by majestic pines as the sparkling water is tinted by the sunset, or you can enjoy cocktails while drinking in nature's beauty. Afterwards, your guests can easily move inside through the glass doors to the lounge-style Bar Area for butler-passed appetizers and the restaurant's signature seafood raw bar, a spectacular array of the week's freshest catch. With its polished wood floor and comfy sofas, this area provides a great clubby atmosphere for dancing, and its massive stone fireplace is a perfect photo backdrop for cutting your cake or even staging your ceremony during the winter months.

Dinner is served in the Dining Room, built on two levels to take advantage of that ever-present view, which now faces some strong competition from the highly acclaimed, mouth-watering presentations from their culinary staff. Dishes emphasize fresh seasonal produce, and are extremely flavorful and light. The restaurant also offers their signature Santa Maria-style, open-pit barbecue, featuring tri-tip and chicken cooked over red oak and served with salad, garlic bread, and other sides. The "BWG" (Big Water Grille) Barbecue is mobile, too, so if you're hosting an event within 30 miles of the restaurant, they can cook their fabulous comfort food to order at your location.

To complement your meal, Big Water Grille's wine list includes a variety of wines from around the world in a range of prices. In fact, if you're planning an intimate reception or rehearsal dinner, wine lovers in your party will appreciate the Wine Cellar, a sophisticated private setting separate from the Main Dining Room.

And since this is Nevada, where there are no restrictions on when to end your music or have last call, if you buy out the restaurant they will let you set your own hours so you can start later in summer to catch the sunset and then party the night away.

CEREMONY CAPACITY: The restaurant holds 100 standing guests indoors in front of the fireplace and 30 seated or 100 standing outdoors.

EVENT/RECEPTION CAPACITY: The restaurant accommodates 120 seated or 135 standing indoors and 30 seated or standing outdoors on the deck.

MEETING CAPACITY: Meeting spaces hold 100 seated guests.

FEES & DEPOSITS: 50% of the food and beverage minimum is required to reserve your date. The balance is due at the end of the event. Rental fees range $0–750 depending on your event needs. Meals range $48–100/person. Tax, alcohol and a 20% service charge are additional.

AVAILABILITY: Year-round, daily, anytime. Call for details.

SERVICES/AMENITIES:

Catering: provided
Kitchen Facilities: n/a
Tables & Chairs: provided
Linens, Silver, etc.: provided
Restrooms: wheelchair accessible
Dance Floor: provided
Bride's Dressing Rooms: CBA
Meeting Equipment: some provided

Parking: large lot
Accommodations: no guest rooms
Telephone: emergency use only
Outdoor Night Lighting: provided
Outdoor Cooking Facilities: no
Cleanup: provided
View: panorama of Lake Tahoe and mountains
Other: event coordination

RESTRICTIONS:

Alcohol: provided
Smoking: not allowed
Music: amplified OK

Wheelchair Access: yes
Insurance: not required

North Tahoe Event Center

8318 North Lake Boulevard, Kings Beach

530/546-7249

www.northtahoeevents.com
sales@northtahoeevents.com

Lakeside Event Center

- Rehearsal Dinners
- Ceremonies
- Wedding Receptions
- Corp. Events/Mtgs.
- Private Parties
- Accommodations

The North Tahoe Event Center, located in an enviable spot on the lake's less-crowded North Shore, is a modern facility with nothing between it and the deep blue waters of the lake except a wide stretch of pristine beach. Both large and small events are welcome here.

During those glorious months from late spring to early fall, have your entire celebration on the center's expansive Lakefront Terrace, right next to the sand. The serene, azure lake and jagged mountain silhouettes form a stunning backdrop, highlighting the importance of the moment. No matter where you are, gentle breezes flow off the water, and you feel like a part of the breathtaking panorama all around you. After, why not stroll along the shore with your new spouse, wriggle your toes in the sand, and let your photographer capture candid moments for you to look back on in the years to come? For your reception, continue to embrace the great outdoors, and dine on the spacious terrace, a premium spot to savor a romantic sunset or watch as the moon rises above the Eastern Sierras, casting a golden shimmer upon the lake.

The center also has several options for indoor gatherings year round. The contemporary Lakeview Suite overlooks the deck through floor-to-ceiling windows, and the neutral décor doesn't distract from the mesmerizing view of the lake and surrounding peaks dusted with snow. The 4,800-square-foot Timberline Room, with its hardwood stage and audiovisual equipment, is perfect for an elaborate gala. Other nice features include a large bride's room, roomy commercial kitchen and in-house catering. You're also free to bring your own alcohol, and use your own caterer.

Both you and your guests will love the chance to experience Tahoe's year-round recreation—skiing, fishing, golf and hiking—as well as less strenuous but equally satisfying activities like fine dining, shopping and visiting art galleries.

With its prime location, flexibility, and glorious view, the North Tahoe Event Center has developed quite a following for those who wish to celebrate in one of the country's most desirable destinations.

CEREMONY CAPACITY: Several rooms accommodate up to 350 seated or standing guests indoors. The Lakefront Terrace holds 350 seated or standing outdoors.

EVENT/RECEPTION CAPACITY: Various rooms hold up to 350 seated or 500 standing guests indoors. The Lakefront Terrace can seat 250 and accommodate 350 standing guests outdoors.

FEES & DEPOSITS: A 50% deposit is required to confirm your date. The balance is due 2 weeks prior to the event. Rental fees range $1,100–9,000 depending on guest count and space reserved. If you bring your own caterer, there is an extra $3–7/person fee. Use of the in-house caterer requires a deposit (applied to the final catering invoice) to retain those services. In-house catering starts at $30/person. Tax, alcohol and service charges are additional.

AVAILABILITY: Year-round, daily, 9am–2am.

SERVICES/AMENITIES:

Catering: provided or BYO
Kitchen Facilities: commercial
Tables & Chairs: provided
Linens, Silver, etc.: place settings and glassware provided with in-house caterer
Restrooms: wheelchair accessible
Dance Floor: portable provided
Bride's Dressing Area: yes (large or small available)
Meeting Equipment: large screens, LCD projectors, easels, A/V, wi-fi, conference calls, high speed internet available

Parking: large lot, extra fee
Accommodations: available nearby
Telephone: house phones
Outdoor Night Lighting: yes
Outdoor Cooking Facilities: BBQ grill
Cleanup: provided
View: Lake Tahoe and Sierras
Other: wedding and event coordination, vendor referral list available

RESTRICTIONS:

Alcohol: provided or BYO
Smoking: designated areas
Music: amplified OK indoors

Wheelchair Access: yes
Insurance: required
Other: no rice, confetti or artificial flower petals

Sugar Bowl Resort

Sugar Bowl Ski Area, Norden
530/426-6769
www.sugarbowl.com
mshrewsbury@sugarbowl.com

Tahoe Area Ski Resort

- Rehearsal Dinners
- Ceremonies
- Wedding Receptions
- Corp. Events/Mtgs.
- Private Parties
- Accommodations

Sugar Bowl Resort leads a double life. In the winter, thousands of skiers descend upon its well-groomed slopes, anxious to make the most of the ample snowfall. In summer, however, visitors discover a quiet, awe-inspiring, high-alpine resort that's custom-made for an exclusive mountain wedding, retreat or family reunion.

Built in 1939 at the base of Mt. Disney, the original Lodge at Sugar Bowl is still the resort's focal point and the site of most special events. When you host your celebration here, you have exclusive use of the entire venue, including bar, lounge, dining room, decks and lawn. You also get the 27 guest rooms, which are quite cozy—especially the spacious suite where the newlyweds usually spend their wedding night.

The Lodge's décor is steeped in Old Tahoe charm with a European flair. A large stone fireplace and oak Craftsman-style furniture welcome you into the lounge, where creamy white board-and-batten walls are covered with vintage prints depicting Donner Summit's rich history and storied past. Most rooms have a wall of windows overlooking scenic Mt. Disney.

While the lounge and dining room are often used for rehearsal dinners and indoor receptions, the Lodge's expansive wooden deck is the standout site. Facing majestic mountains and a flower-studded hillside, it offers plenty of space for dining and dancing. It can also be partially covered with a white canopy or set with umbrella-shaded tables. Below the deck is a manicured lawn bordered by tall trees, a custom-built fire pit ringed by Adirondack chairs, and a gently flowing stream. It's a lovely spot for exchanging vows and taking photos.

The secluded Lake Mary Cabin offers a different but equally stunning setting. Built at the water's edge, the peaked cabin has its own generous deck facing a quintessential alpine vista of the sparkling lake and Mt. Disney. This is a wonderful place for a Friday night rehearsal dinner, an intimate ceremony on the adjacent lawn, or a relaxing afternoon spent on the private beach.

If you want to get married at Sugar Bowl but don't plan to stay over, reserve the Judah Day Lodge, a large, contemporary venue featuring wraparound windows that provide mountain views from every table. You can tie the knot outside on the vast brick patio that runs along the front of the room, with the ever-present mountains as a backdrop.

And don't miss the opportunity to invite your guests to the top of Mt. Disney for champagne and appetizers. As family and friends gather on the deck of the mountaintop station and take in the spectacular panoramas all around, they'll be thanking you for bringing them to such a magical place.

It's true, weddings simply shine here. Sugar Bowl's natural assets, Old Tahoe charm and impeccable service impress everyone who visits, no matter what time of year.

CEREMONY, EVENT/RECEPTION & MEETING CAPACITY: The Lodge at Sugar Bowl can accommodate up to 300 guests outdoors and 150 guests indoors, the Judah Lodge up to 400 guests indoors or outdoors, and the Village Hall up to 110–125 guests, indoors only. The Lake Mary venue holds up to 100 guests outdoors.

FEES & DEPOSITS: For weddings, a $1,000 nonrefundable deposit is required when the event is booked. Half of the estimated food and beverage cost is due 30 days prior to the event; the balance is payable at the event's conclusion. Catering costs start at $42/person. Tax and an 18% service charge are additional.

AVAILABILITY: June through October.

SERVICES/AMENITIES:

Catering: provided, no BYO
Kitchen Facilities: fully equipped
Tables & Chairs: provided, extra fee
Linens, Silver, etc.: provided, extra fee
Restrooms: wheelchair access limited
Dance Floor: deck or lounge
Bride's Dressing Area: yes
Meeting Equipment: TVs and VCRs
Other: event coordination and referrals

Parking: ample
Accommodations: 27 guest rooms for Lodge at Sugar Bowl functions only
Telephone: pay phone
Outdoor Night Lighting: limited
Outdoor Cooking Facilities: BBQs, no BYO
Cleanup: provided
View: mountain peaks

RESTRICTIONS:

Alcohol: provided
Smoking: designated areas
Music: amplified OK

Wheelchair Access: limited
Insurance: not required

The professionals in the back of this book are the best in the business. How do we know? Read page 637.

627

PlumpJack Squaw Valley Inn

1920 Squaw Valley Road, Olympic Valley
800/323-7666, 530/583-4158
www.plumpjacksquawvalleyinn.com
kedmundson@plumpjack.com

Inn & Event Facility

- Rehearsal Dinners
- Ceremonies
- Wedding Receptions
- Corp. Events/Mtgs.
- Private Parties
- Accommodations

Tucked in a quiet valley at the base of the majestic Sierra Nevada Mountains is a world-class hotel with all the charm of a mountain lodge. The PlumpJack Squaw Valley Inn boasts a truly original look—one you won't find anywhere else in Tahoe. The Lobby and guest rooms are done in muted earth tones and sumptuous fabrics, and display an exceptional melding of decorative elements: innovative metal sculpture, eye-catching furnishings and striking light fixtures that combine whimsy with copper, glass and chrome.

The ambiance of the main building continues through the adjacent event facility. Here a split-level ballroom features huge natural wood beams that crisscross beneath a high peaked ceiling, giving the entire space the feeling of an elegant cabin in the woods. Natural light, rich hues on the walls, and blond wood wainscoting create an understated sophistication. The highlight of the ballroom is the floor-to-ceiling views: snow-dusted mountains that seem close enough to touch, and a garden landscape bursting with springtime colors. The lower level holds the dining tables, while the upper level is often used for dancing or cake cutting. If you're planning an intimate get-together, the ballroom can be divided into four sections by luxurious tapestry panels.

During the warmer months, as the snow melts and the wildflowers and waterfalls regain their glory, the inn becomes a haven for outdoor celebrations, held on the sun-splashed pool patio. Bordered by the event facility, the PlumpJack Cafe, and lofty aspens and pines, the patio has the rustic appeal of a village courtyard. Wedding ceremonies are staged against the dramatic backdrop of trees, rugged peaks and open sky. After the vows, have a cocktail hour and reception next to the pool on the patio's raised level. Adjacent to the pool deck is a more secluded site for intimate ceremonies: Couples can wed atop a cut-stone deck on the bank of Squaw Creek, where pine trees, boulders and a mountain slope create a natural milieu.

Wherever you hold your event at the inn, it will be handled by a professional staff, known for their dedication and attention to detail. All event catering is provided exclusively by the inn's renowned restaurant, the PlumpJack Cafe. Their menu focuses on innovative California cuisine, incorporating locally sourced, organic and seasonal ingredients. The Cafe also boasts an extensive wine list, which has received Wine Spectator's Award of Excellence for the past five years.

Your destination wedding at the inn treats your guests to luxuriously appointed accommodations, complete with complimentary gourmet breakfast buffet. And the inn makes a perfect base camp for exploring the breathtaking surroundings, including a jewel of a lake just a few minutes away. Recreational activities abound—biking, hiking, fishing and more.

PlumpJack's designers have conceived something unique: a mountain inn, banquet facility and restaurant with both the avant-garde distinction of a cosmopolitan city and the fresh simplicity of a mountain retreat. Whether you dream of a winter wonderland wedding or exchanging vows in the pine scented summer air, PlumpJack Squaw Valley Inn lets you celebrate in the lap of nature any time of year.

CEREMONY CAPACITY: Each of the two banquet rooms accommodate 200 seated or 400 standing guests; the pool deck holds 250 guests, the Creekside room holds 200.

EVENT/RECEPTION CAPACITY: The site holds 220 seated guests indoors and 300 seated outdoors.

MEETING CAPACITY: Each conference room holds 300 seated theater-style or 200 conference-style.

FEES & DEPOSITS: For weddings and special events, a deposit is required to reserve your date. Site fees start at $2,000 and vary depending on time of year. Catering fees for weddings and special events start at $55/person for dinners or buffets. Tax, alcohol and a 20% service charge are additional.

AVAILABILITY: Year-round, daily.

SERVICES/AMENITIES:

Catering: provided
Kitchen Facilities: n/a
Tables & Chairs: provided
Linens, Silver, etc.: provided
Restrooms: wheelchair accessible
Dance Floor: provided
Bride's Dressing Area: Penthouse Suite
Meeting Equipment: fully equipped

Parking: large lot, complimentary
Accommodations: 48 guest rooms, 8 suites including penthouse
Outdoor Night Lighting: no
Outdoor Cooking Facilities: n/a
Cleanup: provided
View: Sierra Nevada Mountains
Other: event coordination; activities such as tram rides, hikes, horsebackriding, skiing, sledding, golf, mountain biking, etc.

RESTRICTIONS:

Alcohol: provided, corkage $25/750 ml bottle or $50/magnum
Smoking: outdoors only
Music: amplified OK

Wheelchair Access: yes
Insurance: not required
Other: no rice or balloon releases

Resort at Squaw Creek

Ski Resort

400 Squaw Creek Road, Olympic Valley
530/583-6300
www.squawcreek.com
info@squawcreek.com

- Rehearsal Dinners
- Ceremonies
- Wedding Receptions
- Corp. Events/Mtgs.
- Private Parties
- Accommodations

Spectacular Squaw Valley is a land with two faces: Its winter countenance is pristine white and icy cool, with mountain peaks, pine trees and chalets half-hidden beneath a blanket of snow; the milder months are a blush of wildflowers and sunlit meadows, of balmy star-speckled nights and emerald mountain slopes. One of the best places to savor the Valley's dual personality is the Resort at Squaw Creek, 195 hillside acres of relaxation, indulgence and breathtaking beauty.

Decked out in glass, wood and granite, the resort's interior spaces are designed to be lived in, not just walked through. Step into the spacious lobby practically any time of day, and you'll find guests making themselves at home in the cozy seating areas. Some are curled up with a book in front of the large stone fireplace, others are chatting away, and a few are soaking up the mountain view through a wall of glass.

Outdoor areas are equally welcoming, whether you're taking a siesta in a patio lounge chair, or hosting a special event for hundreds of guests. From spring to fall, wedding ceremonies and receptions simply belong on the resort's multilevel terraces. Most couples get married on the Spa Deck, where they exchange vows against a gorgeous backdrop of tree-covered mountains. Large weddings are held at the Pavilion. Perched above the green valley floor, this sunny patio seems to embrace nature, reaching beyond its perimeter of colorful blooms and lacy greenery out towards the majestic High Sierras. A magnificent 250-foot waterfall cascades alongside the Pavilion and into a stream that ripples through a water garden just below.

There are plenty of indoor options, too. The Alpine and Grand Sierra Ballrooms host larger groups, and the latter comes with a prefunction space that's great for a cocktail hour. For a more rustic ambiance, consider holding your reception in the view-filled Cascades Restaurant, with its charming Tahoe-inspired furnishings. Take over one or more of its stylish dining areas, or reserve the striking private dining room in Six Peaks Grille for your rehearsal dinner. If you'd like to host an indoor/outdoor reception, have it in Ristorante Montagna, an elegant California-Italian eatery whose expansive dining room adjoins an outdoor deck. Yes, it is a relief to know that whatever your event weekend entails, from the rehearsal dinner through the ceremony, reception and post-wedding brunch, this resort offers a diverse selection of venues.

No matter how much fun everyone is having, you have to sleep sometime, and the resort's 365 well-appointed accommodations include suites with kitchens, fireplaces and flat screen TVs.

When they're not relaxing in their suites, your guests will find quite a few things to do here. Besides the world-class spa and fitness center, boutique promenade, distinctive restaurants and myriad of banquet options, there are activities for every season. Summer choices include a challenging championship golf course, tennis, biking and hiking. In winter you can downhill or cross-country ski (they have ski-in/ski-out access), snowshoe, ice skate, and take a sleigh or dogsled ride. Heated swimming pools with Jacuzzis and free shuttle service to Squaw Valley are available year-round. When we visited, however, we just wanted to unwind. As we walked around the grounds, breathing in the fresh, delicately pine-scented air, we decided this is one destination resort we wouldn't mind revisiting.

CEREMONY CAPACITY: The Spa Deck holds 200 guests theater style or 160 theater style with a cocktail reception; the Pavilion holds up to 500 seated theater style.

EVENT/RECEPTION CAPACITY: The Ballrooms accommodate 200–600 seated or 700 standing guests; Cascades Restaurant holds up to 160 seated guests.

MEETING CAPACITY: Event spaces accommodate 20–600 seated guests.

FEES & DEPOSITS: 25% of the estimated food and beverage total and facility fees is required to reserve your date. An additional 25% is due 6 months prior to the event. The balance is due 3 working days prior. Rental fees start at $2,000, and vary depending on the day of the week, time of day and space rented. Packages start at $115/person. A 22% service charge and tax are additional.

AVAILABILITY: Year-round, daily, flexible hours between 6am–2am.

SERVICES/AMENITIES:

Catering: provided
Kitchen Facilities: n/a
Tables & Chairs: provided
Linens, Silver, etc.: provided
Restrooms: wheelchair accessible
Dance Floor: provided
Bride's & Groom's Dressing Areas: CBA
Meeting Equipment: provided, extra fee may be required

Parking: large lots; valet available, extra fee
Accommodations: 365 guest rooms & suites
Telephone: house and office phones
Outdoor Night Lighting: yes
Outdoor Cooking Facilities: BBQ CBA
Cleanup: provided
View: mountains, forest, fairways, meadow
Other: children's program, spa services, heated swimming pool, Jacuzzis, bike rentals, golf, tennis courts, guided hiking

RESTRICTIONS:

Alcohol: provided, or BYO with corkage fee
Smoking: outside only
Music: amplified OK with restrictions

Wheelchair Access: yes
Insurance: recommended

Lake Tahoe Golf Course

Golf Course & Clubhouse

2500 Emerald Bay Road, South Lake Tahoe
530/577-0788 x3
www.countryclubreceptions.com
eventdirector@laketahoegc.com

- ● Rehearsal Dinners
- ● Ceremonies
- ● Wedding Receptions
- ● Corp. Events/Mtgs.
- ● Private Parties
- Accommodations

Your family and friends will be thrilled to come to your destination wedding—especially if you pick a compelling location like South Lake Tahoe. This High Sierra resort area, known for its stunning scenery, boasts a range of attractions that will appeal to everyone on your list. And if you host your celebration at Lake Tahoe Golf Course, you'll be able to enjoy the experience along with them: The venue's accommodating staff will handle all the details so that you can take a deep breath of alpine air and relax.

The setting here is spectacular. Located on a verdant meadow within a California state park, this 18-hole golf course and clubhouse is spread out beside the Truckee River, offering an intriguing mix of landscaped grounds surrounded by natural woods. The clubhouse, distinguished by a river rock base and steep pitched roof, has the flavor of a mountain lodge with the iconic Mt. Tallac visible behind it.

On the other side of the building lie the manicured greens and far-reaching vistas of the Sierra landscape that form an amazing backdrop for your ceremony. Guests seated on the 10th tee watch you walk down the aisle towards a beautiful tableau: a wrought-iron arch festooned with flowers in front of twin peaks joined together in the distance. And it doesn't matter what time of year you schedule your wedding—this vista is gorgeous in every season, whether it's showcasing pale alpine flowers, deep rich greens, a blaze of red and gold, or the shimmer of snowcaps.

There's no shortage of great spots for photos, and you may want to start by posing on the long wooden bridge that spans the river or at the edge of the boulder-strewn Truckee itself. Meanwhile, your guests can mingle over cocktails and hors d'oeuvres at the Reception Tent adjacent to the clubhouse. Light and airy with a high, peaked ceiling and dropdown chandelier, its windowed canvas walls let everyone drink in the view; in warm weather the walls can be tied back to completely open the tent up to the outdoors. The wraparound Garden Terrace, planted with flowers, makes a nice al fresco alternative for cocktails, with dinner and dancing inside the tent. (Larger groups often party at a more expansive tent on the 10th fairway, with equally terrific views and a clear ceiling for celebrating under the starry night sky.) Either of the tents can also be used in combination with the clubhouse Dining Room.

If the weather is inclement or the couple prefers an indoor wedding, both the ceremony and reception may be held in the Dining Room. It features a cathedral ceiling, exposed wood beams and high dormer windows, as well as its own bar. The glow from forged iron wall sconces gives the space a sense of warmth, while a wall of windows frames the beauty outside.

From start to finish, you're in good hands here with an on-site wedding planner who will help you choreograph your event, customize your menu, match you with the local vendors who best suit your needs, and do it all within your budget. Plus, they can arrange lodging for your guests and suggest nearby activities from boating on the crystalline lake to gambling and shows at nearby casinos.

CEREMONY CAPACITY: The site holds 150 seated indoors and 300 seated outdoors.

EVENT/RECEPTION CAPACITY: The facility accommodates 100 seated or standing indoors and 100 seated or 200 standing guests outdoors.

MEETING CAPACITY: Meeting rooms seat up to 200 guests.

FEES & DEPOSITS: 25% of the total event cost (nonrefundable) is required to reserve your date and the balance is due 14 days prior to the event. Rental fees range $500–2,500 depending on the day and time of the event. Meals start at $40/person. Tax, alcohol and a 20% service charge are additional. Packages are available that include DJ, minister, florals, cake, photobooth and photographer.

AVAILABILITY: Year-round, daily.

SERVICES/AMENITIES:

Catering: provided
Kitchen Facilities: n/a
Tables & Chairs: some provided
Linens, Silver, etc.: provided
Restrooms: wheelchair accessible
Dance Floor: portable provided
Bride's Dressing Area: CBA
Meeting Equipment: some provided
Other: on-site wedding cake

Parking: large lot
Accommodations: no guest rooms
Telephone: guest phone
Outdoor Night Lighting: provided
Outdoor Cooking Facilities: BBQ on site
Cleanup: provided
View: fairways, river; panorama of mountains, canyon, forest

RESTRICTIONS:

Alcohol: provided
Smoking: designated areas only
Music: amplified OK

Wheelchair Access: yes
Insurance: not required

Want to know WHAT TO ASK a potential location or vendor? Check out our Questions to Ask starting on page 17.

Part Two: Event Services

All our Event Services have been

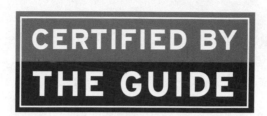

1. ### We only represent the best professionals in the biz.

The professionals featured in our Service Directory aren't plucked from the *Yellow Pages* or a random Google search. They're a carefully selected group of vendors who we'd recommend to our friends and business associates without hesitation.

2. ### Because we're picky, you don't have to worry about who to hire for your event.

We've thoroughly checked the professional track record of our advertisers so you can be as confident about their abilities as we are. The companies we highlight have passed our reference check with flying colors, and we're honored to represent each of them. They've all been *Certified By The Guide*.

3. ### Getting into Here Comes The Guide is tough.

The service providers we represent are topnotch. We put each one through a rigorous reference check, which involves interviewing up to 30 other event professionals and brides. We call every single reference and ask about the professionalism, technical competency and service orientation of the advertiser in question.

When you invest 7–10 hours talking to that many brides and professionals, you get a crystal clear picture of who's doing a superb job and who isn't. Those candidates who received consistent, rave reviews made it into *The Guide*. Those who didn't were (nicely) turned down.

Working With Professionals

Hiring a Caterer: Get References and Look for Professionalism

If you're selecting your own caterer, don't just pick one at random. Get references from friends and acquaintances or, better yet, call the caterers listed in the *Here Comes The Guide* Service Directory. We've thoroughly screened these companies and can assure you that they're in the top 5% of the industry in terms of quality and service. We keep all of their references on file, so you can call us and ask questions about them.

Every caterer is different. Some offer only preset menus while others will help you create your own. Menus and prices vary enormously, so know what you want and what you can spend. After you've talked to several caterers and have decided which ones to seriously consider, get references for each one and call them. Ask not only about the quality of the food, but about the ease of working with a given caterer. You'll want to know if the caterer is professional—fully prepared and equipped, punctual and organized. You may also want to know if the caterer is licensed, prepares food in a kitchen approved by the Department of Health, or carries workmen's compensation and liability insurance. Although this level of inquiry may seem unnecessary, responses to these questions will give you a more complete picture of how a caterer runs his or her business, and will help you determine which caterer is best suited for your event.

Facility Requirements for Caterers

Facilities often have specific requirements regarding caterers—they may have to be licensed and bonded, out by 11pm or fastidiously clean. Before you hire a caterer, make sure that he or she is compatible with your site. In fact, even if the facility does not require it, it's a good idea to have your caterer visit the place in advance to become familiar with any special circumstances or problems that might come up. You'll notice throughout *Here Comes The Guide* the words "provided" or "select from list" after the word *Catering*. Sites that have an exclusive caterer or only permit you to select from a preferred list do so because each wants to eliminate most of the risks involved in having a caterer on the premises who is not accustomed to working in that environment. Exclusive or preferred caterers have achieved their exalted status because they either provide consistently good services or they won the catering contract when it went out to bid. Whether you're working with one of your facility's choices or your own, make sure that your contract includes everything you have agreed on before you sign it.

Working with an Event Planner or Wedding Coordinator

Opting to hire a professional planner may be a wise choice. A good consultant will ask all the right questions, determine exactly what you need, and take care of as much or as little of your affair as you want. If you'd like to feel like a guest at your own event, have the consultant manage everything, including orchestrating the day of the event. If you only want some advice and structure, hire a planner on a meeting-by-meeting basis.

Most of the principles used in selecting a caterer apply to hiring an event coordinator. Try to get suggestions from friends or facilities, follow up on references the consultants give you, compare service fees and make sure you and the consultant are compatible. The range of professionalism and experience varies greatly, so it really is to your advantage to investigate each consultant's track record. You can save a lot of time by starting with the coordinators featured in *Here Comes The Guide*.

Again, once you've found someone who can accommodate you, get everything in writing so that there won't be any misunderstandings down the road. Although engaging a professional to "manage" your event can be a godsend, it can also be problematic if you turn the entire decision-making process over to them. Don't forget that it's your party, and no one else should decide what's right for you.

For a list of questions to ask potential wedding venues and vendors, go to page 17 in this book. You can also find them on HereComesTheGuide.com.

Event Services by Category

Marriage Preparation Workshop

Photo Booths

Photographers

Videographers

MELONS CATERING & EVENTS

WEDDINGS · CORPORATE · PRIVATE

3963 CALLAN BOULEVARD, SOUTH SAN FRANCISCO, CA 94080
650.583.1756 ph.
650.583.0329 f.
WWW.MELONSCATERING.COM

Coordinators

maxine andrew   designs · orchestrates · inspires · creates · simplifies

weddings are amazing when Maxine coordinates the details...**instead of you** *You!*

800.361.6809   ·   insteadofyou.com

Strawberry Fields DJs take pride in making your celebration sparkle. From Sinatra to Bublé to the Black Eyed Peas, we'll play the music YOU want to hear and get the dance floor moving. Your guests won't want to go home!

CLASS · QUALITY · COMMITMENT

Established 1982 · Owner/DJ: Don Fitzsimmons

www.strawberrydj.com · bookings@strawberrydj.com · (800) 499-3460

Our Fun, Professional DJs

Floral & Event Designers

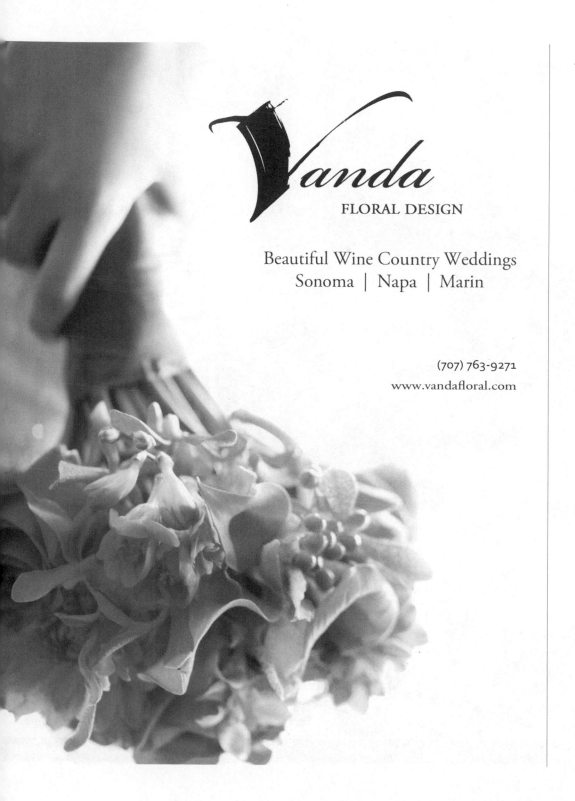

Vanda
FLORAL DESIGN

Beautiful Wine Country Weddings
Sonoma | Napa | Marin

(707) 763-9271
www.vandafloral.com

Arlene Boyle   415.771.7508   violettaflowers.com   violetta05@aol.com abcdefghijklmnopqrstuvwxyzabcdefgh ·

· marriage vows · moving cards · stationery · monograms · thank yous ·

· invitation design · envelopes · placecards · announcements · menus ·

Calligraphy

english · עברית

Adrienne D. Keats
(415) 956·5006
adriennekeats@yahoo.com

abcdefghijklmnopqrstuvwxyzabcdefghijklmnopqrstuvw

Marriage Preparation Workshop

"This workshop was one of the best time and money investments we've made for our relationship...it should be on every couple's wedding to-do list." JULIE & PAUL

Marriage Prep 101

"It was amazing to see how certain assumptions that we had about each other's feelings and perceptions got totally turned on their head, just by learning to communicate in a new way." VICTORIA & CHRIS

Marriage Prep 101 is an award-winning workshop for engaged, seriously dating and newlywed couples. Taught by Drs. Patrick and Michelle Gannon—husband-and-wife psychologists/relationship experts—the class will help you:

- Focus on the strengths of your relationship.
- Learn positive communication.
- Develop conflict resolution and intimacy enhancement skills.
- Lay the foundation for a successful, satisfying marriage.

The Gannons have conducted over 90 workshops for more than 1400 couples. They welcome people of all backgrounds, ages and faiths.

Featured on the CBS Early Show *and* Evening Magazine TV, *as well as in the* SF Chronicle, Huffington Post, Time, *and many more publications. Great reviews on* Yelp.com.

Drs. Michelle & Patrick Gannon

"The Gannons' sense of humor, honesty, and experiences from fifteen years of marriage made it seem like we were learning from good friends." KRISTA & JEREMY

MarriagePrep101.com · drmichellegannon@gmail.com · 415.905.8830
Facebook.com/MarriagePrep101 · Twitter.com/DrMichellexo

PHOTO BOOTHS DESIGNED FOR WEDDINGS

Classic Photo Booths
Affordable Portable Photo Booths
Custom Backdrops
Designer Graphics
And so much more...

San Francisco PHOTO BOOTH.com

a division of denon & doyle entertainment

800.944.9585
SanFranciscoPhotoBooth.com

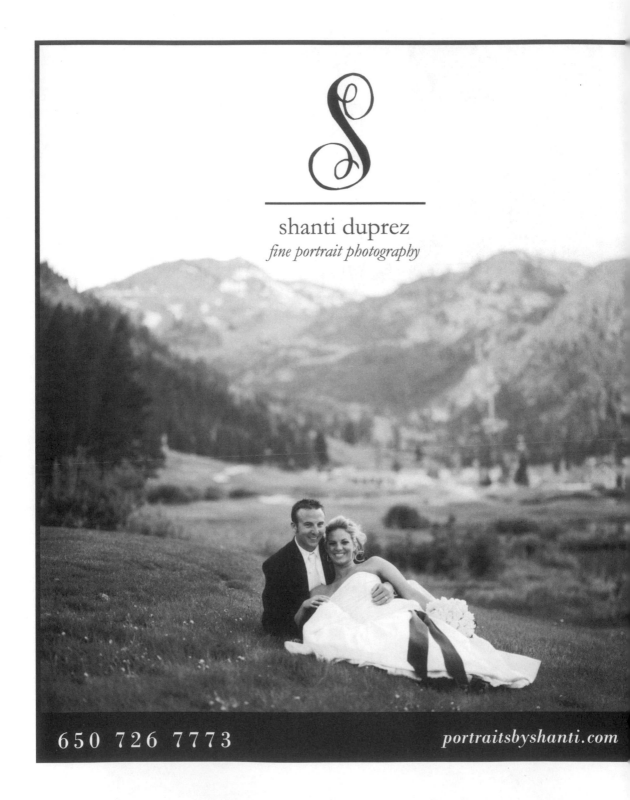

shanti duprez
fine portrait photography

650 726 7773

portraitsbyshanti.com

Photographers

www.darcyweddings.com

Photographers

www.LionPhotography.com
415.215.2579
707.766.6955

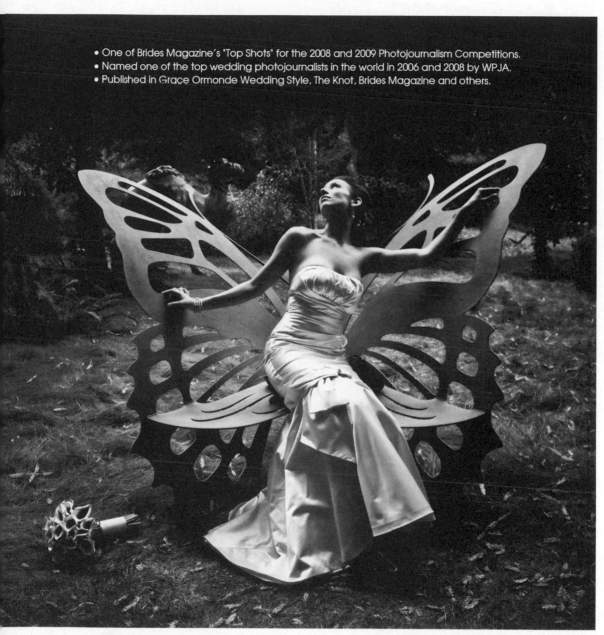

- One of Brides Magazine's "Top Shots" for the 2008 and 2009 Photojournalism Competitions.
- Named one of the top wedding photojournalists in the world in 2006 and 2008 by WPJA.
- Published in Grace Ormonde Wedding Style, The Knot, Brides Magazine and others.

- Named the snuggliest mama in the world by her 7-year old (her 30-something husband agrees).

rhee bevere
PHOTOGRAPHY

www.rheebevere.com

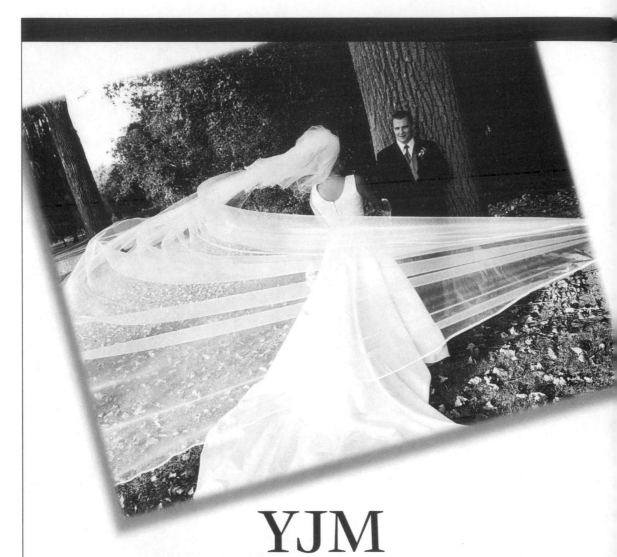

YJM

PHOTOGRAPHY

SERVING THE GREATER BAY AREA

925·362·0280

www.yjmphotography.com

DIGITAL FILES AVAILABLE UPON REQUEST

WEDDINGS - SPECIAL OCCASIONS

Photographers

WWW.JASMINEWANGPHOTO.COM

Photographers

Photographers

a moment.   unscripted.   unforgettable.

A MOMENT CAPTURED.   FOREVER.

415.596.3646 / tara@arrowoodphotography.com

Arrowood
PHOTOGRAPHY

a smile. a teardrop. a kiss. an instant.

www.kiphotography.com

Videographers

Videographers

Videographers

THOMAS HUGHES
FILMS

Photo © Todd Rafalovich

Indexes

Event Locations

a

b

C

d

e

f

g

i

j

k

l

m

n

o

S

t

u

v

Event Services

j

k

l

m

r

s

t

V

W

Y

Bridal Salons

Salons We Love

It's not easy to make our list of favorite Northern California bridal salons. First, we check each one out and evaluate their reputation and dress selection. Then we ask brides and wedding professionals what THEY think. The result is this exclusive list of bridal salons that collectively offer a wide range of fabulous wedding attire to suit a variety of budgets.

Don't forget to visit HereComesTheGuide.com, where you can browse by wedding and bridesmaid dress designers, as well as services such as custom dress design and alterations.

Want extra savings & style? HereComesTheGuide.com also lists designer *Trunk Shows and Sample Sales!*

SAN FRANCISCO

Bridal Galleria
3 Embarcadero Center, Lobby Level
San Francisco, CA 94111
415/362-2277
www.BridalGalleria.com

Encore Bridal
By appointment only.
San Francisco, CA 94108
310/545-1409
www.EncoreBridal.com

Glamour Closet
114 Columbus Avenue
San Francisco, CA 94133
415/391-1515
www.GlamourCloset.com

JinWang
300 Grant Avenue, Penthouse
San Francisco, CA 94108
415/397-9111
www.JinWang.net

Jinza Couture Bridal
1933 Union Street, 2nd Floor
San Francisco, CA 94123
415/351-1588
www.Jinza.net

Joan Gilbert Bride, European Collection
By appointment only.
San Francisco, CA 94118
415/752-1808
www.JoanGilbertBride.com

Marina Morrison
30 Maiden Lane
San Francisco, CA 94108
415/984-9360
www.MarinaMorrison.com

Novella Bridal
557 Pacific Avenue
San Francisco, CA 94133
415/981-9373
www.NovellaBridal.com

Siri Boutique
540 D Barneveld Avenue
San Francisco, CA 94124
415/431-8873
www.SiriInc.com

SOUTH BAY

Gabrielle's Bridal Atelier
422 East Campbell Avenue
Campbell, CA 95008
408/370-4999
www.GabriellesBridal.com

Haute Bride Couture Bridal
40 N. Santa Cruz Avenue
Los Gatos, CA 95030
408/827-4775
www.HauteBride.com

Iridescence Bridal Couture
By appointment only.
San Jose, CA 95126
408/688-4877
www.IridescenceBridal.com

SWATI Couture
3458 Janice Way
Palo Alto, CA 94303
510/610-5990
www.SwatiCouture.com

TRUDYS Brides and Special Occasions
The Pruneyard Shopping Center
1875 S. Bascom Avenue, Suite 134
Campbell, CA 95008
408/377-1987
www.TrudysBrides.com

TRI-VALLEY AND LIVERMORE WINE COUNTRY

J'aime Bridal
719 Main Street
Pleasanton, CA 94566
925/846-8459
www.jaimebridal.com

PENINSULA

Nouvelle Vogue
241 South San Mateo Dr., 2nd Floor
San Mateo, CA 94401
650/347-3444
www.NouvelleVogue.com

Perfect Details
Retail Showroom, by appointment only.
851 Burlway, Suite 301
Burlingame, CA 94010
650/576-4927
www.PerfectDetails.com

EAST BAY

Janene's Bridal Boutique
2418 Central Avenue
Alameda, CA 94501
510/217-8076
www.JanenesBridalBoutique.com

MONTEREY/CARMEL

Epiphany, a divine bridal boutique
Mission Street between Fifth & Sixth
Carmel, CA 93921
831/626-7700
www.Epiphany-Boutique.com

Virtual tours let you visit event sites without leaving home!

Use your computer to visit hundreds of venues without ever leaving home. Each tour gives you a 360-degree view of a location's event spaces—it's like standing in the middle of the room and turning in a complete circle so you can see everything. By taking a "tour" online, you can quickly decide if the location you're viewing is a good fit for you.

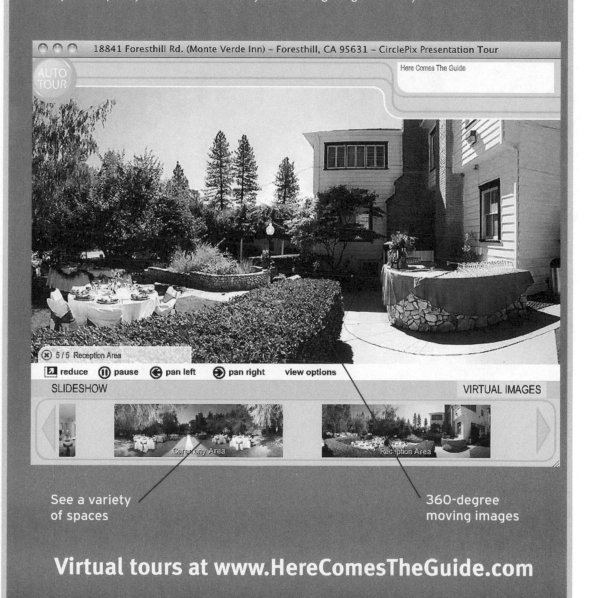

See a variety of spaces

360-degree moving images

Virtual tours at www.HereComesTheGuide.com

About the Authors

Jan Brenner has co-authored and edited all of Hopscotch Press' books. Although she received a BA in English from UC Berkeley, she backed into writing only after spending ten years in social work and four in publishing. Along the way she got a couple of other degrees that have never been put to official use. A lifelong dilettante, she's quasi-conversant in 3.1 languages, dabbles in domestic pursuits, and travels whenever she gets the chance.

Jolene Rae Harrington has been with Hopscotch Press since she first fell in love with their groundbreaking publications while planning her own beach wedding in 1995. In addition to co-authoring and editing the *Here Comes The Guide* books, she serves as Director of Creative Content for HereComesTheGuide.com and is a frequently quoted expert on the bridal industry. Beyond her work at Here Comes The Guide, Jolene's writing credits range from an award-winning television script to a best-selling children's computer game. She lives in her native Southern California with her husband and various animal children.

About the Founder

Lynn Broadwell is an author, publisher and former marketing professional for the special events industry. Her company, Hopscotch Press, provides a website and publications designed to meet the needs of the general public and special event professional. Ms. Broadwell has been featured in many articles and has appeared on radio and TV.

Ms. Broadwell is a graduate of UC Berkeley, with both an undergraduate degree in landscape architecture and a masters degree in business.

Notes

Notes

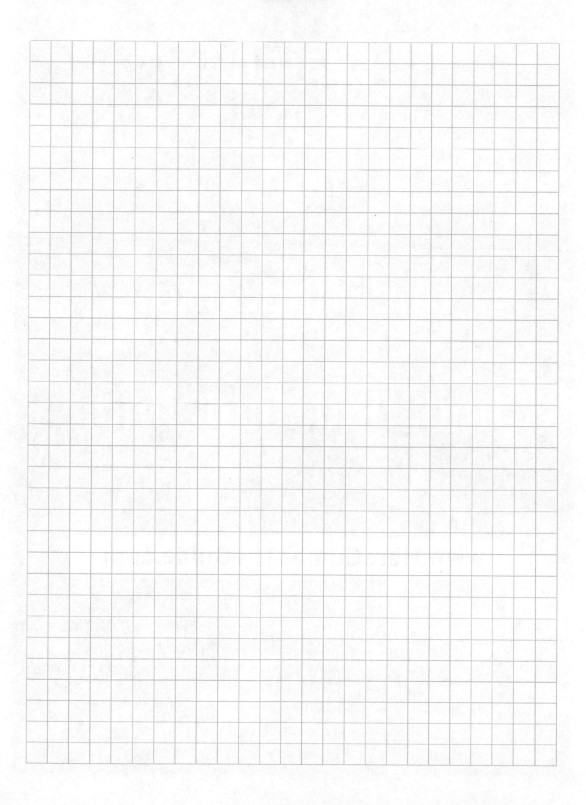